JUMPING THE ABYSS

JUMPING THE ABYSS

Marriner S. Eccles and the New Deal, 1933–1940

Mark Wayne Nelson

The University of Utah Press | Salt Lake City

The Defiance House Man colophon is a registered trademark of The University of Utah Press. It is based on a four-foot-tall Ancient Puebloan pictograph (late PIII) near Glen Canyon, Utah.

21 20 19 18 17 1 2 3 4 5

Library of Congress Cataloging-in-Publication Data

Names: Nelson, Mark Wayne, author.
Title: Jumping the abyss : Marriner S. Eccles and the New Deal, 1933-1940 / Mark Wayne Nelson.
Other titles: Marriner S. Eccles and the New Deal, 1933-1940
Description: Salt Lake City : The University of Utah Press, [2017] | Includes bibliographical references.
Identifiers: LCCN 2016049587| ISBN 9781607815556 (cloth : alk. paper) | ISBN 9781607815563 (ebook)
Subjects: LCSH: Eccles, Marriner S. (Marriner Stoddard), 1890-1977. | New Deal, 1933-1939. | United States—Economic policy—1933-1945.
Classification: LCC HC106.3 .N457 2017 | DDC 332.1/1092 [B] —dc23 LC record available at https://lccn.loc.gov/2016049587

Printed and bound in the United States of America.

In Memory of Ella and James Gowan

CONTENTS

ACKNOWLEDGMENTS

It is customary, when authors express gratitude, to emphasize that the scholars to whom they are indebted bear no responsibility whatever for any deficiencies that may be found within the forthcoming work. I do likewise. I know, in fact, that one or two people cited below do not share my general approval of most of the New Deal. They, nonetheless, genially contributed time and energy in providing me with assistance. Of one thing I am quite certain, this is a much better book because of the people who generously gave their time to read and comment on it.

This book had its genesis at Pepperdine University when I was working on my master's degree. I owe a great debt to the history faculty there. I would like to thank Herbert Luft and David Baird. I owe a special debt to Stephen Sale—the first person to suggest that my preliminary efforts were worthy of being published—and especially to the wonderful John McClung, who offered both knowledge and kindness in overseeing my efforts. In addition, Roger McGrath, while visiting Pepperdine, was greatly helpful and encouraging.

While working on my doctoral degree at Claremont Graduate University, I was fortunate to make the acquaintance of Rick Wartzman at the Drucker Institute. Rick's willingness to become involved in this project occurred just as I was feeling discouraged and seriously considering abandoning it for other academic pursuits. Also at this time, I reached out to Phillip Harvey, at Rutgers University, who was equally encouraging and helpful and graciously contributed his extensive knowledge on the history of social welfare. Both were instrumental in my research becoming a finished product. I owe a special thanks to Janet Brodie for allowing me to leave the realm of social history and take up once again the economic and political affairs of the New Deal. Janet was also instrumental in putting me in contact with Hans Palmer and Jean Schroedel, who provided invaluable scholarly input. I also sought the advice of Roger Sandilands in Scotland, whose expertise on Lauchlin Currie and the economic thought of this period is impressive. I can't thank him enough for his munificent sharing of information and his willingness to read the chapters I sent to him.

I have never met a historian who did not feel a special fondness for librarians and the directors of special collections. In this regard, I want to express my deep appreciation to Paul Mogren and the wonderful staff at the Special Collections division of the J. Willard Marriott Library at the University of Utah in Salt Lake for all of their assistance. Many thanks also to John Alley and the staff at the University of Utah Press, and to Ginny Hoffman for her careful copyediting of this volume.

I reserve my most heartfelt thanks to my friends and family. My longtime friend Don Ingalls, while working all week on the "big issues" of health care, took time in the evenings and on weekends to review a good deal of this manuscript. The book is dedicated to my in-laws, Ella and James, who provided invaluable support in numerous ways. Most of all, I thank my son, Gowan, and my wife, Katherine, whose love and inspiration are there for me always.

INTRODUCTION

We capitalists have got to decide how much we are going to pay for capitalism.
—Marriner S. Eccles, *New York Times*, May 1935

This is the crowd that wants power rather than recovery—the crowd that for 12 years was in power, that tried the very policies which ended in the greatest smash in our economic history; the crowd that willed this administration a debt of 20 billions and a demoralized, prostrate country; yet they have the sublime audacity to propose that we go back to the very policies which wrecked the country. They have been proved false prophets on their own record.
—Marriner S. Eccles, memo to FDR, December 1935

This book presents the first comprehensive and independent analysis of the career of one of the most important public officials in the history of the United States. More than a decade ago, I began to research and write about the role played by Marriner S. Eccles during the New Deal as a leader in the Civil Works Administration, a special assistant to the secretary of the treasury, and as the chairman of the Federal Reserve Board of Governors. Since that time I have come to learn far more about his participation during those years and, indeed, a good deal more about the vexed political and economic milieu in which his stint as a public servant unfolded. Although this work is clearly intended to amplify the contributions that Eccles made in these important policy areas, it also seeks to correct common inaccuracies in the historical record about the details of that participation.

Although this book does not aspire to biography, it does furnish an account of Eccles's early family history and some details of his life as a businessman before the onset of the Great Depression. It is interesting how barren his personal papers appear to be in regard to his personal life. This is certainly true of his memoir as well. After a frank acknowledgment that his consuming interest in both his business and public affairs rendered him "guilty of neglect" both as a husband and as a father to his three children, there is scarcely another reference to family matters.[1] While what follows is an assessment of Eccles's activities covering the years from 1933 to 1940, his fiscal and monetary involvement and interests were so far ranging it may persuade some readers that this work might better be described as an account of the New Deal with Eccles simply as the focal point. The narrative lingers occasionally to explore some of the fundamental questions that have occupied scholars of the Great Depression since the 1930s, but it does so with Eccles's perspective never far removed.

There can be little doubt that Eccles was at the very center of the New Deal disputations over the efficacy of fiscal policy measures. While reflecting upon the early years of the so-called Keynesian Revolution, no less an authority on America's economic history than John Kenneth Galbraith would assert that it was not John Maynard Keynes, but rather Eccles who played the most active role in the widespread dissemination of "Keynesian policies" throughout the land.[2] One might be hard-pressed to find many matters upon which Milton Friedman and his fellow economist John Kenneth Galbraith agreed. Although Galbraith in large measure embraced Keynesianism—inclined though he was to fear that it had traveled down a "one-way street"—Friedman viewed it as a rather lamentable development. On the pivotal contribution played by Eccles in advancing its precepts, however, they were entirely of one mind. "Yours is the only revolution on record," Galbraith once wrote to Eccles, "that entered government by way of a central bank."[3]

Eccles was possessed of what Galbraith liked to term "the primitive instincts of a businessman"; so primitive, in fact, it appears he failed to obtain a high school degree.[4] He emerged as a figure in national life not from the charmed surroundings of Bloomsbury, but from the Mormon Zion in the great American basin. He came to his unorthodox economic views not while a professor at Oxford but as a rough-and-tumble participant in the American business scene. From the mid-1930s on, Eccles was something of a household name. He was the ubiquitous advocate of deficit spending; quoted in countless newspaper and journal articles; seen on newsreels, at business conventions, and in union halls; heard frequently on radio; and pictured on the cover of *Time* magazine. Large numbers of pre–World War II Americans, who had little familiarity with the name John Maynard Keynes, knew of this irascible Mormon from Utah.

Alas, before the Great Recession clouded the nation's economic horizon in 2007, Marriner Eccles was largely forgotten. In the minds of many historians he was considered—when considered at all—as something of a curiosity, a homespun Keynesian who, as a Republican businessman from Utah, advocated deficit financing and played an important role in refocusing the power of the Federal Reserve from New York to Washington.[5] For the growing number of academic economists who championed free-market capitalism and viewed the New Deal as an impediment to economic revival—while claiming to have the mathematical models to prove it—Eccles was dismissed as the embodiment of all the inimical fallacies of the Keynesian age. Writing in 1987, Robert Lucas, the highly acclaimed champion of the "rational expectations revolution" in economic thought, stated dismissively that "what we now call macroeconomics" was centered on a series of controversies that had simply been outgrown: "the liquidity trap, operation twist, the loanable funds doctrine, and all the other macroeconomic issues that seemed so important as they were occurring and are so hard to remember now." Thus Keynes and those who followed his lead "were obliged to rely on Marshallian ingenuity to tease some useful dynamism out of purely static theory," while "the modern theorist is much better equipped," observed Lucas, "to state *exactly* the problem he wants to study and then study it." Hence, the very debates that had so consumed Eccles and that had engaged public policy makers for more than half a century were deemed somewhat antediluvian.[6]

To those economic historians who were disposed to consider the New Deal favorably, Eccles was viewed as a noble figure who made an ultimately fruitless effort to persuade President Franklin Roosevelt to dramatically increase spending in the prewar years, but who also failed to realize the monetary possibilities available to him as the head of a central bank. To such economic historians, the abandonment of the gold standard and the tremendous growth of the money supply—developments such as the massive importation of gold from abroad—with which Eccles had no connection, brought the impressive increases in the Gross National Product from 1933 to 1937 (a growth that averaged approximately 9 percent a year). For example, Christina Romer (appointed the first chair of President Obama's Council of Economic Advisers) gave Eccles a rather poor grade for his comprehension of the efficacy of the Fed's monetary mechanisms.[7]

While there are clearly legitimate reasons for Romer's assessment—especially, as we will see, in terms of Eccles's cluelessness about the role of gold inflows—such pronouncements, nonetheless, appear a tad uncharitable when one considers that the 1935 restructuring of the Federal Reserve, an alteration that significantly heightened the degree to which these mechanisms are effective, can be attributed more to him than to any other individual. Fittingly, as the present chair, Janet Yellen, arrives at work each morning to apply the tools of monetary policy, she enters the Marriner S. Eccles Building.

The 1982 building dedication notwithstanding, Eccles's role in the Depression years rarely receives sufficient historical exploration. This study attempts to address this oversight by elaborating upon the rather unique perspective he brought to the Roosevelt administration in the years before the onset of the Second World War. If Eccles was the bellwether of what he termed "compensatory economics," who were his principal allies and who were his most ardent detractors? Why did such advocacy largely fail until the exigencies of war production belatedly fulfilled his fiscal objectives?

Although many of the fiscal and monetary issues in dispute throughout this period have been thoroughly investigated by others—one thinks here of Herbert Stein's excellent *The Fiscal Revolution in America* and Allan Meltzer's classic volume one of *A History of the Federal Reserve*—they have largely evaluated Eccles's fiscal and monetary positions in isolation from each other. Moreover, both works have somewhat neglected to explore the rather sophisticated economic conceptions furnished to Eccles by his staff at the Federal Reserve, led by a brilliant young economist from Harvard, Lauchlin Currie. Outside of scholarly articles in academic journals, the Eccles/Currie relationship and its importance in the nation's economic history have been generally overlooked.[8] Likewise, the controversy surrounding Currie and the famous Communist espionage charges of Elizabeth Bentley have been largely forgotten (see note for further details on that controversy).[9] If Eccles failed to grasp all the intricacies of his economist's views, he nonetheless understood many of their core tenets and articulated them for the president, the Congress, and the American public; the degree to which these positions may have varied a bit from the traditional understanding of "Keynesianism" ought to be noted.

But even histories that delve into Eccles in some detail are almost entirely concerned with the part he played in the Banking Act of 1935 and the Roosevelt Recession of 1937. Eccles's involvement in the Civil Works Administration, the Housing Act of 1934, the Agreement on Bank Supervision, the Works Financing Bill, and other matters is virtually always overlooked.

This lack of attention to the extensiveness of Eccles's involvement in the affairs of the New Deal is, of course, not generally the case with the two works of history that make him the focal point. These notable exceptions are Eccles himself in his 1951 autobiography, *Beckoning Frontiers*, and Sidney Hyman in his 1976 authorized biography, *Marriner S. Eccles: Private Entrepreneur and Public Servant*. A valuable source of information for anyone interested in the

New Deal era, *Beckoning Frontiers* occasionally displays a tendency—hardly an uncommon dimension of any autobiography—to interpret events in a self-serving fashion. At certain points it achieves this by simply neglecting crucial details. Although some of these omissions appear designed to enhance his reputation as a sagacious participant in the unfolding events of the 1930s, others, interestingly, had they been referenced, would have tended to redound to his benefit by mitigating his culpability in what many regard as the monetary miscues of 1937. (Why Eccles would have preferred to leave such matters obscure is unknown. I can merely offer a speculation in a later chapter.) Although providing some degree of critical analysis and greater clarification, Hyman's book, written with Eccles's full participation, too frequently adheres to his subject's historical account without, it seems, a careful inspection of vital primary sources of information and the conflicting accounts of others.

The most neglected source of information about Marriner Eccles's career is to be found in the former Fed chairman's own personal papers housed at the University of Utah. Perhaps the most important contribution of this study, therefore, is the introduction into the historical record of a significant amount of material drawn from forty-five boxes of documents in this archive. Interestingly, some of the more revelatory information included in this work derives from a full examination of documents that Eccles selectively cited in his memoir. Thus, occasional discriminating editing on Eccles's part—especially the crafty use of ellipses—has led many scholars of the 1937 recession to reach a few erroneous conclusions about his role in that economic calamity. Although most of the material revealed in this inspection is hardly subject matter that Eccles wished to keep hidden away, much of it is nonetheless of significance. For example, unmentioned in both Eccles's memoir and Hyman's biography or, it appears, anywhere else, is evidence of the part he played in the short-lived Civil Works Administration. (As this work argues, the CWA has been a widely underappreciated aspect of the New Deal.) It was gratifying to stumble across documents that connected him to this remarkable agency. Clearly, then, Eccles's personal papers have been indispensable.

Newspapers have proven to be a precious source of information. What Eccles was stating publicly—to large, official audiences and in press releases and interviews with reporters—reveals insights on his political strategies and his occasional political missteps. They are especially revealing of the degree to which he was willing to side with or to transgress the policy positions of the Roosevelt administration. (As we will see, even while the Fed chairman, he viewed himself as a member of the administration.) Moreover, these comments are in some instances at odds with his autobiographical accounts. Not surprisingly, the two most utilized journalistic sources found herein are the *New York Times* and the *Wall Street Journal.* Although these papers occasionally carried exclusive articles, most of Eccles's important public commentaries can be cross-referenced for general accuracy with Associated Press and United Press accounts. I discovered that Utah newspapers were especially helpful in that they were particularly aware of all issues in which Eccles was involved. This was certainly the case with the *Salt Lake Tribune* and his hometown newspaper, the *Ogden Standard-Examiner.* These publications were quite valuable in discovering some important details about his business interests in Utah.

A survey of popular magazine articles in publications such as *Time* has helped in gaining some perspective on how Eccles was portrayed to the nation. (His membership in both the Republican Party and the Mormon Church clearly intrigued readers and added to his mystique as a New Deal progressive.) This kind of insight can also be garnered from an array of syndicated columnists and editorial writers, both those who admired him and those who considered him a threat to Western Civilization. His appearance in more specialized publications—frequently as an invited author—allowed him to express his views in a more exacting fashion. This was certainly the case with his frequent contributions to *Bankers' Magazine* in which he presented the more technical aspects of his financial positions.

Of course, congressional testimony—and Eccles gave a good amount of it—is an excellent means by which to understand a number of his positions on issues that were left unmentioned or only slightly touched upon in his memoir. It is also an excellent way to become familiar with the views of his political adversaries who always appeared before the same committees to counter his arguments and economic reckonings.

A good deal of information included here comes from government reports and publications. This is certainly the case with the subject matter that deals with housing. In addition to the President's Conference on Home Ownership, the annual reports of the United States Housing Administration are quite valuable. With the affairs of the Fed, the minutes of the Reserve's Open Market Committee and the monthly Federal Reserve Bulletin furnish some insight about how economic developments were being evaluated and why certain courses of action were taken.

Chapter 1 (Balance the Budgets of the World) uses as its title the very words spoken by the extraordinarily influential Bernard Baruch before the Senate Finance Committee in February 1933. The famous financier's comments reflected the overwhelming consensus that governments at all levels must place their expenditures in alignment with their revenue. As the chapter makes clear, this hue and cry for the balancing of public budgets and governmental austerity was a worldwide antidote for economic ills. A rather detailed depiction of how this issue became the focal point of the 1932 presidential campaign, embraced by both political parties, sets the stage for the first appearance in the national arena of Marriner Eccles. His testimony before the Senate Finance Committee in early 1933 was a stunning refutation of all that was accepted orthodoxy. Eccles's insistence that he was merely proffering "logical radicalism" is intrinsic both to his economic argument at the time and to an important assertion in this book. Had it not been for the experience of the First World War, Eccles stated to the committee, his extreme spending proposals would seem highly irrational. (Ironically, the debt ceiling limit first imposed by Congress in 1917 was motivated not by the need to curb expenditures but to allow the Treasury to increase spending unencumbered by the need for constant Congressional approval. Congress had given its approval for a much greater level of debt—$43 billion—than the $25 billion actually incurred.)[10] The assumption of a vastly greater fiscal burden in the very recent past, however, rendered his suggested level of outlays meager by comparison. In fact, the federal debt-to-GDP ratio was 40 percent in 1936—less than half of its 2010 level. The nation, Eccles believed, could very well have been brought to accept a growing debt if it concomitantly witnessed the benefits of employment and economic growth. Although a similar argument about the size of government debt could be made in 2016, the fact that robust economic growth—essential to Eccles's perspective—has yet to recur is problematical. As an avid reader of the latest macroeconomic theorists, one wonders how Eccles might react to Robert Gordon's highly regarded 2015 book, *The Rise and Fall of American Growth*. At least it could be argued, however, that public opinion was simply not an insurmountable obstacle to the implementation of an effective fiscal policy throughout most of the 1930s.[11]

Although chapter 2 (To Set the World Aright) inserts some important biographical information about the Eccles family experience, its primary emphasis is upon the various influences that transformed a rather conservative Republican banker from Utah into a driving force for progressive activism in Franklin Roosevelt's administration. Eccles liked to say that he arrived at his new economic and political sensibilities as a consequence of his empirical experience as a businessman weathering, and learning from, the hardships of the Depression's early phase. And yet he had an active mind and was clearly influenced to some degree by a number of economic thinkers, especially the writings of William T. Foster. Foster authored, with Waddill Catchings, the very popular tract *The Road to Plenty*. This 1928 book is an important work in the "underconsumptionist" economic thought that Eccles came to espouse. The book is worthy of a good deal of attention.

In his association with Harvard economist Lauchlin Currie, who is introduced in chapter 2, Eccles was following a not uncommon tradition reminiscent of John Hobson and Albert Mummery's collaboration between an academic economist and a well-to-do man of business. It is important to observe that although Eccles made for a rather solitary presence before the Senate Finance Committee, his position on government spending and an activist agenda was far from unique. The chapter takes note, therefore, of the growing public chorus of those clamoring for such a course of action by 1931.

Chapter 3 (The Established Rules of Decency) examines Eccles's affirmation that he derived the foundation of his intellectual and moral sustenance, not from the progressive theorists of his age, but from the chair of moral philosophy at the University of Glasgow, Adam Smith. It was Smith who provided the foundation for Eccles's humanistic conviction that it was government's role to establish, as Eccles himself phrased it, "minimum standards of decency" below which no American who labors faithfully should be allowed to fall.[12] Eccles, and to no lesser extent FDR, considered themselves heirs to a centuries-old desire to realize a vibrant commercial society that cared about the welfare of human beings. It forms the very core of "New Deal liberalism" and neither the president nor the chairman considered this pursuit of capitalism with a human face as in any way the product of an alien or unfamiliar set of beliefs. This chapter makes a vital deviation from the tactual issues of the Great Depression to trace the thread of this sentiment through the industrial age from Adam Smith and Robert Owen (at least his earlier years) to the leaders of twentieth-century reform. It is there, in Herbert Croly's *The Promise of American Life*, written when Eccles was a boy of nine, that this vision may have found its most intellectualized expression. "It has a large economic side," Theodore Roosevelt insisted when he adopted Croly's New Nationalism and placed the contours of the New Deal before the American public in 1912, "but it is fundamentally an ethical movement."[13]

Chapter 3, therefore, insists that the New Deal be considered in its historical context. It is acknowledged further on that both FDR and Eccles may have lacked direct exposure to some of these thinkers; as Keynes once insisted, however, all leaders, even delusional ones "who hear voices in the air, are distilling their frenzy from some academic scribbler of a few years back."[14]

Chapter 4 (Salvaging the Human Element in All of Us) deals in large part with what economic historian Bradford DeLong has identified as a "counterfactual pessimism" that is commonly found in New Deal historiography: a conviction among a large number of scholars of the Great Depression that there were such powerful political and economic encumbrances at play in those years—especially the public's disfavor with the accumulation of government debt—that the implementation of many effective public policies was either short-circuited or never even seriously considered. In weighing the implications of such a perspective, DeLong suggests that its acceptance "has quite possibly led economic historians further away from a balanced view of the Great Depression and from indicating to noneconomic historians how the Great Depression might provide useful analogies for thinking about the economic problems of today." (The fact that the Obama administration understandably believed it unrealistic to clamor for a larger—or second—fiscal stimulus in 2009 comes readily to mind. "Look, I get the Keynesian thing," President Obama was reported to have stated, "but it's not where the electorate is.")[15]

One of the more recent examples of such a perspective might be seen in George Akerlof and Robert Shiller's recent book on the psychological forces that drive economic life. After noting that New Deal spending was "orders of magnitude short," they sound an oft heard explanation that FDR lacked both the "inclination" and the "political legitimacy to go far enough."[16] This chapter challenges at least the latter of those assumptions by examining the stunning, if exceedingly brief, life of the Civil Works Administration. Created by executive order in November of 1933, the CWA was a public works project that was intended to help the nation survive the winter of 1933–1934. Placed in the hands of the remarkable Harry Hopkins, the program demonstrated the remunerative power of well-compensated labor upon both aggregate demand and the human spirit. Born on November 9, 1933, the CWA put some 4 million Americans to work by Christmas and nearly 4.3 million by mid-January of 1934. It may be one of the most underappreciated accomplishments in U.S. history. Often viewed as a precursor of the Works Progress Administration (WPA) created in 1935, the CWA was no such thing. Although budgeted for $400 million taken from the Public Works Administration, the program quickly surpassed that amount and was spending money, said one disapproving observer, "like a drunken sailor." Despite garnering widespread public support and demonstrating discernible economic benefit that could have sustained the agency's political viability, FDR ordered its disbandment in the spring of that year. Marriner Eccles headed the CWA in Utah and made an effort to keep it in existence. Although he trumpeted the program at the time, he included only one positive but rather parenthetical reference to the CWA in his memoir and failed to make any mention of his direct association with it. It is worthy of a brief speculation about why that is so.

Chapter 5 (A Man in the Treasury) is concerned with the short but quite important stint Eccles spent as a special assistant to Treasury Secretary Henry Morgenthau. It has never been certain how Eccles managed to go to work for someone with whom he had both personal and ideological antipathy, although such couplings were far from rare in the New Deal. This animus between the two seemed to begin at their initial meeting and continued through their careers. The main focus of this chapter, however, describes his role in the formation of the National Housing Act of 1934. The material presented here supports Eccles's contention that housing construction was far and away the most essential element of a full economic recovery. The mechanism for putting vast numbers of construction workers back on the job was set in place with the formation of the Federal Housing Administration that Eccles championed. The story of how the opportunity to end high unemployment in the 1930s through housing construction was left unrealized might legitimately be called tragic. Nonetheless, the emergence of a modernized construction industry that followed in the wake of the National Housing Act that Eccles advocated, managed to produce, *marred as it was by the racial injustice of American society*, a volume and quality of moderate housing by the post–World War II years that, as historian Gail Radford has acknowledged, "seemed impossible at a mass level" as late as the 1920s. Moreover, the financing, planning, and land-use improvements that the FHA fostered allowed housing to play a crucial role in economic stability and may, suggests economic historian Alexander Field, "have contributed to the postwar moderation of the business cycle as much as did the much-vaunted role of fiscal and monetary policy."[17]

The role that Eccles played—after his 1934 appointment to the Board of Governors—in altering the Fed's structure in order to transform it into what he termed "A Real Central Bank," is the topic of chapter 6. It is essential to provide a bit of background, however, about the country's historical relationship with the ideological conception and previous implementation of central banking. This is especially important in regard to western attitudes toward eastern financial interests. Eccles believed, and the chapter supports the contention, that the Federal Reserve's initial incarnation in 1913 was designed to fortify the influence of New York City as the paramount source of monetary control. This role was heightened with the growing importance of the Fed's open-market purchases and sales after World War I. For this reason, therefore, during his confirmation process, there was a good deal of emphasis placed on the fact that he was a westerner.

It is also during his confirmation hearings that Senator Carter Glass, who was known as the "father of the Federal Reserve" and who resented Eccles's encroachment upon his domain, attempted to discredit "that Mormon missionary" by bringing a number of his business connections into public view. Although these details failed to derail Eccles's appointment, they do reveal some interesting aspects of his personal career that neither he nor Sidney Hyman bothered to discuss. As Eccles was advocating various governmental courses of action, he continued to maintain many of his business investments, and was clearly impacting corporate decisions in a number of the concerns in which he had once been officially in charge.

It would be deeply unjust to suggest, however, that Eccles was a venal opportunist who arrived in Washington in pursuit of an agenda designed for his own personal enrichment. He was an extremely successful businessman before he entered government service and would have most certainly continued being so. While he believed wholeheartedly that a revived housing sector would salvage American capitalism, he was also a man, coincidently, whose concerns sold mortgages, lumber, and construction services. And yet, despite what one might feel about his political vision, it would seem difficult to deny that he was a man—although possessed of overabundant doses of ego and ambition—driven by an abiding sense of concern for his country's welfare.

Although most of the issues surrounding the debate over the Banking Act of 1935 that are discussed in this chapter have been thoroughly explored in the past, there is one episode that has been nearly lost to history. Inexplicably, Carter Glass introduced an amendment to Title III of the proposed law that would have largely repealed the separation of commercial and investment banking enshrined in his own Glass-Steagall Act of 1933. The effort failed, but not before FDR weighed in on the issue in an interesting way.

Chapter 7 (Our Best Gun) examines Eccles's role in the Roosevelt administration. Although Eccles did indeed refer to himself as a member of the administration, which in turn considered him as such, Lauchlin Currie's observation that he was "with" but not "of" the New Deal is a fair appraisal of his association. His Fed responsibilities seemed divorced from White House interference; however, the chairman's relationship with the president was distinguished by its singularity, unlike any before or since. What makes this interaction unique was not merely that Eccles supplied FDR with advice aplenty, often drafting entire speeches that he urged the president to deliver, but that he was also willing to publicly comment when he thought the course being followed was wanting. On most occasions, but certainly not all, these rebukes provided little sustenance for the conservatives in Congress, because they found Eccles's ideas even more objectionable than FDR's.

There are two important policy matters discussed in chapter 7 that Eccles believed were misconceived by the administration. There were few in Washington more adamant about the need to institute a more progressive tax structure than Eccles. He was dissatisfied with a number of the suggestions that emanated from FDR's Committee on Economic Security. As we shall see, he despised the implementation of the payroll tax to fund Social Security for its regressivity, and argued constantly that the New Deal was not effectively using the tax structure to achieve a fairer and more market-friendly distribution of national income. The key to achieving this, Eccles insisted, was to sufficiently tax what historian Mark Leff terms the "subplutocrats." This was something FDR was reluctant to do until the war.

Eccles believed it would be difficult to design a poorer public works project than the Works Progress Administration. The WPA may have been particularly irksome to him because he had sent to the White House a somewhat detailed memo on how an effective works program ought to be structured. Although chapter 7 will discuss the varied ways he considered the program defective, the main flaw was that it simply was failing to spend enough or to pay workers anything beyond a mere subsistence wage and would, therefore, have a marginal impact on aggregate demand. Moreover, although Eccles thought a program that resembled the CWA would be far more preferable, he really favored one that operated on a contract basis with private developers. In any event, the government needed to get more stimuli into the economy. Eccles was fearful at the time that FDR was planning to improve his chances of reelection the following November by severely cutting the deficit to demonstrate that the administration was serious about balancing the budget and reducing the nation's debt. This, he sternly warned the president in December 1935, would be a tragic mistake. Not surprisingly, Eccles's entreaty led to a confrontation with the fiscally conservative Henry Morgenthau, who discussed the memo from the Fed chairman with his ally, Budget Director Daniel Bell. Together they set out to dissuade FDR from listening to Eccles and to get him to reaffirm his goal of fiscal restraint. What is noteworthy about this incident is that virtually all who write about it are of the mistaken belief that it occurred exactly a year later, in December of 1936. Why this is so will be explained in chapter 7.

It will be clear in chapter 8 (The New Deal Recession) how this error in chronology influences to some degree any explication of the "Roosevelt Recession" of 1937. This recession is an enormously important event in New Deal historiography. Beyond the human suffering that accompanied this startling economic collapse, is the political impact it would have on the composition of the 76th Congress as a result of the 1938 midterm elections. There can be little doubt that the loss of seventy House seats to the Republicans in the fall election limited the administration's options in the years before the war. The macroeconomic lessons of the recession and the debate over what those lessons actually happen to be are explored in the chapter. Eccles has been faulted for agreeing to an increase in the reserve requirements that many have identified as an important culprit in the reversal of economic fortunes in mid-1937. The events of the recession, and of his career more generally, do seem to illustrate that Eccles, unlike Keynes, had much more faith in acting pursuant to "reasonable calculation." It seemed, Sidney Hyman wrote of him, that he considered the "very word 'economic' as though it were a synonym for 'rational' and 'intelligent.'" He was less inclined to believe that there is at times what Keynes described as a "delicate balance of spontaneous optimism" that could be adversely impacted by developments that a rational observer might think innocuous.[18] A common perception of Eccles's role in the 1937 recession is that he was wrong in his monetary position—increasing reserve requirements—while his fiscal position of maintaining high federal expenditures was correctly propounded. As we shall see, however, by the early months of 1937, his advocacy was on the right side of the former and the incorrect side of the latter. In short, at a crucial point in time, he got the monetary policy right and the fiscal policy wrong. The case is made, however, that the mistakes were widely distributed throughout the administration and that it might be far fairer to identify this economic collapse as the "New Deal Recession."

The title of chapter 9 (A Drop at a Time) features the precise words that Eccles used to describe the manner in which he believed the Depression was fought. In 1938, FDR was persuaded by Eccles and the "spenders" in the administration to take on a quasi-Keynesian aspect to fight the recession, and the country, assisted by the initial emergence of war production, began to spend its way to recovery. FDR's State of the Union address in 1939 included bits and pieces of memos that Eccles had been sending off to the president for all of five years. That same January, Eccles was elaborating on many of the points the president had touched upon when the chairman participated in a nationwide debate with Senator Harry Byrd over the soundness of deficit spending on the

NBS radio network. It was a case he made at every speaking event across the country. He had become, as Sidney Hyman assessed, "the John the Baptist of the new dispensation."[19]

A good deal of chapter 9 chronicles Eccles's efforts to win over the president and Congress to the idea of consolidating all bank regulation in a single agency. In Eccles's opinion this would constitute a major impetus for economic revival, and although he failed in the attempt he managed to gain acceptance of a Uniform Agreement on Bank Supervisory Procedures, which, among other things, dispensed with the use of mark-to-market assessments of bank portfolios.

Another important concern of chapter 9 is the central recommendation of the Fiscal and Monetary Advisory Board that FDR created in 1939. The committee was a typical Rooseveltian orchestration. He selected Eccles and Frederick Delano, the two leading advocates of deficit financing, and teamed them with Budget Director Daniel Bell and Secretary Henry Morgenthau, the two most vociferous critics of such spending, and fully expected that something productive would emerge from their efforts. What they did compromise upon was the Works Financing Bill. The legislation was a complicated way to shift infrastructure spending off budget as investment loans. It was a noble attempt that, had it been adopted by Congress, would have done a great deal to bring about full employment before U.S. entry in World War II, and would certainly have placed the country in a far better situation when confronted with the need to ramp up production to meet the challenges of that conflict.

The failure of the Works Financing Bill and other initiatives in 1939–1941 left Eccles in a rather discouraged state. He was not unmindful, however, of the New Deal's significant achievements. As Christina Romer has observed, real GDP in the United States grew at the "spectacular" annual rate of nearly 10 percent between 1933 and 1937. In the year 1936, a nation of 128 million people benefited from the creation of nearly 1.5 million *private-sector* jobs. (By contrast, the 308 million Americans of 2010 witnessed the addition of a somewhat robust 1.2 million private-sector jobs.) Once the administration regained its bearings in mid-1938, the economy grew at more than 10 percent a year until the country entered the war and, Romer argues, was largely back on trend *before* the stimulus the conflict provided. This level of growth outpaced by a wide margin any other *peacetime* period in the history of the United States.[20]

For Eccles, however, all that was simply not good enough. In May of 1940, when the "phony war" in Europe turned stunningly real—as demonstrated by the photograph on the front pages of American newspapers of a beaming Adolf Hitler posing before the Eiffel Tower—and American unemployment fell to slightly more than 9 percent as the United States accelerated its production of the implements of war, Eccles wholeheartedly rejected what he sensed was a pervasive complacency by both the president and Congress. "As a democracy," he lectured the Economic Club of New York, "we can't afford to take the position that because conditions are satisfactory for many of us, others who are less fortunate can be shunted aside . . . until economic revival develops at some unpredictable future time." Aside from humane considerations, he argued, "it is not good government, good democracy, or good economics to lose the productivity of millions of workers." He suggested to his listeners that "fine phrases" about American institutions "are a meaningless mockery to a man who could not find a job."[21]

The speech was a clear reflection of Eccles's conviction that Americans had social rights as well as political ones. He was reminding FDR that, only weeks before, the president had addressed the nation to say that "he would ask no one to defend a democracy which in turn would not defend everyone in the nation against want and privation." This was, as chapter 3 will examine, an ethical standard that many in the New Deal considered foundational to all they sought to achieve. His advocacy of income redistribution; his insistence that the scourge of high unemployment and its accompanied suffering must not be countenanced; his conviction that decent housing, a national health care system, and equal educational opportunity must be translated by government from "basic rights into realities," have marked him as one of the New Deal's most progressive participants.[22] The chairman clearly identified with John Maynard Keynes's assertion that economics itself was a "moral science" that must "deal with introspection and with values." Nor would the Utah banker have dissented from the famous British economist's much-neglected observation that "in the short run we are all still alive. Life and history are made up of short runs."[23]

Following the outbreak of World War II, while Eccles was demonstrating that he could be every bit as avid a crusader against inflation as he had been against high unemployment—with fiscal policy once again the preferred weapon of choice—he could not resist sending off a letter to Senator Harry Byrd of Virginia. In the course of their very public debate over the merits of deficit financing during the Depression, the conservative Democrat had often made the point that Keynes's "fantastic fallacies of spending, borrowing, and lending" were rejected by his own country, and that in England he was "a prophet without honor." Eccles, motivated he claimed "by no mean spirit," wanted to make sure that Byrd had not missed the fact that Keynes had recently been elaborately celebrated by the king of England for his many contributions to the nation and that he was now "Lord John Maynard Keynes." Eccles then conveyed to Byrd his confidence that when peace once again returned to the world, the United States would enjoy full employment without the need to resort to "continued deficits and growth of the public sector." Nonetheless, the day would no doubt arrive when he would be aligned with "this now honored prophet" in calling for fiscal policies that the good senator would oppose, and they could then return to being "friendly enemies." As for the English economist, Eccles concluded: "Time has a curious habit of justifying this man Keynes."

In relating the details of this letter in his 1976 biography of the Fed chairman, Sidney Hyman wrote that the "curious habit" of time would likely be "justifying" Marriner S. Eccles as well.[24]

So it would seem.

1

BALANCE THE BUDGETS OF THE WORLD

"The Rock of Gibraltar"

As the Great Depression deepens, the importance of fiscal balance emerges as a worldwide fetish. It is the driving theme of the 1932 presidential race in the United States.

On October 11, 1932, in the midst of the presidential campaign, former chief executive Calvin Coolidge addressed a gathering of the Republican faithful at a large rally held in New York City's Madison Square Garden. "If there is anything which a government could do to prevent the decline in business the world has experienced," reasoned the staid New Englander, "it must be that some government somewhere would have been wise enough to apply a remedy." He continued, "If no such remedy anywhere has been found the inference is practically certain that the present economic condition was brought about by forces no government could foresee and prevent." Yet, while expressing this near fatalistic view, Coolidge was quick to remind his audience that economic well-being could best be restored by prudently eschewing debt. "The answer comes back according to the words of Holy Writ," he cautioned, "that they who drink of that well will thirst again."[1]

With this latter sentiment President Herbert Hoover was in complete accord. In his acceptance speech of his party's renomination in August 1932, he affirmed that the elimination of debt was "the foundation of all public financial stability and of all public confidence." Throughout the summer and fall, he sounded this goal in virtually every campaign speech he delivered, along with its necessary corollary, the crucial necessity of a "drastic reduction of government expenditures."[2]

Upon the exposition of such a sound economic principle, the party of Jefferson and Jackson was determined not to be outshone. To the immense satisfaction of *Barron's* and other financial journals, the Democratic Party platform, composed under the guidance of fiscally conservative A. Mitchell Palmer, matched its Republican counterpart in heralding the need to economize. Circulated among many of the party's insiders, as something of a testament to such determination, was a guideline for governing drafted by the former Wilson administration official and soon to be New Deal administrator, General Hugh Johnson. An acolyte of renowned Democratic financier Bernard Baruch, the West Point graduate's "Proclamation" was written under the non de plume Muscleinny; he was identified merely as the "Dictator pro tem." "Sickened" by the accumulation of massive debt, the "buying power" of the American people had been obliterated by a Hoover government that had "literally beaten public confidence to death." It was essential, therefore, insisted Johnson's Muscleinny, that the expenditures of the federal government be reduced by at least 25 percent.[3]

This suggested cut in the national budget was taken to heart by the convention's nominee. In the course of the campaign, Franklin Roosevelt would occasionally imbue his rhetoric with the ideological benchmarks of modern progressivism that his distant cousin, Theodore Roosevelt, had elucidated in his New Nationalism speech more than two decades before. Time and again, however, he succumbed to the blandishments of Bernard Baruch, Felix Frankfurter, and other fiscally conservative supporters, and sounded the deficit alarm. In Pittsburgh he warned that the per capita debt of the federal government was simply unsustainable, and that Hoover's "unprecedented deficits" were "the most reckless and extravagant" ever witnessed.[4] Recriminations abounded. "I accuse the present Administration of being the greatest spending Administration in all our history," charged the Democratic challenger.[5] The incumbent's rejoinder was a simple reminder that, under the Constitution, the body that initiates fiscal policies, the House of Representatives, was controlled by the spendthrift Democrats under the firm rule of its speaker and their vice-presidential nominee, John Nance Garner.[6] Garner responded that Republican "errors in the delicate balance of taxes and spending [had] upset the stability of business."[7]

Certainly, one of the "errors" that Garner referenced was Hoover's refusal to raise taxes until well into 1932, when the shortfall of revenue was estimated to exceed $900 million. (The front pages of the nation's newspapers announced the shocking news in June of 1931 that for the first time since the war the U.S.

Treasury was authorizing a long-term bond issue to meet the government's expenses.)[8] Roosevelt, too, charged that taxes should have been increased earlier and placed significant emphasis upon what he considered to be the Hoover administration's failure in judgment.[9] "Cut and balance" thus became the catch phrase of the 1932 presidential contest. Indeed, the principal matter of contention revolved around the issue of which political party would most effectively achieve what nearly everyone conceded was a laudatory goal.

In his willingness to risk deficits in fiscal 1931 and 1932, Hoover was joined by the most unlikely of figures, the Republican chairman of the Finance Committee, Senator Reed Smoot of Utah. Smoot stated publicly that it was "impossible" to raise taxes in the midst of such depressed conditions and thus supported Hoover's conviction, stated in his December 1930 State of the Union speech, that to increase taxation to pay for construction work "defeats its own purpose, as such taxes directly diminish employment in private industry." Indeed, Smoot had supported Hoover's decision a year earlier—before the magnitude of economic decline was understood—to actually lower taxes in fiscal 1931 for both individuals and corporations. Economic historian Peter Temin has emphasized that this cut was planned in the previous summer and was less a product of demand management than it was a "reflection of balanced-budget ideology."[10] Nevertheless, as a partial consequence of this fiscal decision, tax revenue declined by nearly 50 percent as expenditures rose by 60 percent—an increase due in large measure to expenditures on public works projects and the payment of veterans' certificates.[11] The payment to veterans in 1931 amounted to the significant sum of $1 billion. The veterans' annuity was established by Congress in 1924 with yearly contributions to a trust fund to be distributed in 1945. Although Hoover opposed the early payment of the "bonus" to veterans in 1931, he was unable to sustain a veto of a compromise measure that allowed vets to borrow as much as 50 percent of their 1945 payment at low rates of interest.[12]

Inadvertent as it may have been—due in large measure to badly calculated budget estimates and a veto override—the Hoover administration had, nonetheless, engaged in what would come to be termed "fiscal stimulus." In fact, a study by economist E. Cary Brown came to the incongruous conclusion that the stimulating impact of fiscal policy in the first two years of the Depression was larger than any other two-year period of the 1930s. Brown also found that the fiscal stimulus furnished by local, state, and federal governments in 1931 exceeded any other year of that decade.[13] Peter Temin has expressed a contrasting view of Hoover's fiscal actions, noting that they expanded aggregate demand by a meager 0.3 percent of GNP. He agrees with Brown that the budget in 1931 was more expansive than any other year of the Depression, but points out that any percentage change must be measured against the relatively small size of the federal government in 1931 and the diminished level of national income that year.[14]

The 1932 campaign would present an even more acute irony. Two days after Calvin Coolidge's Madison Square Garden speech, in which he cited the ominous onslaught of "forces no government could foresee and prevent," Franklin Roosevelt delivered a major radio address from the New York governor's mansion in Albany. Roosevelt said he believed public works should be used as an aid to fight unemployment. He was quick to remind his listeners, however, that public works "cost money" and that the "thoroughly unsound financial policies" of the present administration and its accumulation of debt left him limited leeway if he were elected. "From the long range point of view," stated the governor, "it would be advisable for governments of all kinds to set up in times of prosperity what might be called a nest egg to be used for public works in times of depression. That is a policy which we should initiate when we get back to good times."[15] "If we had brains in this country," stated Governor Roosevelt's own industrial commissioner, Frances Perkins, less than a year earlier in a public address, "we would have had a long-range plan of public works." The blueprints for construction projects, she argued, should have been on the desks of governors all across the nation in December of 1929.[16]

This suggestion proved particularly galling to President Hoover. He responded to Governor Roosevelt in a speech delivered from Cleveland two days later. He noted that in the matter of the proposed "nest egg," Roosevelt "either ignores or is ignorant of the fact that as far back as 1922 we developed the idea of making use of public works to assist in the stabilization of employment in times of depression and laid the foundation for its operation." (For a 2012 recommendation of this idea, see note.)[17] The nest egg idea was one he had long before propounded. As secretary of commerce under Warren Harding in 1922, Hoover labored to prevent the spending of hundreds of millions of dollars appropriated for federal construction projects. The money had been budgeted in 1921 when the nation was in the throes of a severe recession. In the recovery of 1922 he had argued that the funds should be set aside in anticipation of a future economic downturn. Later in the decade he advocated for a $3 billion reserve fund for previously approved projects that would be activated when certain indexes seemed to suggest a looming period of stagnation.[18]

This anticipatory policy, which Hoover encouraged state and local governments to adopt, is one of a wide array of efforts that lend some credence to those who point out the fact that the defamed Hoover was not entirely a prisoner of classical economic thought. As commerce secretary in 1927, he appointed a Committee on Recent Economic Changes that issued a report—"Consumption and the Standard of Living"—that emphasized the role public policy needed to play in the maintenance of suitable levels of mass purchasing power.[19]

One of Hoover's first acts to counter the Depression, to the chagrin of Andrew Mellon, his treasury secretary, was to reject the orthodox view that a reduction in wage levels was a necessary corrective development. Meeting with leaders of American industry in December of 1929, Hoover extracted a pledge—short-lived though it may have been—to hold the line on any reduction in pay. Hoover placed Col. Arthur Woods of New York in charge of the president's Emergency Committee for Employment. Woods was advised by the famous public relations guru Edward L. Bernays, who undertook a radio and newspaper campaign to spread the notion far and wide that it was morally incumbent upon large corporations to maintain their workforce and keep wages intact. (Of course, if nominal wage rates were maintained in a deflationary economy it would mean that real wages were increasing.) The degree to which this campaign proved efficacious in sustaining wages is difficult to discern. As Ben Bernanke has pointed out, the belief in "wage stickiness" in the face of deflation is "consistent with the Keynesian tradition" and might have occurred to some extent despite any action taken by President Hoover. The issue is further complicated by the fact that in 1929–1932 real wages in Germany were falling as its economy experienced a severe decline, while real wage increases in Britain coincided with its recovery. This would tend to indicate that there were forces at play that were far more vital than wage levels. The fact that Hoover contributed to the severity of the economic crisis, however, by preventing the corrective influence of declining labor costs, continues to be an article of faith among conservative critics. This, along with his notorious increase in tariff rates (the injurious impact of which, as discussed below, quite a few economists now believe has been significantly overstated), led to the widespread conviction that Hoover, as journalist Walter Lippmann observed at the time, was both "inactive" and "meddlesome."[20] This mixed assessment lingers to this day.

Hoover did indeed attempt to disassociate himself from what he termed the "economic fatalists," positioned to his political right, by reminding these "pessimists" that "exactly the same thing was once said of typhoid, cholera, and smallpox." Certainly his passion for "associationalism" and the role of government as a coordinating agent among business interests resonated with the underlying rationale of what would become the early New Deal's national recovery efforts. Moreover, Hoover's creation of the Federal Farm Board, the Reconstruction Finance Corporation, and the Home Loan Bank Board were suggestive of the agencies that would soon emerge under FDR. Historian Ellis Hawley has perhaps substantially understated the distinctions between the two administrations by labeling the New Deal as merely "Hooverism in high gear." He legitimately observes, however, that the Hooverites were clearly "not the laissez-faire fundamentalists excoriated in New Deal rhetoric."[21]

In the fall of 1932, however, as the presidential campaign drew to a close, it was not legislative innovations but rather fiscal prudence that appeared to be the prescribed bipartisan bromide. In an effort to close the budgetary gap and "restore confidence," President Hoover and the Democratic Congress passed on June 6 the Revenue Act of 1932. In addition to a significant increase in the marginal tax rates on personal income, it raised estate, corporate, and nearly all existing excise taxes on items such as tobacco and theater tickets. (It is important to keep in mind that until 1943 there was no withholding tax. The increased payment of income tax, therefore, was not due until March of 1933, after FDR had become president.) In addition, it created a whole array of new taxes, including ones on gasoline, tires, and lubricating oil.[22]

In October, to ensure that budgeting accountability would, in fact, come to fruition, a number of the nation's most prestigious citizens, of both political persuasions, formed the Economy League (not to be confused with the anti–New Deal American Liberty League founded in August of 1934). Included among its members were Al Smith, Elihu Root, and Gen. John Pershing. As chairman of the league, Rear Adm. Richard Byrd publicly read a statement signed by members of his advisory council. "In two decades we have seen the cost of government rise from about $3,000,000,000 to about $14,000,000,000," it warned after this ominous display of zeros. "The general public," it concluded, "will find itself in a condition of servitude unless government costs are reduced." Indeed, the *New York Times*, in a threatening headline, quoted the league's admonition that "anarchy" was the clear alternative to such austerity.[23]

Any account of this resolute faith in fiscal austerity as the necessitous path to economic renewal would prove remiss if it failed to note that this was a course of action annunciated across the globe. The self-proclaimed socialist premier of France, Joseph Paul-Boncour, announced in 1933 that all plans for his nation's future would prove bootless if they failed to eliminate a looming budget deficit. The Japanese finance minister made a similar assessment in 1930, warning that the government's viability depended upon fiscal soundness;

so stated the inflation-obsessed rulers of Czechoslovakia, the fascist Getúlio Vargas of Brazil, and the finance minister of Republican Spain, Jaime Carner. The latter responded to an inquiry about his most desirous governmental objective by offering up three: "a balanced budget, a balanced budget, and a balanced budget." And closer to home, few embraced the imperative need for spending cuts and tax increases as strenuously as the Canadian government of Prime Minister William Mackenzie King. He was then defeated at the polls in 1930 by the even more conservative R. B. Bennett, who, as his biographer noted, was a veritable "rock of Gibraltar" on fiscal balance until he proposed a belated Canadian New Deal in 1935. Alas, even Sweden failed to completely sever its tether to traditional notions of fiscal prudence.[24]

"Starvation and Dire Need"

In a remark that will set the tone for the remainder of the New Deal, FDR asserts that there are human needs that may well trump fiscal responsibility.

Although politicians of both parties kowtowed to the league's dire admonishment, Franklin Roosevelt, it seems, was determined to set an unassailable standard of fiscal prudence. He boasted in his radio address on October 13, 1932, that he led the way for New York to become the first state to funnel money to localities for unemployment relief; he proposed funding this generous outlay with a *doubling of the state's income tax*.[25] Three days after the Economy League's pronouncement, he dispatched a letter to veterans' activist Dominick DeLucco of Hartford, Connecticut, explaining that the unsettled state of the budget precluded the early payment of bonus benefits. On this matter he was now publicly on record as siding with Herbert Hoover. "Let me remind you," he wrote to the disenchanted veteran, "that a nation is like a family—it cannot spend more than it receives without going bankrupt." As if to emphasize his determination in this regard, Roosevelt concluded his missive by pledging that his administration would slash federal expenditures by a stunning 25 percent immediately upon assuming office. The *New York Times* published the letter on October 18.[26]

The very next day, at a rally at Pittsburgh's Forbes Field, the Democratic nominee reiterated his rash budgetary goal and the unfortunate necessity of denying premature cash bonuses to veterans. (FDR would remain steadfast in this position until Congress overrode his veto of the payment in 1936.)[27] "I regard reduction in Federal spending as one of the most important issues in this campaign. In my opinion," he continued, "it is the most direct and effective contribution that Government can make to business." FDR then lashed out yet again at the Hoover administration's maladroit handling of fiscal matters, intoning, "Now my friends, I am going to give you a real shock. Instead of the estimated deficit of $150,000,000, the [actual] deficit on June 30, 1932, for two years was $3,750,000,000." To help rectify this startling imbalance, Roosevelt, anticipating the imminent ratification of the Twenty-First Amendment, advocated a tax on beer to produce several hundred million dollars of revenue. The next morning the "bonus, budget and beer speech," as it was dubbed, became the lead story in most of the nation's newspapers. The banner headline in the *New York Times* exclaimed:

> ROOSEVELT OPPOSES CASH BONUS NOW;
> URGES BEER TAX TO BALANCE BUDGET

It was, as intended, a powerful statement of fiscal discipline. Franklin Roosevelt would reject increased spending and increase taxation. Those in attendance at Forbes Field that evening, and the diligent readers who pursued the story to page nineteen, however, discovered Roosevelt's oration contained this rather important proviso:

> If starvation and dire need on the part of any of our citizens make necessary the appropriation of additional funds, which would keep the budget out of balance, I shall not hesitate to tell the American people the full truth and recommend to them the expenditure of this additional amount.[28]

Interestingly, many of the nation's smaller newspapers, such as Santa Monica, California's *Evening Outlook* and Connecticut's *Hartford Courant*, while taking note of the rejection of veterans' bonuses and the proposals for balanced budgets and beer taxes, made no mention whatsoever of the potential altering nature of "starvation" and "dire need."[29]

Although never explicit about the parameters of the "New Deal," FDR's campaign rhetoric did contain some clear-cut proposals. He supported, for example, some form of federal aid for unemployment insurance, a lowered tariff, and a vigorous public utilization of hydroelectric power.[30] For the most part, however, his offer of "bold, persistent experimentation," and his vow to use the might of the federal government for the benefit of the "forgotten man at the bottom of the economic pyramid," although vague, seemed sufficiently inspirational to a desperate nation. His election victory over President Hoover in November was overwhelming, winning forty-one states and more than 57 percent of the popular vote.

An acute observer of that 1932 election might have understandably anticipated a schizophrenic application of governing principles. This uncertainty was heightened perhaps with the publication of *Looking Forward*, a compilation of FDR's articles and speeches that was released the same week as his inaugural, in March of 1933; *Looking Forward* went to the top of the nation's best-seller lists and required a fourth printing in its first month in publication. The book was so popular that MGM, with FDR's permission, changed the name of an inspirational Depression film that premiered in April of 1933 to *Looking Forward* and inserted a quote from the book in the movie's opening.[31] The New Deal planned, said the newly elected president in the pages of *Looking Forward*, to place the "relations between government and business" in a "process of redefinition during the coming years." There was a clearly stated intention to insure the unemployed, end "old age want," and "bring about a wiser, more equitable distribution of the national wealth."[32]

Coursing through the entirety of the book, however, was a rather sober reality: "Hard necessity drives us now." The title of the book played upon the famed *Looking Backward*, Edward Bellamy's utopian work of 1889. The future held, FDR affirmed, not the ease and comfort of life unveiled in *Looking Backward*'s resplendent America of 2000, but rather a "long and arduous" process of transformation; and it all demanded that revenue equal expenditures. To be sure, farmers must receive adequate prices for their labor, but whatever plan was adopted to achieve this end must "finance itself." It amounted to a "sacred obligation" to their children and grandchildren, he informed the country, "to hand over to them cities, villages, counties, states and a nation which will not be a series of millstones about their necks."[33]

As the presidential campaign of 1932 unfolded, William Randolph Hearst's Hollywood production company was filming *Gabriel Over the White House*. Hearst, who was then an avid Roosevelt supporter, made the film available for FDR to view before his inaugural; the president-elect is reported to have suggested a number of changes.[34] In the film, an uninspired president—something of a cross between the worst features of Warren Harding and Calvin Coolidge—is divinely inspired, after he is badly injured in a car crash, by a visitation from the archangel Gabriel. The chief executive, played by Walter Huston, then assumes the temporary role of a benevolent dictator who sets out to realize a progressive agenda of social reform. A president who previously deemed unemployment—and virtually every other problem brought to his attention—a "local matter," now informs a mass gathering of unemployed men that he will offer them a place in an "army of construction" until the "wheels of industry begin to turn again," at which time they will be gradually "retired to private employment." To a disbelieving cabinet secretary who disapproves of his actions, the president responds, "This is War! The enemy is starvation." Yet, even this cinematic leader, intent upon such far-reaching social goals, pays homage in the film to the essential need for a balanced budget.[35] "The inescapable consequences of debt," the president lectures an assemblage of foreign dignitaries, "is that it must be repaid." As his government is attempting to balance the budget, he informs them, so must they.[36]

One wonders how many moviegoers in March of 1933 considered how the new president was to engage upon massive public works projects, as well as a host of other humanitarian pursuits, and manage to balance the federal budget.

Saving the Rich

The unknown Marriner Eccles appears in Washington to argue for a policy of "logical radicalism," a phrase that is central to his New Deal advocacy.

On January 4 of that year, exactly two months before President-elect Roosevelt's inauguration, the United States Senate passed a resolution directing the Committee on Finance "to make an investigation and study of the present economic problems of the United States." The committee was authorized to obtain the views of economists, financiers, and "other persons" who, in the members' opinion, "may be able to offer constructive suggestions with respect to the solution of such problems." The resolution was initiated by Senator Bryan Patton "Pat" Harrison of Mississippi. A conservative Democrat, Harrison's seniority meant that he would assume the chairmanship of the Finance Committee from Republican Reed Smoot as a consequence of the 1932 election, which had placed the Senate under control of the Democrats. (The Democrats had previously gained a House majority in 1930.) Harrison was hoping to ward off any radical economic solutions and light the prudential road to recovery for Roosevelt's administration by furnishing a sounding board for rational financial leaders and captains of industry.[37] The transcript of the hearings provides a valuable tool for gauging the mindset of the nation's most influential citizens in the days immediately preceding FDR's ascension to the presidency.

The first witness to appear before the committee was celebrated financier and former head of the War Industries Board Bernard Baruch. A loyal son of South Carolina and the Democratic Party, Baruch was something of a Wall Street legend. Although a Democrat, he was viewed as one who stood above the political fray, and was considered something of an authority on everything from mining and railroads to agriculture and international relations. It seemed quite understandable, therefore, that his counsel would be sought before all others.[38]

The imperious "adviser to Presidents" cautioned the senators at the outset that his lengthy testimony should not be interrupted by questions until he had concluded. What caused the Depression, Baruch insisted—an assertion that found widespread approbation in the course of the hearings—was the "inflation, debt, taxes and national self-containment" engendered by the Great War. While he observed that the present condition of the country "has been said to be like war," it was "worse than war." The insidious enemy they had to confront, he continued, was "everywhere, even within us." For the proponents of what was soon to be known as deficit financing, desirous of high governmental expenditures and low taxation, Baruch's orthodox exhortation was nothing short of calamitous. "No nation is living within its income now and the money of all is unsound and suspect," he said. If there were a single banner under which they must march, Baruch advised, it would be: "*Balance the Budgets of the World!*" They must slash government spending, "cut it as rations are cut in a siege," he implored, and "tax—tax everybody for everything." (He would later cease to analogize the Depression with war believing that it allowed a rationale for reckless spending.) Only such fiscal sacrifice could restore business confidence and "take the hungry man off the world's pavement and let him smile again."[39]

A sampling of the testimony of those who followed Baruch provides some appreciation of the pervasiveness of this line of thought.

Henry Haskell, editor of the Kansas City Star: "I have found everywhere strong approval for the suggestion to invest the President with almost dictatorial powers to balance the budget."[40]

Edward Duffield, president of the Prudential Life Insurance Company: "I do not question that, speaking generally, every member of Congress agrees with me as to the necessity and desirability of balancing the budget . . . people need confidence." The Depression, Duffield asserted, should be allowed to run its course with government providing only emergency relief to keep people from starving. "We have grown so accustomed to expect government to provide," he stated dejectedly.[41]

P. W. Litchfield, president of Goodyear Tire & Rubber Company: The cause of the Depression, said Litchfield, "might properly be lumped together under the embracing title of extravagance."[42]

Myron Taylor, chairman of the United States Steel Corporation: "If the government would put its own house in order as an example to the community, balance its budget and live within its income, it would go a long way towards reviving public confidence." Why then, asked the incredulous Senator Robert La Follette, was there no semblance of restored confidence the previous spring when the president, Congress, and the American people were under the false impression that the budget had been placed in balance? "It seems to me that the simple rules that we apply in our own lives are those to apply here," Taylor responded, ignoring the question while employing what economists would come to ruefully label the "fallacy of composition"—assuming what is true for a part is equally true of the whole. "When our resources begin to shrink," Taylor cautioned, both a family and a nation must "live more simply."[43]

H. C. Dickenson, president of the Society of Automotive Engineers: "The underlying cause leading to all national disasters, such as those of Rome and Spain and Europe, during the dark ages," Dickenson informed the committee, had developed from the burden of debt that had "reached such dimensions that savings of business were all absorbed in the payment of returns on capital."[44]

David Franklin Houston, president of Mutual Life Insurance Company: That the First World War caused the Depression "seems obvious," Houston maintained. "It would be offensive to the intelligence of the committee to dwell on the need for a balanced budget."[45]

Perhaps to establish the semblance of balance, some spokesmen of labor and farm organizations were invited. Of the forty-six individuals who testified before the Senate Finance Committee, only six were so affiliated. Even some of these witnesses joined the balance-the-budget bandwagon. Master of the National Grange, L. J. Taper, while lamenting the nation's "maldistribution of wealth," acknowledged that his organization believed in "the reduction of the expenses of the government." Farm spokesman George Peek, while citing the disturbing decline in farm income, highlighted the need to reduce local, state, and federal budgets.[46]

Not surprisingly, the real point of contention in the hearings was between the "sound money men" and the "inflationists." Advocacy of the latter position and the need to balance government budgets, however, were not mutually exclusive. Howard University economist Herman Arendtz, while detailing the wondrous benefits to be derived from the remonetization of silver, emphasized the need to cut government expenses and bring the budgets into balance.[47]

With few exceptions, the mantra of fiscal prudence droned on for a full two weeks.

One of the last to be summoned before the Finance Committee was Marriner S. Eccles. As he strode to the witness table in a purposeful manner, Washington, D.C., got its first glimpse of a figure who would soon gain prominence upon the political stage and remain as an influential player upon it for the next two decades. That morning, however, other than the fact that he was a Mormon banker from Utah, not a single member of the committee knew the slightest detail about him, how he had managed to obtain an invitation to testify, or what he was expected to say. With his black hair slicked back atop his wiry frame, he displayed all the characteristics of a finishing nail. As his one distinguishing feature—a physical manifestation of his independence from the eastern establishment—he sported a bolo tie. He was impersonal, cantankerous, intense, unflinching, and, by his own admission, wholly immodest.

He structured his opening remarks to deflect any notion that his statement was in the least bit theoretical. He was Marriner S. Eccles of Ogden, Utah, he told them. He was a banker and president of the First Security Corporation, the first bank holding company in the nation; president of the Utah Construction Company, one of the Six Companies, a joint venture presently constructing the Boulder Dam; he was president of the Stoddard Lumber Company, the Amalgamated Sugar Company, and a director of the Salt Lake branch of the Reconstruction Finance Corporation. He was a man of business.[48]

"It is incomprehensible," Eccles lectured the members of the committee, that the American people should continue to suffer from a depression that the federal government could end. "We shall either adopt a plan which will meet this situation under capitalism, or a plan will be adopted for us which will operate without capitalism," he said. "We have done nothing in the last three years?" interjected Senator Thomas Walsh, a conservative Democrat from Massachusetts. "I think not," was Eccles's tart reply.

He then suggested a program he would term "logical radicalism." The plan was designed to pump billions of dollars into the American economy. He called for the federal government to furnish half a billion dollars to the states in the remainder of 1933 on a per capita basis to assist with unemployment. He called for $2.5 billion—and far more if unemployment remained unacceptably high—to be funneled to state and local governments for public works in 1933 alone. He called for billions to be spent implementing a domestic allotment program to pay farmers so agricultural production could be regulated, although he insisted it must not be financed by regressive taxation. He proposed as much as $5 billion be granted to the Federal Land Banks to reduce both interest and principal payments on farm mortgages. "Where does the Federal Government get this money to give to the states?" inquired an incredulous Senator Thomas Gore of Oklahoma. "Where," shot back Eccles, "did it get $27 billion during the war to waste?" At a few points, it seemed clear that some members of the committee were unaware that Eccles was proposing deficit financing. "Isn't it true," asked Senator Walsh, "that such payments can be made only by imposing the hardship of increased taxation upon the American people?" "No, they would not pay now," insisted Eccles, invoking the cardinal principle of what he termed compensatory economics, "There are times to borrow and there are times to pay." Now, he affirmed, was the time to borrow.

Although some of those who testified before the committee suggested that the Allied war debt owed the United States should be reduced, Hoover had announced a holiday on the payment to the United States by the Allies if they suspended German reparations; Eccles advised it would be preferable to cancel the debts altogether. "What?!" shouted Senator James Shortridge of California, "Cancel all those debts?" Eccles went on to explain that since the Allies did not have the gold with which to pay—the United States, he pointed out, owned 40 percent of the world's supply—and since restrictive tariff policies made it difficult to sell their products abroad, they simply did not have the financial wherewithal to meet this obligation; to demand its fulfillment merely exacerbated the world's economic turmoil, he argued. To make the case for cancellation of this debt to an American public clamoring for its payment, he acknowledged, would require some element of political courage; such courage, he informed the esteemed members of the Finance Committee without, it seems, the slightest degree of conciliation, was clearly lacking.

The Utah businessman concluded his testimony with an appeal for "national child labor, minimum wage, unemployment insurance and old age pension laws" and high-income and inheritance taxes to control capital accumulations. "Such measures as I have proposed may frighten those of our people who possess wealth," Eccles acknowledged. And yet, he insisted, "This is not soaking the rich, it is saving the rich." Moreover, he stated indignantly, "It is a national disgrace that such suffering should be permitted in this, the wealthiest country in the world."[49]

The following day Eccles's hometown paper, the *Ogden Standard-Examiner*, proudly extolled his remarks and took note of how "refreshing" it was to have "one of our bankers take a position so bold and positive for a change in our capitalistic system . . . to assure the nation against these repeated cycles of inflation and depression which are so destructive and are productive of so much misery." The *New York Times*, however, interpreted his comments differently, and reported on page two of its financial section that a "young Utah banker" had urged a "broad program of socialization" before the Finance Committee. The article went on to state that the witness "apparently irritated some members of the committee."[50]

The reporter also observed that the intensely focused businessman smiled when he announced, "I am a capitalist." It must have occurred to more than a few readers of the *Times* that morning—understandably—that these were peculiar views for a Republican banker from Utah. What, one imagines many of them contemplating, might explain it?

2

TO SET THE WORLD ARIGHT

Adam Smith in His Soul

Eccles's father instills in his son an appreciation for the majesty of American capitalism. But David Eccles's claim on "self-made" manhood is tempered by assistance from the Mormon Church.

In the spring of 1910, David Eccles wrote to his son in Scotland. He was delighted that Marriner was "feeling the spirit of the Lord," and that he appeared to be enjoying his Mormon missionary work. In a subsequent letter to his parents, just before requesting the financial "where-with" that would allow him to set off with a Mormon friend on a visit to Ireland, Marriner described how deeply he relished the rather raucous gatherings of citizens on Glasgow's green. His proselytizing method was to wait until some other speaker had assembled a sizable crowd and then leap into oratorical fray at some propitious moment. "I put my tracks on the ground," he wrote, "and laid my silk hat on them and started to preach."[1]

Before the conclusion of Marriner's two-year mission, David Eccles joined him for a time in Glasgow. It was a nostalgic visit for his multimillionaire father. In his childhood, David had wandered the streets of his native home in dire poverty. While touring the city with him, Marriner was more keenly appreciative than ever that his father's transformation was as quintessential an American rags-to-riches saga as one is likely to encounter.[2]

Born in 1849, in what was arguably the most abject slum in all of Europe—the Kacadens area of Glasgow—David Eccles joined his siblings in the workforce at the tender age of eight. While the Eccles children labored in coal mines and factories, their principal task was to hawk the kitchen utensils that their blind father fashioned on a wooden lathe. Thus, through the sporadic sale of wooden potato mashers and rolling pins, the grim and very real prospect of starvation was held meekly at bay. To further supplement the family earnings,

David learned how to purchase trinkets at a wholesale outlet and sell them throughout Glasgow at a 100 percent markup, thereby displaying, while still a child, a rough-hewn business prowess; it was a facility for the cleverness that a free market demanded, an ability that would last the remainder of his life.

In 1863 the Eccles clan came into contact with American missionaries from the Church of Jesus Christ of Latter-day Saints. Less persuaded, perhaps, by the nature of the gospel of "continuous revelation" than the certainty that any existence would be a profound improvement upon their dire circumstances, the family members consented to migrate to the "state of Deseret" adjacent to Great Salt Lake. Their passage would be paid for by the church's Perpetual Emigration Fund, which the recipients, once settled, were expected to refund. The Eccleses—seven children and two adults—made the journey to the shores of America in the nearly airless hold of a ship with no water for bathing and no toilet facilities. The only food available was what they had managed to carry aboard themselves. They were forced to sleep upon this supply at night to keep it from the ravenous rats that scurried throughout the vessel. Scurvy and communicable diseases ravaged the voyagers, making sea burials a nearly daily occurrence. After six weeks of horrific hardship, David Eccles disembarked at Castle Gardens in the battery of Manhattan on July 1, 1863, as the first day of the battle at Gettysburg was raging. He was fourteen years of age, malnourished, penniless, and illiterate.[3]

Upon arrival in Utah, the family was assigned, wrote Marriner, by the "central planning agency" of the Mormon Church to a nearby uninhabited canyon some fifteen miles east of Ogden. Allocated sixty acres, the Eccles family members found they needed to hastily master the skills of farm life. They soon discovered that they had merely exchanged the precarious life of the Glasgow slums for the even more dangerous challenge of the American wilderness. In their second winter in Utah, they narrowly avoided starvation when David dragged a sled loaded with unground wheat through fifteen miles of waist-deep snow to a miller. On the return journey of two days he nearly froze to death while sleeping in the snow. Also that winter, one of the Eccleses' two oxen died. The remaining ox was brought into their log cabin to ensure its survival. Before the winter concluded, every member of the family had ripped open their straw mattresses to provide the beast with feed. The family was fortunate to be alive in the spring of 1865.

David Eccles was hardly content with mere survival. "The Adam Smith in his soul," Marriner would one day write of him, "wanted hard cash." While his family left the wilds of their isolated canyon for the safety of Ogden, David journeyed to Oregon where he obtained work as a lumberjack and learned the rudiments of the logging business. In his early twenties, he obtained his own logging contract and from that moment on, he never again lived a day in poverty, never again worked for another man, and never borrowed another cent. Employing his acute and innate business instincts, he branched out into everything from banking and insurance to railroads, sugar refining, and construction. At the time of his death in 1912, he was the president of eighteen companies and a prominent director of nine others. The poor boy from Glasgow was an American millionaire many times over.[4]

David Eccles, unlike most Mormons, was also a polygamist. At the age of twenty-six, he married Bertha Marie Jenson who would bear him six sons and six daughters. This family came to be identified as the "Ogden Eccleses." Ten years after taking his first wife, he defied federal law and took a second. In 1885, with federal officials swarming throughout the state to crack down on polygamy, he married Ellen Stoddard in Logan, Utah. Ellen would give birth to nine more children. The first of these "Logan Eccleses" was Marriner Stoddard, born in September 1890 and named after an apostle of the church who had officiated at his parents' marriage.[5]

The eldest child of David's second marriage was imbued from early childhood with his father's firm belief in hard work, thrift, and self-denial. David was convinced, as evidenced by his own life experience, that if a child was eventually to enter the world of business, formal or prolonged education was of slight worth. What was of inestimable value was the exposure of children to gainful employment. To provide such edification, and to eschew the noxious vices of "idleness" and "high living," Marriner was put to work at the age of eight. From that year on, when not in school, he worked ten hours a day, six days a week, in one of his father's enterprises. His first job was carting boxes for a factory that was a part of the Oregon Lumber Company for five cents an hour. That same year his father presented the eight-year-old with his first business proposition. If he managed to save $100, he would be awarded one hundred shares of Oregon Lumber stock at its par value. Three summers later, in the proudest moment of his childhood, he was awarded the stock after he had saved the requisite amount. "Son, you are now a capitalist," pronounced his father, "because you have saved more money than you have spent."[6] Indeed, an abiding financial principle that David instilled in his son was the necessity to scrupulously avoid debt. He was particularly proud of the fact that he furnished his own capital needs without ever turning—as so many western interests did—to eastern bankers to sustain business ventures.[7]

Young Marriner's maturation as a full-fledged capitalist coincided with the emergence of the Progressive movement upon the American scene. His father, of course, had "no ear," Marriner reflected, for "voices that spoke of dangers inherent in the concentration of productive forces in fewer and fewer hands." The admonishments of the New Nationalism and the New Freedom left his father slightly aghast. "He saw no reason why other men could not or should not recreate themselves in his image, providing of course, they were left free to use their wits and will without government interference."[8]

In his autobiographical reflections on his father's passion for rugged individualism, however, Eccles makes no mention of the fact that David arrived in Utah at a time when the Mormon Church was encouraging cooperative networks and "wished to guard against the development," writes historian Leonard J. Arrington, "of a moneyed class among the Latter-day Saints themselves which would rend the social fabric and destroy cohesion and unity."[9] Members of the church leadership, it seems, were hardly adherents of a process of creative destruction. They were quite willing to "take hold" of a fledgling business and support it out of tithing resources until those engaged in the industry were capable of making a successful go of it. It is wonderfully ironic that the sugar beet industry, from which both David and Marriner would gain significant wealth, owed its initial capital investment and development to the central planning efforts of the church government.[10] Of course, the hostility that enveloped Mormonism from its founding in New York through its turbulent sojourns in Ohio, Missouri, and Illinois produced an economic life that developed somewhat apart from the economic and social environment of the 1830s and 1840s, and would have necessarily placed a greater premium upon cooperative endeavors. "The social ideal of Mormonism," notes Lowell Bennion, in his analysis of the business ethic of world religions, "is the law of consecration or 'united order' in which surplus property and earnings are held in common to be distributed according to the needs of the individual." It seems clear, however, that traditional economic individualism was predominant by the time Marriner Eccles entered the world of business in Utah. A history student at the University of Illinois, who composed a master's thesis under Marriner Eccles's "supervision" in 1950, wrote that it would be an "interesting speculation" to consider how his views about the interplay of government and business "may have been influenced by a study of Mormon history, especially the careful planning of early Mormon leaders in Utah." One can only wonder why he simply did not abandon the need for "speculation" and directly question Eccles about such influence.[11] It was not a matter that Eccles explored in his autobiography and may not have been an issue he wished to discuss with a graduate student.

Also missing from his memoir is any discussion of his personal sense of religiosity, or lack thereof. Other than a reference to the fact that he enjoyed an alcoholic beverage from time to time, there is no information divulged to assist in discerning his standing in the Mormon Church.

Marriner's empirical business training under his father's tutelage culminated when, at the age of nineteen, he was placed in charge of the commissary for a large construction project. Following his two-year stint as a missionary, during which he met his future wife, May Young, Marriner returned to Utah in 1912. He barely had time to unpack when he was sent by his father to oversee the construction of a hydroelectric power plant ten miles southwest of Logan.[12]

Later that year, shortly after Marriner's twenty-second birthday, David Eccles died of a heart attack. As the eldest of the Logan Ecceses, Marriner became the steward of their interests, and in the process confirmed his father's conviction about the efficacy of advanced education. The following year, while he was still twenty-two, he gained his first experience in banking when the Thatcher Brothers Banking Company made him a director. By the dint of hard work, the exercise of acute business sagacity, the forcefulness of character, and, of course, a careful cultivation of his father's extensive business connections, Marriner would soon find himself at the helm of many of the business concerns over which his father had presided. By the close of the 1920s, Marriner Eccles was not merely the president of the First Security Corporation, he was also president of the Eccles Hotel Company, the Sego Milk Products Company, and the Stoddard Lumber Company; vice president and treasurer of the Amalgamated Sugar Company with assets in the neighborhood of $10 million; president of the Utah Construction Company; and a director of the Utah-Idaho Central Railroad, the Lion Coal Company, the Anderson Lumber Company, the Mountain States Implement Company, the Utah Power and Light Company, and numerous others. He was also the owner of a three-hundred-thousand-acre ranch that contained forty thousand sheep and some twenty-five thousand head of cattle.[13]

For the young Mormon businessman, life was good.

The Pioneer

As an aggressive businessman in the 1920s, Eccles is heralded as an innovative banker. He is publicized as the first to apply a holding-company structure to banking.

In the 1920s, before the shadow of the Great Depression darkened the national landscape, Marriner Eccles, as his father before him, worshiped devoutly at the temple of laissez-faire. On matters of broad economic policy he was content to defer to the great business and financial titans of the East. A member in good standing of the Republican Party, he had with considerable enthusiasm supported the candidacy and election of Herbert Hoover to the presidency in 1928. He could, in the finest Rotary Club tradition, cite a litany of GOP achievements: the large debt from the Great War had been slashed by $7 billion; the economy was growing at a rapid pace; prices were stable and unemployment was exceedingly slight, even though millions had been added to the work force; corporate profits were up by more than 75 percent; and, sans inheritance levies and three reductions in the marginal income rates, taxes were exceptionally low.[14]

The nation's overall good fortune seemed to parallel Eccles's own personal success. In 1925 the thirty-four-year-old businessman and father of three was elected president of the Utah Bankers Association. Three years later he became the initial president of the First Security Corporation, a holding company that owned and operated twenty-eight banks throughout Utah, Idaho, and Wyoming. Essentially a mechanism to circumvent Jacksonian prohibitions on branch banking—a policy that Eccles considered economically inimical—it was the first time such a contrivance was used in the United States in the field of banking and for that reason garnered a good deal of national attention.[15]

In May of 1930 the *New York American* published an article about a "39-year-old pioneer of a new style of group banking in the United States." Eccles explained in some detail the merits of the bank-holding "technique." It combined "centralized guidance and supervision with local self-management of unit banks." In what may not have been an insignificant advantage, centralized supervision gave local loan officers a convenient excuse for "turning down neighbors who made a sentimental appeal." It provided greater liquidity while also improving each bank's diversification. In much of the four-state region in which First Security operated, many of the best borrowers were forced to turn to Chicago banks. This was necessitated by either a lack of resources or laws that prohibited more than 10 percent of a bank's capital from being loaned to a single entity. This could now be circumvented by divvying the loan among the banks in the chain. The article ended by observing that Eccles's bank-holding format would surely sweep the country. One thing is certain: Marriner Eccles was intimately familiar with the various ins and outs of banking.[16]

The article failed to acknowledge, however, the crucial role played by Eccles's younger brother. Like Marriner, George received on-the-job training, working as a teller during his high school years. Quite unlike his brother, ten years his senior, George obtained a stellar higher-level education at Berkeley and then Columbia University where he graduated in 1922. At Columbia he became a student of H. Parker Willis, who, as an economic advisor to Senator Carter Glass, would come to deem Marriner's 1935 banking restructure "the worst and most dangerous measure . . . perhaps at any time in American history." Interestingly, then, in addition to matching his older brother's acumen in formulating the success of First Security Corporation, George would reject his academic indoctrination to enthusiastically embrace the macroeconomic positions Marriner would come to espouse in the 1930s.[17]

In the late 1920s, however, the Eccles brothers would confidently assert that the achievements both they and the country were enjoying were not accidentally or casually acquired, but rather the product of individual initiative, thrift, and a spartan determination. In civic orations that he delivered in these years, Marriner extolled such traits and sounded a note of profound optimism. Clearly, he observed, the panics that had so regularly marred the nation's past were no longer to be feared. Hard work, patience, and the practice of "greater economy in government," he assured his listeners, would usher in an age when the problems of "life and growth" would permanently supplant those of "death and decay."[18]

"Show No Signs of Panic"

Eccles weathers the economic storm. He does so, however, with government assistance from the Reconstruction Finance Corporation and a government contract for the largest construction project in the world.

The downturn that began in the summer of 1929 would strike the nation with a stunning ferocity. The details may scarcely be necessary to state. By the summer of 1932 more than 25 percent of the labor force was unemployed and millions more had their working hours drastically reduced. Steel plants were operating at 12 percent of their capacity. Between 1930 and 1933, a record 7,149 state-chartered banks had failed along with 1,947 that were national banks; they dragged down with them more than nine million savings accounts. Remarkably, 45 percent of all American farm mortgages—comprising 52 percent of the total value of farm mortgage debt—were in delinquent status. In these years real Gross National Product declined by nearly 35 percent. Millions had lost their homes and businesses.[19]

Marriner Eccles's first reaction to the downfall in the nation's economic fortunes was to fight back with all the cold skill and business acumen he could summon in an effort to keep his business interests on sound financial footing. His experiences in these years would have a crucial impact on the policies he would come to advocate in his time in public service. This is especially so in regard to a sanctified banking practice known as the real bills doctrine, a topic that will be explored in the following pages.

One weekend in the summer of 1931 Eccles was informed that his principal banking rival, the Ogden State Bank, had failed and would not reopen its doors that Monday morning. Eccles was by now thoroughly familiar with the mass psychology of bank depositors. The Ogden State Bank was an old and highly esteemed institution and its collapse would most definitely have a ripple effect and lead to a massive run on First Security banks as well. That Sunday he summoned a meeting of officers and directors of his banks. At nine o'clock the following morning, he instructed them, they were to appear at the offices of Ogden State Bank's largest commercial depositors. They were to inform the officials of these businesses that Ogden State Bank had failed and that they were there to offer them First Security's banking services. It was vital, he stressed, for them to channel a large number of these accounts into First Security's coffers.

The next morning Eccles had all the personnel of the savings group meet at eight o'clock and he warned them of the coming storm. "Go about your business as though nothing unusual was happening," Eccles cautioned them. "Smile, be pleasant, talk about the weather, show no signs of panic." Rather than open three teller windows as was customary, all the windows were to be manned every minute of the day. Sandwiches would be brought in and no one was to go to lunch. Then, as he recalls, he gave them the following instructions:

> We can't break this run today. The best we can do is slow it down. People are going to come here to close out their savings accounts. You are going to pay them. But you are going to pay them very slowly. It's the only chance we have to deal with the panic. You know a lot of depositors by sight, and in the past you did not have to look up their signatures, but today when they come here with their deposit books to close out their accounts, you are going to look up every signature card. And take your time about it. And one other thing: when you pay out, don't use any big bills. Pay out in fives and tens, and count slowly. Our object is to pay out a minimum today.[20]

By early morning the lobby of the bank was brimful of anxious depositors. The throng spilled outside and down the street in tense anticipation. The nerves of all became increasingly frayed as the afternoon wore on toward the traditional three o'clock closing. People began to push and shove one another and increasingly one could hear the disconcerting sound of voices raised in anger. Earlier in the day Eccles made an emergency call to the Federal Reserve Bank in Salt Lake City requesting the delivery of additional currency. Just in time the armored car arrived from the Federal Reserve. Eccles would liken the moment to the dramatic and timely arrival of the U.S. Cavalry in some Hollywood western. As the crowd parted to make way for the guards bringing the currency to the nearly depleted vault, Eccles spotted Morgan Craft, the deputy manager of the Salt Lake Federal Reserve who had ridden as a passenger in the armored car to Ogden. Grabbing Craft by the arm, Eccles threaded his way through the lobby to a marble counter. Climbing atop the counter, Eccles raised his hand into the air. "Just a minute!" he shouted. "Just a minute!" The restless swarm of depositors fell to rapt attention. Eccles gazed down upon their worried faces. They had stood in line for hours determined to salvage what was for many the savings of a lifetime. Eccles informed them that the bank would not close at three o'clock but would in fact remain open "just as long as there is anyone who desires to withdraw his deposit or make one." Therefore, he suggested, "you people who have just come in can return later this afternoon or evening if you wish." Surely, he continued, they had all witnessed the arrival of a large amount of currency only moments before. This would take care of all of their requirements, he said, and then added, "There is plenty more where that came from." At that moment Eccles reached down and lifted Craft up to stand upon the countertop beside him. Eccles identified him as an officer of the Federal Reserve and said that he would verify what had just been stated. "Mr. Craft," Eccles said, "say a few words to the folks." Yes, Craft responded, he could verify what Mr. Eccles had just told him. A large amount of currency had indeed just been delivered and, yes, he affirmed that "there is plenty more where that came from."

This was most certainly the truth. The Salt Lake Reserve was overflowing with currency. But as both men were fully aware, not a cent of this plentiful supply belonged to First Security nor did the corporation have access to it. Nevertheless, "in a split instant," said Eccles, "the faces before me relaxed in relief." As numerous people withdrew from the lines, one could hear the reassuring buzz that made its way to the assembled depositors outside. "They are going to stay open, they are going to stay open." Disaster had been temporarily averted.

At the close of the day, Eccles assembled his staffers once again and provided them with new instructions:

> Now listen. A lot of people who have been at work will only hear about this run for the first time when they get home tonight. Tomorrow there will be the makings of another crush, and we are going to meet it by doing the opposite of what we did today. Instead of opening at ten, we are going to open at eight. Nobody is going to have to wait outside of the bank to start any sort of line. When people come in here, pay them very fast. Don't dawdle over signatures. Pay out the accounts in big bills. Above all, don't let any line form. It will mean a continuation of the panic.[21]

The following day, Tuesday, many people came into the lobby of the bank and, observing no evidence of a panic, turned and left. However, the bank would actually pay out more money than it had on Monday, but the run was over and the bank survived. "I thanked God," he said, "for the nerves I had inherited from my father and mother."[22]

Eccles's dramatic moment atop the counter in his bank's lobby conjures the cinematic George Bailey calming distraught depositors in *It's a Wonderful Life*. It played upon the classic tale of the "animal spirited" panic that emptied the vaults of essentially sound institutions and furthered a domino effect of financial ruin. It is a scene deeply ingrained in the American historical memory, and as Eccles must surely have known, it depicts a sequence that, for the most part, never really occurred. When Eccles's staffers at the Federal Reserve examined the cascade of bank failures that had engulfed the nation only a few years before, they discovered that the turmoil did not originate with the average small depositor. Lauchlin Currie, the assistant director of research who would play such an important role in Eccles's career, reported that contrary to the "popular impression" their investigation revealed "that in bank after bank the damage had been done by large withdrawals by people with inside information considerably before the final runs started." In his memoir Currie went on to lament: "This abuse of trust by directors and their friends is not a pretty chapter in American financial history."[23] Indeed, a careful reading of Eccles's account of the 1931 banking crisis in Utah largely substantiates Currie's finding. It was, he wrote in *Beckoning Frontiers*, often large "commercial accounts" engaging in what he termed a "concealed run," rather than panicked individuals, that "hastened the collapse of countless country banks."[24]

Eccles often noted that his business interests survived the economic turmoil in relatively fine fashion. Not a single depositor in any of the First Security Corporation banks, he often stated proudly, would lose a cent in the course of the Depression. One of his loan officers would describe his banks as "run on the most conservative basis," and that Eccles himself was "as a disciple of the gospel of big reserves and a high degree of liquidity." Moreover, the Eccles brothers "shunned conspicuous consumption in their style of life," wrote Sidney Hyman, and "insisted on strict budgetary and accounting procedures" to track every dollar that emerged from their institutions. The fact that he was able to weather the economic turmoil unscathed was a significant component of his allure when Marriner entered the public spotlight. Typical of the many portrayals of him that appeared in the press when he was appointed to the Fed was a February 1935 *Fortune* piece that praised his ability to bring his banks through the Depression unharmed, and a *Time* article that same month that commended him as a banker "who has made and kept a fortune in his own right." In point of fact, however, contrary to some of his statements, a number of Eccles's banks received a significant amount of assistance from the federal government's Reconstruction Finance Corporation.[25]

Indeed, some of his concerns would thrive in the early 1930s. In 1930 the Utah Construction Company (Eccles had become its president) was awarded the principal contract for the building of Boulder Dam. The company was part of a syndicate called the Six Companies; W. A. Bechtel was its president and Henry Kaiser its public relations chief. Congress gave its approval of the massive project a full year before the advent of the Depression. The contract was awarded in 1930 and construction began in March of 1931.[26]

"True Optimism" to "Economic Catastrophe"

A nation that had not experienced a prolonged depression in decades transits from confidence to deep gloom in 1931.

The country began 1931 with a general display of confidence. As Benjamin Bernanke has explained, by the end of 1930 the downturn began to flatten out and although it had been severe, it was comparable to the short-lived recession of 1920–1922, and "it would have been reasonable to expect a brisk recovery, just as in 1922."[27]

"No one disputes the certainty of eventual recovery," wrote A. D. Noyes, the financial editor of the *New York Times*, wrote on New Year's Day. "All economic history settles that." Citing the "absolute soundness of the American currency" and the fact that "money is easier on Wall Street than at any time in twenty-two years," the front-page editorial prophesied that recovery could not be far distant. While acknowledging that the government had indeed been profligate, Noyes reminded his readers that the Treasury was already taking "in sail" and "until this present fiscal year there had been no actual deficit in public revenue since the war." He concluded the piece by stating that "nobody in or out of Wall Street entertains the least doubt of eventual and complete reversal of the present economic trend."[28]

The pages of the *Times* that New Year's Day abounded with auspicious prognostications confirming Noyes's assessment. One article discussed how all twelve Federal Reserve districts had just filed optimistic reports. The same page contained a story about Wall Street movers and shakers expressing great optimism. On the following page was a piece about how very positive the presidents of major corporations were. Two pages later, there appeared a full-page advertisement by the Loyalty Group, an association of eleven fire insurance companies; atop the advertisement in bold lettering were the words "TRUE OPTIMISM." The copy below it read: "Do not be ashamed of your true optimism, and do not be afraid to express it because you fear some pessimist may ridicule it and tell you that some day he will say 'I told you so.'"[29]

The confidence of business and financial interests were based, to some extent, on the encouraging macroeconomic forecasts of academic economists. Both Irving Fisher at Yale and the Harvard Economic Service used the 1920 downturn as an indicator of imminent revival. In both 1920–1921 and 1929–1930 real GNP declined by 10 percent. That there were significant distinctions between these two events—Peter Temin, for example, identifies the latter decline as sparked by a "failure in aggregate demand" rather than a mere "shift of demand" that took place a decade earlier—were left for future economists to explore.[30]

Nor was this auspiciousness confined to New York City's financial interests. When Youngstown, Ohio, mayor Joseph Heffernan predicted that the Depression could take five years to run its course, local business leaders ridiculed him. Heffernan's suggestion that a $1 million bond issue be passed for unemployment relief was met with chastisement by an influential newspaper which stated that the Depression would be over before such relief was needed. The voters of Youngstown agreed with that assessment and defeated the bond issue in November of 1930. "Thus," said Heffernan, in the sobering spring of 1932, "we passed into the early days of 1931—fourteen months after the first collapse—with no relief in sight except that which was provided by orthodox charities."[31]

So confident were many in Congress that the corner had been turned on the economic doldrums that they began to redirect their attention to the perceived threat of impending inflation. In January of 1931, Louis T. McFadden, the chairman of the House Banking and Currency Committee, sounded the alarm that the Federal Reserve's lowering of the discount rate to 3 percent was now providing the economy with excessive stimulus.[32]

The Fed, with little understanding, it seems, of real and nominal interest rates, was certain that it had pursued an easy-money policy and took note of a rise in industrial production and worried about the inflow of gold from Europe. "The Federal Reserve," writes Allan Meltzer, "never discussed using monetary policy to support the modest recovery."[33]

As stated previously, President Hoover refused to request a tax increase to cover revenue shortfalls, so assured was he that the federal coffers would be filled in the course of 1931 by a rejuvenated economy.

That the nation was, in fact, entering a period during which unemployment would remain above, or slightly below, double digits for the entirety of the following decade was simply unimaginable to the vast majority of Americans in January of 1931. This general expectation of imminent improvement can be explained in large part by the fact that there was only a dim recollection in the nation's collective memory of sustained economic turmoil. The prolonged depression of the 1890s occurred before the wheels of financial memory had begun to turn for many Americans. Eccles, for example, was an infant and toddler during its debilitating reign over America. That downturn began in very late 1892 and *unemployment by some estimates reached well over 18 percent in 1894 and did not fall below 10 percent until 1899!*[34]

Such an extended period of economic malaise was certainly not an aberration in American history. The Depression of 1837 was among the longest periods of economic contraction in the nation's history, lasting some seventy-two straight months. The "Great Depression" (as it was then called) of 1873 continued for at least six years, and may have intensified after 1875. (It is indeed sobering to consider that a sixty-five-year-old man who died in 1935 would have spent a quarter of his life living in an economy suffering the pains of economic depression.) Although many older Americans, and those possessed of some sense of economic history, were well aware of these extended periods of economic decline, there was significant confidence that the Federal Reserve System would short-circuit such a drastic reoccurrence.[35] When President Woodrow Wilson signed the Federal Reserve into law in 1913 he lauded its stabilizing abilities. The economic history of the twentieth century appeared to furnish support for such confidence. Not only had the recessions of the previous three decades been short-lived, but in only one, 1921, had the unemployment rate (11.9 percent) risen above 10 percent.[36]

As the year progressed, however, with few signs of economic recovery, the nation became considerably less sanguine. In April of 1931, John Maynard Keynes, who had attained some level of notoriety in the United States for his critical bestseller about the Treaty of Versailles, written more than a decade earlier, delivered a national radio broadcast from London, in which he predicted that there would be no speedy return to prosperity. "The problem of recovery," said the economist, "would be severe." He estimated that it could take five years to overcome the economic slump. "The spokesmen of the business world," he observed, "are not so gay and foolish as they were a year ago."[37] Months earlier, in December of 1930, Keynes published an article in which he described the events of the previous year as "one of the greatest economic catastrophes of modern history." This assessment was beginning to look considerably less hyperbolic.[38]

At the close of 1930, the peculiarly named Bank of United States (it was not allowed to use the name "Bank of *the* United States") was in deep distress. Founded on New York City's East Side, the bank had fifty-seven "affiliates" across the city that served the needs of the garment industry and had, in fact, the largest number of depositors of any bank in the United States. On the night of December 10, an emergency meeting at the offices of the New York Fed failed to arrange a guarantee of the bank's liabilities—it appears it was saddled with far too many bad mortgage loans—and as a consequence no other institution could be persuaded to take it over. At four a.m. the following morning, the conference adjourned with the Bank of United States deemed insolvent and closed by the Fed. Rather remarkably, this decision was reached in the same building, and quite possibly in the very same room, where the determination was made to allow Lehman Brothers to fail some eight decades later in 2008. Some argue that anti-Semitism played a significant role in the refusal of officials to carry out a plan of assistance for the Jewish-owned and operated bank.[39]

In early 1931, the Fed seemed to have successfully managed to avoid a panic among other New York banks. In retrospect, the psychological impact of the BUS failure was clearly underappreciated. A crowd of some twenty thousand had gathered at its Bronx branch when word spread that the institution was in trouble. The high profile of the BUS led to a subtle but steady drain of deposits that, due to a negative multiplier effect—loan portfolios were diminished by as much as three or four dollars for every dollar in withdrawals—led to the loss of billions in bank credit by mid-1931. Shortly before a Senate investigation revealed that the BUS had used its affiliates to take bad loans off its books as a way to foil unfavorable bank examinations.

The banking situation worsened in September of 1931 when the British—the champions of a reconstituted gold standard in the 1920s—abandoned the gold standard. The fear that the United States would follow such a course compelled numerous European governments to convert dollar holdings into gold. The United States witnessed a massive outflow of gold, and within a month from the British abandonment of the gold standard, 522 American banks closed their doors. By the fall of 1931, the economy was clearly nose-diving.[40]

Dissatisfaction with this intensified suffering began to manifest itself in increased and more vehement demands that government at all levels cut expenditures and balance budgets. Numerous state governments displayed diligence in this effort, with Mississippi leading the way by reducing its budget by a full 30 percent, and thus exacerbating the nation's economic catastrophe.[41] This damaging policy was followed by hundreds of relatively large municipal governments. The city of Dallas, for example, took extreme measures to cut its budget by $1 million a year. Not to be outdone in fiscal austerity, Houston created surpluses throughout the 1930s including one of $368,000 in 1935.[42] Remarkably, with massive numbers of his countrymen standing in soup lines and sleeping in doorways, President Hoover informed Congress in his annual address, given on December 9, 1931, in what surely ranks as one of the most insensitive and out-of-touch remarks ever delivered by a political leader in all of American history, that the evidence from the Public Health Service indicated an actual improvement in sickness and general mortality. "No greater proof could be adduced," he informed the ailing country, "that our people have been protected from hunger and cold and that the sense of social responsibility in the Nation has responded to the need of the unfortunate."[43]

The Business Man and the Economist

The public pronouncements of John Maynard Keynes in the early part of the Depression resemble what will become Eccles's newly formed economic catechism.

The enormous human suffering that accompanied the state government cutbacks gave Eccles immense consternation. The parsimonious credit policy and stern collection system his banks were compelled to employ and the layoffs in his lumber mills he was forced to approve caused him guilt and embarrassment.

As a leader of the business community he had come at times to perceive the crisis as almost a personal affront. He was, he would later write, "at the bottom of a pit without any known means of scaling its sheer sides."[44]

As the Depression lengthened and deepened in intensity, the assurances of those who proffered orthodox responses began to ring increasingly hollow to the frustrated entrepreneur. He noted that the same voices that only a few years before had—in this grouping he included himself—spoken of a depression as a phenomenon of the past, now referenced it as an inevitable economic force that had simply to be endured. Indeed, it was not uncommon for Eccles to hear the nation's plight set down as a God-given development evidenced by its own biblical citation of Joseph and the seven cows—lean years must necessarily follow fat ones. As was continually asserted, moreover, lean years—the nation had in its past experienced some forty downturns in prosperity—always dissipated in time with the application of self-corrective forces.

Eccles began to question it all. By 1931 he would reach the unsettling conclusion—at odds with previously cherished principles—that efforts to seek "individual salvation" were contributing to "collective ruin" and that the remedy to the country's ills resided in *an activist government*.[45] The economic collapse, he would inform Utah Rotarians in early 1932, had created conditions that were "more critical than a war" and should be fought with a commensurate level of intensity.[46]

Years later when Eccles composed his autobiography, *Beckoning Frontiers*, he left the reader to form the distinct inference that these newfound economic convictions were the unrefined product of his own untutored but worldly observance. He attributed his unorthodoxy, in part, to the fact that he never attended college and did not, therefore, have to unlearn petrified economic doctrines. Although it is true that Eccles owed no great debt of gratitude to the world of academe, he seemed to purposely cultivate the specious notion that he was uninfluenced by the economic musings of others. In his official biography of Eccles published in 1976, Sidney Hyman wrote that in the fall of 1933, Eccles "had not yet read a word of Keynes."[47] Actually, as will be discussed, by that time Eccles had quoted Keynes at length in his speeches.

After conducting a personal interview with Eccles, Herbert Stein wrote in *The Fiscal Revolution in America* that by the time he became a participant in public life Eccles had not "read anything by Keynes," and was "not aware of deriving his views on fiscal policy from anything he ever read or heard." This seems rather unlikely. Throughout 1931 and 1932 Keynes was mentioned in some detail on dozens of occasions in both the *Salt Lake Tribune* and the *Ogden*

Standard-Examiner. By 1933 Keynes's advice for American policymakers came with greater specificity and even more exposure. For anyone keeping abreast of economic thought in the early 1930s—as Eccles clearly was—exposure to the British economist was nearly unavoidable. This seems all the more likely since Keynes was espousing the very same economic credenda that Eccles was learning to embrace. In June of 1931, for example, just about the time Eccles's views were transiting, the press covered Keynes's talk to the New School for Social Research in Greenwich Village. In Keynes's estimation, the *New York Times* reported, "more than 90 percent of the depression in America was due to a falling off of construction." Keynes's remediation for this debilitating state of affairs was soon to become Eccles's: a *government-induced* building program not paid for through taxation. In what would emerge as a continual bone of contention shared by both men until gathering storm clouds rendered it moot, Keynes rejected the oft-made assertion that only a war could salvage the American economy. In fact, he emphasized, "there is nothing that President Hoover can do that an earthquake could not do better."[48]

In Keynes's well-publicized open letter to FDR at the end of 1933, which even a casual observer of the political scene might well have encountered, he cautioned the president that a failure on his part would mean that "rational change will be gravely prejudiced throughout the world, leaving orthodoxy and revolution to fight it out." The reform measures the administration was pursuing were laudatory, stated Keynes, but should take a backseat to economic recovery. (It brings to mind the more recent criticism of President Obama's decision to attempt health care reform before an economic recovery was clearly underway.) It was for this reason that he assessed the centerpiece of the New Deal, the National Industrial Recovery Act (NIRA), as "a wrong choice in the order of urgencies." He feared that the legislation—discussed further on—"probably impedes recovery." As we shall see, Eccles was contemporaneously inveighing against the NIRA for essentially the same reasons. The Keynes letter to the president also touched upon yet another theme that Eccles would make his own; he described the "fallacies" that he feared arise "out of crude economic doctrines commonly known as the quantity theory of money." Attempting to raise output and income by focusing on the volume of money rather than the "volume of expenditure," Keynes mused, was "like trying to get fat by buying a larger belt."[49]

In addition to his public addresses, and his newspaper and magazine articles, Keynes published a few widely circulated pamphlets in 1932 and 1933. In March of 1933 he wrote a series of lengthy articles for the *London Times* that were gathered into a short book that made the rounds among policymakers and academics on both sides of the Atlantic. Keynes was hoping to influence the tone of the World Economic Conference scheduled for later in the year. For the delegates to "issue pious resolutions concerning the abatement of tariffs, quotas, and exchange restrictions would be a waste of time." These things, he insisted, were merely "symptoms" not "causes" of the world's economic strife. Presaging his role at the Bretton Woods Conference at the close of the next world war, Keynes modified his previous "barbaric relic" assessment of gold and suggested an "international authority" that would allocate notes to governments on some gold-based adjusted formula that could then be used by central banks as reserves against domestic circulating currency.[50]

The general thrust of the pamphlet, however, was directed at more prosaic suggestions. On sale in the United States at the end of April 1933 under the title *The Means to Prosperity*, it sold out its first printing in four days. The world's economic predicament comes not from an absence of material things, he informed his readers, but "from some failure in the immaterial devices of the mind" that prohibit "the acts of will necessary to put in movement the resources and technical means we already have." The principal requirement now was "a little, a very little, clear thinking."[51]

Much of what Keynes elaborated upon for his fellow economists three years later in *The General Theory of Employment, Interest and Money* is present in this pamphlet designed for a wider audience. Keynes likens increased taxation to achieve a balanced budget in an economic downturn to a manufacturer who, "wrapping himself in the rectitude of plain arithmetic," reacts to declining sales by increasing his prices. "A reduction of taxation," he asserts, "will run a better chance, than an increase, of balancing the budget"; that's assuming, of course, that the tax reduction is not offset by some foolish government spending cut—"by reducing teachers' salaries, for example." He writes about the "velocity of the circulation of money" and of a "multiplier" of "loan expenditures"—government spending financed by borrowing rather than taxes—that result when the newly employed in turn spend and forward their wages on to others to consume. He points out, however, that such spending is subject to a "certain proportion of leakage" at each stage, a consequence of some portion being saved, some spent on imports, and some part causing an increase in prices and thus diminishing to some degree consumption elsewhere. Nonetheless the net result, he happily reports, is a multiplier of "at least two." For caution's sake he is willing to reduce this expectation and maintain that the employment through loan expenditure of two men would "lead indirectly to the employment, not of two further men, which represents my own belief, but of one further man." Here too, Keynes places the greatest emphasis on *the need to build housing*.[52]

The Aggregate Demanders

The underconsumptionist perspective and its adherents are explored.

In the summer of 1936, as the United States endured its seventh straight year of double-digit unemployment, a young economist at Harvard University, seeking to augment his modest income, consented to employment as a private instructor. His tutorial services in macroeconomics were for the edification of one Henry Dennison, a wealthy Massachusetts paper-products manufacturer. Dennison, in alliance with three other successful businessmen with discernibly leftist political predilections, was determined to author a monograph that would provide President Franklin Delano Roosevelt with both staunch support and sage advice. The college instructor, John Kenneth Galbraith, was to furnish economic guidance for this entrepreneurial foursome and to assist in crafting its manuscript.[53]

Upon moving into Dennison's Juniper Hill home for the summer, Galbraith quickly discovered that the energetic manufacturer was in possession of his own fully formulated and well-entrenched theory of what ailed the American economy. The professor soon learned that there was a "spending stream" and a "saving stream." The depression they were experiencing was caused—as indeed were all business downturns—by the nonspending of savings. Quite simply, there was an acute shortage of purchasing power in the economy; the spending stream had turned into a trickle. The requisite solution to this sad economic state was for the government to jump-start the economy by offsetting the deficiency of private purchasing by substantially increasing its public expenditures. Failure to rectify this purchasing shortfall would consign the economy to an indeterminate economic limbo.

It fell now to the young economist to disabuse the experienced businessman of his homespun and unrefined economic theory; this, he clearly understood, would be a daunting task, considering that these views were held with some constancy.[54]

In the early part of the nineteenth century, French political economist Jean Baptiste Say firmly established that producers initiated the cycle of economic life. As a consequence of their felicitous decision to produce, they correspondingly generated, in the form of wages, interest, rent, and profit—the capacity to consume. Hence, Say's Law: supply produced its own demand. Any shortage of purchasing power, therefore, was merely a temporary stall, corrected in due course by the economy's built-in adjusters. Thus, as savings accumulated, investment was eventually assured by the lure of declining interest rates. Similarly, a temporary state of unemployment was rectified by the attraction of producers to lower labor costs. Moreover, the recurring but transient "boom" and "bust" phases of the "business cycle" were the unfortunate, but inexorable, components of a market system. All of this, of course, was by the 1930s a well-worn economic pedagogy. And so, despite the darkening shadows cast by the Great Depression, prominent economist Joseph Schumpeter could proffer the following view to an assemblage of Harvard economic students in his pronounced Austrian accent: "Chentlemen, you are vorried about the depression. You should not be. For capitalism, a depression is a good cold douche."[55] (Schumpeter favored the university's reduction in staff pay as economically remedial, while fully supporting the decision to leave the salaries of professors untouched. "A gentleman," he reasoned, "could not live on less than $50,000 a year.") This route to economic recovery found its quintessence in President Herbert Hoover's treasury secretary Andrew Mellon's infamous dictum: "Liquidate labor, liquidate stocks, liquidate the farmers, liquidate real estate."[56]

To be sure, as referenced above, there was already a loose alliance of academicians and liberal businessmen who took arms against this sea of orthodoxy. And as we shall see further on, a group of economists at—of all places—the University of Chicago had been advocates of fiscal stimulus for half a decade. Indeed, as economic historian David Laidler, among others, has demonstrated, an "engine of analysis" in the area of formal economic thought was well underway. Galbraith himself was hardly at ease with classical theory, but he attributed the country's economic woes to the power of oligopoly and monopoly. "The remedy," he informed Dennison, "was more competition."[57] And yet, in that summer of 1936, he reflected in later years, "No candidate for a Ph.D. at a major American university who spoke seriously of a shortage of purchasing power as a cause of depression could be passed." This belief among the senior faculty at most universities, he adjudged, was not so much "doctrine" as it was "theology," and the preponderance of American economists—at least those who desired tenure—genuflected at its altar.[58]

As the professor dealt with his pupil's heretical economic convictions, a controversial book was making the rounds among his Harvard colleagues. Published only months earlier, it bore the title *The General Theory of Employment, Interest and Money*, and was authored by John Maynard Keynes. As Galbraith turned the pages of the highly esteemed British economist's tome, what emerged—largely in the erudite vernacular of the economists' trade—was a clear vindication of the views of Henry Dennison. Supply did not always create its own demand, nor were the widely touted built-in adjusters always poised to rectify the oversupply of saving. The notion that an economy could be stalled at underemployment equilibrium was hardly chimerical, and governments needed to actively implement remedial policies and willingly incur significant budget deficits in the process. "Our criticism of the accepted classical theory," Keynes wrote, in an assertion that Henry Dennison had long before espoused, was that its "assumptions" simply "could not solve the economic problems of *the actual world* [my emphasis]."[59] He cautioned, moreover, about "waves of irrational psychology" directing economic life by means of "whim or sentiment or chance" and overriding, from time to time, "strict mathematical expectation."[60]

"I was shaken," Galbraith would later write. "This was not the primitive instinct of a businessman; this was the sophisticated case of a greatly renowned economist." One evening over cocktails, Galbraith decided to inform his student of Keynes's views. Dennison, who—like Marriner Eccles—spent his whole life "in the actual world," was not in the least bit surprised.[61]

This relationship between economist and businessman, which the Dennison/Galbraith vignette illustrates, has played a significant role in economic history; it certainly figures prominently in the account of the New Deal that this work explores.

It is probable that Dennison—like Eccles—had some exposure to Keynes before the advent of *General Theory.* Keynes, moreover, was far from the only formal economist whom Eccles became aware of on the eve of his arrival on the national political stage. He was introduced to Professor Paul Douglas of the University of Chicago at a seminar held at the University of Utah in 1933. That year Douglas, with a few of his University of Chicago colleagues, published *Balancing the Budget*—a seminal work in the development of fiscal policy. Douglas espoused, as did Eccles, an underconsumptionist view of the Depression's origins. Moreover, in 1931, according to Sidney Hyman—in a fact left unmentioned in his autobiography—Eccles attempted to mitigate his "economic illiteracy" by "carefully" reading the work of William Trufant Foster. Foster's prescient book *The Road to Plenty* was an important work in fostering belief in underconsumption as a root cause of economic collapse and of the limits of monetary policy as a rectification for such conditions.[62]

The Road to Plenty was written by Waddill Catchings, an iron manufacturer and partner in Goldman, Sachs, and William Trufant Foster, a past president of Reed College in Portland, Oregon. In the early 1920s the former Harvard classmates established the Pollak Foundation for Economic Research. Citing the Greek mythological figure of Sisyphus, who was condemned for eternity to roll a huge stone to the top of a hill only to see it roll down again, they posed this question: "Must business forever suffer under the curse of Sisyphus?" They argued that it did not, and in a series of books published in the course of the 1920s, they rejected what they termed the "economics of despair." In 1926 they composed a paper, "The Dilemma of Thrift," in which they argued that the deficiency of demand for goods and services during a recession could be rectified by a "Federal Budget Board" that could unleash public works projects. This publication gained sufficient attention that it inspired a countering pamphlet from the Austrian School economist Friedrich Hayek. Hayek, who spent a year studying at New York University in 1923–1924, was troubled that the idea won the endorsement of Commerce Secretary Herbert Hoover. Hayek published "The Paradox of Saving," a lumbering publication written in German that upheld the validity of Say's Law and asserted that a government-implemented works program would merely "bring grave disturbances" to the natural flow of the economic system.

The Road to Plenty, however, was the most important work of Foster and Catchings; it was published over a year before the calamitous 1929 stock market crash. John Maynard Keynes made generally favorable reference to the two amateur economists in his *Treatise on Money* in 1930. In an attempt to subject their book to "rigorous examination," the authors offered a $5,000 prize to the person who provided the best "adverse criticism" of their theories and appointed Owen Young, then chairman of General Electric, to act as principal judge. This brought forth 431 replies from distinguished economists and businessmen the world over.[63]

The Road to Plenty bears a closer resemblance in style to an Upton Sinclair novel than an economic text. The book is composed of a lengthy series of dialogues about economics among passengers of various professions on a train bound from Boston to Chicago. Perhaps as a means of deflecting accusations of ivory-tower theorizing, Catchings and Foster make the intellectual star of their book "the Business Man." Their introductory description of him is worth citing:

> [A fellow traveler] recognized him as a leading citizen of the Commonwealth; a director of the Federal Reserve Bank; a benefactor whose generosity was well known to the inner circle of social workers; the leader to whom every one had turned, with a common impulse, in Liberty

> Loan and Red Cross drives. First of all, however, he was a business man, a business man of wide and successful experience. A self-made man—very much so—but *this* one did not worship his creator.[64]

That the authors had unwittingly crafted a prototype of Marriner Eccles becomes increasingly apparent. Although numerous men of business partake in the conversation as purveyors of conventional economic wisdom, the Business Man, to the surprise of all, proceeds to challenge cherished assumptions. His principal antagonist in these Pullman car colloquies is none other than a professor of economics whose cocksure pontifications the Business Man finds at variance with his work-a-day experience.[65]

By the time the train arrives in Chicago, the Business Man—and a few acquired allies—has set forth, in a kind of horse-sense exegesis, virtually every major tenet of neoclassical economics including the innocuousness of growing a substantial government debt to remedy a recession. After all, they reasoned, the American people merely owed the money to themselves. In taking issue with Say's Law, they argue that the flow of money to the consumer is at an inadequate level to keep pace with productive capacity. As confirmation of this fact they bring attention to the badly worn shoes of the train porter, who, when asked why he does not purchase a new pair, replies, "Ain't got money enough, suh. That's all's the reason."[66]

Along this line the authors were quite determined to debunk the prevailing 1920s conviction that the decade-and-a-half-old Federal Reserve System would prevent any severe economic setback. In April 1926, in fact, Foster testified before the Banking and Currency Committee of the House of Representatives and warned that the Federal Reserve could not "with its present powers" prevent a recession of price levels and that when it occurred the Fed would be "unjustly blamed."[67] The Business Man makes just this point when he asserts that no mechanism exists to increase the flow of money to consumers. "Was not the Federal System established for that very purpose?" asks an incredulous companion. "No," the Business Man laments. "It was established to provide producers with money."[68]

It is when the Business Man proposes an institutional solution to rectify these systemic problems that one senses how crucial an influence the work may have played in Eccles's future career. It was essential to establish a government agency similar to the Federal Reserve; it would be responsible for examining all forms of economic data and indexes, including foreign trade, income distribution, and the volume of money. It would then advise the government on the proper policy to follow in regard to all manner of fiscal and monetary policies that should be pursued, including the nature and scope of public works projects, the degree and form of taxation, and the appropriate levels of monetary activity. It was, as we shall shortly see, the very kind of agency that Eccles thought he was running when he assumed the chairmanship of the Fed only a few years later.[69]

In the following decade, when Eccles was occupying his seat as the chairman of the Fed, he engaged in a bit of correspondence with the coauthor of *The Road to Plenty*, William Foster. Moreover, Eccles invited Foster to speak in Ogden on at least three occasions before he (Eccles) commenced his career in Washington. Foster enclosed with his letters, articles, and testimony he [Foster] gave in the 1920s on the underconsumptionist perspective, and his dire forecast if the condition were left unaddressed.[70] Was he, perhaps, seeking to remind Eccles of his early role in the history of the New Economics?

In a public address in 1941, Eccles would acknowledge that in these early years of the Depression, two books—*The Road to Revival* and *Recovery: The Second Effort*—had made "the deepest impression" upon him. The authors of both works were in attendance to hear Eccles's attribution. *The Road to Revival* was written in 1932 by a British economist named F. Cyril James who taught for a time at the University of Pennsylvania. A graduate of the London School of Economics, he advocated government support of social programs such as public works and poverty assistance. Eccles had underlined a passage from *The Road to Revival* in which James stated that "the final aim of economic activity is the enriching of human life" and that a "redistribution of national income on a sounder basis" would help engender for "the average man and woman a standard of living more worthy of economic civilization." In a passage that Eccles became quite fond of, James wrote that there could not have been much unemployment during the wise reign of King Solomon after he enriched the poor city of Jerusalem by engaging upon a "large number of extravagant improvements." It is quite possible that Eccles encountered James at one of the numerous gatherings of American bankers, where the young academic economist made presentations. The fact that James worked as a banker while attending graduate school would likely have enhanced Eccles's estimation of his economic analysis.[71]

In the same speech, Eccles revealed that he also read in the "depths of the depression" the work of another academic economist, Sir Arthur Salter. "The role of finance," wrote Salter, in words underscored by Eccles in his personal copy of the book *Recovery: The Second Effort*, "is to be the handmaid and servant of economic activity." Salter argued that competition and individual enterprise could be enhanced by government oversight and regulation. The secret, he insisted, was to find a way to minimize the "abuses" of both government and free markets. On the eve of Franklin Roosevelt's election to the presidency, Salter joined Keynes, Arthur C. Pigou, and four other prominent British economists to urge their fellow countrymen to do the patriotic thing and boost consumption. By the following year Salter realized that recovery was beyond the scope of the private sector. In September of 1933, economic journalist Harold Callender cited Salter as a staunch proponent of "extensive capital expenditures by governments."[72]

Eccles brought both books to his office at the Fed where they remained for the entirety of his tenure. There seems little doubt, therefore, that his insistence that his reconstituted economic thinking was not shaped by anything he had read seems overstated. Moreover, Eccles was hardly alone in his growing acceptance of the underconsumptionist school of economic thought.

In 1919, two businessmen, the manufacturer Henry Dennison and the retailer Edward Filene, became the founding members of the Twentieth Century Fund, a foundation dedicated to fostering equity in industrial relationships between labor and management. Both would help design the Wisconsin Plan, the only unemployment plan in the nation until the advent of the Social Security Act. Filene, like Eccles, prided himself on his real life pedagogy in economic affairs. Filene entered the world of business after his father's illness precluded a college education. "Instead," he reflected, "I began to study subjects with which my work brought me into contact in a practical way—that is, subjects that would correct or amplify the theories I was applying to the problems of my business."[73] Filene's 1924 book, *The Way Out*, struck the underconsumptionist chord before Catchings and Foster. "Unemployment," he insisted, "unlike death, is preventable." Filene even argued the very Keynesian position that unemployment insurance was not merely a humanitarian necessity, but a vital component of a successful effort to restore aggregate demand.[74]

Historians have identified a cadre of businessmen of this era who prematurely shared a "'Keynesian' concern with the dynamics of mass consumption." Included among them were industrialist Morris Leeds, shoe manufacturer Milton Florsheim, Beardsley Ruml of Macy's Department Stores, Robert Johnson of Johnson & Johnson, and Ernest Hood of the Naumkeag Steam Cotton Company. Historian Steve Fraser associates them with a "new, rising milieu of mass-market-oriented producers, distributors, and financiers" who were "far more amenable to 'Keynesian' approaches to shoring up aggregate demand."

There was also the Committee of the Nation led by Vincent Bendix of the Bendix Corporation and James Rand Jr., the president of Remington Rand. Also among its leaders were Lessing Rosenwald of Sears, Roebuck and the company's president, Robert E. Wood. A long-time Republican, Wood voted for FDR in both 1932 and 1936 and would develop a close relationship with Eccles when he was on the board of the Chicago Fed. Many of these interests had their ventures underwritten by Lehman Brothers and Goldman Sachs. A number of these progressive businessmen sat on Lehman's board, and the aforementioned Waddill Catchings, after all, was Goldman Sachs's lead economist; the firm's Sidney Weinberg became the single largest fundraiser for FDR's 1936 reelection campaign.[75]

The economic notions opined by these "aggregate demanders" did not emerge entirely bereft of modern foundational academic precedents. In the previous century, another felicitous relationship between a scholar and an entrepreneur—highly reminiscent of the Galbraith/Dennison pairing and the connection that Marriner Eccles was soon to establish with the economist Lauchlin Currie—produced a vital inspirational link with these pre-Keynesian men of business. In 1886, a report by a twenty-three-member Royal Commission, assigned the task of reporting on the causes of the recent economic decline, failed to satisfy the intellectual demands of a young lecturer on political economy, John A. Hobson. The son of a middle-class newspaper editor from rural England, Hobson was inspired by the social theories of Henry George and deeply disturbed by the grinding poverty he witnessed in London after his graduation from Oxford. His skepticism of the commission's findings, laying the blame for the depression upon overproduction that was accentuated by high foreign tariffs on British exports, was shared by his good friend Albert Frederick Mummery.[76]

A successful entrepreneur, Mummery had for some time attempted, without initial success, to convince Hobson of the inimical impact of that most esteemed of human endeavors—saving. "This man entangled me in a controversy," the economist would later write of the businessman. Their 1889 collaborative work, *The Physiology of Industry*, was something of a play on Alfred Marshall's *Economics of Industry* published a decade earlier. The authors took issue with the John Stuart Mill's staunch defense of Say's Law. "All sellers are inevitably, and by the meaning of the word, buyers," Mill asserted, while insisting that if the productive powers of the country could be doubled "we would by the same stroke, double the purchasing power." In challenging the automatic connection between these two economic activities, Hobson and

Mummery also took aim at Adam Smith's famous dictum: "What is prudence in the conduct of a private family can scarce be folly in a great nation." To the contrary, what is often good for the part is often bad for the whole; thrift, they wrote, often stalled consumer demand, the real driving force of economic prosperity, and saddled society with disastrous levels of unemployment. To make such an assertion at that time, notes economic historian Robert Heilbroner, was viewed as "nonsense of the most arrant kind." Indeed, Hobson recalled that one Oxford professor "considered it as equivalent in rationality to an attempt to prove the flatness of the earth." In paying tribute to Hobson, who "flung himself with unflagging, but almost unavailing, ardor and courage against the ranks of orthodoxy," John Maynard Keynes identified his work as "an epoch in economic thought." (One might assume that Keynes left out any assignment of personal courage to the mountain-climbing Mummery on the understanding that an independently wealthy man of business had far less at stake in the duo's endeavor than an academic economist.) Inserting this comment into his *General Theory*, Keynes was quick to add that while his contemporaries might not state their adherence to Say's Law in as "crude a form" as was done in the previous century, it "still underlies the whole classical theory, which would collapse without it." Fidelity to what he called a "Robinson Crusoe economy" remained vibrant.[77]

In the aftermath of his attack upon accepted economic orthodoxy, Hobson lost both his lecturing position and his opportunity to join the influential Political Economy Club of London. Nevertheless, the scorn of his peers did not prevent him from pushing his heretical ideas further still. In his 1896 book, *The Problem of the Unemployed*, he blamed the maldistribution of income for the frequent failure of aggregate demand.[78]

This income inequality argument clearly had its share of adherents in the early 1930s. Eccles, as we shall see below, developed one of the more colorful ways of making this case. Siding with this perspective as well was publishing mogul William Randolph Hearst. Had the profits of the 1920s, Hearst argued, been "distributed in wages, prosperity would have been maintained and increased."[79] Hearst became perhaps the most important advocate of public works projects. Taking to the airwaves in June of 1931 at the personal invitation of William S. Paley, president of the Columbia System, Hearst called for the federal government to appropriate $5 billion to provide public works jobs for the unemployed. "It is time to increase the national debt and increase expenditures," Hearst maintained. Restoration of prosperity was assured, he informed his radio audience, provided the government expended this appropriation "and did not sit on it perpetually like a deluded hen on a porcelain doorknob." Hearst then proceeded to orchestrate an editorial campaign by his newspapers to clamor for jobless relief.[80]

Although many progressive economists in the 1930s looked upon J. A. Hobson with an abiding sense of respect and inspiration, and were concerned with the equity of income distribution as an important component of boosting aggregate demand—especially in light of the growing acceptance of a "marginal propensity to consume"—not all shared a belief in the causal nature of such inequality in terms of the Depression. As Peter Temin has pointed out, the fact that consumption expenditures throughout the 1920s remained steady as a percentage of national income, and declined only in 1930, renders the underconsumption explanation "untenable."[81] Even Keynes in the *General Theory*, although sympathetic to the goal of income redistribution, and aware of the enhanced average propensity to consume that would result, stated that this school of thought "may lay a little too much emphasis on increased consumption" while "neglecting" the area of investment. More recently, in drawing a comparison between the Great Depression and the Great Recession in regard to income inequality, Paul Krugman makes the same point. The "popular story—that the rising share of income going to the rich has undermined overall demand, because of the shrinking purchasing power of the middle class—just doesn't work when you look at the data," he writes. The "'underconsumption' stories," Krugman continues, depend on consumer spending lagging as income becomes more concentrated. In reality, in the years preceding both economic declines consumer spending "remained strong despite growing inequality." Krugman, however, then references the work of Cornell economist Robert Frank, who has explored the development of "expenditure cascades" in the decade before the 2007 recession, during which the nonrich kept pace as consumers by engaging in an unsustainable level of borrowing. This, as we shall see, is the very condition that Eccles believed prevailed in the 1920s.[82]

The legacy of Hobson and Mummery may not have been far from the mind of ninety economists who signed a statement on January 4, 1931, that endorsed a plan put forth by an organization calling itself the Emergency Committee for Federal Public Works. The committee was essentially supporting legislation introduced in Congress the previous fall by Senator Robert Wagner of New York, which called upon Congress to issue a $1 billion "prosperity loan" to finance needed public improvements. In supporting the plan the economists affirmed that they were "simply approving . . . a principle accepted by leading economists and socially-minded businessmen for a generation past." The federal government, the economists' statement continued, should do its part "in restoring the *purchasing power* [emphasis mine] of the masses of people." It is important to note, however, that the statement was not advocating that these projects be funded by deficit financing, but rather by "equitably distributed" taxation. The fact that many of the signers were academic economists, and that they acknowledged the existence of deficient purchasing power as a macroeconomic problem, seems to undercut John Kenneth Galbraith's 1975 recollection, cited in this introduction, that no PhD candidate in economics at a major American university who made such an assertion could be passed. In fact, at least one of the signers of the public works statement, T. N. Carver, was teaching at Harvard at the time. It is clear, however, that many of these men came to such an understanding after their student days were behind them and before they assumed full professorships.[83]

A growing number of economists were becoming increasingly vocal by the spring of 1931; the news media reported these defections from economic orthodoxy. "Just as we saved our way into the Depression, we must squander our way out of it," said Virgil Jordan, an economist employed by McGraw-Hill Publishing Company, in an address to the Pennsylvania State Chamber of Commerce. In an article titled "Should the Budget Be Balanced?" in *The New Republic*, Harvard economist Sumner Slichter argued that only increased spending could restore prosperity. Early in the New Deal, a group of six untenured instructors of economics at Harvard, including, and in fact instigated by, Lauchlin Currie, signed a letter to the White House praising the abandonment of the gold standard and encouraging increased government expenditures. (This action must have displeased seven senior members of the economics faculty at the school, the "Seven Wise Men," who were at that time in the process of publishing a book that was critical of the New Deal. None of the six young upstarts, including Currie, were offered tenure.) In a publicly released letter to Wagner, University of Illinois economist Edward Berman maintained that the senator's public-works proposal was, if anything, vastly underfunded.

Joining the assault upon balanced budgets was a band of economists at the University of Chicago. Dubbed the "Chicago School," they made the case that although monetary mismanagement clearly caused the Depression, "*inadequate, temporary stimulation might well leave conditions worse than it found them*" [emphasis mine]. Rather than utilizing government deficit financing as merely a tool of recovery—what was beginning to be termed "pump priming"—they advocated a permanent role for compensatory fiscal policy as an agent of *stabilization*. That year Paul Douglas of the University of Chicago (technically, as an underconsumptionist, he was not a member of the Chicago School) published *The Problem of Unemployment* and, as a member of then New York governor Roosevelt's Committee to Stabilize Employment, was credited by Frances Perkins with being the deciding influence in FDR's newfound enthusiasm for unemployment insurance. Douglas also taught Paul Samuelson at Chicago, who was destined, in Douglas's view, to "become the ablest modern economist in the world" and a Nobel Prize–winning advocate of the New Economics.[84]

Money Matters

A group of economists at the University of Chicago stress the importance of monetary policy as a corrective to economic decline, but acknowledge, along with John Maynard Keynes, the role of fiscal action.

Many of Douglas's colleagues at the University of Chicago, however, were firmly convinced that the Depression had been triggered by monetary tightening. The "quantity of money" in the economy was the real determinant of the business cycle. Moreover, they believed that correct monetary policy *usually* could furnish the wherewithal to lead the economy back to prosperity. The severity of the downturn, and the failure of the Fed to act quickly and aggressively, however, rendered these tools insufficient and persuaded these economists to call for deficit expenditures by the federal government. In 1956, Milton Friedman, although he did not share their faith in deficit financing, would credit these "Chicagoans" with pioneering his essential view of the "quantity theory of money." As economic historians Roger Sandilands and David Laidler have pointed out, however, the economic ideas at Chicago were hardly unique. There were numerous others who proffered similar ideas. Teaching at Harvard at this time was British economist Ralph Hawtrey. Hawtrey was an unwavering believer in the potency of monetary policy. In his 1932 book, *The Art of Central Banking*, he expressed the conviction that, no matter the severity of a depression, "there must ultimately be a limit to the amount of money that the sellers will hold idle, and it follows that by this process the vicious circle of deflation can be broken, however great the stagnation of business and the reluctance of borrowers may be." In fact, it was Harvard's Lauchlin Currie who may have first arrived at the core of the quantity theory. (In the early 1990s Friedman conceded that he was remiss in overlooking Currie's role.) Currie was also a much more enthusiastic purveyor of a belief in government spending than any of the Chicagoans. His outspokenness in that regard would make him something of a heretic at Harvard and lead him from academia to Marriner Eccles.[85]

In any event, it could be safely said that some Americans were slightly ahead of John Maynard Keynes in the advocacy of such fiscal measures. When Keynes spoke at the University of Chicago in May of 1931, he urged the United States to focus primarily on monetary stimulus; this was a case he made a year earlier in his *A Treatise on Money*. As the keynote speaker at the Harris Foundation Lectures, he observed that the "cure of unemployment involves improving business profits." Central to this achievement was the adoption of a means of increasing "the volume of investment." Although "restoring confidence" and implementing some degree of public works projects as a "reserve weapon" would be helpful, the real solution to the current economic predicament, he emphasized, was a vigorous policy of open-market purchases. Keynes, going back to his criticisms of the Treaty of Versailles, seemed to offer sage advice. In 1928 he argued that the Wall Street boom in stock prices should not compel the Fed to pursue restrictive policies because there was no evidence of inflation accompanying it. In fact, he suggested quite presciently that the Fed might consider expansionary policies to offset the diversion of credit from industrial concerns to security speculation.[86]

As he stated in his *Treatise*, however, the gold standard (which Britain was still on) proved something of a fly in his monetary ointment. A too-vigorous engagement—often to the extent required—could result in a precarious outflow of gold. Because Britain was more dependent upon "international trade and international lending" than the United States, it necessitated a greater level of government expenditures. The United States functioned, he asserted, as more of a "closed system." In the round-table discussions that followed his address, he mused that a policy that favored interest-rate reduction over government spending was more conducive to the nature of American "individualism." He noted that he was speaking "in the country that was the last home of individualism." To economist Don Patinkin, who would come to know a number of the participants in the conference, Keynes's endorsement of a mostly monetary effort in the United States may have had more to do with the fact that the country was a more suitable locale from which to prove his "magic formulas that could solve the world's economic ills." This need for verification was no doubt heightened by the offer he made to the head of the Bank of England to have his "head chopped off" if his policy proved ineffectual. As many economic historians have observed, however, the hallmark of Keynes's experience as an economist was his allegiance to altering theory based on real-life developments. By the close of 1931 he was beginning to respond to events by altering his emphasis on monetary and fiscal matters. Although Keynes would retain his head, the persistence of economic malaise even after Britain jettisoned the gold standard that September compelled him to write another book—one in which public expenditures would not be relegated to the status of a "reserve weapon."[87]

Although still a small minority, those willing to abandon the sanctified fetish of balanced budgets were increasing. Starting in mid-1931, the publisher and editor of the *Philadelphia Record* and the *Camden (NJ) Courier Post*, J. David Stern, began a constant assault on the wisdom of such perceived fiscal prudence. "Balancing the budget is a bookkeeper's phrase," stated Stern, "This country cannot afford to be ruled by bookkeepers." If the nation was willing to incur a $26 billion debt to win the World War, he reasoned, why not resort to such wartime measures to defeat the Depression?[88]

When Marriner Eccles testified before the Senate Finance Committee in February of 1933, therefore, he could hardly be described—as he sometimes seemed to prefer—as a lone wolf howling in isolation. In 1931 he was an avid follower of the nation's political and economic crosscurrents. To what extent he was aware of, and influenced by, all of these developments, is a matter of some uncertainty. He would simply describe in epiphanous terms the new field of thought and action he adopted as a consequence of the country's dissolving economy. "On a morning toward the first of 1931," he would reflect, "the scales suddenly dropped from my eyes."[89]

"What Is an Economic System For?"

Eccles comes to espouse the notion that a market economy must not merely enrich individuals but enhance the quality of life in a society.

As previously mentioned, Eccles had been a frequent speaker at various associations throughout Utah where he extolled the robust economy of the 1920s. As early as March 1931, however, he took to the lecture circuit as an exponent of a vastly altered sentiment. That month he went before an assembly of bankers in Salt Lake City and ridiculed the "vast quantities" of optimism that business leaders had "pumped into the air" in the fallacious notion that all the economy needed was a good dose of positive psychology. "There is only one agency in my opinion that can turn the cycle upward," he stated to another incredulous assembly of bankers the following summer, "and that is government." The more unreceptive an audience appeared at the outset to his newfound theories, the more he seemed to relish the challenge of conversion. "As the pursuit of money had been the organizing principle of my life for almost twenty years," Eccles would state, "the pursuit of an idea of economic balance now replaced it."[90]

He came in time to title his address, "Reconstructing Economic Thinking." He would begin these talks by acknowledging that although he had no pretension of being an economist, he was certainly no stranger to business and financial life. Previously, however, he "had been so absorbed by the fascination of the financial and business game," he "had not stopped to consider the fundamental and underlying purpose of it all." He would request that his fellow Utahns entertain the question the Depression had forced to the forefront of his own consciousness: "What is an economic system for?" Should it not, he reasoned, be a vehicle "to give men who are able, worthy, and willing to work, the opportunity to work and to guarantee to them sustenance for their families and protection against want and destitution." If so, the system had clearly failed.[91]

Moreover, Eccles maintained, there was no guarantee that this failure would be short-lived. The Depression in which they were immersed should not be viewed as just another series of busts that periodically afflict the economy. This Depression, he cautioned, was transitional in nature and not an ordinary cyclical downturn. In the past, spontaneous recovery inevitably resulted due to the lure of large-scale, highly profitable fields of investment. Capital that had accumulated during depressions or recessions was, in time, unleashed to build railroads, construct from scratch the infrastructure of a newly conquered continent, and transform an overwhelmingly agricultural economy into an industrial behemoth. These vast demands on accumulated capital, he alleged, were in large part no longer extant. With no profitable outlets, warned Eccles, these funds could remain indefinitely idle. Here, Eccles was expressing some allegiance with the not uncommon view of many progressive thinkers in the 1930s: the notion that historic channels for investment had in large part dried up—what some began to term the "secular stagnation thesis"—and would need government assistance in reimaging. (As we shall see, World War II and the economic potentialities left in its wake would lead to the abandonment of such a perspective by Eccles and virtually everyone else.)[92]

In Eccles's view, therefore, it was distressing to see the predominant economic debate in America unfolding as a hostile contest between the country's "sound money theorists" and its "inflationists." Both camps, he argued, were exponents of policies inimical to economic health. Inflationist schemes came in essentially three forms: decreasing the number of grains of gold in the dollar, the issuance of fiat money, and the remonetization of silver. Due to Utah's substantial mining interests, the last proposal gained some currency there. Eccles's empirical banking experience, however, provided ample evidence in his mind of the shallowness of such a monetary panacea. "Contrary to the view of many people," he contended, "there is no shortage of currency in circulation at the present time as the volume of currency outstanding now is substantially more than in 1929." The velocity of money, meanwhile—its turnover as shown by checks drawn against individual accounts—had declined from more than $70 billion per month in 1929 to less than $30 billion per month. This had enormous implications for the nation's economic vitality, Eccles insisted, since 90 percent of all purchases were made, not with currency, but by checks drawn on bank money. Monetary inflation therefore would have slight impact upon the only thing that truly mattered: increasing the purchasing power of the nation.[93]

The deficiency in the nation's purchasing power, Eccles affirmed, was caused—as was the Depression itself—by a wholly inadequate distribution of the national income. Eccles would come to employ a metaphor that he believed ideally captured the American economic scenario. The United States, in the 1920s, was engaged in a gigantic poker game, and as the game progressed, the chips became concentrated in fewer and fewer hands. The only way for many to remain as players was to borrow, and when their credit ran out, the game stopped. To firmly establish this point, Eccles would often shower his audience with figures from the statistical department of the Federal Reserve. Of all accounts in the Reserve System, 99.3 percent held less than $10,000, he instructed. Yet, such accounts amounted to less than 40 percent of total deposits. Even more sobering, he pointed out, was the fact that accounts of $50,000 or more, although a mere 0.1 percent of all accounts, contained 44.6 percent of total deposits.[94]

It was clearly not the fault of bankers, declared Eccles, that this vast reservoir of idle funds was not finding its way through the nation's financial veins. "Nothing would be more agreeable to the bankers," he assured his listeners, "than to be able to lend or invest money safely or profitably." How, he reasoned, could bankers "finance the building of more factories and more rental properties and more homes when half of our productive property is idle for lack of consumption?" Lack of confidence by business interests, therefore, was well founded. "Confidence itself is not a cause," Eccles would insist. "It is the effect of things already in motion." What was deemed a "lack of confidence" was merely a prudent business assessment that additional investment was not needed.

The only escape from the Depression, therefore, Eccles decreed, was increased spending by the federal government. Before the Utah Educational Association in October 1933, Eccles quoted the following passage by "the great British economist" John Maynard Keynes:

> Formerly there was no expenditure out of the proceeds of borrowing that it was thought proper for the State to incur except for war. In the past, therefore, we have not infrequently had to wait for a war to terminate a major depression. I hope that in the future we shall not adhere to this purist financial attitude, and that we shall be ready to spend on the enterprises of peace what the financial maxims of the past would only allow us to spend on the devastations of war. At any rate, I predict with an assured confidence that the only way out is for us to discover some object which is admitted even by the deadheads to be a legitimate excuse for largely increasing the expenditure of someone on something.[95]

To argue that government could not achieve prosperity, continued Eccles, is to deny "what governments have done in the past and what our government has done in every period of war." Alluding to the structural nature of the Depression, he maintained that the Great War, far from causing the Depression, as was commonly maintained, actually postponed it. "The world very likely would have sunk into a deep depression possibly worse than this one had the war not come," he commented. A failure to create commensurate purchasing power in a time of peace would be tantamount to a failure to govern, "and a people which will not support a government spending adequate to their needs must come to grief."

Next, Eccles posed the crucial question: "Where will the government get the money?" The answer, he would tell his largely resistant audience, was to borrow. The reason that the government failed to embark upon such a course was because "orthodox financial business and political leaders think this will destroy the government credit and make our money unsound." But America's currency, Eccles would point out, was already "painfully sound" and its leaders seemed on a quest to make it so sound that every credit institution in the country would close as a consequence. "The great struggle in America today," the banker pronounced, "is between the people who believe what they call sound money and the people who believe in the right to eat and the right to work." He continued:

> Sound money arguments are appealing to those selfish and economically ignorant people who have money and feel sure of getting more while millions grow poorer. Such arguments have no appeal to those government employees who were thrown out of work so that the Government could balance its budget in order to keep the dollar sound. It

> has no appeal to the farmer and the home-owner who are burdened with debt and taxes and are about to be foreclosed.[96]

If his Utah audience members were largely disenchanted with the advocacy of intentionally incurred government debt, they found their native son's next proposal even more distasteful. What revenue government did raise must be acquired through progressive taxation. Taxes that fall heavily on consumers—sales taxes, real-estate taxes, tariffs, and public-service charges—must be reduced or eliminated, Eccles urged, and replaced with "heavy income taxes . . . in upper brackets [and] heavy taxation of undistributed corporate profits." Achieving this, Eccles stated, was "fundamental." There was, he suggested, an alternative: communism. This was a form of social organization, however, that "the American people at the present . . . are not willing to try."[97]

Although his polemics failed to garner widespread support in Utah, Eccles found solace in an organization of business and professional men who designated themselves "the Freidenkers" and proclaimed their determination to promote innovative thought. The group members believed it prudent to abandon their intellectualized name, however, when detractors in Utah began referring to them as "the Free Drinkers." It did not take long for Eccles to become a driving force in the organization. Writer Darrell J. Greenwell attended one of the bimonthly Monday night discussions for the first time in January 1932 and promptly wrote to Eccles afterward to inform him that he was now a "disciple" who wanted to "spread the gospel of the master." Other members were equally enthused in their desire to obtain a wider venue for their star iconoclast.[98] One of the association's founders, Robert Hinckley, used his influence with his uncle, U.S. senator William King, to obtain an invitation for Eccles to testify before the Finance Committee in late February 1933. (King, while a Democrat, had distinctly conservative views—although he was a major critic of what he viewed as U.S. imperialism abroad—and would come to oppose most of the New Deal's legislative agenda.) Earlier that same month, Hinkley sponsored a lecture series at the University of Utah, where he was a regent, on the catastrophic state of the American economy. Eccles was invited to attend the lectures and it would prove one of the most momentous events of his life.[99] The featured speaker at the symposium was the erudite journalist Stuart Chase. In 1932 Chase had written a series of lengthy articles in the *New Republic* called "A New Deal for America" that later in the year were published as a book titled *A New Deal.* Presidential speech writer Samuel Rosenman inserted the line "I pledge you, I pledge myself, to a new deal for the American people" into FDR's

1932 presidential acceptance speech. (Twenty years later, however, Rosenman could not recall being inspired by Chase's words.) Many of the economic positions taken by Chase—although certainly not all—bore a close resemblance to Eccles's own. If Eccles read either the articles or the book, he seems not to have publicly acknowledged doing so. It is worth noting, however, that the first chapter of Chase's book is titled "What Is an Economic System For?" This is, of course, the very question Eccles posed to his audience when delivering his speech "Reconstructing Economic Thinking."[100]

Delayed by a snowstorm, Chase missed a luncheon address he was scheduled to deliver before an assembly of Utah's commercial and financial leaders at a downtown hotel. Chase consented, however, to meet with a few of these businessmen while he consumed a late lunch. At that time, the rapid-fire questions posed to him by Eccles, a member of the contingent, rendered eating a difficult task. Eccles had an acute interest in President elect Roosevelt's "brain trusters": Rexford Tugwell, Raymond Moley, and Adolph Berle. As if to gain respite from the distracting inquisitiveness, Chase invited Eccles to offer his own assessment of the nation's economic plight. Being as he was in one of the country's most conservative states—home, after all, to the continually reelected Reed Smoot—and speaking as he was to business interests, the progressive Chase must have fully expected to hear an orthodox incantation about the sanctity of balanced budgets and the essential need for revivified business confidence. Such, of course, was not the case. The local banker proceeded to provide the worldly journalist with an only slightly condensed rendition of the speech that he had been delivering throughout Utah for the previous two years. Chase, a bit nonplussed, encouraged Eccles to seek a wider audience. When informed of Eccles's upcoming appearance before the Senate Finance Committee later that month, Chase suggested that Eccles make his way to New York City and meet with Professor Rexford Tugwell, still teaching at Columbia University. Chase volunteered to write a letter of introduction.[101]

Within hours of giving his testimony to the Senate Finance Committee in February of 1933, Eccles was on a train bound for New York City. The following day he had lunch with Professor Tugwell—an appointment arranged by Stuart Chase—at a drugstore on the Upper West Side. Eccles brought a copy of the statement he had delivered in Washington the day before. Although Tugwell was surprised that a banker from Utah would express such views, the meeting exposed some fundamental differences between the two men that will be explored below. Eccles left believing the encounter, "while pleasant, was fruitless."[102]

Eccles returned to Utah and resumed his heretical economic lectures. Not long after he delivered such a talk to the Utah Bankers Association, and shortly before he went to speak in Washington, E. G. Bennett, a business associate, visited him. Bennett informed Eccles he was speaking for the board of directors of First Security. The members were worried about him, concerned that he was overwrought. They feared the impact his expressed views would have on business. Eccles told Bennett to inform the board members that if they did not approve of what he was saying they could get a new president.

"I find some pleasure in noting," Eccles reflected many years later, "that if I was a traitor to my own class, I earned that distinction long before Franklin Roosevelt."[103]

"Wrecked on the Rocks of Loose Fiscal Policy"

FDR begins his presidency with a show of fiscal restraint.

The man of the hour was Lewis William Douglas. On the very day Marriner Eccles testified before the Senate Finance Committee, President-elect Roosevelt announced at a Hyde Park press conference that he was appointing the congressman from Arizona to be director of the budget. This position, Roosevelt informed the nation on the front pages of its newspapers, would be "of Cabinet rank" and no member of his "official family" would be in "closer and steadier contact with the President." Douglas was, FDR related to a political confidante, "the greatest find" of his administration.

Conservative lawmakers and members of the financial community immediately hailed Douglas's appointment. The selection was a clear indication that the president was intently serious about government austerity. The Democratic legislator had a sterling reputation as the most steadfast advocate of budget balancing in the Congress. A year earlier Douglas had stood in the well of the House and delivered an impassioned plea for fiscal balance, concluding his remarks with a dramatic request for all members willing to pledge themselves to such a desirous end to rise to their feet. Nearly the entire assembly did so. He was the ideal choice to bring to fruition Roosevelt's campaign promise to slash federal expenditures by a full 25 percent. If this were to be achieved it would most certainly mean a vast reduction in payments to veterans which comprised nearly a quarter of all federal expenditures. In this regard, Douglas's record as a highly decorated war veteran would render him less vulnerable to charges of insensitivity. If the budget director's plan to achieve balance failed, the *New York Times* advised its readers, "it will be because the President, or Congress, or both, do not support him."[104] Douglas would, no doubt, display "ruthlessness," the *New York Tribune* wrote approvingly; ruthlessness, the paper concluded, was what was necessary. Remarkably, Douglas would inform the members of the advisory board for the soon-to-be-created Public Works Administration that there was no legal obligation upon them to spend a nickel of the PWA's appropriation of $3.2 billion. In fact, he argued, the economy would be far better off if they simply decided to leave the entirety of their funding idle.[105]

Alternatives to Douglas's conservatism on fiscal policy had few proponents among Roosevelt's inner circle. "None of us," wrote Raymond Moley, the ringleader of the "brains trust" and, like Tugwell, a professor at Columbia (but of political science), "was a member of the 'borrow and spend' school." The conviction "that spending was an economic blessing had few supporters," Moley noted, either across the nation or within the administration. Adolph Berle of Columbia Law School, yet another member of the brain-trust nucleus, warned FDR repeatedly of the alarming burden the rising debt placed on the credit of the United States. Even Tugwell, viewed by many as the Robespierre of the New Deal, paid lip service to the sound objective of a balanced budget in a *New York World Telegram* interview in January 1933, a month before his first meeting with Marriner Eccles.[106]

Franklin Roosevelt's expositions on budget balancing, while not unmindful of considerations of political expediency, were, nonetheless, heartfelt. Like Herbert Hoover, Roosevelt was a product of a strain of progressivism whose emphasis was as much moralistic as economic—its essence being a fierce determination to sanitize government and promote its greater efficiency. Both men had lent enthusiastic support to passage of the Budget and Accounting Act of 1921, which streamlined budgeting methods and created a director of the budget to assist the president in preparing an annual budget and a comptroller general to audit all executive accounts. The act thereby placed acute emphasis upon the locution "a balanced budget," soon to become the most shopworn phrase in the American political lexicon and one that both Hoover and Roosevelt would embrace. To intentionally resort to fiscal deficits would, in Roosevelt's own mind, said Rexford Tugwell, be "doing wrong, and he was sensitive to criticism." In Tugwell's view, FDR "operated within somewhat the same [ideological] limitations as Hoover." Both men served together in the Wilson administration and appeared, at the time, to regard each other favorably. There were, however, glaring differences that the Columbia professor cited: FDR was much more of a pragmatist and a vastly better politician.[107]

On March 5, the day after his inauguration and a full week before his first official "fireside chat" with the nation over the banking crisis, FDR delivered his initial radio remarks to the country. Speaking on an American Legion radio show, he addressed the budget deficit and cautioned veterans that they must help in the attack upon the unflattering traits that allowed the insidious foe of debt to encroach upon American life. This slackness was an enemy with whom the country must "never conclude an armistice."[108]

On March 10, 1933, six days following his inauguration, Roosevelt sent a special message to Congress. National recovery depended upon "the unimpaired credit of the United States government," he stated. "Our government's house is not in order," pronounced the president as he proposed what would come to be termed the "Economy Act" granting him the discretion to reduce veterans' benefits and cut across the board the salaries of all federal employees. To those who advocated a "pump-priming" role for the government, he had these words of caution: "Too often in recent history liberal governments have been wrecked on the rocks of loose fiscal policy."[109]

The Economy Act, drafted under the guidance of Lewis Douglas, officially entitled the "Economy Act to Maintain the Credit of the United States Government," became law on March 20, 1933. The act received the support of sixty-nine conservative Republicans in the House of Representatives, while nearly a third of the chamber's Democrats voted against it. The law gave the president the authority to slash federal salaries by up to 15 percent and to dramatically revise the benefits of veterans.

On April 1, FDR, who had consistently refused throughout the 1932 presidential campaign to specify where his economies would be achieved, signed an executive order reducing or eliminating the benefits of 1.4 million veterans, thereby reducing governmental expenditures by more than $400 million. These cuts reduced disability payments by as much as 25 to 80 percent to current recipients, and removed well over 500,000 veterans and their dependents from payments altogether. (It also instituted more stern guidelines for establishing a legitimate disability.) In addition, federal salaries were reduced by $75 million while the Post Office Department was subject to a commensurate cut. Along with a scheduled government reorganization that would save $250 million, the Economy Act savings amounted to over $850 million—not quite a 25 percent reduction in government expenditures, but in the minds of fiscal hawks, an encouraging start. Lewis Douglas was immensely satisfied and completely confident that the law had laid the "foundation for recovery."[110]

The Usual Orthodox Manner

Eccles, disenchanted with the fiscal conservatism of FDR, begins to communicate with administration insiders in Washington about adopting a different course of action.

"My heart sank," said Marriner Eccles, when he read the text of the president's Economy Act proposals. He quickly drafted a circular letter for his Utah allies and sent copies to Senator Robert La Follette (the lone member of the Finance Committee favorably disposed to Eccles's testimony) and Rex Tugwell. "It seems to me," Eccles wrote, "that if the proposed policy is carried out, it can only result in further drastic deflation." La Follette wrote back in agreement; the Economy Act had "launched an engine of deflation." A crisis would develop as a consequence, he said, "unless a program is launched to counteract it."[111]

Perhaps Eccles's strongest booster in the administration was the secretary of war, George Dern. The secretary was not only a resident of Utah, but also a director of Eccles's First Security Corporation. He was a successful mining entrepreneur who was elected to the Utah State Senate as a progressive Democrat in 1914. After championing a variety of progressive legislation, including a workers' compensation law for the state, he went on to win the governor's seat from a Mormon, incumbent Republican. Dern, who was a Congregationalist, won reelection in 1928 and was selected to be the chairman of the National Governor's Association where he made the acquaintance of Governor Franklin Roosevelt. FDR would make him the first Utahn to be honored with a cabinet position. Three days after the president's address to Congress, Eccles received a letter from his business associate. "I shall appreciate it very much," wrote Dern, "if you will write me from time to time, giving me your views." The secretary of war went on to relate that the president was handling economic affairs with the Treasury with slight consultation with members of the cabinet.[112]

Eccles, of course, hardly needed prompting. On March 30 he sent off a lengthy memorandum to Dern detailing the essential need for increased spending. "It seems to me that the government is attacking our economic problems in the usual orthodox manner," observed Eccles. "And I see little fundamental change in the methods they are pursuing and those pursued by the

Republican administration." Dern wrote back to Eccles on April 20 to apprise him of the fact that although he had discussed his views at a cabinet meeting, the administration, nevertheless, seemed bound and determined to pursue its frugal path. The secretary of the treasury, William Woodin, Dern informed Eccles, was even opposed to the guarantee of bank deposits; so, in fact, was FDR himself.[113]

The day after his memo to Dern, Eccles drafted yet another involved communication for the benefit of Rexford Tugwell and La Follette. In this memo he voiced his concern for the manner in which the government was floating its bond issues. When the Treasury resumed these sales in mid-1931—the first such series since the Liberty Bond drives of World War I—it did so by placing the bonds with the Federal Reserve banks for marketing. To assure that they would be widely available to the public, they were issued in denominations as low as fifty dollars.[114] "It is a mistake," scribed Eccles, to allow the Treasury to float a "large popular bond issue through the public." Depositors, he cautioned, would withdraw deposits to buy them and this would "raise havoc with thousands of banks."[115]

Also in April 1933, Senator John G. Townsend Jr., a member of the Senate Banking and Currency Committee, wired Eccles for advice on various currency inflation measures. Eccles used this opportunity to further his theory on the proper way of selling government bonds. When he wired Townsend back he also strongly advised that the best way to inflate the economy was to issue $5 billion in bonds to be purchased directly by the Federal Reserve Banks. (During the inflationary years of World War II, he advocated the very opposite strategy.) If purchased by the public, he emphasized, no inflation would result.[116]

Eccles continued to stress the importance of this matter of bond sales even after La Follette had written back to him to say that, in his view, the manner in which government bonds were sold was less important "than just getting it done." He did agree, however, that the direct sale of bonds to Federal Reserve Banks was a good suggestion—one that he himself "had been enamored [with] for some time." Moreover, Secretary Dern communicated Eccles's suggestion to Secretary Woodin who rejected the idea, certain that the money used to purchase securities would get back to the banks soon enough. Undaunted, Eccles continued to energetically stress the importance of this method as a vital instrument of compensatory economics. In doing so, he was displaying what many who knew him would agree was a lifelong trait: a bulldog determination in pursuit of any course he deemed sound public policy.[117] "I made life uncomfortable for all who came near me," Eccles recalled about these months. "I was irritable and impatient." Unlike Hamlet, said Eccles, "I did not curse my fate that I was born to set the world aright."[118]

While clearly eager to play a meaningful role on the national scene, Eccles had to content himself with improving the affairs of his home state. As the chairman of the Utah Committee on Relief in 1933, he lobbied to substantially bolster the meager payments made to Utah's destitute citizens. The state's relief payments, however, were roughly in alignment with the rest of the country, averaging less than five dollars a week per family; this at a time when an unskilled laborer earned somewhere in the area of twenty-six dollars a week.

Even though he was generally opposed to the federal government providing assistance for relief, President Hoover signed the Emergency Relief and Construction Act authorizing the Reconstruction Finance Corporation (RFC) to make $300 million available to the states for such purposes. The RFC, assigned the task of providing loans to banks, railroads, and insurance companies, had become operational less than two months earlier.[119] The agency was inspired by the War Finance Corporation established by the Wilson administration during the war. The five-member board of the RFC was mandated by legislation to be bipartisan. One of the two Democrats appointed to the board of directors was a fellow Mormon from Utah and a life-long friend of Eccles's, Wilson McCarthy. Although generally conservative in his public-policy positions, McCarthy had been a great supporter of Al Smith and was a political ally of George Dern. Like Eccles he was involved in both banking and ranching in the West and did his best to direct more of the RFC's resources toward agriculture and livestock interests. To Eccles's dismay, the RFC payments for relief were made in the form of loans bearing 3 percent interest to be deducted from federal highway appropriations beginning with the fiscal year 1935. Moreover, the agency was, he wrote, taking action "on behalf of creditors and investors," and largely transgressed the stimulative tenets of compensatory economics.[120]

Eccles was determined, however, to infuse Utah with as much money from the RFC as possible. To "disguise" the federal money distributed by the RFC from those that felt Washington should not play any role whatsoever in such assistance, the funds were given to the Utah Committee on Relief to pass on to private charities. As the director of the Salt Lake branch of the RFC under President Hoover, and as chairman of the Utah Committee on Relief, Eccles was in a good position to accomplish this. He and Robert Hinckley, who operated the day-to-day operations of the relief effort, wisely concluded that the money would probably never need to be paid back and that they should acquire—totally insufficient as it may have been—as much federal money as possible for the people of Utah. At a meeting of the state relief committee sometime following this, Wilson McCarthy, who was on a tour of western states, spoke. In an unintentional testament to the efforts of Eccles and Hinckley, he informed the committee that he was embarrassed by the fact that his home state used more RFC relief per capita than any other state in the union. Incensed, Eccles lambasted McCarthy; how dare he suggest that recipients of such meager assistance were guilty of some moral lapse. These were men and women willing and determined to work who, he felt, should harbor no sense of guilt whatever. Too many public officials in the United States, he instructed McCarthy, were still living in the nineteenth century. Interestingly, when Eccles wrote about this incident in his memoir, he neglected to mention his friendship with McCarthy or that his fellow Utahn modified his austere views during the New Deal years.[121]

The perception throughout the country, as Eccles was aware, was that the Mormon Church could "take care of its own." While the church did its best, the need was simply overwhelming. Moreover, as long as members of a church paid taxes, Eccles insisted, they should expect the federal government to "take care of its own," not with a dole but with jobs.[122] On one occasion he emphatically argued to Senator Reed Smoot, who had represented Utah in the United States Senate since 1903 and had been a close friend of his father's, that federal assistance was imperative. The Mormon Church's contributing members, he informed the senator, were themselves distressed. Eccles recalled that Smoot, who was an apostle of the church, looked at him "with cold eyes that received light but no images."[123]

The desperate situation in Salt Lake City is demonstrated by the establishment of an organization known as the Natural Development Association (NDA). By early 1933 there were as many as ten thousand citizens in the NDA, which, like numerous other such organizations across the nation, issued its own currency—the vallar. The NDA also founded its own newspaper titled the *Progressive Independent*, which proclaimed a populist slogan on its masthead: "A New Economic System: For Human Welfare, Man above Money."[124]

When FDR created the Federal Emergency Relief Act (FERA) in May 1933, it marked the first time in U.S. history that the federal government provided direct aid to the unemployed. Since FERA was considered an emergency response to the inability of state and local governments to cope with the dire unemployment conditions, it was not considered as a permanent agency, and it received funding for a two-year period. Half of the money was distributed in the form of matching grants with one federal dollar for each three spent by the state. The other half was placed in a discretionary fund from which payments could be furnished to states that were particularly hard hit by the economic downturn, or whose matching provision was deemed too onerous. This federal intervention induced state and local governments to double their relief contributions. On occasion FERA cajoled states to increase expenditures by threatening to cut off federal funding completely. The actual administration of relief was left to localities that were supervised by state administrators.[125]

The most onerous aspect of this new relief effort, Eccles believed, was the utilization of a means test for recipients. As the chairman of the Utah Relief Committee, he benefited, he said, from "a grass-roots observation post."[126] The regulations required local social workers to visit the homes of relief applicants to make an assessment of each family's financial wherewithal: the extent of their possession of real property as well as any savings they might have accumulated. In addition, they were to interview friends and relatives to determine what outside assistance might be available. It was also the social workers' task to report the family members' needs to their church and to their children's school to seek out all possible assistance of which they might avail themselves. The social worker was to return—technically, at least—to the home on a monthly basis to keep an ongoing account of the level of need. Once a family's "budgetary deficiency" was determined, its level of weekly compensation, a factor of hourly wage and hours employed, was established.[127]

Although FERA director Harry Hopkins hoped to alter in some fashion the traditional philosophy in which a recipient of assistance must, as he phrased it, "be made to feel his pauperism," he was forced to concede that his agency failed in this regard. "If we had not become so accustomed and, in a sense, so hardened to the fact of poverty," he wrote in 1936, "we should even now be astounded at our effrontery."[128] More importantly, argued Eccles, from the standpoint of fiscal stimulus, by merely allowing a recipient to barely afford rent and food, FERA proved to be totally ineffectual. "It checked starvation and death," he wrote, "but it did not create new jobs." A real jobs program, he constantly insisted, was desperately needed.[129]

While Eccles approved of much of the legislation that flowed from the New Deal's celebrated "hundred days," he continued to level harsh criticism at endeavors he deemed not merely ineffectual, but deleterious. In the former category, he listed FDR's adoption of Cornell professor George Warren's plan for lowering the gold content of the dollar as a means of raising commodity prices. This was the "scheme," as Eccles termed it, that FDR selected from the three inflationary alternatives available to him in the spring of 1933. As previously noted, Eccles expressed great incredulity about such a course of action. It failed in his view to achieve the objective of raising commodity prices and merely resulted in the United States becoming the recipient of more than three-fourths of the world's supply of gold, "for which," he insisted, "we had no use."[130]

In fact, the monetary gold supply almost doubled between December 1933 and July 1934. This massive influx is attributed initially to devaluation—the United States officially abandoned the gold standard in April of 1933—and later in the 1930s to the increasingly precarious political situation throughout Europe. Far from being useless, as Eccles maintained, this massive monetary expansion was, in the view of many economic historians, largely responsible for the level of recovery throughout most of the New Deal years. Quite aside from any specified Federal Reserve action, an "inflationary regime," to employ Peter Temin's term, replaced a deflationary one, lowering real interest rates while altering expectations and leading to significant increases in durable goods expenditures. In Christina Romer's analysis, it was the aggregate demand stimulus furnished by the massive monetary influx *before* the onset of hostilities in 1939 that allowed the American economy to reach its pre-Depression trend level *before the fiscal stimulus of World War II spending kicked in.*[131]

It is hardly surprising that Eccles failed to even make passing reference in his memoir to the World Economic Conference that convened in London in June of 1933. FDR shocked all sixty-six nations in attendance—including the delegation from the United States—by rejecting any notion that the United States would merely reset the dollar and consign the world to a revived gold standard. "I would regard it as a catastrophe amounting to a world tragedy," stated the president, if the conference concerned itself with satisfying the "old fetishes" of internationalist bankers. Those nations that followed suit and depreciated emerged from the economic morass at a significantly faster pace than those that remained stubbornly attached to gold. Although often perceived, then and now, as a "beggar thy neighbor" policy, as Ben Bernanke has pointed out, the abandonment of gold redounded to the benefit of most of the world. In affirming that FDR was "magnificently right," John Maynard Keynes proclaimed in an article in the *Daily Mail* that the stage had been set for the exploration of "new paths: paths new to statesmen and to bankers, but not new to thought." And in expressing a concern that Marriner Eccles believed exceeded all others, Keynes urged governments to now "put men to work by all means at our disposal."[132]

Although generally a free-trade advocate, Eccles devoted only a modicum of criticism toward the notorious Smoot-Hawley Tariff. In his testimony before the Senate Finance Committee in early 1933, he made mention of the difficulty that high tariffs presented to foreign debtors who needed to sell goods to finance repayment to the United States. His preferred solution to this policy, however, was simply to permanently cancel these debts. When Eccles elaborated upon the causes of the Depression, however, the issue of the Smoot-Hawley Act seemed not high on his list of culprits; while it may not have been the wisest course of action, perhaps, he certainly did not contend, as did FDR's secretary of state, Cordell Hull, that the tariff was "at the very heart of this country's economic dilemma."[133]

It is possible that Eccles's tacit acceptance of the tariff was somewhat related to his agricultural interests. With farm income plummeting throughout the course of the 1920s, Herbert Hoover pledged in the presidential campaign of 1928 that his administration would render assistance and protect agricultural products from ruinous undercutting by international markets. The Republican Party had historically supported high tariffs; indeed high tariff rates were already in place with the 1922 Fordney-McCumber Act. What helped to foster agricultural protectionism toward the late 1920s was the growing willingness of southern cotton producers to align with the farm block. The South had traditionally feared that foreign markets would retaliate against high tariffs. With an enormous surplus of cotton already overflowing in southern warehouses, the threat of retaliation lessened and encouraged an "alliance of corn and cotton." Nevertheless, although the 1930 act, signed into law in June of that year, boosted the tariff on agricultural products rather significantly, it brought relatively mild increases to a variety of other products.

As the president of the Sego Milk Products Company, the Amalgamated Sugar Company, and a lumber concern, Eccles was not unfavorably disposed to some level of tariff protectionism. Senator James Couzens of Michigan would raise this issue with Eccles during his Senate confirmation hearing when he was selected to head the Federal Reserve. Indeed, the beet sugar industry owed its very existence to governmental interference into the "free market." The U.S. Department of Agriculture, soon after its 1863 creation, turned its attention to funding research that helped make beet sugar a viable alternative to cane sugar. The bounties that the government showered upon the industry during these years also proved crucial to its emergence as a money-making enterprise. This assistance presumably did not alter David Eccles's fervor for laissez-faire.

As early as 1789, Congress had imposed a tariff upon sugar imports. The protective nature of these tariffs, however, was diminished considerably by political considerations. With a significant amount of sugar production essentially in the control of Americans, numerous foreign interests began receiving special consideration, and sugar from Cuba, Hawaii, Puerto Rico, and the Philippines intermittently entered the country duty free. Sugar prices plummeted to less than three cents a pound in the early 1930s—Eccles's company suffered some $500,000 in losses—leading to renewed outcries from domestic producers about unfair foreign competition, especially in regard to cheap labor. The Smoot-Hawley Tariff—Senator Smoot of Utah was, unsurprisingly, aware of beet-sugar problems—raised the duty on raw sugar imports from Cuba from 1.76 cents a pound to 2 cents a pound, more than offsetting the lower production costs between western beets and Cuban cane. Eccles led a movement, however, calling for some form of an international allotment plan that would guarantee an adequate supply of sugar to satisfy consumer needs while establishing a fair price for producers. This plan became a reality with the passage of the Jones-Costigan Sugar Act in May of 1934. It is touched upon in a later chapter.[134]

The notion that the 1930 Smoot-Hawley Act prolonged and significantly intensified the Depression gained credence as early as 1934 with a popular book by Joseph Jones. Jones reminded the nation that 1,028 economists were signatories to a front-page letter in the *New York Times* in May of 1930 that urged President Hoover to veto the act. The nation was punished, Jones argued, when the rest of the world retaliated with countervailing restrictions on American imports. Economist Paul Krugman, who was awarded his Nobel Prize for his work in international trade, and a wide array of other economists have pointed out the many flaws in this still popular interpretation. Paul Krugman deems the claim "incredible."

Those who assert that Smoot-Hawley adversely affected the economy nearly always cite the significant rise in *ad valorem* (percentage of import value) tariff rates. The act, however, really imposed nominal dollar amounts upon specific products. Between mid-1930 and the third quarter of 1932, the volume of both U.S. imports and exports declined by a little more than 40 percent. This was accompanied, however, by a stunning degree of deflation that would have significantly raised *ad valorem* rates even in the event that the Fordney-McCumber tariff remained in effect. (A $10 import fee on a product worth $100, for example, would produce a 100 percent increase in the *ad valorem* rate if its price declined to $50.) Hence the claim, frequently noted in

U.S. history textbooks, that Smoot-Hawley raised the tariff on imported goods by as much as 60 percent. Although countries did retaliate and impose higher fees on some U.S. goods—this is especially true of Canada—exports amounted to an estimated 3.34 percent of real GNP. (Exports amounted to 13 percent of GDP in 2011.) Indeed, if one factors into this a shift of consumption from imports to domestic goods, it is possible that Smoot-Hawley had, as economist Barry Eichengreen's 1989 analysis asserts, a positive impact on U.S. GNP. More probable perhaps is the 1998 assessment by Douglas Irwin that "Hawley itself appears to have been a very small direct shock to trade and therefore, it is likely, to the economy at large." Nonetheless, the persistent textbook censure of Smoot-Hawley remains what Eichengreen has aptly termed "bad history in the service of good policy."[135]

Trumpets, Parades, and Placards

The adoption of the National Industrial Recovery policy was entirely predictable and, in Eccles's view, entirely foolish. Although he did not share brain truster Rexford Tugwell's faith in planning, he thought there was much to appreciate in Adolph Berle's work.

In the classification of those early developments he did view as inimical, Eccles placed the National Recovery Act (NRA, officially known as the National Industrial Recovery Act). Passed on June 16, 1933, the NRA ambitiously set out to standardize behavior in industries by allowing trade associations to formulate codes of fair competition under the auspices of the federal government. Anyone who closely followed the testimony in February of those who spoke before the Senate Finance Committee hearings on the problems and cures of the Depression could have anticipated such a legislative development. While Bernard Baruch spearheaded the proposal in his appearance before the committee, he was merely restating a plan he had detailed three years earlier.[136] "It is lunacy," he declared in May of 1930, "to decree unlimited operation of a system which periodically disgorges indigestible masses of unconsumable products." From his vantage, Baruch was envisioning a capitalist system that, because it eliminated antitrust interference, engendered a "relaxation of the grip of government." In the immediate aftermath of the war, Baruch actually put forth the concept of a quasipublic "Supreme Court of Commerce" intended to place limits on reckless and wasteful competition, by hearing arguments presented by various industrial rivals and rendering judgments on price levels and acceptable business practices. After all, he reasoned, wasn't such an organization—the Fed—already setting the price of money? Remarkably, Baruch had enough influence to get the proposal into the Democratic Party platform of 1920. Indeed, as far back as 1919, noted Baruch's underling, Gen. Hugh Johnson (who would be appointed to head the NRA), Baruch, and a wide array of other businessmen and economists, had promulgated a similar plan that would build and refine the administrative structure that was deemed so successful in the Great War. It was Johnson's intention to dispel the popular notion—which persists to this day—that the NRA was "an after-thought or an unexpected brain-storm conceived in the confusion of early 1933."[137]

In fact, in the course of the 1920s, spurred on by the Federal Trade Commission, well over a hundred "codes of fair competition" were adopted by businesses in various fields. One of the first of this kind was the American Construction Council (ACC) established with the active encouragement of Commerce Secretary Herbert Hoover and headed by the young vice president of the Fidelity & Deposit Company, Franklin D. Roosevelt. By 1930, a plan for cooperative associations had been introduced by the United States Chamber of Commerce and the president of General Electric Corporation, Gerard Swope. After Bernard Baruch advocated his "policy of enlightened cooperation" before the Finance Committee in early 1933, he included a number of labor-friendly provisions.[138] Following Baruch, two influential labor leaders lent strong support for national planning. "The economy needs to be managed," avowed United Mine Workers' president John L. Lewis, claiming his was the "voice of millions." The nation, chimed in Sidney Hillman of the Amalgamated Clothing Workers of America, was desperate for "legislation which will establish an instrumentality to coordinate the industries of this country."[139]

In a speech before the United States Chamber of Commerce on May 4, 1933, and three nights later, in the second of his fireside chats, FDR explained the NRA to the American people. When he had assumed office the country had been "dying by inches," and it was time now to "bring order out of chaos" and eliminate "cut throat prices and unfair methods of competition." It was wrong, said the president, to consider the proposal as "government control." It was rather a "partnership in planning."[140]

What is striking about the NRA is the widespread support the concept received from the American people throughout the remainder of 1933. "Those who are not with us are against us," cautioned its chief administrator, Hugh Johnson. More than two million employers agreed to its provisions. Even Herbert Hoover initially pledged fidelity. (Henry Ford would flummox the administration by surpassing the minimum labor standards of the act while refusing to sign the industry's code, or display "Roosevelt's buzzard.") The Blue Eagle parade in New York City contained a quarter of a million *participants* (as opposed to onlookers who lined the parade's path). "Life insurance men and telephone linemen; stock brokers and chorus girls," wrote historian Arthur Schlesinger Jr., energetically marched up Fifth Avenue.[141]

Marriner Eccles was not among the NRA's enthusiasts. From his perspective it was all grounded on the false postulate that free enterprise had played itself out and that the technocrat could in some fashion supplant the businessman as the linchpin of economic progress. That cooperative planning among industrialists could end the Depression was foolhardy in the extreme. It was, after all, not an "indigestible mass of unconsumable products" that confronted the nation, but rather a staggering deficiency of aggregate demand. While section 7(a) of the act provided for organizing rights, maximum hours, and minimum wages—goals for which labor had long struggled—the 550 codes (and 200 supplementary agreements) that affected a staggering 2.3 million employers brought economic benefits that Eccles deemed largely chimerical. The NRA, with all its "trumpets, parades and placards," he maintained in his memoir, failed to achieve the essential goal of increasing the purchasing power of the American people.[142]

It is worth taking note here of the fact that Eccles's views on the National Recovery Administration were shared by the NRA's own chief of research and planning. Alexander Sachs came to this position from his job as the director of economic and investment research at Lehman Brothers. Although Hugh Johnson always referred to him as Dr. Sachs, the Jewish refugee from Lithuania possessed only an undergraduate degree—and not in economics—from Columbia. While working on Wall Street during the 1920s, Sachs gained notoriety by cautioning that the prosperity of the decade was thinly supported, not widely shared, and heading for a collapse. After the crash he was elected to Lehman's board of directors. Like Eccles, Sachs felt wedged between New Dealers who advocated planning and those who were austere budget balancers. Referring to himself as "a lone wolf New Dealer in the menagerie of economists," he accepted the position at the NRA on the expectation that the public works provision would be the NRA's saving grace by activating spending that would "liberate private capital goods." He was as disappointed as Johnson when FDR assigned this half of the NRA to Harold Ickes at the Interior Department. After a year of working to unsuccessfully limit the deleterious aspects of the program, he resigned. While Sachs proceeded to corresponded with Jacob Viner, Isador Lubin, John Maynard Keynes, and other critics of state planning, he would go on to accept future roles in the New Deal. It appears, however, that he refrained from taking his dim view of the NRA to the public.[143]

Eccles debated with himself over the wisdom of openly making his views on these matters public. After all, he reasoned, at least something was now being attempted. He questioned, moreover, if a public expression of dismay would be somewhat disloyal. Although the possibility of such a concern on his part cannot be dismissed, one cannot help but suspect that he also considered how a public disavowal of the NRA might affect his chances of being offered a position in Washington. Ultimately, as would hold true throughout his career in public life, he simply could not abide remaining silent about government policies he deemed injurious. And so, in a series of speeches in Utah he attacked the NRA as falsely premised on the conviction that "the nation is suffering from overproduction" when, in fact, it was simply a case of tens of millions of Americans having "no effective purchasing power." In addition, it could not be gainsaid that the endeavor was "another name for monopoly practices." It was important, he stated, to "call things by their right name."[144]

To be sure, there was an economic upswing in the months following the NRA enactment. (Of course, he supported the Title II provisions of the act that created the Public Works Administration, but lamented the glacial pace at which its funds were expended.) It was apparent, Eccles reflected, to those "inside the business community" what was, in fact, occurring: businessmen were frantically increasing inventories before the higher wages and production standards of the NRA were imposed. Following quickly upon the heels of this "beat the code" upsurge of the summer months was a precipitous economic downturn in September. This, Eccles asserted, was the first—but not the last—"Roosevelt Depression." (It is worth noting, however, that the National Bureau of Economic Research does not consider this downturn a bona fide recession. The GDP for the fourth quarter of 1933 did decline, but the first quarter of 1934 showed gains that surpassed the third quarter of 1933.) He would one day recollect sitting beside the president and Mrs. Roosevelt at Warm Springs, during the bleak days after the economic catastrophe of 1937. "I suppose," the First Lady reflected, "people will call this 'the second Roosevelt Depression.'" Clearly perturbed, FDR curtly insisted that it was the first. "But Franklin," Eleanor calmly responded, "aren't you forgetting the depression in the fall of 1933 after you tried to balance the budget and the NRA codes went into effect?"[145]

Yet another striking aspect of the NRA is the extent to which historical analysis has buried this central policy of the "first New Deal" in criticism similar to Eccles's. As early as December 31, 1933, the *New York Times* published an open letter to FDR from John Maynard Keynes. Expressing precisely Eccles's view at the time, Keynes explained that it was a "technical fallacy" to expect that an increase in prices, derived from the restriction of supply rather than an infusion of demand, would bring recovery. While some New Deal champions have agreed with such assessments, arguing that the New Deal was successful despite this experiment in business code-making, its detractors often cite it as among the most egregious transgressions of the 1930s. "Only later on could people see that the cloth of gold being spun before their eyes was spun of air," Eccles recalled, "and that the king, after all, was naked as the day he was born."[146]

Eccles's derisive perspective, however, seems hardly consistent with those academic economists who consider the first New Deal contractionary. The fact remains that—the brief "first Roosevelt Depression" notwithstanding—the two years in which the NRA was in existence witnessed considerable economic growth. One can imagine Eccles at least entertaining the arguments of some recent economists who maintain that, as a temporary "emergency" measure—which, after all, is how the NRA was presented to the American people—the supervised monopoly power of firms and workers had beneficent effects. A policy that would have been injurious in normal circumstances, it is argued, was both inflationary and expansionary in the extreme conditions of 1933.[147]

That something along the lines of the NRA would emerge from the brain trusters—Moley, Berle, and Tugwell—was hardly a surprise. Very early in the campaign for the presidency, the three had collaborated on a memorandum to FDR that urged a centralized plan of national action. (This is the same memo referenced earlier that called for both a large investment in public works and a balanced budget.) Ray Moley may have been the least enthused of the trio when it came to the conceptual basis for this strategy of recovery. And yet the Columbia professor, whose national renown won him the cover of *Time* that May of 1933 as the most influential of FDR's wise men, would demonstrate his fidelity to the NRA when he would lead the charge to revive the act after the Supreme Court ruled it unconstitutional two years after its inception. The law could be continued, he suggested, on a voluntary basis, or a constitutional amendment could be drafted to meet the court's concerns.[148]

Rex Tugwell's support was understandable. A protégé of the social theorist Thorstein Veblen, Tugwell argued that "competition and democracy were not Siamese twins." This should have been apparent decades before, he maintained, but now, thanks to the Depression, "The jig is up. The cat is out of the bag. There is no invisible hand. There never was." Savage capitalist competition, at those times when the power of oligopoly did not fix prices, was "tragically wasteful" and "led to disaster." It was essential now "to supply a real and visible guiding hand," said Tugwell, "to do the task which that mythical nonexistent, invisible agent was supposed to perform, but never did."[149]

Eccles clearly shared some common ground with Adolf Berle Jr.—at least in the 1930s. The grandson of a German Catholic "Forty-Eighter" who migrated to the United States in the wake of the failed revolutionary fervor of 1848, Berle grew up steeped in the social gospel. His father, a Boston Protestant theologian, was an acolyte of Louis Brandeis, and, in fact, testified at the first Jewish Supreme Court justice's confirmation hearing in 1916. The senior Berle was at the time a member in good stead of Brandeis's Anti-Merger League. In 1909, Adolf Jr. was accepted into Harvard at the age of thirteen, although the decision was made to postpone his entrance until he was fourteen; he graduated with both bachelor's and master's degrees in history in 1914. (His decision to take extra courses delayed his graduation by a year.) Two years later he became the youngest graduate ever of Harvard Law School. After assuming a career in corporate law he joined the army during the First World War. His bunkmate at a training camp for officers in the Adirondack Mountains was a young man from Maine named Gardiner Means. Means would earn a PhD in economics at Columbia University, and coauthor with Berle a seminal work in American economic thought a decade and a half later. The army stationed Berle in the American-occupied Dominican Republic, where he was assigned the task of stepping up that nation's sugar production. After the war Berle represented sugar interests—something he shared, of course, with Eccles—for many years as a corporate attorney.[150]

Berle's emergence as a New Dealer would bring him into direct conflict with an old adversary, Felix Frankfurter. Their personal dislike for each other began at Harvard Law, where the intensely self-confident Berle was a confrontational student in Professor Frankfurter's classes. The animus between them was exacerbated by the inveterate disagreement among progressives over the issue of how best to cope with the power of modern corporations: break them apart or regulate and oversee their societal influence. Although Frankfurter generally favored the former, the latter became a crucial component of Berle's conception of sound statecraft.[151]

In the 1920s, Berle lived on Henry Street—directly next door to Lillian Wald's famous settlement house—and left the Lower East Side each morning for his Wall Street office. As he gained a national reputation for his knowledge of corporate law, he was increasingly discomfited by the fact that the corporate institution that he was positioned to know so intimately had already become, as Thorstein Veblen described it, "the master instrument of civilization." Seeking to direct attention to the implications of such a development, he partnered with Gardiner Means to write *The Modern Corporation and Private Property*.

In their 1932 book, Berle and Means, while affirming that the corporation's role in modernity was a fait accompli, cautioned that as the "dominate institution of the modern world" it posed a clear threat to numerous societal interests and had, therefore, to be regulatively corralled and assigned a more reasonable role in economic and political life. Their concern had less to do with the productive workings of such business enterprises or their efficiency as it did with the alarming fact that such institutions were near the point of replicating the "religious power of the mediaeval church or the political power of the national state." Indeed, corporations had already reached a point where they could "compete on equal terms with the modern state." The principal threat, they argued, came in the form of the now dominant role played by professional technocratic managers, whose self-interest often drove corporate decisions. The problem—one recognized as such today—was that many of these managers were instrumental in selecting the membership of the boards assigned with their supervision. In such a setting the gifted entrepreneur who largely drove commercial success and innovation had given way to a self-sustaining corporate bureaucracy. The fidelity to an unencumbered corporate structure by many who considered themselves market fundamentalists was—and remains—a peculiar loyalty in light of the fact that the individual investors had, in return for the "wages of capital," largely "surrendered" their ownership to this bureaucratic elite.

Interestingly, then, although the industrial revolution had placed large numbers of workers under the control of an "industrial manager," it had done so as well for the ostensible owners of the same companies in which such workers toiled. (In 1926 Berle wrote an article in the *Harvard Law Review* that accused companies of issuing below-par offerings of stock to weaken stockholders' power.) In his discussion of this issue, economic historian Paddy Ireland notes the acute irony that while Adam Smith viewed the emerging corporate structure with a good deal of suspicion, Karl Marx looked on with considerable satisfaction. The rise of the modern corporation amounted to, as Marx phrased it, "the abolition of capital as private property within the framework of capitalist production itself," and represented "private production without the control of private property." It is worth keeping this perspective in mind when considering Berle's desire to win for himself the appellation of "the American Karl Marx—a social prophet." While Marx had a proletarian revolution in mind, writes *New Dealers* author Jordan Schwarz, Berle believed "the middle class needed a revolution against corporate concentration"; like Eccles, he wished to redirect "the flow of power from corporate managers and financiers in Wall Street toward popular control in Washington. Between the proletarian revolution and monopoly capitalism lay a middle way of which he was the prophet: corporate liberalism"; or, as in the more politically charged phrasing of Berle—"people's capitalism."[152]

Berle and Means's book became quite well known in academia. John Kenneth Galbraith, in fact, was somewhat under its spell when he began tutoring Henry Dennison in early 1936. Galbraith, however, would later recollect that the work was largely ignored by economists; he speculates that this was due in part to the fact that Berle was a lawyer by trade and thought academically unsuited for attention, and because the book's focus—unlike a simple diagnosis of monopolistic competition—on "power without property" was simply too alien a criticism for scholars to address within the context of classical economic thought. This seems an unwarranted conclusion since, as Galbraith must have been aware, there was in the 1930s a concerted attempt by a group of statisticians at Harvard to disprove much of the statistical evidence put forth by Means and Berle (although the facts and figures were provided by Means—who was at the time a PhD candidate—while the general argument was Berle's). Beyond academic economists, the authors' intention was to gain credibility with corporate lawyers, investment bankers, government regulators, and the myriad of actual players in the American business scene. They sought, Schwarz asserts, "to take the study of big corporations from the hands of muckraking popularizers and give it the authenticity of serious modern scholarship." The work, however, appeared to attract significant attention in the mainstream press. In an analysis that appeared on the front page of the *New York Herald*'s book review, Charles Beard pronounced the work "a masterly achievement" and ranked it as the most important contribution to "American statecraft" since the *Federalist Papers*. Nonetheless, it failed to satisfy the grievances of the far left while it heightened the apprehensions of free marketers. That the *Modern Corporation* laid the foundation for much of the criticisms of corporate misfeasance for decades to come is perhaps substantiated by a 1982 Hoover Institute seminar commemorating the book's fiftieth anniversary. Terming the work the "intellectual grandfather" of corporate capitalism's antagonists, the conservative think tank lamented *Modern Corporation*'s role as "one of the most influential books of the twentieth century."[153]

Eccles would profess to be quite familiar with the book. In regard to Berle and Means's emphasis upon the need for internal shareholder oversight, he may have possessed some firsthand experience. Eccles claimed that as a young businessman he demonstrated to investors in the Oregon Lumber Company that its managers—led by his half-brother David—were diverting substantial sums of money for their personal use. By resorting to proxies he gained a controlling interest in the company. After being invited to join the board of the Utah Construction Company, Eccles insisted upon close examinations of all statements and demanded that the board have a voice in the major policies that the company's managers promulgated.[154]

Berle's assertion that much of what he was proposing in his capitalist revolution was merely "the logical working out of our system" was precisely how Eccles framed his own proposals. Recall that in his testimony before the Senate in 1933 Eccles chose to characterize his blueprint for recovery as "logical radicalism." As we will see, in the late 1930s, when both men were New Deal veterans, they joined forces to propose what they framed as a common-sense plan to induce the Reconstruction Finance Corporation to adopt a much more aggressive posture as an agent of economic stimulus. This, in fact, had been a goal of Berle's since he had been appointed legal counsel to the RFC in 1933.[155]

Although it would never become quite as innovative as either Eccles or Berle wished, there is no question that the RFC—created hesitantly by Herbert Hoover—was transformed under the remarkable New Deal leadership of Jesse Jones. As Eccles surveyed the preeminent figures in the administration in that first year, he had to feel a certain agnation with the tall, whitehaired Texan. Jones had abandoned his family's lumber business to enter the world of banking and, like Eccles, he came to appreciate how the federal government, working in conjunction with private interests, could foster dynamic economic development. Two decades earlier Jones led a successful campaign to coax the Wilson administration to build a fifty-mile ship channel to link Houston to the Gulf of Mexico. The American taxpayers thereby made Jones's city the most vital commercial center in the American South and—thanks to wise anticipatory real estate purchases—made the young banker exceedingly rich.[156]

Moreover, Eccles shared what Jordan Schwarz has identified as Jones's "anticolonial attitudes toward Wall Street" that typified western bankers. Ultimately, the Texan's reputation as a fiscal conservative would make him more acceptable to the eastern banking establishment and was destined to foster numerous policy confrontations with Eccles and other progressives. As chair of the RFC, however, Jones took full advantage of the authority given the agency by the Emergency Banking Act of 1933, to eschew saddling banks with more debt in the form of loans in favor of infusing them with capital by compelling them to sell preferred stock to the RFC. By 1935 the agency had in its portfolio over a billion dollars of preferred stock in half the banks in the country, including some of Marriner Eccles's.[157]

From Eccles's vantage, in the nascent days of the New Deal, Berle's ideas about government utilization of credit, money, and regulation to foster a more ebullient and reliable capitalist structure, were, for the most part, not being addressed. Indeed, he wondered whether Tugwell had "brought himself abreast of the broad conceptions" his colleague from Columbia was proposing.[158] In light of the fact that Rex Tugwell was an avowed champion of a planned economy, and fully expecting that the professor would seek to pursue a course very much in the planning tradition, it is not terribly surprising that Eccles left their drugstore meeting in February believing that a productive relationship was unlikely to materialize. Nevertheless, there was much upon which both men agreed, and Eccles seemed determined to keep a line of communication open with the presidential advisor. Until the fall of 1933, however, there seemed to be no substantial exchange between them. In his autobiography, Eccles makes mention of an "unexpected letter" from Tugwell on October 10, 1933, in which Eccles was encouraged to come to Washington to discuss "things which are rather pressing problems at the present time."[159] This account seems mildly disingenuous, however, since Eccles himself had reinitiated contact with Tugwell before this. Traveling to the nation's capital in August, he called on Tugwell who happened at the time to be out of town. Tugwell actually extended his invitation on October 18. Eccles promptly responded that he could be in Washington on the thirty-first of that month. He may have excluded some details to avoid the impression—a correct one, perhaps—that he [Eccles] was earnestly soliciting his services.[160]

It would have been excruciating for someone as prepossessing as Eccles to merely watch contentedly from the sidelines as the exciting whirlwind of political events swept by. "Legions were rushing to Washington to save the nation," mused the acerbic journalist John T. Flynn of these months, "with the sense of joyous dedication with which the old-fashioned volunteer fireman rushed to a saloon fire." The Utah businessman, with firehose in hand, would arrive upon the national scene with precisely that spirit. He sought to douse the country, not with socialism as the *New York Times* discerned in its assessment of his January 1933 testimony to Congress, but rather with capitalism with a human face. In this conception of his role he was not far afield from the president himself. It was a vision whose beacon furnished the guiding light for all that both men sought to achieve in the realm of public policy. The following chapter seeks to explore this undertaking and to take stock of its heritage.[161]

3

THE ESTABLISHED RULES OF DECENCY

"I Am Talking Straight Dutchess County Americanism"

Speaking to his "neighbors," FDR articulates the fundamental beliefs of the New Deal.

"The New Deal is no revolution," wrote Louis M. Hacker in the January 1934 pages of *Harper's*. As the nation evaluated the efficacy of the CWA, the historian asserted that what FDR had wrought was far too complicated to be categorized as such. "Revolutions," he observed, "are very simple things." To a nation engulfed in the "alphabet soup" of government initiatives, however, it certainly looked as though significant change was underway. Viewing from the British Isles, and favorably sensing a revolutionary tenor, H. G. Wells suggested that the future held a potentially laudatory place for the new president. Ignominy awaited him, he prophesized, should he choose to embrace the destructive capitalism of the past. Some six years later, Wells would somewhat tepidly maintain that the New Deal had done its best to steer clear of that checkered past and was "plainly an attempt to achieve a working socialism and avert a social collapse in America." Of course, he ruefully observed, "Americans shirk the word 'socialism' but what else can one call it?"[1]

Roosevelt had a different name for it. Speaking to his "neighbors" at Vassar College in August 1933, not far from his family home at Hyde Park, FDR insisted that the "great national effort to set our national house in order" was largely following the path previously blazed by some progressive state governments. Not long before the New Deal commenced, renowned social philosopher John Dewey, looking out at a ravaged America, wrote censoriously of the nation's incantation of the "older creeds" of "our essential Americanism." By "repeating them often enough," he observed, "we hope to ward off the evils of the new situation, or at least to prevent ourselves from seeing them." It was, he pronounced, "our great abdication." Possessed, it seems, with a sense of this national delusion, FDR was determined not merely to sermonize upon the "older creeds" but to use them as a springboard for action. To be sure, they were setting out to alter the "old order" that allowed the country to drift "down the hill," but they were not tampering with the core principles inherent in American life. Indeed, by abandoning some of the rules of a "bygone age" they were merely adapting—as Americans had always done—to new realities. And although it could be said that there were "drastic changes" in some of the governmental methods it chose to employ, the New Deal, far from infringing upon personal liberty, was actually enhancing it for millions of Americans. It "all ties in," he explained, with "the old theme" of being a good neighbor. "I am talking straight Dutchess County Americanism," FDR intoned.[2]

It is not an uncommonly held belief that Roosevelt deliberately eschewed pontificating about political philosophy in much the manner that Ben Franklin eluded the prospect of an afterlife: they were not topics either man cared to "dogmatize upon." Frances Perkins rather famously recorded his response to a young man's query about his philosophy: "Philosophy? I am a Christian and a Democrat—that's all." The quote can often be found in support of the typical assessment that FDR's was "almost totally unencumbered and unenriched by conceptual thought" and could therefore be persuaded to "change course" with some frequency since he "rarely committed to a single ideological position." This understanding is seen in Richard Hofstadter's view ("The Aristocrat as Opportunist") that one found at "the heart of the New Deal" not "a philosophy but a temperament." But such appraisals tend to assume that political strategy (flexibility) necessarily excludes an underlying allegiance to a societal vision; the latter was something he most definitely possessed. FDR was far less the masterful practitioner of "the principles of politics," Eliot Janeway suggested, than he was the craftsman of a "politics of principles." Roosevelt's was a deceptive pragmatism, said Janeway, "which mere politicians and, indeed, mere idealists cannot understand." Political scientist Sidney Milkis concurs with such an appraisal, insisting that "the New Deal needs to be taken more seriously as a *political program*, based upon firmly established values, rather than a series of hastily contrived reactions to social developments."[3]

To that end, FDR's penchant for connecting the New Deal with the American past—a modernizing, if you will, of "Dutchess County Americanism"—may have been minimally esoteric but amounted nonetheless to a genuine creed that his speechwriters (Sam Rosenman, Tom Corcoran, et al.) did understand

and captured for him throughout the expanse of his presidency. To be sure, this New Deal rhetoric had a realpolitik dimension that helped in no small measure to counter the incessant associations with various isms that were hurled its way. The uniform-clad Civilian Conservation Corps, the supervised cartelization of the NRA, the government employment offered by the jobs programs, and the increased discussion of government pensions for elderly Americans inevitably engendered associations with both fascism and socialism.

FDR rather brilliantly addressed any fears that might arise among Americans in regard to these matters in his June 28, 1934, fireside chat. "A few timid people, who fear progress," he instructed, "will try and give you new and strange names for what we are doing." Those who make such connections, FDR informed the country, "are trying to make very complex and theoretical something that is really very simple and very practical." While he was away for the summer, he explained, the White House was to undergo a renovation to install modern piping and electrical wiring. He had every confidence, however, that upon his return he would not discover that the architects had added "some strange new Gothic tower or a factory building or perhaps a replica of the Kremlin or the Potsdam Palace." He had no such fear because the men in charge knew full well that any new alteration must "blend with the essential lines of the old." It was the harmonious blending of the old and the new, he noted, "that marks orderly peaceful progress not only in building buildings but in building government itself." The new structure, he assured the nation, "is a part of and a fulfillment of the old." The New Deal he saw as a commitment to the "historic traditions of the American people." It was simple: a Rooseveltian "city on a hill" that infused John Winthrop's plain admonition of 1630, that the "rich and mighty should not eate up the poore" and that the public must be "knit more nearly together in Bonds of brotherly affection." It was a philosophy often delivered in the most casual of ways; perhaps that explains why a preponderance of Americans had so little difficulty in their visceral understanding of it.[4]

What FDR set out to do that day in Dutchess County was to place the New Deal within the context of American Progressivism. By following in the path of both Theodore Roosevelt's New Nationalism and Woodrow Wilson's New Freedom, he was satisfying Edmund Burke's distinction between "change and reformation." As William Clyde Dunn quotes Burke: "Change is 'novelty,' a wholesale disregard for traditional circumstance. Reform is 'a direct application of a remedy to the grievances complained of.'" A "disposition to preserve [as FDR thought he was doing with capitalism] and an ability to improve, taken together," Burke stated, "would be my standard of a statesman." In this regard,

Roosevelt may have been welcoming of the appellation Burke assumed for himself—a pragmatic "philosopher in action."[5]

Jefferson at Fontainebleau

The Founding Fathers cared deeply about extreme inequality and understood its importance in maintaining a viable republic.

In their analysis of the evolution of "the core commitments" to social welfare in the United States, social scientists Theodore Marmor, Jerry Mashaw, and Philip Harvey have identified a general acceptance of the following duality: an understanding that there is a level of subsistence that all Americans should remain above, concentric with a promise of social and economic opportunity. A commitment to both would become the pillars upon which the New Deal was constructed, and each was explicitly stated in FDR's Vassar speech and implicitly embedded in a quotation from Jefferson that FDR included in his national bestseller of 1933, *Looking Forward.*

> We have no paupers, the great mass of our population is of laborers, our rich who can live without labor, either manual or professional, being few and of moderate wealth. Most of our laboring class possess property, cultivate their own lands, have families and from the demands for their labor are enabled to extract from the rich and the competent such prices as enable them to feed abundantly; clothe above mere decency, to labor moderately and raise their families.[6]

These sentiments of Jefferson's—his expression, if you will, of *the promise of American life*—would have been easily identifiable to all of the founders as crucial elements of James Harrington's model commonwealth of *Oceana.* The work of this seventeenth-century English theorist occupied a prominent position in the political thought that swirled around the establishment of the American Republic. The distribution of property, Harrington observed, was the ultimate determinant of political power. This law of "the balance or dominion of property" dictated that in republics, the balance of property—to prevent any cause for internal "commotion"—must be "substantially" in the hands of the many. "He argued," writes historian Richard Olson, "that Aristotle and Machiavelli had both recognized special cases of the general law in discussions of why republics cannot long survive the rise of great inequalities of wealth between the many and the few." While Harrington believed that men were quite capable of altruistically comprehending that the public interest must often supersede their own private concerns, they must often be compelled by law to act in accordance with such an understanding. But as C. B. Macpherson has emphasized, when Harrington referred to Oceana as an "equal commonwealth," he was not speaking arithmetically, but rather in terms of the equality of opportunity. All citizens are equal in terms of believing they have a stake in society—their allegiance will redound to their own material well-being. It is clear to the great Harrington scholar J. G. A. Pocock, however, that in Harrington's conception of a "democracy of landholders" the *demos* must possess land "in relative equality." Nor was he averse, Pocock informs us, to the notion that legislation could rectify an imbalance.[7]

This may not have been far from James Madison's reasoning when he suggested that it was prudential for a government to discourage an "immoderate" acquisition of property "by the silent operation of laws, which, without violating the rights of property, reduce extreme wealth towards a state of mediocrity." This statement is suggestive of Jefferson's famous letter to his fellow Virginian from Fontainebleau some years earlier. Jefferson asserted that legislators could find "means of silently lessening the inequality of property" when such conditions arose. His "train of reflections" on the "unequal division of property" had been set in motion, he informed Madison, by a stroll he had taken with a poor peasant woman, during which "enquiries into her vocation, condition, and circumstances" were made. Disturbed by the woman's plight, he suggested that the very existence of such "unemployed poor" in a land of wide abundance amounted to an ipso facto acknowledgment that "the laws of property have been so far extended as to violate natural right." Contemplating his country's future, Jefferson cautioned his fellow Virginian: "If, for the encouragement of industry we allow it [land] to be appropriated, we must take care that other employment be furnished to those excluded from this appropriation." He remained "conscious," of course, that an equal division of property was "impractical." Nevertheless, the "misery" engendered as a consequence of "enormous inequality" in wealth must encourage lawmakers to formulate corrective "devices" that are harmonious with the "natural affections of the human mind." Jefferson's contemplation of the troubles that future industrial development might cause in terms of social dysfunction was not something to which his political counterpart, Alexander Hamilton, gave much thought.

Jefferson's comments, while hardly reflective of a tolerance for some governmentally orchestrated social transformation, do convey a clear concern for some measure of economic equity when wealth distribution is deemed to be substantially unbalanced.[8]

From Jefferson's vantage in the late eighteenth century, however, the United States seemed to be fulfilling Harrington's requisite for a free republic. Charles Pinckney agreed, writing in 1787 that the United States presents a "greater equality than is to be found among the people of any other country and an equality which is more likely to continue." Noah Webster, the rock-ribbed Federalist, shared this view and considered this essentially balanced distribution of property to be the nation's greatest strength. According to economic historian J. Bradford DeLong, in the aftermath of the American Revolution, the wealthiest 1 percent of American households held some 15 percent of national wealth (although, as the footnote below reveals, Jefferson's Virginia—even when only white males are concerned—may not have been the best exemplar of an egalitarian paradigm). Life in the early 1930s, however, convinced both Franklin Roosevelt and a significant number of Americans that the national government was failing to fulfill its part in the contract with its people. DeLong estimates that the richest 1 percent of American households held some 45 percent of national wealth in 1929.[9] "The terms of the contract," FDR reminded his fellow Americans, "are as old as the Republic and as new as the new economic order." When Jefferson employed the standard "above mere decency" in praise of American life, he was prematurely articulating a New Deal litmus test of societal progress. As commented upon above, the word "decency" was one that New Dealers applied repeatedly. "The objective of all these plans," wrote Frances Perkins, "was to make human life on this planet in this generation more decent." It was, she observed of the president, "the word he often used to express what he meant by a proper, adequate, and intelligent way of living." While lauding the historic Fair Labor Standards Act, for example, FDR announced that it was premised on the conviction that goods produced under "conditions that do not meet rudimentary standards of decency should not pollute the channels of interstate trade." In his 1935 State of the Union address, the president spoke of the incontestable necessity of "a decent living" and the "security of decent homes" for all Americans. Government, Marriner Eccles stated, "can and should insist on minimum standards of decency in the mode and conditions of life for its people." (In this minimum standard, he included maximum employment, minimum income, and virtually every other social benefit of the New Deal.) Harry Hopkins put it simply: "A new standard of public decency was being set."[10]

Commensurably ubiquitous in the rhetoric of the New Deal—stated often by Marriner Eccles—was a commitment to an "equality of opportunity." What distinguished Herbert Hoover's use of the locution from FDR's was a fundamental disagreement over what actually constituted equality of opportunity and, moreover, what governmental measures impaired or enhanced individual liberty. For example, when he delivered his address to Congress on tax reform in June 1935, President Roosevelt quoted his cousin Theodore's address of 1907. Calling for a heavy progressive tax upon large fortunes, he scorned the notion that it constituted a levy upon "thrift or industry." To the contrary, he affirmed that "such a tax would preserve a measurable equality of opportunity" for generations.[11]

Here, too, FDR was adamant that efforts to achieve such equality be framed as harmonic with American political ideology. In November 1933, his Thanksgiving Day Proclamation called upon Americans to remember those who "fought to keep pure the ideal of equality of opportunity." In the industrial age, however, "clear sighted men," as he observed earlier that year, "saw with fear the danger that opportunity would no longer be equal." In this need to preserve cherished American ideals by reimagining the strategic responses of government, he claimed Thomas Jefferson as an ally. "He did not deceive himself with outward forms," said FDR. "Government with him was a means to an end, not an end in itself; it might be either a refuge and a help or a threat and a danger, depending on the circumstances."[12]

Jefferson certainly displayed distaste for ideological rigidity in governance. In writing on this issue long after his political life had passed, he reflected that the age that established the core principles of American life was one that he knew intimately. "I belonged to it, and labored with it," noted the famed Virginian, referencing his fellow founding brothers who inhabited the age with him. "It was very like the present," he continued in words that captured the very essence of FDR's New Deal defense of experimentation, "but without the experience of the present; and forty years of experience in government is worth a century of book-reading, and this they would say themselves, were they to rise from the dead."[13]

It seems probable, moreover, that Jefferson would acknowledge the accuracy of historian Joseph Ellis's assertion that the country was not so much founded on the "proposition" he presented in the Declaration of Independence, as it was on "an argument about what that proposition means." FDR's most profound—and irrecusably his most successful—attempt to win that argument, and unite the nation's political heritage with the efforts of his administration, occurred in June 1936 as he accepted his party's presidential nomination in Philadelphia. He instructed his speechwriters to infuse the acceptance with the rhetoric of the Revolution and the Declaration of Independence. He was especially desirous that they touch upon a sense of "self-evident truths."[14]

More than a quarter of a century earlier, when Theodore Roosevelt stood upon a kitchen table in an open field to address tens of thousands of Kansans in the town of Osawatomie and professed that Americans possessed social as well as political rights, he too touched briefly upon reverential moments of the nation's past. But the former president, inspired by journalist Herbert Croly's 1909 work *The Promise of American Life*, framed the assertion that day as a "moral wakening" conveying the sense that he was speaking of a novel conception without which the nation "cannot go forward." Containing many of the essential elements that would come to fruition in the New Deal, TR's New Nationalism seemed to suggest a future that would be achieved when "public men" became "genuinely progressive." He had, perhaps, placed too much emphasis on Croly's insistence that "the better future which Americans propose" was an idea that must "in certain essential respects emancipate them from their past." Responding to a significant wave of negative reaction, TR conceded in a personal correspondence that he "had no business to take the position in the fashion that I did."[15]

By contrast, FDR's address was drenched in the lineage of an esteemed past and posited as a call for redemption. "Philadelphia is a good city," he began, "to restore to the people a wider freedom." Speaking before an immense gathering of one hundred thousand at Franklin Field, he was determined that his remarks would be widely distanced from any suggestion of socialism. As the embattled farmers at Concord Bridge had taken up the struggle against a privileged aristocracy that had no legitimacy in American life, so Americans of the 1930s must dislodge from power the contemporary "royalists of the economic order." This privileged order had conceded government's role in maintaining "political freedom" but considered that "economic slavery was nobody's business." Could it be that government could protect citizens in their right to vote but not in their "right to work" and "right to live"?[16]

"Today we stand committed to the proposition that freedom is no half and half affair," FDR proclaimed that June night in Philadelphia. "If the average citizen is guaranteed equal opportunity in the polling place, he must have equal opportunity in the market place." As Lincoln had called the American experiment with democracy "the last best hope of earth," Roosevelt went on to state that the New Deal was "fighting to save a great and precious form of government for ourselves and for the world." What he meant, wrote historian Arthur Schlesinger, was clear: "On the success or failure of the American attempt to make industrial society livable might rest the future of free society everywhere."[17]

That November, FDR, in conjunction with the Democratic Party, went on to win the most overwhelming political victory in American history. (The implications of the election, and the manner in which it signified a change in the overall direction of the New Deal, will be touched upon in the next chapter.) It seems highly doubtful that among the great number of Americans who cast their ballots for Franklin Roosevelt in that election, there were many who were of the mind that in doing so they were abandoning, or in any fashion mitigating, the essential principles of their economic and political heritage.

The groundwork for that 1936 campaign had long before been established. If TR did not sufficiently articulate the genuine Americanism of the New Nationalism in his 1910 address in Osawatomie, it was not a failing of his 1912 presidential bid. His Bull Moose run was, by a wide margin, the most successful third-party candidacy in all of U.S. history. In 1909, when Croly articulated his vision of a leader who could meld Hamiltonian means with Jeffersonian ends, and thereby ennoble a vigorous federal government to act as the champion of individualism, he specifically singled out Theodore Roosevelt. "An individuality such as his," Croly suggested, was ideally suited to the task. TR was dedicated, writes John Morton Blum, "to the virtues of the rural America of his forebears, to hard work, self-control, duty, honesty, sobriety, bravery, to the sum qualities he called character."[18]

If TR tethered Progressivism to an "individualist ethic" by embodying such estimable traits, his Democratic opponent in 1912 did so by the dint of elaborate scholarship. As early as 1898, with the publication of *The State*, Woodrow Wilson had begun a philosophical assault on the notion that a conservative states'-rights perspective he had once espoused was a bulwark against the erosion of individual liberty. He had come to see that the work of the founders was as much a product of experience as of deliberation; "government," he writes, "is a part of life, and, with life it must change, alike in its objects and its practices." The only principle that must be left "unaltered" in a system of meaningful liberty, he insists, is the ability of a people to respond to historical circumstances. "Political liberty," Wilson tells us, "consists in the best practicable adjustment between the power of the government and the privilege of the individual." He had now come to understand that government, in fact, had it within its power to unshackle an individual from dehumanizing farm debt, disease-ridden tenement walkups, life-threatening work environments, and the madness of cyclical banking panics. Government, therefore, functions in this Wilsonian conception as "the indispensable organ of society." Indeed, an enhancement of society by creating conditions that facilitate the self-development of all, Wilson avers, might properly be termed *socialism* had the word not already been appropriated by a "radically mistaken class of thinkers."

However, when FDR came to incorporate what historian Scott Zentner has labeled Wilson's "new politics of individuality," he understood that it would be far safer to explain it as merely a revised Dutchess County Americanism.[19]

"Adam Smith's Fervor"

As a moral philosopher and an economic theorist, Adam Smith could indeed prove inspirational to a New Dealer; it requires, however, a reconnection of the severed ties between morality and political economy.

As we have already seen, by the election of 1936 Marriner Eccles had long been on record that Americans should expect their government to be actively engaged in assuring social rights for its citizens. In the immediate aftermath of the election, he delivered conciliatory speeches to banking associations and, as Sidney Hyman writes, made an "appeal to them to join in a common struggle to support the indivisible relationship between human rights and property rights." This was a self-evident proposition, for Eccles, and for FDR.[20]

Like Roosevelt, Eccles defended his convictions as firmly rooted in the past and representative not of some wide-eyed social theorist, but a historical personage whose probity was beyond question in mainstream American life—Adam Smith. Smith appears in the very first sentence of Eccles's memoir. There can be little doubt that in his eighteenth-century understanding of the workings of a market economy, Adam Smith would *generally* embrace the tenets of Say's Law. Eccles drew from Adam Smith, however, perspectives far more encompassing than any narrow chicken-or-egg polemic over the issue of supply and demand. To his father, and to the vast majority of those who revere his name, the Scottish philosopher remains the acknowledged high priest of laissez-faire. The fact that Smith never once employed the phrase that seems inextricably connected to his name is somewhat indicative of the extent to which his famous book has been insufficiently perceived. "As my father in his youth may have heard that doctrine explained by those who could read," Eccles wrote,

> they did not tell him that Adam Smith's fervor ran strong on behalf of apprentices, laborers, and Farmers—so strong, in fact, that he was the

> first to suggest that labor was the sole source of value in commodities. That his attack on monopolies was a double-edged one, applying equally to those who plundered the wealth of a nation under a royal charter, and those who plundered it in the name of liberating all commercial efforts from the trappings of state control. That the very title of his work, *The Wealth of Nations*, asserted the paramount standard of the *national* welfare, and not the wealth of *men*, as the one by which all economic activity was to be judged.[21]

His father, he recollected, was too busy building his business empire to bother reading the actual text of *The Wealth of Nations*. "The edited version," he assumed, "the one that read 'no government interference'—suited him better." One can only wonder when Marriner Eccles availed himself of the actual text. When did he take notice of passages in Smith's vast tome, published in 1776, that seemed at variance with the overwhelmingly accepted interpretation? He has left behind no tattered, notated, or underlined copy of the work in his personal library. Nor did he seem to present a more nuanced view of the book when he began his abandonment of a strict free-market vision of economic development.[22]

Nonetheless, *The Wealth of Nations* does indeed present frequent evidences that would appear somewhat better suited to the sensibilities of New Dealers than avid free-marketers. In discussing, for example, the distinction that a society makes between the commodities that are "necessaries" to its inhabitants and those that are mere "luxuries," Smith invokes what emerged as the common New Deal standard of "decency." He informs his readers that necessaries, beyond being indispensable to support life, encompass "whatever the custom of the country renders it indecent for creditable people, even of the lowest order, to be without." He goes on to reiterate that "those things" that all should possess are not merely dictated by "nature" but are prescribed by "the established rules of decency" that a society has "rendered necessary to the lowest rank of people." Does Smith believe, therefore, that it is incumbent then upon the state to be proactive and orchestrate the means by which such indecencies might be remediated? The answer, of course, is yes. This he believes can be achieved in numerous ways, but principally, as we will explore below, through taxation. Smith was greatly influenced by Henry Home's (Lord Kames) 1774 work *Sketches of the History of Man*. One of Home's general rules of taxation was "to remedy the inequality of riches as much as possible, by relieving the poor and burdening the rich." This was a way, Home asserted, to combat one of the "many vices that poison a nation." Thus the suggestion by Smith for a removal of taxes on necessaries and its imposition upon luxuries.[23]

This point is not an unimportant one for it goes to the very core of Milton Friedman and Rose Friedman's criticism of a New Deal conception of "fairness." If a government is to take measures to promote "fairness," they argue, it has entered a muddle, for it is a vague notion "that is difficult, if not impossible, to define precisely." But is "fairness" any more elusive than "liberty"? Indeed, if a government decides that it is an infringement of the latter to enter a citizen's abode without a warrant, why can that government not decide that it is a violation of the former for a citizen not to have an abode? In fact, as we have seen, the venerable moral philosopher from Scotland tells us that each society must make such determinations. Milton and Rose Friedman, who shuddered at the possibility that they and their fellow Americans were perilously close to being residents "in George Orwell's *Animal Farm*," were, as Marriner Eccles suggested, merely denizens of a society employing a coda detailed in Adam Smith's *Wealth of Nations*.[24]

Smith's concern that workers be treated fairly is revealed throughout the book. Indeed, in his lifetime, writes historian Emma Rothschild, he had a well-deserved reputation as a great "friend of the poor." Thomas Malthus went so far as to criticize Smith's excessive preoccupation with "the happiness and comfort of the lowest orders of society." While most are aware that he lauded the gains in productivity associated with the division of labor, few appreciate the concern he expressed for the social costs associated with such manufacturing, in which a worker performed a repetitive task day in and day out. "The labouring poor, that is the great body of the people" that he fears could fall into a sluggishness of mind "*unless government takes some pains to prevent it.*" In addition to a system of compulsory public education, Smith stresses the need for the state to give "entire liberty" to those who could entertain the people "by painting, poetry, musick, dancing; by all sorts of dramatic representations and exhibitions." Perhaps the theatre and arts projects of the WPA, or the National Endowment for the Arts, would be seen by him as profitable public endeavors. (He at least, unlike a suspicious inquisitor of HUAC's 1938 investigation of Hallie Flanagan's WPA theatre projects, would not suspect that one "Christopher Marlowe" was a Communist subversive.) He favored the law that required masters to compensate their laborers in money and not in kind and yet objected to one that limited the wages that could be paid to apprentices of various trades in and around London. Legislation, Smith noted, was nearly always structured for the benefit of the proprietors; however, "when the regulation . . . is in favor of the workman, it is always just and equitable."[25]

Employers would do well, he maintained, to listen "to the dictates of reason and humanity" and provide labor a "liberal reward," for it "increases the industry of the common people." If this penchant in favor of labor surprises some today, it was hardly revelatory to Smith's contemporaries. When minimum-wage legislation was introduced in Parliament in 1795, its sponsors cited passages from *The Wealth of Nations* in support of their proposal, with Samuel Whitbread arguing that Smith was prepared to favor "legislative interference" to further the cause of equity. "No society can surely be flourishing and happy," he quoted Smith, "of which the far greater part of the members are poor and miserable. It is but equity, besides, that they who feed, clothe and lodge the whole body of the people, should have such a share of the produce of their own labour as to be themselves tolerably well fed, clothed and lodged."[26]

Although it is entirely possible that Eccles found such passages while engaged in a thorough reading of the historic book, it seems more likely that at some point in the transformation of his economic views he availed himself of an analysis that introduced him to this unfamiliar perspective. There are, of course, a number of such writings that he might have read. When Eccles went to work for the Treasury Department in early 1934, however, he came into contact with the eminent economist from the University of Chicago, Jacob Viner. Perhaps the most influential revisionist look at the legacy of Adam Smith was provided by Viner's lectures in the 1920s and his introduction to the commemorative 150th-year publication of *The Wealth of Nations* in 1926. Viner had been an advocate of deficit spending since 1931. Indeed, the term "compensatory economics" that Eccles was so fond of using may have been coined by him in 1931. Viner had come to the Treasury to work as Secretary Morgenthau's advisor. In what would prove an enormously important event in Eccles's life, Viner brought into the Treasury a young economist he greatly admired from Harvard named Lauchlin Currie. Currie became Eccles's academic alter-ego, and they would build a close working relationship for the next several years.[27]

Adam Smith was well aware, insisted Jacob Viner, that the natural order arranged by the "invisible hand"—a phrase he used but once in the book—was capable of rendering conditions that could be quite injurious to the general welfare. However, he was also keenly conscious of the fact that the government of his time was in the hands of an incompetent and corrupt clique that operated for the benefit of an aristocratic few. Therefore, observes Viner, the "evils of unrestrained selfishness" *might* be preferable to the malfeasance of the state. But this preference for laissez-faire was not warranted, in Smith's view, by an unflappable conviction that some beneficent natural order would inevitably become operational; rather, government ceded its role by default. Here Viner makes a crucial assertion: "The modern advocate of Laissez Faire who objects to government participation in business on the grounds that it is an encroachment upon a field reserved by nature for private enterprise cannot find support for this argument in *The Wealth of Nations*."[28]

What is surprising about the book, however, is the frequency with which Smith was willing to concede that governmental intervention was warranted. He was especially solicitous of the well-being of tenant farmers, for whom he had a palpable sympathy. He urged that rents in kind should be taxed at a greater rate than money rents, due to the fact that "such rents are always more hurtful to the tenants." He favored government involvement—not an invisible hand—to discourage landlords who burdened tenants by prescribing for them a particular mode of cultivation. It was advisable, moreover, for the state in numerous instances to actively protect consumers. Government stamps, for example, could verify the quality of plate and linens. Having observed the collapse of large banking concerns in the 1770s—dare we characterize them as "too big to fail"?—he gave his assent to curtailing "the natural liberty" of those "which might endanger the security of the whole society." It was axiomatic that they be "restrained by the laws of all governments." He was certainly conscious of the fact that one could cite certain "operations" that would prove "profitable to the bank as a mercantile company; yet the country could derive no benefit from it, but, on the contrary must have suffered a very considerable loss by it." It was acceptable, therefore, for the government to have some degree of control over rates of interest and the conditions of mortgages. There were, in fact, many such things that he was unwilling to allow the marketplace to shape haphazardly, or to form by way of some "spontaneous order" that Friedrich von Hayek and Milton Friedman praised him for discovering.[29]

Even more notable was Smith's willingness to permit government to be an agent of wealth redistribution. This is implicit in a number of his proposals, especially his convictions concerning taxation. "It is not very unreasonable," he wrote, "that the rich should contribute to the public expense, not only in proportion to their revenue, but something more than in that proportion." Luxury carriages, for example, should pay a heavier rate on toll roads, so that the rich can be "made to contribute in a very easy manner to the relief of the poor." Smith's penchant for finding ways to "extract from the rich" (Jefferson's wording quoted above) to assist the poor, was so well known in his own time that some cast blame on him for inciting the Scottish peasant revolts of the 1790s.[30]

"He saw a wide and elastic range of activity for government," Viner writes of Adam Smith, "and he was willing to extend it even farther if government, by improving its standards of competence, honesty, and public spirit, showed itself entitled to wider responsibility."[31]

In the view of many scholars who have considered Smith as something far more than a doctrinaire free-marketer, it is hardly surprising that a man who occupied the chair of moral philosophy at the University of Glasgow, and whose most celebrated work in his own time was *The Theory of Moral Sentiments*—written seventeen years earlier—would have infused *The Wealth of Nations* with considerations of justice and equity. Central to the former work is a "beneficent order" the properties of which have been "implanted in man by nature." Although self-interest is a powerful and omnipresent component of man's makeup, it is "regulated by natural justice and tempered by sympathy and benevolence." The orchestrator of these varied internal drives within the human breast is alternately termed by Smith the "Director of Nature," the "great judge of hearts," and even "God." (He eliminated the one passing reference to Christ from the final edition of the book.) The most fascinating of these designations in *Moral Sentiments*, however, is the use of the phrase "an invisible hand." Is it possible, therefore, that the "invisible hand" that corrals self-interest in the 1757 book is the same "invisible hand" that gives it free reign in the 1776 *Wealth of Nations*? Thus we have the famous inconsistency the Germans termed "Das Adam Smith Problem."[32]

While some scholars are determined to reconcile the two works, arguing that the latter must always be read with the former firmly in mind, Viner is perfectly content with the fact that they are occasionally contradictory. That Smith did not seem to sense an ideological conflict is evidenced by the fact that when he made revisions to *Moral Sentiments* in his last years of life, he made no attempt at any reconciliation. The great man, Viner reasoned, was quite as capable as anyone else in holding positions that seem in conflict. To illustrate, Viner included in his lectures and writing on this matter a bit of personal experience. One imagines that had Eccles heard the tale—although Viner's remembrance of Eccles was that he was a "voluble talker" who, rather than listening, "talked for hours at a time"—he would likely have appreciated it. In the morning session of a conference on financial regulation, Viner heard a private banker vigorously inveigh against governmental intrusion in the private sector. That afternoon the very same banker heaped praise upon a public bank commissioner for wisely "enacting sound regulations governing the entrance into the banking field" of concerns that were "irresponsible" and "fraudulent." There is little doubt, Viner observes, that the man "was as sincere in the morning as in the afternoon."[33]

The story captures the very essence of what Eccles's private and public experience would teach him: government interference in the private sphere was neither intrinsically good nor bad. He well understood that the law prohibiting branch banking had exacerbated the financial panic at the onset of the Depression. He was equally aware, however, that prudential government action could render such catastrophic economic downturns a relic of the past. The challenge of governance was to discern between the two.

Adam Smith understood this distinction as well. Needless to say, in his day and age, he retained far more skepticism than did Marriner Eccles about government's ability to impact society in a beneficial fashion. Although Eccles came to his convictions empirically, it would not be unfair to consider Smith a rather isolated academic who largely employed deductive reasoning. He did, however, spend a productive two years living in France where he made the acquaintance of numerous "physiocrats" with whom he shared some important economic beliefs—most significantly a contempt for mercantilism and an advocacy of free trade in corn. In her analysis of the "close intellectual connections" that Smith forged with the Marquis de Condorcet and Anne-Robert Turgot, Emma Rothschild has come to a conclusion that is not dissimilar from Jacob Viner's: categorizing these political economists as merely adherents of laissez-faire is simply ahistorical. As she points out, "18th-century political economy presents a different and more complex view of the relations between commerce and government—and one which is of continuing importance in modern economies."[34]

Although largely remembered in history as the instigator of an ill-fated plan to lift controls on grain when he was Louis XVI's minister of finance in 1776, Anne-Robert Turgot was something approaching an eighteenth-century rendition of Harry Hopkins. He achieved acclaim for his remarkably successful stint as the intendant of the poverty-stricken—indeed famine-stricken—province of Limoges in 1770. Poverty, Turgot wrote, should be "not only relieved, but respected." It is not "alms" the people want, he insisted, but dignified and sufficiently salaried work to enable them to purchase the necessaries of life. While private property was to be respected, there must be a commensurate acknowledgment for what he called the "most sacred of all property . . . the property of man in the fruit of his labour." He scorned the idea of "soup or bread" lines as an "authorized mendacity" and requested funding for a large-scale jobs program to "spread money among the people." When the controller general provided the aid, he stipulated that 80 percent be used to purchase rice and 20 percent for public works. Turgot accepted the funding but inverted the ratio. He substantially reduced taxes upon the poor while imposing new levies upon rich proprietors. He issued an ordinance that prohibited landlords from displacing tenants until the following harvest was concluded, and required them to take back those already dismissed. Finally, because merchants would not bring grain into a province where they could not make a profit, he lifted controls on prices, while granting low-interest loans to importers. It was government's responsibility, he argued, to open up avenues of free enterprise. He introduced to the people of Limoges an eighteenth-century rendition of the WPA, the RFC, the AAA, the FSA, and the Surplus Relief Administration in one fell swoop.[35]

Across the English Channel in early 1776, Adam Smith, who both knew and admired Turgot, prepared to publish his assault upon the old order in the pages of *The Wealth of Nations.* That same year, Turgot, as the newly appointed minister of finance, was attempting to disassemble an entrenched order that he felt had impaired France for generations. "Because he saw the imminent threat of a great revolution," writes John Kenneth Galbraith of Turgot, "he sought to forestall it with a small one, while his enemies, as so often in history, preferred to risk the greater one." His action to quickly end the old Colbertiste policy of state-supported corporations, to dissolve the guild system and eliminate the *courvee,* to destroy in short the very underpinning of the *ancien regime,* quickly alienated the powerful interests in France with a vested concern in its preservation, and they soon overwhelmed him. Turgot was replaced in May of 1776.[36]

Adam Smith possessed a copy of Condorcet's *Life of Turgot,* and the *Proces-Verbal* that Turgot himself sent to the Scottish political economist outlining his reformist plans for France. Years afterward, Smith wrote that it served "as a most valuable monument of a person whom I remember with so much veneration," the "ever to be regretted Mr. Turgot."[37]

It seems unlikely, of course, that Marriner Eccles was aware of the political career of Anne-Robert Turgot and his association with Adam Smith. It does seem likely, however, that he would have admired the skillful manner in which Turgot orchestrated the intervention of the state in the marketplace. Although the French official dedicated his efforts to eliminating the inimical governmental intrusions that characterized the mercantilist system, he was cognizant of the beneficial role that well-structured public policy could play in the building of a just society. As a real-life practitioner of Smithian tenets, Turgot stands as a pioneering, indeed, seminal figure in the history of humane capitalism.

In the United States, the awareness of such a governmental capacity was long in coming. Although Jefferson never actually voiced the famous pronouncement consistently attributed to him—that "government governs best which governs least"—it was, nonetheless, a sentiment being echoed by the Jacksonians a half-century later.[38] And for most Americans at the close of the eighteenth century, and beyond, Adam Smith remained the great expostulator of the "obvious and simple system of natural liberty." As historian Tony Judt has recently noted: "Until the late 19th century, government was simply the apparatus by which an inherited ruling class exercised power."[39] It is not hard to fathom, explained Henry Steele Commager, how the lessons of the "Old World" were left revealed for all to see with great clarity: government was the enemy of religious toleration, the cause of incessant warfare, the perpetrator of inequity, and the exploiter of the poor and powerless. Nor is it surprising, writes Commager, in a country without the competition of the crown, the church, the aristocracy, the guilds, or a standing army, that commerce, trade, and business would come to reign supreme.[40]

By the middle of the nineteenth century an influential corps of clerical economists, led by Baptist minister and president of Brown University Francis Wayland, had labored quite effectively to reconcile for Americans the drive for personal profit with the spirit of scripture. His *Elements in Political Economy*, first printed in 1837, became one of the most widely used American textbooks of all time, and presaged the Austrian school of Ludwig von Mises by over a century. The introduction to the 1886 edition informs the reader that Wayland's "aim was to put into simple statement . . . the doctrines of Adam Smith, Say, and Ricardo." It is God, Wayland maintained, who made man a creature of desires. But they are wants that "unfold with the exercise of our rational faculties." The "means of gratification" are purposefully hidden and yield only to "the toil of the contriving mind and muscular force." How foolish, therefore, to ameliorate the struggle with legislation that will merely effect a "stagnation of business." The "plentifulness or scarcity of money," for example, on no occasion "requires the interference of government, but that it is a matter, which, if left alone, will regulate itself"; from Wayland's perspective, any unnecessary government spending can justifiably be termed "evil."[41]

In a world of such expositors, Adam Smith, the moral philosopher who expressed concern with what would happen to the mind of a worker who devoted a lifetime to some repetitive task, was left to wither. In the earlier part of the nineteenth century, when foundational courses in moral philosophy preceded courses in political economy, it is likely that students were introduced to the Adam Smith of *Moral Sentiments.* In the aftermath of the Civil War, however, when universities initiated specialized departments of "economics," morality became increasingly peripheral to the new science of supply and demand.[42]

"The Anvils of Experience"

A businessman in Eccles's ancestral Scotland demonstrates the efficacy of capitalism with a human face for the entire world to see, and The Theory of Moral Sentiments *proves foundational for Charles Darwin and Lester Frank Ward—"the Father of the American Welfare State."*

The connecting thread from Adam Smith's eighteenth-century writing to Marriner Eccles's New Deal sensibilities wound its way down unappreciated pathways. It seems altogether fitting, however, that the Industrial Revolution's first real template of a capitalist enterprise capable of embracing both profits and equity should emerge from the realm of the Scottish university tradition of moral philosophy in which Adam Smith played such a central role. A decade after the publication of *The Wealth of Nations*, an enlightened banker and founder of the Glasgow Chamber of Commerce began production at his textile plant on the River Clyde. When David Dale handed over ownership and management to his twenty-seven-year-old son-in-law, Robert Owen, New Lanark had more than eighteen hundred people employed. Owen would make the enterprise even bigger and create the largest textile plant in the world.[43]

The son of a saddler in rural Wales, the poorly educated Owen had trained as a draper's apprentice before he set out to achieve better things in Manchester. Learning the rudiments of the spinning trade, he was appointed at the age of twenty to manage a plant employing some five hundred workers that he soon turned into the most productive manufacturer of high-quality yarn in all of Britain. Within a few short years of assuming control of New Lanark, in January 1800, Owen's harmonious fusion of entrepreneurial skill and humanitarian concern would make him famous across the globe. Thousands of visitors each year, including the Russian czar and scores of prominent Americans, came to witness the daily operations of a plant that eliminated and curtailed child labor, reduced workers' hours, increased compensation, and instituted nursery care, progressive education, free health care, and consequential grievance procedures. Most crucially, of course, he did it all while vastly increasing productivity and profits. Upon his first visit to the United States, it was the moral force and innovative nature of this New Lanark enterprise that won him an invitation to speak in the Hall of Congress and private audiences with President James Monroe, President-elect John Quincy Adams, former president Thomas Jefferson, and future president Andrew Jackson.

Like Marriner Eccles, Owens used his entrepreneurial success to authenticate unorthodox economic views. "Like you, I am a manufacturer for pecuniary profit," he informed an audience of fellow capitalists in an address delivered as the nation was sinking into a severe economic downturn. The tone of the remarks bear a clear similarity to Eccles's "Reconstructing Economic Thinking" speech delivered to Utah businessmen in the darkest days of the early 1930s. "Let us not," Owen pleaded, "perpetuate the really unnecessary evils, which our present practices inflict on this large proportion of our fellow subjects." It was in their self-interest to join him in fostering the "progressive improvement" of the living standards of the working class.[44]

Like Eccles, Robert Owen spent little time acknowledging in his written reflections the influence others had on his development. The depression that stuck Britain in the aftermath of the Napoleonic Wars found Owen comfortably situated financially and stoutly arguing—from his experience and observations—that the slump had been triggered by an inequitable distribution of wealth. His adherence to an underconsumptionist argument was every bit as strong as Eccles's, and his solutions essentially the same. It was necessary to increase the purchasing power of the people by temporarily providing them with public employment. It would, no doubt, "prove an interesting calculation, and useful to government," Owen thought, "to estimate how much its finances would be improved by giving proper employment" to those wasting away in idleness. Put to work "under the direction of an intelligent government" the infrastructure of the entire country—"roads, canals, harbors, shipbuilding"—could be repaired or constructed from scratch. Such "persevering attention" is requisite, he insisted, to meet such "occasional" downturns of economic activity.[45]

More fundamentally, however, the depression proved an opportunity, Owen insisted, to forge a new ethic of capitalism. "He firmly believed," writes V. A. C. Gatrell, "that the changes he advocated in the distribution of wealth would 'touch not one iota of the supposed advantages' enjoyed by the governing classes." The moneyed classes needed only to be persuaded that the uplift of the workers to a level of decency would enhance the life of the entire society. Perhaps it was the failure of Parliament to enact any meaningful change, or a dawning awareness that the enlightenment of his fellow capitalists was not in the offing, that explains how, in his later years, his mind became, as Margaret Cole describes it, "enveloped in utopian fog." Convinced that the hoary customs of the Old World would prove less receptive to the new communal order he was now certain needed to be established, he purchased twenty thousand acres on the lower Wabash River in Indiana for his ill-fated community of New Harmony.

And so Robert Owen, who had come to believe that religion was the source of a "great proportion of the miseries which exist in world," had chosen a country in which to build his backwoods utopia—what Arthur Bestor described as history's first secular attempt to build a communistic society—that was rapidly becoming the most devoutly Christian place on earth.[46]

To be sure, when the call for meaningful social change would come in the United States in the aftermath of the Civil War, it would be sounded by committed Christians of the Social Gospel, who asked and answered the Reverend Charles Sheldon's plaintive question, "What would Jesus do?" They stood in opposition to the conservative thought that embraced Herbert Spencer's application of evolutionary concepts to social organization and which championed "the survival of the fittest." The extent to which this belief, termed "Social Darwinism," amounted to a profound misnomer was revealed with the publication of Charles Darwin's *The Descent of Man* in 1871. In *The Descent of Man* Darwin turned his attention to humans and the process of group selection. In this regard, he maintained, the survival of the fittest among primeval tribes had everything to do with highly developed social instincts, connected primarily to a "moral sense" that prized cooperation and an altruistic concern for all their members. In his examination of *The Descent of Man*, historian Richard Olson notes the "crucial" impact that Adam Smith's doctrine of "sympathy" played in Darwin's thinking.[47]

Indeed, the very first sentence of Smith's *Theory of Moral Sentiments* identifies "some principles" in man's "nature" that "interests him in the fortune of others, and render their happiness necessary to him, though he derives nothing from it, except the pleasure of seeing it." This inherent "sympathy," Smith observes, "this correspondence of the sentiments of others with our own appears to be a cause of pleasure, and the want of it a cause of pain."[48] Darwin was well aware that there were some inherent dangers in taking on as beneficiaries of societal sympathy some who would not otherwise survive. "Unlike Spencer, however," writes Richard Olson, "Darwin saw these negative consequences as the necessary price to be paid for something more important: a 'nobility' that was a condition for the emergence of civilized nations out of barbarism."[49]

However, as Smith famously illustrated in *Moral Sentiments*, great compassion notwithstanding, it is far more probable that one would experience a sleepless night over the impending loss of the tip of one's little finger than the loss of myriads in a Chinese earthquake. Indeed, in the latter development, he suggests, one would "snore with the most profound security." Sympathy, while potent, does not trump self-interest as one of the "original passions of human nature." As Smith's next book would elaborate upon, there are notable benefits—and yet sizable costs—to be derived from the pursuit of such passion for self-interest. As with the "characters of men," so with "the institutions of civil government": they may "be fitted either to promote or to disturb the happiness both of the individual and of society." Hence, the great philosopher issued this touchstone in *The Theory of Moral Sentiments* which might well serve as a preface to the New Deal's Security and Exchange Act: "The fatal effects of bad government arise from nothing, but that it does not sufficiently guard against the mischiefs which human wickedness gives occasion to."[50]

Few Americans grappled with the societal interplay of self-interest, altruism, and sympathy—the issues that had so occupied Adam Smith—in a more meaningful fashion than Lester Frank Ward. The thrice-wounded Civil War veteran and Brown University professor is, in fact, the connecting link between such concepts and modern progressivism. His 1883 tome, *Dynamic Sociology*, became the hallowed fount for critics of laissez-faire. "None contributed more to undermining Social Darwinism and laying the foundation of the welfare state," argues Henry Steele Commager. According to historian Sidney Fine, "It was Ward, as much as any individual who undermined the Spencerian do-nothing social philosophy and laid the scientific basis for the positive state."[51]

The notion of the "positive state"—the conviction that the government could reverse the baneful estimation of the founders and become not merely the guardian of liberty but, as Ward phrased it, "direct natural forces into channels advantageous to man"—was the core affirmation of *Dynamic Sociology*. Writing as he did amid the extremities of the Gilded Age, Ward insisted that social conditions demanded that government needed to assume this positive role, before the possibilities of human advancement were exhausted "and the night of reaction and degeneracy set in."[52]

Ward conceded in the book's introduction, however, that "almost everything that has been said by advocates of laissez faire about the evils of government interference is true." The explanation for this poor performance was simply that the United States was "living in the 'Stone age' of the art of government." The implementation of public policy was narrow and unimaginative; it was dominated, much the way mercantilist governments were, by powerful special interests. Most crucially, legislation was not yet *socially dynamic*. Social statics, the title of Herbert Spencer's first book, reflected the stagnant laws of the social order; *social dynamics*, on the other hand, was really a developing process that regularly necessitated reevaluation and was "progressive" in nature. The art of governing, therefore, had its analogue in the science of astronomy or physics. A participant in dynamic sociology constantly learned from prior legislative efforts and formulated new theories. So, he insisted, it should be with a future president and Congress that will be mandated to craft new social legislation.[53]

It seems appropriate to ruminate here on the degree to which Ward would have relished FDR's campaign pronouncement that the country would "take a method and try it, if it fails, admit it frankly and try another. But above all, try something." Ward would certainly have delighted in the exhortation for "bold, persistent experimentation" carried out with "enthusiasm and imagination" that would leave behind, hopefully forever, what the Civil War veteran termed "the gospel of inaction." Indeed, in his Madison Square Garden address, FDR reflected on the developments of his first term with the assessment that his administration was "hammering out" its programs "on the anvils of experience."[54]

The argument over the benefits that accrue to society when a precise segment of its population is assisted by social-welfare legislation is one that persists to this day. Like Darwin, Ward—often identified as the founder of "Reform Darwinism"—had little doubt about the long-term implications of fostering humane governmental activism. "If nature progresses through the destruction of the weak," he declared, "man progresses through the protection of the weak." A month before his death, Lester Ward heard Woodrow Wilson assert in his inaugural address that "there can be no equality of opportunity" if the nation stood by and allowed any of its "constituent parts" to be "crushed" or "weakened" by "societal processes." To permit this—and, of course, Wilson's adherence to Jim Crow tragically did—would be tantamount, one might say, to an "indecent" transgression of a cherished precept of American life that extends back to the country's founding.[55]

It has been the intention of the above pages to establish that both Marriner Eccles and Franklin Roosevelt attempted to connect the philosophical underpinnings of the New Deal to a long-accepted American conviction that an equality of opportunity and the certainty of a decent life should be available to all. Hence, FDR could describe the New Deal as a "crusade to restore America to its people." That neither the president nor the chairman was entirely familiar with those who laid the intellectual groundwork for that crusade is hardly surprising. "Practical men," John Maynard Keynes reminds us, "who believe themselves to be quite exempt from any intellectual influences, are usually the slaves of some defunct economist."[56]

Nothing "New or Revolutionary"

The notion that government could legitimately take action to diminish the gap between the very rich and the very poor had never been—even among many conservatives—an earth-shattering proposition.

Finally, because both Eccles and the administration perceived it to be a crucial element in the attainment of an equitable society, one New Deal objective warrants singular discussion: the use of the progressive income tax to achieve some level of income redistribution.

Of all of the accusations leveled at the New Deal by conservative critics during the 1930s, few were as common and virulent as the association of the progressive income tax with communistic/socialistic notions of wealth redistribution. The charge was often accompanied by the observation—still very much a part of conservative discourse—that such a tax appears as a stated objective of Karl Marx in *The Communist Manifesto*. And yet, Jefferson's musings from Fontainebleau have been echoed since by the most politically temperate of Americans. "I do not think there is anything new or revolutionary about the redistribution of wealth theory," confided Alfred Landon, reacting to such allegations the year before he became the presidential standard bearer of the Republican Party in the election of 1936. "Every wise statesman in every period of history," continued the then-governor of Kansas, "has been concerned with the equitable distribution of property in his country." Although Landon offered these thoughts in a private correspondence, he publicly endorsed such beliefs in his gubernatorial inaugural to the people of Kansas that same year. He spoke that day of a national "goal" to achieve "a wider spread of prosperity and opportunity."[57] This was the sentiment behind his insistence in his presidential nomination acceptance speech to his fellow Republicans in 1936 that caring for those unable to find jobs was simply a matter of "plain duty." It was an "obligation" that he pledged "will never be neglected"—although he may well have been tempted to insert never "*again*" neglected—by "our Party."[58]

As a Kansan, Landon was certainly aware that he was hardly introducing novel benchmarks of social progress. The call for a fairer distribution of national wealth was not an import from some remote part of the globe. It was a familiar hue that resounded throughout the very heartland of America; its inspiration, moreover, came not from some esoteric tract propounding alien concepts, but from an intrinsically American sense of egalitarianism. In 1908 Kansas's *Emporia Weekly Gazette* lauded the decorous Republican, William Howard Taft, for his unequivocal support for the progressive income tax, and his "stubborn adherence to certain old fashioned notions which is bound to engage the attention of intelligent voters of both parties in all sections." The soon-to-be president was leading a contingent of fellow Republicans, the paper was delighted to announce, who, though men of substantial means, were as little "concerned with getting rich" as they were with the characterization of their programmatic solutions as "socialistic." The *new* ideas they proposed, the paper noted, were not in fact new at all, but rather "as old as man. It is the curbing of greed." These ends, the *Emporia Gazette* informed its readers, were "moral rather than economic."[59]

Earlier that very year, in March of 1908, Cordell Hull, a twenty-six-year-old Democratic congressman from the Cumberland Mountains of Tennessee, delivered his maiden speech on the floor of the House of Representatives, where he denounced the tax structure of the United States for allowing the wealthy to shirk its share of the country's burden. The "father of the American income tax," Hull also labored passionately for the implementation of the estate tax.

Far from being imbued with socialistic ideas acquired from Saint Simon or Karl Marx, the young legislator considered himself a devoted Jeffersonian. As a student of the third president, he had committed to memory large segments of the Declaration of Independence and the entirety of Jefferson's first inaugural address. Like the aggrieved American farmers of the Populist movement, who, sixteen years earlier in Omaha, Nebraska, called for the adoption of progressive taxation and for the power of the government to be expanded, Hull believed he was transfiguring Jeffersonianism, not betraying it. In the matter of taxation, the congressman could very well have summoned the third president's own sentiments. An effective way to lessen the inequality of property possession, Jefferson had suggested from Fontainebleau, is to "exempt all from taxation below a certain point, and to tax the higher portions of property in geometrical progression as they rise."[60]

In the national debate that swirled around the adoption of a progressive income tax, its proponents could have marshaled the support of Adam Smith who, as noted above, favored progressive levies; but the like-mindedness of an even more surprising source could have been utilized: Jean Baptiste Say. His *Treatise on Political Economy* competed with Francis Wayland's as the most widely used "economics" textbook of the nineteenth century. Like Wayland's, it was indeed a bastion of laissez-faire principles. Upon close examination, Say argued, nearly all economic "convulsions" are the consequence of "avarice or ignorance of [government] authority." With the "political disease removed" from playing its ruinous role, he assured his readers, normal economic activity could resume. Not surprisingly, Say's scorn applied in a general sense to taxation, which often is an "engine of national depression and misery."[61]

And yet, there are passages in Say's *Treatise* that Marriner Eccles would no doubt find agreeable. Like Adam Smith, Say favored government expenditures for certain public works, and like Smith, he strongly urged education for all levels of society—including females—at public expense. It would be "unpardonable," he wrote, for those countries that fancied themselves as refined to neglect to do so.[62] (Since Say was first published in the United States in the 1820s, before the advent of Horace Mann's advocacy of public education, one wonders how conservative American students received such a judgment.) Therefore, a government was in need of raising revenue to pay for such expenses.

But Say expressed a clear concern with what he defined as the "evil of the inequality of fortune." As did Adam Smith, he wrote of the need for a well-functioning society to concern itself with the distinction between "necessaries and superfluities" and to be mindful, as was Smith, that the definition of both must always be relative: a factor of "time" and "place." Like Smith, Say maintained that replacing regressive forms of taxation with "proportionate" ones still failed the test of fairness. "For my part," he continued, "I have no hesitation in going further, and saying that taxation cannot be equitable, unless its ratio is progressive."[63] Nearly as surprising—this presumably failed to mar his system of "perfect liberty"—he endorsed the use of tax policy to effectuate positive social behavior. The burden of taxation could check "all kinds of unproductive consumption." Loathing conspicuous consumption, "the love of display," he recommended "discouraging the costly and insipid indulgences of the wealthy, and promoting the simpler and cheaper enjoyments of the poor and industrious." Implicit in filling the state's coffers with such selective taxation of the wealthy is the redistribution of income. One suspects that had Marriner Eccles, or Franklin Roosevelt, delivered the following disapprobation from Jean Baptiste Say, it would have generated an accusation from the *Wall Street Journal* that he was resorting, yet again, to class warfare.

> It is time for the rich to abandon the puerile apprehension of losing the objects of their sensuality, if the poor man's comforts be promoted. On the contrary, reason and experience concur in teaching that the greatest variety, abundance, and refinement of enjoyment are to be found in those countries where wealth abounds most, and is most widely diffused.[64]

No New Dealer could have said it better.

4

SALVAGING THE HUMAN ELEMENT IN ALL OF US

"The Big Spender Group"

Eccles arrives in D.C. to meet the New Dealers with whom he will build alliances. While he will join the "spenders," he is not a "planner."

In point of fact, Eccles's invitation to come to Washington to meet with prominent New Dealers in late October 1933 may have been indicative of the faltering confidence many of them had in the National Recovery Act. The Federal Reserve Board's adjusted index of industrial production, which had fallen from the 1929 high of 125 to 58 at the time of FDR's inaugural, then rebounded to 100 in the "beat the code" summer of 1933, had fallen back to 72 that November. Disgruntled labor leaders began to call the NRA the "National Run Around," while some businessmen offered the epithetical "No Recovery Allowed."[1]

The attention Eccles received in Washington was an indication of the esteem Tugwell had for the Utah Republican. (The *Los Angeles Times* was soon to identify him as Tugwell's "protégé.") Before he left the Capital, the professor even offered to have him make the case for compensatory economics directly to FDR. Eccles mysteriously demurred, saying an administration insider might be a better choice to make such an entreaty. Tugwell revealed to Eccles that he had designs on making him an insider and suggested that he take a position leading the new Public Housing Authority. Insisting that he knew virtually nothing about the housing issues of large cities, Eccles declined. Moreover, since his business associate in the First Security Corporation, E. G. Bennett, was already in Washington helping for a limited time to set up the Federal Deposit Insurance Corporation, he deemed it irresponsible to leave as well.

It is possible they agreed that when Bennett returned to Utah, a more suitable position would be found for Eccles in the government. Tugwell then proceeded to introduce him to those in the administration most receptive to the application of deficit financing to restore the nation's prosperity. At his hotel, Eccles and Tugwell had dinner with Secretary of Agriculture Henry Wallace, his legal counsel and future Securities and Exchange Commissioner Jerome Frank, and the indubitably street-smart Harry Hopkins, whom FDR placed in charge of the Federal Emergency Relief Administration (FERA). Born a mere twenty-one days before Eccles, Harry Lloyd Hopkins would become his most important ally among what columnist Drew Pearson came to designate "the Big Spender group" of the New Deal. The son of a leather-merchant father and a devout Methodist mother, Hopkins left his home in Iowa after graduation from Grinnell College and went to work for the Christodora House in Manhattan. A member of no church, an imbiber of whiskey, a denizen of the racetrack, and devotee of the poker table, Hopkins was, as *Time* magazine noted, "no typical settlement worker." And yet, he had spent the entirety of his adult life in the field of social work, first gaining eminence in the progressive administration of New York City Mayor John Mitchell. Hopkins worked for the Red Cross before Governor Roosevelt designated him New York's relief administrator.[2]

Like Eccles, Hopkins had a well-earned reputation for direct, confrontational verbal exchanges. One day, while publicly extolling the many worthy endeavors that a government jobs program might achieve, his speech was interrupted by an indignant voice that demanded to know who was to pay for it all. "Never above a certain amount of hokum," writes his biographer and granddaughter, June Hopkins, the New Dealer "pulled a piece of business that would delight any stage manager." After slowly removing his jacket and rolling up his shirt sleeves, he glared in the direction of the voice and replied with a thunderous "You are!" Following a dramatic pause, he added "and who better?" Indeed, "who could better afford to pay for it," he continued. "This is America, the richest country in the world. We can afford to pay for anything we want. And we want a decent life for all the people in this country. And we are going to pay for it."[3]

While Eccles possessed kindred views about the capacity of the nation to realize a "decent life" for all its people, his emphasis differed from Hopkins's defense of spending in two somewhat significant ways. First, he would certainly have modified the final sentence to say "we are going to pay for it *in time*." Secondly, he nearly always framed his advocacy of public spending as ultimately a fiscal savings by driving home the tremendous costs associated with high unemployment and economic inertia.

Such distinctions notwithstanding, among such company the Utah banker was now preaching to the choir. As Eccles recollects the dinner, it was generally agreed that a policy of deficit financing should be rigorously pursued. Eccles, it seems, was to assist in selling an aggressive spending agenda. The major impediment to such a course—that is to say, those who were most influential in convincing FDR that it was the road to ruin—were the budget balancers Lewis Douglas at the budget bureau and Will Woodin, the treasury secretary. Aware of Woodin's ill-health, the participants agreed to attempt to influence the undersecretary of the treasury, Dean Acheson. The following night, Eccles, Tugwell, and Secretary Dern had a dinner meeting with Acheson. Although many considered him a fiscal conservative, Eccles found Acheson open to persuasion and he was confident that he could be brought into the spenders' alliance. This seems to have been an accurate analysis of the undersecretary, who, although old friends with Lewis Douglas, was something of a blank slate when it came to these kinds of matters. This endeavor was rendered moot when Acheson was soon thereafter dismissed by FDR for, what Eccles would term, his "justifiable" opposition to the administration's gold policy.[4]

The next day, Tugwell arranged for a meeting with the secretary of the interior, Harold Ickes. Ickes, a lawyer from Chicago who was also a disaffected Republican known for having a penchant for bluntness (in 1943 he would title his memoirs *The Autobiography of a Curmudgeon*), had been placed in charge of Title II of the NRA, which created the Public Works Administration (PWA). FDR's separation of the spending mechanism from the code-writing function of Title I of the law enraged NRA director Hugh Johnson, who had planned to use the funds available in Title II as a persuasive tool in gaining compliance from recalcitrant sectors of the business community.[5]

Although some of the PWA's appropriation of $3.3 billion was funneled to other government agencies—the navy built the carriers *Enterprise* and *Yorktown*—a significant amount of the funds went to state and local government projects in the form of loans and grants. The loan to the sponsor of the project covered roughly 70 percent of the estimated cost and carried a 4 percent interest rate, while the grant provided the remaining 30 percent. (The amount of the grant was increased to 45 percent in 1935, a measure that Eccles, then at the Fed, urged.) Moreover, there were a significant number of strings attached. A contractor hired by a locality could employ a certain number of its own workers if they possessed specialized skills. They were mandated, however, to give preference to local veterans first, and then to union members. A Labor Advisory Board set rather high PWA regionalized wage levels. Skilled workers in the North received $1.20 an hour while the unskilled received fifty cents.[6]

While Eccles had long called for a public-works endeavor that operated on such a contract basis, he had also been critical of reliance upon financially devastated state and local governments that were burdened with both an eviscerated tax base and constrictions upon their debt levels. The PWA attempted to skirt the latter predicament by assisting localities in the formation of special districts that were free from such restrictions. How much easier it would have been, not to mention quicker, to simply activate the program entirely with federal dollars. At least the PWA was not committing the error that Eccles would adamantly assert the soon-to-be-created Federal Housing Authority would be guilty of: letting fear of default unduly restrict its lending policy. The PWA's advisory body was willing to lend even when the estimated chance of repayment was merely fifty-fifty. All things considered, it was deemed to be worth the risk. As it turns out—and as Eccles insisted would have been the case with FHA loans—the default rate was low.[7]

Eccles also believed that Ickes's famous obsession with reviewing every detail of a project to weed out any semblance of impropriety, although admirable in its way, was somewhat excessive and was preventing a swift outflow of stimulative spending. (Eccles's official biographer, Sidney Hyman, was most likely expressing his subject's views, as much as his own, when he suggested that the recovery would have benefited if their roles had been reversed and Ickes's deliberateness had been brought to code formation and Johnson's impulsiveness to the green-lighting of PWA projects.) The day he visited the interior secretary, he found him "as always, plodding through a mass of work" and, therefore, only available for a short meeting. Eccles recalled that a longer meeting seemed unnecessary since "he expressed general agreement with what I said to him."[8]

Although Eccles made no mention of it, one wonders if the conversation with Ickes did not include at least a fleeting reference to the subject of the Pineview Dam project. Located a mere seven miles from his home in Ogden, the proposed dam was to be the centerpiece of the larger Ogden River project. The plan was approved the previous August when Eccles made his trip to the nation's capital. Needless to say, he would have wanted his Utah Construction Company to obtain the contract for the work. Did he make an effort to hasten the "plodding" interior secretary along? If so, it seems he was successful; the

Ogden Standard Examiner announced a little over a week later that the federal government was finally ready to accept bids for the construction contract for the $3 million project. The Utah Construction Company did build the Pineview Dam. Among other things, the initial irrigation of twelve thousand acres made it viable to grow sugar beets in the region.[9]

"Efficiency and Humanity"

As a Republican businessman Eccles finds he fits the CWA mold.

While it is understandable that Eccles would refrain from including his business concerns in a memoir that essentially chronicles the political developments of his time, his omission of another matter from the account of his sojourn to Washington that fall of 1933 is simply baffling. Eccles's dinner with Henry Wallace and Harry Hopkins appears to have occurred on November 2. That very afternoon, FDR gave his approval for what would prove to be one of the most remarkable government endeavors in American history—the Civil Works Administration (CWA).

Although Hopkins had done his best to shed the image, the work relief performed by FERA continued to conjure in the public mind the notion of a "make-work" project: removing people from the dole to labor on some task—digging holes and refilling them—that had no intrinsic value. Indeed, on some occasions FERA functioned in much this fashion. The CWA, however, would be drastically different. Gone from the program would be the means test that both Eccles and Hopkins found contemptuous. Hiring would essentially be handled by the United States Employment Service (USES), created that previous June as a bureau of the Department of Labor to coordinate federal hiring with the operations of all state and local employment agencies. Gone were the demeaning interactions with social workers to establish a family's "budgetary deficiency." Most importantly, the adoption of the PWA's pay scale proved to be a "boon to workers," notes economic historian Nancy Rose. Although employment was limited to thirty hours a week—as was the case under PWA contracts—the CWA would more than triple the national average pay that a worker received under FERA, from $17 to $60 per month.[10]

There was a crucial, and somewhat tragic, caveat to President Roosevelt's endorsement of the CWA. Hopkins, and his principal aid, Aubrey Williams, sold the idea to the president as a stop-gap measure to tide the country over for the first winter of his administration. Hopkins had posited his argument in terms of humane necessity rather than economic sagacity. "Hunger," said

Hopkins, steeped as he was in the liturgy of the social gospel, "is not debatable." The CWA was to terminate in the spring of 1934.[11]

When FDR addressed a conference of local, state, and federal leaders from all over the country at the Mayflower Hotel on November 15, he specifically stated that the program was for the "winter months." The president, however, characterized the CWA in terms that would become somewhat problematical when a furor arose over its termination months later. Of the four million to be employed, he stated, some two million would be transferred from FERA work rolls. These recipients, he declared, "are today on what we might just as well call, frankly, a dole." He went on to observe: "When any man or woman goes on the dole, something happens to them mentally and the quicker they are taken off the dole the better it is for them during the rest of their lives." The other two million "workers" would be largely recruited, he hoped, "from the ranks of people who perhaps ought to have been on the dole—those who may have been too proud to ask for assistance." It seemed clear to the president, as it would to the four million that were soon to be brought into the ranks of the CWA, that they were not the beneficiaries of government largess, but rather government employees who were rejoining the active work force.[12]

Despite the imposed limitation on the program's duration, Hopkins left the White House that second day of November "fairly walking on air." He had given the president the assurance that a mind-numbing four million workers would be gainfully employed under the CWA by December! It seems almost unimaginable that the program was not discussed that evening when Hopkins and other New Dealers met for dinner with Eccles. It seems unlikely, moreover, that any other topic would have significantly encroached upon the conversation. They were embarking upon something that had never been done before; there would have been a great deal to discuss. The logistics of employing so many, so quickly, was a daunting task. How would the workers' paychecks be produced? FDR publicly announced the project on November 9. The General Accounting Office informed Hopkins that with the first payday of this new agency due in a mere three weeks, it was simply a physical impossibility to engrave and distribute hundreds of thousands of paychecks—and, indeed, a million of them a week later—on such short notice. Although the CWA would reverse the ratio of PWAs expenditures by planning to commit 70 percent of its funds to labor and only 30 percent to material costs (Hopkins would later assert that the ratio was 80/20), the fact remained that an extraordinary number of tools would have to be obtained. But from where? How could banks be encouraged, or compelled, to cooperate and pay the face value of CWA checks?

Where would the personnel come from to run these projects in an efficient manner? Most importantly, where would the money come from?[13]

Eccles had strongly held views about such issues. The administration decided the first $400 million of the CWA's money would be diverted from the PWA's appropriated funds. Eccles favored a separate appropriation, but looked favorably on the speedy application of spending that this utilization made possible. While Harold Ickes, the PWA's administrator, was reported to be completely supportive of this plan when FDR made his public announcement the following week, one wonders when this idea was revealed to him. Was he made aware of this on November 3 or 4, around the time Tugwell scheduled his meeting with Eccles? Sidney Hyman wrote—with insight he seems to have acquired from Eccles—that the "news had to be broken gently to Ickes." Was Eccles, therefore, to be part of some persuasive cadre if the interior secretary proved recalcitrant? Moreover, wouldn't Eccles have been eager to express an opinion about how banks processed the CWA's paychecks? It was decided that identification cards would be distributed to all workers and federal regulations were promulgated, pursuant to an executive order by FDR, to prohibit banks from charging to cash CWA checks.[14]

Such questions are entirely speculative, of course, because Eccles never wrote about his participation in the planning stages of the CWA. He gave the impression in his memoir that he left Washington soon after his meeting with Ickes. In fact, as was widely reported in Utah's newspapers, he remained in Washington to attend a Civil Works Administration gathering of over one thousand civic leaders from around the country at the Mayflower Hotel that was noted above. By the middle of November he was still in the city where he was joined by his good friend from Utah and fellow Freidenker, Robert Hinckley. Also in the nation's capital with Eccles was Henry Blood, the Democratic governor of Utah. Blood, a strong supporter of the New Deal, spent six weeks in Washington meeting with Harry Hopkins and George Dern drumming up support for a "flood of applications" for federal projects that he hoped to garner for Utah.[15]

Not only is Eccles's memoir, and Hyman's biography, silent about his contribution to CWA planning, but neither makes any mention of the fact that before he left town he was appointed the chairman of the CWA in the state of Utah. (Even odder is the fact that Eccles made only a single, parenthetic reference to the program in his memoir.) As a Republican businessman, he in some sense typified the kind of leadership the agency had across the country. Historian Bonnie Fox Schwartz, who wrote an excellent account of the CWA, notes this discovery:

These businessmen and efficiency experts, many of them independent Republicans and holdovers from the Herbert Hoover "New Era," came to dominate the CWA from Washington down to the state and county offices; and they ran the program more like an emergency employment corporation rather than charitable make-work. By January, 1934, the social work initiative had given way to the priorities of industrial management, as CWA orders called for engineering standards, systematic safety campaigns, accurate data collection, and unit-cost accounting. Labor policies permitted union hiring for skilled jobs and representations on local boards to determine wage rates and redress grievances. In the eyes of these efficiency types, CWA employees had rejoined the active work force and were no longer relief clients.[16]

"Daddy Came Home with the First Real Money in Years"

In spite of charges of corruption and misuse of funds, the CWA harmonizes social justice and economic growth, while gaining great popularity with the American people.

There was certainly no shortage of Americans eager to receive real jobs at real wages. Jobs, stated Harry Hopkins, where "fellows have to be hired and fired like everybody else"; jobs that paid workman's compensation to anyone injured or killed. Over 9 million people applied for the 2.4 million new placements that were created. In Chicago people began to line up the night before the initial recruitment. Dawn found some 70,000 filed in front of forty-one park field houses that registered applicants.[17] Of course, when Hopkins spoke of "fellows" being hired, he meant essentially that; women were largely excluded from CWA participation. Of the nearly one million women who applied, a mere 217,000 found positions. The vast majority of these jobs were still under the auspices of FERA, where means tests and low pay prevailed. In addition, despite regulations that technically prevented it, racial discrimination was widespread throughout nearly all of the New Deal work programs. It was common, for example, for skilled nonwhite workers to be designated as unskilled and paid lower wages. While Harold Ickes was taking some action to prevent such discrimination on PWA projects, CWA administrators in Washington largely turned a blind eye to such developments.[18]

Despite these blemishes upon the CWA's record, Harry Hopkins made good on his November 2 promise to FDR about the scope of his creation. By

Christmas an astonishing 4 million people were at work on the agency's projects, and by early January another 265,000 were added. At that time some 8 percent of the American labor force were employees of the Civil Works Administration. FERA spent $60 million a month; the CWA outlays exceeded $200 million per month. Washington was furnishing three-fourths of the funds to states on the basis of population with one-fourth determined by the number of each state's relief recipients. To hasten the development of projects and hiring, Hopkins informed state CWA chairmen that any unused portion by mid-December would be directed to other states.

Eccles, therefore, intended to waste little time in getting the CWA up and running in Utah. He arrived back in Utah on the night of November 19, 1933. He made the journey home with Robert Hinckley who was appointed the Utah director of the CWA. Not surprisingly, they spent nearly the entirety of the journey discussing their plans in great detail for an array of projects that could be immediately unleashed. The following day, a Monday, Eccles announced that "substantial" numbers of Utahns would be hard at work by Friday, and he gave his assurance that at least eighteen thousand would be employed within a month.[19]

It should be acknowledged that in addition to Governor Blood, Utah had other representatives in D.C. who were enthused with the CWA. As a consequence of the 1932 election, the entire Utah congressional delegation—both senators and both of the state's congressmen—were Democrats. Senator Elbert Thomas, a prolabor professor of political science at the University of Utah, won his seat by defeating the legendary Reed Smoot. Congressman J. Will Robinson replaced a long-term Republican as did Eccles's own representative, Abe Murdock. With George Dern, and such eager elected officials, the state was well positioned to take in federal dollars.

Although Harry Hopkins considered that the pump-priming benefits of the CWA endeavor took a secondary place to human welfare, Eccles felt that the two were inextricable. On his first day on the job he could hardly resist laying out the case for compensatory economics. President Roosevelt had indeed bestowed a "gift" upon the states. "If such spending is continued by the government long enough and in sufficient volume," Eccles lectured in a pronouncement that appeared in nearly all of the state's newspapers, "purchasing power will gradually increase until most of the unemployed will be absorbed in the normal business channels." For those concerned with fiscal extravagance, he offered the assurance that an irrefutable consequence of economic growth was a filling of the tax coffers with the necessary revenue to pay down the national debt.[20]

Utah met its quota with a fair amount of ease—Eccles was not about to allow funds to be allocated somewhere else. By Thanksgiving the *Ogden Standard-Examiner* was praising the "surprising speed and efficiency" with which Weber County was constructing badly needed roads. On Christmas Eve the *Salt Lake Tribune* noted with great satisfaction that eight thousand men were working in Salt Lake County alone. This included 180 working on George Washington Memorial Park and a contingent of artists painting murals atop the dome of the state capitol under the guidance of the famous portrait artist Lee Greene Richards. A badly needed drainage project in Salt Lake's west end resulted in the added benefit of an idle local cement plant becoming activated. The CWA, the newspaper editorialized, was adding "a cheerful note and a hopeful spirit to the eve of Christmas." The average weekly disbursement of $13.50, and the gratification of productive work, were instilling "faith in the hearts of little children and hope into the hearts of distressed and troubled grownups." The earnest editorial concluded: "What is happening in Salt Lake under the patronage of the Civil Works Administration is but typical of what is transpiring in other parts of the State and Country."[21]

The accuracy of this final assertion would prove difficult for any scholar to dispute. Bonnie Fox Schwartz has assembled a sampling of the remarkable tributes that American workers expressed about the CWA. "The happiest group of painters you ever saw" thanked FDR "for salvaging the human element in all of us." A long-unemployed structural engineer with six children from Michigan wrote about his first check of fifteen dollars. "Dear President, how I wish you could have seen the smiles of joy on the faces of my loved ones when 'daddy' came home with the first real money in three years." Plasterers in Cleveland, Ohio, informed the president of what an "honor" it was to repair walls in a school for disabled children, and assured him that they were "trying to turn out the best job in the city." After witnessing workers putting in sewers in Sioux City, Iowa, journalist Lorena Hickok was told by a city engineer, "You just can't believe these are the same men who were listlessly and unwillingly doing their time a week ago on work relief projects to get their grocery orders." On (Theodore) Roosevelt Hill in Richmond, Indiana, a group of laborers posed for a photograph to send to the president as a token of "heartfelt thanks . . . for the work they are now receiving."[22]

In Robert and Helen Lynd's *Middletown in Transition*, they recorded the "blessed rain" of CWA funds falling upon the "parched taxpayers" of Muncie, Indiana. "It was too good to be true," they wrote about the city's reaction to the program:

> And under the C.W.A. the golden stream was not confined to persons on relief. Good old Uncle Sam! Nobody was talking then about the unbridled waste of Washington spending in the hands of "brainless bureaucrats." It was manna direct from heaven, and Middletown came back for more, and more, and more.[23]

In early January 1934, FDR left the White House in a top-down convertible to tour CWA projects in Washington. The variety of work he witnessed would have been a common sight in communities all across the nation. Included in this presidential outing were a swimming pool and recreation park being constructed, the *New York Times* informed its readers, "for the exclusive use of Negroes." At his final stop at the Municipal Zoo, he observed the erection of new structures and murals being painted by CWA artists in the reptile house.[24]

The swimming pool that FDR witnessed being constructed that day was, in fact, one of 350 public pools that the CWA built, the playground but one of 2,000; the artists were a mere handful of the 3,000 painters, sculptors, and etchers the agency put to work on public art projects. In addition, Civil Works laborers gave the nation 44,000 miles of new roads, 2,700 miles of sewer lines, 1,000 miles of water mains, 400 sewage and water pumping stations, 2,000 miles of levees, and 469 new airports, while erecting or repairing 7,000 bridges and 4,000 schools. Golf became a considerably less elitist pastime as municipal courses were contoured in every part of the country. The CWA gave employment to 33,000 idle schoolteachers to conduct adult education classes for the benefit of 800,000 Americans, and 33,000 unemployed nurses to assist in health studies and render badly needed care for hundreds of thousands of people who had not seen a health care professional in years and in some cases never at all. In its four months of life, however, the Civil Works Administration did vastly more than this. It was, as Robert Leighninger has demonstrated, an extraordinary long-range public investment.[25]

For Marriner Eccles the best part of it all was that 4.2 million people were now earning a decent income and were wasting little time in spending it. However, one of the frequent complaints leveled against the CWA—and there were quite a few—was that wages were too high and were draining workers away from private labor. This was a widespread accusation among southern agricultural interests. When Georgia governor Eugene Talmadge voiced such a concern, it drew a caustic response from Harry Hopkins that the governor was "always yapping." He went on to lament that "some people just can't stand to see others making a living wage." There were some instances, as both Hopkins and Eccles knew, when CWA wages were slightly above those established in the NRA codes. This prompted the president to announce that such disparities would be modified when revealed. With the exception of menial labor, however, it seems unlikely that many workers chose to abandon a private-sector job for one in a program that was scheduled for termination within a few months.[26]

There was a notable exception to Eccles's indifference to the accusations of excessive CWA wage levels. It was while he was the chairman of the Utah committee that he began a verbal battle with the building-trade unions that would continue throughout the 1930s. He felt the wage demands of the Salt Lake Building Trades Council were far in excess of those for other trades and, if met, would mean that fewer other jobs could be created. Skilled carpenters in Salt Lake and in much of the country earned $1.20 an hour. Later, when he went to the Fed, he would cite excessive wages in the building trades as a primary cause of weak housing construction.[27]

In addition to employers who accused the CWA of unfair wage competition, the program drew the ire of a wide array of other interests. Some on the far left argued that far too much money was being spent to enhance the pleasures of the leisure class, or asserted, as did *The Nation*, that pay was far too low and that the effort could charitably be characterized as merely "a civilized form of unemployment relief."[28] Private contractors—especially paving contractors—argued that they were losing out on a substantial amount of public work. Social workers felt aggrieved that their services had been passed by, while local and state Democratic Party operatives objected to the CWA's extensive use of Republicans. In Nevada, for example, Democrats were certain that the state's Republican director, Cecil Creel, was capitalizing on his position to make a run for elective office. (He did run unsuccessfully for the U.S. Senate in 1942.)[29]

Aside from the claim of fiscal conservatives that Harry Hopkins was spending money "like a drunken sailor," the most difficult criticism for CWA officials to deal with were the widespread reports in the media alleging gross inefficiency and outright graft. These delighted members of the Republican National Committee. In mid-January 1934 the RNC issued a pamphlet titled "CWA Scandals" that charged the program with "gross waste of public funds," conducted with "rank political favoritism" and "downright corruption." Harry Hopkins claimed to be caught off-guard by such graft. "I never anticipated anything of the kind," he informed the press. "I suppose I'm naïve and unsophisticated, but I didn't, and I feel badly about it."

Indeed, more than a few of the 177,600 projects undertaken by the CWA were hastily conceived and poorly executed, and corruption could hardly be said to be nonexistent. As historian Forrest A. Walker has clearly demonstrated, however, these reports were vastly overstated. Hopkins, although essentially aware of this, felt compelled to display concern and decisive action. Despite the protestations of the Pennsylvania state director and chairman that they were quite innocent, Hopkins ordered the removal of two officials in that state's program for misappropriation of funds and taking kickbacks. While this incident was widely reported nationally, the fact that they were shortly exonerated, and that Hopkins wrote a letter of apology, received considerably less attention. Similarly, it was front-page news when Hopkins sent officers from the Army Corps of Engineers to take over the CWA in Los Angeles County. Here, too, charges were soon dismissed against the nine men indicted.[30] The most bizarre incident occurred when Hopkins sent federal relief administrators to take over the North Dakota program after Governor William Langer was accused of soliciting contributions from CWA employees. Although Langer was convicted by a federal district court and went to jail for a time, the conviction was reversed on appeal in early 1935, and the enormously popular governor resumed his political career. (Interestingly, the Langer case continues to be cited by conservative critics of New Deal work programs. The Cato Institute's Jim Powell, in his 2003 book *FDR's Folly*, simply states that Langer was convicted and "went to prison.")[31]

The Utah CWA had its own difficulties with fraudulent accusations of graft. On February 7, 1934, Eccles and Hinckley were shocked by an allegation in the *Salt Lake Telegram* of "sensational disclosures" unveiled in Washington that Utah was one of nine states being investigated by a grand jury for irregularities. The article stated that an enlarged PWA investigating staff—the CWA did not have the capacity to investigate itself—had obtained sufficient evidence to warrant prosecutions in the state. Caught off-guard, Robert Hinckley could only reply to the press that any civil works graft in Utah must be of a "petty nature." A special CWA field agent had previously described the state as "well organized" and affirmed that he had found, in fact, no irregularities.[32]

Hinckley quickly sent off a telegram to Washington inquiring about the matter and was informed in a return telegram from Hopkins's assistant administrator, Aubrey Williams, that they were just as mystified over the accusations.

Hopkins had ordered no such inquiry, nor was there one underway by the Justice Department. The newspaper story, Williams concluded, must be a "fabrication."[33]

Eccles and Hinckley served tirelessly for the CWA without financial compensation, and for them these public slanders warranted a more vigorous rebuttal from the administration. Hinckley felt that Hopkins's defensive press releases acted as an encouragement to the agency's enemies across the country who wished to portray it as "honeycombed with graft." Eccles, then in Washington, wrote to Hinckley in mid-February informing him of a phone conversation with a sympathetic Hopkins. Hopkins told Eccles that certain newspapers simply wished to damage the CWA. Eccles related their conviction that no one in Washington seemed to be sufficiently making the case for the "great economic and social value" of their efforts. He further stated that Washington "was allowing minor and inconsequential matters of irregularities to capture the front pages and discredit the program." Hopkins simply told him that they were "doing all they can to prevent such publicity."[34] Of course, these matters were hardly helped when FDR stated on February 7 that he might prefer to replace the CWA with a "structure that would do away with the present machinery, with its alleged petty graft and political favoritism."[35]

Eccles's conversation with Hopkins occurred just prior to the February 19, 1934, issue of *Time* magazine that featured the plain-speaking Hopkins on its cover. The story was surprisingly sympathetic to the CWA and its national administrator. He was portrayed as a no-nonsense man who cut through red tape—"snip, snip, snip"—and got things done. He successfully put over 4 million people to work with an efficient staff of only 122 and a monthly payroll of $22,000. With the need for haste, and reliance upon local initiative, it was hardly surprising that some of the money was unwisely and fraudulently spent. But Hopkins was depicted as quite a hands-on administrator with competent investigators and accountants who "supply him with complete reports of every cent spent in every state." Moreover, the article stated that he had been "quite candid" about "occasional" misuse of funds. While acknowledging that the issue of graft may "loom large in the public mind," he insisted it amounted to very few cases. "It may be my own fault," he reasoned. "I may have made a mistake in kicking a lot of this stuff outdoors. But I don't like it when people . . . finagle around the back door." This last sentence, a classic Hopkinsesque reflection, was placed in quotation marks below his portrait on the front cover.[36]

Time's understanding of the misuse of funds largely reflected the overall sentiment in the country about the CWA; it is indicative as well of historical reality. Of all the accusations PWA investigators looked into, Forrest Walker discovered a mere seventy-seven were referred to the Justice Department for prosecution, and only twenty-two of those resulted in a conviction. Even in Chicago—aside from the occasional misuse of funds for snow removal and garbage collection—the instances of graft proved negligible (this to the surprise and dismay of Colonel McCormick who fully expected his *Tribune* would report an extravaganza of corruption). When one takes into consideration that nearly $1 billion was spent in a four-month period, that 4.2 million people were employed, supervised by over 70,000 administrators, the fact that there were only twenty-two proven instances of criminal wrongdoing is rather remarkable.[37]

It is ironic, therefore, that what was one of the notable achievements of the CWA has been frequently viewed as a demerit in its historical legacy. Even some who are disposed to view the program as a successful effort to bolster both human dignity and economic activity, often concede its unfortunate dalliance with corruption. It is significant, for example, that the word "boondoggle" is often associated with the CWA. In fact, the term did not enter the American lexicon until a full year after the program's demise. In the course of a hearing by a hostile interviewer in April 1935, a FERA worker in New York City who taught an arts-and-crafts course at a recreation center explained that one of the activities in which he engaged was to instruct people on how to creatively use everyday items to fashion some functional gadget, or what was called in frontier days a "boondoggle." The next day the *New York Times* placed the word in the headline of a story that ridiculed the use of taxpayer dollars for such trite purposes. Shortly thereafter, the Republican National Committee highlighted the word in their new pamphlet, "Roosevelt the Waster." By June, the department store J. W. Robinson Co. was advertising the "daringly original" Boondoggle hat, which featured an open crown that was laced with strips of silk.[38]

By the fall of 1935 the word, and what it signified, was widely known in the country. In December, President Roosevelt and other dignitaries, were entertained at the Gridiron Dinner with a skit on boondoggling. As early as July of that year, the syndicated columnist Rodney Dutcher wrote that the Roosevelt administration wished to distance the new works program it was formulating—what would become the Works Progress Administration—from any affiliation with the "leaf-raking," "boon-doggling" Civil Works Administration.[39]

One wonders if this association, which seems to have grown in the decades following the New Deal, could be the reason that Eccles chose to avoid any discussion of his role in the CWA when he wrote his memoir in 1950.

He was certainly eager to defend the works program in 1934. It is important to note that although the CWA drew a significant degree of opprobrium, it also generated tremendous support. On February 1, 1934, Eccles left Utah to accept a position as a special assistant to the new secretary of the treasury, Henry Morgenthau. Shortly after arriving in Washington, he received a congratulatory letter from the CWA committee in Utah thanking him for serving the works program "unselfishly, without stint, and with patriotic devotion." Eccles wrote back to say that the "success" of their CWA efforts "would not have been possible but for their fine cooperation."[40]

By the time of Eccles's departure for Washington, there was a powerful sentiment in the country that the CWA should remain operational until the economy had substantially improved. Eccles's own congressman, Abe Murdock, assured the Salt Lake Chamber of Commerce in mid-January that there was "no possibility" that the CWA would be abolished.[41] Few felt more strongly about this than Eccles himself. Upon the announcement of his appointment to the Roosevelt administration, his hometown newspaper, the *Ogden Standard-Examiner*, proclaimed that he was their city's "contribution to the welfare of the nation." As a "vigorous champion" of the CWA he would herald its vital role in fostering national recovery. "If Marriner Eccles does nothing more than add his full weight of influence to the expanding of the morale-sustaining, hope-creating CWA," the paper's editorial stated, "he shall have served to great purpose." To allow the program to expire, the paper argued, in a sentiment that was palpable across the country, would be to go "back to the dole system." This notion, that the CWA offered work while all previous efforts had amounted to imposed work relief, was one of the more potent arguments that could be channeled in its favor.[42]

An indicator of how favorably disposed the nation was toward the CWA occurred in February 1934, as its initial appropriation of $400 million was nearly depleted. Following a forty-minute debate, the House of Representatives voted 382 to 1 to provide the additional funding that would carry the program through the month of April. The lone vote in opposition was cast by a seventy-one-year-old Democratic representative-at-large from Texas, George Butler Terrell. Most of his fellow congressmen, and Terrell himself, believed that his vote would very likely cost him his office. "Everyone knows the quickest way to commit political suicide," wrote the *El Paso Herald*, "is to vote against a CWA appropriation." The city council of Terrell's own hometown of Alto sent off a telegram to FDR stating that he did not represent their feelings. Convinced, however, that the jobs program was a clear violation of constitutional authority, Terrell was determined to vote his conscience while conceding that a revolution might ensue if the program were ended. He was spared a defeat at the polls that fall when illness prevented him from seeking reelection. In 1936, however, he suffered his only electoral defeat, losing a race to be the state agriculture commissioner.[43]

Support for continuing the program beyond its spring deadline was also widespread. At the time that the additional funds were approved, Hopkins announced that it was nevertheless necessary to begin the process of scaling back work hours and hourly pay for the workers. As these cutbacks went into effect in mid-February, thousands of CWA workers in New York City stormed the program's Madison Avenue office in protest. Weeks earlier Mayor LaGuardia had addressed a mass crowd of over ten thousand gathered at the Cathedral of St. John the Divine to discuss the importance of continuing the CWA. Led by Bishop William Manning, the meeting began with an interdenominational procession of over one hundred clergymen. New York governor William Lehman made public a telegram he had sent to the president urging him to endorse additional congressional funding and warning him that private industry was not yet prepared to absorb the workers that would be left idle if the program were ended. Minnesota's popular governor Floyd Olson made a personal appeal to the president at the White House. Kansas governor, and the next Republican presidential candidate, Alfred M. Landon wrote personally to FDR. "This civil-works program is one of the soundest, most constructive policies of your administration," he stated, "and I cannot urge too strongly its continuance."[44]

At the local level the pleas for continuance of the CWA were somewhat more desperate. "It has been a Godsend to this community," wrote Ogden's mayor Harman Peery to Senator William King. King, the most conservative member of Utah's delegation, wrote back that he would gladly work for the program's continuance. Such advocacy was especially vocal in the South where the demobilization was initiated. The mayor of Winston-Salem, North Carolina, pleaded for the program to remain operational, as did the Wilson, North Carolina, Chamber of Commerce. In Alabama, the mayors of both Montgomery and Mobile made appeals. All across the country there were protest marches in support of the works program. In Washington, D.C., protesters marched to the Capitol under a banner reading "We Want Jobs Not Charity." In a single week some fifty thousand letters of support for the program flooded Washington.[45]

The belief that the CWA was providing the economy with a significant boost was widespread. The California Chamber of Commerce credited the

CWA with "putting money in circulation, reviving manufacturing plants, and providing worthwhile public improvements." "Nevada Reviving under CWA Relief" proclaimed a *New York Times* headline in February. "Texas Is Moving toward Recovery" yet another read, while giving the CWA significant credit along with the rising prices of cotton and oil. (Oil, the article stated, had risen to the staggering price of a full dollar a barrel.) The *Altoona Mirror*, which celebrated the CWA when the city's "public spirited citizens gratefully accepted" their first paycheck in November, praised the program again in April for assisting in the economic improvement in central Pennsylvania. In January, the National City Bank's bulletin revealed that the Christmas retail trade surpassed all expectations, and cited "the stimulating effects of the Civil Works Administration." Sears, Roebuck and Montgomery Ward reported significant increases in sales, as did S. S. Kresge and W. T. Grant. The tool industry, although advised in November of the tremendous need for wheelbarrows, picks, and shovels, was certain that their huge inventories would meet the demand. By December they were delighted by the need to step up production when backlogs were depleted. In Columbus, Ohio, shoe stores were completely sold out after CWA workers there cashed their first paychecks, while buyers at the Annual Shoe Fair in St. Louis placed the highest orders in years. A South Carolina furniture store placed a series of orders for three hundred mattresses, after ordering fifty in all of 1932. In Chicago the clear economic improvement benefited the Kelly/Nash machine that won an overwhelming political victory in that city's spring primary. "We'll tie this ticket to the tail of the Roosevelt kite," stated boss Pat Nash, "and soar to victory."[46]

The Fed's Adjusted Index of Industrial Production may have been positively influenced, increasing a full 20 percent from November 1933 to April 1934. "All sections of the country are participating in the recovery of buying power," observed the *Wall Street Journal* in early January. The *Chicago Daily Times* cited the CWA influence upon heightened sales, and *Business Week* credited the program for the "sharp improvement" in consumer buying.[47]

Despite what the CWA was doing to enhance the lives of millions of Americans, despite the benefits it seemed to be bestowing upon aggregate demand, despite the very vocal support it received from key political figures across the country, there seemed little chance during those early winter months that the administration would decide to extend its lifespan. Harry Hopkins made this clear to his staff early on when he informed them that he thought it "humanly impossible for anybody to inject any chance of permanence in this thing." It seems probable that it was part of the bargain he struck with FDR on November 2, when the bold plan was green-lighted, that he would not waver in his public commitment that the CWA would not continue past the spring of 1934.[48] The president said repeatedly that he would be reliant upon the reports sent to him by his budget director, Lewis Douglas. Everyone, of course, was well aware that this spelled doom for the CWA. The budget director's hostility to the program was hardly a secret. Indeed, the only comment Eccles made about the CWA in his memoir was a simple assertion that Lewis Douglas was responsible for its demise.[49]

This, of course, along with the disastrous fiscal action he would take in 1937, is a sad reflection of FDR's fidelity to a balanced budget. In these early years of the New Deal, before polls had developed a higher degree of scientific respectability, the president's primary gage of public opinion was an extremely close analysis of newspaper editorials and especially of the extraordinary number of letters he received from the American public. (The White House mailroom worked diligently to keep a daily tally of support of or opposition to any particular endeavor, and even made sure to identify and weed out all "pressure mail" that resulted from organized efforts.) The president would have undoubtedly known, therefore, how much support the CWA had throughout the country. Indicative of the close connection many in the business sector had with the CWA, the agency's last checks in Salt Lake were distributed at the city's chamber of commerce.

It seems clear that this political support for the CWA was more than sufficient to sustain its continuance had the president chosen to vigorously come to its defense. Instead, he elected to actively oppose such an option. When a bipartisan coalition was formed in Congress to advocate for funding in fiscal 1935, FDR pulled out all the stops to kill the movement in its tracks. Inviting lawmakers to meet with him at the White House, he made a personal appeal to them, warning that the attainment of a balanced budget—a goal that was imperative to him—would be sacrificed if the present level of CWA spending continued. It would have been a perilous political position for members of Congress to publicly support the continuation of a program that both Harry Hopkins and President Roosevelt were calling fiscally irresponsible. Nevertheless, fourteen members of the Senate stood steadfast for at least $1.5 billion for the following year.[50]

For Marriner Eccles, soon to be a bona fide member of the administration, the demobilization of the Civil Works Administration, and the return of

FERA—a "dole" as FDR himself had termed it the previous November—was completely unacceptable. It was their duty as public servants, he believed, to bring about the permanent restoration of work and prosperity for all Americans; and central to that achievement was another governmental program, one better and even bigger than the CWA.

FIGURE 1. Marriner Eccles about the time he began his New Deal career at the Treasury Department in 1934. He was soon to run afoul of Treasury Secretary Morgenthau's notions about fiscal prudence. It was from this position that Eccles would oversee that year the National Housing Act which would alter forever the mortgage structure of the United States. Marriner S. Eccles Papers, Special Collections, J. Willard Marriott Library, University of Utah.

FIGURE 2. The irreverent Harry Hopkins holds a press conference in 1934. Earlier that year, despite the protestations of many businessmen—including Eccles—political leaders of both parties, and countless laborers, he followed FDR's dictate and shut down the Civil Works Administration. Harris & Ewing Collection, Library of Congress.

FIGURE 3. Eccles's greatest rivals in the New Deal: Virginia senator Carter Glass, seated on the left, and Treasury Secretary Henry Morgenthau Jr. standing behind him. A conservative Democrat who considered himself the father of the Federal Reserve, Glass resented Eccles's changes to the System. Morgenthau, a fervid believer in balanced budgets, considered Eccles an interloper in matters of fiscal policy. Harris & Ewing Collection, Library of Congress.

FIGURE 4. FDR signing the historic Banking Act of 1935 ("Eccles's Bill") that restructured the Federal Reserve System. Eccles stands second from right. To his right, Henry Steagall, Jesse Jones, Henry Morgenthau Jr., Fletcher Duncan, J. F. T. O'Connor, and Carter Glass. Harris & Ewing Collection, Library of Congress.

FIGURE 5. The Federal Reserve Board meets in October 1937 to discuss the sudden downturn in the U.S. economy. The chart behind them in the center tracks "Industrial Production." It indicates the disastrous decline between 1929 and 1933 and the impressive uptick from 1933 to mid-1937. The chart had yet to be updated, however, to record one of the more precipitous declines in industrial production in U.S. history that began late that summer and would continue well into 1938. Left to right, Menc Szymczak, John McKee, Ronald Ransom, Eccles, Chester Davis. Harris & Ewing Collection, Library of Congress.

FIGURE 6. Eccles (far right) attends a conference of congressional leaders and New Deal administrators in January 1937. To his right, Pat Harrison of Alabama, the Senate Finance Committee chairman; Carter Glass of Virginia, the chair of the Senate Appropriations Committee; and Jesse Jones of Texas, the director of the Reconstruction Finance Corporation. Only weeks prior to this gathering, Glass had cautioned Jones about the "power-mad" Eccles, and during this meeting reminded Jones that the Appropriations Committee would be considering continuation of funding for the RFC. Harris & Ewing Collection, Library of Congress.

FIGURE 7. Eccles corners Senate Finance Committee chairman Pat Harrison to drive home a point. He was consumed at the time with pushing his plan for unifying all bank regulation under the purview of the Federal Reserve. Harris & Ewing Collection, Library of Congress.

FIGURE 8. The imperious Democratic financier Bernard Baruch (on the right) gives advice on fiscal responsibility to Senator James Byrnes of South Carolina, the chairman of the Senate Unemployment and Relief Committee, in 1938. When he appeared as the most celebrated witness before the Senate Finance Committee as the New Deal began, Baruch proclaimed that they must all march under the banner "Balance the Budgets of the World!" His advice in 1938 was unchanged. Harris & Ewing Collection, Library of Congress.

FIGURE 9. Appearing before a Senate committee on March 23, 1939, Eccles issued a stunning statement that made the front pages of newspapers all across the country the following day, including the *New York Times*. With a clear undertone of sarcasm, he recommended—since so many felt that a balanced federal budget would lead to prosperity—that Congress assume "full responsibility" and take measures to immediately cut expenditures. It would lead, he believed, to "disastrous results," but, he said, they were living in a democracy after all. Here, his exasperation unmistakable, he takes a pause in his testimony. Harris & Ewing Collection, Library of Congress.

FIGURE 10. Lauchlin Currie testifies before the National Economic Committee in May 1939. Eccles met the Harvard economist when they worked together at the Treasury Department. Here, he joined fellow Harvard economist Alvin Hanson in echoing Eccles's constant lament that the government was acquiring far too much revenue from regressive consumption taxes. In this hearing Currie also laid the groundwork for Eccles's testimony later that year in favor of the Works Financing Bill to help further "income-producing expenditures." Harris & Ewing Collection, Library of Congress.

FIGURE 11. Eccles's "friendly enemy," Senator Harry Byrd of Virginia, in 1939. Earlier that year, Byrd and Eccles engaged in a nationally broadcast debate on the merits of deficit financing and what Eccles termed "compensatory economics." Harris & Ewing Collection, Library of Congress.

FIGURE 12. Eccles (left) greets FDR and his son James upon arrival at the new Federal Reserve Building for the dedication ceremonies on October 20, 1937. Eccles was soon to recruit James as an ally in his attempt to persuade the president to engage in greater fiscal stimulus. James, appointed as his father's personal secretary, would meet with Eccles each Monday, beginning in early 1938. Marriner S. Eccles Papers, Special Collections, J. Willard Marriott Library, University of Utah.

FIGURE 13. Near the close of his career in Washington, Eccles poses in front of the Federal Reserve Building. In October 1982, the structure on Constitution Avenue was rededicated the Marriner S. Eccles Building. Marriner S. Eccles Papers, Special Collections, J. Willard Marriott Library, University of Utah.

5

A MAN IN THE TREASURY

"Put Up or Shut Up"

The decision to enter government constitutes a challenge for someone who has spent a lifetime as an executive in the private sector. Eccles begins his strained relationship with the fiscally conservative treasury secretary.

On New Year's Day 1934, Marriner Eccles left Utah for a short visit to the nation's capital. Only days earlier he had received a telegram from Thomas K. Smith, assistant to the acting secretary of the treasury, Henry Morgenthau Jr., requesting that he come to Washington to "talk over monetary matters" with the secretary. Following his encouraging encounter with the spenders, and the enthusiasm Rex Tugwell expressed in finding a place for Eccles, this was hardly a surprise. Considering Eccles's views on fiscal issues, however, the soon-to-be permanent secretary of the treasury seemed an unlikely boss.[1]

The son of Woodrow Wilson's ambassador to Turkey, Morgenthau had been the head of the Farm Credit Administration, and while he possessed rather progressive views on a range of issues, he was a noted fiscal conservative. A Dutchess County neighbor of FDR's, he had purchased a thousand-acre farm there in 1913, and he and his wife became close friends of the Roosevelts.

Not surprisingly, Eccles characterized his two interviews with Morgenthau as "unsettling." Although this might seem expected considering the divergent views they held on essential economic and financial policy issues, it seems from the very beginning of their relationship that there existed a rather pronounced mutual dislike between the two men on a personal level as well. "The more we talked," Eccles wrote in his memoir, "the less I understood why I had been called to Washington." Eccles was clearly annoyed when Morgenthau, whom he felt was somewhat inattentive throughout their discussion, requested that he draft a report on what initiatives he felt should be pursued in the area of money and banking. After several days passed without any word from Morgenthau, Eccles left in a pique to transact business in New York City, leaving behind word of his dissatisfaction with the manner of treatment he was receiving, and that he fully intended to head back to Utah. He promptly received a message from the secretary asking for a second meeting at his home on Saturday afternoon. This turned out to be an interview where Morgenthau made numerous inquiries about Eccles's business interests. At the conclusion of the meeting he offered Eccles a position in the Treasury as one of his assistants, where he would "fit in somewhere." Eccles asked for some time to think the matter over.[2]

Shortly after Eccles notified his associates that he would be taking a job with Secretary Morgenthau, they demonstrated the improbable nature of such an arrangement by staging a comedic skit at a farewell dinner for him. To the amusement of all, the spoof depicted Rex Tugwell selling Eccles to an appalled treasury secretary and an incredulous distributor of New Deal patronage, Postmaster General James Farley. It is a fair assumption, however, that Morgenthau was acting at the behest of the president—not a cast member in the Utah parody—who had been successfully persuaded by the spenders to procure a position for Eccles. The new secretary of the treasury had a reputation for willingly succumbing to FDR's wishes. "He is servile," stated Vice President John Nance Garner of Morgenthau. "I don't mean loyal. I mean servile to Roosevelt."[3]

For any serious student of the New Deal, however, this juxtaposition of Morgenthau and Eccles strikes a familiar chord. Time and again Roosevelt brought into his administration participants to work with one another whose convictions were sure to harmonize as congenially as oil and water. "So far as I could see," said Raymond Moley, "there was neither a well-defined purpose nor underlying principle" to this generally acknowledged penchant. Moley wished future historians well in establishing that it amounted to anything more than happenstance. For the ubiquitous 1930s journalist and unremitting Roosevelt critic John T. Flynn, the administration was a portrait of sheer chaos: "a great harlequinade of government." While speculating that Roosevelt may very well have enjoyed the discomfiture the practice of engaging opposites engendered, Tugwell concluded that FDR was simply "of two minds about so many matters." Hence, conflicting policy initiatives such as the pledge to economize and assist the unemployed operated side by side. In New Deal historian and participant Joseph Lash's view, it amounted to a "technique of governing" by keeping power divided among his subordinates in such a way that all served his purposes rather than he theirs." Arthur Schlesinger Jr. agreed with this assessment, labeling it "the competitive theory of administration." Although it led invariably to "confusion and exasperation," it ensured "that in a bureaucracy filled with ambitious men eager for power the decisions, and the power to make them, would remain with the president." On the other hand, by dispersing authority to the extent he did, FDR had created, writes one trio of historians, a "planetary system wherein many would have a place in the sun."[4]

Eccles recollects some uncertainty about accepting a position under Morgenthau. Any diffidence, he would claim, was resolved in the course of a conversation with his business associate E. G. Bennett. About to leave his position with the FDIC, Bennett informed Eccles that it was time to "put up or shut up." Bennett advised that Eccles would likely come to regret that "in a time of emergency when you had a chance to work in public service you ran away and hid yourself in your private affairs."[5]

It seems barely plausible that Marriner Eccles, at virtually any point in his adult life, gave the slightest bit of consideration to hiding himself away in private life. However, there seems to be a good deal of probity in the thoughtful reflection he inserted into his book concerning the challenges that confront successful businessmen when they decide to take a position in government. After struggling for many years to figure out how to "put the pieces" together in a workable fashion, they are entering an environment where they may not even suspect where the pieces are located. They are exchanging a world where the measure of success is clearly delineated on the bottom line for one where success is often elusive, and in any event, is rarely agreed upon. They must operate in a framework designed by others, and where all ultimate decisions are made on high by others. Moreover, they are risking their status in society as men of achievement. Although it is a cause for some apprehension, wrote Eccles, the fact remains that "most other things afterward seem flat or jaded."[6]

Eccles informed Secretary Morgenthau that he would take a position in government for a year and a half. After he returned to Utah he received a perfunctory letter from Morgenthau. Dated January 29, 1934, it announced in one sentence that Eccles had been appointed as Morgenthau's assistant. He wasted little time in getting to the nation's capital. Marriner Eccles, who had not worked for another man since he was twenty-two years of age, became a special assistant to Henry Morgenthau on February 1, 1934. The spenders had their man in the Treasury.

CHAPTER 5

"The Eagle Has Two Wings"

Eccles's views place him with the liberals in the New Deal. He continues to communicate with his business associates in Utah about their mutual interests, and sympathizes with banks in the drafting of securities legislation.

In early February, Eccles wrote to Lawrence Clayton, who ran his First National Bank in Ogden, telling him that he loved his new job—"working every minute"—and asked if he would kindly deposit his "first check from Uncle Sam" that he had enclosed. Clayton, who began working for Eccles ten years earlier as an assistant cashier and would come to Washington before the end of the year as his assistant at the Fed, wrote back to say that he was "very pleased" to take care of the matter while adding: "Inasmuch as this carries the stupendous sum of $47.21, we are all uttering a little prayer that this is not your regular month's pay." His monthly salary, in fact, was well in excess of $700.[7]

After two weeks on the job, Eccles wrote to his brother George back in Utah. He was, he said, "getting along satisfactorily" and had "made quite a number of good friends." A few days before, he had been invited to a stag dinner at Harry Hopkins's apartment and he provided George with a list of the revelers: Henry Wallace, Rexford Tugwell, Jerome Frank, Robert Wagner, Fiorello La Guardia, and Robert La Follette. The newly arrived assistant from Utah was rubbing elbows with a virtual who's who of the country's most progressive governmental officials.[8]

An April issue of *Fortune* magazine recognized that these men were "birds of a feather." An article titled "Mr. Roosevelt's Men" was accompanied by a drawing of a nesting eagle with spread wings (the symbol for the NRA). The feathers of the left wing were labeled with the names Wallace, Hopkins, Frank, Tugwell, Wagner, and Eccles, while those of the right bore the names Douglas, Johnson, Jones, and Morgenthau. That a mere assistant in the treasury would be included in such a litany of important players is significant. Although it seemed hardly necessary, the caption informed readers that "The Eagle Has Two Wings." Identifying Eccles as one of Morgenthau's chief assistants, the article failed to speculate on why the treasury secretary would choose someone from the opposite end of the eagle's ideological expanse. While Eccles was described as a "Utah banker with a special point of view," Morgenthau was depicted by *Fortune* in a less-than-flattering light as an "honest and hardworking individual of very average mental ability" whose weaknesses included "his suspicion of the motives of those who do not agree with him." The article revealed that Morgenthau had imposed gag rules on all Treasury employees and demanded that all utterances be approved by his press secretary, Herbert Gaston.[9] While Morgenthau would later suggest that this directive on press contacts was activated at the behest of FDR, it was clearly directed primarily at Eccles.[10]

This hardly dissuaded Eccles from spreading the gospel of compensatory economics throughout the Treasury. He drafted a memo highly critical of the Federal Advisory Council's recommendation that government spending be curtailed. Only days before he began working as a special assistant, the Treasury offered a $1 billion sale of securities to finance the deficit that the president had regrettably informed the nation of in his budget message to Congress in January. The first offering was instantly sold and, to Eccles's immense satisfaction, was oversubscribed many times over. He believed this was grist for the argument that a balanced budget was clearly not determinative in establishing the confidence that American investors had in the credit of the federal government. It was also indicative of the substantial funds laying idle for want of investment opportunity.[11]

One of the important issues before Congress at the time was the Fletcher-Rayburn Bill that would become the Securities and Exchange Act of 1934. FDR sent a message to Congress calling for stock-exchange regulation in Eccles's first week on the job. The overall objective of the law was to maintain the exchange as an institution that facilitated investment for capitalists rather than a gambling den that produced gains for speculators. Many of the specific ideas for achieving this emerged from the well-publicized hearings of the Senate Banking and Currency Committee directed by its legal counsel, Ferdinand Pecora. The Pecora hearings, which had been underway for a full year, stunned the American people with front-page details obtained from subpoenaed Wall Street insiders. "From their reluctant testimony," writes Arthur Schlesinger, "emerged the portrait of a world of insiders where for years businessmen had greedily stuffed their pockets at the expense of the innocent and dumb American citizen." One of the more damming revelations of this kind was the J. P. Morgan "preferred list," where shares were sold at prices considerably below market value to many of the nation's leading citizens who realized massive profits by promptly unloading the stock for the price that everyone else was paying. The committee also reported that investment banks floated billions of dollars of foreign bonds that they absolutely knew were destined to end up in default, and thereby transgressed "elementary principles of business ethics." The committee report stated that it amounted to "one of the most scandalous chapters in the history of American investment banking."[12]

The legislation was geared to eliminate, or curtail, such untoward manipulations, to saddle the sellers of securities, as FDR termed it, with "the burden of telling the whole truth" about the nature of their products, and to regulate the margin requirement demanded of purchasers.

Most of Wall Street attacked the legislation with a level of vitriol and line of argument that would sound wholly familiar to anyone following the debate over the Dodd-Frank Act of 2011. While many agreed, wrote the *New York Times*, that "some of the practices indulged in" during these speculative days were unjustified, many were "perfectly honorable dealings" that were "made to appear questionable by the manner in which the testimony concerning them was taken." Richard Whitney, the president of the New York Stock Exchange—soon to be a prison inmate for his own misdealing—accused Ferdinand Pecora of misusing statistics. If enacted, Whitney and other Wall Street interests argued, the legislation would accomplish little more than driving American investment to foreign markets. The U.S. Chamber of Commerce cautioned the bill was "deflationary" and was clearly drafted by "a few inexperienced individuals whose idea of desirable procedure to arrest evil is to impede or stop legitimate business practices." (In fact, the principal author of the legislation, Benjamin V. Cohen, in addition to being a brilliant Harvard-trained attorney, had played the market to his great advantage. Like most others, however, he lost his shirt in the crash.) Besides, "German efforts to regulate trading on stock from 1895 to 1908 ended in failure," one historically minded financial analyst pointed out in the pages of the *New York Times*. "Those old Wall Street boys," observed Will Rogers in his typically keen fashion, "are putting up an awful fight to keep the government from putting a cop on their corner."[13]

In early March, barely a month after Eccles assumed his position at the Treasury, the nationally syndicated columnist Rodney Dutcher reported that there were some in the administration who were "standing with Wall Street" and attempting to exert their influence with FDR to weaken the bill. Some feared this group, led by Henry Morgenthau, was gaining influence with the president. Among those "liberals" providing "inspiration" for the legislation remaining "rigid," Dutcher identified "Treasury fiscal adviser Marriner Eccles."[14] For Morgenthau it must have been annoying to discover that newspapers all across the country were printing the news that his newly hired adviser was taking issue with his positions. It was this incident that may have prompted Morgenthau's gag order on the department, although it was probably not the first, and most certainly not the last, public disagreement between them.

For Eccles, and for many other New Dealers, speculation conjoined with underconsumption to constitute what historian Steve Fraser has characterized as the "Siamese twin sins of the old order." As Fraser notes, there was a pervasive view throughout the administration that government oversight would play a vital role in redirecting the flow of capital "to where it was most economically and socially useful if not most immediately bankable." This was part and parcel of what Eccles had been exploring in his "Reconstructing Economic Thinking" lecture, discussed earlier, where he emphasized that the sheer "pursuit of money" must be supplanted by "an idea of economic balance." As he would always ask, "What is an economic system for?" And for that matter, what was a stock market for?[15]

The degree to which the Securities Exchange Act was weakened was a matter of some disagreement. While many of the nation's financial interests continued to grouse about unnecessary regulation, the *New York Times* pronounced the act "far less drastic" than had been supposed. Pleasing to many free marketers was the fact that control of margin requirements had been taken from the Federal Trade Commission and given to the Federal Reserve Board. The legally actionable occasions when fraudulent provisions in a prospectus—or a "mistake" as Wall Street termed it—were reduced, as well as the potential penalties that could be mandated as a consequence. A significant number of other modifications pleased even the financial attorney Eustace Seligman, who estimated that some "four-fifths" of the onerous proposals had been deleted. At the signing of the act, the *Times* observed that "Mr. Pecora was particularly happy," but more than a few leftists thought the lawmakers sold out.[16]

The fact remains, however, that securities were now under government supervision, and many of the unsavory dealings that had become a part of everyday life would not resurface until "free-market triumphalism" returned to capture Wall Street nearly a half-century later. Perhaps it was chimerical to believe that the stock market would ever merely serve the needs of commerce and not, in historian Steve Fraser's words, act as "a playground for the middle classes." Yet who can doubt that under the Securities and Exchange Commission of the 1930s, the likes of a Bernie Madoff would have been unimaginable?

If Marriner Eccles was among those attempting to keep securities legislation from being diluted in the spring of 1934, there was at least one area where he viewed governmental oversight as unwarranted. Interestingly, the Securities Exchange Act exempted securities issued by both national and state-chartered banks. The ostensible reasoning behind this exclusion was that at the state and national level, banks were already subject to a significant degree of regulation.

For the most part, however, the regulatory protections in regard to banks concerned the depositors in these institutions, not their stockholders. The thinking here was that if the soundness of banks were established for their creditors it would translate as protection for investors as well. There was also a concern that the public disclosure of certain financial positions could precipitate bank runs.[17]

The hearings before the Senate Committee on Banking and Currency, however, reported that, historically, "commercial banks have consistently issued financial statements to stockholders which obfuscated the true conditions of the banks affairs." The exclusion of commercial banks from the securities legislation, however, failed to garner a great deal of public attention. Although Eccles had more than a few disagreements with the American Bankers Association, he was in complete accord with its assessment that such inclusion would gain nothing "except confusion, duplication, and multiplicity of unnecessary regulations." As an advocate of centralizing bank regulation, he certainly was not willing to bring in the SEC as yet another agency that banks had to deal with. (This would remain essentially the case until the 1964 amendments to the Securities Act.) This was a view he would continue to hold throughout his tenure with the Federal Reserve. Moreover, although he spoke very little about the issue, he did not seem to favor the separation of commercial and investment banking stipulated in the Banking Act of 1933.[18]

Eccles did not entirely set aside all of his business concerns when he took up government service. Not long after his arrival in Washington, he received a letter from Stephen Richards, a business associate and official in the Mormon Church. Eccles had persuaded the conservative Republican to partake in a CWA project that Richards was "not very well satisfied" that he had accomplished. He was writing, however, on behalf of many of their fellow businessmen who believed, as did he, "that this whole 'New Deal' business" had lost sight of the importance of "profit" and its importance as the driving force in the "life of business." Richards was contacting Eccles to assure him that his colleagues were well aware that no one was more "legitimately persuaded" of this view, and they were delighted that he was in Washington to "stabilize matters" and bring some empirical business sensibility to the government. When Eccles wrote back, he assured Richards, "I have kept in rather close touch with this entire sugar situation as it relates to our company as well as from a political standpoint."[19] In fact, only a week into Eccles's tenure at the treasury, Henry Morgenthau was clearly annoyed when during a cabinet meeting with the president, Secretary of War and Eccles business associate, George Dern, began reading a lengthy report on the sugar beet industry that Eccles had written.

"After he had been reading about *fifteen minutes* [emphasis mine]," Morgenthau recorded in his diary, "I could not stand it any longer and wrote to the President the attached note." On a small piece of White House stationery, which he preserved for his files, the secretary had scribbled "May I sing some soft music?" FDR then inscribed below, "Yes Chamber music or a Potpourri."[20]

The political "standpoint," to which Eccles alluded in his letter to Richards, was perhaps the recognition that the administration was intent on fulfilling the free-trade wishes of Secretary of State Cordell Hull by lowering trade barriers. To quell internal unrest in Cuba, and satisfy American corporate interests that were invested there, it was a certainty that tariff levels on sugar from that country would be lowered. What Eccles desired, therefore, was something of an international allotment program to curtail production. By the end of February, it was announced that Java and Cuba, the world's largest producers, would restrict sugar output.[21] Eccles's Amalgamated Sugar Company had beet growers throughout Utah, Idaho, and Montana under contract to supply sugar for their refineries. Although some in that region thought an allotment plan would prove disastrous, in March 1934 the growers adopted a resolution favoring passage of a production quota system. The law passed in June. When Secretary of Agriculture Henry Wallace announced in late October that they were lowering the quota for Idaho, it produced a protest from that state's governor. Amalgamated Sugar, meanwhile, wasted little time in acting the role of prudent capitalist, and moved an Idaho refinery to California, where the quota had been increased. In words that would become increasingly familiar to American workers a generation hence, the *Ogden Standard-Examiner* sounded the defensive explanation of Amalgamated Sugar and assured readers that the relocation was "brought about by irresistible economic pressure."[22]

"Coming South to Rescue the Republic"

Eccles meets Harvard economist Lauchlin Currie, who will serve as his principal economic advisor and who will introduce him to some finer points and intricacies of compensatory economics.

Even before he was officially hired by Henry Morgenthau, Eccles made the rounds at the Treasury and met a good number of the department's personnel. It was clear that there would be some fundamental differences of opinion if he joined on. For example, Morgenthau appointed Thomas Jefferson Coolidge as undersecretary of the treasury. Coolidge was a Boston banker whom Eccles characterized as possessing economic views that "were to the right of President McKinley." Eccles spent three hours in conversation with the economists George Warren and James Harvey Rodgers. Rodgers, on leave from Yale, joined Eccles in his skepticism of the efficacy of Warren's plan to increase prices through gold manipulation. Rodgers, Eccles was pleased to discover, was an enthusiastic advocate of public works expenditures. Rodgers, however, had made it very clear that the high wages of the CWA were inimical to recovery by raising costs to industry. With the exception of the building trades, this was not a conviction that Eccles shared. On the contrary, the penurious pay of the Works Progress Administration—founded the following year—Eccles viewed as a much more serious impediment to recovery.[23]

Inexplicably, neither Eccles nor Hyman make any mention of the most influential economist at the Treasury in 1934, Jacob Viner. Both, of course, make reference to the arrival of Lauchlin Currie, whom Viner brought to the Treasury from Harvard later that year. In fact, while Eccles makes four references to Currie in the course of his New Deal memoir, he substantially underplays his significance. Alan Brinkley has accurately identified Currie as the "intellectual leader" of the fiscal liberals and "simultaneously one of the most anonymous and most influential figures of the late New Deal."[24]

Like Eccles, Currie came from Scottish ancestry, although his family, from the Highlands, remained Roman Catholic. Born in 1902 in Nova Scotia, he recalled that the little fishing village in which he was reared identified much more with New England than with the rest of English-speaking Canada. While his father acquired a substantial fleet of sailing vessels, an achievement that left the family "well off," he described the region as largely free of class consciousness. It approximated, he would write, Longfellow's "idyllic" Evangeline "where the rich were poor, and the poor had abundance." In 1922 he began his studies at the London School of Economics, just as the Fabians were losing their grip upon its academic direction, a development that he claimed tempered somewhat the socialist thrust of his academic exposure. He recalled, however, being deeply influenced by R. H. Tawney's *Elements of Social Justice* and Graham Wallas's *The Great Society*, two of the landmark works of Fabian thought.[25]

Currie, wrote fellow Canadian John Kenneth Galbraith lightheartedly, was yet another of his fellow countrymen who, "in their selfless way, had come south to rescue the republic." It was at Harvard that Currie would earn his PhD in 1931. It is quite revealing that in his dissertation on bank assets in the United States and Britain, he would examine a number of issues that became quite important to Eccles. Currie took devastating aim at the Federal Reserve's misguided—indeed, he argued, catastrophic—adherence to the "Real Bills

Doctrine" (explored in chapter 6). Although Allan Meltzer, in his history of the Fed, credits Currie with awakening Eccles to the injurious impact of this practice, it would seem that this was a lesson that Eccles had learned to a large extent as a real-life banker in the dark days of the Depression. It might even be argued that western bankers had been long familiar with this deficiency.[26]

Interestingly, while Currie was a staunch proponent of deficit spending long before the appearance of Keynes's *General Theory* in 1936—it was this advocacy that made his future as a teacher at Harvard somewhat tenuous, and prompted his acceptance of a position at the Treasury—he was not accepting of Eccles's underconsumptionist convictions concerning the causes of the Great Depression. To a casual observer of economic developments in this period, Currie's differences with Keynes seem rather slight, and more than a little arcane. Currie, however, brought a different emphasis to the fiscal policy argument. Influenced by Allyn Young, his teacher at Harvard, Currie did not seek to relegate "Say's Law" entirely to the trash bin of history. The mistake of its proponents, he argued, was the assumption that overproduction was an impossibility. Maladjustments between supply and demand could occur at the macro level and in times of economic collapse, traditional supply-side mechanisms would prove insufficient and required active monetary and fiscal stimulative measures. Although it was not a concept he would fully develop until later in his career, rather than a strict Keynesian approach to increasing aggregate demand, Currie favored identifying certain "leading sectors" in the economy and employing active policy measures to promote their growth. In this sense, then, Currie was identifying a deficiency of supply in these areas that resembled somewhat the concepts of J. B. Say. As Currie, in fact, came to designate it: "Sayian demand." It is easy, Currie would explain, to confuse such demand with a purely monetary demand.[27]

Moreover, to simply increase aggregate demand in all segments of the economy—what some termed the "Big Push" strategy—would dissipate any fiscal impact and prove less effectual. It was also important, moreover, to identify leading sectors where demand was not weak, but rather held in check by certain "structural and institutional obstacles." To unleash these "constraints on the side of supply" would be particularly effective. In addition, a sector's potential for releasing "latent demand" was heightened if it was heavily dependent upon borrowing that was amortized and paid off over an extended period. All of this meant, of course, that housing and construction were prime targets for consideration. As already noted, Eccles felt that the problem in this sector was not insufficient demand, but rather the barrier imposed by the unrealistic wage demands of the building trades. This, of course, was a position that Eccles was espousing well before he encountered Lauchlin Currie. The Harvard economist would reflect in his later years when he served as an economic advisor to the Colombian government that the "first empirical establishment" of these views dated to his work at the Fed in the 1930s. It is quite likely that Eccles failed to grasp the complexities of Currie's concept of Sayian demand. Indeed, it is safe to conclude that its distinctions remain elusive to many trained economists. Nevertheless, what Currie would come to refer to as "demand management" made total sense to Eccles.[28]

Yet another crucial element of Currie's understanding of an efficacious application of fiscal policy—one that Eccles had no difficulty in comprehending—is illustrated by his eventual rejection of the use of the term "pump priming." Currie used the term in the title of one of his 1935 papers where he evaluated the impact that an array of expenditure and revenue options—both qualitatively and quantitatively—would have on the restoration of full employment. The optimal choice, of course, was one that spent the greatest amount and directed the most resources to construction. While the paper stressed that it was essential to *make a sustained effort* until recovery was solidly underway, the use of the terms "pump priming" and "spurt" had a tendency to convey the impression that a one-time demand shock would open the nation's economic pipeline.[29]

Later that year, with the assistance of Martin Krost, a young economist he brought from Harvard, Currie elaborated upon his "pump priming deficit" in an analysis contained in a work titled "Federal Income Increasing Expenditures, 1933–1935." The paper pointed out that the simple notion of deficit spending—what the entire world would in time call "Keynesianism"—was an inadequate, and often misleading, barometer of the extent to which government budgets were impacting the economic life of the nation. For indeed, some expenditures were "income-increasing" while others amounted to mere transfers that contained minimal or no stimulative value. The same distinction applied to the revenue side of the budget, where "non-income decreasing" taxes were preferable—at least in a downturn—to taxes that were deflationary. What was important, therefore, was to focus attention, not on deficits, surpluses, or balanced budgets, but rather the "net contribution" that resulted from the choice of revenues and expenditures. It was at least theoretically possible that a budget in cash surplus could provide a greater degree of stimulus than one running a deficit. In Currie's view, therefore—as with aggregate demand, discussed above—not all deficits were created equal.[30]

There was little doubt in the minds of either Currie or Eccles, however, that the woeful unemployment conditions of the 1930s demanded an optimum of "income-increasing expenditures" and "non-income decreasing taxes": in other words, very high deficits.

No Self-Respecting American Ought to Say: "We Cannot Do It Here"

Convinced that housing was the key to recovery, Eccles—aware of European programs—inserts himself at the very center of the New Deal's plans to resuscitate that sector of the economy.

Sidney Hyman writes that while Eccles's economic ideas were "deduced from his experiences," they were nonetheless "rough hewn" and in need of "the refinements that presently came with the help of gifted young economists" with whom he came into contact at both the Treasury and the Fed.[31] While Currie would most certainly top that list in terms of such influence, in regard to creative ways to stimulate housing, it would appear that it was Eccles who provided some of the refinement. Lauchlin Currie would meet Marriner Eccles for the first time some two months after the economist's arrival in Washington in July 1934. By June, however, Eccles had already played a crucial role in the transformation of the mortgage structure in the United States. It was this development, affirmed Roger Sandilands, that would come to shape Currie's ideas about housing functioning as a "leading sector" in economic recovery.[32]

On Eccles's fifth day on the job, February 5, 1934, he received a letter from James Taylor, a builder from Salt Lake. Taylor implored Eccles not to get so involved with his assigned duties "as to lose sight of the importance of using your influence with the president and his advisors in bringing about early provision for making available federal funds for financing new home construction and renovation." Taylor confessed that he did not know what could be done, but expressed confidence that Eccles was "one of the few who can solve the problem of accomplishing the right presentation at the right time and in the right way." Eccles wrote back the following week to say that while there has been "a good deal of talk on the subject," they had yet to work out a comprehensive plan which would "even approach or in any way meet our national requirements" in regard to housing construction. He assured Taylor, however, that no one was more determined to figure out a way to achieve this.[33]

As we shall see, Eccles would soon become a driving force in the formulation of housing policy in the New Deal. Many of the details of that involvement which follow in this chapter transpired long after he had taken up his position with the Federal Reserve at the close of 1934. As stated previously, Eccles had a very expansive understanding of what his duties entailed as chief monitor of the nation's monetary mechanisms. He believed, in fact, that he was in some fashion the overseer of the nation's general economic well-being. A whole range of policy issues, therefore, he considered well within the parameters of his role as diagnostician and advocate of sound economic health. All of these matters he found vastly more interesting than the raising and lowering of discount rates and reserve ratios; and nothing consumed his attention more than the intricacies of government's proper relationship with the housing industry. He remained in near-constant contact with officials in the Federal Housing Administration—an agency that he legitimately felt he had helped to father—and spewed forth his housing positions in a continual stream of memos, letters, and addresses throughout the entirety of his career in government service.

His first connection with housing issues occurred shortly after he was officially assigned the task of representing Secretary Morgenthau in dealings with certain government agencies, principally the Reconstruction Finance Corporation and the Home Owners' Loan Corporation (HOLC). For Eccles this proved highly frustrating. While the RFC made large loans available to railroads, it did nothing to stimulate car loadings. The HOLC, by rewriting mortgages, stymied the massive wave of foreclosures that had afflicted the country, but failed to produce a single new home. Both were effective agencies of *relief*, but Eccles's interest was in *recovery*.[34]

In early March, Eccles met Winfield W. Riefler, a Federal Reserve economist on loan to the president's Emergency Committee on Housing. The committee was created by FDR earlier in the year, with Frank Walker appointed its chairman and Riefler its economic advisor and secretary. For hours Eccles and Riefler discussed the nation's housing crisis and the pivotal role housing construction could play in bringing about economic recovery. In late March 1934, Eccles began attending meetings of the Committee on Housing as the Treasury's representative and quickly became discouraged by what he encountered. For the most part the committee seemed the captive of what Eccles termed "social service–worker thinking"—a preoccupation with government-financed "public housing." Overcoming the newcomer's reticence to speak out—never a serious impediment for him—Eccles began to insist that they devise a policy that would encourage private investment in housing. They should strive, he felt, to fulfill what he had come to believe was the credo for government's proper role in an economic downturn: "generating a maximum degree of private spending through a minimum of public spending"; albeit the minimum amount could very well necessitate massive government deficits.[35]

In addition, Eccles felt that the committee was too large and cumbersome and met too infrequently to formulate a cohesive plan of action. Heeding his concerns, the committee created a subcommittee and installed Eccles as its chairman. Eccles, along with Riefler, recruited an eclectic staff to provide technical assistance for the subcommittee. The most essential of these participants were Albert Deane, a consumer credit expert from General Motors; J. M. (Matt) Daiger, a housing expert; and a young economist and lawyer from the RFC, Frank Watson.

Because FDR and Frank Walker were leery about creating yet another New Deal agency, they wanted any legislative proposals to be implemented under the aegis of the Home Owners' Loan Corporation. The HOLC was being very successfully run by a newspaper publisher named John Fahey. As the committee proceeded, however, it became evident to Eccles that Fahey did not look favorably on their efforts, and Walker consented to their recommendation that their committee form a separate governmental entity. In the end, the committee pursued a course of action for new homebuyers that resembled the rewritten mortgages the HOLC sponsored—where mortgages were amortized and significantly extended.[36]

In time, Fahey, whom Eccles believed had a narrow New York perspective on real estate development and a too-cozy relationship with the building-and-loan industry, became a leading critic of the housing program that emerged from Eccles's committee. As touched upon below, Fahey came to support the initial legislation only after he successfully lobbied FDR to include provisions that Eccles adamantly rejected. After passage of the measure, Fahey would oppose its renewal, and reverted to the view that while homeowners hit hard by the plummeting of land values needed assistance, the free market was perfectly able to substantially increase residential construction. After all, he reasoned, the 449,000 new family units that came on line in 1921 required no assistance from the federal government. What was crucial, he believed, was that interest rates must be "fixed high enough" to encourage investment, which, if sufficiently remunerative, would even spur building in "second and third-class neighborhoods where risk is higher."[37] This free-market perspective, when contrasted with the criticisms of progressive housing experts, highlights the middle road that Eccles wished to travel. Edith Elmer Wood, an influential author and housing-reform advocate with roots in the settlement-house movement, had long extolled the public sector efforts of European governments. In Belgium, she pointed out, noncommercial loan associations allowed workers to borrow 90 percent of a property's value while paying interest as low as 3.2 percent over a period as long as twenty-five years. All workmen were also given lower rates if they purchased a life insurance policy on the unpaid portion of the loan. The program was overseen by local housing committees whose members were appointed by the national and local governments.

Eccles believed, however, that any approach that strayed too far from generally commercial solutions to housing problems was something of a political nonstarter in the United States. In his efforts to formulate an American housing plan, he would prove to be highly selective in regard to foreign experiences, touting those aspects of plans from abroad that he judged would make the case for his vision of a public-private partnership. He was, however, certainly on record as generally agreeing with Edith Wood's assessment of European accomplishments in the area of social welfare: "If a thing needs to be done," she wrote, "and a host of British, German, Belgian, French . . . officials have proved honest and efficient enough to do it successfully, no self-respecting American ought to say: 'We cannot do it here.'"[38]

Indeed, Eccles had long believed that, left completely to its own devises, commercial forces could not adequately furnish the requisite housing the country needed. Frank Watson prepared a report for the committee that revealed some surprising shortcomings of the free market in this regard. The roots of America's housing problem predated the Depression. Since the end of the First World War, America's housing stock had been deteriorating faster than it was being rebuilt. While there was a construction boom in the mid-1920s, its emphasis was not on the provision of affordable housing. A high percentage of the private homes constructed in those years were high priced. Moreover, residential housing construction of all kinds reached its zenith in 1925, when it amounted to a remarkable 8 percent of GNP. (By contrast, at the peak of our recent housing boom in 2005, residential construction was at 6.2 percent of GDP.) By 1929, there was already a shortage of affordable housing—at least according to the 1934 study done by Watson for Eccles's subcommittee—which was, of course, drastically accelerated by the onset of the Depression. In the years 1921 to 1929 the total dollar amount of residential construction in 257 cities averaged $1.8 billion annually. This figure had fallen to $426 million by 1931 and to an astonishingly anemic $76 million by 1934! Some traditional lenders practically left the field of home mortgages. For example, life insurance companies, which committed $525 million to such mortgages in 1929, committed only $10 million in 1933.[39]

Eccles and the subcommittee were keenly aware of the enormous economic stimulus that a rejuvenated housing market could provide. It was estimated that well over 3.5 million of those out of work had been directly engaged in construction activities. This amounted to nearly 30 percent of the country's unemployed. The committee further recognized that renewed housing construction would have an enormous ripple effect on related industries; everything from lumberyards to drapery factories stood to benefit. Absolutely nothing was more important to economic recovery.[40]

The members of the committee were also cognizant of the fact that any suggestion of government involvement—especially the federal government—in the area of housing struck some segments of America as a dangerously socialistic endeavor. By the turn of the century, progressives had struggled to merely put in place minimal governmental standards as to construction and maintenance. But despite the growing severity of urban crowding, and the constant insistence of activists who pointed to European innovations in the field of housing that utilized both public and private initiatives, housing in the United States remained almost exclusively at the whim of market developments.

While highly beneficial, the increasing imposition of building, safety, and health codes was certainly one of the factors that pushed up building costs in the years prior to the First World War. In the decade before the war, the cost of residential housing increased by 50 percent. This rapid rise in costs continued after the war; a unit of housing in 1929 cost 21 percent more than in 1922. While the cost of living had nearly doubled between 1885 and 1925, observes historian Gail Radford, "the price of an entry-level new house had grown five and one-half times." This necessitated an increase in debt financing in the field of housing construction. Where previously over half of all purchasers paid out of personal savings, or from loans of friends and relatives, by 1930 two-thirds of buyers resorted to institutional lenders.[41]

This in turn encouraged financial innovation of sorts. A new instrument known as the mortgage bond was created as part of an overall attempt to lure small investors into the housing market. The bonds were backed by a single mortgage or the bundling of several mortgages, and were marketed in denominations as low as $100. Without adequate government supervision, however, the marketing of securities backed by real estate was potentially rife with abuse. As Eccles's subcommittee began its meetings, newspapers and financial journals were reporting on a massive fraud of three hundred thousand investors by a number of bond and mortgage companies. Overwhelmingly, the holders of these certificates were small investors—many of whom lost their life savings—who had been assured of the complete safety of the investment by an array of government officials. The directors of these companies were subsequently described by the New York district attorney as "men of high standing," and included in their ranks W. Averell Harriman of the New York Title and Mortgage Company. As it so happens, most of the real estate against which the certificates were marketed was next to worthless. In fact, a very large proportion of the mortgages were already in default at the time most investors bought in. The Westchester Title and Trust Company possessed roughly $1.5 million of mortgages in 1932 of which $1.1 million were in default at the time certificates were issued. Many of these companies transferred these foreclosed properties to subsidiaries and thus relieved themselves as official guarantors. "We didn't bring it up if they didn't ask," responded the vice president of one of the companies to an inquiry about what details were revealed to their customers. In all, a total in excess of $800 million was lost. It amounted to a colossal failure of government oversight, asserted *The Nation*.[42]

Ironically, as Gail Radford has demonstrated, it was during the building boom of the 1920s—a period that many see reverentially as the golden age of the free market—that a national debate emerged over the extent to which government should assert some authority to influence housing conditions. For an extremely brief period during the war, the federal government entered the housing market directly when Congress hesitantly allowed the Labor Department to create the United States Housing Corporation to contract directly with contractors to build homes for defense workers. This effort, prompted as it was by the exigencies of the war, ended as abruptly as the conflict itself, and the small number of federally owned homes was quickly sold to private owners.[43]

However, the postwar shortage of housing, and the drastic upswing in its cost, prompted a bevy of suggestions about what government could actively do about it. Other than the American Federation of Labor and progressive housing experts, there were few advocates of direct government construction. Frederick Law Olmstead Jr. led a movement to encourage the government to provide low-interest loans to developers and funds for research into developing improved materials and building methods. On the state level, a number of property-tax exemptions for new construction were enacted, and despite howls of protest from free marketers, rent-control laws became widespread. (Even President Coolidge supported rent control in the District of Columbia.) As secretary of commerce in the 1920s, Herbert Hoover acknowledged that homeownership was simply beyond the means of the nation's working class. In the midst of the severe recession of 1921, he established a Division of Building and Housing to work with the National Association of Real Estate Boards to find ways to foster the construction of small homes to spur economic recovery. That Hoover thought that it was incumbent upon government to address this issue—despite his insistence that the solution should reside in somehow making it commercially feasible for the private sector to satisfy the housing needs of the working class—is a good illustration of why he is viewed by many as a transitional figure in the evolution of the social-welfare concerns of the public sector. The most useful thing that could be achieved, in his estimation, was to standardize building codes and construction material. One of his notable achievements in this regard was the construction industry's adoption of a single, uniform brick size, abandoning the dozens of different-sized building bricks.

Among the more pertinent conceptions to emerge in the 1920s, in terms of the work of Eccles's subcommittee, was the Labor Department's suggestion to "tilt capital flows toward residential construction" by creating a secondary mortgage market in the United States. The federal government could establish regional banks that would purchase mortgages and market tax-free, mortgage-backed bonds. This would allow banks to convert illiquid mortgages—its most troubling characteristic—into a liquid asset. To a large extent this system had been implemented with farm mortgages when the Farm Loan Bank system was created under Woodrow Wilson. Although the concept, as applied to the general homeowner, never came to fruition in the 1920s, it presaged legislation enacted in the 1930s.[44]

The fact that this plan remained merely speculative, and that the nation's mortgage structure remained unchanged, was recognized by Eccles's committee as the principal impediment to a reenergized construction sector. In the early 1930s, a significant majority of home purchasers needed to secure more than a single mortgage. Throughout the nation, lending institutions were restricted to granting mortgages that did not exceed 50 percent of the appraised value of a home. In addition, the duration of these loans was exceptionally short, rarely exceeding ten years. Federal law prohibited federally chartered banks from granting a mortgage loan that was longer than five years. These policies cannot be attributed solely to the presence of restrictive legislation since it was generally deemed a poor business decision to exceed these limits. Proof of this is to be found in the significant percentage of home loans that were well within the confines set by law both as to amount and duration. Three-year mortgages, for example, were quite common. Building-and-loan associations (soon to be more commonly termed "savings and loans") were able to provide better terms than banks and insurance companies, but interest rates were quite high—ranging from 8 to 12 percent on a mortgage up to twelve years—and these institutions simply did not control a significant portion of potential mortgage money. While there were some eleven thousand building-and-loan companies in the country, they generated well under 20 percent of the nation's mortgage value.[45]

Such terms necessitated, therefore, that most people resort to a second, third, or even a fourth mortgage to purchase a home. While the interest rate on a first mortgage generally was less than 6 percent, the secondary, or "junior mortgages," nearly always carried higher rates. "We all know of cases," FDR complained in a publicly released letter, "where even first mortgage interest rates were as high as 8, 10, or 12 percent." Moreover, many incidental expenses of a first mortgage also accompanied junior mortgages and some costs, such as brokerage fees, were often steeper. Consequently, the total charges imposed upon home purchasers were prohibitively high.[46]

The problems posed by such home-mortgage financing had not, as noted above, gone previously uncommented upon. In 1931 President Hoover summoned a conference on homeownership that produced a massive multivolume study. When he addressed the conference, Hoover waxed on about the central role that homeownership played in the American consciousness. "That our people should live in their own homes is a sentiment deep in the heart of our race and of American life." He went on to observe that the American people "never sing songs about a pile of rent receipts," and observed that "we do not in our imagination attach to a transitory place that expression about a man's home being his castle, no matter what its constitutional rights may be." Hoover's secretary of commerce, Robert Lamont, struck a particularly Harringtonian note—the necessity, that is, for a republic to have propertied citizens—when he stated that it is "doubtful that democracy is possible where tenants overwhelmingly outnumber homeowners."[47]

Indeed, from the days of Jamestown the prospect of land ownership had long been a driving force among immigrants to America's shores. If this hunger made newly liberated indentured servants exploitable purchasers of "sour land," it also rendered the Homestead Act settlers, the immigrants of Upton Sinclair's *Jungle*, and the more recent seekers of subprime mortgage terms in the 2000s, easy prey for unscrupulous marketers and speculators. This danger was not entirely unrecognized by the authors of President Hoover's report on homeownership. To some extent they conceded that government had a role to play in both safeguarding against the exploitation of the desire for homeownership and ensuring that it became a widespread reality. It has proven to be a tricky balance to achieve.

The philosophical and psychological importance of homeownership notwithstanding, Hoover seemed quite mindful of the stimulative economic impact that housing construction would generate. Although the Hoover report concerned itself with a significant amount of minutia—including the need for more flexible plaster and sound insulation in home construction—it did identify the nation's mortgage market as highly troublesome. Typical of the Hoover administration's attempts at reform, the conference tended to view the problem more from the perspective of lenders than borrowers. Agencies, it was reported, would be more inclined to loan, for example, if foreclosure costs could be reduced and redemption periods shortened. It was further suggested by the Hoover conference that usury laws, which restricted interest on junior mortgages, be eliminated. This, it was reasoned—typifying a trickle-down sensibility—would relieve the homeowner by infusing additional money into the second-mortgage market.[48]

Eccles's committee, on the other hand, was intent on revolutionizing the mortgaging of homes in the United States. Their goal was to establish a mortgage market that eliminated what Eccles denounced as "the second mortgage racket" and relied upon a single, amortized long-term, low-interest loan that allowed a homeowner to furnish a low down payment. This was a goal that had already been effectuated in many parts of Europe. In Britain, as Eccles liked to point out, thanks to government guarantees, a 10 percent down payment was required on a privately built home that carried a thirty-year amortized mortgage at an interest rate of a mere 4.5 percent! (In fact, the "builder's pool" mortgages in Britain merely required a 5 percent down payment on a thirty-year mortgage.)[49]

With near-lightning speed, the committee formulated a legislative proposal that was placed before Congress in the second week of May as the proposed National Housing Act. The heart of the legislation was the Title II provision creating the Federal Housing Administration (FHA) to insure mortgages of homes and large-scale or low-rent housing projects. To be eligible, a prospective beneficiary of an FHA mortgage needed to be a resident of a home that did not contain over four dwelling units—although a sizeable majority was granted to single-home purchasers—and had a principal obligation that did not exceed $16,000. Since the median price of a home in the United States was approximately $4,800, the act was not crafted solely for the benefit of those of modest means, although, in the first years of the program, only 10 percent of

FHA homes were in excess of $9,000 and only 6 percent of mortgagors had incomes in excess of $6,000. In the 1930s, a full half of these mortgagors had incomes at or below $2,500. The FHA would guarantee mortgages granted for 80 percent of a home's appraised value (raised to 90 percent in 1938) and were amortized for durations of up to twenty years (raised to thirty years in 1938). The interest rate on an FHA mortgage was not to exceed 5 percent per annum—some had rates below 5 percent—or 6 percent under "some special circumstances." Mortgagees were allowed to charge one-half of 1 percent on decreasing balances as a service charge, and a 1 percent insurance fee was to be paid into a Mutual Mortgage Insurance Fund that would be deposited with the Treasury and invested in U.S. securities. Payments on defaulted loans would be paid from this fund in the form of debentures paying 3 percent interest and maturing three years after the maturity date of the mortgage.

Title II also addressed the need to encourage low-rent housing developments. The act required that these loans could only go to properties held by municipal, state, or federal agencies or by private dividend companies that were founded for this purpose and that were subject to public regulation in regard to rents and rate of return. In the case of low-rent housing by municipal authorities, many of the limitations in the act were waived. Administrators could insure mortgages up to the full value of the property. In addition, the maturity of such mortgages was allowed to exceed the twenty-year limit, nor was there a limit imposed as to the dollar amount of these loans.[50]

Eccles was quite enthused over what he judged to be the sound business principles to be found in Title I of the act, which established a $200 million federal fund to insure up to 20 percent of all loans made by all qualified institutions for property modernization and repair. These low-interest loans would not be secured and could range from $100 to $2,000 to be paid back in small payments over a period of five years. In light of the fact that 80 percent of American families had yearly incomes below $1,800, the upper limits of the loan provision indicated that Title 1 was not merely for the small homeowner, but, as Eccles expressly stated, for anyone desirous of improving or repairing a real estate investment. If 20 percent of $1 billion in loans were lost—a percentage he assured lawmakers was "almost inconceivable"—it would deplete the government fund. However, if $200 million could "act as a cushion to create the effect of a billion," Eccles pronounced, "it seems to me it is good business and good economy."[51]

Title III of the National Housing Act addressed the problem created by the nonliquid nature of mortgage loans. The severe panics of the early years of the

Depression heightened the desire of banks to keep their assets in readily convertible forms. Holders of mortgages could obviously not demand immediate payment to produce a flow of badly needed cash. If, however, as some pointed out in the 1920s, mortgages could be shifted from owner to owner, in much the way stocks and bonds are sold in an open market, it would do much to enhance the attractiveness of such investments. Title III attempted to achieve this end by authorizing the creation of National Mortgage Associations which would operate under a federal charter and be empowered to purchase insured FHA mortgages. The associations could then issue debentures against these assets. The associations would be assured that any defaults would be guaranteed by the U.S. Treasury's Mutual Mortgage Insurance Fund. Perhaps the most important aspect of this proposal, Eccles stated before Congress, is that it would "channel funds from what are termed the creditor sectors" of the country where large credit funds accumulate, such as the eastern states, to those regions starved for investment. This would also encourage more home loan participation by nationally chartered banks and make a good deal more money available for home purchases. In this prognosis, Eccles was proven entirely accurate. Until 1916, in fact, national banks had been prohibited by law from making real estate loans and proceeded after that date with great caution. After passage of the National Housing Act, national banks issued more FHA mortgages than state banks and nearly twice as many as the nation's savings and loans.[52]

Fearful of the competition that the act would surely engender, building-and-loan associations voiced profound reservations about the legislation. As noted above, in an attempt to mollify the opposition of John Fahey and the building-and-loan community, Title IV was added to the law, creating the Federal Savings and Loan Insurance Corporation under the auspices of the Home Loan Bank Board. Although it appears a simple leveling-the-playing-field compromise, Eccles fought this development fiercely, arguing that the industry had already been bailed out by taxpayers with the creation of the HOLC. (It was in debate over this issue with John Fahey at the White House that Sidney Hyman suggests that Eccles may have first met FDR.) When the president sided with Fahey, the law had to accommodate their concerns. By providing deposit insurance, the associations' principal argument was undermined: that because they were left out of FDIC protection, they needed to charge higher interest than the FHA would allow. This hardly silenced the attacks upon the legislation. In addition, many commercial banks, especially the larger ones, were less than eager to see the commercial banking system enter the field of long-term mortgage financing, although the act limited insured mortgages by banks to 60 percent of their time funds.[53]

In his statement before the House Banking Committee in May 1934, Eccles could not resist delivering a lecture on the economic necessity of such an endeavor. "There is no lack of money," he informed the members of the committee, heretofore obsessed with increasing its volume. "A volume of money will not increase, or will not create inflation," he advised, "except it gets in circulation." It was "velocity" of money, therefore, that should properly occupy their deliberations. "There is one of two ways, or a combination of two ways, of getting this money into velocity," he continued, framing his proposal as a sagacious business proposition. The government could continue to sell securities to pay for such programs as the recently defunct Civil Works Administration, or it could entice the excess funds of the private sector into circulation with the federal government incurring possibly no cost whatsoever. (Of course, he felt Congress should do both.) The legislation before them was in large part a "self-sustaining proposition," he assured the lawmakers. Even if 25 percent of all insured mortgages defaulted, the expense could be met by the government merely selling the properties at 50 percent of their appraised value—a task that would be easily achieved—and tapping into the insurance fund. Hence, the taxpayer would not be responsible for a single cent of such a resolution.

Despite fierce opposition, Congress promptly passed the legislation. The act was adopted as a temporary federal program that would expire on October 31, 1937. (Eccles campaigned fiercely to successfully achieve renewal of the legislation that year.) The main selling point of the FHA was that the government was not competing with private capital, but rather unleashing it and allowing market forces to once again operate. On June 27, 1934, approximately three months after Eccles convened his subcommittee on housing, President Roosevelt signed the National Housing Act into law.

One Great Opportunity Lost

Although the structure for housing revival was established, the United States fails to follow Britain's example and leaves the FHA's promise unfulfilled. Sufficient home construction will have to wait till the postwar years.

FDR then needed to designate an administrator of the FHA. Although Harry Hopkins was initially considered, his candidacy was withdrawn after widespread business opposition to his nomination arose. NRA administrator Hugh Johnson (soon to resign) was rejected by influential forces on the left. To Eccles's chagrin, FDR ignored the recommendations that he and other members of the committee offered and appointed an oil executive named James Moffett. Eccles quotes FDR's remark that he was in search of "window dressing" for the new agency. It was widely reported that Moffett was leaving a $100,000 job at Standard Oil to take the FHA position. The inference was that the president felt he needed someone with well-known business credentials. Moffett, according to Eccles, had candidly admitted that he had never heard of the FHA until the president contacted him to request that he become its administrator.[54]

Eccles and others successfully lobbied Moffett to appoint Albert Deane, a member of the subcommittee, to run Title I of the act. The president of a General Motors subsidiary and an expert on consumer credit, Deane did a spectacular job of administering the extension of loans for repair and renovation. Slightly over a month after passage of the act, institutions began issuing loans under the Title I provisions; 72,658 were made before the close of 1934. The law was amended in the spring of 1935 to permit loans of up to $50,000 for improvements to commercial property and the purchasing of equipment and machinery. By the first week of December 1934, over four and a half thousand community chairmen had been put in place to oversee publicity campaigns that included newspaper ads, millions of mailers and films, and an extremely popular national radio show, "The Master Builder," which flooded stations with fan mail. By mid-1937, loans had been made in all but 30 of the 3,073 counties in the nation. Under Deane's leadership $1 billion' worth of loans—54 percent for improvement of single-family residences—were issued, of which only 5 percent were lost. These defaults cost the government a mere $50 million of the $200 million that had been set aside for that purpose. Even accounting for the fact that some percentage of that money would have been spent anyway—a consideration that Eccles failed to mention in his memoir—the stimulative benefit of this aspect of the law is difficult to deny.[55]

One of the most underappreciated developments of the New Deal years, in terms of both stimulating economic growth and transforming American life, emerged as a byproduct of the National Housing Act, and particularly from the impetus of Title I. As historian Ronald Tobey's work has demonstrated, the sales boom in home appliances, contrary to popular belief, did not occur in the 1920s, but rather in the 1930s, and especially between 1935 and 1941, when, as Tobey writes, a "true mass market in electrical household goods existed for the first time." To some extent, this can be attributed to the expansion of electricity to previously unelectrified regions and to the lowering of electric rates to homeowners—both notable achievements of New Deal policies.[56]

An electrified home in the 1920s, however, often entailed merely a ceiling outlet in each room that could accommodate a couple of 40-watt bulbs. The fact is that a majority of homes did not have the heavy wiring capacity for appliances such as stoves, refrigerators, and washing machines; nor did most building codes require such capability. Moreover, many homes simply did not have convenience outlets in which to plug in even an electric iron. A good deal of the increased electrical ability of homes in the 1930s came as a result of modernization loans granted under Title I. In addition, these loans were often used to purchase large electrical appliances. (The act, until the 1938 revisions, even allowed renters to take out loans for appliances.) Thus a refrigerator—its average price reduced to well under $100 by the mid-1930s—could be purchased for as little as $3 or $5 a month, and was thereby transformed from a luxury item to an everyday necessity. Most importantly, the FHA building guidelines made heavy electrical wiring mandatory and established a standard that was quickly adopted for nearly all construction thereafter.[57]

The centerpiece of the National Housing Act, however, was the mortgage provisions of Title II; its impact on economic growth cannot be assessed as favorably. For many on the political left, the National Housing Act was merely viewed as a vehicle for speculative real estate interests. A housing advocacy organization composed of a variety of labor unions and the Labor Housing Conference described the act as a "thoroughly bogus measure" that could actually prove injurious to American workers. *The Nation* pronounced the legislation "the Anti-Housing Act" which placed housing for the people who needed it most on the nation's back burner.

Yet another frequently heard criticism that quickly arose was that Title II, which even a *Wall Street Journal* article touted as having enormous potential for coaxing idle funds into action, was simply not making homes available at a fast enough pace. A December 1934 *Ladies' Home Journal* editorial, after declaring that "women want homes," lamented that they could not get them. The FHA, the magazine contemptuously observed, was "ballyhoo." Months later, *Fortune* pronounced: "The Administration has let slip its one great opportunity to attack the Depression by the revival of the construction industry." Marriner Eccles was largely in agreement with this sentiment. The actual stimulus provided by Title II fell considerably short of the *Wall Street Journal*'s calculus of over a billion dollars of private money. The failure to fully utilize the tremendous potential of the FHA was, in Eccles's view, the single greatest failing of the New Deal.[58]

It was slightly unreasonable, however, for the *Ladies' Home Journal* to have expected many FHA-insured mortgages to be available in December 1934. It was not until the very end of that year that the Title II provisions of the act became operational. This delay was understandable since it was necessary for the FHA to send representatives to the legislatures of all the states to secure legislative approval for state institutions to invest in FHA mortgages. Underwriting offices were set up in all of the states and in Hawaii and Alaska, and underwriting manuals needed to be drawn up and printed. Moreover, there were thousands of staff members who needed to be hired and trained. In light of these obstacles it is not surprising that a mere 102 mortgages had been accepted by the end of 1934. In fact, one could marvel somewhat at the speed with which the government operated when considering that there were families living in FHA homes at Christmas, when the program hadn't even been discussed until after Saint Patrick's Day. By Christmas of 1935, over 42,000 mortgages had been approved. From June to December of that year, residential construction as measured by the value of building permits reported to the Bureau of Labor Statistics showed an average monthly increase of 207 percent over the same months of 1934. In 1935 somewhere in the area of 16 percent of all new, single-family, nonfarm residences were constructed by way of FHA financing. The following year this figure rose to 23 percent.[59]

Although a modest achievement given the degree to which the market had bottomed out, when coupled with the home improvement program, it must be acknowledged that the National Housing Act played at least some role in the sustained economic recovery that lasted until the late summer of 1937. As early as June 1935, the National Lumber Manufacturers Association issued a proclamation in which it lauded the FHA as "practical, businesslike and sound, and as having already made a substantial contribution to national recovery."[60]

Nonetheless, Eccles's bleak assessment that the program fell far short of what it could have achieved seems warranted. A graph provided to the Federal Reserve by the National Bureau of Economic Research at the beginning of 1938 dramatically demonstrated for Eccles the anemic growth of new nonfarm housing units. While it shows significant percentage increases each year between 1933 and 1936—the "New Deal recession" would cause a near 50 percent decline of new units in 1937—it visually highlights the stark shortfall when compared to any year of the 1920s.[61] Economic historian Alexander Field has explored the construction sector of the United States in the context of overall economic development in the 1930s:

> By 1937 long-term interest rates had fallen almost a third. Real consumption was higher than in 1929, as was manufacturing employment. Passenger vehicle production had risen to within 12 percent and producer durables to within 5 percent of their 1929 highs. Yet real spending on construction was just 59 percent of its 1926 peak: spending on new nonfarm housing was barely 36 percent of its 1925 peak. What idiosyncratic factors differentiated construction from other components of capital formation, making it less responsive to monetary ease and reviving aggregate demand? Why did construction behave so differently in comparison with the post–World War II period, when it typically led upturns in aggregate activity?[62]

In searching for an explanation for this failure of construction activity to play its role in replenishing aggregate demand during the New Deal years, Field finds—as did Eccles—the standard narrative that the lack of vitality in this sector was related to the vast "overbuilding" and "overinvestment" that occurred in the boom years of the 1920s invalid. In Field's view it was not so much the "quantitative excess" of the 1920s so much as it was the unplanned, uncoordinated, and unregulated nature of that development that presented both "physical and legal obstacles to construction recovery." Developers in the 1930s discovered that many prime sites on the outskirts of cities had been marred by poorly distributed plots and badly planned streets and water mains. In many instances the costs of redevelopment were prohibitively high. The land speculation of the 1920s often left areas with a hodgepodge of owners, many of whom had walked away from their mortgage and tax obligations. Often localities did not possess the financial wherewithal to initiate legal proceedings to take possession. Moreover, the title to land was often obscure. These matters had been exacerbated, Field asserts, by the incestuous relationship between savings and loans and the real estate developers who sat on their boards of directors. Such conflicts of interests, Field suggests, bears some resemblance to the savings-and-loan debacle of the 1980s.[63]

Although one can imagine Eccles being somewhat receptive to Field's "uncontrolled land development" theory, his explanation for the lackluster construction of the 1930s lay elsewhere. One of the problems he identified as early as November 1934 was the fact that the FHA had failed to sufficiently lower the effective interest rate on many of the mortgages it insured. Any interest rate in excess of 5 percent, he wrote in a memo, was "unwarranted." He was critical of the annual service fee that the FHA allowed, noting that "no such charge was even contemplated by the committee."[64]

Most crucially, Eccles considered the steep rise in construction costs as a major impediment. The Watson study, done for the subcommittee on housing, indicated, however, that the increased expense of building material was not the culprit. The study estimated, for example, that a 10 percent increase in lumber would add a mere 1 percent to the cost of a home. Watson believed that excessive wages paid in the building trades were a leading factor in hindering the expansion of housing and construction projects. As discussed above, this was an issue Eccles had been speaking about publicly since 1933 when, as chairman of the Utah Civil Works Administration, he criticized the Salt Lake Building Trades Council for what he considered its unreasonable wage demands.[65] For Eccles, Watson's report was merely a formalized verification of this conviction. The study indicated that, even as early as the spring of 1934, wage rates in the building trades were 116 percent of what they were in 1921, while general commodity prices were 67 percent and building materials were 79 percent. In June, 1935, a *Fortune* article observed that the Federal Employment Relief Administration reported that in May, 1934 that there were 7,000 builders and contractors on the urban relief roles. The article cited the Watson report and reasoned that "wages for a bricklayer at $14 a day are a serious deterrent to a $25-a-week clerk who wants to build a house, even though the bricklayer, only working a day and a half a week, makes but $21." *Fortune* then suggested that if the bricklayer earned $7 a day he might work a full week and earn a substantially greater yearly income. These sentiments so closely parallel Eccles's own that one cannot help but wonder if he communicated with *Fortune* in some fashion.[66]

A Federal Reserve report provided details of a successful plasterers' union strike that shut down a PWA project when plans were revealed to install ceilings of finished concrete rather than plaster. This attempt to scale back on the use of plasterers was attributed to the new union contract which called for a pay boost from $12 a day for eight hours to $14 for a six-hour day. The same file contains a report that aggregate building labor costs in 1937 had increased approximately 25 percent over 1936. These salary increases were won, it was reported, by the formation of united councils of building trades that "worked in sympathy" with one another's strikes.[67]

In November 1937, Eccles received a memo from the second director of the FHA, Stewart McDonald, which disputed other reports citing rapid increases in some building materials as a substantial impediment. He forwarded information from an index of basic building materials ("lumber, paint, cement, etc.") which largely updated Watson's findings in 1934. "On the basis of 1926 as 100, this index, in September 1937, was 97.2 or 3.3% below the level of 1936." (Presumably these prices had essentially reached the 1926 level the previous year.) However, he reported, the Bureau of Labor Statistics indicated that the average weekly earnings in the building trades were substantially higher than the average industrial worker.[68]

The salaries in the unionized building trades were indeed princely compared to those of many American workers. Nonunion lumber jacks in the Southeast were earning $10 a week for ten-hour days in 1937. This included a five-hour day on Saturdays.[69] The wages achieved in the building trades greatly outpaced even other segments of organized labor. The average yearly salary for a worker under a United Autoworkers contract in 1936 was only $1,356. (Consider that a bricklayer who settled for—as *Forbes* suggested—$7 a day would earn over $1,888 a year.) The CIO's United Electrical Workers negotiated a pay raise from Westinghouse in early 1937 that increased the hourly wage to 55 cents. This would have provided their workers $4.40 for an eight-hour day.[70] In one of the first memos Eccles prepared for the president when he left for the Fed, Eccles included information on this wage disparity. In France, Germany, and England, the hourly wages of skilled factory workers, he stated, were only slightly lower than those prevailing in the building trades. In the United States the average wage ranged from $1.20 to $1.65 in construction trades while skilled industrial workers received 65 to 90 cents.[71]

Eccles's papers are strewn with anecdotal accounts that reinforced the statistical evidence about the limiting impact of building-trade salaries in the 1930s. Included is a letter from a Portland realtor who describes a combine of union plumbers who, in the summer of 1936, demanded a 60 percent increase in salary to finish a building job. The president of a New York construction company wrote to Eccles in the fall of 1937 suggesting ways to reduce housing construction costs. He confirmed reports that labor costs, and not building materials, were the difficulty he was encountering. He was paying skilled workers in the building trades $12 a day but employing them irregularly. These workers average only 140 days of work a year, he reported, and are limiting their income to $1,680. It would be in everyone's interest, therefore, to effectuate more reasonable pay scales.[72] A Toledo, Ohio, building-and-loan president stated that his association's FHA loans of $350,000 could be twice that amount if labor costs had not "increased tremendously."[73]

Even this obstacle, however, could have been surmounted, Eccles felt, had the FHA not been led by inept and recalcitrant leadership. James Moffett, he believed, installed as his deputy to oversee Title II a commercial banker who made no secret of his opposition to the goals which the legislation espoused. When rules and regulations were promulgated "they were so rigid and restricted in their text and application," Eccles later recalled, "that about the only people who could avail themselves of the program were those who did not need it." Matt Daiger, the housing expert who worked on Eccles's housing subcommittee, had become a senior advisor to the Federal Housing Administration. In the summer of 1935, Daiger wrote a memo to Eccles insisting, "I think the FHA people need to realize that they have only scratched the surface of eligible mortgages."

Both men agreed that deficient salesmanship and overcautiousness had resulted in the enlistment of only a fraction of the potential eligible home buyers. Eccles's papers provide substantial evidence that the conservative underwriting policies were largely a response to the widespread fear that, as one *New York Times* financial writer assured readers in early 1937, the program "will prove over a period of time a great stimulus to unsound speculation in real estate and a serious factor in the lending of hundreds or millions of dollars on a weaker basis than ever before." Thus, apprehension about asset bubbles and the specter of inflation—a fear that was omnipresent in the New Deal years—continued to stifle stimulative policies. There was also the fact that mortgages were viewed as a perilous investment in 1934. The press was continually reminding Americans of the enormity of the existing residential debt. In November 1934 this debt was in excess of $21 billion, second in size only to the federal government's debt. There is little doubt that this formed a psychological barrier against further capital formation to service this economic sector.

Yet another concern was the extent of mortgage moratoria enacted by twenty-eight states. Some, like the New York moratorium, while requiring continued payment of interest and taxes on the mortgaged property, allowed for suspension of all payment of principal. Nor did the law rely on judicial discretion, but applied to all home, commercial, and farm payments. While such laws were essential during the high-water mark of foreclosures, they were becoming, Eccles and Daiger believed, increasingly counterproductive as a drag on new mortgage loans to those wishing to enter the housing market. New York State extended its law for another two years in 1937. On the other hand, any abrupt end to moratoria could present an overwhelming number of foreclosures becoming simultaneously overdue.[74]

Nonetheless, FHA records reveal that by the end of 1935, 67,029 mortgages had been appraised, but only 42,147 had been accepted. Roughly half of the total value of these loans was for newly constructed homes, although, as Eccles made clear in his testimony to Congress, the sale of existing homes was of crucial importance since such sales often made the construction of new ones possible.[75]

The refusal to act boldly, even after a much more sympathetic Stewart McDonald took charge of the program, continued to prove maddening to Daiger and Eccles. (McDonald was a businessman from St. Louis and was an acolyte of Jesse Jones for whom he had previously worked at the RFC.) A statistical review of the FHA's development makes this frustration thoroughly comprehensible. Remarkably, by the end of October 1937, the FHA's insured mortgage program reported that its losses were "less than $10,000." The director of the New Jersey FHA announced earlier in the year that of the over twelve thousand mortgages it had insured from private lending institutions in its three years of operation, only *three properties* had been turned over to FHA administrators. Meanwhile, the national Mutual Mortgage Insurance Fund established to meet such losses *had grown to more than $20 million*. It is important to keep in mind, as Eccles was quick to remind everyone at the time, this fund was not created from taxpayer contributions, but rather from a charge attached to the mortgages themselves. Obviously this meant that the entirety of the fund could be depleted without costing the federal government a dime.[76] (Remarkably, as Shaun Donovan, President Obama's HUD secretary, reported in 2011, since its creation in 1934, the Mutual Mortgage Insurance Fund has never required an appropriation from Congress to support FHA loan guarantees.) Yet another indication that the FHA potential was not being fulfilled was that while the act permitted loans up to 80 percent of the appraised value of a home, by the end of 1937 a mere 38 percent of all mortgages reached that level.[77]

The implementation of the law was also hampered by the refusal of a single financial interest to come forward to form a mortgage association to purchase mortgages from lending agencies. Eccles speculated that this was an attempt by large banks and insurance companies to sabotage the legislation. This strategy, he believed, sprang from the conviction that the Depression would end of its own accord and they could then resume the practice of high interest rates and the old terms with which they felt comfortable. The reality may have been far less conspiratorial: the secondary-mortgage market may simply have been too new, and potentially dangerous, for private investment to risk. In addition, Congress eliminated the proposal that exempted any mortgage association from income tax liability. Coming to the rescue of the FHA was the RFC, which announced on July 30, 1935, that it would assume the role of a mortgage association and purchase FHA mortgages. In 1938, at the behest of the president, the RFC formally created the Federal National Mortgage Association which came to be known as Fannie Mae. It is important to note here that it was not until the Housing and Urban Development Act of 1968 that the conversion of Fannie Mae into a privately owned entity run by a shareholder elected board committed to profit maximization began. The Emergency Home Finance Act of 1970 completed this transformation by allowing Fannie to purchase conventional mortgages as well as those insured by the FHA and VA.[78]

Throughout the remainder of the 1930s, the reluctance of the FHA to take full advantage of the potential economic stimulus of home building, despite some obstacles, continued to act as a constant irritant to Marriner Eccles and Matt Daiger. In a despairing memo to Eccles, Daiger wrote that FDR "had brought this on himself" by placing people in positions of authority who possessed "limited" vision and who were "utterly unfamiliar" with the complicated matters of housing policy.[79]

Nonetheless, Eccles never ceased pouring out a steady stream of letters, memos, and speeches decrying this recalcitrance, while heralding the FHA's possibilities. In a March 1935 letter to FDR, he praised the aggressive efforts made in Germany and in Britain to facilitate housing construction. In one year, he reported, German unemployment in the building trades fell some 70 percent. The Bureau of Economic Research reported in November that in the previous year 300,000 dwelling units were built in the United Kingdom in contrast to less than 50,000 in all of the United States. To an assembly of Ohio businessmen he observed: "In the past five years the number of houses built in England and Wales totaled 1,179,294, [while] the number built in the United States during that same period is estimated at about 700,000." Had the United States built at the same rate in proportion to its population, he pointed out, "we should have produced during that same five years five times as many houses, or 3.5 million." It was largely due to this factor, he informed the New York chapter of the American Institute of Banking in 1938, that national income in Britain was at 110 percent of its 1929 level, while the United States was at 75 percent of its 1929 level. It is also worth noting that in 1930, the per capita national income in the United States was a third larger than that of Britain; by the close of the decade they were essentially the same.[80]

The primacy of housing construction to the U.S. recovery was a matter that both Keynes and Eccles emphasized. "It should not be difficult to perceive," the British economist observed in 1933, "that 100,000 houses are a national asset and 1,000,000 unemployed men a national liability." There are, moreover, numerous contemporary scholars who have given credence to such an assessment. As Peter Temin and John Garraty have noted, only after 1936, following enormous investments in housing and infrastructure, did the Nazis turn toward war production. By that time they had long before achieved full employment. Alexander Field has written as well that the better recoveries made by Britain and Germany during the Depression are clearly related to the housing "booms" that both countries experienced in the 1930s. In fact, Richard Harris and Chris Hammett have observed a convergence in homeownership between Britain and the United States during these years. The percentage of homeownership in England and Wales was as 10 percent in 1914 compared to 46 percent in the United States. By 1938 that figure had risen to 35 percent in England and Wales and had fallen to somewhere near 40 percent in the United States. It is highly significant, and deeply instructive, for anyone interested in public policy, that a good deal of the British increase, and the entire American decline, took place during the Depression. Although balanced budgets in these years hampered a more thorough recovery, writes Robert Skidelsky, "cheap money" and 3.5 percent long-term interest rates fueled a "housing-boom-led recovery" in Britain. And yet, as Jordan Schwarz has noted, without the FHA the economic conditions in the 1930s would have been bleaker.[81]

Of course, if the construction industry had, in fact, reached its full potential in the United States, the problem that would have then presented itself was a shortage of skilled labor. Numerous memos arrived on Eccles's desk cautioning that the administration should make plans to address this development. Eccles believed that a sizeable component of the new jobs program should make building-trades work training a priority. Sadly, the level of new home construction was such that this never became a crucial problem in the 1930s.[82]

"Social Service Worker Thinking" and "the Possibility of Escape"

Eccles opposes the construction of large-scale public housing while maintaining these needs can be achieved through private incentive. He fails, moreover, to address issues of race.

There was one aspect of the National Housing Act to which Eccles seemed to pay slight heed—with the exception of six words, it was otherwise left uncommented upon in his memoir. As mentioned above, included in the Title II provisions of the act was a provision for the creation of a Large Scale Housing Division to construct housing for low-income Americans. Eccles and Matt Daiger made no secret of their conviction that the low-income housing provisions of the act were simply not "practicable." Eccles was, however, clearly aware—as his housing committee's report acknowledged—that the nation's poor were not the beneficiaries of the 1920s construction boom. Surveys done under the auspices of the CWA in the early part of 1934 highlighted the enormous extent of substandard housing throughout all areas of the nation. Daiger drove this point home to Eccles by repeatedly reminding him that a "rent crisis will appear" if this problem was not addressed. It became quickly apparent, however, that the low-rent housing provisions of the FHA were not going to provide low-rent housing. Two and a half years after the law was enacted, a mere thirty-one projects had been accepted for insurance. To be affordable to low-income Americans, moreover, monthly rents in most parts of the country could not exceed eight dollars per room. Slightly over 6 percent of all the apartments constructed under FHA-insured projects rented units that fell within that range. In fact, a very high percentage of FHA apartments rented for monthly rents in the range of sixteen to eighteen dollars per room. In other words, the program was servicing the needs of roughly the same income group that would benefit from the construction of FHA single-family homes. The benefits of federally backed insurance could simply not offset the real estate, construction, and operating costs associated with large-scale developments without some form of additional subsidy.[83]

Eccles would continue to stubbornly cling to the belief that the nation's housing needs, in terms of the construction of more rental properties, could be met by merely coaxing private capital investment into activation. In early 1935, as the administration was contemplating a works project—what would emerge as the Works Progress Administration—Eccles drafted a memorandum for FDR that offered an alternative course of action that relied upon subsidizing efforts of the private sector. The centerpiece of his proposal was a 20 percent subsidy for housing developers. (This alternative course of action is discussed in greater detail in chapter 7.) His suggestion for increasing such construction after the onset of the 1937 recession was to enhance the rental provisions contained in Title II of the National Housing Act.

It was clear as early as March 1935 that no amount of modifications to the law could make such housing possible without subsidization. This was a point acknowledged by the National Association of Real Estate Boards in the summer of 1937 when it cited the fact that families earning in the area of $1,200 were not having their housing needs addressed by Title II provisions. Housing conditions by 1939 seemed to confirm *The Nation*'s suspicion that the federal government seemed content with lower-income groups "waiting for the deterioration" of housing abandoned by higher-income groups. This "filtering up" process, as housing expert Arthur Weimer noted in 1937, was viewed by many as a legitimate way to improve housing conditions. The increase in the housing supply that resulted from the construction of one- to four-family homes would create vacancies in older housing that would both lower rents and, just as importantly, make better residences available to lower-income families.[84]

The beneficial features of the "filtering up" process were complicated by the penchant many in the New Deal had with slum clearance. While Eccles inexplicably remarked in a 1935 memo that he did not think low-cost housing "offers very good prospects as a recovery measure," he seemed confident that slum clearance did. When he composed his 1935 alternative to the WPA he suggested, as part of his plan for housing stimulus, that "government might pay the costs of demolition of existing properties" for developers. (He did include in his program a 20 percent subsidization of low-income projects that would be administered, although not constructed, by the PWA.) During the 1937 recession he reiterated that it would be quite sensible for bonuses to be offered for the demolition of slum areas. The housing act passed by Congress that year (legislation that is discussed below) contained an "equivalent elimination" provision that required any federally financed housing projects include commensurate slum clearance. It was not uncommon in these years for residents of urban centers to pay out half their income in rent. Destroying housing before an adequate supply was made available, therefore, incensed many progressive housing activists such as Lewis Mumford and Catherine Bauer, who felt that it primarily satisfied the desires of realty interests. This point was forcibly made in a memo from Matt Daiger in mid-March of 1937. The "apartment building boom" of the 1920s, he wrote, "emptied a great many slum dwellings" and made the housing shortage particularly acute for the nation's poor. "Ironical as it may seem," he lamented, the industrial recovery precipitated by the New Deal exacerbated the problem by increasing a demand for workers in areas that could least afford to accommodate them.

In May 1935 the *New York Times* published Ernest Kahn's assessment of the U.S. housing situation. A housing expert who had served as head of municipal housing in Frankfort, Germany, Kahn had cautioned in an extensive article in the *Survey Graphic* that the United States should follow the lead of the British government and relegate slum clearance to a much later second phase of a major new housing effort. The United States could also learn from the British that private capital alone could never bring about a suitable solution to the nation's "critical" shortage of housing. He observed, moreover, that the successful and "radical" British effort was being overseen by a conservative government.[85]

While Daiger attempted to convince Eccles that slum clearance should be held in abeyance until the housing shortage improved, he also had doubts about using British public housing as a template. He advised Eccles that the way to respond to critics who argued that U.S. public-housing efforts should replicate the British pace of construction was to remind them that "the U.S. is not a compact little island" that can easily implement a nationwide, uniform housing program. Moreover, he said, critics should be reminded of the array of differences in the United States, ranging from diverse climates to the presence of "racial groups."[86]

There can be little doubt, however, that the effort of the federal government in the area of public housing—motivated by what Eccles derided as "social-service worker thinking"—was wholly inadequate throughout the entirety of the New Deal. The National Industrial Recovery Act did contain a provision for a federal housing program that Secretary Harold Ickes created. His PWA Housing Division built what one architectural historian has described as "the finest urban housing" put up in America for "many decades." The high-quality buildings it constructed—over one-third of which were for African Americans—did not impose a means test for its occupants. It drew the ire of one congressman who observed that the PWA's housing seemed indistinguishable from private developments. Presumably, housing built by the government should look like housing built by the government.[87] Like everything Ickes presided over, of course, the Housing Division moved at something of a glacial pace. (This was exacerbated when FDR impounded over $100 million from the program to use for relief payments in late 1934.) After describing the three PWA housing projects near completion in New York City in early 1937, journalist Victor Bernstein observed: "Here then, is what has been accomplished toward housing rehabilitation for nearly 2,000,000 New Yorkers who need it: the building of three low-rent units sufficient to house 2,150 families or about 7,500 persons. At this rate, it is pointed out, New York City will be rid of its slums in a little over 270 years."[88]

The demise of the PWA housing program, after a four-year life span, marked the end of the only occasion in the peacetime history of the United States when the federal government directly built public housing. In anticipation of this development, FDR issued a plea in late 1936 to twelve hundred delegates attending the National Association of Real Estate Boards to cooperate in providing proper housing for low-income families. As we shall see further on, Eccles frequently sent memos to FDR suggesting the tone of certain public speeches, and on a number of occasions actually took the liberty of drafting the president's address himself. These comments, read to the convention by the new head of the FHA, Stewart McDonald—with whom Eccles was in frequent contact—sounds suspiciously Eccles-like. He was fully aware, the president informed the convention, of their desire to keep all levels of government out of direct participation in housing construction. He went on to tell them that it was their "responsibility," therefore, "to help us discover the ways in which private capital can cooperate with public authorities in improving the housing conditions of the nation as a whole."[89]

Roosevelt's letter to the real estate convention was quite similar to an address Eccles delivered to a convention of bankers only months earlier. He sounded a similar alarm and cautioned that they must enter the mortgage market to keep government involvement at bay. The FHA, he assured them, had only "just begun to scratch the surface" and he urged them to "keep up with the times."[90]

For two years in succession Senator Robert Wagner's public-housing legislation failed to pass in Congress. It received little support from Eccles, who described the bill in a March 28, 1935, memo as "a delusion and a snare." In September 1937, however, after slight progress had been made in corralling private-sector investment in large-scale housing, FDR signed into law the United States Housing Act. With the economy falling into recession, the president thought a commitment to public-financed housing would help revive the construction industry. Eccles, of course, was critical and attempted unsuccessfully to forge an alliance with Frank Walker and others, to persuade the president to instead alter the National Housing Act of 1934 to encourage more large-scale housing projects by private interests. If some of the restrictions placed upon mortgages were removed, and if National Mortgage Associations were permitted to insure twenty times their capital in debentures rather than just twelve times, and if they could be permitted to originate loans on large-scale projects as well as purchase FHA-insured mortgages, it would do a great deal to encourage action in this area. Moreover, as Daiger insisted, "the FHA should focus on cheap homes"; a good deal more three- and four-unit homes could be built if the FHA's $16,000 limit were lifted. Eccles was even successful in getting Senator Wagner to agree to attach the recommended FHA changes as a rider to his housing bill. After all, the New York progressive reasoned, his act and these FHA revisions were not mutually exclusive propositions. The Senate, however, ruled this amendment out of order and not germane to the legislation.[91]

Passage of the Wagner Act—a far cry from what Wagner himself desired—"ignored the basic fact," Eccles reflected in his memoir, "that only through the expenditures of private funds on a variety of forms of housing could the economy as a whole as well as the construction industry make any recovery." To make matters worse, numerous provisions of the housing law mitigated its stimulative impact substantially. Led by Senator Harry F. Byrd, a conservative Democrat from Virginia (soon to become Marriner Eccles's most vociferous critic in Congress), a contingent of budget hawks attached a cost-limitation amendment to the act. This provision forced an unreasonable cap on what could be spent per family unit. The first two projects built in New York City by the United States Housing Authority (USHA), the freestanding agency created to administer the law, spent half as much per unit on these projects as did the PWA's Housing Division. Public housing for the poor in the United States was now guaranteed to look like public housing for the poor. The entire amount appropriated under the act amounted to a mere $500 million to be spread over a three-year period. It was as Eccles described it: "just a drop in the bucket as far as need went."[92]

Undaunted, Eccles, as the chairman of the Federal Reserve, continued to lead a coalition of business and government officials who worked to alter and expand the reach of the FHA. The following year he won FDR's support, and Congress adopted many of the changes that were rejected in 1937. It clearly played a part in the rapid economic recovery that commenced in the middle of 1938.

There is one major failing of the FHA that Eccles, and very few others at the time, even bothered to mention. In President Hoover's 1931 conference on homebuilding, his secretary of commerce, Robert Lamont, in describing the grim conditions in many of the nation's cities, identified "the Negro" as "the worst sufferer." Lamont wrote the introduction to a separate volume for the study that specifically addressed "Negro" housing. The difference between the immigrant and black populations inhabiting substandard housing, he noted, is that in the case of the former, "there is the possibility of escape, with the improvement in economic status in the second generation." That the FHA would play a leading role in the "escape" of massive numbers of Americans to decent housing can hardly be denied. That this opportunity was denied to black Americans is equally certain. Historian Lizabeth Cohen has cited statistics from the northeastern states which reveal that in the immediate post–World War II period, a mere 0.9 percent of FHA mortgages went to African Americans.[93]

From the very beginning of the FHA, observes David Freund, there was a "racial calculus built into its housing and mortgage operations." The notorious phrase inserted into the FHA's *Underwriting Manual* that prohibited the introduction of "inharmonious racial groups" into neighborhoods was, Freund informs us, merely viewed as a manifestation of the scientific principles that the agency intended to apply to sound real-estate management—"professionalism" that routinely eschewed actuarial risk. Racial exclusion was a given. It is worth noting that an examination of the 1934 issues of the leading African American newspaper of that time, the nationally distributed *Chicago Defender*, reveals numerous articles concerning the newly created FHA. Interestingly, virtually every reference explains only the home-repair provisions contained in Title I of the act. A reader who availed himself only of the *Chicago Defender*, it appears, would have remained unaware that the FHA was making homeownership itself more accessible to the American people. It is of little wonder, therefore, that when the new FHA administrator, Abner Ferguson, was scheduled to speak to the Negro Business Conference, his assistant essentially apologized for tying up his time; he assured him, however, that his comments need not exceed "five or ten minutes."[94]

How much time Marriner Eccles spent addressing black business leaders is uncertain. If newspaper accounts, which seemed to faithfully chronicle his many public appearances, are any indication, it would seem he never did. Any concern about racial justice contained within his papers (with the notable exception of relocated Japanese) is not readily apparent. One of the rare connections with such issues occurred when Eccles received a complaint from Congressman Donald O'Toole of Brooklyn, who was indignant that a provision asking about ancestry was included on the Reserve Board's employment application, Eccles promptly ordered that the question be removed. In a public letter to O'Toole the chairman confidently insisted that there "never has been any discrimination because of religion or ancestry" in the Reserve System.[95]

In those files that deal with the events and concerns surrounding the National Housing Act there are no letters, memos, studies, or public speeches that address the critical housing needs of African Americans. In his autobiographical account, *Beckoning Frontiers*, however, Eccles mentions that one of the businessmen invited along with him to provide economic advice to the Finance Committee in early 1933 was a millionaire oilman named George W. Armstrong. Armstrong, a former judge who had once run a chain of banks in Texas, stirred up a storm of protest in the fall of 1949—approximately the time

Eccles was compiling his book—when he offered to donate millions of dollars to the financially desperate Jefferson Military College, provided they pledged to never admit anyone who was black, Asian, or Jewish. Eccles parenthetically mentions this incident and derisively refers to the "Honorable" George Armstrong as one who wished to "teach racism." It is the sole occasion when an issue of race is discussed in his memoir.[96]

Eccles's inclusion of the Armstrong story hints at a general distaste for overt racism. It is possible, of course, that his general attitude may have approximated FDR's: a terrible injustice that must be dealt with at some future date and that must not be allowed to interfere with the advancement of other vital issues of social welfare. The Depression, in other words, was no time for tilting at windmills. To suggest, however, that race simply did not enter his field of vision is problematical. When Harold Ickes assumed command at the Department of the Interior, he was appalled to discover how few African Americans were employed by the Six Companies—and primarily Eccles's Utah Construction Company—at the Boulder Dam project. Ickes, who demanded a nondiscrimination clause in all PWA contracts, and who created a post of special advisor on Negro matters within his department, found that these hiring policies were beyond his reach. In the summer of 1934, fifteen of the 5,251 workers on the dam were black, and all were employed at the lowest pay grade. This employment situation was publicly opposed by the NAACP and its details were covered in the mainstream American press. If Ickes was powerless to alter it, Eccles may not have been. "He is still the moving power" in the Utah Construction Company, a *Forbes* piece informed its readers in 1935. Ironically, an official with the company stated that *housing accommodations* made it "impractical" to hire a greater number of black laborers.[97]

If the National Housing Act failed in terms of racial equity, it also failed in terms of accommodating the poor of any color. Indeed, as has often been pointed out, the ultimate success of the FHA in providing a massive amount of affordable residential housing, and its semblance of doing so within the parameters of a market economy—the very aspect that Eccles touted—rendered the poor as the only clients of noncommercial public or nonprofit housing. As a consequence, an astonishingly small amount of such housing was constructed, both during the New Deal and beyond. By the 1980s, while nearly a third of housing units in the United Kingdom were provided by public or nonprofit agencies, a mere 3 percent were in the United States. And, of course, virtually the entirety of such housing was cheaply constructed and located within the confines of central cities.[98]

Eccles began his involvement with the housing committee with the full intention of driving a stake through the heart of the short-term, high-interest mortgage. By 1940 some 40 percent of all new residential construction came under FHA insurance and such loans had transformed the way all homes were built and marketed. The 10-percent-down, 30-year mortgage would soon become relatively common. (The GI Bill would allow for zero down payments.) Increasingly new home construction was being built by large developers and housing prices began to fall significantly. Nearly 40 percent of homes built in 1940 were selling below $4,000—substantially below the cost of an average home before the Depression. By the late 1930s, nearly a third of families receiving FHA loans had incomes at or below $2,000, and two-thirds of all FHA families were paying less than 15 percent of their monthly incomes in mortgage payments; this, of course, at a time when many renters were spending half of their incomes on rent. So proficient had home construction become by 1940 that the FHA was announcing the construction of homes in the $2,500 range that required only a 5 percent down payment. While this made homes affordable to the working class, the FHA cautioned that there were "definite limitations to the locations where they can be built with FHA approval." Soon the agency's Land Planning Division, in cooperation with suburban zoning boards and in tandem with the high cost of inner city real estate, would occlude the possibility that a great deal of such housing would be built.[99]

Nonetheless, the NHA was transformative. In 1930 roughly 47 percent of American families owned the home in which they lived. This figure, which had remained nearly unchanged for the previous half-century, began to fall swiftly in the Depression-racked early 1930s. With the intervention of the federal government and the revamped mortgaging terms introduced by the FHA, which effectively socialized such debt, this percentage began to climb rapidly and consistently. According to U.S. Census Bureau figures, this number registered 43.6 percent in 1940 and rose to 55 percent in 1950 and to 61.9 percent by 1960. It reached its peak at 69.2 percent in 2004—three years before the subprime disaster struck.[100]

While the stimulative impact of FHA housing was clearly felt before the U.S. entry into the Second World War, the full potential of this altered mortgage structure to produce housing was not experienced until the postwar period. By then, Eccles—who lamented that it did not occur before the war—was worried that in the absence of constant vigilance, it could all get out of hand and that easy lending terms could fuel a dangerous inflationary situation in housing. (Interestingly, mortgage debt rose rapidly after the war to some 14 percent of GDP.

By 1960 it was at 25 percent, and it reached 48 percent by 2000. Four years later it topped 60 percent.)[101]

In early 1937, Matt Daiger sent Eccles a memo expressing some skepticism about whether a "more respectable construction industry than we had in the 1920s" was in the making. He observed that "high costs and high prices have never restrained house buyers from being foolhardy, have never arrested a building boom until supply had far outrun demand and smashed the market; and the practical thing for the man who set the pace in the construction industry to do is to push up prices and 'make his pile.'"[102]

6

A REAL CENTRAL BANK

A "Tame Millionaire"

Eccles's success as a Republican businessman becomes an asset in his ascent.

On September 4, 1934, Lewis Douglas's name once again surfaced on the front pages of the nation's newspapers. The previous day the budget director announced his resignation from the administration. "The break between Mr. Roosevelt and Mr. Douglas," the *New York Times* reported, "has been no secret." Speculating on the cause of this disaffection, it was noted that a good deal of the Economy Act that Douglas had sponsored with such intensity had been repealed by Congress—after overriding a veto by FDR. Two-thirds of the pay cut that the act had imposed upon federal employees had been restored. Mr. Douglas "sent word that he had nothing to say," the *Times* stated. "His resignation," the newspaper's editorial page dolefully pronounced, "will be taken as removing a strong, if not the only remaining defender of sound public finance in the administration." The following summer, as President Roosevelt was about to sign the Social Security Act, Douglas published a book comprised of lectures he had delivered earlier that year at Harvard. America, he said, had scrapped its system "for the plan used by the Soviets." Not surprisingly, the spenders shed not a tear at his departure. "Awful" is how Tugwell described Douglas to Eccles.[1]

Of course, Eccles was keenly aware that Douglas's exit from the administration hardly signified that the president had jettisoned the misbegotten desire to prematurely balance the federal budget. In the aftermath of the passage of the Housing Act, Eccles busied himself with activities that Secretary Morgenthau found objectionable. On a return trip to Utah, the *Standard Examiner* reported that he "spoke his mind quite freely" at a Chamber of Commerce luncheon on the need for increased deficit spending by Washington.[2]

In August Eccles authored a memo that was highly critical of a recent Federal Advisory Council admonition that government spending must be curtailed to offset the specter of inflation. "It is amazing," he wrote, "that banking leaders should give such prominence to these views after their experiences in going through several years of the most severe deflation this country has ever experienced." Counteracting the Depression, he continued, presented the country with a sufficient challenge without the need "of worrying about an inflation that might develop in the future."[3]

This dogged insistence that not enough was being done to end the Depression endeared Eccles to many of the leftists in the Roosevelt administration. Detractors found it difficult to label him pejoratively. He was not an "ivory tower academic" like Rex Tugwell, or an eccentric like Henry Wallace, or a "bleeding heart" social worker like Harry Hopkins. He was a Mormon businessman—one who openly acknowledged a fondness for a cocktail or two and whose sincere religious convictions seemed never to be publicly adjudged—a self-described "tame millionaire," who had the knack of issuing forceful pronouncements that for many had the ring of good old-fashioned horse sense—a New Dealer who could meet a payroll. "He really doesn't calibrate as a non-dues paying bolshevist," mused the well-known journalist John T. Flynn.[4]

It may well have been such factors that first won him favor with FDR. In the contentious White House meetings over the Housing Act, the president no doubt bore witness to what George Creel once observed as a forcefulness that "glowed with a certain incandescence"—what a *Fortune* writer described as "intense rather than domineering." While it was Rex Tugwell who most admired this pugnacity, it was, Eccles tells us, Henry Morgenthau who may have been the first to suggest his name to the president as a replacement for Eugene Black, who resigned as governor on the Federal Reserve Board in June 1934. Eccles mentions in his memoir that Morgenthau first broached the subject with him briefly on a "blistering day in August." When the secretary again asked him what he thought of the prospect several days later, Eccles records that he responded that he had "given it no thought." In light of a clearly ambitious nature, the suggestion that the offer to head the Federal Reserve would have simply escaped his attention is almost comical. As early as August 7 his hometown paper, the *Standard Examiner*, somehow discovered that he was a leading candidate for the job.[5]

In his memoir Eccles avoided any consideration of why his chief adversary in the administration sought his advancement to such a prestigious position. One suspects that the secretary of the treasury may have considered Eccles less of a threat to his fiscally conservative objectives if he were relegated to the world of monetary affairs. One of the few areas of agreement between the two men, moreover, was the need to maintain "easy money" conditions. Morgenthau sought an active, open-market policy of Fed purchasing of outstanding federal issues to assist in issuing of new securities. As Allan Meltzer has demonstrated, the level of monetary activism the Federal Reserve System provided in the early part of the New Deal was motivated more by a strategy to stave off what it deemed to be dangerous inflationary schemes than by a sound understanding of its expansionary role.

In terms of monetary policy, therefore, Eccles's derision of the "bugaboo" of inflation would ensure that he would not prematurely pursue a restrictive course of action. One wonders if Morgenthau ever entertained the thought that Eccles would use his position at the Fed as a bully pulpit from which to proselytize the gospel of compensatory economics. The treasury secretary was not averse, therefore, to some of the fundamental alterations in the System that the determined Eccles made no secret of favoring. While the most vital of these changes was situating open-market decisions within the exclusive purview of the Federal Reserve Board in Washington, Eccles desired in a larger sense to shift the "unbalanced" locus of power in the Fed from New York City to Washington, D.C. When FDR broached the subject of the Fed position directly to Eccles at a White House meeting in September, Eccles bluntly informed the president that he would not "touch the position of governor with a ten-foot pole unless fundamental changes were made in the Federal Reserve System." Roosevelt was receptive and agreed to review a detailed memorandum that spelled out the changes he considered so vital.[6]

Eccles's Fed memo was actually drafted by the Treasury economist Lauchlin Currie. This collaboration between them would be the first of many. While Eccles exuded enormous confidence, he was often conscious of his lack of formal education and the degree to which that hindered a formalized presentation of his ideas, especially in written form. In addition to serving Eccles in this regard, Currie acted as both a tutor and a sounding board for Eccles's ideas. "He had an excellent analytical mind," Currie recalled, "one of the best I have encountered." He agreed, however, with Jacob Viner's assessment of his loquaciousness. Eccles was a "fluent talker."

> His mind was so active that one thing would suggest another, and this a third, and there was always the danger that the original point would get lost in the shuffle. . . . He would doubtless be astonished if someone

> told him that he was not the easiest man to work with or under. I had to smile—though ruefully—in reading his stories of his difficulties in getting over a point to the President, as I experienced exactly the same difficulties with him. He liked to think out loud, as did the President, and he thought continuously. The preparation of a speech was an ordeal.[7]

"Rarely," Currie nonetheless stated, "had two people with such varying aptitudes which complemented each other so well been so suddenly catapulted into a strategic spot at a critical moment which enabled them to make an impact." The first product of their collaboration would lead to one of the most important laws in American monetary history—the Banking Act of 1935. They would go to the Fed together.[8]

Eccles's official resignation from his Treasury post, addressed to "Dear Mr. Secretary," was as terse as the one Morgenthau has sent to hire him: "I hereby tender my resignation as Assistant to the Treasury, effective as of November 16, 1934."[9]

The Money Kings of Wall Street

As a westerner, Eccles's appointment to the Fed reinvigorates historical conceptions of eastern banking.

On November 4, 1934, the day following congressional elections in which the Democrats added to their already substantial majorities in both houses, Eccles presented his memorandum, "Desirable Changes in the Administration of the Federal Reserve System," to the president in a two-hour meeting at the White House. With FDR's commitment to work for these changes, the announcement of Eccles's appointment as governor of the Fed occurred six days later. On November 11 it was the name Marriner Eccles that appeared in banner headlines across the nation. While noting that the forty-four-year-old Utah banker and industrialist, "of Mormon ancestry," was "a wholehearted supporter of the New Deal policies," the *New York Times* quoted Eccles's statement that he considered it "a pleasure and a privilege" to follow FDR's "leadership." The article speculated that his appointment signaled that the administration had abandoned any thought of "far-reaching changes such as the establishment of a government central bank," but that a strengthening of the Reserve Board seemed likely.[10]

To ward off criticism that he was dangerously radical in other respects, Eccles issued a statement the day after his appointment in which he alluded to his February 1933 testimony before the Senate Finance Committee. The *New*

York Times had earlier that year characterized his statement as "so far out of the beaten paths of economic thinking that there were few who really understood it." He had never voiced a need for a "redistribution of wealth," Eccles insisted, "that is perfectly impossible under the capitalist system." Rather he sought "a better distribution of wealth production"; meaning—as he better articulated on other occasions—that it was vital to get income into the hands of those American workers who lacked a sufficient amount of it. Hardly satisfied with what it viewed as the subtleties of this clarification, the *New York Times* editorial page made reference the following day to Eccles's "high strung and extravagant assertions" about economic affairs. Such statements, the editorial pontificated, are "to be regretted in an appointee to an office of such dignity and responsibility." In a heartening conclusion, however, the editorial advised readers not to despair since the preponderance of power in the System—thanks to the "wise and effective" Federal Reserve Act of 1913—resided not with the governor and his board, but with the twelve regional Federal Reserve Banks. Leading the way, it noted, was the Federal Reserve Bank of New York, presided over in the past by the legendary Benjamin Strong and at present by his competent successor, George L. Harrison. Not surprisingly, the *Wall Street Journal* shared this poor estimation of Eccles's suitability for the position.[11]

A somewhat more reasoned perspective of any proclivity Eccles might display for radical economic policies was furnished by the economist Roger Babson. Babson, who, in contradistinction to Irving Fisher, was enjoying some renown for his prescience in forecasting the great crash, wrote a lengthy piece of economic analysis that found its way into the newspapers in early 1935. "Here is a man worth watching," Babson said of Eccles. While the *New York Times* and American bankers might view him as a radical, Babson assessed the new Fed chief as "a true friend of progressive conservatives." In Eccles he claimed to see a true believer in using government influence to foster a resurgence of market capitalism. He wished that "there were more like him in Washington," and "every progressive employer and corporation" should feel likewise.[12]

One of the more frequent comments about Eccles's elevation to Banker in Chief was the fact that he was a westerner. "It is said," the *New York Times* reported about FDR's selection, that the president "sought a man who was not closely associated with the great financial centers in the East." The following week, the business writer Frank Kluckhorn praised Eccles's "enthusiasm and frontier fearlessness in meeting big problems with action." A *Fortune* magazine article on Eccles, after citing his western origins, observed that the West traditionally "ran on debt" and that banking had always been "dominated by the eastern seaboard."

Eccles grew up in a part of the country, wrote Francis Brown, where there has "always been a dislike bordering on hatred for eastern banking and bankers." This largely explains, he states, "his readiness to advocate a socially controlled capitalism." Eccles's statement that our economic system is "not an exact science" and that experience alone can determine the proper course of action, Brown assessed as "a reflection of the West and of a pioneer heritage." Writing from Denver, Colorado, journalist John Farnham opined that Eccles's appointment was "perhaps the most encouraging thing the Roosevelt administration has done, so far as this section of the country is concerned." He, too, wrote of the western lack of appreciable capital and its constant indebtedness to Wall Street financial interests. "On the whole," he asserted, "the Federal Reserve System . . . has been of less use to the western banks than to those in the East, because too many classes of paper that the western banks take are not rediscountable as 'self-liquidating.'"[13]

While Eccles was inclined to consider this something of a nationwide predicament, the restrictive notion of what constituted a sound asset was, as we shall see, precisely one of the problems he identified in his memo to FDR. Eccles certainly agreed with Farnham, however, that the West experienced this more acutely and that as a westerner he had sensitivity to this issue that none of his predecessors possessed. He recalled in his memoir, for example, that there was little clamor for an agency like the RFC in the early days of the Depression: "Eastern institutions could still safeguard their protective layers of fat by calling in the obligations owed them in the West and the South. But when those obligations were no longer collectible and the eastern institutions lay exposed to a fall against rock bottom, then they demanded the RFC, and it came into being." This seemed merely a reprise of a longstanding pattern in American financial history.[14]

"Westerners," writes New Deal historian Jordan Schwarz, "made resentment and grievances an ingrained part of their culture." The determination to end their "colonial subservience to New York" and to take possession of "their share of the economic pie" had engendered what he termed the "peculiar chauvinism of Westerners." The Roosevelt administration was keenly in tune with this sensibility and, as Schwarz notes, even those New Dealers who had never stepped foot beyond the 98th Meridian were "Westerners at Heart. They would make the Federal Treasury the West's best banker." Walter Lippman believed that FDR's connection with the landed gentry fueled typical prejudices of what Jefferson called the "paper aristocracy." Installing thc bolo-tie-clad Marriner Eccles at the Fed was part and parcel of this affirmation.[15]

The hostility for the "Money Kings of Wall Street" was deeply rooted in the American past and hardly restricted to the American West. "I believe," Thomas Jefferson wrote to his treasury secretary, Albert Gallatin, "that banking institutions are more dangerous to our liberties than standing armies." This was especially evidenced in Jefferson's resistance to the centralized banking represented in the form of Hamilton's Bank of the United States (BUS). It was a legacy of distrust continued in Andrew Jackson's legendary opposition to Nicholas Biddle's reincarnated second BUS. As historian Sean Wilentz has emphasized, Jackson's sometime opposition to government—and his vehement animus for the governmentally sponsored BUS—was not motivated by a passion for laissez-faire, but rather a determination to sever the connecting links between public officials and the "moneyed aristocracy." Wilentz informs us of Jackson's and his followers' "willingness to wield federal power forcefully over economic issues . . . when they thought doing so was necessary to protect the democratic republic."

Ironically, this opposition to "the Monster" was prompted less by a fear that "hard money" was endangered than a concern that an eastern elite would use its financial wherewithal to promote its own interests while stifling the credit requisites of western expansion. Indeed, what historian Bray Hammond derisively termed the "reckless booming anarchy" that ensued after Jackson used the power of government to prematurely kill the BUS by moving funds into numerous state-chartered "Pet Banks," nevertheless, did infuse the West with financial credit. In Henry Myers view, in the final analysis, the reckless overextension of loans did have a positive impact upon economic development in the 1830s. What is crucial to consider about this well-known episode in American history is the underappreciated fact that before his exit from the presidency, Jackson gave serious thought to forming a third BUS that would be centered in Washington and that would report regularly to Congress. Thus even at this early date—and even by Andrew Jackson—consideration was given to the possibility that a centralized government bank that was unequivocally under government control and supervision could enhance economic conditions and operate for the benefit of what Jackson deemed "the laboring classes."[16]

To be sure, however, the Jeffersonian/Jacksonian agrarian conviction that eastern financial interests were the power behind federal government banking laws maintained a clear resonance with western farmers in the first decades of the twentieth century. The prohibition on real estate investments imposed upon national banks by the National Banking Act of 1864 lasted for half a century, and thereby rendered as much as four-fifths of western bank assets ineligible for mortgage loans. The void was largely filled by Wall Street mortgage companies such as Mercantile Trust and Equitable Trust that were dominated by bankers like James A. Roosevelt and the infamous J. P. Morgan. Interest rates on farm and home mortgages in the early 1890s ranged from 5 percent in Manhattan to 8 percent in Louisiana, and in excess of 12 percent in western Kansas. Similarly, even rates on prime commercial paper saw ranges of 3.83 percent in Boston to 8.34 percent in Dallas and 10 percent in Denver. To escape from this burden of indebtedness and high interest, many in the West were often eager to embrace a variety of inflationary schemes. It was, Eccles lamented, "a debtor's counterpart to a creditor's dogma."[17]

Although discoveries in numerous parts of the world doubled the world supply of gold around the turn of the century and for a time dampened the clamor for inflation, the adherence to the gold standard would continue to hamper attempts to instill flexibility into the money supply. Moreover, the structure established by the National Banking Act remained problematic for western agriculture. The law required the thousands of nationally chartered banks to make deposits into "reserve banks" located in forty-seven cities across the country. These larger reserve banks were themselves mandated to place reserves in still larger "central reserve" banks located in Chicago, St. Louis, and New York City. Not surprisingly, New York City banks—which competed among themselves in terms of paying interest on the funds of rural banks—accumulated a disproportionate amount of the nation's reserves. Indeed, at the beginning of the century a full two-thirds of the nation's cash was held by banks in the thirteen eastern states. That they paid high interest, and the fact that these large city banks were required by law to maintain a 25 percent reserve ratio in vault cash, placed increased pressure on the performance of their portfolios. Increasingly, this meant taking on higher risk and placing funds into stock-market transactions.[18]

Logistically, the system was not well suited to provide the kind of flexibility in the money supply that the seasonal demands of agriculture made upon it. All too often the financing needs of western farmers reverberated in New York City, where its largest banks were the terminus of a cascade of credit demands. When the surge was unexpectedly strong and the financers on Wall Street could not coordinate an infusion of liquidity, a national banking panic could ensue. On occasion, the U.S. Treasury would make a cumbersome attempt to stem a run on banks by shifting funds out of its subtreasuries to banks or regions in need, or make advance payments of interest and principal on its bond obligations.[19]

The stopgap nature of these mechanisms was placed on alarming display in the course of the "Panic of 1907." On this occasion, the hoarding of cash, the payment of payroll in scrip, the freezing of commercial loans, and the general loss of liquidity was felt not merely in farm regions, but across the nation. In the previous decade, J. P. Morgan and an assemblage of fellow financiers had come to the rescue of the United States Treasury when the 1893 depression resulted in a troubling depletion of the nation's gold reserves. In 1907, however, the American economy had grown in both size and complexity and the worldwide extent of the crisis clearly outstripped any solution that even the most powerful Wall Street banks could proffer. With the New York Clearing House overwhelmed, with the stunning failure of the city's prestigious Knickerbocker Trust Company—a savings bank of sorts for many of New York's high and mighty—and with J. P. Morgan presiding in panic mode over nerve-racking round-the-clock meetings of financers, the inadequacy of the U.S. banking structure had come home to the money kings. It was now the federal government that came to the rescue. After Morgan met President Theodore Roosevelt in an emergency conference, tariff receipts were directed to the necessary institutions and the secretary of the treasury, Charles Cortelyou, rushed to New York to oversee the further transfer of federal funds. Ironically—and in a clear demonstration of the need for some entity to command an overall perspective on the changes in the economy—Cortelyou and his predecessor at the Treasury had for a year been removing liquidity from the economy by building up gold reserves. This was at a time when the San Francisco earthquake and fire made heightened demands on greater liquidity.[20]

In his landmark reevaluation of the impetus behind the founding of a new central bank that followed in the wake of the 1907 panic, historian Gabriel Kolko takes note of the vulnerable position in which the Wall Street banks found themselves during that crisis and interprets it as an indication that their financial dominance was beginning to wane. Indeed, Kolko reasons, had they possessed the degree of power that many of their contemporaries—and some present-day historians—believed they did, they would have acted to frustrate the development of competition in a variety of sectors in which they had vested interests. He expends a good deal of effort demonstrating that this influence never came into play. This is especially so in the area of steel production, where J. P. Morgan's mammoth U.S. Steel Corporation was losing market share throughout the opening decade of the century. This had much to do, he asserts, with the increased tendency of industrial corporations to finance their rapid growth by using their own burgeoning profits rather than the intermediary services of investment banks. In the first decade of the century, a full 70 percent of the new capital invested in manufacturing concerns came from internal sources. The growing geographical dispersion of these industries, moreover, redounded to the benefit of regional banks, many of which were newly established. Remarkably, from 1900 to 1912, the nation's ten thousand banks grew to some twenty-five thousand. This growth, and the depository volume that accompanied it, was disproportionally centered in western regions.[21]

Kolko thus presented a fundamentally altered perspective on the power relationships at play in 1910. Far from imposing a restrictive governmental supervisory structure upon the leading financial powers of New York, writes William Greider, "the results were nearly the opposite." He goes on to observe:

> The money reforms enacted in 1913, in fact, helped to preserve the status quo, to stabilize the old order. Money-center bankers would not only gain dominance over the new central bank, but would also enjoy new insulation against instability and their own decline. Once the Fed was in operation, the steady diffusion of financial power halted. Wall Street maintained its dominant position—and even enhanced it—until the trauma of 1929.[22]

In the aftermath of the 1907 Panic, Congress created a National Monetary Commission charged with studying the monetary system of the nation and making corrective proposals. Headed by the patrician senator from Rhode Island, Nelson Aldrich, the commission departed for a tour of European central banks. Acting as advisors on this expedition were two men—one a close associate of J. P. Morgan and the other the president of the American Bankers Association—who exercised great influence upon the commission's members. The hybrid legislation that the commission recommended—a decentralized/centralized/public/private bank—bore the clear earmarkings of the nation's disputatious history on the subject of monetary control.[23]

Upon returning from Europe, Aldrich invited a select cadre of powerful financers to a clandestine gathering on the implausibly named Jekyll Island off the coast of Georgia in 1910. There, the "Aldrich Plan" for the creation of a new central bank was discussed in great detail. Why Aldrich felt the need to conduct this meeting sub rosa is uncertain. It was in no way a secret that he and his banker friends were the commanding figures in the Monetary Commission.

It seems hardly surprising, therefore, that the Federal Reserve plan would draw criticisms from several quarters. The role of eastern bankers and Aldrich's reputation as a leading foe of tariff protection for agricultural interests meant that western opposition was particularly acute. When he accepted his party's nomination for president in 1912, however, Woodrow Wilson made it clear that he was a sympathizer with the old populist imputation that "vast confederacies" of banks and corporations were in control of the nation's credit, and he intended to do something about it. Considering that the presidential campaign was unfolding amidst the revelations of Congressman Arsene Pujo's highly publicized investigations of the "money trust," Wilson's rhetoric proved expedient. Among Pujo's revelations was that J. P. Morgan & Company had officers who served as directors of 112 large corporations. Wilson was ultimately successful in convincing a preponderance of the American people—and, it seems, some historians of the Progressive Age—that this new Fed Board, on which the secretary of the treasury and the comptroller of the currency were to sit, was to oversee the financial workings of the banking system and render it all less unseemly.[24]

Wilson was also successful in making the law slightly more amenable to populist sentiment. The discounting of agricultural credits, for example, which was prohibited under the original Aldrich Bill, was permitted under the law for agricultural loans of up to six months. Unlike the initial provisions, which allowed for the use of Federal Reserve notes only within the System, the law now made the notes legal tender and an obligation of the U.S. Treasury. These changes came far from quelling all opposition; the act would not prohibit interlocking directorates, nor would it place the regional reserve banks or their branches firmly under public control. Enough had been done, however, to overcome enough agrarian opposition to pass the measure. As historian Arthur Link has observed (and as Marriner Eccles and FDR were to become quite aware), the selection of those who would occupy positions in the Fed was capable of generating nearly as much critical attention as the formation of its formal structures. By 1914, when the Fed was preparing to commence its operations, Wilson was attempting to repair his relationship with big business. "Wilson climaxed his little campaign to win the friendship of the business classes," writes Link, "by turning over control of the Federal Reserve Board, in effect, to their representatives, as if he were trying to prove the sincerity of his recent professions." The banking community was delighted by Wilson's announced appointments of International Harvester director Thomas Jones and Wall Street banker Paul Warburg. While both men drew the outrage of progressives, Warburg—whose banker son would emerge as one of Marriner Eccles's staunchest antagonists—was able to barely win confirmation to the Board, but the animus of agrarians, who accused Jones of plotting to organize an illegal combination in farm production, foiled his appointment. A bitter Woodrow Wilson castigated members of the Senate for fostering "class antagonism."[25]

Less remarked upon was the appointment of Benjamin Strong to be the first governor of the Federal Reserve Bank of New York. Though few were fully aware of this at the time, the Federal Reserve Act had elevated the young president of the city's Bankers Trust to the summit of economic power, not merely in the United States but across the globe. By 1915, the flow of banking deposits, which had been gradually trending toward western regions of the country, was now disproportionally filling the coffers of New York banks. That year a conservative estimate found some 53 percent of the nation's bank balances were stored in that city. The New York Fed was designated the agent of all foreign transactions of the United States government and the securities purchasing agent for the entire System. In the aftermath of the Great War, the New York Fed performed the majority of open-market operations and it pretty much set the discount rate for all the other branches. In Benjamin Strong's view, the Fed was essentially a financial alliance of private reserve banks that were supervised, but not directed by, the Board. For all its pretense of diffusion, the Federal Reserve Act had centered monetary power—and it wasn't in Washington, D.C.[26]

In a recent examination of the Panic of 1907 and the reforms that emerged as a consequence, business historians Robert Bruner and Sean Carr reach a conclusion not far from what Gabriel Kolko espoused nearly a half-century earlier. "Ironically," they write, "the Fed, one of the landmark achievements of the Progressive Era, was a child of the 'money trust' that Progressives feared."[27]

Marriner Eccles in large part agreed, and set out in 1935 to give the Fed new parentage.

"The Smell of Cordite in the Air"

As the new leader of the Fed, Eccles makes a few enemies with his undiplomatic actions, while maintaining fiscal policy as his primary interest.

From Eccles's vantage in the fall of 1934, the recently passed Housing Act and the Federal Reserve revisions that lay in the immediate future would engender a vastly improved allocation of the nation's financial resources. Although he continued to feel that the real solution to the nation's economic health, both in terms of its present doldrums and its soundness in future years, resided with the fiscal choices made by its government, Eccles was gaining a deeper appreciation for the role of money. While Allan Meltzer is quite right when he writes that Eccles did not cast any blame upon the actions of the Fed for causing the Depression, the influence of Lauchlin Currie soon led Eccles to accept the belief that its policies significantly "intensified" the downturn. Ironically, as touched upon in chapter 2, with Currie, Eccles had as his principal advisor on economic affairs one of the most influential adherents of a monetary interpretation of the Depression. Indeed, David Laidler goes so far as to state that the interpretation that is so closely associated with Milton Friedman was "undoubtedly pioneered" by the Harvard scholar. In fact, Milton Friedman himself acknowledged that Currie's role in this regard has been given insufficient attention. The Canadian economist was among the first to trace the status of money stock from 1921–1933, which demonstrated a 24 percent decline for 1929–1933. Throughout the entirety of his years in the New Deal—for the remainder of his life, it seems—Currie never wavered from the conviction that Fed missteps brought on the Depression and that its policy of "complete passivity" prevented the possibility of an early extrication. (This assessment is something of an irony in light of the fact that some use just these words to describe the Fed policy during the New Deal.) Like Eccles, however, Currie considered monetary policy as part of an overall macroeconomic plan of attack. If he taught Eccles that "money matters," the working banker in turn may have assisted the Harvard economist to come to grips with the stubborn confines of a "liquidity trap," and to see that "spending matters."[28]

Within two weeks of his appointment as governor of the Fed, Eccles granted an interview with the *New York Times* in which he spent virtually no time speaking about the intricacies of monetary oversight of the banking system. Rather, he elaborated on the need for government to come to the rescue of business with "a great public works program." To ensure its success, the works program must have *no restrictions placed upon it in regard to either its duration or its level of expenditures*. It need simply be big enough and last long enough "to provide employment for all persons capable and willing to work" (although, as mentioned earlier, Eccles was not an advocate for the construction of public housing). It was of crucial importance, he stressed, that the program begin in a speedy fashion. The Fed's role was to furnish a "harmonious" climate for the sale of U.S. securities to fund it all and to thereby "avoid financing on a currency or some other inflationary basis." Equally important, he assured readers, the Fed had a variety of mechanisms at its disposal to check any advance of inflation that might occur in the future.[29]

It is hardly surprising that on Eccles's very first day as a member of the Federal Reserve he issued a memorandum to the White House that had virtually nothing to do with monetary affairs. It is extremely unlikely that a president ever received anything remotely like it from the head of the Fed. Dated November 11, the memo expressed concern over "the appearance of instability in administration policies" which were doing a great deal to "neutralize the effects of its constructive efforts." Psychological factors in the process of recovery, the memo continued, are of crucial importance. "The battle would be half won, were the public convinced that the administration knew exactly what it was doing." Ironically, of course, Eccles's own outspokenness about the need for a vigorous jobs program and deficit financing, while the president was himself enamored with the idea of balanced budgets and had recently indicated that no big jobs program was under consideration, hardly helped to foster clarity about public policy goals.

It was crucial, the memo continued, not merely to appropriate money for programs but also to spend it in a timely fashion. "Speed" was of the utmost importance. A following memo made reference to a front-page *New York Times* article from October 30, which reported that the PWA, in its sixteenth month of existence, had managed to spend only a third of its original $3.3 billion appropriation. "Fighting a depression is like jumping over an abyss," the memo cautioned. "If the cleft is ten feet wide, even a nine foot jump is worse than no effort at all."[30] Five days later, Eccles bothered to send off a similar cautioning memo to the treasury secretary. In addition to finding it irksome, it may have disabused Morgenthau of any hope that the new Fed governor was now wholly engrossed in banking reform. "It is essential," wrote Eccles in the memo, "to have larger expenditures."[31]

Eccles's New Deal rivalry with Henry Morgenthau, and his encroachment into the realm of fiscal budgetary matters, has long been commented upon. The *New York Herald Tribune*, observing the public tussle that developed between the two, provided a poor assessment of both men in 1935. While "the Secretaryship of the Treasury" has gone "to seed" under Mr. Morgenthau, "the head of the banking system," the paper asserted, "is a man who loses no opportunity to appropriate any financial prerogatives that are not nailed down."[32]

In fact, the Treasury had hardly "gone to seed" under Morgenthau's tenure. When Congress overwhelmingly passed the Gold Reserve Act in January 1934 (the vote was 370 to 40 in the House of Representatives), it sanctioned the president's order of the previous December directing the Treasury to take possession of all of the System's gold, and in return to issue gold certificates at $20.67 to the reserve banks. The day following passage of the legislation (January 31), Roosevelt fixed the price of gold at $35 an ounce. The Treasury then established an Exchange Stabilization Fund with $2 billion of its profits—obtained, of course, from the possession of gold valued at $35 an ounce that was acquired at $20.67 an ounce—from which, among other things, it funded industrial loans by reserve banks and engaged in market transactions. (The Industrial Advances Act of 1934 added section 13(b) to the Federal Reserve Act, allowing Federal Reserve district banks to make *working-capital* advances to sound businesses that were unable to raise capital. In 1932, Congress, over Herbert Hoover's veto, adopted section 13(3) which allowed the Fed Board to make direct loans to "any individual, partnership, or corporation" under "unusual and exigent circumstances.") The fund, equivalent in value to the Fed's open-market portfolio, allowed the Treasury to counteract Federal Reserve actions. It allowed the department, writes Allan Meltzer, "a strong hand in setting policy toward interest rates, money, and debt, and it used its power." Indeed, he asserts, in its relationship with the Fed, the "Treasury remained the dominant partner" for the remainder of Eccles's tenure.[33]

These details contain, therefore, an appreciable irony. While one cannot help but consider that the nation may have fared better had Eccles and Morgenthau been appointed to the other's respective position, it seems doubtful that Morgenthau would have fulfilled the forceful role that Eccles played in the historic adoption of the Banking Act of 1935 and the reshaping of the Federal Reserve System that occurred in the 1930s. "The main thing to keep in mind in regard to Eccles's appointment," wrote Frank Shelton, a Fed official who had some familiarity with him, is that "he will dominate the Federal Reserve and the Reserve Banks."[34]

Eccles wasted little time in validating the expectation expressed in this internal Fed memo. In his first week on the job as a recess appointee (he had been sworn in but Senate confirmation was months away), while still occupying his office at the Treasury, George Harrison, governor of the New York Federal Reserve Bank and the man whom the *New York Times* had only days before lauded as the de facto leader of the Federal Reserve, paid Eccles a welcoming call. This proved a rather awkward visit since the restoration to the Washington board of the power that had been "usurped" by the New York Fed was the most vital element of Eccles's proposed banking legislation. Until Benjamin Strong's death in October 1928, Harrison served as the legendary governor's deputy. When officials of foreign central banks came to the United States to discuss monetary affairs, more often than not they headed not to Washington, but to Strong's office—now Harrison's—at the New York Federal Reserve. Eccles found this troublesome since the governor of this bank was placed in power by "the private banking interests of New York." The forty-eight-year-old Harrison, known for his affability and diplomacy, followed a very different route to central banking than had Eccles. A member of Skull and Bones during his days as an undergrad at Yale, he went on to receive his law degree from Harvard, where he graduated near the top of his class. Prior to going to the Fed as a legal counsel in 1914, he served a clerkship on the Supreme Court for Oliver Wendell Holmes. From Eccles's perspective, this was not a terribly impressive background from which to understand the workings of banking, industry, and commerce.[35]

What is interesting to observe, however, is that Harrison receives accolades from contemporary economic historians for the actions he took in the immediate aftermath of the 1929 stock market crash. Under his direction, the New York Fed, without the approval of the Washington Board, took aggressive action by purchasing $150 million of government securities. This, as Barry Eichengreen stated, "was impressively fast action even by the standards of Ben Bernanke." The Board, however, incensed that Harrison had acted without their sanction, took actions to rope him in. Eichengreen gives little credence to the suggestion of economic historians Friedman and Schwartz that Harrison —unlike Benjamin Strong—did not have a forceful enough presence to confront the Board.[36]

Eccles's recollection was that Harrison dropped by "ostensibly to offer his congratulations." Following a brief exchange of pleasantries, Harrison invited Eccles to attend the meetings of the Legislative Committee for the Federal Reserve System. The committee, which Harrison chaired, was composed of private bankers from the System who framed and initiated legislation affecting the Federal Reserve. In fact, the committee was newly formed. Established only that past June, it was clearly attempting to offer a much more modest legislative alternative than what was expected from the new governor. It certainly would have attempted to keep power in the reserve banks. Eccles, employing what he described as "primitive and blunt words," informed Harrison that he would most definitely not be attending the meetings of his committee because he intended to immediately abolish it. All legislative proposals of the Federal Reserve Board, he informed what must have been a rather shocked and offended George Harrison, would emanate henceforth from the Board itself. From that moment on, Eccles recalled, "the war between the two of us was on in earnest."[37]

On November 19, Eccles continued with his charm offensive when he attended a meeting of the Federal Advisory Council. A creature of the 1913 Federal Reserve Act, the council was composed of twelve bankers, each of whom was elected by the directors of their respective Federal Reserve banks. The council was instructed to "confer and advise directly" with the Federal Reserve Board. Over the years, however, the council had essentially usurped much of the Fed's role in terms of providing public information. In the minds of many Americans, the opinion of the Federal Advisory Council was believed to be officially that of the Fed itself. The deference which the media paid to the council Eccles found quite bothersome; this was especially true of their most recent pronouncement decrying deficit financing.

Dispensing with opening pleasantries that everyone must have anticipated in an introductory meeting, Eccles leveled the type of brusque verbal offensive for which he had already gained a reputation. The function of the council, he pronounced, was to serve the Board in an advisory capacity and not to be a purveyor of political propaganda. From this moment on, he continued, the council should release no public statement until it had first submitted it to the Federal Reserve Board for review. In response to the chorus of protestation that arose from council members that their organization was a statutorily recognized, independent agency, Eccles reminded them that the Board was also independent and could choose to ignore the council and deny it access to the Fed's staff and resources. Moreover, he did not intend to discuss the matter with them any further and suggested that the council meet the following day to decide upon their future course of action. With, as he recalled, the smell of cordite in the air, he concluded the meeting as unceremoniously as it had begun. Twenty-four hours later, the Advisory Council essentially agreed to follow Eccles's procedure for releasing its public statements.[38]

"Why Thomas Jefferson Would Not Speak to These People"

Eccles and Senator Carter Glass commence their adversarial relationship.

Eccles's confrontation with the Advisory Council was sure to displease the redoubtable senior senator from Virginia, Carter Glass, who considered the Advisory Council as his personal conduit for receiving and conveying banking information. Often referred to as the "father of the Federal Reserve," the seventy-seven-year-old Democrat had been the chairman of the House Banking and Currency Committee, which had overseen the Fed's creation in 1913, and he looked upon the institution with something approaching a proprietary right. "Next to my family," he once confided, "the Federal Reserve System is nearest my heart." Glass, a newspaper editor from Lynchburg, and a leader of the effort to disenfranchise African Americans in Virginia, found himself assigned to the House Banking Committee when he came to the Congress in 1903. Completely unfamiliar with banking issues, the young congressman immersed himself in the world of finance through reading countless books and engaging in continual interrogatives with influential participants in the field. He felt confident that he had gained sufficient expertise when the committee he chaired began drafting the legislation to create the Federal Reserve System in 1912. Glass went on to serve as President Wilson's second treasury secretary, where, pursuant to the 1913 law, he served as ex-officio member of the Fed Board, and assumed the role of chairman when he attended meetings.[39]

Although widely considered the congressional oracle on banking matters, Glass had been persuaded in 1933 by the incoming Roosevelt administration to forego leadership of the Banking and Currency Committee and assume the chairmanship of the Appropriations Committee. This was done to deny the appropriations chairmanship to the highly intemperate Senator Kenneth D. McKeller of Tennessee, who was viewed as an unrivaled spoilsman and the last man FDR wanted in such a post. Nominally the chairmanship of the Senate Banking Committee went to Duncan Fletcher of Florida. The de facto chairman, as everyone understood, was Carter Glass, who exerted control by chairing a full subcommittee that reviewed all vital legislative proposals.[40]

Throughout the fall of 1934 it was an open secret in Washington that FDR was considering nominating Marriner Eccles as governor of the Fed. At no time, however, did the president—perhaps because he was certain of the response he would receive—seek the advice of Carter Glass on this matter. Nor was it a secret that the administration was working on banking revision. On this matter as well, the administration chose to ignore the esteemed senator from Virginia.[41]

As if these facts alone were not enough to engender an invidious response from the proud senator, Eccles proceeded to ensure his enmity by waiting until December 17, after Congress had adjourned, to write a conciliatory letter to Glass in Lynchburg. While a hosanna to Glass's achievements in the field of banking, the contact may have been a little tardy to sufficiently soothe his animus. The following day, Glass responded by thanking Eccles for his "courteous personal allusions" and recognition of his "persistent efforts to maintain the independence of the Federal Reserve System." Since Eccles's letter, while highly praiseworthy, made no such reference to "independence," this response was blatantly revealing.[42] Their personal relationship continued its downward spiral when, in their first face-to-face encounter, shortly before Congress reconvened in January 1935, Eccles provided a somewhat lame excuse about why he could not discuss with Glass some specifics of the banking bill as it was then constituted. At this meeting Eccles promised that the senator would be furnished a copy of the legislation prior to its arrival on Capitol Hill. The bill would be sent to the House on February 5 and to the Senate the following day without Glass being provided an advanced copy. When Eccles attempted an explanation, Glass called him a liar. The battle lines, both personal and ideological, were clearly drawn.

In his memoir Eccles attempted something of a defense of this slight by observing that in Carter Glass's book, *An Adventure in Constructive Finance*, where he recounted the events of the 1913 Federal Reserve Act, Glass stressed that while drafting the law, he kept the details secret from everyone except President Wilson and Treasury Secretary McAdoo. This, he insisted was a strategic necessity since the "revolutionary provisions" of the act would be endangered if prematurely disclosed. The old Virginian now had little sympathy for such a strategy.[43]

In fact, Senator Glass had long before turned a jaundiced eye, not merely to Eccles's appointment, but to many of Roosevelt's endeavors. Glass would lead a significant cadre of conservative southern Democrats, most especially his fellow Virginian, Senator Harry Byrd, who would become the most forceful critics of liberal policies. An avatar of fiscal conservatism, Glass had recoiled in horror at the administration's prodigal ways. Once, overhearing a reference to the democratic nature of the administration, he shot back, "Why, Thomas Jefferson would not speak to these people." By mid-1935 his animus was greater still. "The New Deal is not only a mistake," he pronounced, "it is a disgrace to the nation. I would rather die than live to see the disgrace of this era." In regard to Eccles, not only was FDR elevating a man with a besmirched fiscal reputation, he was placing him at the helm of an institution that he revered.[44]

"Useful Servants of the National Welfare"

Eccles delineates the key alterations that he believes will make the banking system serve the nation's needs.

In reading Eccles's account of the history of the Banking Act of 1935 in *Beckoning Frontiers*, one might infer that the far-reaching effects of the law would have lain legislatively fallow were it not for Eccles's September 1934 encounter with FDR, when he made his acceptance of the Fed position conditional upon the president's pledge to seek fundamental changes in the System. The generalized need to invest the Federal Reserve Board with a greater concentration of power, however, had long been on the New Deal to-do list. At a meeting in Warm Springs, in May of 1932, the need to achieve this was recognized. Of course, they also acknowledged at that time, as Ray Moley remembered it, that to move toward a central bank "carried us pretty far from ancient moorings."[45]

Nevertheless, Eccles clearly prioritized the banking issue, and it is perhaps accurate to state that absent his presence in the administration, the effort to alter the System would probably not have occurred in 1935. In that case, had reform been delayed to a later phase of the New Deal, it is possible that its sweeping dimensions could have been curtailed, or possibly stifled altogether. If such a counterfactual consideration is justifiable, what is historically unquestionable is that the legislation that emerged, both as to policy alterations and specific structure, was to a great extent the handiwork of Lauchlin Currie and Marriner Eccles.

The memo that Eccles delivered to the president at their November 1934 meeting was, like so many that would follow in the next three years, drafted by Currie, but specifically contoured by the new governor. It cited a number of changes that would "introduce certain attributes of a real central bank capable of energetic and positive action without calling for a drastic revision of the whole Federal Reserve Act." While the memo displays a keen awareness that deference needed to be paid to the nation's historic suspicion of centralized monetary control, it also expresses a clear amount of disingenuousness on this matter. Hence Eccles suggests that while his revisions preserve "private ownership" and "local autonomy" on "really important questions of policy authority and responsibility," power needed to be "concentrated in the Board." Thus, he maintains, "effective control is obtained, while the intense opposition that greets every central bank proposal is largely avoided." It seems, therefore, only a mild overstatement to say that the plan would create a central bank through some degree of misdirection and sleight of hand.[46]

Not surprisingly, the memo begins by stressing that the control of aggregate demand is the key determinate of national income. The "effect of an increased rate of spending may be modified by decreasing the supply of money, and intensified by increasing the supply of money." What "experience shows," however, is that without "conscious control" the money supply moves in a procyclical direction. Of its own momentum the money supply contracts when "the promotion of business stability" requires its expansion and expands when economic health necessitates its curtailment.

"Far and away" the most effective weapon in the Fed's arsenal to control the money supply, the memo emphasizes, is the buying and selling of securities on the open market. It should be interjected here that it is simply not the case—as is sometimes asserted—that this was a financial mechanism that was largely unheard of prior to the post–World War I period. The practice of open-market purchases of previously issued government securities by the government actually dates to the 1850s. Witnessing large surpluses accumulate—the government was then using a subtreasury to deposit its funds—James Guthrie, Franklin Pierce's secretary of the treasury, suggested that the administration could get money back into circulation by purchasing government bonds. By this time, such a policy had been ongoing in England for over thirty years, where the Bank of England assisted the Exchequer in refunding the public debt by purchasing and selling its outstanding obligations. As Allan Meltzer has pointed out, only weeks after the System became operational the Board authorized the reserve banks to purchase government securities at their own discretion. A section of the act that did permit this was largely motivated by the desire to keep banks in the System somewhat in debt to the reserve, so the discount rate (the interest they charged banks to borrow) would remain a viable tool. In fact, the first meeting of governors in 1915 deliberated on the wisdom of such uncoordinated activity.[47]

While the exercise of such transactions was obviously contemplated, the fact that no formal provision was incorporated into the Federal Reserve legislation that regulated or coordinated it is revealing. It is clear that in 1913 the ramifications of open-market activity were not apparent. Much of this oversight is explained by the paucity of the federal debt at the time the System was established. For this reason, the Fed's congressional sponsors could hardly be faulted for failing to imagine the potential potency of this activity. The debt of the federal government at the time was well under $1 billion and seemed on its way to becoming expunged. Most of this debt was in the form of bonds authorizing national circulation or held by estates, thus only about $100 million of U.S. bonds were available for purchase. By the close of the First World War, however, this debt had ballooned to an astonishing $27 billion, and it became readily apparent that buying and selling these securities would have profound effects on monetary affairs. Purchases or sales would first lower or raise the federal funds rate—the interest rate at which banks lend to each other overnight—and the infusion or depletion of money would initiate a ripple effect throughout the economy and ultimately affect the spending decisions of households and businesses. "It is not too much to say," Eccles's memo informed FDR, "that who controls this power controls the money system, and, in large measure, the supply of money."[48]

In an attempt to bring some centralized control to market operations in the 1920s, the Fed eventually settled on a body known as the Open Market Investment Committee (OMIC) that excluded from participation the seven southern and western Federal Reserve banks. Membership consisted of the governors of the New York, Boston, Philadelphia, Cleveland, and Chicago Fed banks. The OMIC established a trading desk operated by the New York Fed to execute a coordinated plan of action. This was a likely choice since the New York Fed, not surprisingly, controlled a full third of such securities. Any policy agreed upon by the committee, however, needed the approval of the Board in Washington. Moreover, participation in the OMIC was voluntary and the Board lacked the legal authority to prevent any reserve bank from doing whatever it wished in terms of the open market. While representatives of all twelve banks were added to the committee (now called the Open Market Policy Conference) in 1930, it was not until the Banking Act of 1933 that any structure became written law. The act mandated that each year the board of directors of all twelve banks elect a representative to what was now designated a Federal Open Market Committee. While the 1933 act gave the Board the power to approve or disapprove the committee's recommendations, and prohibited the reserve banks from following their own course in terms of purchases and sales in the open market, it still allowed them to obstruct any coordinated plan by simply refusing to participate.[49]

The changes made by the Banking Act of 1933, Eccles maintained in his memo, fundamentally altered nothing of any real importance. The Federal Open Market Committee continued to be "dominated" by twelve privately selected men who "by the very nature of their appointments, duties and associations, cannot help but be profoundly influenced by a narrow banking rather than a broad social point of view." It was "essential," he insisted, that the Federal Reserve Board assume "complete control" over "the timing, character and volume of open market purchases and sales of bills and securities." The diffusion of power and responsibility, the memo stated, played a crucial role in the Fed's maladroit handling of monetary policy in the past. It was essential to concentrate authority and responsibility in "the hands of a small policy formulating body."

It was also necessary to bring the governors of the reserve banks—who, he reminded the president, were not even mentioned in the Federal Reserve Act—under some form of public control. He urged, therefore, that the Board be given the power of approval over all appointments to the reserve bank governorships; it would also be a good idea, furthermore, to bring the salaries of the Fed Board in closer alignment with their counterparts in the reserve banks. This, he believed, along with control of the open-market operations, would allow the Fed to acquire the "respect and prestige" it was presently being denied.

Eccles recalls that FDR was quite attentive and interactive in the course of their two-hour meeting where he presented his banking memorandum. As he both elaborated on its specifics and added additional suggestions that were not contained within the memo, the president on occasion leapt ahead of him to finish his train of thought, while all the while silently calculating the political feasibility of each proposal. Previously, he stated, FDR had semantically assaulted the financial barons of Wall Street. Eccles assessed these attacks as "largely theatrical in character," and they had been followed by scant substantive policy initiatives. The Banking Bill of 1935, however, offered the opportunity to "make the nation's financial centers useful servants of the national welfare."[50]

Scholars usually refer to Eccles's banking memo as including eight points. Indeed, there are eight numerals listed, but they are essentially restatements of the same issue: an empowered central bank that had control of the money supply needed to be created. Other than the restructuring of the open-market operations and giving the Fed Board the power to approve the selection of the governors of the individual reserve banks, the memo contained no specific recommendations.

"Credit that Is Kept Sweet and Clean"

Eccles argues that the Fed must consider both price stability and high employment as its goals. It will come to be known as a "dual mandate."

Both Eccles and Currie—who actually drafted the memo to the president—were clearly operating within realpolitik constraints. In fact, the whole necessity for the schematic division of twelve reserve banks—by 1935 it seemed an inviolate structure—made "little sense" to Currie. While at Harvard and during his tenure with the Treasury Department, he advocated a fundamental corrective for the nation's banking system: the supply of money should be separated from the lending of money. This could be achieved by instituting reserve requirements of 100 percent on demand deposits, while time deposits would have no reserve requirements at all. Currie realized that such a radical alteration was a political nonstarter, and there appears little evidence that he sought to persuade Eccles of its merits.[51]

There was, nonetheless, an array of banking changes that Eccles and Currie were mutually eager to see enacted. Much of Eccles's November 4 discussion with the president delved into these specific alterations to the System. As a recent practitioner in the field, Eccles was keenly aware of the precariousness of unit banking. Of the eleven thousand banks that failed or merged between 1929 and 1933, roughly 90 percent were small banks without branches. In Canada, where nationwide banking was allowed, there were virtually no failures at all. Moreover, it was clear that the failure of some seven thousand banks during the pre-Depression 1920s was indicative of structural complications that could not be attributed merely to depositor panics.[52] When the Banking Act of 1933 permitted national banks to establish branch banking in those states where branch banking was allowed, Eccles consolidated his banks under First Security to five with twenty-three branches. When FDR immediately rejected his suggestion that the legislation incorporate nationwide branch banking, Eccles, uncharacteristically, dropped the matter with apparently little hesitancy. In his confirmation hearing cited below, he stated his strong support for branch banking; not wishing to annoy the president, however, he stressed that he was not recommending it be part of the banking act.

Although Eccles appears to have also shared Currie's view that the Glass-Steagall Act's separation of commercial and investment banking was unnecessary, he seems never to have even broached the subject with FDR. The power of the Senate Banking Committee hearings, conducted by legal counsel Ferdinand Pecora, which had concluded early that year—encompassing over eleven thousand pages of testimony—had so solidified the rationale for such separation that it would remain a difficult political proposition to challenge for half a century (as proponents of repeal would discover in the summer of 1935). In addition, an influential group of investment bankers—many of whom supported FDR in the election—proved to be a driving force behind the law. Led by the leaders of Chase National Bank, including the president's cousin Vincent Astor, it was a coalition that included many of the leading investment banks in the country. The major exception to this support, of course, was J. P. Morgan & Company, which had used the dual banking functions to acquire its sizable power.[53]

Moreover, while deposit insurance was Henry Steagall's prized legislative accomplishment, the separation of commercial and investment banking was Carter Glass's bailiwick. Indeed, Glass, who had long opposed deposit insurance, accepted this feature to assure passage of his banking act. There seems little doubt, however, that to argue—as future scholars like George Benston have done—that the abuse of securities operations was not at the heart of the banking crisis, may very well have risked derailing the entire effort at restructuring the System.[54]

It was of utmost importance, both Currie and Eccles believed, to convey to the president the absolute need to centralize power. In a proposal that was guaranteed to set off fireworks, Eccles argued that it was of vital importance to change the legislative mandate given the Fed from the prosaic assignment to "accommodate the needs of industry, commerce and agriculture" to the expansive duty "to exercise such powers as it possesses in such manner as to promote conditions conducive to business stability and to mitigate by its influence unstabilizing fluctuations in the general level of production, trade, prices and employment so far as may be possible within the scope of monetary action and credit administration."[55]

In the view of many—especially Carter Glass—it is precisely because banks strayed from their mandate to serve the needs of commerce that the nation fell into a financial crisis to begin with. Had banks continued to merely accommodate the short-run credit needs of productive local businesses by issuing loans backed by *real goods*, instead of speculative stock-market securities, it would have allowed them to liquefy this "eligible paper" at Federal Reserve banks when panic conditions overwhelmed them. Adherence to this "Real Bills Doctrine," Glass insisted, would have permitted the mechanisms of the Fed—a structure that the senator felt he had installed—to function effectively to keep thousands of banks afloat. Moreover, Real Bills—"credit that is kept sweet and clean"—was considered an essential safeguard in the never-ending preoccupation with the phantom of looming inflation. Any loan that was matched by an increase in real output, it was assumed, would not be contributing to an increase in excess money. Indeed, when the creation of the Federal Reserve was being debated, those who feared the inflationary potential of its loans—"elastic money"—were assured of the self-liquidating nature of discounted commercial paper, as businesses paid back their loans and the money went back into the System and was extinguished.[56]

The experience of the previous five years, however, had convinced Eccles that the Real Bills Doctrine—what Currie termed "The Commercial Loan Theory of Banking"—had played a key role in the nation's massive number of bank failures. "During the Depression," Eccles maintained, "many banks were forced into bankruptcy not because their assets were bad but because they could not meet the narrow and essentially unrealistic eligibility requirements" when they went to the reserve banks for assistance. In other words, the problem was that a good number of banks were not insolvent but illiquid. (That this was the principal cause of Depression bank failures was asserted by Milton

Friedman and Anna Schwartz and is challenged by others. See Calomiris and Mason, "Consequences of Bank Distress.") Ironically, Currie argued in his PhD dissertation that commercial loans, far from being the safest and most liquid of assets, were frequently the most difficult to unload in the market and thus the least liquid. It was essential, in Eccles's view, that the law allow advances to member banks, not on the basis of "eligible paper," but rather "any sound asset." This expansion of acceptable collateral—allowed on an emergency basis by the 1932 banking act—was a virtual necessity, he argued, since the total amount of self-liquidating paper in the entire country amounted to a mere $2 billion—far too meager for commercial banks to operate profitably.

As a corollary to this revision, Eccles informed FDR, it was of vital importance to encourage greater activity in the construction industry by liberalizing the provisions on real-estate loans. The amount that member banks were allowed to lend in mortgages, both in terms of total volume of their portfolios and the percentage of appraised value of the real estate, must be increased. Here again, Eccles felt he was making a case for the nation's smaller banks that could not operate profitably on the basis of their demand deposits alone. Member banks had in excess of $10 billion in time deposits that badly needed long-term investment opportunities.[57]

Although open-market operations were gaining importance, the control of reserve requirements remained an important weapon in the Fed's arsenal. The effectiveness of this mechanism, Eccles believed, could also be heightened by reform. While Currie would have preferred to make vast changes in the control of reserves, Eccles was willing to settle on somewhat less radical modifications. The current law permitted an adjustment in requirements only when the president was acting pursuant to an emergency and when at least five Board members gave approval. Eccles wanted the Board to have the unlimited authority to change reserves for both demand and time deposits by majority vote, absent any participation by the president or any necessity of a declaration of emergency conditions.

It was also important, Eccles believed, to have all of these changes managed by a streamlined board of five technically competent members. The individuals should be selected merely for their education or experience in monetary and financial affairs, with the present requirement that the Board be balanced geographically abandoned.

Roosevelt, Eccles remembers, concluded the meeting with a forceful slap upon the table prior to pronouncing, "It will be a knock down and drag-out fight to get it through. But we might as well undertake it now as at any other time." Had he known at the time how virulent the opposition to the bill would become, Eccles wrote, "I don't know if I would have had the courage to take the job. But at the time, Roosevelt's pledge of support was all I needed to hear."[58]

If Eccles approached the congressional hearings on the banking bill certain of the president's full support, Carter Glass was of a different view. The "old warrior," as FDR designated him, had apparently been informed by the president that he was not entirely committed to the reforms that Eccles sought. This would, of course, have been shocking news to Eccles, especially since it was the president who devised the strategy to shepherd the bill into law. FDR suggested that the banking bill reforms (Title II) be sandwiched between two other provisions that were widely desired by the banking community. Title I of the bill required all member banks to join the FDIC after July 1, 1935, but favorably improved the assessments and rates for doing so. Title III would extend the deadline for bank officials to either repay any loans they had previously received from their own institutions or face termination.[59]

By early February of 1935, the president was describing the banking proposals of Title II as "tentative." Carter Glass was quoted as saying that same day that it was "impertinent" to assume that he would support a piece of legislation that he had not yet had the opportunity to fully read. The pressure on FDR to sever Titles I and III from the bill was quite forceful. Leo T. Crowley, the head of the FDIC, J. F. T. O'Connor, the Comptroller of the Currency, and Jesse Jones of the RFC, all attempted to dissuade Roosevelt. In the end, however, the president's tentativeness seemed designed to intimate to those who led the entreaty against Title II that they had made inroads with him against the provision. FDR worked craftily behind the scenes, however, to support the measure, including persuading the Senate to appoint three new favorably disposed members to the banking committee. *Time* informed its readers that "it was the Washington consensus" that the administration was using the banking bill to divert the "peppery little Virginia senator" from attacking the new $4 billion public-works bill that FDR finally decided to support.[60]

With guidance provided by Chairman Henry Steagall, and second-ranking member T. Alan Goldsborough, the banking bill was swiftly and favorably approved by the House Banking and Currency Committee. The two men had marshaled an array of favorable witnesses before his committee, including an only mildly challenged Marriner Eccles. The hearing gave life to a seminal lesson in macroeconomics when Alan Goldsborough analogized Eccles's description of what today would be termed a liquidity trap to the futility of "pushing on a string." That exchange, and the assessment of the congressman as an ally of Eccles and the banking bill, often encompass Goldsborough's political legacy in most New Deal historical accounts. A closer look at the colloquy between the two men, however, illustrates the extent to which some in Congress—and throughout the nation—viewed these revisions of the Federal Reserve System as constituting a modest alteration of policy.

"Placid and friendly at home," *Time* magazine wrote of the Maryland Democrat from the rural eastern shore, "he is an energetic, fist-clenching, table thumping speaker in Congress." A fervent populist, first elected in 1920 and defying the Republican onslaught of that year, the fifty-eight-year-old attorney had supported a good deal of radical inflationist policy that Eccles had decried. These political sentiments were clearly on display during the Banking Committee's hearings and it reflected the American sensibility about banking, and bankers, that was explored previously. The reforms that were being proposed, Goldsborough declaimed, were insufficient to rectify the credit system or bring an acceptable level of prosperity to the American people. "The present banking system is artificial and built up by bankers to control money. Society should take the control back from the bankers." Eccles's rejoinder that "under communism or socialism" this goal might be more easily achieved brought a sharp rebuke from the congressman that he had said nothing about either. "A tremendous banking class absolutely runs this country," Goldsborough insisted. "It must take its place in society or it will swallow us all up." Eccles, while giving some acknowledgment that there was an imbalance of power, insisted that the bill before them was "a step forward." Somewhat soothed by such reasoning, the lawmaker, serving his seventh term, conceded that the banking act was "infinitely better than anything we have had before." After adding that the nation must somehow rid itself "of this debtor-creditor complex," Eccles reminded him that the "whole system of capitalism" is built on precisely such a relationship.[61]

Goldsborough was striking a chord that resonated with many of his countrymen. Discussed previously, it has proven itself a timeless American grievance, its rhetoric as familiar to the denizens of the 1830s who heard the Jacksonians assail the machinations of Nicholas Biddle, as it was to Americans of 2011 condemning Henry Paulson and Timothy Geithner's Troubled Asset Relief Program. Eccles was making the point—also entertained previously in this work—that Andrew Jackson considered: the way to combat this private power is with government control.

Eccles would get a better sense of the extent of such sentiment later that year when Texas congressman Wright Patman garnered 150 House members to cosign his bill ordering the Congress to take over the Federal Reserve by purchasing all of its stock. In Eccles's estimation Patman represented a distinctly separate danger: giving elected officials total control over the System. "We are extremely dubious," stated the *New Republic*, representing a somewhat more sophisticated perspective about the chances that the alterations in the System would effectuate meaningful change. In an article titled "Giannini Fights Morgan," Sassoon Ward, writing for the *Nation*, pronounced the bill at some level a power struggle by regional financial interests with much at stake. Taking note of the San Francisco banker's strong support for the bill, and the massive extent of his real-estate holdings that the new law would now make eligible for discount, he suggested that "the bill might be called a Giannini bill." And yet, Ward's conclusion was one that many on the left would reach: "Mr. Eccles would put an end to dictation of Federal Reserve policy by the New York banks against the Roosevelt program." And surely, taking power from Wall Street was not a thing to be taken lightly. It was rightfully considered, Ward opined, "the most important piece of banking legislation laid before Congress since the Civil War."[62]

Like Father and Son

In congressional hearings, Eccles and Carter Glass go to battle over the merits of the Banking Bill and matters of personal hegemony.

Although the bill, now being referred to publicly as "Eccles's," was reported out of the House committee on April 8, it had at that date yet to be considered by Glass's Senate subcommittee. A week following the House committee's approval, Glass's subcommittee—which had delayed consideration for months—kept the matter in abeyance and took up the matter of Eccles's confirmation. Senator Glass hoped to strike a blow at the bill by discrediting Eccles, and assuring his rejection by the subcommittee and the full Senate.[63]

Eccles began his testimony by revealing that a substantial amount of his time in business was dedicated to his banking interests. He had been president of a bank holding company, the First Security Corporation, now run by E. G. Bennett and his younger brother, George. Senator Glass reminded him that the Federal Reserve Act required that all members must certify that they have disposed of all bank stock holdings and that they have given up any position as an officer or a director of a banking institution. One imagines that Eccles may have suspected at this point that Glass was setting him up to appear crafty and disingenuous. Perhaps because he refused to acknowledge anything untoward, Eccles let the questioning proceed along the path that the senator preferred.

What follows is the portion of the testimony highlighted in the *New York Times* the following day.

—May I ask if you have disposed of all your bank stock?

—I have.

—In a bona fide sale?

—I have.

—Without any reservation at all?

—Without any reservation.

—Do you consider the First Security Corporation of Utah a banking institution—the one that owns these five banks?

—I do.

—Do you have any interest in the First Security?

—I have not.

—Is it owned by the Eccles estate?

—A portion of it is.[64]

Eccles then went on to elaborate. The estate—established as the Eccles Investment Company—owned some 15 percent of the First Security Corporation, and Eccles owned less than 9 percent of the Eccles Investment Company. Because the stock was not listed on any exchange, and because there was no market at the time for bank stocks, he explained, he sold the stock to the Eccles Investment Company at a net capital loss of $90,870. Eccles brought with him to submit into the record a lengthy opinion from the Federal Reserve's legal counsel affirming the legality of all of Eccles's transactions.

The *New York Times* account, on the front page the next day, was scant about any extenuating details. The sale seemed to closely resemble the circumstances of former Republican treasurer Andrew Mellon, who was accused of merely transferring his stock to his brother. The paper reminded its readers that in a tax-evasion proceeding against Mellon, Robert Jackson, the general counsel for the Bureau of Internal Revenue, had asserted that the Mellon transaction did not amount to a real sale and that Mr. Mellon was still the actual owner.[65]

Other revelations from Eccles's testimony garnered less attention. He was asked by Glass if his financial interests had ever received loans from the Reconstruction Finance Corporation. After stating that none of his companies had received any such loans, Eccles was forced to concede, after Glass pressed the issue, that the Western Investment Company, owned by his First Security Company, had received an RFC loan of nearly $1 million in 1932. When Glass once again persisted, Eccles acknowledged that a number of his banks had received funds from the RFC by selling the agency preferred stock. "Well that is what I mean," Glass responded. In fact, the senator was well equipped with all pertinent facts about the extent of such assistance. Most notably, the First Security Bank of Rock Springs, Wyoming, capitalized at a mere $10,000, had preferred stock of $150,000 with the RFC. Eccles seemed to fumble for reasons to explain why a number of his banks had accepted this infusion of RFC money, stating at one point that the RFC "tried to get all the banks to take preferred stock." Although this was indeed the case—an exceeding high number of banks had been so encouraged by the RFC—Eccles gave the appearance, yet again, that he was attempting to be evasive.[66]

To Glass's annoyance, none of these matters seemed the least bit important to the American public. Although there were accusations about other "activities" of the First Security Corporation, Senator James Couzens, the progressive Republican from Michigan, stated that he did not favor denying an appointment on the basis of a "whispering campaign." The subcommittee voted to confirm by a vote of 6 to 2. The full committee unanimously approved the appointment. "Purposely missing," when the vote was taken, observed *Time*, was "Eccles's warm foe, Carter Glass . . . who mortally hates Eccles's plan for tightening government control of the Reserve System."[67] When the full Senate voted on confirmation, Glass cast the only dissenting vote. "As so frequently happens now," the dejected Glass informed fellow lawmakers, "my sound opinions do not count for much."[68]

Despite Glass's pitying assessment of his political standing, his opposition still posed a formidable force, and passage of the Banking Bill was hardly a foregone conclusion. Analyzing the 74th Congress in January 1935, political commentator Mark Sullivan predicted that the lower House would follow FDR anywhere. With all the Democrats in the House coming up for reelection in two years it would have taken a brave representative to buck the president. Of the sixty-nine Democrats in the Senate, however, fully fifty-five could safely be labeled—so Sullivan believed—as "conservative." Foremost among them were the Virginia Democrats, Carter Glass and Harry Byrd. Only nineteen of these members were running for office in 1936. The Senate might give the president a free ride on appointments, but if the legislation could be displayed to the public as radical, its passage would not be a certainty.[69]

When Glass's full subcommittee finally did convene to consider the banking legislation on April 19, it became quickly apparent that the smooth sailing the bill encountered in the House would not be replicated. The chairman had scheduled an influential array of witnesses eager to sound a public alarm about its perilous provisions. First to testify was Paul Warburg, the vice chairman of the Bank of Manhattan. Warburg's father had been a member of the Fed for years—his appointment by Woodrow Wilson, it will be remembered, was viewed as a betrayal by many progressives—and like his son, a good friend of Carter Glass. While the transparency of the tactic to sandwich Title II of the bill between two popular provisions was scarcely referenced in the House hearings, Warburg made immediate mention of it:

> I shall confine myself to a discussion of Title II, which deals with the proposed amendments to the Federal Reserve Act. I shall do this for the same reason that if someone were to say to me, "I am going to do three things for you: buy you dinner, buy you a drink and cut your throat." I would not waste very much time choosing my drink or ordering my dinner.[70]

The kernel of the banking proposal, said Warburg, quoting Eccles's House testimony, was the essential need to bring about a "conscious control of the nation's supply of money" and amounted therefore to nothing more than "Curried Keynes." If Eccles and Currie prepared the sauce, Warburg asserted, the main dish was John Maynard Keynes "whose theories find more support in this country than in his own." Indeed, he maintained, Governor Eccles was asking Congress to approve a theory of monetary policy that enjoyed negligible support from the world's recognized authorities. Moreover, said the prestigious banker, the Fed would be utilizing—here a thought and selection of phrase to make Brandesians cringe—"the people's money" in their "willy-nilly" decisions to alter reserve requirements or engage in open-market operations; and all of this to achieve an end whose efficacy was highly questionable. It was not the specious economics embedded in the bill that was "charged with dynamite," warned Warburg, but rather its dangerous political ramifications. The legislation proposed giving the Executive an unwise amount of influence since the governor would hold office at the president's pleasure. Allowing "the long arm of the Treasury" to control credit machinery, Warburg argued, was "the favorite device of spendthrift governments." After assuring the committee that he was not one to see a Communist under every bed, he resorted to quoting Lenin: "the first step in the direction of Communism must be the nationalization of banks." Warburg then wondered if the authors of the proposed banking legislation realized "whose game they are playing."[71]

Overseeing the testimony of his sympathetic witnesses, like a demanding and corrective father, was Carter Glass, asking leading and provocative questions whenever he glimpsed an opportunity to exploit a fertile topic, hastening to add remedial information to bolster a weak line of reasoning and interposing an opinion to sidetrack a colleague's inopportune line of inquiry. As bank president Frank Ferguson gave notice of the grave danger of political influence inherent in the bill, he was queried by Senator Bankhead: has there ever been a time, asked the senator, when the Federal Reserve Board was "not subject to the influence of the administration in power?" When Ferguson began to furnish an equivocal answer, the chairman leapt into the exchange. "Yes, I can name a time when they were not." In the eight years of the Wilson administration, Glass affirmed, the president eschewed even social contact with Board members for fear that it might be erroneously interpreted as political manipulation. Nor could he recall a single instance in which President Coolidge ever made such an overture.[72]

When Frederick Snyder of the United States Chamber of Commerce momentarily departed from his diatribe against the bill to favorably entertain the suggestion that a committee of experts might be assembled to study the issues dealt with in the legislation, he was chastised for his backsliding by the elder senator who asked reprovingly, "Could you get a better group of experts than this committee?"[73] Although essentially aligned with Glass's position, Adolph C. Miller, a member of the Federal Reserve Board since its inception, clearly felt the chairman had overreached when he stated that the Banking Bill "converted the Federal Reserve System into a spoils system—nothing else on earth." In response, Miller began to wax philosophically. "Does it not all come down to this, that men, after all, are the stuff of which governments . . . are made?" The enactment of laws ultimately mattered little, reasoned Miller, "if you have men who are either intellectually or morally incapable of fulfilling those functions." With Glass's exasperated rejoinder that government could, at the very least, refrain from statutorily encouraging malfeasance, Miller replied, "I quite agree."[74]

With a wide number of witnesses, however, Glass needed to exert little cajolery. "This is not liberalizing the Federal Reserve System," claimed Winthrop Aldrich, the chairman of the Chase National Bank. "It is making it over into an instrument of despotic authority." Aldrich launched the most effective challenge to the economic foundations of Eccles's proposal. Open-market operations were ineffective, he argued, pointing out that between March 1932 and November 1933 the Federal Reserve banks bought $1.6 billion in government securities from which the economy derived little discernible benefit.[75]

Encased between a bevy of hostile witnesses came the testimony of Marriner Eccles. Eccles was called before the subcommittee on May 10, 1935, nearly a month after it had begun deliberations. Only the day before, the House passed the Banking Bill by a vote of 271 to 110, placing Carter Glass in a particularly churlish mood.[76]

Eccles began his testimony by reading a statement that sought to downplay the broad dimensions of his bill. The proposals were "not revolutionary" but rather "definite and limited" in scope, he stated. Nor were they theoretically conceived but arose from "the experience of the past twenty years." Those who criticized its provisions as an attempt to subordinate the country's banking system to political control, Eccles maintained, were not merely falsely interpreting the present bill but were demonstrating "a lack of clear understanding of existing law and of the proper relationship between the Reserve System and the government." For those members of the press who attended the hearing desirous of witnessing a clash between the governor and the chairman, this statement must have drawn wry smiles of satisfaction. Here was Marriner Eccles, in typically fine form, apprising the widely acclaimed "father" of the "existing law" that, despite his parentage, he did not quite comprehend its significance.

Glass, however, remained tight-lipped as the governor continued his lecture by delving into the Federal Reserve's history. Since the system was first proposed it was recognized, stated Eccles, that "matters of national credit and monetary policy should be under public control." To substantiate this point, Eccles cited a 1913 report of the Senate Committee on Banking and Currency (it should be remembered that in 1913 Glass chaired the House Banking and Currency Committee) which emphasized that supervision of the banking system was a governmental function and that "private interests have no right to representation, except through the government itself." As further proof, Eccles went on to quote a part of President Woodrow Wilson's address before a joint session of Congress in June 1913:

> The control of the system of banking and of issue which our new laws are to set up must be public, not private; must be vested in the Government itself, so that the banks may be instruments, not the masters, of business and of individual enterprise and initiative.[77]

It was clear, Eccles concluded, that the wishes of the Fed's 1913 proponents formed "the guiding principle of the legislation, which is now under consideration." For Carter Glass whose idolatry of Woodrow Wilson was well established, and who considered himself a bona fide arbiter of the former president's legacy, this assertion must have been especially grating and it brought the senator's silence to an end. "Well, of course, Governor, that is your peculiar interpretation," intoned the chairman who then brought attention to what he claimed was Eccles's insufficient emphasis on the word "supervisory" in his recitation of the congressional report. "The Federal Reserve Board was to be a supervisory censor body," Glass pronounced, "totally devoid of any acquisitiveness to supervise the administration of the law." Then followed this exchange in which Senator Couzens participated.

> *Senator Couzens.* Do you see a distinction there, Governor?
>
> *Senator Glass.* Evidently not; but I do, a very grave distinction.
>
> *Governor Eccles.* Of course, there is a distinction between the use of the word "supervisory"—I suppose you would have to read the entire—
>
> *Senator Couzens.* (interposing) Report.
>
> *Governor Eccles.* (continuing) The entire report.
>
> *Senator Glass.* Inasmuch as I wrote the report, I know what "supervisory" means.
>
> *Governor Eccles.* The reading of the statement of President Wilson here [reading]: "The control of the system of banking and of issue which our new laws are set up must be public, not private—"
>
> *Senator Couzens.* (interposing) Did you write that, Senator?
>
> *Senator Glass.* What?
>
> *Senator Couzens.* Did you write that too?
>
> *Senator Glass.* No. Woodrow Wilson wrote that. Nobody ever wrote anything for him that I know of. Nobody ever wrote anything for me.[78]

Eccles then resumed his rereading of the Wilson passage, seemingly ignoring what may well have been a veiled insinuation by the senator that the governor's staff and not Eccles himself had composed the statement he was presenting.

To further his position—and to perhaps further antagonize the chairman—Eccles trotted out a quote from Glass's old ally, the late Paul Warburg (the father of Paul Warburg referenced above) who once stated that the "management of the central reservoir" of reserves "must be free from the dangers of private interests." What Warburg meant, said Glass, interrupting, was the deposits in the respective reserve districts. "The Federal Reserve Board had no reservoir. It has none now," declaimed the senator. "He is speaking, of course," responded

Eccles, matching the chairman's authoritativeness, "of the control of the reservoir of Bank reserves."[79]

If viewed from the proper perspective, Eccles continued, his proposal seemed "almost a non-controversial matter." Who would deny, he stated, that the Congress is constitutionally vested with the power to coin money and regulate its value. Indeed, this idea that "control over money is a matter of national concern" and must therefore be retained by the sovereign power is as old as government itself. The Banking Bill of 1935, he explained, sought merely to adopt this venerable tenet to the modern world. Fully 90 percent of the volume of payments made by Americans on a daily basis were made by check rather than cash. This substitution of credit for cash currency, Eccles said, had been a gradual development but one that must now be fully appreciated. The government could not genuinely fulfill its monetary responsibility, he argued, without the power to control credit availability. All of the newer central banks of the world, the chairman informed the committee, recognized the necessary relationship between the government and the central bank, most especially the Bank of England and the Chancellor of the Exchequer. "On the contrary," the chairman interrupted, reliable sources had informed him that the Exchequer would not "dare to tell the Bank of England what to do." As if he had anticipated Glass's comments, Eccles then read an excerpt from Viscount Snowden's book (Snowden was a former Chancellor of the Exchequer) in which he had elaborated upon the intimate relations between the bank and the government. "For all practical purposes," Snowden wrote, the Bank of England was "a State Bank." Since the governor seemed to view the conversion of the Bank of England to a State Bank as such a desirable achievement, asked Glass, "Are you in favor of a [U.S.] Government Central Bank?" Eccles responded that he was not. "Why not?" Glass demanded to know. "Are you in favor of Father Coughlin's bill?" (The radical radio-priest had called for the federal government to purchase all of the Federal Reserve's stock.) "No," responded Eccles, "I am not." "Why not?" Glass sharply asked. The ownership of the stock, said Eccles, was, in and of itself, not the vital matter. The vital matter was who had "responsibility for management."[80]

Eccles appeared eager to temper these issues of centralized government control with the emphasis he felt his bill placed on increasing the "regional autonomy of the Reserve banks in matters of local concern." In this regard, he pointed out the banking bill loosened the grip of the Fed upon the System's twelve Reserve banks. At that time, Eccles reminded the committee, the Reserve Board in Washington appointed three of the nine directors of each of the Reserve banks, one of whom was its chairman. The chairman, who had significant responsibilities, was the Fed's representative at the Reserve banks. Eccles's bill proposed fusing the role of each bank's chairman with that of its governor (to be selected by the Reserve bank's board) and making the position subject only to the Fed's approval. In that case, said Eccles, the Reserve banks would now control the chairman's duties and would, as a result, have increased responsibility in dealing with member banks. This, he suggested, would more properly create a Federal Reserve System that both President Wilson and the proponents of the original act had intended.

Any time Eccles invoked the name of Woodrow Wilson, it was a sure-fire guarantee to elicit a foul-tempered retort from the chairman. This time was no exception. "Another thing in the mind of President Wilson and of the proponents of the Reserve Act," an irritated Glass maintained, was a steadfast determination to prevent "speculative investment transactions." Here occurred one of those interesting transitions that happen from time to time in American politics where the proponents and detractors of centralized governmental power exchange positions. Without the firm rules set down by the Board in Washington, Glass maintained, "member banks might engage in speculation to their heart's content." When Eccles stated that he did not think this was the case, Glass abruptly interrupted with a defensive charge that suggested, yet again, that the governor had been programmed by his staff. "Evidently," said Glass "the counsel to the Board does not think that the chairman knows anything about the Federal Reserve Act, but the chairman thinks he does."[81]

Eccles was proposing that the Reserve banks be allowed to lend to the banks in their districts on the basis of "sound assets." He was keenly aware from his own experience under fire as a bank president that many financially sound institutions went under during the panics of the early 1930s because, as discussed previously, Reserve banks would only lend on the basis of a bank's "commercial paper"—its highly liquid assets. These assets, referred to as "eligible paper" consisted of ninety-day commercial obligations or nine-month obligations on agricultural paper.[82] Many of these institutions, however, had a large percentage of their holdings in long-term, nonliquid but quite sound investments. The Banking Bill would expunge the requirement that Federal Reserve banks consider as eligible paper only short-term loans related to commerce, industry, and agriculture.

When Eccles made the case for changing these requirements, Glass insisted that to do so "opens the facilities of the Federal Reserve Banks for speculative investments." Eccles responded that "sound assets do not necessarily mean speculative investments." When banks fear that loans will not be issued by the Fed on sound assets, Eccles alleged, they confine their loans to commercial paper thus handicapping the entire economy. "The total amount of commercial paper in the banking system today," he instructed, "is less than 8 percent of their [banks] total loans and investments." When Glass responded that such figures must be due to the unprecedented business downturn, Eccles was ready with a sharp reply. "In 1929, Senator, the total was only between 12 and 13 percent." Glass was incredulous. "After the crash?" he asked. Eccles, who doubtless relished playing the schoolmaster with the veteran lawmaker, replied, "No, before the crash; and it has declined from a little over 4 billion to approximately 2 billion." Such restrictions, moreover, favored the larger banks, the governor pointed out, since commercial credit sought the lowest cost market. This was all the more the case with banks large enough to sell their paper in the market. Consequently, commercial or eligible paper tended to accumulate in the larger banks disproportionately located in the nation's urban areas, resulting in a drain of investment funds from rural areas.[83]

Perhaps Eccles's most uncomfortable moment in the Senate hearings resulted from a question posed to him by Senator Couzens. "Governor Eccles, assuming that your bill had been enforced in 1928 and 1929," the senator asked, "what procedure would you have taken?" Eccles seemed curiously ill-prepared to answer the question and remarked that he felt it too broad. "What I'm trying to find out," Couzens persisted, "is how this bill of yours effectively changes existing conditions so that no future evils arise." Senator William Gibbs McAdoo, Democrat from California (Wilson's first treasury secretary), appeared to come to Eccles's assistance by suggesting that the answer to the question would most likely be found in the course of the governor's statement if only the members allowed him to finish it. (McAdoo and Glass were clearly not fond of one another, an animus that may have originated in 1913 when McAdoo unsuccessfully attempted to supplant Glass's Federal Reserve plan with his own.) Eccles approved of McAdoo's suggestion and expressed the desire to finish his statement and field questions afterward. Glass, however, sensing his nemesis was on the ropes, leapt into the exchange:

> *Senator Glass.* Well, you may do that, so far as I am concerned, except that I would like to supplement the question that the Senator from Michigan asked. He asked what you would have done—
>
> *Governor Eccles.* Yes.

Senator Glass. (continuing) In 1928 and 1929. I would like to ask what the Federal Reserve Board did do in 1928 and 1929, because you propose now to charge it with supreme authority in this matter. What did it do in 1928 and 1929?

Governor Eccles. I do not know that I can tell you exactly what they did, Senator.

Senator Glass. The record is perfectly clear.

Governor Eccles. Yes.

Senator Glass. I assume that you do not know. If you do not, you will find it in your own records that the Federal Reserve Bank of New York for, I think four consecutive weeks, proposed an appreciable raise in the rediscount rate, and that the Federal Reserve Board, I think for the same number of weeks, positively refused to sanction that action. Now state what you would have done. I do not know, but I do know what the Federal Reserve Board did do.

Senator Couzens. Of course, if Governor Eccles does not want to answer this, I submit in all humility to the two former Secretaries of the Treasury and will let them run the meeting.

Governor Eccles. I would prefer to read this and I would be glad to answer the questions later.

Senator Glass. I do not want to run the meeting, but as a member of this committee, I am going to take the privilege of asking questions.

Senator Couzens. I asked a question and did not consult the chairman or the Senator from California, but an effort was attempted to estop an answer to my question at the moment because of the austerity of the two former Secretaries of the Treasury.

Senator Glass. As a matter of fact, so far from attempting to estop an answer to your question I supplemented your question so that the answer might be more complete.

Senator McAdoo. I may say for the record that I had no thought of preventing an answer to the question of the Senator from Michigan. My only purpose was to expedite the hearing, perhaps, by allowing him to complete his statement and then have him answer the question. I have no objection to his answering the question.

Senator Couzens. The Senator from California knows that after the reading of a long statement many of the thoughts and questions we desire to have answered are forgotten by the time the statement is completed. If the Senator from California does not want me to interrupt, I will not interrupt any more.

Senator McAdoo. I do not care, but I think, and I am quite sure that the Senator from Michigan underrates his mental processes if he cannot retain in his memory the questions he wanted to ask until after the statement is concluded.

Senator Glass. Proceed, Governor. Or if you prefer, answer the question by the Senator from Michigan, and my supplemental question.

Senator Townsend. I think the Senator from Michigan is entitled to an answer to his question, if the Governor is prepared to answer.

Senator McAdoo. Certainly he is. I only made the suggestion for the purpose of trying to expedite the testimony.

Governor Eccles. Will you repeat the question?[84]

In point of fact, Couzens was never furnished with a suitable response. Apparently at a loss, Eccles merely conceded that monetary control alone could not cure economic problems and that other factors, such as the poor distribution of national income and imprudent fiscal measures, had played a decisive role in the 1920s. For example, said the governor, income taxes in that period should have been increased rather than reduced. All of that may be true, responded Couzens but that had nothing to do with the operations of the Federal Reserve. "That is right," Eccles conceded, "and as I say, there is a limitation as to what the banking system could do toward maintaining stability." When Senator McAdoo attempted to ask a question, he was abruptly interrupted by Couzens. "Just a minute," said the frustrated Republican from Michigan, who asked once again, "If this bill had been a law, what should the Federal Reserve Board have done?" In an admission that Carter Glass must have found gratifying, Eccles said simply, "I could not answer that, Senator." Couzens asked expectantly, "Well, just why this bill?"[85]

It proved to be an interesting exchange. Eccles, who had been so intent upon repelling the hostile interrogatories of Carter Glass, was caught flat-footed by a simple question from a politically neutral senator seeking only clarity. Why Eccles was not more substantively responsive to Couzens's question is mystifying. It was not an issue he addressed in his autobiography. Lauchlin Currie may have been as puzzled as anyone. Only a year earlier he published a detailed article in the *Journal of Political Economy* on the missteps taken by the Fed. One can only speculate that to have spoken of specific monetary measures would have provided Carter Glass the opportunity—one he managed to take advantage of nonetheless—to make the point that it was the much maligned New York Federal Reserve Bank and not the Board in Washington that proposed the appropriate monetary course of action in the late 1920s.

Ten days later, as he had promised Couzens, Eccles submitted a lengthy statement to the committee in which he addressed the policy followed by the Fed in 1929 and how his bill would improve its monetary options. A couple of points that were made in this supplemental report should be mentioned. The Fed in 1929 was prevented from pursuing a vigorous open-market operation, the report stated, because the System could not buy government securities freely due to the fact that they were not eligible as collateral for Federal Reserve notes, and, as Eccles had gone to great pains to point out in his testimony, there was an inadequate supply of commercial paper eligible for such purposes. Moreover, even if Carter Glass was accurate in stating that the New York Federal Reserve Bank's wish to pursue a tight money policy in 1929 was stifled by the Board in Washington, the Banking Bill, by centering responsibility, would put an end to all such indecisiveness and subsequent buck-passing contentiousness.[86]

While Eccles may have wished he had had the presence of mind to make these points in his exchange with Senator Couzens, his appearance before the Senate Committee on Banking was on the whole extremely impressive. If Carter Glass had hoped to derail the Banking Bill by demonstrating the deficiencies of its author, he had clearly failed.

Some years later, Eccles conceded that his difficulties with Carter Glass may have stemmed from the fact that they had many deep-seated traits in common. They even looked alike. Eccles, in fact, was somewhat startled on one occasion upon viewing a photograph of Glass and himself side by side. "We seemed to be father and son," he perceived, "which, perhaps accounts for our troubles."[87]

Standing between the "Do-Nothing" and the "Do-Anything" Crowd

With the help of Elliot Thurston, Eccles is successful in selling the banking measure as a moderate public policy change.

As Congress debated his banking bill, Eccles took his case to the American people. He added a former newspaperman, Elliot Thurston, to his staff. Thurston worked for Eugene Meyer's newspaper when the editor was governor of the Fed. Meyer's intention was to avoid the press as scrupulously as he could. Thurston's job with Eccles, on the other hand, was to "establish cordial relations with the press" and to get him as much media exposure as possible.[88]

Thurston did this rather well. On Saturday, May 22, 1935, Eccles addressed a national radio audience on the National Broadcasting Corporation. "With the banking cataclysm so fresh in our memories," he began, the country should fully expect its government to rectify the defects in the banking system "that contributed to bringing untold distress to millions of our people and threatened to plunge our entire economy into the abyss.... We should profit by the lessons we have learned from the emergency." He continued, "If after all this nation has gone through during the past five years, you still believe that we can leave our monetary system to chance or fate, then it would be futile for me to try to persuade you that our present system can and should be improved." In layman's terms the governor explained the mechanisms of monetary control available to the Fed. There were, he instructed, reserve requirements that member banks were required to meet that could only be altered by a declaration of emergency by the president. But this was a power, Eccles reasoned, that should be available to the Fed "in the normal course of events for the very purpose of preventing an emergency." Indeed, he reasoned, "Even if an emergency did not exist the declaring of it would almost certainly create one." He attempted to demystify the process of open-market operations and emphasized that it was a power that should be managed for the benefit of the commonweal. And who were those who opposed his bill? They are, Eccles insisted, "the same interests that have repeatedly been against all progressive social and economic legislation such as the income tax ... child labor laws and the Federal Power Commission." They are, he charged, the same interests that have been "against all that enlightened legislation which has long since been accepted and now forms the basis of such economic and social advances we have achieved."

Toward the conclusion of his radio address, Eccles cited a passage from the "authoritative and illuminating book" on the founding of the Federal Reserve by Senator Carter Glass. Glass had written of a meeting between President Wilson and the nation's leading bankers. "Will one of you gentlemen tell me," the president asked, "in what civilized country of the earth there are important government boards of control on which private interests are represented?" Should, the president asked rhetorically, "the railroad select members of the ICC?" And what of the charge one heard repeatedly by the bill's detractors that the legislation was merely a scheme by the Roosevelt administration to "force" upon the American people the sale of government securities to finance its budget deficits. How can this be so, reasoned Eccles, when the demand for government bonds was so great that the average interest rate the government paid on such securities had declined by more than 25 percent since President

Roosevelt assumed office? It is worth noting that Eccles, not surprisingly, began his talk that evening by affirming that while control of the money supply was an important factor in future economic stability, it was spending that would provide the immediate relief that the country so desperately needed.

The following morning the *New York Times* printed the entirety of Eccles's address and carried a story about it on its front page, as did many newspapers across the country.[89]

Thurston also obtained favorable cover stories in the *Saturday Evening Post* and the *Literary Digest* for his new boss. *Time* stated that many Americans were of the mind that "Marriner Eccles is all that stands between the nation and disaster." In an issue that followed quickly on the heels of this laudatory claim, the magazine helped deride the notion that Eccles was anything but a "practical businessman" seeking commonsense reforms he learned on the shore of the Great Salt Lake. *Fortune* ran a very favorable article that featured a family photo of Eccles with his wife and their two teenage children. *Barron's* allowed Eccles to author a lengthy article on the banking law. The intention was to play down any semblance that the bill was in the least bit revolutionary. They were pragmatic changes "that did not alter the fundamental character of the System."[90]

Throughout the summer of 1935, Carter Glass inveighed just as vigorously against the bill from the floor of the United States Senate. "I speak of it simply as the Eccles bill," said the senator, "because nobody, with a single exception, who appeared before the Banking Committee has advocated this bill." The proposal would wreck completely the regional banking system of the nation and place its control completely in the hands of a Washington bureau, he warned, "a bureau which has never had a magician in its membership, and does not have one now." Glass then pointedly attacked Eccles:

> It is simply shocking, it is appalling to think that newest member of that Board, who never had a day's association with the Federal Reserve System in his life, proceeded within less than ninety days after his nomination to propose revolutionary changes in all the fundamental provisions of the law.[91]

Eccles, for his part, took the battle directly to the banking community and spoke before the Ohio and Pennsylvania Bankers Associations and met with a committee of the American Banking Association. Some ground was gained. The Bank of America president, A. P. Giannini, echoing Eccles's phraseology, praised the bill as the outgrowth of "twenty years of practical experience." It was not, he stressed, "a radical document."[92] Nevertheless, the opposition of bankers, on the whole, remained steadfast. Meeting with bankers individually, Eccles proved quite convincing, "but when they return to their own camp," he later reflected, "they went native again, and accepted the party line." Indeed, at the Philadelphia bankers convention at which Eccles spoke, George Norris, the governor of the Federal Reserve Bank in that city, charged that the bill would create "an oligarchy, utterly repugnant to every American principle." After all, he insisted, the assistance of the RFC and the security furnished by the FDIC had sufficiently rectified the banking problems that beset the nation. Besides, he added, would it be prudent to expect "that men could be possessed of the superhuman wisdom to use such powers wisely?"[93]

As the debate wore on, additional voices furthered the argument that the banking bill was distinctly less radical than many alternatives that might gain ground. Addressing a large gathering of bankers at the end of May, the coauthor of the underconsumptionist *The Road to Plenty*, William Foster, cautioned that "Roosevelt and Eccles stand staunchly between the impotent do-nothing crowd on the right and the irresponsible do-anything crowd on the left." While no doubt displeased by the former characterization, the bankers seemed to heed Foster's warning that there were those willing to lead the country on a spree of "drunken joy-riding."[94]

As the Senate hearings wore on many who had vigorously opposed the bill, fearing perhaps that the House version or some even more radical alternative might gain strength, appeared increasingly willing to accept a compromise measure. In his confused and bungling testimony before Glass's committee, Secretary Morgenthau was reported to favor government ownership of all stock in the Federal Reserve banks and concentration of credit in, as the *New York Times* characterized it, "a supreme court of finance." This apparent endorsement of the populist proposals of Texas congressman Wright Patman and his colleagues caused some commotion when FDR, informed of Morgenthau's comments at a press conference later that day, reacted somewhat favorably. This matter may have been particularly annoying to Eccles because in an April meeting with Morgenthau, Eccles gained the support of Treasury Undersecretary T. J. Coolidge, who agreed that government stock ownership of the Fed was meaningless.[95]

Eccles, who had spent a great deal of time refuting the fear that a revised Fed was simply a ruse to have the System fund extravagant budget deficits, must have been wildly disenchanted with some of the secretary's comments. When Senator Glass queried Morgenthau about whether Eccles's bill could be used for just such fiscal exuberance, he responded with a noncommittal "I'll have to take your judgment for that." The secretary appeared surprisingly ill-informed, about not only the details of the proposed legislation, but the most rudimentary aspects of monetary policy. The bottom line for Morgenthau was expressed in his statement that the "fireman" and the "engineer" needed to work together. "In crisis," he testified, "it shouldn't be that the engineer wanted to have full steam ahead and the fireman didn't want to put coal in the boiler." He confided that he had been displeased with the Fed's lack of open-market purchases in the past year and a half. "I must say they have played a very unimportant role." He went on to say, however, that he had a good relationship with the present FOMC and that they had "nothing to have a row about." As he prepared to leave, Morgenthau was heard to mumble something about "experts." This prompted Glass to ask if he had "ever come in contact with inexpert experts." Pointing to his chest Morgenthau replied "here's one." As everyone who heard the exchange must certainly have known, it was not the flustered secretary of the treasury Glass had in mind when he made the inquiry, but rather the man he called "that Mormon missionary."[96]

A few days later, R. S. Hecht, the president of the American Bankers Association, called Morgenthau's comments a "distinct shock" to American bankers and referenced President Jackson's farewell address where he sounded the warning about the "despotic sway" of a central bank. Nevertheless, Hecht's comments were now somewhat conciliatory in regard to Eccles's bill. The ABA soon made it clear that if the interests of private bankers, especially in regard to participation on the Open Market Committee, were accommodated, a compromise measure would be acceptable. In addition, both the *New York Times* and the Eugene Meyer–owned *Washington Post* that had editorially opposed the bill, called for a compromise solution.[97]

The bill that emerged from the Senate subcommittee in late June, however, was hardly in a form that Eccles fully approved. While a *New York Times* editorial described the public statement he issued in response as by "no means unfriendly," the syndicated columnist Drew Pearson wrote that Eccles was nearly apoplectic with anger and informed the administration that he would go public to expose the "mutilated measure." He was, Pearson reported, calmed by FDR who assured him that the conference committee would rectify some of the features altered by Carter Glass. In his memoir, Eccles suggests that merely keeping Glass from breaking the legislation into three separate bills and preventing attempts to hold off on passage until the fall session—an achievement in which he says he received FDR's assistance—was a significant victory.[98]

Marching Down the Hill Again?

A movement is instigated in 1935 to end the Glass-Steagall separation of commercial and investment banking.

While Eccles's concern with the bill continued to be focused upon its Title II provisions, the Glass subcommittee inserted an amendment to Title III that, as the *New York Times* described it, "dwarfed interest" in all other aspects of the banking legislation. Somewhat remarkably, Carter Glass was fully supportive—indeed, it seems, the instigator—of a provision that permitted banks of deposit to once again engage in the underwriting of securities. Although the news leaked a few days before the subcommittee made it official, the news that day engendered a significant degree of incredulity. "Well, why not?" the crotchety Glass shot back when questioned about it. "There's been an outcry that banks will not make loans. Now the Morgans can go back to underwriting, but with these restrictions." The limitations, he insisted, would assure that "things will not go back to what they were." The proposal limited commercial banks to underwriting only new issues and prevented them from engaging more than 20 percent of a single issue over $500,000. Sales, the amendment stated, "could not be made to the customers of the banks," nor could underwriting commitments exceed 200 percent of a bank's "unimpaired capital and surplus."[99]

These provisos notwithstanding, the proposal produced a whirlwind of reaction. Bank stocks soared as many financial writers praised the action as one that would reopen capital markets and fulfill the needs and requirements of American industry. The *Los Angeles Times* opined that the return of the big New York banks, especially J. P. Morgan, may give "new stimulus" to the economy by "making available large aggregations of capital to assume the underwriting risk."[100] It was a chance, penned Earle Crowe in his syndicated "The March of Finance" column, for banks of deposit to finally earn "a few dollars profit" at a time when the financial rewards for such banks were at a "low ebb." It signaled, he hoped, that American bankers will return once again to "aggressive new business tactics." It might even prove the first step in the elevation of banking to its "former stature and dignity."[101]

Of course, not all of Wall Street was entirely of one mind. Many of the same investment banks that had waved good riddance to the House of Morgan—although Henry S. Morgan formed the investment bank Morgan-Stanley with other partners from the commercial bank—only a couple of years before, were hardly eager to welcome them back to the underwriting fold. While the Investment Bankers Association came out in opposition to the restoration, the American Bankers Association was caught off-guard. In its last gathering the prospect of such a development was not even on the agenda as a topic of conversation; in fact, at no time in the early days of the bill's formulation had anyone put forth such a suggestion.[102]

For Henry Steagall, chairman of the House Committee on Banking and Currency, opposition to this new addition to Title III now became his central concern. In a statement and an exchange with reporters on July 4, he offered no opinion of the Senate's Title II revisions, but lamented the proposal to permit banks to do "business at the same old stand." It brought to mind, he stated, the "camp meetings" in Alabama where everyone "got religion, promised to be good and then proceeded to backslide." In fact, the *New York Times* subheadline that quoted Steagall reflected a widespread sentiment: "Looks as if We Marched Up the Hill and Are Going to March Down Again." For many on the political left, the fact that the measure also exempted these banks from any civil liability pursuant to the Securities Act of 1933 made it all the more unacceptable.[103]

The most important perspective on this development, of course, was the president's. According to news accounts, a "skeptical" FDR had conferred on two occasions with Joseph Kennedy, the first chairman of the Securities and Exchange Commission. He was reported to be in conferences about this issue with George Harrison, of the New York Fed, and Yale economics professor Irving Fisher. Harrison was known to favor the accommodation to commercial banks. As for Fisher, he may have importuned the president with even more frequency than Eccles, having written thirty-five letters to FDR in 1933 and 1934 alone. At this time he was perhaps best known—aside from his famously inaccurate 1929 prognosis that the stock market would stay permanently elevated—as the author of "The Debt-Deflation Theory of Great Depressions," a 1933 article that explained the vortex into which an economy is drawn when vast numbers feel compelled to engage in an acceleration of debt retirement, thus forcing a deflationary cycle that intensifies the very burden of the debt they are seeking to unload: "The more the debtors pay, the more they owe." Fisher's solution was not large-scale public-works projects—the operational details of the newly created Works Progress Administration were at the time underway—but rather monetary policies that would foster private sector development.[104] For this reason he was enthusiastic about Marriner Eccles's appointment to head the Federal Reserve System and generally looked favorably upon the Banking Bill's alterations as enhancing the efficacy of monetary policy. (He would become disenchanted, however, with Eccles's lack of boldness with the

Fed's newfound influence.) Now, Fisher was preoccupied with jettisoning, as Lauchlin Currie favored, fractional reserve banking. Since Currie abandoned the idea as politically infeasible, the concept was gaining adherents. Secretary of Agriculture Henry Wallace presented the idea in a favorable way to FDR, and the progressive economics professor at the University of Chicago, Paul Douglas, endorsed it as "sound, even ideal in principle."[105]

Only a couple months earlier, in April 1935, Fisher published his book *100% Money* where he put forth ideas that resembled those that Lauchlin Currie had proposed in his book. Fisher wanted all commercial banks to have both a demand-deposit wing and a time-deposit wing. Demand deposits would have a 100 percent reserve requirement that could produce profit only from the interest it would produce in reserve and any charge to depositors. The time deposits would have no reserve requirements at all and banks would be at liberty to use those funds for normal banking activity. It was a practical way, he felt, to "divorce the demand deposits business from investment business." This, of course, would have rendered the whole argument over the Glass-Steagall repeal a moot issue. Fisher, like Currie, no doubt thought that the commercial and investment separation was unnecessary and possibly deleterious. Since Fisher's proposal would also mean that the taxpayers would be relieved of any responsibility in terms of deposit insurance, it would allow the entire Glass-Steagall Act to be done away with. While it seems a safe assumption that Fisher was making this point to the president, there appears to be no indication that FDR was giving 100 percent money serious consideration.[106]

Had FDR thrown his support behind this attempt to repeal the Glass component of the Glass-Steagall Act, its success might have been a possibility. That there existed significant congressional support for the underwriting measure was indicated when the full Senate adopted the Glass subcommittee bill and voted down an amendment by Robert La Follette (39 to 22) that would have taken the controversial addition to Title III out of the bill. It was clear, however, when the seventy-six-year-old Steagall and the seventy-seven-year-old Glass convened the conference committee that the measure was unacceptable to the House conferees. "I don't dare take this bill back to the House," said Steagall, who expressed the fear that his colleagues would "tar and feather me." In early July FDR wrote to Glass to assure him that while the senator had "a long period of intimate contact with banking legislation" he had witnessed "more rotten practices among the banks of New York City than you have." When Carter Glass continued to push the matter, FDR drafted a more forceful missive to the senator. Considering the ardent expression of his convictions, it is doubtful that the president gave much credence to the arguments proposed by those counseling him to support the amendment. This letter of August 9, both for the light it sheds on FDR's views and for the delightful display of his sense of humor, is deserving of being included in full.

> Dear Carter:
> I am just off for Annapolis. I am sorry not to see you before I go. As to underwriting of securities by banks, I am, frankly, wholly opposed. The provisions in the Senate bill for a so-called safeguard through open market sales is not a safeguard. If you were not of such a trusting and unsuspicious nature, and if you had had my experience with certain elements in certain places, you would know that the old abuses would come back if underwriting were restored in any shape, manner or form.
>
> One other thought—two years ago you and I were agreed that the underwriting of securities never was and never should be a legitimate right or action on the parts of the commercial banks. I honestly think a great question of principle is involved and I cannot change my opinion, especially as it is based on a great many years of practical experience in connection with conducting such underwriting in the past. Do please accept this principle from an old and experienced lawyer and businessman who will ever be your affectionate friend.

One can certainly imagine Eccles and FDR, who at times joked about Glass in their meetings, having a mirthful exchange over the president's sardonic reference to Glass's "trusting and unsuspicious nature." A few days later, parts of the letter were liberally quoted in papers across the country. When the bill emerged from the conference committee a week later it was shorn, not surprisingly, of the commercial bank underwriting amendment.[107]

What seems conspicuously absent from this somewhat peculiar flurry in American economic history is any comment by Marriner Eccles. While he had praised the Glass-Steagall Act in the past, his favorable attitude seemed clearly directed toward the deposit insurance component of the law. As will be discussed below, Eccles gave indications that he shared the views of his economic advisor. Perhaps he feared the measure might endanger the entire act. In any event, in the summer of 1935 it was one battle that he appears to have—at least publicly—sat out.[108]

The Eccles Bill

Termed by Eccles a step toward the Fed's "rehabilitation," the Banking Act makes significant changes in the System.

In his memoir, Eccles writes that he met with his allies in the House and agreed to acceptable alterations of his original proposal. In fact, the bill that emerged from the conference committee was essentially the same one that left the Senate. The bill was passed by the 74th Congress and on August 23 President Roosevelt signed into law the Banking Act of 1935. As FDR inscribed his name, he presented a pen to Marriner Eccles and then handed one to Carter Glass. As he did so, Eccles recalls someone whispering loudly "he should have given him an eraser instead."[109] When FDR handed the pen to Glass he joked that "he might be the only one who really understands its contents." This was a comment that Eccles failed to record.[110]

Glass would claim a significant political victory—that he had rewritten Title II of the act. If the administration seemed unwilling to disabuse the public of the accuracy of Glass's assertion, Eccles suggests, it was possibly because no one actually believed it. It was, as Eccles phrased it, a victory "dressed up as a defeat." While some Washington insiders shared this assessment, it is clear that in much of the country Glass was viewed as the victor. A number of the syndicated financial writers considered the outcome to be significantly in Glass's favor. "Glass won the most sweeping victory of his long career," the *National Whirligig*—a nationally syndicated political column—informed its many readers. This was a view expressed by many newspapers across the country. Even Marriner Eccles's sympathetic hometown paper the *Standard-Examiner*, proclaimed Glass's triumph in a banner headline on its front page. The Provo *Evening Herald* reported Glass's smiling response to an inquiry about his satisfaction with the new law: "Am I pleased or am I not?"[111]

The senator's smugness may not have been unwarranted. As mentioned, it was essentially the Senate bill that was enacted into law. Moreover, one of the act's most important achievements, the initiation of open-market operations in Washington, was something—along with the removal of the secretary of the treasury from the Federal Reserve Board—that Eccles acknowledged Glass desired as well. Nonetheless, nearly all of the fundamental changes that Eccles wished to make in the System were achieved to one extent or another. Although neglectful of Lauchlin Currie's contribution, Arthur Schlesinger Jr.

did not err when he wrote that the Banking Act of 1935 was "in every essential respect Eccles's original idea."[112]

That the Banking Act of 1935 failed to satisfy many who had endorsed it is apparent from some of the tepid endorsements it received. It was, the ABA stated, an "acceptable piece of legislation." The *New York Times* was slightly more generous when it deemed it "a fairly useful and workable piece of legislation." It was, as nearly all economic historians would affirm, one of the most important pieces of financial legislation in the nation's history. In the fall of 1935, Irving Fisher, the well-known economist at Yale, assessed the Banking Act as the "greatest benefit growing out of the depression" because it made a "managed economy" possible.[113]

The day before FDR signed the act into law, Eccles sent him a memo detailing its provisions. Its language bears the markings of Lauchlin Currie. The public had lost faith in "monetary administration" because it had proven "unequal to the requirements of modern life." The Federal Reserve had "failed to measure up to its responsibilities." The powers of the System, the memo informed the president, "are centralized in the Board, which will now have an inescapable responsibility for the manner in which they are exercised." The Fed's "adherence to an obsolete tradition" that rendered it a "passive agency for the accommodation of commerce and business" was now a thing of the past. "An important phase" of the Fed's "rehabilitation," the memo emphasized, was the selection of "a strong Board that will command the respect and confidence of the country." The legislative change in structure had placed the Fed in a "more rational relationship to the country's economic life"; its benefits would be squandered, it intimated, if the president failed to appoint qualified and energetic members who possessed a broad understanding of the national economic scene. The memo then highlighted the fields of expertise that particular members should possess: commercial banking experience; the security investment market; foreign exchange and foreign conditions; interpretation of business and financial developments; and experience in bank credit.

It was as polite a way as possible to stress the inadequacy of the present Board. It demonstrated, moreover, that the new chairman was clearly interested in playing the role of arbiter of the qualifications of their replacements. In delineating the "tasks" that would confront the new Board, specifically the "problems of branch banking" and the "problem of the proper relationship between commercial banking and investment banking," Eccles was indicating an intention to revisit concerns he had allowed to fall by the wayside when the Banking Act of 1935 was coursing its way through Congress. Leading the to-do list of this newly energized Board was "a study of the reforms necessary to bring about unified banking under Federal control, a unification of banking supervision and administration in Washington." In this renewed environment, Eccles was wasting little time in placing before the president an issue that he felt was of paramount importance, and one he would struggle to implement for the next decade.[114]

On the same day Eccles gave the president a separate memo that detailed the specific alterations to the System. Beginning February 1, 1936, the Federal Reserve Board was to be known as the Board of Governors of the Federal Reserve. The Board would be reduced from eight to seven members, all of whom would be appointed by the president and confirmed by the Senate for terms of fourteen years. Their salaries were to be increased from $12,000 to $15,000 per annum. The secretary of the treasury and the comptroller of the currency would cease being members of the Board. One member of the Board was to be designated by the president as chairman (previously called the governor) and was to act as the executive officer and another member of the board as vice chairman. Both the chairman and the vice chairman were to serve a term of four years.

The senior executive officers of the twelve Federal Reserve banks were previously known as governors and deputy governors and their positions were not subject to Federal Reserve Board approval. Effective March 1, 1936, they were to be known as presidents and vice presidents and elected by the Federal Reserve banks for terms of five years. Now, however, these appointments were expressly made subject to the approval of the Board of Governors of the Federal Reserve System.

All of the Fed's three principal instruments of monetary control were significantly revised. Eccles's original intention was to jettison the technical distinctions between eligible and ineligible paper and permit discount loans to member banks on "sound assets." Since Carter Glass found this phrase objectionable, the term "any satisfactory security," was adopted instead. Moreover, national banks that previously were confined to short-term loans and to real estate loans only in the area in which the bank was located were now released from such restrictions. Moreover, real estate loans that were not insured by the FHA were now permitted for up to 60 percent of appraised value for a period of ten years. The total amount of real estate loans as a percentage of its time and savings deposits was increased from 50 to 60 percent.

Hereafter, by the affirmative vote of four members of the Board, and without the need to declare an emergency or obtain presidential approval, reserve requirements could be raised or lowered. To accommodate yet another reservation of Carter Glass's, however, restrictions were placed on the degree of such changes. Required reserves could not be decreased below the amount then required by law or increased to more than twice that amount. Eccles had striven to place no restrictions whatsoever on the Board's reserve requirement power.

With little doubt the main concession made to gain passage of the act was in the reformulation of the Open Market Committee. Previously, it will be remembered, the committee was composed of representatives of the twelve Reserve banks. Eccles wanted the workings of the committee placed exclusively in the hands of the Federal Reserve Board with a committee of bankers from the Reserve banks acting in a solely advisory capacity. The act, however, created an Open Market Committee (FOMC) composed of the seven members of the Board and five representatives from the Reserve banks. Boston and New York would select one member as would the combined directors of Philadelphia and Cleveland, and the combined directors of Chicago and St. Louis. The banks in Richmond, Atlanta, and Dallas would each make one selection as would the banks in Minneapolis, Kansas City, and San Francisco. The meetings of the FOMC were to be held in Washington on at least four occasions each year upon the request of the chairman or any three members of the committee. Unlike the previous open-market operations, no Federal Reserve bank was permitted the right to accept or reject the committee's decisions about security sales or purchases or to engage in open-market operations except in accordance with the FOMC decisions. The law now required that the Board keep minutes of each FOMC meeting and to record all votes and submit the details in an annual report to Congress.[115]

Missing from the Banking Act of 1935, however, was a provision that Eccles felt was of enormous significance. Before the Subcommittee on Banking he had lobbied for the adoption of "a definite mandate" that proclaimed the Fed an active agent in the exercise of compensatory economics—in fact, its primary *raison d'être* was to promote "business stability and moderate fluctuations in production, employment and prices." While such a mandate was included in the House version of the bill, it was excised by Carter Glass and his Senate colleagues. Left in its stead was the old and, as Eccles lamented, "indefinite" command that the System was to "accommodate agriculture, commerce and industry."[116]

The Drive of a Bullet

Eccles sells the Banking Act with verve and self-confident knowledge.

Throughout his life Marriner Eccles appeared to derive immense pleasure from standing before a hostile crowd with a fierce determination to achieve a transmutation of his audience's political or economic thought. These remonstrations were in no way quixotic. He was a thorough pragmatist hardly given to expending effort in dubious battle. The struggles in which he partook he deemed to be assuredly winnable. George Creel once depicted Eccles's countenance as "undertakerish" upon first glance—an estimation that invariably underwent a rapid reevaluation as one remained in his presence. Creel described his talks as "electric" and noted that he was possessed of a "gift of intense incisive speech" that gave "every idea the drive of a bullet." In the pages of the *New Republic*, John T. Flynn deemed Eccles "a curious phenomenon; a banker with an immense curiosity about the economic system in which we live; who is genuinely disposed to know what it is all about." This trait he assessed as being "full of promise."[117] Financial writer Herbert Corey once observed Eccles at a luncheon gathering of "heavy browed" bankers who conveyed an "impression of suppressed fury." Eccles, he noted, however, "was as free of awe, humility and self-consciousness as a wet dog is of discretion." Corey continued:

> Some of the bankers were intentionally rude to Eccles. They evidently proposed to put him in his place with a thump. Most men in Eccles's position would have been either hurt or angered. Eccles was so much interested in the ideas he wished to put over, and in the questions he wanted to ask that he did not even notice they were trying to take him for a ride. At first, he aroused my protective instinct. He made me think of a nice, gentle little boy surrounded by high school bullies, and I was sorry for him. Before he got through, I was sorry for the bankers. He knew everything about banking—by periods, details, totals, panics, causes, and effects.[118]

Although the American Bankers Association (ABA) officially endorsed the Banking Act, it did not enjoy extensive support among its membership. The law was viewed by many of them as merely a mechanism that would assist the further growth of yearly deficits and never-ending government debt. Most bankers, in John T. Flynn's estimation, were "violently opposed" to the banking legislation and none too pleased that their representatives seemed "afraid to come out with an attack commensurate with their rage." This timidity was spawned perhaps by the banking leadership's understanding that they were still "supposed to be repentant and chastened."[119] The conservative sensibilities that dominated the ABA were highlighted in September of that year when the organization's educational director described the "current social security propaganda" as "an enemy of the savings banks," and a fraudulent attempt to "promise abundance for all by robbing selective Peter to pay collective Paul."[120]

The extent of this rank-and-file disaffection was quite apparent when the American Bankers Association held its annual convention in New Orleans two weeks later—only two months after the Banking Act became law. When the name E. G. Bennett, Eccles's old business associate, was placed in nomination as vice president (a position that carried the right of succession to the presidency in two years), the convention of 3,600 bankers rose up in fierce indignation. In a "stormy meeting" the convention selected as vice president Orval Adams, also of Utah. Adams had previously described the New Deal as a "disease" and American bankers, he asserted, needed to "provide the remedy." Since the administration could not spend without using the bankable funds of the nation, Adams called for an "embargo" of government securities until a regime of balanced budgets and "sane tax programs" was adopted. (Indeed, local banks throughout the nation demanded drastic budget reductions and employee layoffs by municipal governments before they would grant loans.) On the closing day of the ABA convention, Harper Sibly, the president of the United States Chamber of Commerce, endorsed Adams's sentiments and rued the fact that sacred traditions as "self-evident as the Ten Commandments" were being challenged by the New Deal.

It was before this hostile crowd that Marriner Eccles appeared to deliver the convention's closing address. The expenditures of the federal government, Eccles decreed, were "insignificant" when compared to the rise in national income it had helped revive. Government bonds, "far from being a burden, have been a Godsend," the new Federal Reserve chairman informed the unreceptive convocation. He then stressed the point he returned to time and again throughout the remainder of the decade. The federal government, he reminded his audience, had incurred a massive debt in the course of a two-year period of the war. Between 1920 and 1930 this debt of some $26 billion was then massively reduced by nearly $10 billion while the economy grew at a rapid pace and while taxes were reduced four times. "Those who talk of boycotting government bonds" said Eccles in reference to Adams's plan, "suggest a drowning man to whom a life line is thrown but who objects that it is an interference with individual right and liberty to drown." Placing aside his prepared statement, Eccles looked out at the irate delegates. If they wish the government to get out of business and banking, he adduced, they must, themselves, get in.

In this regard it could be said that Eccles literally put his money where his mouth was. "A bank has a responsibility to the community," he had lectured his employees, while reminding them that "its success depends largely upon the success of the community." His banks significantly outpaced the general level of lending between the trough of the Depression and the summer of 1937; and even when the economy plummeted in the following year, and lending fell concomitantly, First Security's loan portfolio continued to increase.[121]

The very day Marriner Eccles held forth before his fellow bankers in New Orleans, the front pages of America's newspapers carried a story that seemed to suggest that the future plans of the administration in Washington were more in harmony with the bankers' wishes than those of the Federal Reserve chairman. FDR announced that the deficit for fiscal 1937 (which would begin on July 1, 1936) would be slashed by $1 billion, half of which would come from cuts in federal spending and half from increased revenues. The *New York Times* reported that many of the alphabetical agencies of the New Deal were precariously hanging in the balance.[122]

It was clear what this signified to Marriner Eccles; the most important battle—the struggle for economic recovery—had yet to be won.

7

OUR BEST GUN

"With" but Not "Of"

Although Eccles is clearly engaged in the affairs of the Roosevelt administration, his participation is qualified.

Campaigning for the Banking Act of 1935, Eccles had deflected criticism that the proposal tied the Fed too closely to the president by responding, "The Fed is not to act as the captive of any administration, but in the public interest."[1] While at no point in his tenure could Eccles be properly described as a captive of the administration, he, nevertheless, viewed himself as a member of it.[2] A good number of the media accounts about him made just such an assessment. Journalist George Creel described him as "an authoritative spokesman for the New Deal, sitting at the right hand of the Great White Father."[3] Evidence that members of the administration felt similarly is scattered throughout Eccles's collected papers—correspondence, the nature of which one would hardly expect to discover in the files of a contemporary Fed chairman. In July 1935, Press Secretary Stephen Early sent Eccles a letter informing him that New Deal "spokesmen" needed to polish their public relations techniques with members of the press. Early suggested that it might be wise to take such measures as providing the press corps with advance copies of speeches to enable them to meet deadlines. He even suggested that Eccles's speeches be sent to the White House "before delivery."[4] A letter Early wrote to his colleague Marvin McIntyre in early 1935 provides further evidence that Early viewed Eccles as a member of the New Deal team. Early observed that for some weeks Eccles had remained publicly silent on important policy issues. "We are under attack with our best gun silent," he complained to McIntyre. This sense that Eccles was in some fashion a part of the Roosevelt team was widely held by outside observers. "He is definitely in the inner most ring," observed the *New Republic* of Eccles's place in the New Deal.[5]

The fact that Eccles was the chief executive officer of an independent regulatory agency did not dissuade Democratic Party officials from continually requesting financial contributions from him. "I want you to send me a strictly voluntary contribution," wrote Democratic national committeeman A. S. Brown, "and I want you to make it just as liberal as you can." While Eccles seemed to feel at times imposed upon by such requests, he stoically viewed them as an unsavory fact of political life. "I cannot afford to be on the black list," he wrote to a friend back in Utah about such solicitations. After enclosing a $1,000 check in a letter to James Farley, he discouragingly instructed the Democratic National Committee chairman to "substitute some other name than mine—I don't care whose."[6]

Although he is not forthcoming about some of these matters in his memoir, Eccles is surprisingly candid about his collaboration with the administration on numerous issues that would doubtlessly raise eyebrows today. For example, FDR sought Eccles's counsel in designing an adroit plan for rejecting candidates to the Fed Board that both men found undesirable. In the course of the negotiations with Carter Glass over the Banking Act, the president had agreed to allow the senator to select three of the seven members of the newly crafted Board. About one such candidate favored by Carter Glass, Eccles advised that the president write to the senator and inform him that unfortunately his man was too old and that he must, by necessity, "refuse men over sixty." When FDR informed Eccles that he was receiving strong political pressure to reappoint Judge J. J. Thomas of Nebraska to the Board, the chairman wrote back rejecting Thomas while suggesting the president write to him to say "how much you have appreciated his services and his contribution to the Board." He could then suggest that since Senator Norris was not running for reelection that Thomas should attempt to win his seat. That way, said Eccles, the judge would not be "much disturbed and inclined to be resentful and retaliatory."[7]

The selection process would provide a sobering ringside seat from which to view the political machinations of national politics. FDR confided in Eccles about the political pressure placed upon him by Vice President John Nance Garner to select a Texas businessman named Ralph Morrison for the Fed Board. Garner had even telephoned Eccles to push his appointment. The president agreed with Eccles about Morrison's unsuitability. "I know Morrison. He's no choice of mine," he recalled the president telling him. Reconsidering a week later, however, Roosevelt informed Eccles that he had succumbed to Garner's resort to the familiar line "I've never asked a favor of you before"—although Roosevelt assured Eccles that Garner had made, and been granted, many favors previously. While the new chairman conceded to the political realities surrounding Morrison's appointment—though the media was somehow made aware of his distaste for the selection—the Texan's stay on the Board was short-lived; he resigned from the board two months after his confirmation and left for Mexico reportedly to escape his financial troubles. Eccles writes parenthetically in his memoir of rumors surfacing that Morrison only received his appointment as recompense for campaign payments to the president.[8]

Here, Eccles was circumventing some rather embarrassing and noisome political developments that Drew Pearson's "Merry-Go-Round" column called at the time "one of the most unusual and important inside stories of the New Deal." Theirs was, he informed readers, "the day of the big campaign contributions to both parties and the case of Morrison illustrates what campaign contributions may do." In fact, Morrison gave $50,000 to FDR's war chest in 1932, making him the third-largest single contributor behind Bernard Baruch and Joseph Kennedy. The president then named him as one of the six American representatives to the London Monetary Conference in 1933. The conference acted to increase and stabilize the price of silver, and the administration followed up with support for the Pitman Silver Purchase Act of 1934 (named for Senator Key Pitman of Nevada). The law directed the Treasury to purchase silver until the silver reserve reached one-fourth of the gold reserve. Morrison at the time, it seems, was in possession of nearly eight hundred thousand ounces of the metal.[9]

A man with many business interests including finance and ranching, it was his involvement with a power development project on the lower Colorado River that garnered the attention of a federal court. Morrison attempted to complete the Hamilton Dam abandoned by an Insull Utilities company that had gone into receivership. After being turned down by the RFC for a loan, Morrison was also refused assistance from Harold Ickes who explained that PWA money could not go to a private power development. Morrison quickly persuaded the Texas Legislature to create a Lower Colorado Power Authority. With a little help from FDR, who, according to court records, contacted Ickes on Morrison's behalf, the PWA allotted $4.5 million for the project to the governmental agency that Morrison created. The receiver for the Insull company filed a report in a federal court that they had received only $800,000 of the $1.6 million Morrison was to pay for the cost of the unfinished dam. The story faded quickly from the national scene and press attention became focused upon the confirmation of Chester Davis, the former director of the Agricultural Adjustment Administration, to the Board.[10]

Eccles must surely hold the record for the most visits to the White House by a Fed chairman. On the Saturday afternoon he arrived to discuss the matter of the suitability of Ralph Morrison, he discovered FDR sitting in front of a radio with his mother and his two well-known secretaries, Grace Tully and Missy Lehand. He motioned for Eccles to be silent and take a seat. Eccles's expectation was that their meeting would commence with the merciful interruption of the intermission. The president, however, filled that entire time with reminiscences of his childhood vacations throughout Germany. The frenetic Fed chairman, whose musical tastes were gratified by little more than bagpipes, was a painful captive for the entirety of a Wagner opera. The story is indicative of the somewhat deputized status that Eccles occupied in the New Deal. On another trip to the executive mansion to finalize the composition of the Fed, an unexpected Carter Glass dropped by to discuss that very matter. To deny the senior senator further ammunition for his claim that the new chairman was an operative of the White House, Eccles was hastily spirited to an adjoining playroom for FDR's grandchildren. Amidst the scattered toys, the chairman waited impatiently for the duration of Glass's visit.[11]

The close relationship between Eccles and FDR seemed to some extent suppositional with many Americans. One would hardly expect, for example, that Alan Greenspan or Ben Bernanke would be queried in their public appearances about the general health of George Bush or Barack Obama, as Eccles was with President Roosevelt. And yet, perhaps Lauchlin Currie supplied an apt description of the chairman's "peculiar" relationship with the administration when he wrote that Eccles was "with" the New Dealers but not "of" them. Few members of an administration would feel at liberty to level the kind of substantial criticisms of its policies as Eccles did on a variety of matters. As Fed chairman, of course, he steered clear of any electoral endorsements of either the president or his congressional allies. This was especially true of the 1936 election when he resisted the efforts of some of FDR advisers—but not the president himself—to take a direct role in the reelection campaign. However, Currie conceded that after Leon Henderson, their intellectual ally, had become the first economist appointed to the Democratic National Committee during the 1936 campaign, Eccles directed him to furnish Henderson with as much technical support as he could. On matters of reserve requirements, discount rates, and open-market purchases, however, it could be safely stated that he simply did not take marching orders from the White House. Illustrative of this was his rejection of FDR's desire to have reserve requirements increased in May of 1936, to illustrate before the political conventions that inflationary danger was under control. On the other hand, it is somewhat revealing that the president felt at ease making such a request of the chairman in the first place, and that Eccles felt compelled to meet with him in July—after the party convention—to inform him of an increase in requirements before a public announcement was made.[12]

Moreover, the president felt quite comfortable in seeking Eccles's advice on an array of policy decisions. More often, however, the chairman's advice was unsolicited. Upon learning in August 1936 that Jesse Jones, the RFC administrator, intended to address the annual convention of the American Banking Association in November (the very convention that Eccles himself had sternly confronted the year before), he promptly wrote to Marvin McIntyre about the matter. Eccles insisted that Jones, who had worked to eliminate the Title II provisions from the Banking Act, was "playing the bankers game and should be called off," and that no other administration official should address an organization "which supports and tolerates" such harsh criticism of the New Deal.[13]

On numerous occasions the chairman took it upon himself to draft whole speeches for the White House. Not long into his tenure at the Fed, Eccles drafted a speech for FDR to deliver at the annual Gridiron Club. The speech contained a number of Eccles's favorite monetary points. As proof that banks had not lost faith in the federal government, the president could cite the fact that they were purchasing federal securities at 2.8 percent, down from 3.5 percent two years earlier. He wanted the president to make mention of yet another of his most frequently cited facts: the proportion of Great Britain's bank assets that were in government securities was much larger than in the United States. "Yet," Eccles's recommended speech continued, "we hear no outcry about the unsound position of the British banks." While FDR did scatter many of these facts in other speeches, it is doubtful that he would have marred the satirical nature of the Gridiron event with such dry political observations.[14]

A few weeks before FDR was scheduled to deliver a Homecoming Day address in Atlanta, Eccles sent Steve Early some detailed "suggestions" to "prepare" the president. He wanted FDR to shower his audience with a myriad of indicators that would substantiate an improved life in the South: crop values had risen 51.5 percent between 1933 and 1934; the number of automobiles in Georgia had risen from 288,000 in 1932 to 377,000 by 1934; construction in the Atlanta Federal Reserve District had risen 160 percent since 1932. "How was this recovery brought about?" the president should ask. It was not due to the "lazy fairies" of "laissez faire," but was brought about because "your Federal Government intervened vigorously."[15]

This was not the speech the president delivered to "the enthusiastic gathering of more than 50,000 which greeted him" in the Georgia Tech stadium. Rather, the southern press reported that FDR, after a brief mention of the benefits of the WPA, touted the end of "the dole" and that the government's deficit would soon be headed steadily downward.[16]

Wright Patman and "The Wheel of Wealth"

A Texas congressman's hostility to the Fed proves a continual irritant to the Fed chairman.

FDR did actively seek Eccles's advice after receiving a letter from Congressman Wright Patman in July 1937. Patman informed FDR that he had 150 cosponsors of a bill that called for the federal government to purchase the $130 million of stock that member banks held in the twelve Federal Reserve banks. Doing so, he wrote, would give the government possession of some $300 million in surplus which those banks had on hand. The bill also proposed that the Fed Board be altered to give the "administration complete power and control of the monetary system, which is very much needed." The congressman trusted that the president would publicly call for the chairman of the House Committee on Banking and Currency to give the bill a "full and complete hearing at the earliest possible date."[17]

Identified as a "soft-voiced but persistent Texan" by the *New York Times*, Patman had been proposing "populist" legislation since his election to Congress in 1928. A hardnosed district attorney, he began as a cotton farmer and possessed a firsthand understanding of the challenges confronting small-scale agriculture; he considered the Fed a conspiratorial enterprise designed to assist in keeping farm interest rates unnaturally high. Patman, in fact, possessed views that were quite representative of a significant segment of the Democratic Party. While convinced that the Depression was caused by underconsumption, he was equally confident that the economic situation was rooted in a restricted money supply that could be rectified by monetary expansion. Why, he argued, would the government sell interest-bearing bonds to finance a deficit instead of simply printing "cost-free" greenbacks? This proved a long-lasting point of contention with Eccles, who avoided a detailed response to Patman until he finally drafted a public letter to the congressman in early 1941, where he described such "printing press money" as a step toward an inflationary state that would virtually "mean the end of the capitalist system." By borrowing from banks the government was tapping into accumulated savings and thus, at a time when increased war production was fostering an overheated economy, was reducing the lending power of these institutions. Moreover, discontinuing payment on the public debt would amount to "so much income cut off from savers, trusts, institutions, and individuals that require the safest type of investment." "Your plan," he wrote the congressman, "is inconsistent with the nature of our capitalist democracy."[18]

This was an interesting response when one considers that in 1935—in a very different economic environment—when answering a similar inquiry from Congressman Cross, Patman's colleague from Texas, Eccles painted a different picture of the dire economic consequences that would ensue from such a practice. An inflationist member of the House Banking and Currency Committee, Cross wanted to know why it would not be a good idea for the government to retire all outstanding government bonds by paying for them in currency, thus saving annual interest charges. Eccles, in testimony before the committee, speculated that to prevent the threatened credit inflation that would result from the increase in excess reserves, the Reserve Board, under the expanded authority vested in the Fed by the new banking legislation, would increase reserve requirements. The average holdings of government bonds by System banks amounted to 39 percent of their assets. Such institutions would have little difficulty meeting higher requirements. Many banks, however, especially the smaller banks that were in possession of far fewer government bonds, would have to liquidate other assets to bring their reserves up to required levels. "It would be terribly deflationary," Eccles reasoned. "The change would be so revolutionary," he explained, "that it would bring about extreme deflation—a condition as bad as the bank holiday." Cross failed to ask an obvious question: Couldn't this predicament be avoided if the Fed simply refrained from taking such action? Indeed, in an economy struggling to regain economic growth, would it make sense to increase reserve requirements?[19]

The following day, March 16, 1935, Eccles returned to the issue of meeting expenses of government by way of printed currency, rather than borrowing, by pointing out the paradoxical fact that, at the time, the government could borrow so cheaply that it actually cost more to print currency. The various costs associated with printing—ink, paper, shipping, insurance charges, etc.—exceeded the expense of financing through discount bills. Discount bills with maturities ranging from ninety days to one year were bid for competitively at denominations that varied from $1,000 to $1 million. Short-term bills were sold by the Treasury at an average rate of only 0.06 percent while greenback costs were in the range of 0.15 percent. While Eccles failed to persuade Cross and Patman to abandon their greenback alternative to borrowing with this argument, he seems to have never raised with the Texas populists—either in 1935 or 1941—what must surely have been one of the more worrisome aspects of their scheme: the direct payment of currency by the Treasury would, of course, effectively eliminate the need for the sale of government bonds and would thereby adversely impact the Fed's open-market operations.[20]

If the plan for currency financing was never a serious consideration, Patman's emphasis on increasing public control over the Fed was a far more resonant issue. The congressman considered the rationale that monetary policy needed to be insulated from politics as farcical. In his estimation, the quasi-private arrangement under which the System functioned merely permitted powerful financial interests to control public policy. He also was highly critical of the notion that some mechanisms utilized by the Fed could not operate effectively in public view. Why, for example, should the Fed be allowed to audit its own accounts without a government agency or even an outside accounting firm furnishing scrutiny? To focus public attention on the private nature of the Fed, Patman mischievously insisted that since the government did not own the Federal Reserve's stock, its new headquarters on Connecticut Avenue should therefore be subject to taxation by the District of Columbia. The city government sent a tax bill to the Fed and threatened to place the building on public auction if the Fed refused to pay. To settle the issue, it was necessary for all twelve Reserve banks to execute a quitclaim deed attesting to the fact that the building was, in fact, owned by the federal government.[21]

While Patman engaged in such antics, he was not to be taken lightly. He was the driving force in the seven-year struggle to pass—over FDR's veto—the Veterans' Bonus Act, and he was the author of the anti-chain store legislation (the Robinson-Patman Act) that became law the year before. (Patman would fall short the following year in his proposed "Death Sentence Bill" that would have virtually taxed most chain stores out of existence. Eccles publicly opposed the effort.) The fact that he had already gathered 150 cosponsors for his Fed bill was worrisome to both the president and the chairman. "This is becoming a hot potato," FDR wrote to Eccles. "How do you think I should answer it?" Eccles wrote back that while it was indeed a "hot potato," it amounted to "legislation of the crank variety" and was founded on the agrarian notion that "the millennium can be achieved by monetary manipulation." (Interestingly, Patman favored Lauchlin Currie's idea that demand deposits be subject to 100 percent reserve requirements.) Although Eccles had some sympathy with Patman's desire to provide the federal government with a greater degree of control over the System, adopting a "shotgun method" of making the Fed a creature of the administration was a step in the wrong direction. Patman's bill would restore membership on the Board for the secretary of the treasury and the comptroller of the currency. Worse still, in Eccles's view, it would add the chairman of the FDIC as a voting member.

Eccles drafted a somewhat curt letter that the president could utilize in his reply to the congressman. He could tell Patman that while he had taken note of his points, inasmuch as he does not support such legislation, he could hardly be expected to call for hearings. He should, of course, thank Patman for his interest and thank him for keeping the White House informed.[22] Nevertheless, the Fed could not treat Patman's demands with too much caprice.

The views he was expressing were important, and Eccles felt it incumbent to furnish the public with a satisfactory rejoinder. The conspiratorial notions that swirled around the Fed had been with the institution since its founding, and, indeed, still resonate with a certain segment of Americans today. Joining Patman as a congressional critic of the Fed was Louis T. McFadden of Pennsylvania. A Republican congressman, McFadden spoke of the Fed as "evil" and designated it "the most corrupt institution the world has ever known." The central bank's "moneyed vultures" had cost the country enough money to retire the national debt several times over. Only a few years before, McFadden presided as the chairman of the House Committee on Currency and Banking and served as president of the Pennsylvania Bankers' Association. Like Patman, McFadden could boast of significant legislative achievements. In 1927 he championed a law that bore his name and which mandated that national banks had to adhere to the branch banking restrictions imposed by the state in which they were located. (The McFadden Act would stifle interstate banking for over half a century, and make it more difficult for the banking system to become fully "loaned up" by preventing banks with excess reserves from placing them in out-of-state branches that could better utilize them.) Foremost of the nefarious schemes perpetrated by the Federal Reserve, he believed, was the secretiveness of its founding. The Jekyll Island meeting loomed large in his conspiratorial notions. As with most conspiracy theories this one contains an element of fact. That this cabal of bankers was led by the German-Jewish immigrant, and president of Wells Fargo, Paul Warburg helped fuel the anti-Semitic tone of much of the suspicion levied at the Fed.[23]

With this political backdrop, the Fed staff prepared a very detailed exploration of what it considered the principal misconceptions contained in the Patman bill. Most essentially, of course, was the need to establish that the Fed operated in the public interest, and not as a money-making apparatus for private banks. "Who owns the stock [in the System] is relatively unimportant," it stressed. During its twenty-three-year existence the Federal Reserve System had earned in the neighborhood of $1.2 billion. Of that sum a full half had been used to meet operating expenses incurred in the process of providing currency to the banks and to the public, clearing and collecting checks, analyzing and reporting upon economic data, and a host of other services. Of the half earned above such expenses, one-quarter went to the payment of the franchise tax to the federal government, while another quarter was appropriated by the federal government as a capital contribution to the Federal Deposit Insurance Corporation. The Fed was statutorily obligated to pay a 6 percent dividend payment (which Eccles conceded was a bit "out of line with current rates" and could be reduced) on the nontransferable stock holdings that member banks were required to subscribe to in proportion to their capital and surplus. The remaining 25 percent of funds, the memo explained, were held in a surplus account that could be appropriated by the federal government whenever it so desired.[24]

The experience of other countries, the report maintained, indicated that it was "advantageous" to keep a separation between the regulation of credit and the fiscal arm of the country. Why it was not beneficial, as Patman insisted, to have a consistent and coordinated fiscal and monetary policy that could be altered through the political process whenever the nation felt it operated inimically, was not specifically addressed. (On this matter Lauchlin Currie actually agreed with Patman.) The report noted that by abandoning locally elected officials of district banks in favor of permitting Washington to handle all such appointments, as the bill provided, it would destroy "local pride and local interest in the System" and harm the "confidence" that the "business community" had in its administration.[25]

Administration officials and congressional allies used the Fed report—what today would be termed "talking points"—to oppose the bill. Patman, however, continued his populist assault on the influence of concentrated banking. He carried with him to all public addresses his handmade "wheel of wealth" poster that visually illustrated the financial resources of the nation's top twenty-four banks. "It's hard to believe it, unless you've checked up as I have," said Patman, pointing out that 484 men who comprised the aggregate board of directors of those banks controlled over one-third of all banking resources. It illustrated, in his view, the still-potent truism of Jefferson's cautionary observation that "banking institutions are more dangerous than standing armies." What the third president termed the "issuing power" must be, Jefferson insisted, "taken from the banks and restored to the government and the people to whom it belongs."[26]

Carter Glass, who led the charge against "going French"—adopting, as did the socialist government of Premier Leon Blum, political control of its central bank—must have been incensed to read that Marriner Eccles was expressing sympathy for some of Wright Patman's concerns. Eccles "does admit," wrote the *New York Times*, "that complete control [by Washington] is desirable." What Eccles meant, of course, was that he agreed with Patman's distaste for private bankers sitting on the all-important Open Market Committee. This was a policy that Eccles attempted to foil when the Banking Act of 1935 was being crafted. It was certainly possible, the chairman stated, for the private bankers on the committee to align themselves with a few reserve members to "nullify" the credit policy approved by a majority of the Federal Reserve Board.

Patman's bill was soundly defeated in Congress, but the congressman's desire to eliminate the Open Market Committee, thereby leaving its functions exclusively to the Fed Board, seemed like a perfectly fine idea to Eccles.[27]

"The Safest Policy Is the Boldest Policy"

Eccles is greatly dissatisfied with the WPA. At the close of 1935, while suggesting a more robust effort, he gives FDR a prophetic warning.

"The policy of laissez faire has gone forever," Marriner Eccles informed members of the Ogden Rotary Club in the summer of 1935. He was quick to add, however, that none need say obsequies for capitalism; it would continue on, albeit in a "modified form" with the government "acting as a compensatory agent to effect distribution when private capital fails to assure employment." He showered his luncheon audience, which included both Lions and Kiwanis Club members, with an array of statistics to verify his assertion that the nation was making consistent economic progress. He was "tremendously well satisfied" with the better management of money and credit which the recently passed Banking Act had made possible. And while he was not entirely pleased with the form it took, he was encouraged by the fact that a national jobs program was about to commence, although the extent of his disfavor with the emerging Works Progress Administration (WPA) was left uncommented upon.[28]

Next to the construction of housing, Eccles believed, the most essential endeavor for the federal government was a massive commitment to public works. In June of 1934 FDR formed, by executive order, a cabinet-level committee to formulate a plan to address the issues of unemployment and old-age insurance. Headed by Labor Secretary Frances Perkins, it assumed the name Committee on Economic Security and included the secretaries of agriculture and treasury, the attorney general, and the head of FERA, Harry Hopkins. In addition, the president would appoint a fifteen- to twenty-member advisory council comprised of "national leaders" in various walks of life. The advisory council was to hold hearings and solicit the input of labor, business, agriculture, and state and local governments and submit their findings to the committee for consideration. While the primary focus was to be the creation of a program of old-age pensions and unemployment insurance, the committee was also charged with looking at vocational training, health insurance, and the creation of a large-scale public-works program. It was the intention of the committee, FDR stated, to "constitute the most comprehensive treatment of the problem of economic and social well-being ever presented to the people." If the Constitution "tells us" that our national government was established among other things "to promote the General Welfare," FDR informed the nation, it was then "our plain duty" to provide security from the "hazards and vicissitudes of life" that foster so much "social unrest and economic demoralization." At a White House meeting of the committee on November 15, 1934, FDR spoke of health insurance as "highly desirable" and expressed his confidence—one that Eccles shared—that the nation would come "to this form of insurance sooner or later." He was confident, he proclaimed, that "we can devise a system which will enhance and not hinder the remarkable progress which has been made in the practice of the profession of medicine and surgery in the United States."[29]

Eccles presented a memorandum for FDR titled *A Suggested Works Program*. It was a way to light a different path down which the forces of progressive action might travel. The twelve-page document was drafted with the assistance of Henry Edmiston, a young economist who, at Eccles's request, left the Brookings Institute to work at the Fed. Eccles makes mention in his memoir that he "argued the problem" or the direction that a public-works program should take with both FDR and Harry Hopkins. It would appear that these were largely verbal exchanges. The memorandum was not sent to the president until March 8, 1935, well after the Committee on Economic Security had formed its recommendations. Why Eccles waited so late in the game to put forth a formal proposal is somewhat puzzling. Of course, during the previous months he was nearly consumed with the issues surrounding the Banking Act of 1935. They were ideas, however, that Eccles had long "pressed on Roosevelt."[30]

The document stresses the importance of public-works expenditures as a mechanism for *recovery* rather than being viewed from—as he contended

Hopkins and Ickes did—"the standpoint of great human sympathies." The problem of recovery, the report states, is primarily that of bringing about a large expansion of expenditures by "corporation men, municipalities, and home builders." It was important to emphasize that this was not something the private sector was generally prepared at the time to do. Unfortunately, the memo begins, industrial plants and equipment were then greatly in excess of current needs. It would be entirely unwise for businesses to add to their productive assets until existing capacity was utilized.

The report conveys some element of sympathy for the predicament of both the public utility and the railroad industry. With the Public Utility Holding bill about to be formulated—the "death sentence act" as many in the industry termed it—it was understandable that the half-billion dollars that the industry annually spent on construction would be held in abeyance. (In the end, the act, drafted by Ben Cohen, would provide regulation of the "evil features" of holding companies rather than their extinction.) Expected expenditures by the railroads on maintenance and equipment would no doubt be hampered by still-diminished revenue, wage increases, and new pension obligations. The Wagner-Hatfield Act had been signed into law the previous summer and required a 2 percent payroll deduction from workers and a 4 percent contribution from the rail corporations. While this would induce retirements and open up employment opportunities, it would hardly make up for the employment that would arise from fixed capital investments.

Nor could there be any reasonable expectation that the construction expenditures of municipalities—which had fallen from over $2 billion before the Depression to a paltry $600 million—would see any unaided improvement until tax income increased. There remained, therefore, but one solution that was underscored in the memo: "*The National Income Must Be Increased by Government Spending.*"[31]

The document states flatly that the $4 billion the administration intended to spend on a works program in the coming fiscal year of 1936 was "totally inadequate." (The stated amount was $4.8 billion, but it was assumed that $800 million would be expended prior to the beginning of the fiscal year in July.) The national income of 1929, which exceeded $80 billion and had plummeted to $40 billion in 1933, had rebounded to approximately $55 billion. (According to recent figures used by the Bureau of Economic Analysis, a GDP of $87 billion fell to $64 billion in 1933.) The goal was to quickly reach and surpass the 1929 level and achieve a national income of some $90 billion. However, Eccles insists, there was no reason "to expect any substantial improvement with the expenditure of such a small amount." The memo then sounds what would prove to be—in regard to unacceptable levels of unemployment at least—a prophetic warning:

> In this case the safest policy is the boldest policy. If we spend some every year, but not sufficient to give the required stimulus to private expenditures, we can build up a large debt and still not be out of the depression. This has been the history of the deficits of 1931–1934.[32]

The manner in which Eccles recommended the government spend this money was in some respects not what was generally considered a "jobs program" at all. Since the administration seemed "committed" to the insufficient figure of $4 billion, the challenge was to use this sum as leverage to bring about $9 billion' worth of "new expenditures." (Eccles uses the expression "prime the pump" in the memo; so it had clearly not yet been discarded.) The document furnishes as good an example as any other of how his ideas were distinct from those being bandied about "in the administration." Virtually the entirety of a successful program of recovery, he affirms, could be reduced to one single objective: that of increasing the incomes of the American people.

> A piece-meal program which seeks to remedy the debt problem by forcing prices higher through redistribution of output; to remedy the unemployment problem by taking people off of straight relief and putting them on work relief; to remedy the railroad problem by economies and reduction of capital structures; to remedy the real estate problem by the government taking over mortgages; and to remedy the international trade problem by negotiating international treaties, is doomed to failure *unless the national income is increased.*

The essential question then became: what is the best way to increase individual incomes? In his 1935 State of the Union address, delivered only weeks before, the president spoke in vague terms of the coming jobs program. (The committee delivered its recommendation to FDR eleven days later.) In the course of his remarks that day, he emphasized that "no wise man" would proffer "any intention of destroying the profit motive." In structuring its jobs program, however, Eccles felt that the administration must not lose sight of its primacy in American economic life. "Ours is a profit economy and in order to get recovery we must work through the profit motive." Eccles suggests the government undertake "on a *contract* basis billions of dollars' worth of public works of a wide variety." Most of these projects could be selected by state and local entities who must receive subsidies—not loans—of at least 50 percent. This would entice localities to obtain the remainder through the flotation of municipal securities, the market for which, Eccles pointed out, was quite strong in early 1935. The administration of grants would be overseen by the Public Works Administration with the directive that all projects needed to be commenced "within a reasonably short period after applications are approved." Presumably, Eccles felt such a directive—and perhaps the approaching election of 1936—would instill a sense of haste into Harold Ickes's administrative style. Of course, the optimal result would emerge from an admixture of something resembling Ickes's administrative structure and Harry Hopkins's boldness.

Not surprisingly, the most important aspect of a recovery program, the memo argues, was a massive revival of residential construction. Once again, Eccles felt the need to point out to the president the beneficial effects that increased housing had brought to the British and German recoveries. A recent headline in the *New York Times* proclaimed "Britain's Recovery Held Remarkable." This despite the fact, the story reported, that it had a balance-of-trade deficit with "practically every country" and a "very significant" one with the United States. Britain also demonstrated that a greater debt could be incurred without the sky falling. Figures on the total public debt per capita came to $433 in the United States and $1,030 in Britain.

Here, too, it was now crucial—and financially viable—to provide subsidies for new or repaired housing projects of at least 20 percent. This was a figure that could be increased or reduced depending on conditions. Also, construction must be expeditious and no subsidies would be granted if construction did not commence within three weeks of an application's approval. The administration of the subsidies would be overseen by the FHA with demanding affidavits of performance and hefty punishment under the criminal code for attempted fraud. Contracts for low-income housing subsidies would be administered by the PWA. The intention was to use $1 billion of government money to entice at least $4 billion of private money into residential construction. When one considers, Eccles wrote, that loans insured by the FHA had so far amounted to a "negligible" $40 million, the success of this inducement would prove significant.

Similar subsidies of $100 million should be made available for rural electrification and another $900 million allocated to the CCC—above its projected budget—and the Bureau of Public Roads and the engineering department of railroads. All of the latter should be in the form of grants and not loans.

While most of these endeavors would involve taxpayer money to generate profits for private concerns, it would relieve the government of day-to-day operations and deny conservatives the claim that government was displacing private enterprise. "If a sufficient stimulus is now applied," Eccles concluded, "we can rely upon the momentum thus generated to pull us out of the depression and enable us to utilize our enormous physical capacity to produce."[33]

The works program that did emerge from the committee, the Works Progress Administration (WPA), proved a great disappointment to Eccles. The very manner in which the president described the program in his April fireside chat, not as a fuel to set the engine of commercial life at full throttle, but rather the somewhat charitable-sounding intent of a "crusade to destroy enforced idleness," reflected, it seemed, a variant of the tired rubric of past efforts. The WPA "can be described with a fair degree of accuracy," writes economic historian Philip Harvey, "as 'CWA Lite.'" In Eccles's view, this was largely the problem: the program presented emasculation rather than an improvement upon the CWA. It was "inadequate" both in terms of the numbers of idle Americans it would employ and the pecuniary compensation they would receive. "At no time," he would later reflect, "was it able to care for more than three million people, though its existence ran concurrently with periods when there were ten million unemployed." That the administration persisted in seeing the program as a relief measure rather than an instrument of recovery was highlighted in the winter of 1937–1938 when, in the midst of the severe recession that hit the country earlier that year, a decision was made to reprise the foolishness of the CWA experience and hire an additional three hundred thousand workers on the understanding that they would remain employed only for three months to get them through the winter.

In addition, the compensation the WPA provided its workers, Eccles observed, "barely maintained families at subsistence levels." Most significantly, the WPA failed at what he asserted was its most essential task—activating private-capital goods industries that were dormant for want of sufficient consumer demand. Unlike Ickes's Public Works Administration projects that created as many as two hundred jobs in private industry for every one hundred workers employed, the WPA was credited with less than sixteen private jobs for every one hundred it employed. The agency's internal restrictions on the use of large equipment, Eccles complained, "forced WPA workers to use picks and shovels as though they were Chinese coolies." Moreover, by imposing what he termed a "dehumanizing" means test, it also failed to replicate the great boost in self-esteem and pride engendered by the CWA. "In every individual case," Eccles lamented, for those entering the WPA's ranks, "this was a public proclamation that the man was a failure and a pauper who had exhausted his insurance, savings, credit, friends, and relatives." In this regard the president failed to follow the policy suggestions of his Committee on Economic Security which sought to achieve what it termed "employment assurance" for all, not merely those receiving public assistance.[34]

To be sure, as Eccles was quick to acknowledge, the WPA was a vast improvement over FERA. (Recognizing the "need for speed," it might have sufficed as an emergency measure, he thought, until private sector stimulation gained steam.) Any stigma associated with relief status notwithstanding, WPA workers were employees and not charity recipients. The program wisely allowed for a great deal of local participation and control. A large majority of the WPA's projects were selected by local governments which paid some 20 percent of its costs on average. Its extraordinary list of accomplishments—especially in terms of infrastructure—laid the groundwork for the nation's breathtaking productivity in both World War II and the postwar years. It is also clear, however, that it was encumbered by endless complications. (On these issues Eccles would have had a valuable source of inside information from his good friend and associate Robert Hinckley, who was placed in charge of administering the WPA in Utah and ten other western states.) The program opened itself up for political infighting by requiring—pursuant to its enacting legislation—that all positions that paid $5,000 or more per year be submitted for Senate confirmation. Throughout the nation there were in excess of four thousand pay schedules. Constant bickering from private sector contractors—who Eccles believed could have been the biggest boosters of increased government spending—led to a policy that forced WPA workers to accept private jobs at the lowest possible pay levels. By paying its workers a livable wage, the CWA graphically demonstrated the extent to which producers and retailers of basic consumer goods would benefit when CWA paychecks were cashed. By contrast, WPA employees had barely the wherewithal to pay the bare necessities of food and rent.

Dean Brimhall, a labor relations advisor to Harry Hopkins and a former Freidenker fellow from Ogden, kept Eccles informed on WPA issues. "It may surprise you to know," he wrote Eccles in a memo, "that we have many thousands of workers employed at 15 cents per hour. We have carpenters and similar tradesmen working for 40 cents per hour." Thus, highly skilled construction workers were receiving some $48 a month in income. Under the WPA therefore, workers were not purchasing clothing but producing it. Catherine Cleveland, the director of the program's sewing projects, was identified by the *New*

York Times as the head of one of the largest garment-manufacturing organizations in the country (producing in one year over fifty-five million garments). This was a state of affairs sure to alienate both clothing manufacturers and the organized unions that struggled to ensure garment workers went home with a sufficient income to lead decent lives.

The clamor for WPA positions by Americans on relief led to a wooden-headed provision that terminated work for anyone employed for eighteen straight months. This understandably caused disruption on sites in various states of completion, where knowledgeable workers were replaced by those unfamiliar with the project. A dismissed worker was prohibited for thirty days from reapplying for an assignment to another location. For many, of course, this meant a prolonged return to relief. A study of nearly eight hundred thousand people let go as a consequence of the "18-month rule" reported that only 13 percent were employed some six months later. It was nonsense of this kind that Eccles felt could have been avoided if employment hiring and project completion were contracted to a private contractor with close public supervision.[35]

Eccles's reservations about the WPA did not appear prominently in his public pronouncements in 1935. Still relatively new in his position at the Fed, the chairman was relatively circumspect about airing his disagreements with his New Deal associates. Considering the nature of Eccles's temperament, it was a reticence bound to be short-lived.

The Man Too Well Remembered?

FDR's 1935 Revenue Act is philosophically powerful but fails to achieve a substantial alteration of American income.

Eccles asserted in an address before the Commercial Club of Boston, in early 1935, that in the competition of the various "isms" that thrived in the world, capitalism must be defended on the grounds that it is the best guarantor of "the good life." If it could not be so defended, if it could not in an "equitable fashion" meet the material needs of mankind, it was "doomed." Before capitalism's eminence could be safely established as an unassailable truism, its "inherent instability" must be confronted and eliminated, he asserted. He assured the Boston businessmen they had at their disposal three "compensatory instruments" that could render severe swings of the business cycle a relic of the past. Varying governmental expenditures, taxation rates and methods, and monetary levels could permanently establish economic stability, he told them. If they failed to properly utilize these instruments, said Eccles, then "as surely as I am standing here, you will not have *compensatory* but direct controls in every important sphere of economic activity."[36]

As Eccles stated in his Boston address, the taxation policies of government formed a crucial component of the holy trinity of compensatory economics. On March 7, the United Press International reported his testimony before the House Banking Committee, only the day before his remarks in Boston. "Redistribution" of income, the UPI proclaimed, "burst forth today as a fast-rolling ball of political dynamite headed toward the 1935 election contests." The article insinuated that an acute irony was at play when a leading force behind such a stated goal emanated from "the very throne of banking control." The most efficacious tool to achieve a "better balance," stated the newly appointed head of the nation's central banking system, was the income tax. Some speculated, the UPI report continued, that Eccles was acting as an emissary from the Roosevelt administration who felt compelled to answer the populist clarion of Huey Long's Share-Our-Wealth demands and the fiery rhetoric of Father Charles Coughlin. Only a week earlier, the radio priest delivered one of his more memorable political sermons, cautioning that if the tide were not soon turned—largely by way of progressive taxation in extremis—to safeguard and empower the "little fellow," the nation would approach in coming decades a state of corporate "feudalism" that operated for the benefit of its ruling elite. Eccles made it clear, however, that he was not animated by some need to temper such views and that he spoke only for himself. Moreover, he said, his recommendations were not a siren to the barricades, but rather a call to preserve a market economy and the "good life."[37]

While ambivalent about raising taxes in what was still an economy in need of increased stimulation, he felt progressive taxing policies quite justifiable, and in harmony with the ideas that Lauchlin Currie was developing—what would come to be termed, as we have noted previously, *"the net federal contribution."* To the greatest extent feasible, if "income-decreasing receipts" could be obtained from those with an elevated propensity to save, while "income-increasing disbursements" made their way to those with an overwhelming propensity to spend, then the net federal contribution would be maximized and the economy would reap the benefit. Eccles repeatedly drove home—both in speeches and articles to the American people and in memos and personal conversations with the president—the dire economic consequences that ensued from the fact that in 1929 nearly a quarter of the national income went to the wealthiest 1 percent of the American population.[38]

There was little doubt that Eccles was expressing these views in a nation where a "soak the rich" mentality would hardly diminish political support. Very early on in the Depression such sentiment was palpable. Indeed, it will be recalled that FDR sounded the underconsumptionist theme and the need for a "wiser, more equitable distribution of the national income" on the campaign trail in 1932. Surprisingly then, prior to 1935, both the president's rhetoric and actions in this regard were rather circumspect. The administration did respond, however, to the public furor to curb excessive corporate salaries that followed in the wake of Albert Wiggin's testimony before the Pecora Committee in June 1933. The former president of Chase Manhattan Bank, Wiggin revealed how an inner cadre of executives sat around and assigned extraordinary payouts to one another at the very time the bank was enduring massive losses. Wiggin's own "retirement pay" amounted to $100,000. (The decisions made by these salaried executives, to the detriment of shareholders, confirm Adolph Berle's assertions in his recently published *The Modern Corporations and Private Property*.) Not only was Wiggin compelled to forego this sum, but shortly after, Jesse Jones, the administrator of the Reconstruction Finance Corporation, demanded as a condition of its loan to the Southern Pacific Railroad that its management reduce their salaries by as much as 60 percent. He then announced that similar requirements would be demanded of all corporations that availed themselves of RFC assistance. Some historians have surmised, however, that the administration was simply staving off more severe demands by lawmakers. In fact, a congressional act set a salary limit of $17,500 for any insurance executive of a company receiving RFC funds.[39]

Such sentiment, however, did not significantly influence the tax policy that emerged from the White House. When Eccles assumed his position at the Fed, the strongest calls for the adoption of more progressivity in the federal tax structure emanated from the halls of Congress. These demands were proffered more in terms of equity than economic stability. For Eccles, to derive such a large percentage of government revenue from such regressive sources was largely a matter of economic wooden-headedness. In 1935 the federal government derived more revenue from tobacco taxes ($425 million) than it did from the individual income tax ($420 million). The gasoline tax raised nearly twice the amount ($203 million) of the estate tax ($104 million). In fact, nearly 60 percent of federal revenue came from taxes on consumption.[40]

While Eccles generally supported the agricultural allotment programs of the Agricultural Adjustment Act—it did indeed significantly boost farm income and sugar-beet producers benefited—the processing tax that furnished its funding was in his view a significant drag upon consumer purchasing power, and he campaigned strenuously for its elimination. The tax was levied upon the first entity that initiated the transformation of certain designated agricultural products from their raw state to an item of retail sale. Virtually no one questioned the fact that the tax was essentially borne by consumers and was therefore undeniably regressive. Agriculture Secretary Henry Wallace feared that subjecting the program to general-fund financing would too graphically highlight its cost and render its continuing funding precarious. The processing tax, on the other hand, was "a comparatively painless way," writes historian Mark Leff, "to extract substantial revenues from an unwitting public." While some liberal publications such as *The Nation* decried the processing tax, calling it the "most indefensible tax ever," it seemed to engender slight public reaction. This lack of public resistance was certainly not due to the fact that the tax was insubstantial; it was responsible for generating nearly 13 percent of the federal government's revenue.[41]

The first significant attempt to derive greater tax receipts from progressive sources emerged from Congress in 1934 and enjoyed only lukewarm support from the White House. Eccles supported the effort, led by Senator Robert La Follette, to cut the estate-tax exemption from $50,000 to $25,000. (In Britain the exemption was $500.) This high level meant that only slightly more than 1 percent of estates owed any tax whatsoever. (With the current $5 million exemption this percentage was actually lower in 2011.) While this effort failed, they were able to enact higher payment levels for estates that were susceptible to the tax. The act added only slightly to the income-tax burden of the wealthy; it eliminated a few filing advantages that the tax code provided large corporations, and graduated somewhat the levies upon capital gains. If all of this failed to sharply increase taxes for the wealthy, Congress at least took the bold step of reducing regressively by repealing the tax upon candy and soft drinks.[42]

Even after the stunning Democratic success in the 1934 congressional elections—which defied the traditional midterm losses to the incumbent president's party—in which the Democrats managed to increase their already large majority in the House by seven seats and their Senate representation by nine, FDR maintained a reserved tone toward redistributive taxing policies. This despite the fact that many in Congress ran on the pledge to pursue such a legislative accomplishment. The president's State of the Union address in January 1935 offered no suggestion that major tax reform would be proposed. By early spring, however, plans were afoot for a dramatic announcement. The traditional explanation for the administration's support for a revised tax structure in 1935 is no doubt accurate: the growing influence of Huey Long needed to be counteracted. The president, as he reportedly informed Ray Moley, intended to "steal Long's thunder."[43]

On June 19, 1935, FDR's tax proposals were read aloud to a wildly approving House of Representatives and a somewhat less enamored Senate. (The act would win an overwhelming victory in the House by a vote of 282–96 and a less impressive tally in the Senate of 57–22. There was little bipartisan support, however, with a total of just 25 Republican members of the House voting in favor.) The rhetoric of the speech, and the clear political strategy that motivated it, have too often evoked a cynical and rather dismissive attitude from historians. But the realpolitik circumstances surrounding this address should not obscure the fact that FDR seemed to sincerely feel that he was proposing a heightened level of economic justice. It was, he informed Harold Ickes, his finest presidential achievement. Moreover, the speech, crafted by Felix Frankfurter, may well be the finest defense of progressive taxation ever articulated by an American politician.[44]

"A careful study of our own and other countries revenue systems," FDR begins, demonstrates the need for revision. To be sure, at Henry Morgenthau's insistence there is a reference to an enhanced ability to raise money and to move the government toward a balanced budget and a reduced national debt. The remarks emphasize, however, that equity and economic growth and development are mutually reinforcing. The present tax structure is "operated in many ways to the advantage of the few." Altering this system to place a greater emphasis upon "ability to pay" is a "wholesome" guide for public policy. It was of vital importance to make the case that to levy taxes in such a manner was not a betrayal of American individualism but rather an addendum that could be utilized to provide a greater measure of "equality of opportunity" so that all Americans had a genuine shot at developing their individual talents to the greatest extent possible. More importantly, however, it was essential to point out that "wealth in the modern world does not come from merely individual effort." Rather it was the collective labor of generations, Roosevelt insisted, that established the foundation of a decent society in which wealth could be made and enjoyed; "the people in the mass have inevitably helped to make large fortunes possible." Moreover, "creative enterprise," which so distinguishes American life, "is not stimulated by vast inheritances." No one understood this better than Andrew Carnegie. "Where wealth accrues honorably," the president quoted the steel magnate, "the people are always silent partners." (That Carnegie, in fact, favored completely confiscatory estate taxes was left unmentioned.)

Above all, stated FDR, the country must recognize that "social unrest and a deepening sense of unfairness are dangers to our national life which must be minimized." Although it seems unlikely to have been in the forefront of Felix Frankfurter's consciousness, the last was a sentiment right out of the pages of James Harrington's *Oceana*.[45]

While FDR attempted to avoid an antibusiness tone by including small corporations as the beneficiaries of a graduated corporate tax, it was inevitable that numerous business interests from the United States Chamber of Commerce to the National Association of Manufacturers would react unfavorably. Most pronounced, not surprisingly, was the chorus of protestation which poured forth from the nation's wealthiest citizens. The act, after all, raised the top marginal tax bracket to 79 percent—although for three years only John D. Rockefeller qualified—and reduced the estate-tax exemption from $50,000 to $40,000. Even prior to the revenue address, *Fortune* magazine financial writer Roswell Masil maintained that 25 percent of the $4 billion that would be collected that year would come from the richest one-seventh of the population. This "minority," Masil claimed, felt itself ill-used and overburdened. "If the Arkansas share-cropper would like to claim the title of the forgotten man," he wrote, "the New York City banker would like to claim the title of the man too well remembered."[46]

Eccles, in fact, wished the New York City banker to be better remembered still. The problem that both Eccles and Robert La Follette had with the revenue revision of 1935 was that it essentially failed at the goal of income redistribution. In a well-publicized exchange of public letters between FDR had and Roy W. Howard, the conservative publisher the Scripps-Howard newspapers, who accused the New Deal of implementing a tax policy that was more intent on "revenge" than "revenue," the president pointed out that the newly passed tax law "affects only those individuals who have incomes over $50,000 a year." Of course, when the distribution of income in the country during the 1930s is analyzed, this tax emphasis becomes problematic. In 1935, 74 percent of American households had annual incomes of less than $2,000 and a full 38 percent earned less than $1,000. The tax code provided that the first $2,500 of family income was exempt from taxation, and allowed a $400 exemption for each child, along with a 10 percent earned-income credit. This meant that a couple with a single child and an earned income of $3,200 would have a federal income tax liability of zero. This becomes more meaningful when one considers that an income of only $4,000 would have placed that family in the richest 5 percent of American households, while

$12,000 would have earned them the exalted distinction of being among the richest 1 percent.

After noting such statistics, historian Mark Leff has explored the lack of political will by the administration to raise taxes on the "subplutocrats" and thereby achieve a meaningful redistribution of national income by invigorating the income tax through "building up its base rather than by decorating its summit." A full 96 percent of Americans paid no income tax whatsoever. This need to broaden the tax base was certainly apparent to Eccles and many others who occupied the political left. Eccles spoke about this issue publicly throughout the 1930s. After he addressed a group of St. Louis bankers and called for lower exemptions and higher rates to be applied to incomes between $5,000 and $50,000, the AP reported that the heat between the Treasury Department and the chairman had "fanned into open flames," and a White House spokesman issued a statement that Eccles was not speaking for anyone in the administration. "What we need is a new definition of wealth," Clarence Darrow agreed in the pages of the *Progressive* magazine, "and a mighty radical one." World War II would achieve in the 1940s what elective politics prevented in the 1930s.[47]

The Calamity Howlers

In his December 1935 memo to the president, Eccles suggests explaining the details of the nation's debt level to the American people, and he cautions against a premature effort at balancing the budget.

Looking ahead to the 1936 presidential election, FDR expressed the concern that the Republicans would nominate someone who, while a social progressive, was fiscally conservative. (By raising only an additional two dollars per capita, the Revenue Act of 1935 offered poor prospects for assisting in balancing the budget.) Such an opponent, felt FDR, would prove quite challenging, having the ability, as Harold Ickes phrased it, "to run with the hares and hunt with the hounds." The realization of such a strategy seemed a likely development when William Randolph Hearst—now thoroughly alienated from the New Deal after the Revenue Act—met with Kansas governor Alfred Landon in November 1935. Landon, who styled himself a "practical progressive," was well positioned to level a barrage of criticism at what Roosevelt still believed was his Achilles heel—large budget deficits.[48]

That the need for a balanced budget seemed likely to be the focal point of the 1936 presidential race was a disquieting prospect for the advocates of compensatory economics. When Eccles returned to Washington from his rather confrontational speaking engagement with the American Bankers Association in New Orleans, discussed earlier, he had a conversation with the president about his concerns and followed up with the longest (twenty pages) and certainly the most impassioned entreaty he would ever write to FDR. He sent it to the White House on December 28, 1935. "The political tide is running against the administration," Eccles warned in the memo's opening sentence. (A Gallup poll in September indicated that FDR's personal popularity had fallen to 50.5 percent.) The public and the press, he wrote, were fixated upon the New Deal's internecine conflicts and occasional failings instead of its notable achievements. The administration inherited, Eccles continued, "the most chaotic conditions in the peacetime history of America," and in two years the country had been rescued from this unprecedented prostration and over $25 billion had been restored to the national income. This achievement and the New Deal's case, he argued, were "not being effectively made" to the American people. They should constantly be reminded that the budget was unbalanced in large part to provide relief to the very banks, insurance companies, and railroads whose leaders now were deriding the government's efforts to aid its distressed citizens. "Since it is the habit of our people, if not all peoples," he averred, "to vote against rather than for," the president should direct the coming campaign against the forces of reaction.

> This is the crowd that wants power rather than recovery—the crowd that for 12 years was in power, that tried the very policies which ended in the greatest smash in our economic history; the crowd that willed this administration a debt of 20 billion and a demoralized, prostrate country; yet they now have the sublime audacity to propose that we go back to the very policies which wrecked the country. They have been proved false prophets on their own record.

Moreover, Eccles insisted, the public must be made aware of the fact that the size of the debt had been "grossly distorted and magnified by ignorant or irresponsible alarmists, such as the Warburgs and Douglases." It was also foolish to compare as they did the debt of a nation with that of an individual. He noted that the gross debt of the nation ($30 billion) was commensurate with a mere four months of the national income. In addition, the $8 billion of that amount for which the Roosevelt administration was responsible amounted to slightly more than one month of the national income. Can it be seriously contended, Eccles asked, that a government should not spend a month's income to effectuate economic recovery? Nor, he instructed, should "borrowing from itself and paying interest to itself" financially embarrass the nation. The way to balance the budget, he argued, was to bring about a growing, dynamic economy. How is it that it could be acceptable in some minds for the country to add massively to the national debt—$9 billion in one year and $13 billion the next—during the World War, but it amounted to a moral outrage to incur a couple billion dollars of debt to restore a decent life to the American people? The mistake had been to lower taxes drastically in the course of the following decade, instead of paying down more of the debt incurred. The "calamity howlers," who warned repeatedly of the dangers of the public debt, brought to mind, Eccles said, the "'shallow politicians'" whom Lord Macauley described in his *History of England*, whose caustic criticisms were only silenced by the massive growth of British wealth, which "exposed their needless alarms as baseless."

To listen to the administration's critics, therefore, and to attempt a "premature" balancing of the budget, Eccles reiterated, would "impede recovery and invite another onset of deflation." The New Deal, he implored, should stay the course and reaffirm its commitment to bring to "fruition" the aspirations of "the forgotten man and the underprivileged."

> To turn back now, to revert to the opposition policies which were tried and which failed disastrously, would be a fatal mistake. To slash the budget in capitulation to critics, would be not only to confess error where there had been none, not merely to admit that the critics are right . . . but most of all and worst of all it would be politically and economically wrong. It would set back the recovery, perhaps fatally. . . . The danger today is not from the meager handful of Reds in this country, but from the blind reactionaries whose policies all but brought us to public revolt and would, if reinstituted, jeopardize the very things of which they prate but are too blind and greedy to understand how to protect.[49]

We know from comments made subsequently by Secretary Morgenthau that Eccles's memo made quite an impression on FDR. The very day he received Eccles's memo, the president met with Morgenthau and Budget Director Daniel Bell. John Morton Blum, the historian who formulated a historical narrative from Morgenthau's personal and professional papers and published it in *From the Morgenthau Diaries* in 1959, discovered in these files a detailed summary by Morgenthau of what the secretary termed Eccles's "December memorandum." Blum describes the distress of Morgenthau and Bell—a fellow fiscal conservative—when FDR admiringly read passages of Eccles's memo aloud in their meeting on the twenty-eighth. Morgenthau, Blum writes, viewed the memo as a clear threat to his efforts to impress upon the president the necessity to make real inroads toward a balanced budget. His fear may certainly have been, moreover, that Eccles—and, of course, Currie—might become central economic advisors to the White House. Morgenthau and Director Bell agreed, therefore, to do whatever they could to "dynamite Eccles's point of view."[50]

It seems appropriate here to provide some clarification of what has been a chronological error in some historical accounts of this New Deal episode. John Morton Blum, who never viewed the original Eccles memo, relied upon Morgenthau's detailed summary to describe the memo and the reaction it engendered. While it is obvious that Morgenthau's summary is a description of the December memo just described, Blum identifies this development as having occurred a full year later, in *December 1936*. Numerous scholars, citing his book, have furthered this mistake. It is interesting to note that the president's calendar indicates that he had a meeting with Morgenthau and Bell on December 28 in 1935 and 1936. There can be little doubt, however, that this memo was given to the president in 1935. Since Blum was reviewing a document that was misdated, his error is understandable. Nonetheless, a close look at the diary entry reveals unmistakable evidence of that misdating. Morgenthau, for example, writes that Eccles's position, although reckless, might furnish positive campaign rhetoric for FDR. This would make no sense if it were written in December 1936, two months after the campaign had concluded in FDR's reelection. Moreover, after mention of Eccles's memo, Morgenthau states that the president wanted to plan for a contingency in the event the Supreme Court struck down the Agricultural Amendment Act—something that had occurred nearly a year before December 1936.

Had Professor Blum had access to the actual memo written by Eccles, he would have immediately recognized the error. Beyond the fact that the memo is dated 1935, it contains numerous references that prove conclusively that it could not have been written a year later.[51]

A couple of examples should be demonstrative. The very first sentence—referenced in Morgenthau's summary—warning that the political tide was turning against the administration, is hardly consistent with the aftermath of the 1936 election, which gave FDR and the Democrats one of the most overwhelming victories in U.S. history. Alf Landon was mentioned in the memo as a looming threat, which, of course, he would not have been in December 1936. Most importantly, as we shall see, in December of 1936 there would have been slight need for Morgenthau to "dynamite Eccles's point of view" in regard to the budget, since it was, by that time, essentially in harmony with his own. Indeed, only days earlier, on December 22, 1936, Lauchlin Currie prepared a memo for Eccles which informed him that the coming year "will mark the transition from a governmentally supported recovery to a self-generating upswing." On December 17, 1936, Eccles affirmed before a bank management conference in Boston that the budget would be balanced and that the federal government would need to borrow very little in the near future.[52]

A number of scholars who have explored the events leading to the recession of 1937 have referenced Eccles's memo to FDR, while citing *The Morgenthau Diaries* as a source. Herbert Stein, for example, does so in *The Fiscal Revolution in America* and, thereby, names Eccles as one of the few "dissenting voices in the administration" to plead for a continuation of deficit financing.[53] In his book *The End of Reform*, Alan Brinkley cites Blum when he writes about the end of 1936: "Others in the administration—among them Marriner Eccles—argued vigorously that reductions in federal spending were premature, that the economy was not yet healthy enough to be able to absorb a major drop in government support."[54]

Interestingly, one writer who fails to discuss "Eccles's December memorandum" is Eccles himself in his autobiography, *Beckoning Frontiers*, published seven years before Morgenthau's account. Eccles explores the 1937 recession in some detail without any mention of a cautionary memo he sent to FDR in December of 1936. If he did read the *Morgenthau Diaries*—and it is a bit difficult to believe that he was uninterested in doing so—he would have known that the author had mistakenly applied his 1935 state of mind to 1936. The latter date would have been only six months before the economy displayed its first signs of turning sour. Since many attribute the downturn to a premature attempt to achieve a balanced budget—the very thing Eccles had cautioned against in the memo—it certainly appears to make the Fed chairman seem quite prescient indeed. If Eccles failed to read the *Morgenthau Diaries*, he most certainly read Sidney Hyman's biography of his public career, *Marriner S. Eccles: Private Entrepreneur and Public Servant*, where, citing the *Morgenthau Diaries*, he discusses the 1936 memo to the president. Hyman began his collaboration on the book with Eccles in 1971 when the former Fed chairman was eighty-one years of age; the work was published in 1976, a little over a year before Eccles's death in 1977. Throughout this period Hyman tells us that Eccles remained vibrant and "was spared" any "decay of the mind and will." One must ask, therefore, if Hyman wondered why Eccles did not include this 1936 memo in his own account of these years. Perhaps it was Sidney Hyman who penciled in a question mark below the 1935 date on the December memorandum in Eccles's files?

Politics All the Way Through

To Eccles's chagrin the payroll tax—a political device in FDR's view—is used to fund the Social Security system. The Fed chairman fights it privately and publicly as a regressive drag upon recovery.

When all was said and done, it was the devilishly sly FDR who ran with the hares and hunted with the hounds. Throughout 1936, wrote Arthur Schlesinger, he tempered "a policy of moderation" with "a garb of militancy." The president most certainly fulfilled Eccles's wish that he go aggressively on the offensive. In his annual message to Congress in January, Roosevelt boasted that he had "earned the hatred of entrenched greed." Those "autocrats" sought, he proclaimed, "power for themselves and enslavement for the public." Before the annual Jackson Day Dinner, the president observed that, like Jackson, "the material power of the nation" was arrayed against him. Placating the left with his rhetoric, he comforted moderates with a continued determination to bring the budget into balance. In the election of 1936, he trounced Alf Landon, winning the electoral votes of all but two states.[55]

The economy, which improved throughout 1936, doubtlessly played a role in FDR's enormous victory. To the proponents of compensatory economics, however, these favorable economic developments—the payment of bonus benefits to vets and the court-decreed demise of the AAA processing tax—were due not to the president's initiatives, but rather in spite of them. The despair Eccles displayed in his December 1935 memo to FDR was a response to the headway that the balance-budgeters were making in 1935. "I have made a real start towards changing the whole picture of expenditures of the government," Harry Morgenthau confided in his diary in the summer of 1935, and he was confident he was succeeding in putting "this country back on a sound financial basis."[56]

Morgenthau counted among the successes of that year—and Eccles's among the setbacks—the final structure and financing of the Social Security system. FDR considered the payroll tax a crucial aspect of its continued political viability. As he famously stated to the social scientist Luther Gulick, the tax, while it may have had deficiencies in terms of progressivity, was "politics all the way through." The sense of a paid-in pension benefit would mean that "no damn politician can ever scrap my social security program." (The ultimate validity of this prophecy was borne out when the supposed civil libertarian, Ayn Rand, accepted Social Security and Medicare benefits with the rationale that she had already paid for them; which, of course, would certainly not have been the case with the relatively newly created Medicare.) It appears that Eccles never entertained the notion—nor does there seem to be any evidence that it was a commonplace assertion—that since the payroll tax amounts to a forced saving that replaces or reduces the need for an individual to make such a diversion of income, it should not be viewed as a tax burden.

The dangers associated with a worker-financed system seemed to play out in Germany when economic tailspins buffeted the system and saddled it with an unsustainable burden. To guard against such a development, the payroll tax would be evenly divided between employer and employee. Beginning with a 1 percent deduction from payrolls in 1937, it would increase in stages to 5 percent by 1956. Morgenthau's enthusiasm for the payroll tax, however, had everything to do with fiscal prudence and the desire to keep large deficits at bay. In fact, when the bill was near its final form, the treasury secretary suddenly balked at the solution arrived at to compensate for workers at or near retirement who would receive benefits with insufficient time to pay in: an infusion of revenue from the general fund would need to be pumped into the system in 1965. To the great annoyance of many, Morgenthau indignantly led a successful effort to double the tax's initial split contribution to 2 percent of payrolls. To Eccles's dismay, what he considered a bad tax was thereby made twice as bad in one fell swoop. The less regressive alternative of raising the level of income subject to taxation substantially higher than the stipulated level of $3,000 appeared not to be entertained.[57]

In Eccles's view, neither FDR's political reasoning nor Morgenthau's fiscal sanctimony could justify the inequity and macroeconomic malfeasance of the tax. He made numerous appeals to the president; in one memorandum he called the tax a $1 billion-a-year "deduction from consumer buying power," and entreated FDR to rethink the financing of the system and to look again at funding trends in foreign countries. (A number of nations used payroll taxes but supplemented their funds with general revenues.) Hardly content with internal memoranda, Eccles would publicly inveigh against the payroll tax with regularity, designating it before a Texas bankers' convention as "one of the most deflationary taxes that this country has ever put on."[58]

Better than Nothing

Once again, Eccles becomes embroiled with a fiscal-policy measure by becoming a proponent of an undistributed-profits tax designed to coax stockpiled corporate earnings to be paid out in dividends. The most controversial of New Deal taxes, it was never implemented in the form Eccles desired or suggested.

The need to add a more favorable mix of revenue options was a frequent source of conversation and scholarly review in the Federal Reserve throughout 1935. The expectation that the Supreme Court might deprive the Treasury of half a billion dollars in revenue from the AAA processing tax became a reality when the Court suspended the tax late in the year and officially struck it down in *United States v. Butler* on January 6, 1936. Pleased by this development, Eccles assisted in stonewalling an effort within the administration to rewrite the tax to gain the Court's approval. From a fiscal-stimulus perspective—though Eccles was diffident about it—there was more good news when the House of Representatives voted to override the president's veto of an immediate payment of the veterans' bonus and was joined by the Senate in early 1936, thus allowing the Adjusted Compensation Act to place $2 billion into the pockets of American veterans.[59]

On July 23, 1935, Lauchlin Currie sent Eccles a detailed analysis of what was being termed an "undistributed profits tax"—touted by some as a means of plugging the imminent revenue shortfall. The tax would come to occupy a controversial place in Eccles's career and, indeed, in American economic history. The central idea behind the tax—that "excess profits" held by corporations should be subject to stiff taxation unless paid out to stockholders—was by no means an invention of the New Deal. The tax was nearly adopted at the close of World War I and a version of the tax passed in the Senate in 1924. Moreover, the tax was by no means enigmatic, with a number of enactments throughout Europe. The first champion of the concept in the Roosevelt administration was Rexford Tugwell who explored the tax in his 1933 book, *The Industrial Discipline and the Governmental Arts.*[60]

Currie's July 1935 memorandum to Eccles was composed at the chairman's request. Currie establishes the rationale behind the tax by noting that the three entities controlled by Andrew Mellon—Gulf Oil, American Aluminum, and Union Trust—retained $117 million of the $146 million in earnings, or 80 percent, in the years 1927 to 1929. While the corporation was technically owned by the shareholders, it was actually controlled by salaried executives who may well have been motivated by considerations other than shareholder interest. Management might be more concerned with gross and net returns than an increasing rate of return for the stockholders; and, as Eccles was quite aware, significantly large liquid cash reserves often translated into greater pecuniary compensation for them. In addition to the benefit of higher dividend payments if corporations were effectively discouraged from holding back a substantial portion of earnings, Currie reasoned that there would be "a much closer calculation of probable costs and returns on any new investment if management had always to borrow or to ask stockholders directly for new money." Moreover, experienced investors were mindful of the fact that the current and prospective earnings of a company are of greater importance in assessing the worth of a stock investment. "If dividends were varied frequently in accordance with variations in earnings," he argued, "the importance of the trend of earnings would be more generally appreciated." This was, he continued, "the standard practice in England." Of course, many shareholders with extremely high incomes enjoyed a significant tax shelter by having earnings retained. Interestingly, Currie expresses sympathy for the "double taxation" argument involved with treating dividend payments as regular income. He suggests—if somewhat parenthetically—that this problem could be avoided by exempting the payment of dividends from a corporation's taxable income. Any loss of revenue from this exemption could be offset by making certain that the windfall provided well-to-do recipients of increased dividends was recovered with a suitably steep progressive income tax. The tax had great potential to "aid in the process of recovery," Currie concluded, by fostering "a desirable increase in spending." It was apparent, however, that another faction of the administration, presided over by Secretary Morgenthau and Budget Director Bell, envisioned the new tax as essentially a mechanism to raise more revenue.

Currie also addressed the "Brandeisian" sensibility that held, on general social grounds, that "bigness" should be discouraged since size begets "vast economic power in few hands." Certainly this conviction was uppermost in the minds of many who wished to deprive corporate managers of massive sums of accumulated profits (although Justice Brandeis considered the tax a far too imprecise tool for diminishing corporate power). Robert Jackson, a rising star in the administration, who was then head of the Justice Department's Tax Division, spoke to a national radio audience in the spring of 1936 to tout the beneficial role the undistributed-profits tax would play in fostering more genuine free-market capitalism. This check upon corporate power was uppermost in the thoughts of Rex Tugwell. FDR sold the tax this way, possibly because it seemed the easiest and most politically viable explanation. It was a rather effective advocacy to take out on the campaign trail. He told the country that the law would impede the ability of huge corporations to "gobble up small business."[61]

While Eccles was primarily concerned with the promise the tax held for generating economic stimulus and full employment, he seemed increasingly sympathetic with the view that the tax would act to retard economic power as well. He received a strongly worded memo supporting this position from E. A. Goldenweiser, the Fed's director of research. (As mentioned earlier, Currie was officially the assistant director.) Goldenweiser seemed to have more confidence than Currie in the beneficent consequences of stifling "intercorporate relationships" and thereby reducing corporate mergers and influence by empowering stockholders. It would, he thought, "be a factor toward economic democracy and away from plutocracy."[62]

Eccles kept among his papers a number of articles from Robert P. Vanderpoel, the financial editor of the *Chicago American*. As the debate about the wisdom of the undistributed-profits tax swirled about, Vanderpoel addressed the frequently expressed concern that the accumulation of "excess profits" made it possible for many corporations to survive the economic cataclysm of the Depression. Vanderpoel demonstrated, however, that, quite to the contrary, many of the nation's largest corporations did not deplete their excess profits to stay afloat, but actually managed to increase their cash holdings during the darkest days of the Depression. He provided these examples:

	End of 1929	End of 1933
General Motors	$27,000,000	$160,000,000
Du Pont	$ 20,000, 000	$ 40,000,000
Westinghouse	$ 22,000,000	$ 39,000,000
International Harvester	$ 22,500,000	$ 33,000,000
Goodyear Tire	$ 15,000,000	$ 24,000,000
Coca-Cola	$ 3,500,000	$ 13,000,000
Chrysler	$ 37,000,000	$ 57,000,000

Vanderpoel hardly needed to add that this accumulation coincided with a period of massive economic hardship in which the savings of millions of Americans withered away. Meanwhile, the "cash in the tills" of the nation's top thirty corporations increased by roughly 114 percent. These figures presented the financial journalist with an obvious question which he was happy to share with his readers: "What is it preparing for with a war chest this size?"[63]

In early 1936, the undistributed profits tax went from the investigatory phase to an official New Deal proposal. With the election on the horizon the administration felt the need to, as Eccles phrased it, "make some sort of show at closing the gap between Federal income and outgo." (This reflection from his memoir should not obscure the fact that at the time his concern was that FDR was deadly serious in closing this gap.) And so Henry Morgenthau and the

Treasury Department placed the tax front and center. Both Eccles and Currie had serious disagreements with the version of the tax drafted by Morgenthau's economic advisor, Jacob Viner, and his general counsel, Herman Oliphant.[64]

On March 3, 1936, Currie sent Eccles another memo on the tax which concluded that the law should make allowances for corporations to make "reasonable" retirement of debt without being penalized. Both men had long before emphasized that—unlike the Morgenthau proposal—the law should not apply to all corporations. They favored an exemption for the first $16,000 of a firm's income. In 1936 this would have exempted 90 percent of the nation's corporations. Large corporations, Eccles maintained, had the ability to access the capital market for new capital; small corporations did not have such access and should be exempt from the tax. Such an exemption would counteract the tax's detractors who maintained that small, innovative companies needed to rely upon retained earnings since banks were reluctant to finance "pioneering" undertakings. The effectiveness of the Fed's monetary mechanisms, he argued, would be enhanced if these large corporations were compelled to borrow in capital markets. Indeed, it seemed a common assertion of the law's supporters that the ability of monopolistic corporations to bypass lenders altogether had created a virtually independent "invisible banking system." This could have procyclical ramifications as well, assuming large corporations were investing earnings in highly priced investments when profits were high and dumping them to finance operations when both investment values and profits were in decline. Eccles believed, however, that the schedule for the tax was far too low to induce a significant distribution of dividends. He proposed that any corporation that retained less than 50 percent of its earnings would pay a stiff tax of 40 percent on the retained portion, and if it retained over 50 percent an even stiffer tax of 60 percent. Perhaps Eccles's major disagreement with the Treasury proposal was its willingness to use the undistributed-profits tax as a replacement for the regular corporation tax rather than simply as a surtax. He felt strongly that the corporate income tax needed to be preserved.[65]

On April 7, 1936, the Democrats on the Ways and Means Committee were delighted when the Republicans called Herman Oliphant to testify on the legislation. Remarkably, they were under the impression that Oliphant opposed the undistributed-profits tax, when he was its author. (A few days earlier the Republicans had their moment of joy when a representative of the Communist Party arrived to endorse the law, despite the amusing and feckless efforts of the Democrats on the committee who did their utmost to point out why he should not be supportive of the measure.) The elimination of the processing tax, Oliphant informed the committee, meant that the Treasury was in need of "real money" which must "come out of the pockets of real people." Far better, Oliphant said, that it come from profits (which were up 40 percent since 1933) rather than wages which were relatively stagnant. At that time, he testified that Marriner Eccles had not participated in the drafting of the proposal.[66]

On May 11, however, as the measure was making its way to the Senate, Eccles arranged for a meeting with the president in which he argued the case for his version of the tax. What may have been his most persuasive point was that the House's modification of the Treasury plan would simply fall short of supplying the revenue that the government needed. In the aftermath of that meeting, Roosevelt supplanted the Treasury bill in favor of Eccles's proposal as the official administration proposal. The bill that emerged from the Senate Finance Committee, however, which was shaped in large part by Virginia's junior senator, Harry Byrd—soon to become the most forceful public critic of the Fed chairman—was, in Eccles's opinion, not merely inadequate but amounted to "a backward step in the growth of tax philosophy." On May 27 Eccles sent a brief memo to FDR detailing how the Senate bill subverted virtually all of the goals of the legislation, it failed to check corporate power, failed to end the tax sanctuary that wealthy taxpayers accessed, and excessively burdened smaller corporations. It is a testament to Eccles's influence that on the very evening that FDR received Eccles's objections he summoned the Senate Finance Committee to the White House to insist that the "Eccles Plan" be reconsidered. The changes that were made to the Senate bill in the conference committee altered the bill somewhat. "The result was better than nothing," Eccles reflected years later, "but not very much better."[67]

In its final version, the law did address some of Eccles's concerns. The normal corporation tax was not jettisoned. Firms would pay it on a graduated schedule: 8 percent on the first $2,000 of adjusted net income, 11 percent on the next $13,000, 13 percent on the next $25,000, and 15 percent in excess of $40,000. After these taxes were paid, another graduated scale would be applied to any amount not distributed in dividends. Corporations would pay 7 percent on the first 10 percent of income retained, 12 percent on the next 10 percent, 17 percent on the next 20 percent, and 27 percent on the final 40 percent. The act exempted banks, insurance companies, and any firm under an order or contract to repay indebtedness out of current revenue. The Revenue Act of 1936 also contained a Title III provision that, in the finest tradition of the New Deal, was officially designated a "Tax on Unjust Enrichment": a levy of 80 percent on any windfall that was refunded after the processing tax was invalidated.[68]

The undistributed-profits tax was an unmitigated success in terms of raising money. Bringing in $800 million in its first full year of operation, it more than offset the loss of revenue from the AAA processing tax. Since the latter was significantly regressive and the former significantly progressive, to the extent that taxes needed to come from somewhere in a depressed economy, the tax had some stimulative and redistributive benefits. While generally critical of the New Deal's inclination to use its tax structure to achieve either of these results, Mark Leff describes the undistributed-profits tax as an "uncharacteristically bold innovation, designed to bring about a fundamental reorientation of the government's relationship to corporations."[69]

The act undoubtedly had unfortunate flaws. It failed to exempt small corporations from its restrictions, and Eccles's assertion that the schedules were not sufficiently stringent to make a real change in the payment of dividends appears to have been accurate. In fact, studies have indicated that it did not alter the distribution of earnings. The percentages of earnings distributed in 1936–1937 were essentially the same as the averages for the previous sixty-seven years. The ratio of dividends to earnings was greater in 1931–1932 than in 1936–1937.[70]

A reader of the *Wall Street Journal* and other conservative publications in 1936, however, would be left with considerable doubt that Western Civilization could survive the imposition of the undistributed-profits tax. It was a "share-the-wealth proposal in disguise"; a "penalizer of thrift" designed as a "direct attack upon capitalism" and a "promoter of monopolies" rather than its foe. In January 1938, Senator James Byrnes, the chairman of a committee investigating the rise in unemployment that had suddenly engulfed the nation beginning six months earlier, spoke, he claimed, on behalf of the beleaguered businessmen of America. It was abundantly clear, said the South Carolina Democrat, that "fear" on the part of capital and investors had essentially paralyzed the nation's commerce; and "that fear was due in great measure to this [undistributed-profits] tax." It is a claim that has reverberated with New Deal critics ever since.[71]

History would seem to indicate otherwise.

8

THE NEW DEAL RECESSION

How's Business?

The signs of a rejuvenated economy are everywhere as the year 1937 begins.

There was an indisputable "rising tone of optimism" in the nation at the beginning of 1937, wrote financial journalist John T. Flynn. "Men in Wall Street and business circles were talking," he said, "about the coming American boom." In the steel country of Pennsylvania, he wrote, "the sky was ablaze with the radiance of the old beehive ovens," while in New England "spindles were humming in the cotton textile mills." The great wave of militant sit-down strikes by labor that swept the country that winter seemed not to have dampened business enthusiasm. (After the sit-down strikes at General Motors and Chrysler, the United Auto Workers membership increased 150 percent by the beginning of May.) Indeed, by March, Flynn claimed, overexuberance might present the real challenge; "there were some business men who were afraid the boom might get out of hand and go too far."[1]

The adjusted index of industrial production, which had fallen from its 1929 high of 121 to 72 in November 1933, registered 97 at the beginning of 1936. Throughout the year it rose encouragingly and ended the year at 114. In 1937 the index continued its rise and by March it reached 118.[2] The *Federal Reserve Bulletin* would report that the national income, which Eccles assured the president was the most vital of all economic statistics, had increased more than 70 percent since the New Deal began, and was quickly approaching its pre-Depression level of $80 billion. A study by the National City Bank revealed that in 1936 the after-tax profits of 940 leading industrial corporations averaged 10.1 percent on their net worth. While the fields of coal mining and railroad equipment showed weak returns of 2.1 percent and 2.2 percent, respectively, automobile companies earned 26.6, drug firms 25.6, agricultural implement concerns 17.5, and chemical companies 14.4 percent. Eccles could point to his own business concerns as validation of a healthy renewal of commerce: by the beginning of 1937 the total deposits in his banks had grown by nearly 60 percent from 1933. The July 1937 issue of the *Fed Bulletin* reported that in the first quarter of 1937 the profits of the nation's largest corporations were 50 percent greater than in the corresponding period of 1936.[3]

In point of fact, as 1937 began—despite the supposed horrors imposed by the undistributed-profits tax—the business sector seemed confident indeed. It looked to the economist Roger Babson, still basking in the glow of his Wall Street crash prescience, like "the first year of real prosperity since 1929." In New York, the commissioner of public markets, the businessman William Fellows Morgan, was struck by how the "irresolute doubt and fear of the past" had given way to "a spirit of genuine confidence." He believed that this "feeling in itself will be a strong factor in carrying us further along next year."

This was a sentiment that was widely shared. The following contemporaneous perspectives on the economic outlook, while clearly related to a desire to enhance share prices, are nevertheless reflective of the fact that there was hardly a crisis of confidence among business leaders in early 1937. Neal Dow Becker, the president of the Intertype Corporation, stated that in the field of printing machinery the outlook for 1937 was "distinctly promising." In the area of office machinery, P. O. Wagoner, the president of Underwood, proclaimed that the recovery had arrived and that "the confidence of the business world has been restored." Hermann Irion of Steinway & Sons thought that the piano business and the music industry in general had "their share in the upturn in business" and had "every reason to feel that the improvement is only in its inception" and would continue far beyond the remainder of 1937. The chairman of William Iselin & Co., a leading textile manufacturer, described textiles as enjoying "an astonishing recovery in sales and profits" and agreed that it was a "universal expectation" in the industry that this would continue. The chairman of Southeastern Cottons, Howard Coffin, agreed and expressed a "feeling of assurance that business will continue its recovery" barring a world catastrophe of some sort. "There is in all probability no more basic barometer of business confidence than that of future advertising commitments," stated ad executive Charles Presbrey, and therefore the forecast for the economy could "not be anything but ultra-optimistic." Louis Comstock, the president of the Merchants Association, observing that "prosperity has again come to many of our consumer industries," saw no reason why this should not continue. The vice president of Guaranty Trust Company, Willis Booth, was also greatly impressed with the "marked gain" that had "occurred in business confidence," as was Malcolm Muir of McGraw-Hill, who was thrilled by the "irresistible upward surge of business which will continue through 1937." Lastly, but certainly not least, liquor distributor Grover Whalen considered that "it took no particularly brilliant effort to forecast a continued trade revival in 1937."[4]

This general tone of confidence was furthered by esteemed financial publications. *Barron's*, after discussing specific economic improvements, informed its readers in its "How's Business?" column that such indicators "grounded the conviction that 1937 will see continued improvement in business and trade." This optimism seemed verified in March when "How's Business?" revealed that *Barron's* gauge of the volume of production and trade, which stood at 75.8 percent of normal only three months earlier, now registered 90.8 percent. The "definite and sharp recovery" that *Barron's* "gauge" evidenced was due in large part, the magazine stated, to the sharp "upturn" in automobile production "*following the strike settlement*" [emphasis mine]. There were some concerns on the horizon—a possible coal strike—but "all in all," it assured its readers, the "spring outlook is promising." Even *The Economist*, not infrequently gloomy in its forecasts, found in February that "the momentum of recovery" in the United States had "gained sufficient force to overcome temporary difficulties." The "process of re-equipment and extension of industrial plants is now in full force." By the end of May the British publication, while noting some looming difficulties, continued its positive U.S. analysis by citing the significant increase in the *New York Times*'s index of business activity from April to May.[5]

Although similar evidence is unremitting, in the interest of avoiding redundancy, the above examples will stand to substantiate Marriner Eccles's contention that a generalized "fear and uncertainty" by business interests played little role in the recessionary conditions that surfaced in mid-1937. (Eccles, however, had a somewhat tangled perspective on this issue. He did suggest, as we shall see below, that "unjustified" price and wage increases in some sectors may have sparked an unhealthy buildup of inventories.) Moreover, he was quick to assert that "confidence," or its lack thereof, is a consequence of economic activity and not its determinant. In this vein, yet another column of Robert Vanderpoel's was clipped from the *Chicago American* for the chairman's files. The journalist was pondering the association of confidence and commercial vitality:

> The peculiar part of it is that history will show that, on the average, business men have the greatest confidence in the future when the future is the darkest and have the least confidence when it is brightest. Business

> men in general were overflowing with confidence in 1929 with the greatest business recession in the nation's history just ahead. In 1932 and 1933 confidence was at its lowest ebb, while as a matter of fact, the greatest upsurge in the nation's history was immediately ahead. Business confidence was at its peak for the five years of Roosevelt in the Fall of 1936 and Spring of 1937. The future was then the darkest since the first year of the Administration.[6]

Vanderpoel went on to explore the often-heard criticism that corporations would be possessed of a good deal more confidence if the government—by way of the undistributed-profits tax—was not bound and determined to deprive them of their financial "cushions." If only in 1929, he reflected, "cushions had been distributed to employees in higher wages, to stockholders in higher dividends and to customers in lower prices, the unhealthy condition would never have occurred, consumption would have been maintained and the depression would have been avoided."

In short, his assessment of the determinative influence of business confidence seemed identical to Eccles's—it was, Vanderpoel pronounced, "a lot of bunk."[7]

Not Shooting the Bulls

With gold pouring into the country and the stock market soaring, Eccles confronts the widespread and unfounded fear that high inflation is right around the corner.

The roots of the New Deal recession of 1937 go back to 1935. As that year began, Marriner Eccles had been the head of the Fed for less than two months. No dramatic monetary policies had been pursued and none were anticipated. Although the open-market portfolio had increased by 25 percent since FDR had come to office, the Federal Open Market Committee (given unambiguous authority by the Banking Act of 1935 to set interest rates by purchasing or selling government securities) had made no purchases in more than a year. In January, however, the discount rate was lowered in five of the System's twelve districts. In addition, Secretary Morgenthau—ever mindful of bond prices—made purchases for the Exchange Stabilization Fund created with the "free gold" nationalization and devaluation in 1933. Indeed, the devaluation was the essential cause of the real monetary development of this period. The nation's monetary gold stock almost doubled between December 1933 and July 1934;

from 1935 on, the increasingly perilous political conditions throughout Europe helped to assure a steady influx. This "scare money," as SEC head Joseph Kennedy described it, continued to flow into the country throughout the 1930s. When banks imported gold they were obligated to sell it to the Treasury, thereby increasing the excess reserves of commercial banks.[8]

With such conditions prevailing, it was hardly surprising that the hobgoblin of inflation—which never entirely left the national stage at any point during the Depression years—would resurface as a major topic of discussion in public life. The issue was raised during Eccles's testimony on the Banking Act in mid-March of 1935. Congressman Cross of Texas expressed concern about the administration's frequent pronouncements about the matter. "If you have any influence at the White House," he requested of Eccles, "I wish you would get them to stop giving out these statements that there isn't going to be any inflation. Every time they do the bottom drops out of Wall Street." Eccles responded to Cross's concern about price stability by providing him with an involved exegesis on the income velocity theory of currency circulation. In any event, he informed the congressman the banking law should contain a provision that the Fed had the "duty" to exercise its powers to promote conditions that will eliminate "unstabilizing fluctuations" in prices and employment. Taking steps to counter inflation, he assured the congressman, was something the Fed was prepared to do, in the event the economy showed signs of overheating. "FEAR OF INFLATION DOUBTED BY ECCLES" was the headline the *New York Times* used in its account of his testimony.[9]

From his first days in the administration as Henry Morgenthau's assistant, Eccles derided those who expressed anxiety about inflation as the nation was still recovering from its massive economic plunge. The word was so ubiquitously used, he said, that he wondered whether people truly understood what it was. "When we get relatively full employment and a full utilization of our productive facilities, then we can worry," he wrote in a critique of the dire warnings about excess reserves by the Federal Advisory Council (composed of an influential banker from each of the twelve Fed districts).[10]

Even as Eccles was issuing his assurances to the House Banking Committee of unfounded fears of inflation, it became clear that some of his fellow Federal Reserve Board members were not so sanguine. On March 21, 1935, the meeting of FOMC concerned itself with the growth of excess reserves. While some expressed concern about the buildup of inflationary pressures, most of the committee seemed quite conscious that any effort to reduce reserves would not only have the possibility of choking off the recovery, but it could be offset by Treasury purchases, or even a decision by the administration to utilize the powers given it under the Thomas amendment to print money. Amid his self-assured testimony before Congress a few days before, Eccles interposed at one point a measure of diffidence by conceding, "We have much to learn about central banking and managed currency." The understanding that they were not dealing with a fine science in the monetary manipulations that were available to them is reflected in a report prepared by Fed staffers. "The memo concluded," writes Allan Meltzer, "that neither past experience nor central bank theory gave any guidance in present circumstances." Events would demonstrate that there was indeed a good deal to be learned about both fiscal and monetary policy.[11]

While the FOMC chose inaction for the time being, in May of 1935 the full Federal Reserve Board, led by the chairman, seeing no "evidence of excessive borrowing or speculative expansion," allowed discount rates to be lowered to 2 percent in ten of the Reserve districts and to 1.5 percent in both New York and Cleveland. In Eccles's view, this remained consistent with the statements he had been making throughout the entire winter and spring. "At present time, we are in the depths of a great depression and beyond creating an easy money situation, there is very little, if anything, that the Reserve . . . can do toward recovery." With this last decline in the discount rate, he was confident that the Board had fulfilled its role to maintain an "easy money situation" that proper fiscal policy could exploit.[12]

In his "pushing a string" analogy he had relegated "monetary action" to the role of junior partner in a depressed economy. He was quick to add, however, that it "could be very effective in curbing undue expansion" if business activity developed to a point of credit inflation. That, he concluded, would be "pulling a string." There were events concomitant with the lowering of the discount rate that would lead some to feel that they were rapidly approaching the moment when the pulling of the string should be contemplated. In March of that year the stock market began to rise and in the second half of the year to rise so steeply that it was soon outpacing, by a considerable margin, the overall growth of the economy. The Standard and Poor's index registered a 40 percent increase for the year and stock prices would double well before the end of 1936. Moreover, the gold influx resulted in a greater increase to the monetary base than had been contemplated. Increasing at an 18 percent annual rate in the first three quarters, it was accelerating at a greater rate by the early fall, and ended the year with a 25 percent annual increase for the final quarter.[13]

In the October meeting of the Fed Board this increase was discussed, as was the fact that there had been a 50 percent swell in excess reserves held by member banks since March. While some members found this threatening and suggested that the Board take action to reduce the reserves, Eccles urged a cautious delay. (On this matter Eccles had the support of Henry Morgenthau.) On November 5 two confidential, internal Fed memos were drafted by the Fed's staff; one expressed the need for raising requirements and the other argued against such action. The former took notice of the fact that demand deposits of member banks not only were greater than they had ever been, but could be "more than doubled on the basis of existing reserves." Furthermore, there was every reason to expect that the excess of reserves would continue to grow. It was therefore prudent for the Fed to absorb "at least a portion of the excess reserves before the bankers have had an opportunity to expand their activities on the basis of these reserves." Since such action would eventually be necessitated anyway, the memo reasoned, it was preferable to rein in superfluous funds gradually so as to avoid a drastic increase in the future—a move that could be economically injurious by causing a deflationary movement. There was also, it added, a "good psychological effect" to be derived from taking such action in that it would indicate that the System was "alert to the situation and prepared to take action." The Fed could not now, as it had in the past, bemoan its lack of authority to act, the memo concluded.

The opposing view echoed Eccles's thoughts at the time. There simply was no indication, it argued, of an expansion of credit and, therefore, "no real reason for taking action of a restraining character." This memo also raised psychological considerations:

> The public should know that when the Federal Reserve System does anything in the direction of restraint that this constitutes a policy of restraint. A simple understanding of red and green signals of credit policy is an advantage which may be lost or impaired by actions that require more or less subtle explanation.[14]

On the same day the memos were issued, the staff also prepared a press statement marked confidential. With the actual dates left blank, the release announced a 25 percent rise in reserve requirements. This increase, the statement declared, was not to be interpreted as a tightening of credit conditions or of lending policies of banks. It was not, in short, a reversal of the Federal Reserve's easy-money policy. Someone clearly considered the rise in reserve ratios merely a matter of time. The Fed was poised to act.[15]

In the meantime fear of inflationary conditions could be mollified by public comments to the effect that the Fed was keeping a watchful eye on developments. Weeks later when Eccles addressed the American Bankers Association in New Orleans on November 14, 1935, he made reference to the need to combat the "twin evils of inflation and deflation."[16]

Mere references of this kind failed to satisfy numerous financial writers. In the *Oakland Tribune*, financial correspondent James McMullen characterized the Board's attentiveness as a "sob to nervous conservatives." The Federal Reserve's advisory council issued a resolution on November 21 calling upon the Fed to take preventive action against runaway credit inflation. The *New York Times* interpreted this statement—as did Eccles—as an accusation that the Fed had "neglected its duty." The very next day, the chairman, speaking for himself and not the Board, issued a public statement to refute such a notion. It was a rejoinder that made headlines across the country, including the front page of the *New York Times*, which read, "WASHINGTON WILL NOT APPLY 'BRAKES' TO BOOM IN STOCKS: ECCLES CALLS IT HEALTHFUL." While Eccles must have been pleased to have his remarks on the front page, the *Times*'s emphasis on Wall Street's bull market typified the coverage the statement garnered across the country. His real objective was to provide a fuller understanding of exactly what inflation was. "I define inflation," the release explained, "as a condition brought about when the means of payment in the hands of those who will spend them increases faster than the goods can be produced." He then went on to ask, "How is it possible to have inflation in that sense when men are idle and plants are idle?" The Federal Reserve Board was carefully watching the inflow of gold from abroad and had at its disposal "ample power" in the form of reserve requirements that could "wipe out the greater part of the present excess" should it become necessary. He apparently thought it prudent to leave unmentioned in the lengthy statement any mention of apprehension on his part that premature action by the Fed might endanger the pace of the economic recovery.[17]

The nation, however, was indeed experiencing "stock market inflation." There were two aspects of this development that he felt it crucial for the nation to understand. First, the fear that this was a reprise of the debacle of 1929 was unfounded. The current purchasing of securities was not being financed by bank credit. In fact, the Fed's reports indicated that since the rise in stock prices began in March, the loans on securities by member banks had actually declined somewhat. There was "an element of safety and strength" in the fact that it was the cash reserves of American and foreign investors that were accelerating the movement in the market. Secondly, the public should understand that outside of the setting of margin requirements, already rather high at 45 percent, there was very little control that the Fed could exert upon stock prices. In fact, the Federal Reserve Act permitted the Board to increase the margin only to prevent "the excessive use of credit," which was not presently the case.[18]

Far from quelling the concerns of the press, Eccles's remarks created something of a mild frenzy. Many financial writers interpreted his comments as an encouragement of the bull market—which they certainly seemed to be—and placed his observations alongside the blessings President Coolidge had bestowed on a feverish market in the previous decade. "After its unfortunate experience with pigs," the *New Yorker* snidely commented, "the government has decided not to shoot the bulls" (a reference, of course, to the Agricultural Adjustment Administration decision to slaughter millions of piglets in 1933). President Roosevelt, sensitive to these developments, sent Eccles a cautionary note from his vacation home in Warm Springs. While he found Eccles's reasoning "entirely sound," he thought it a "real danger" to issue any statement that was even "remotely" related to the actual operations of the market. "This is where Coolidge, Mellon and Hoover got into trouble. A word to the wise!" This advice, Eccles would later relate, "was heeded in the future."[19]

In the months that followed, George Harrison of the New York Fed and other members of the Open Market Committee continued to pressure the Fed Board to take action on reserve requirements. By February 1936 the Federal Advisory Council was now unanimous in its conviction that action should be taken. The strongest opponent of such a course was Henry Morgenthau, who considered the move to be a politically motivated attempt to damage the president. He suggested that margin requirements be increased as an alternative. While nearly everyone at the Fed realized that this was completely ineffectual—and, as noted, technically a transgression of the law—the margin was raised from 45 to 55 percent in January.[20]

Nor would this issue disappear from public discussion and debate. The matter, if anything, began to receive more widespread attention. Eccles took notice of the debate at the end of December 1935 between Winthrop Aldrich, head of Chase National Bank, the largest banking institution in the country, and S. Parker Gilbert of J. P. Morgan & Company. Aldrich described excess reserves as "explosive material awaiting a match." He considered the situation "a far wider speculative abuse than that which culminated in 1929." Gilbert countered with the argument made by Eccles and added his concern that any such curtailment of reserves risked damaging the recovery. Despite any protestations to the contrary, he insisted, the move would be seen as a "reversal of the cheap money policy."[21]

The *Oakland Tribune*'s James McMullen was somewhat mystified by Gilbert's "emphatic dissent" from the rest of the banking circle, who, he wrote, wisely comprehended the peril that excess reserves posed for the economy. That Gilbert was in "substantial agreement" with Marriner Eccles, McMullen mused in his front-page article, "was a breath-taking thought to many in the financial fraternity. After all, you can hardly expect a Morgan partner of being in cahoots with Stalin."[22]

In the course of the following six months, however, Eccles changed his position. It is possible that his rethinking of the reserve policy was underway as early as February of 1936. On the tenth of that month, *Time* magazine placed a portrait of Eccles on its cover. The accompanying article, however, more closely resembled an alarum on the dangers of monetary misfeasance than an exploratory piece about the new chairman. Prior to any mention of Eccles's name, the story makes a hurried reference to "a tremendous potential momentum toward inflation" that has been accruing in the nation's financial system. "If this force is not properly braked," the article cautions, "most disinterested observers" forecast the possibility of "a reckless ride" in the country's monetary future. Following a brief introduction of the new members of the Fed board—all now FDR appointees—*Time* assesses Eccles as the "one remarkable man" among them. After a synopsis of his journey from Mormon businessman to New Deal participant, the article returns to the specter of inflation and makes reference to Eccles's previous assertion that inflation is unlikely in an economy operating below its productive capacity. What "bothers serious economists," the magazine avers, "is whether Chairman Eccles and his fellow money managers will be able to pull the lever before reflation turns into inflation." At least, it was optimistically noted, Eccles "is trying out another set of brakes" with his recent upping of margin requirements for securities. "As it is," the article concludes ominously, "a good many people believe that Marriner Eccles is the only thing standing between the U.S. and disaster."[23]

One might surmise that this article, along with so many others, may understandably have given Eccles pause. With banks buying so many securities at such low interest, enormous losses would surely ensue if inflation did return. Currie began to express the concern that when the recovery began to accelerate, velocity would also recover and the Fed would have to make extremely large sales of bonds to effectuate a significant impact. Eccles agreed to rope in excess reserves. The Board voted on July 14 to institute a 50 percent increase in requirements which would commence on August 15. Of the 6,367 banks in the Federal Reserve System, all but 197 had sufficient preexisting excess balances with the Reserve to meet the increase. This meant, of course, that the new requirement amounted to little more than a bookkeeping notation.[24]

Although "Eccles's Banking Act" authorizing this power stated that it could be implemented without presidential notification or approval, Eccles, as discussed earlier, apprised FDR of the Board's decision a week earlier. He did not, however, inform Secretary Morgenthau who was furious, not merely at being left uninformed, but by the fact that bond yields began to rise the very next week. Subsequent to an extremely heated phone conversation with Eccles, in which he claimed to "put the fear of God into him" for engaging in devious "unilateralism," the secretary flexed his monetary muscles by ordering the New York Fed, which handled the Treasury's stabilization fund, to make purchases. Eccles claimed that he simply assumed that the increase was common knowledge and that he had, after all, forewarned the president. (His additional defense that he was simply out of town when the order was actually issued seemed especially lame.) Morgenthau appeared to be somewhat soothed by the Board's decision to make a limited amount of purchases to support treasuries.[25]

The animus between Eccles and Morgenthau seemed to begin when they first met nearly three years earlier. It was a sentiment that intensified when Eccles circumvented Morgenthau and brought his own version of the undistributed-property tax to the president. Now each considered the other an interloper in his sphere of influence in the New Deal, each certain the other was wedded to policies that would lead the economy astray. It was both personal and political and it would come to a boiling point before the year was out.

While the Fed's August increase in the reserve ratio technically removed $1.5 billion of the System's funds from the credit market, the action was offset by the continued inflow of gold from abroad. The total amount of imported gold since mid-1933 exceeded $4 billion by the fall of 1936. At that time, currency in circulation and the total amount of deposits in banks was approximately $2 billion more than it had been during the boom years of the late 1920s. The phantom of some inflation continued to haunt the country.[26]

Remarkably, consumer prices rose a mere 1 percent in 1936![27]

Laissez-Faire for the Unorganized

Eccles's grouping of certain segments of organized labor with monopolistic corporations, which some view as too avaricious, wins him some praise from conservatives.

As discussed earlier, the nation experienced a rapidly growing economy throughout 1936. "Contemporary data," writes Allan Meltzer, "show national income produced in 1936 rising 15 percent." Marriner Eccles's desperate plea for a more exuberant and stimulative fiscal policy made in his December 1935 memo had materialized largely in the form of a congressional override of FDR's veto of the veterans' bonus ($2.2 billion) and the Supreme Court's invalidation of the processing tax ($620 million). FDR's contribution to fiscal stimulus came in the form of his refusal to raise significantly more revenue and in an authorization of $250 million in Reconstruction Finance Corporation funds to Harold Ickes's PWA (although FDR attempted to sooth the vehement opposition of Henry Morgenthau with assurances that Ickes wouldn't actually spend the money). In total these developments were hardly sufficient to satisfy the demands of Eccles's compensatory economics. They did result, however, in the New Deal's largest deficit heretofore in fiscal 1936, and helped to spawn, in Morgenthau's view, an "inflation psychology."

While Morgenthau had replaced Lewis Douglas as the driving force of fiscal conservatism in the administration, he possessed a distinctly different sensibility than the former budget director toward the New Deal's obligation to pay "decent attention to humane needs." There were indeed times when a balanced budget might be sacrificed. It was this quality that may have ultimately enhanced his influence with FDR. Morgenthau had an acute distaste for organized special interests that he believed continually drove the government toward fiscal profligacy. The veterans lobby was such a group as was the farm bloc whose interests Henry Wallace so diligently served. "What you want is for the Government to keep spending in order to keep business going," he once stated to a fellow New Dealer. "I want business to do the spending in the place of the Government."[28]

Eccles, of course, was thinking somewhat differently in 1936. As the recovery progressed he began to concern himself with the inimical impact concentrated economic power was certain to have on a sustained recovery. In the fall of that year he received a memo from Lauchlin Currie that typified this unease. Currie conveyed his concern over the recent announcement by various large corporations of their ostensibly beneficent intention to tie wage rates to the cost of living. The cost-of-living index, he pointed out, was "being held down by various slow moving prices such as gas and electric rates and rents." The economist cautioned that this would allow certain segments of the economy to restrict wage rates while enjoying excessive profit growth. "That way," he cautioned, "would lie disaster." While both men agreed that while there was little that could be done about the adoption of such policies, they could at least work to ensure that such practices did not receive official favor from the administration. While FDR expressed approval of such cost-of-living wage increases put forward by the steel companies and General Electric, he publicly rescinded his endorsement and stated his opposition if they prevented fair wage advances.[29]

Representative of Eccles's concern was the position of the United States Steel Corporation. The world's largest industrial enterprise, U.S. Steel's profits had increased from $12 million in 1935 to $67 million in 1936 and would go on to register a stunning $130 million in 1937. Despite such profit growth, its board of directors offered, in the fall of 1936, to raise its "common labor" rate from 47 cents to 52.5 cents an hour and to link all future wage increases to the cost-of-living index. After their famous luncheon encounter at the Mayflower Hotel in January 1937, U.S. Steel's chairman, Myron Taylor, and the Committee of Industrial Organizations (CIO) chairman, John Lewis, reached an agreement to raise the basic labor rate from 52.5 to 62.5 cents an hour, thus achieving a five-dollar day for eight hours of work. (The CIO was still affiliated with the AFL and not yet the independent union of industrial workers—the Congress of Industrial Organizations.) The corporation then promptly raised prices sharply and an indignant Marriner Eccles wrote to FDR to argue that the price increase was "greatly in excess of the rise that would be sufficient to compensate for the wage advance." This assertion, that pay raises were not being kept abreast of profit growth, was verified by the Bureau of Labor Statistics and was bound, said the chairman, to exact a deflationary price in the not-too-distant future.[30]

Eccles's apprehension that concentrated power could threaten the recovery by forcing prices to unjustified levels was not confined to large corporations. When the chairman made a few public comments about the damaging influence that certain segments of organized labor exerted on prices, it generated a backlash from many liberals. The *New Republic*, while recognizing his apparent influence with the president, worried that "Mr. Eccles's . . . reputation of being hostile to union labor" could adversely affect the "already damaged relations of Mr. Roosevelt and the CIO." The magazine informed readers that the word they received from Eccles's "associates" was that it was not the CIO that disturbed the chairman, but rather the powerful craft unions of the AFL, and especially those associated with the building trades that he believed were hindering the construction of more housing. These associates also assured the *New Republic* that Eccles was quite sincere about achieving a fairer distribution of income, but that such an achievement was reliant upon a sustained economic recovery and needed to unfold with a greater degree of balance across the spectrum of American labor.[31]

Eccles's "associates" conveyed his feelings about labor fairly accurately. It was an issue he brought up in testimony before a Senate committee; although he was then willing to attribute a good deal of blame for the disappointing performance in construction to the harmful effects of the monopoly power of the building material business. Both, he argued, were "at the bottom of our present difficulties today." He went on: "We have laissez-faire among the unorganized groups . . . and monopoly controlled wages and prices in another part of the economy." According to Eccles these high costs were stifling a great deal of building construction. "I do not want to be misunderstood," he hastened to add. "I am not unfriendly to labor." Workers should, he maintained, get all they possibly could so long as the increase in prices was not passed on to the rest of the population thereby throwing "the economy out of balance."[32]

Eccles's outspokenness on the issue of labor unions not only drew criticism from progressives, it won him praise from unusual quarters. The conservative *Spokesman Review* headlined its positive story on his testimony: "Mr. Eccles' Plain Speaking." The *New York Journal of Commerce* lauded him as the "first important spokesman for the Roosevelt administration to recognize publicly the dangers inherent in the current wave of wage and price increases." A number of businessmen who formed a discussion group at the Faculty Club of Harvard found favor with Eccles's comments. One member wrote to Eccles's old ideological ally William Foster, praising the chairman for criticizing—he noted that FDR never did—"Lewis' and Hillman's means." When Foster passed this commendation on to Eccles, however, he added that the gathering was not "keen" about anything else the chairman had to say.[33]

In the early spring of 1937, Eccles expressed his views about these issues at a luncheon with the president. He left behind a memo that urged the administration to speak out against powerful corporate and labor entities. The CIO's John Lewis, who was also the president of the United Mine Workers, had strongly endorsed Roosevelt in 1936 and contributed an extraordinary sum of money to the campaign. Many attributed the FDR victory in the traditionally Republican state of Pennsylvania—won by Hoover in 1932—to Lewis's influence. It was unlikely, then, that the president would speak out against "unreasonable wage demands." Near the end of a debilitating thirty-four-day strike against Republic and Inland Steel, however, the AP reported an appeal to FDR from the "strike harried" mayor of Johnstown. The mayor called upon the president to confront "the un-American empire that John Lewis is building up." At a press conference shortly after, FDR responded to a question about the strikes with a display of exasperation with both corporations and unions—"a plague on both your houses." This remark, coming shortly after the firing upon peaceful union picketers at a Republic Steel plant in Chicago that killed ten—seven of whom were shot in the back—brought stinging rebukes from many in organized labor, including John Lewis. "It ill behooves one who has supped at labor's table," he stated, "to curse with equal fervor . . . both labor and its adversaries."[34]

The incident may have helped Eccles appreciate the political realities that FDR confronted. Eccles, however, was himself sensitive to accusations that he was antilabor. In the course of a luncheon he once argued his case directly to John Lewis. Shortly afterward, he sent the labor leader a letter that he said was inspired by Lewis's "sense of public responsibility." Eccles's insisted that there were many knowledgeable economists and others who "cannot be charged with either being reactionary or lacking in sympathy with the labor movement" who shared his views. He wrote in part:

> I know that there are a good many cases in which labor has been denied its fair share in the profits of business and has had to battle with every means at its disposal to get a fairer share. I am not talking about those cases. I am talking about what happens when organized minority groups whether of labor or business, take advantage of strategic positions to force their prices out of line with mass purchasing power. Communist and socialist writers agree that democracy is doomed because in the mad rush for profits at the expense of the general public interest, capitalism is bound to generate more and more violent extremes of price inflation and resultant crashes. I am not willing yet to admit that business and labor leadership are incapable of preventing these recurrent disasters, but it is going to take some bold and courageous leadership somewhere to face the realities.[35]

It is worth noting that in this letter to John Lewis, when Eccles wrote of organized unions winning wage increases at the expense of unorganized workers, he only made specific mention of the building trades. In fact, when Eccles touched upon this issue in his Senate testimony and later in his autobiography, one discovers that there, too, he mentions merely the building trades—arguably with good justification—as the culprits. While his missive to Lewis implies a wider application of this disparity, any exploration of the pay received by American workers in any other sector of the economy in these years leads to a dubious consideration of Eccles's overall claim. Even in early 1941, John Lewis's well-organized coal-mine workers received an average hourly wage of 99 cents. The most lucrative compensation for labor outside of the building trades belonged to the automobile workers whose hourly wage averaged a less-than-princely sum of $1.04, thus providing them a yearly income below $2,100. This at a time, it should be remembered, when studies identified that level of income as the minimum necessary for a simple and decent lifestyle. Robert Zieger has written about the lives of "high wage" industrial workers:

> A steelworker family with the statistical average of 2.5 children could afford a new coat for mother and father every six years and a new pair of shoes for each child every two years. The mother could buy two housedresses a year and the father a workshirt annually and two dress shirts every three years. An old used car provided transportation to and from their five-room rented apartment.[36]

John Lewis's answer to Eccles's letter, and the chairman's concern about "organized minority groups," came in his address to the opening session of the CIO's constitutional convention in Pittsburgh eight months later. It was his intention to narrow the disparity among American wage-earners by bringing them all under the protective roof of "a mighty new house of labor."[37]

Any discussion of Eccles's connection with American workers would be remiss if it neglected an important aspect of his own experience as an employer. In August 1932, Senator Tasker Oddie of Nevada called for a congressional investigation of the companies constructing the Hoover Dam. It was a well-known fact that many of the workers were being paid in scrip that was only redeemable at the company stores. In addition to this familiar form of exploitation, the senator charged that the workers were so badly underpaid that they barely had any income left after paying out expenses for room and board. The *Nevada State Journal* accused the employers of ducking taxes and compromising worker safety. These allegations were also made in a series of investigative articles by the *New Republic*. The largest of the Six Companies accused of these transgressions was the Utah Construction Company. The extent of Eccles's involvement with these developments is uncertain. As discussed earlier, however, from his earliest association with the company he was closely involved with all of its operations.

The Six Companies' practice of paying workers in scrip was not ended by public disapprobation or the congressional investigation that followed Senator Oddie's summons. The practice was terminated immediately by the new secretary of the interior in 1933—Harold Ickes.[38]

Beware the Boom

Despite confidential warnings from his friend, Sears president Robert Wood of the Chicago Fed, that it was too soon to pull in the reins on the economy, Eccles agrees to reserve increases and joins the budget balancers by the close of 1936.

In the spring of 1937 *The Nation*'s Oswald Garrison Villard, in his article "What Is the Nation Coming To?" appeared puzzled by the fact that Marriner Eccles, the warhorse of deficit spending, was of a sudden equally plaintive "with his threat of imminent inflation."[39] That very week the *New Republic*'s John T. Flynn thought it "interesting to find New Dealers, all of a sudden and in the very midst of the cheers for returning prosperity, stricken with certain terrors about the permanence of their prosperity." This apprehension was driven, he informed his readers, by the possibility that the good times would turn into an unsustainable "great boom" that would be followed by a "great collapse." He too thought it peculiar that Eccles was part of this contingent. What is more likely to transpire, he wrote presciently, "is that we shall see the collapse of the recovery before the boom begins."[40] While Flynn's economic prognosis was accurate, his description of the boom psychosis as "sudden" was not.

In Eccles's view, the overwhelming victory won by FDR and the Democrats in 1936—a victory enabled by improved economic conditions—validated what he had emphasized from nearly the very beginning of the Depression: the American people were not unfamiliar nor particularly troubled by the assumption of a large sovereign debt if accompanied by economic prosperity. The debt-to-GDP ratio, small perhaps by twenty-first-century standards, registered 40 percent.

The nation willingly assumed a massive increase in the national debt to fight the World War, and they proved to be similarly willing to do so to win the "war against the Depression." Indeed, the conflict proved that the economy could cope with extremely high levels of debt. After all, the deficit in fiscal

1919—which began in July of 1918—stood at $13 billion, nearly twice as much as the New Deal had added to the debt in its entire first four years. The gross debt of the nation had risen from slightly more than $1 billion in 1916 to an astonishing $25.5 billion in June of 1919. As the very different results of the midterm elections in 1938 would graphically demonstrate, the dimensions of the debt—again as Eccles predicted—would only become a political liability when the economy faltered. From the chairman's perspective, it was not simply a matter of economic vivacity trumping fiscal responsibility; rather, economic vivacity *was* fiscal responsibility.[41]

Eccles believed that the most worrisome threat to a sustained recovery in mid-1936 resided with Henry Morgenthau's dogged determination to balance the budget. This was rendered all the more troublesome, he felt, by the monetary powers which Morgenthau had readily available to him. In addition to the manipulation of the stabilization fund, the secretary began to toy with the idea that the Treasury could provide a monetary alternative to raising reserve ratios—an idea that Morgenthau disliked—by sterilizing gold inflows. This would involve the Treasury altering its gold-purchasing procedure. Ordinarily, the Treasury drew on its account at the Fed to purchase new domestically produced and foreign inflows of gold at $35 per ounce and then printed gold certificates for equivalent amounts, that, when deposited to its Fed account, would increase the monetary base. Under a sterilization policy, the Treasury placed gold certificates in an inactive account and thereby prevented any credit expansion.[42]

As Allan Meltzer points out, the same result could have been achieved by the Fed. In the opinion of many, especially Eccles, the Treasury was not simply dabbling in monetary policy, but rather moving to supplant the Fed in a very fundamental way. The omnipresent tension between Morgenthau and Eccles intensified. In the course of discussions over these issues, Eccles sent a strongly worded memo to Morgenthau objecting to his usurpation of monetary policy. The secretary characterized the communication to his associates in the Treasury as "impertinent." According to Morgenthau, Eccles also threatened his resignation when he presented the memo to him. "I was only trying to do something to help Eccles," Morgenthau confided in his diary a few days later.[43]

Lauchlin Currie, who had worked for Morgenthau and was in communication with both men, wrote a letter marked "very confidential" to the chairman in early December 1936, cautioning him of the hazard that a breach with the secretary might entail. The cooperation of the Treasury was vital, Currie reminded Eccles, in coordinating monetary and fiscal policies. Morgenthau "is a person intensely loyal to the President," Currie wrote, "and extremely jealous of the prerogatives of his office." He then assured Eccles that he was fully aware that the chairman put "ideas and objectives above personalities" and that he was in Washington to "make a contribution not to enhance his authority." For these reasons, Currie urged Eccles to make an "overture" to the secretary. Currie's letter to Eccles gives the sense of a wily peacemaker attempting to achieve harmony by imparting the same reasoning to both disputants. Currie was certainly aware of the fact that while Eccles could flood the White House with memos, he did not enjoy the same personal access as Henry Morgenthau, who, as an old personal friend of the president, lunched with him every Monday.[44]

The following day, prompted it seems by Currie's missive, Eccles hand-delivered a conciliatory note to Morgenthau. (This necessitated a mere walk down the hallway since the Fed's offices were then located in the Treasury Building.) He was not motivated by "questions of prerogatives," he assured the treasury secretary. "Now Henry," he continued, "if I have in any way incurred your displeasure it would certainly cause me the deepest regret."[45] On the same day, however, in a separate letter to Morgenthau, Eccles restated his objections to sterilization. Whatever soothing impact the first letter may have had, it was negated by the strong wording of the second. In this letter the chairman reminded the secretary that Congress had placed the power of monetary control with the Federal Reserve. The Board, he informed Morgenthau, was contemplating taking further steps in January to curb excess reserves. The Treasury plan would gum up the works, claimed Eccles, by "introducing a new factor and a new agency into the situation." The public, he argued, would wonder why the Treasury was, at public expense, preempting the workings of the Fed which had yet to fully utilize the monetary methods at its disposal.[46]

There was a strange turn of events two days later on December 17, 1936. In a White House meeting attended by the chairman, the secretary, and the president, Eccles reversed his position entirely and spoke in favor of the Treasury's gold sterilization policy almost as if it were his own idea. If war were declared, Eccles reasoned, foreign governments might sequester the securities of their nationals in the United States, sell them in the market, and take home the gold. This development, he acknowledged, could be avoided by sterilization. It would permit the Fed, he said, to keep its instruments of monetary control in abeyance in case they were needed at a later date. Morgenthau was mystified. Interestingly, in his memoir Eccles mentions the sterilization policy in passing and simply describes it as "part of the effort to prevent further growths in excess reserves." Sydney Hyman, writing in consultation with Eccles, would state that the previous position that Eccles held was actually the Board's and that Eccles finally prevailed upon them to go along with the Treasury policy. When one considers the vehemence of Eccles's earlier opposition, this explanation strains credulity. On December 21, Morgenthau and Eccles held a joint press conference to explain the policy of sterilization. While Morgenthau emphasized that it was exclusively a Treasury program, Eccles stated that the Fed "undoubtedly could have handled the entire situation alone." However, Eccles added that "we don't want to use up all our powers. We should have some in reserve." There was no inkling that there had ever been the slightest disagreement about the matter. The policy was implemented the following week. As discussed below, it would play a crucial role in the coming recession.[47]

Throughout December the Fed Board was in discussions with the Federal Advisory Committee and other Reserve Bank officials over the wisdom of raising reserve ratios yet again. Eccles was ambivalent about doing so.[48] By Thanksgiving the excess reserves, which had been reduced to $1.8 billion by the August increase, were back up to over $2.2 billion. On December 18, 1936, Eccles received a letter from General Robert E. Wood, the president of Sears, Roebuck & Company. Wood, a director of the Chicago Fed, was writing to inform the chairman that the consensus at their last meeting was that there should be no increase in reserves. "I cannot see a boom yet," wrote Wood, espousing a dose of economic analysis that until very recently was Eccles's mantra. "You cannot call the country in the midst of a 'boom' when there are . . . 8 million unemployed." Wood cautioned, as had many others, that small banks would be especially adversely affected, and stressed that an "easy money" policy must not be prematurely abandoned. As for the issue of stock-market speculation, Wood insisted—as Eccles had previously agreed—this was an ineffective tool to dampen it. Wood suggested some other means might be attempted; a tax might be levied on the profits of foreign investors. (This was something Eccles had already publicly endorsed.) Wood enclosed an article from the London *Economist* that supported his view. "You should," he implored, "stop look and listen before you take this action." Eccles wrote back to Wood five days later and emphasized that he had no intention of interfering with the recovery or of creating a "tight money" policy. He urged Wood not to go public with his reservations. If the Reserve banks began to criticize the actions of the Board, wrote Eccles, it would provide "ammo" for their critics.[49]

Undaunted by such warnings—and the opposition of Henry Morgenthau—the Board of Governors, at a January 26 meeting, made the decision to increase reserves again, this time by 33.5 percent. This action thereby exhausted the power of the Board to raise requirements as set by the Banking Act, which limited such increases to not more than twice the 1935 level. On January 30 the Fed announced publicly that this would be achieved in two installments; one-half of the increase would become effective on March 1, 1937, and the remaining half on May 1. This requirement, the Board's statement said, would "eliminate as a basis of possible credit expansion an estimated $1.5 billion of excess reserves which are superfluous for the present or prospective needs of commerce, industry and agriculture."[50] When Morgenthau complained to Eccles that this action would leave a mere $600 million in usable reserves, the chairman assured him that that amount surpassed the level of the credit-crazed 1920s.[51]

For Henry Morgenthau, however, all of these issues took a back seat to bringing the federal budget into balance. Encouraged by the buoyant economy and the opportunity it offered for reaching a balanced budget in fiscal 1938 (which would begin on July 1, 1937), he worked with Budget Director Daniel Bell on spending cuts as the New Year began. They had, he said to Bell, begun to "scrape the barrel clean" by their insistence upon these reduced government expenditures; "Now what I want to do is take the barrel apart so they can't fill it up again." This goal necessitated, both men were convinced, the dismantling of the agencies that served as the vehicles for fiscal extravagance. Morgenthau was pleasantly surprised when a chastened Harold Ickes expressed to the treasury secretary the need to curtail PWA spending. Eager now to balance the budget, Ickes had wearied, he informed Morgenthau, of "being the whipping boy." Also that spring, Henry Wallace acknowledged to Lauchlin Currie the need to raise taxes and cut expenditures.[52]

Morgenthau was most delighted to add to the chorus of budget balancers the strangest of all bedfellows—Marriner Eccles. On April 6, 1937, Eccles stopped by Morgenthau's office and a bemused secretary said he listened as the Fed chairman spoke vehemently of the need to impress the president with the urgency of balancing the budget in fiscal 1938 (which, it is important to emphasize again, would begin in less than three months, on July 1, 1937) and then requested that Morgenthau join him in this endeavor. Morgenthau seemed to suggest that this policy transformation stemmed from a lecture that he heard FDR give to Eccles only a few days earlier. "I wish you'd heard the President talk about balancing the budget to Eccles," said Morgenthau, relating the details of the meeting to members of his staff. "God, if he'd only say publicly what he told him it would be marvelous," he added.[53]

In light of the fact that Eccles had been on the budget balancers' bandwagon for several months when this conversion was to have occurred, this is a peculiar comment. For example, at a March 13 meeting of the Executive Committee of the Federal Open Market Committee, held in Morgenthau's office, Eccles expressed the belief that while an easy-money policy by the Fed should be continued, it "was imperative that assurance be given that the budget would be balanced in 1938 [and] that any experience that would increase indebtedness should be covered by taxation."[54]

Indeed, Eccles would later state in a congressional hearing in 1938 that as early as *December of 1936* he was "advocating the need of approaching a balanced budget." (This, it will be recalled, was the month that Blum, Stein, and others mistakenly believe that Eccles was urging FDR to continue with large deficits.) In fact, Eccles's call for a balanced federal budget predates even this early date. The *New York Times* was surprised to discover that in "off-the-record" remarks to an assemblage of Boston bankers in *November of 1936*, the chairman who "hitherto" had appeared to bankers "almost entirely in the role of a militant advocate of an unbalanced budget" was now insisting that "we have reached a stage of recovery" where the "controls of the government," including curtailing excess reserves and "balancing the budget and retiring government debt," must be activated.[55]

It was in December of 1935 that Eccles had drafted his memo imploring the president to ignore the "calamity howlers" and to continue—in fact, to greatly accelerate—deficit financing. Throughout most of 1936 this was a position he maintained both privately and publicly. As of May it was clear that he had yet to change his mind on this issue. He appeared that month as the principal speaker before the alumni of the Wharton School of Finance. While he reprised his warning about the "twin evils of inflation and deflation," it was clear that the former was not in the forefront of his mind. For the government to decrease its expenditures on recovery prematurely, he cautioned, "would reduce consumer buying power and thus retard, if not reverse, the progress of recovery." To further the growth of the economy, he suggested that "favorable long-term interest rates were available for financing in virtually every field of activity." Of course, he acknowledged, a balanced budget would be essential to achieve when the time was appropriate. One supposes that his audience was more receptive to the comments of Robert Warren, the economist for Case, Pomeroy & Company, who followed him to the podium: "Easy money is regarded as a stimulus, but I am almost tempted to say it is not a stimulus but a narcotic."[56]

As we have seen above, by the end of the year Eccles was prepared to concede that "easy money" had a narcotic potential at least. By early November of 1936, the chairman, who previously discounted the importance of "stock market inflation," was reported by the United Press to be "checking constantly on developments" on Wall Street; one could assume here that the chairman was focused upon stock prices merely for purposes of determining what margin requirements should be applied. It seems rather that the high priest of government spending had begun sinning against his liturgy, and, much like 1929, was conflating stock-market gains with the state of the general economy. It seems clear at least that a preoccupation with the threat imposed by a "boom psychosis" was gradually coloring his perspective. As the year 1937 began, his articles of faith were in a state of apostasy: taxes were being raised; expenditures were being cut; gold was being sterilized; reserve requirements were being raised; and open-market operations were stagnant. The stage was set for the New Deal Recession. It would involve the steepest plummet in industrial production in all of American history.[57]

Monkeying with the Carburetor

Just about everyone is on board for the implementation of bad public policy, and the steepest economic decline in American history begins in the summer of 1937.

In his autobiographical account of the events of 1937, it appears that Marriner Eccles was interested in safeguarding somewhat his reputation as one of the "dissenting voices" cautioning against the abandonment of fiscal stimulus. During the March 11, 1937, luncheon with FDR, he left behind a memo (mentioned briefly above) that reveals how far he had come from his past entreaties to the president. In his memoir, Eccles quotes extensively from this document, including the first two long paragraphs—where he warns of the inflationary power of certain labor and corporate interests—in their entirety. He deleted from this autobiographical account, however, the memo's all-important first sentence: "*The recovery movement is now assured and requires no further positive stimulation by the government.*" Eccles prefaces this long quotation from the memo by stating in his memoir that "on first glance, it did appear that the recovery movement was secure and that no further positive stimulation was required by the government." This conveys the impression that while this may have appeared to be the case, he disabused the president of this notion and went on to warn about "dangers" to the recovery. Moreover, in a self-serving use of an ellipsis, he gives the impression of sagely predicting the impending recession. After warning of the inflationary impact of concentrated power, he states: "If such conditions are permitted to develop another drastic slump will be inevitable." Eccles, however, was not quite as prescient in his prediction as the entire sentence reveals: "If such conditions are permitted to develop another drastic slump will be inevitable *within three or four years, if not before.*" He also writes in his memoir that in early 1937 there were "surface signs that our private economic engine had gained sufficient momentum to move forward without the aid of a government tow car." Here again, he allows the reader to infer that this was an understandable assessment made by others while he continued to warn of "dangers." Yet, as we have seen, that the nation no longer was in need of a "tow truck" was precisely what he told the president.[58]

While expressing apprehension over the cost increases for skilled construction labor, the memo acknowledged that recent wage advances in steel contracts would add only 4 percent to the cost per unit whereas price increases advanced 12 percent. In addition to steel, the memo's chief concern was the price increases in lead, copper, and building materials. Both metals had risen somewhere in the neighborhood of 80 percent since the fall of 1936. The wholesale price of building materials seemed less troubling; falling slightly in the latter part of 1934, it had remained steady until the third quarter of 1936 when prices rose from 86 percent of the 1929 level to nearly 96 percent by the second week of March. The wholesale price of commodities other than farm products and food—as a graph in the memo demonstrated, although Eccles made no reference to it—appeared less troubling still, rising from 79 percent of the 1929 level to 85 percent.[59]

The chairman cautioned that these developments warranted a policy response. He provided FDR with a number of suggestions to ward off the imposition of a more restrictive monetary course of action—although it was something that the administration should be prepared for as a "last resort." A tax increase on income earners between $5,000 and $50,000 was warranted. It might prove effective for the president to announce the formation of a fact-finding commission that would "investigate price advances in important fields and would make appropriate recommendations." Moreover, the Department of Justice and the Federal Trade Commission could threaten to generate "unfavorable publicity" through public pronouncements and discussion of legal options. It might prove quite effective if the president threatened to substantially reduce tariff rates on certain imports. The most-favored-nation clause in trade treaties gave him a good deal of discretionary power in that regard.

In terms of labor costs in the construction field, Eccles revisited old ground. He had for three years emphasized the use of CCC camps to institute "technical training on a broad scale." All public works programs should begin to taper off projects that required skilled labor. They should also devise some strategy to "induce the skilled building trades unions to relax apprenticeship requirements." He felt confident that he had given the president policy options and, most crucially, informed him of the "source of the danger."[60]

That the fiscal tow car was no longer needed by the early months of 1937 became a widespread conviction among many of the administration's previous "spenders." On April 1, 1937, Lauchlin Currie sent the chairman a memo in which he, too, warned of the "emergence of a boom psychology." In some basic industries the supply of skilled labor was "pretty well absorbed." This could create the "danger" that "the demand for goods may increase too rapidly for additional goods to be produced, so that prices will rise rapidly in a sellers' market." To safeguard an "orderly revival" he also suggested tax increases on the intermediate income earners between $5,000 to $50,000. Compensatory fiscal policy dictates, Currie wrote, that tax hikes and debt retirement should be undertaken when a recovery becomes "self-generating and threatens to proceed at too rapid a pace to be sustained. *This stage has been reached*" [emphasis mine]. In a meeting with Henry Wallace later that spring, Currie "made it clear to him" that the chairman "did not favor increased expenditures now." Currie reported to Eccles that the agriculture secretary was in full agreement and expressed the belief "more taxes are needed" and that a "counter-offensive ought to be started."[61]

The new focus on budget balancing and the potential of inflation by Eccles and other progressives in the administration was favorably, if somewhat suspiciously, received by conservative financial observers. *The American Bankers' Magazine*, for example, wrote in a May editorial comment that while well-disposed to recent remarks by the chairman, it was monetary and fiscal irresponsibility that he too often championed that now needed rectifying. Perhaps the most influential journalist in the country, Walter Lippmann, with whom Eccles had a good relationship (the journalist was the main speaker when the University of Utah honored Eccles with an honorary doctorate in 1943) observed in his column in February that the former "darling of the liberals" was now "denounced by the more foolish liberals as a renegade" for adopting budget balancing. But Lippmann informed his readers that he could "testify . . . from personal knowledge that Mr. Eccles has not changed his principles." With the economy now "tending toward a boom," the Fed chairman wished to sensibly "put the overcoat in the cedar chest and turn off the furnace." Eccles, wrote the esteemed journalist, had introduced the notion that "cycles" should be "modified by compensatory measures." The country should "get used to the idea" that a change of course in public policy is not an erratic sign but an indication of an advanced approach by a government that strategically "varies with the economic seasons."[62]

In agreement with the need for a balanced budget was the Brookings Institution. In a study released that spring the liberal-leaning think tank made this the very first of its seven "requirements" for preserving a sustained recovery. Even the very progressive Corrington Gill and Leon Henderson of the WPA, and Mordecai Ezekiel of the Department of Agriculture, addressed the "People's Party" in April of 1937, and while praising whatever wage gains had been achieved by labor, warned that the "alarming" rate of inflation—caused by irresponsible corporate monopoly—might necessitate tighter monetary policies or a balancing of the federal budget.

By the late spring, nearly everyone associated with the administration considered that a fiscal shift toward a balanced budget was either a laudatory objective or a regrettably necessary course of action. In January came the sobering news that the Soviet Union's budget was in balance for 1936. The Soviets viewed it as a significant achievement and proudly proclaimed themselves "the most solvent country on earth."[63]

Despite reports in the press, Eccles wanted to disabuse the public that the Fed had embraced a tight money policy. When he left the president following his March 11, 1937, luncheon he felt his perfunctory comments to reporters had been misinterpreted. He had warned the president about "hot money," the press reported. As Eccles witnessed the growing sense in the nation that the administration was completely refocusing its attention, he issued a press release. "I have been and still am an advocate of easy money," he stated on March 16. "The way to control unjustified price advances is by increasing production." This could be done, he stated, so long as "there is idle labor willing to work." While it was true that a "balanced recovery" now necessitated a "prompt balancing of the federal budget and the subsequent retirement of public debt," he did not favor doing so at the expense of those in need of relief. Taxes could therefore be raised if necessary.[64]

After mentioning his press release of March 16, Eccles states in *Beckoning Frontiers* that "soon thereafter" the bubble burst and "the slump began in earnest." It would be nearly four months, however, before the economy began to show unmistakable signs of a downward spiral. In the meantime the wrongheaded policy decisions continued apace. When a tax shortfall was reported for the first quarter of the year, FDR requested on April 7 that the heads of all executive departments analyze their spending requirements for the remainder of the year and make "a substantial saving" by eliminating all expenditures which were not absolutely necessary. They were required to report back to the director of the budget not later than May 1, 1937. The administration confidently announced in May that as a result of the president's appeal, estimated savings would reach over $100 million for fiscal 1937.[65]

Favorable economic indications continued to dominate the nation's economic news. In May the *Federal Reserve Bulletin* reported that the adjusted industrial index had reached 118 in March, a mere three points below the 1929 level. Output of electrical power and many manufactures including textiles, shoes, leather, and petroleum products were already at rates higher than 1929. The Fed credited an increase in consumer purchasing power with considerably bolstering wool prices. Similarly, cotton prices that had been dormant for years rose approximately 25 percent from the fall of 1936. The Fed reported in the early summer that even the railroads—enduringly one of the sickliest segments of the economy—reported profits for the first three months of the year.[66]

There were some disquieting signs intermixed. On April 25, for example, the vice president of Gimbel Brothers reported that "an alarming impasse has developed in retail trade," while Sears would soon begin to see a falloff in mail-order sales.[67] In August the Fed reported that the adjusted industrial index, which had been on the rise throughout most of the New Deal but had remained stationary since March at 118, had dropped to 115 in June. It also noted that production at shoe factories had fallen considerably in that month. Also in June the level of commercial loans outside of New York City, which had increased throughout the year, began now to decline somewhat. While gold imports from Canada and Japan continued at the same pace, the importation from Europe, which had been tremendous in the earlier part of the year, began to decline sharply at the beginning of July and virtually ceased by the end of the month. In July the Treasury's inactive gold account recorded the first reduction since it was established.[68]

In early August Eccles received a memo from Lauchlin Currie on the decline in purchasing power that would result as a consequence of the fiscal operations of the government. The report attempted to discern how the federal budget would impact the consumer purchasing power, or what the economist termed "total community expenditures." It will be recalled that Currie did not feel that fiscal impact could be accurately determined by merely calculating gross expenditures and receipts of the government. As explored earlier, but worth revisiting, expenditures on such things as debt retirement, payments into the social security trust fund, and gold purchases had no stimulative impact on incomes or business activity. Likewise, there was some portion of taxes where it could be said that "if the government had not collected taxes and spent them, the money might have remained unspent for either consumer or producers' goods." The report attempted to incorporate these facts into its conclusion about the net effect of fiscal policy on economic stimulation. The conclusion was reached that the decline in total community expenditures from fiscal year 1937 to fiscal year 1938 would range from $2.5 billion to nearly $4 billion. A large part of this decline, it was acknowledged, could be attributed to the nonrecurring bonus payments of $1.5 billion. The memo stated that it was "probable" that this sum was spent in the early part of the fiscal year beginning July 1, 1936. Among the cuts in stimulative government spending was a reduction of over 26 percent in reclamation projects (including the TVA), 21 percent in flood control and river-harbor works, 18 percent in highway and rural road construction, and 15 percent in public and institutional buildings.[69]

Although Eccles would in future reflection cite these fiscal developments as the central cause of the 1937 recession, there are really no indications that he was at the time particularly alarmed by this analysis. There were no cautionary memos directed to the president that summer—no press releases or public addresses—objecting to fiscal-policy decisions, nor any reversal of his March assessment that the recovery movement needed no further stimulation by way of government spending.

The recession began in the late summer and by October the industrial index had declined to 102; it would fall to 79 by early 1938. On October 11 the stock market, which had some sell-offs earlier in the fall, began a drastic plunge that culminated in yet another "Black Tuesday" on the nineteenth when seventeen million shares changed hands. Stock prices would decline by half. By the end of December, two million workers had lost their jobs. Before the economy hit bottom in 1938, real GNP fell by over 11 percent and industrial production by an extraordinary 32 percent; this occurred well within a one-year period of time. It was all quite redolent of 1929.[70]

On October 13, General Wood sent an I-told-you-so letter to Eccles. The second rise in the reserve requirements and the sterilization of gold, he maintained, were mistakes. Eccles had already publicly denied that the reserve changes had any adverse effects. Before the House Banking Committee in mid-July, his old friend Wright Patman requested that the chairman admit that he had pursued a "deflationary policy." (Eccles came before the committee that day to testify on his "drastic" suggestion that the securities tax on nonresident aliens be raised from 10 percent to over 22 percent.) Eccles staked out a position that day which he reiterated in a response to Wood; it was a position to which he would adhere for the remainder of his life. There were "nonmonetary" reasons for the downturn, he insisted in his return letter to Wood. An array of "inhibiting factors such as improper taxation and unjustified labor demands" were to blame. "Nobody is more eager than I am to see labor standards and wages increased or more opposed to seeing a few strategically well located . . . groups bid their wages out of line." Look, insisted the chairman, at the plight of the nation's railroads whose meager 1937 profits were swallowed up by wage demands forcing a "cancellation of plans for equipment buying" and the subsequent discharge of thousands of rail workers while railroad securities collapsed.

"I am simply giving you the facts as they stand," Wood wrote back on November 2, as he related the predicament that Sears confronted. Eccles responded with a further elaboration on the recession's causes. "Fear," as Wood suggested in his previous letter, was not a factor, Eccles insisted. Rather, excessive price increases and reduced government expenditures were the real culprits. Reserve requirements and gold sterilization, he reiterated, "had nothing to do with it." Unfazed by Eccles's emphatic response, Wood wrote back once again and implored the chairman to lend his support to the lowering of reserve requirements; this, he added, was "essential." Eccles and his cohorts on the Board in Washington committed "one cardinal error," Wood insisted. "You do not take psychology into account, and it is a tremendous force at the present time."[71]

If Eccles went to his grave maintaining that monetary policy did not instigate the recession of 1937, Henry Morgenthau went to his rest equally insistent that it was not precipitated by fiscal policy. "You people," Morgenthau at one point accused the Fed, "just don't want to admit that you monkeyed with the carburetor and you got the mixture too thin." Both men would also argue to the end of their lives that their particular remedy for the Depression—sufficiently large deficit spending or prompt and continued balanced budgets—was never seriously attempted. Had their policy wishes been faithfully implemented, each man was convinced that the nation would have been spared the prolonged agonies of the Great Depression. That some aspects of this disagreement—the fiscal versus the monetary—are not mutually exclusive and that the recession was the result of an admixture seems never to have been entertained, at least not publicly, by either man.[72]

As will be discussed below, however, in addition to omitting certain details from his memoir that tend to implicate him in the fiscal miscues of these events, Eccles also fails to make mention of a few events that might redound to his benefit if one subscribes to causational monetary missteps. One can only speculate upon the motivation behind these omissions. While it is possible that he considered such details unimportant, it is also possible that inclusion of certain actions on his part would provide ammunition for those who insist that the carburetor had indeed been monkeyed with and that the Fed policies did help bring on the recession.

The leading academic proponents of the argument that monetary mismanagement was crucially connected to the recession are Milton Friedman and Anna Jacobson Schwartz, who, as did General Wood of Sears, point an accusatory finger at the Fed's 100 percent increase in reserve requirements and its lethargic open-market purchases. Eccles's position, as he stated in *Beckoning Frontiers*, was that the downturn did not begin until three months after the final increase in requirements became operable. Friedman and Schwartz, however, make the argument that there is a natural lag before any constricting impact of the policy would be felt. Eccles, it will be remembered, justified the raising of the requirements by pointing out the vast excess reserves that still remained.[73]

Eccles does acknowledge in his memoir that he expected that while the banking system as a whole had great excess reserves to meet the Fed's order, there would be some selling off of U.S. securities by individual banks that were not as loaded up with funds. Moreover, he tells us that he expected that "banks that could buy these securities would defer doing so in the belief that if they waited longer, prices would drop still further." The minutes of the FOMC meeting from April 3, 1937, demonstrate a somewhat different concern on his part. Following the March increase, the sell-off of securities was clearly more significant than he expected; by the middle of that month government securities held by member banks declined by $545 million. Banks were clearly attempting to restore their excess reserves. Eccles observed at this meeting that "banks have been accustomed for a long time to an extremely large amount of excess reserves" and that "the actions of the Board" had "drastically reduced" reserves below a certain level of comfort to which they had become accustomed. (The coming summer would witness certain weeks of what the *New York Times* called "paradoxical circumstances" where there were significant drops in member-bank reserve balances and a rise in member-bank excess reserves. This was brought about by a shifting of deposits from demand funds to that of time deposits that require a much smaller reserve.) Was it possible that he was conceding that despite his protestations an easy-money policy would still prevail, the financial world merely saw—as the internal Fed memo from the previous November warned it would—a flashing red light? Was it possible he had come to realize as Wood stated in his letter, and as Keynes had written less than a year earlier in *General Theory*, that "human decisions affecting the future, whether personal or political or economic, cannot depend on strict mathematical expectation, since the basis for making such calculations does not exist"?[74]

There are additional indications that Eccles had some degree of buyer's remorse on the reserve issue. While he discusses in *Beckoning Frontiers* his willingness to engage in open-market purchases when government bond prices began falling, he fails to convey the vehemence with which he held this position, threatening to resign, in fact, if the FOMC failed to act decisively. On this matter Eccles was allied with Morgenthau, although he strongly opposed the secretary's desire—and threat—to release a significant amount of sterilized gold. To do so, Eccles argued in a meeting with Morgenthau and FDR, would be to concede that the Treasury was running the monetary show and that the changes made in the Banking Act of 1935, designed to strengthen the open-market mechanism, were ineffectual. Eccles even suggested at that White House gathering that if he failed to persuade the Fed to bolster purchases, he would work to cancel the last increase in reserve requirements scheduled for May 1. Viewing the minutes of the previous FOMC meeting in March, Friedman and Schwartz noted that its members were generally unconcerned with the bond-market decline. Eccles, almost alone, they wrote, "took the opposite view." There is something of an irony at play when the leading proponents of the conviction that the recession of 1937 had monetary causes can cite that theory's leading historical detractor as being among the least culpable of the players that set those causes in motion.[75]

As the year progressed, Eccles burnished his record as one of the more *relatively* enlightened members of the Fed in regard to sound monetarism. He favored the lowering of the discount rate throughout the System and especially at the New York Fed which went lower than the rest of the branches, from 1.5 percent to 1.0 percent in August. This was, the *New York Times* apprised its readers, "the lowest rate that any central bank has maintained at any time." Before leaving for his summer vacation—his daughter was getting married that summer—Eccles called for a meeting of FOMC to arrange for the purchases of $200 to $300 million in short-term obligations to be made throughout the early fall. On September 9, however, after a sizeable sell-off on Wall Street, Eccles cut short his vacation—subsequent to his daughter tying the knot—and returned to the Capital. The rumor circulated that he intended to lower the margin requirements from its high of 55 percent.

Actually he had arrived to meet with Henry Morgenthau about gold sterilization. In a phone conversation with the secretary, who was himself vacationing at his "farm" in Dutchess County, the two men agreed that $300 million would be transferred from the Treasury's inactive gold account to its active account at the Fed. By this time—September 12—the nine-month-old fund had accumulated a rather staggering $1.4 billion. The action was in no way related to stock prices, Eccles insisted, but was merely a continuance of "easy money" conditions the Fed had established and a seasonal adjustment to assist the "orderly marketing of crops."[76]

Days later, with the matter of the gold sterilization release settled, Eccles returned to Utah to continue his vacation. On the nineteenth of September he drove with his Utah business associates to Jackson Hole, Wyoming, for several days of fishing. Meanwhile, the statistics being compiled by his staff for the Fed's October report seemed to assure that the coming "boom" was unlikely to be on the immediate horizon. It was expected that industrial activity would see a slight decline. The *Bulletin* released in October would confirm, however, two of Eccles's chief concerns. The net profits of the nation's largest corporations were 20 percent larger than they were in the second quarter of 1936 and the average hourly wage of construction workers had risen 18 percent since then. There was also a somewhat troubling fact that would loom larger in some minds when the recession of 1937 was viewed in retrospect. The October *Bulletin* indicated that a good deal of the operations at the nation's steel mills had been "based on unfilled orders accumulated early in the year." Was it possible that some of the rapid increase in production throughout the previous year was spurred by a desire to build up inventories in the event that labor strife shut down production? If so, the presence of excess inventories when an economy shows sign of slowing is an ominous indication.[77]

Nevertheless, the economy, as already noted, would falter substantially in the months ahead. In slightly more than one year—from June of 1937 to July of 1938—real GNP would plummet 11 percent. Michael Darby has pointed out what is particularly tragic about this development. From 1933 to 1936 the "corrected" unemployment rate fell by 3.6 percentage points a year. Had the Fed not pursued its reserve policy, he points out, there "is every reason to suppose that the natural rate of 5 percent would have been reached by 1938." And had the housing production and works program that Eccles advocated been achieved, perhaps earlier than that.[78]

CHAPTER 8

Turning on the Old Record

While Eccles favors desterilizing gold and spending it, he does not join the "spenders" in late 1937. Rather, he states that deficit spending is not the way out of the recession and offers solutions that he argues will not endanger a balanced budget.

In his memoir Eccles skips the monetary developments discussed above—the lowering of the discount rate and the confrontation over the desterilization of gold—and states simply that "soon" after his cautionary March 1937 meeting with FDR "the inflated price bubble burst and the slump started in earnest." He then proceeds to the events of November 1937 when the battle between the spenders and the budget balancers over how to extricate the nation from the economic downturn began in earnest. It was a battle that Herb Stein has somewhat melodramatically characterized as "a struggle for the soul of FDR." Eccles leaves the reader of these events—and most historians, for that matter—to infer that he had at this point joined forces with the spenders. He had not.

The battle lines were graphically drawn in a speech Secretary Morgenthau delivered to the conservative Academy of Political Science at the Hotel Astor in New York City on November 10. The speech was intended, as everyone knew, to lay the groundwork for what he hoped would be FDR's budget proposals. Both sides had already made entreaties to the president. "What business wants to know is," Morgenthau stated in a cabinet meeting, "are we headed toward state socialism or are we going to continue on a capitalist basis?" Roosevelt responded to this harangue with an insistence that he had "told them again and again." "Well," said Morgenthau, they must be told for "the fifteenth time. That's what they want to know." The secretary was certain that a balanced budget would instill renewed confidence and exuberance to the American business scene. Jim Farley seconded Morgenthau's argument and assured the president that while it was, of course, untrue, the "impression has been created . . . that you have no interest in business . . . a feeling that you have no sympathy or confidence in business—big or little." An exasperated FDR relented. "I will turn on the old record," he consented.[79]

While Henry Morgenthau thought he had won the president over when he stepped to the microphone to deliver his address to the Academy of Political Science, the spenders too thought they had made inroads with him. Two days before Morgenthau's speech of November 10, Isador Lubin, Leon Henderson, and Lauchlin Currie delivered a memo that took issue with everything

Morgenthau espoused. In a four-hour meeting with FDR, arranged by Harry Hopkins, they stressed that it was foolish to believe a balanced budget would bring revival to the economy when the government was running a *cash surplus of $66 million* when the recession began! In October Currie drafted a study that put forth a stunning finding. In 1935 the "net contribution" of the federal government totaled $3.1 billion in a year when the national income grew by $5.4 billion. In 1936 there was a net contribution of $4.0 billion as the national income grew by $8.8 billion. In 1937, however, Currie's study indicated that from February to September the net contribution registered merely $573 million. If the September contribution of only $37 million were replicated for the remainder of the calendar year, the net contribution would total $684 million. The position of the spenders was perfectly clear—the effort to produce a balanced budget was the single most important factor in bringing on the recession.[80]

On the afternoon of Morgenthau's speech, Eccles met with FDR at the White House to present his amendments to the FHA (previously discussed) which he felt would greatly stimulate the economy. The president not only agreed to the amendments, but, as Eccles writes in his memoir, he was also taken with the argument of the spenders, and he recalls stating that they "needed a resumption of government spending and not a curb on it." He states that he was somewhat mystified, therefore, by Morgenthau's paean to a balanced budget that evening. The speech would not have been delivered, he was certain, without FDR's imprimatur. Although recognizing it as an "ungenerous comment," Eccles states: "The contradictions between the afternoon and evening positions made me wonder at this time whether the New Deal was merely a political slogan or if Roosevelt really knew what the New Deal was."[81]

This passage in Eccles's book is suggestive of a rather clever bit of obfuscation. The reader is led to infer that Eccles, too, was advising a resort to increase expenditures with the other "spenders" and was displeased by Morgenthau's remarks which were, in light of the president's comments, "inexplicable." He writes that there had been "persistent rumors" about Morgenthau's balance-budget message that he hoped represented a "passing phase" in the administration's thinking. In fact, the United Press reported on what the secretary's comments would address. "The decision confronting Mr. Roosevelt," they wrote, was whether to "adopt another 'pump priming' program of government expenditures or to maneuver business and finance into private spending operations which would quicken business activity." The story noted that some "influential advisers are urging the latter course." Among those it identified as so urging were Jesse Jones and Marriner Eccles. This would explain why

Currie makes no mention of Eccles in regard to his four-hour meeting with the president.[82]

Indeed, when Eccles met with the president on November 10, he touted as one of the most attractive features of his housing bill the fact that it was fiscally responsible. When FDR delivered his message to Congress about the housing legislation at the end of November—a message that Eccles tells us he drafted for him—FDR stressed this point and the fact that the program would reduce unemployment and thereby "contribute toward a balancing of the budget." The United Press story about the president's statement reported that Eccles "emphasized that no additional spending" would be required. Eccles was clearly of the view that the amendments to the FHA were so vital to the recovery that he was willing to use the fact that it could be achieved without sacrificing the goal of fiscal balance as a necessary selling point. It seems he was willing to place the advocacy of spending in abeyance until passage was secured. Such was his confidence in the stimulative impact of housing construction.[83]

It appears, however, that Eccles stood with Morgenthau on fiscal matters from the very beginning of the slump and throughout the remainder of 1937. On September 28, 1937, the same day FDR proclaimed that the 1939 budget would be balanced, the secretary and the chairman issued a joint statement that they were of one mind on the essential need to get the Treasury out of the red. Doing so, they agreed, would eliminate one of the uncertainties that so troubled the business community and would safeguard against the danger of future inflation. On different occasions that fall, both men also defended the extent of the deficits that had been incurred previously as dictated by the need to provide humane conditions for the American citizenry. "Some persons," Morgenthau stated in his speech before the Academy of Political Science, "contend that another great spending program is desirable to ward off the risk of a serious business depression." This may have been a viable solution for 1933, he stated, for at that time "our whole mechanism was demoralized." Today the "driving force of private capital" merely awaits "favorable circumstances."[84]

Marriner Eccles seems not to be among the "some persons" to whom the secretary made reference. It is true that Eccles sent a memo to the president, dated October 31 of that year, which stated the administration had "everything to gain and nothing to lose by acting." The memo, however, which expressed the conviction that the economic downturn was a "direct consequence" of rapid cost and price increases fostered by labor and business interests in the previous winter and spring, contained no demand that the goal of a balanced budget be jettisoned. It was "imperative," it stressed, that government spending be "maintained" and "if possible" be increased in the coming months. Nonetheless, Eccles continued to state publicly throughout the remainder of 1937 that this could be achieved by means other than deficit financing—principally desterilizing Treasury gold accounts. Sidney Hyman informs us that when Eccles went to meet with FDR at Hyde Park two days after his October 31 memo, he gave the president "a coldly objective memorandum" that stressed the recovery would depend largely upon government expenditures and fiscal stimulus. It is strange, however, that when Eccles made reference to this trip to Hyde Park in his memoir, he made no mention of giving FDR such advice. He refers only to his suggestion that "an expansion of residential construction" would be effective "in checking the deflation."

It was at this meeting that Eccles first presented his proposal to amend the Federal Housing Act. It is also worth noting that the other participants that made their way to the president's estate for this meeting were the budget hawks, Henry Morgenthau and Budget Director Daniel Bell. None of the participants at this economic conference would divulge to the press any specifics of what was discussed.[85]

It is important to establish that Eccles was favorably disposed to budget balancing throughout 1937. Is it any wonder that FDR followed the course he did when so many of the spenders, especially the single most forceful individual among them, were now telling him it was time to work within budgetary parameters. To the extent that a restrictive fiscal policy helped bring on the tragic economic plunge the nation took in 1937, it is richly deserving of the inclusive title "The New Deal Recession."

As the New Year commenced, however, the chairman was poised to become the drum major of the deficit spenders once again.

Economists Laid End-to-End

Eccles appears before Congress and is asked to explain his views on what happened and what path will lead to recovery. These are questions that still persist.

On December 14, 1937, Drew Pearson and Robert Allen's widely syndicated "Merry-Go-Round" published a peculiar column. "Inner circle associates" of the Federal Reserve chairman were "getting jittery for fear he would break out with a speech" that the nation would find disturbing. The recession, they wrote, had left Eccles with a "pronounced fascist slant" and while he had yet to "come out for a totalitarian state," he was of the mind that fascism would be preferable to communism. A "big contractor of labor" he was "heatedly anti-union" and a beneficial development of the slump, Eccles was said to believe, was that it "will bring labor to its knees and teach it a lesson." The "sure fire solution" to the nation's economic woes that he was privately advocating, according to Pearson and Allen, was another large-scale spending program by the federal government using sterilized gold.[86]

The day the "Merry-Go-Round" column appeared found Eccles delivering a speech in Chicago to the American Farm Bureau Federation. His focus—a frequent one by this point—was on the "monopolistic elements" in the American economy that had diminished the "competition" that drives capitalism. Either capital, and some labor interests, must "self-govern" themselves or be prepared for "increased regulation in the public interest." He also interjected what was now a year-long refrain: *"Deficit spending is not the answer."* (This was not inconsistent with what Pearson and Allen wrote about Eccles advocating a spending program since they reported he was talking about using desterilized gold.) His remarks, however, hardly seemed to be those of one plotting to impose a totalitarian regime upon the nation. And yet, as so often occurred throughout his life, he was on the verge of a sharp and sudden change of course. It was an alteration that would indeed involve discussions of fascism, sterilized gold, and large-scale spending programs.[87]

As 1937 came to a close, Senator James F. Byrnes of South Carolina, the chairman of the Senate Committee on Unemployment and Relief, announced that he was intending to hold hearings at the beginning of the New Year on the causes and cures of what the administration logistically euphemized as a "recession." On January 3, 1938, the day before the hearings were to begin, Eccles writes in his memoir that Byrnes called him on the phone to inform him that he was to be the first witness. When Eccles requested more time to prepare his testimony, the South Carolinian informed him that if he could not speak extemporaneously on economic conditions he had no business being the chairman of the Fed. Eccles then expressed the concern that he would most certainly step on the toes of some in the Treasury Department and requested that Byrnes announce at the outset of his testimony that he was a recalcitrant witness. When Byrnes agreed to make such a statement, Eccles agreed to testify.[88]

This account of the preliminary details of his appearance before Byrnes's committee is drawn from the pages of *Beckoning Frontiers* and seems somewhat implausible. That Eccles would, with any degree of determination, seek to avoid an appearance before a national forum where he could defend his actions against a chorus of influential people calling for his resignation is unlikely. That he was unprepared to do so was belied by his detailed testimony often accompanied by charts and graphs. That he would be highly sensitive to the feelings of those in the Treasury lends itself to an equal level of incredulity. Rather, the agreement with Senator Byrnes appeared to provide an ideal way for Eccles to proffer his thoughts to the nation while guarding himself against charges of willfully carping at the administration's policies. Had he so desired, it provided an ideal time to make a clear break with the budget balancers.

In regard to the testimony he gave to Congress, Eccles states in his memoir that he "was forced to challenge the budget balancing philosophy Secretary Morgenthau had advanced on November 10 before the Academy of Political Science." He goes on to observe in his memoir that "Morgenthau's attempt to balance the budget, for all its grand intentions, had made matters worse and not better."[89]

Considering Eccles's own advocacy of this position throughout much of the previous year, this would have been a challenging accusation to make before a Congressional hearing. However, as the committee's opening witness on January 4, 1938, the chairman did sound, once again, the efficacy of government spending. There was only one legitimate way in which the budget could be brought into balance—by increasing the national income. "I am as favorable as anyone could be to the objective of a balanced budget," said Eccles, while acknowledging that "over a year ago I was advocating the need of approaching a balanced budget." (Recall that he did far more than suggest an "approaching" of a balanced budget.) Now, however, to continue with a policy of reducing expenditures or increasing taxes, he insisted, would be highly deflationary.

In regard to monetary policy, he restated his "you can't push a string" theory and cautioned that the nation would be "terribly disappointed" if it was expecting such mechanisms to bring recovery. Other than fostering a favorable climate for business investment there was little the Fed could do. It had already established, he pointed out, the lowest interest rates in the country's history. "I only wish" that the Fed "did have an accelerator," said the chairman.

When asked what would function as an effective accelerator, Eccles brought up the subject of gold sterilization:

> [I]f gold were desterilized, and by "desterilized" I mean deposited with the Federal Reserve System, and the Government given credit, and the Government spent those funds, not using the funds to reduce the debt,

> those funds would go out through the country and would become increased deposits in the banks, and they would also increase the excess reserves. . . . That would be the mechanism of it.

As the testimony was proceeding to a different topic, Senator Henry Cabot Lodge drew the subject back to gold sterilization:

> *Senator Lodge:* Do I understand correctly that you favor putting $1,000,000,000 of this sterilized gold into circulation for public works?
>
> *Chairman Eccles.* I did not express that option. I was merely asked as to the mechanics of the operation. I prefer to express no opinion on that. That seems to be a responsibility of others.
>
> *Senator Lodge.* I thought you said that.
>
> *Chairman Eccles.* No, I did not say that.
>
> *Senator Byrnes.* What you stated was what would be the effect of doing it.
>
> *Chairman Eccles.* That is right. I made no recommendation. I am not recommending. I am merely attempting to outline these things.
>
> *Senator Byrnes.* You did say that you believed it would be a great stimulus, and would be an important factor in ending the recession.
>
> *Chairman Eccles.* That is right.

Senator Lodge's ears had not failed in one important respect. Eccles was once again a spender, and the assumption would follow in the press that he was recommending a renewed effort on public-works projects. (This, as we shall see, was precisely what he would suggest to FDR in a memo at the end of that month.) Lauchlin Currie had written a memo in October of 1937 recommending gold desterilization. Sometime in December Eccles made the suggestion to the treasury secretary. Eccles objected at that time, however, to simply agreeing to desterilize gold, as Morgenthau favored. He was fearful that Roosevelt would see this action "as a panacea." It was not enough to simply desterilize gold, Eccles insisted, it must be spent.[90]

To simply add desterilized gold to excess reserves that he already felt were "plentiful" would achieve little. For that reason, he continued to insist that the increase in reserve requirements had nothing to do with the recession. He was also sensitive to the enormous criticism that the undistributed-profits tax received as a major contributor to the recession. Byrnes informed him that in a questionnaire he sent out to business leaders, they overwhelmingly indicted the tax as an inhibiting factor to investment. Eccles observed that the tax was in effect (although not in the form he advocated) long before the recession began and that no evidence existed that it deterred forward buying or general expansion. "I think the most deflationary thing that could be done would be to repeal completely the undistributed profits tax." It would result, he felt, in the instant discontinuance of dividends. Corporations would merely pay debts and keep funds idle. He was in favor of exempting—as Congress did that year—smaller corporations from the tax.[91]

Of course, he was bound to make mention of the role excessive labor costs, and militancy, had played in both inducing a buildup of business inventories and creating a rather stagnant construction sector. This remark incurred the disfavor of the prolabor senator from Pennsylvania, James Davis. "How," he inquired, did Eccles know that "building labor" was asking for an hourly wage that was too high? This afforded the chairman the opportunity to render what may have been his most satisfying response of the day, and one that allowed him to burnish his tarnished free-market bona fides: "Because no one will buy their services. That is the best evidence of that."[92]

The New Deal recession of 1937 was well tailored for the shopworn adage that all the world's economists laid end-to-end couldn't reach a conclusion. The testimony of Eccles and virtually everyone else who appeared before the Byrnes committee on the causes of the 1937 recession placed issues on the table of economic history that are still largely in dispute. Although Lauchlin Currie conceded in a 1988 correspondence with his biographer, Roger Sandilands, that while in retrospect it may have been better not to have raised reserve requirements in 1936–1937, he still refuted the Friedman and Schwartz contention—which has no shortage of contemporary adherents—that it was a factor in the recession. As Sandilands points out in support of Currie's contention, the 2001 study of L. G. Telser found that there was "no decline in bank lending to the private sector until the end of the first quarter of 1938, hence higher reserve requirements could not explain the decline of business." This view is also on display in Christina and David Romer's analysis, which found "no discernible change in the behavior of reserves as a fraction of deposits until December 1937, seventeen months after the first increase. By this time the declines were nearly complete." As Sandilands concedes, however, the reserve increase "could not have helped matters."[93] Indeed, uncertainty on this matter could be seen in an internal Fed report in the spring of 1940, which concluded that "excess reserves are truly 'excess' only in a legal sense." In the real banking world they met the

System's need for liquidity. "The willingness of banks to hold their present portfolios of Government securities at existing yields," the report asserted, "is dependent on the present supply of reserves." Emanuel Goldenweiser, the Fed's chief of research, penned skeptically in the margin: "That I think is doubtful."[94]

Eccles's notion that the souring of the economy was brought on, at least in part, by rapid cost and price increases in the first half of 1937 has found some academic support. Gene Smiley, for example, has cited the rise in labor costs in the manufacturing industries. This was especially the case, he felt, in the automobile and steel sectors. Christina Romer, however, has written that the explanation of a "supply shock" in mid-1937, caused in large part by unionized wage increases and decreased investment, is "easily disproved." A shock of that kind, she argues, would have been accompanied by a general rising of prices, something which did not occur.[95]

As we have seen, while Eccles was publicly critical of some aspects of the undistributed-profits tax, he rejected the somewhat hysterical accusations leveled against it. According to a *Fortune* magazine poll in 1939, American businessmen ranked only the National Labor Relations Act above the undistributed-profits tax as the most onerous of the New Deal's impositions. (Even the AFL called for its revision.) This, despite the fact that in 1938 Congress revised it in a manner Eccles had always favored. It completely excluded from the tax all corporations with net income of $25,000 or less. This eliminated the tax for 88 percent of all corporations while costing the government only a slight reduction in revenue since the top 12 percent of corporations were in possession of 92 percent of net income. It removed as well the sense that the government was damaging Mom-and-Pop enterprises. The following year Congress ended the tax completely. While the tax has its detractors among economic historians today, Mark Leff defends it and writes that when the tax was eliminated completely in 1939, "Congress cut short one of the New Deal's few significant tax innovations."[96]

Eccles accepted the notion that the business sector's expectation that an increase in unionization and labor militancy would lead to higher future production costs, and thereby incentivized an excessive buildup of inventory. This view—a common one today—was put forth by Charles Kindleberger in 1986. The year 1937 was certainly one of labor unrest; the 560 strikes demanding union recognition in 1935 had grown in 1937 to 2,200 and involved in the neighborhood of one million workers. It can justifiably be asked, however, why the intense labor unrest that followed in the immediate wake of the passage of the Wagner Labor Relations Act in mid-1935 did not prompt a commensurate inventory problem by the third quarter of 1936. Allan Meltzer, in reviewing manufactures' seasonally adjusted inventories, challenges the inventory build-up assumption. The increases in inventory in the final quarter of 1936 and first half of 1937, although steep, are actually slight in relation to economic growth. "A more plausible interpretation," he suggests, "is that the very large decline in final sales made inventories seem excessive." The monetary base, he observes, declined at an 11 percent annual rate in the summer of 1937.[97]

It is in the area of monetary action—or the lack thereof—to prevent or counteract the New Deal recession where Eccles receives his strongest criticism. With troubling signs appearing by midyear, there were no open-market purchases made until November. Even that transaction was made more in support of seasonal commerce than to counteract a badly slumping economy. As explored above, while Eccles failed to support any active fiscal measures when he met with FDR in the fall of 1937—he was still pledging allegiance to a balanced budget—he also failed to discuss a single monetary measure. By insisting that interest rates were already low, Eccles and the Board failed to appreciate that with deflationary conditions prevailing the real rate of interest was rising as the nominal rate remained stationary. Remarkably, following the November purchases another four months would pass before the FOMC acted again.[98]

It may be the issue of gold sterilization where Eccles is open to the most appropriate reproach. There seems little doubt that gold inflows played a major role in the rapid economic growth in the first four years of the New Deal. There appears to be a growing acknowledgment, moreover, that sterilization was a vital policy mistake that helped bring on and intensify the recession and its discontinuance a crucial factor in a rapid recovery. While it is true that Eccles initially opposed sterilization when it was first proposed, his opposition had more to do with the Fed maintaining control of monetary policy than a conviction that it was injurious to economic growth.[99]

His failure to sufficiently appreciate this matter is on display in a letter in wrote to the State Department in February 1938. The chairman described the "unprecedented scale" of gold inflows of the previous years as an essentially problematic occurrence that "required the adoption of special measures by the Board and by the Treasury to prevent excess reserves of commercial banks from becoming dangerously enlarged." Any future movements of gold inflows, therefore, "are to be deprecated" as an "undesirable development."[100]

Owing simply to the insufficient level of federal expenditures in 1936–1937, there are some economic historians who question the degree to which fiscal shock contributed to the recession. There can be little doubt, however, that severely reducing the "income-increasing expenditures" of the federal government before the recovery was secured was an exceedingly bad idea.

There remains another aspect of the New Deal recession that is worth keeping in mind. This chapter began by chronicling the exuberant business climate that prevailed in the nation at the close of 1936 and the beginning of 1937. After citing evidence of a "strong revival in equipment accumulation and large increases in income to capital" that occurred in this period, Alexander Field questions the validity of a "capital strike"—a protest by business interest to demonstrate their general lack of confidence—that some theorists have suggested occurred during the New Deal. While assessing the increase in reserve requirements as unwise, Field writes: "But the very fact that central bank decision makers could think about tightening—could even worry that the economy might overheat—is in a sense testimony to the rapid recovery of the economy during Roosevelt's first term."[101]

After Eccles regained his fidelity to fiscal stimulus, he would resume his frequent assertion that if the nation adopted the mindset of wartime it would quickly vanquish the "enemy" of unemployment. Indeed, who would suggest that an undistributed-profits tax, an alteration of reserve ratios, or increased unionization would have stymied economic growth between the years 1941 and 1945?

If Casablanca's Rick and Ilsa will always have Paris, Keynesians will always have World War II.

A Long, Historic Process

Eccles rejoins the spenders and connects economic success to the growing threat of world fascism. The entreaty made to FDR in 1938 by the spenders also describes the investment of the government in the nation as a part of a role it had always played.

Although Eccles had returned to the fold by the beginning of 1938, it was clear that FDR was indeed turning on the old record of fiscal balance. Eccles was aware, however, that the president was not yet entirely in the grasp of Henry Morgenthau and the fiscal conservatives. The sober meeting FDR had that past November with Henderson, Currie, and Lubin, who, as the *New York Post* described it, "minced no words in giving Roosevelt a hard-boiled review of economic conditions," had left an impression. Currie considered the meeting part of what would be a long educational process for the president.

Throughout the winter of 1938 Eccles met informally with the spenders to devise a strategy to distance the diffident president from the budget balancers. They found strong allies among the members of the National Resources Planning Board, which included as its presidentially appointed chairman, FDR's "favorite uncle," Frederick A. Delano. Delano had a long career as a railroad executive and had served for a time on the Fed Board after his appointment by Woodrow Wilson in 1914. In 1936 he left the board of the Richmond Federal Reserve Bank, where he served as chairman. Other members of the Resources Planning Board who sided with Eccles on spending were Henry Dennison (mentioned in chapter 2 as the industrialist being tutored in economics by Kenneth Galbraith) and Beardsley Ruml. Ruml, who was trained as a psychologist, was a former dean of social sciences at the University of Chicago. He was, among other things, the treasurer of Macy's department store and was appointed by Eccles to the Federal Reserve Bank of New York. While not averse to attacking the recession with increased spending, he was a strong believer in planned deficits achieved by way of reduced taxation. As early as October 1937, Ruml broached the idea, to his friend Leon Henderson, of fostering stimulus by foregoing the December installment of income-tax payments. That these men had acquired their economic philosophy through real world business experience, and not from textbooks, was, no doubt, an important element in their friendship with Eccles.[102]

By the beginning of the year Eccles was also meeting each Monday with FDR's son James. James Roosevelt was appointed personal secretary to the president in the fall of 1937 following the death of Louis Howe. James, who became, as one New Dealer observed, "a sort of intelligence agent for FDR," sympathized with Eccles's objectives; their weekly Monday meetings continued with some regularity well into the summer of 1938.[103] On February 1, 1938, Eccles sent a plan to "combat" the recession to the young Roosevelt. "The longer a spending program is delayed," he cautioned, "the more eventually will have to be spent." It was crucial to desterilize gold, he asserted, and to pump the $1.2 billion then in inactive gold accounts into the economy as government expenditures. "The quickest outlet" for the expenditures, he suggested, was through the WPA. It was advisable, said Eccles, to abolish the agency's means test and immediately expand its rolls to four million. He also proposed allowing all private contractors to be offered free WPA labor to a value of 10 percent of a project's total labor costs and to allow FHA's loans up to 90 percent of the appraised cost of new homes up to $16,000. This was a percentage, he suggested, that could be reduced as the economy recovered. It would also be wise, he added, to accelerate the payment of old-age benefits, not scheduled to begin until 1941.[104]

The following week he furnished the president with the argument that Lauchlin Currie had already made. "The Federal Government is making a negligible contribution to community buying power in comparison to 1934–35," he informed FDR. "We appear to be launched upon a severe *depression* [emphasis mine] of considerable duration," he warned, while rejecting the euphemistic "recession" being employed by many in the administration. "Depression" was a preference that Eccles used in public and it was not one that went unnoticed by members of the press.

Eccles was cognizant that the president was becoming increasingly occupied with the threat posed by world fascism. Indeed, the front pages of American newspapers in these months reveal that this was true of the entire nation. "Democracy is sand driven by the wind," Il Duce had derisively proclaimed. The *Anschluss* was mournfully expected within days, and the assumption of power by Getúlio Vargas in Brazil—on the very day Morgenthau delivered his Political Science speech—demonstrated that fascism was making inroads even in the Americas. Eccles utilized this concern as an additional selling point in his spending advocacy. The initiatives of the New Deal represented, in a certain sense, the last best hope of western democracy and if discredited it would strengthen fascist dictatorships. "The greatest threat to democracy today lies in the growing conviction that it cannot work." He urged the president to exhibit strong, decisive leadership, and insisted that "only in that way can the growing threat of Fascism be overcome."[105]

Joining the spenders in persuading FDR to adopt a spending strategy was John Maynard Keynes. The British economist wrote to FDR on February 1 and again on March 25. The thrust of Keynes's suggestions, to increase expenditures while adopting as conciliatory a policy as possible toward business interests, was largely in keeping with Eccles's views. Roosevelt and Keynes, however, never seemed to forge a fruitful relationship. While Keynes had a low estimation of the president's ability to process economic knowledge, FDR, as a loyal Wilsonian, may never have forgiven Keynes for his assault upon Wilson's role in the Paris Peace Conference. He also seemed to find Keynes's personality irritatingly haughty and his economic explanations arcane. "He left behind a rigmarole of figures," he told Frances Perkins about an earlier meeting. "He must be a mathematician rather than a political economist," he concluded. Proof of his dismissive attitude toward Keynes was evidenced by the fact that he assigned Henry Morgenthau to draft a response. While the treasury secretary looked with favor upon Keynes's suggestion of establishing a probusiness tenor, he ignored his plea for increased expenditures.[106]

Despite these determined efforts, the budget balancers in the administration seemed securely in the catbird seat in the early weeks of 1938. The way to deal with the resurgent forces of economic decline, FDR seemed to feel, was to redouble efforts to balance the budget; but as happened time and again throughout the New Deal years, the president abruptly altered his position.

Visiting FDR at Warm Springs at the end of March, Harry Hopkins attempted an all-out effort to convert the president. He installed Leon Henderson and Aubrey Williams at nearby Pine Mountain Valley to supply him with fresh memoranda to present to Roosevelt. Herbert Stein has surmised that the most persuasive of these communications was actually written by Beardsley Ruml, who joined Henderson and Williams in Georgia. The goal of achieving a national income of $88 billion, said Ruml, was necessary to restore the country to its 1929 level. (It was estimated to have fallen to $56 billion.) This necessitated somewhere in the neighborhood of $7 to $10 billion of additional investment or spending by either the public or the private sector to achieve "reasonably full employment." The economy would be fortunate if private spending amounted to a mere $4 billion of that amount. While it might not be a political possibility for the government to fill that gap with $6 billion, it was certainly feasible to achieve an additional $3 billion.

The Macy's executive then made a plea for historical perspective, noting that from the nation's very inception government had played a vital role in stimulating economic activity, and that the government was the driving force behind the nineteenth century's rapid economic growth. This was an argument quite familiar to Eccles and one that he had incorporated into his "Reconstructing Economic Thinking" speech as early as 1933. "In the past," Eccles then stated, "governments have recognized the necessity of spending great sums of money for the purpose of avoiding the terrific loss and waste through unemployment." This was an effort by government that went far beyond the reach of American history and far beyond the scope of mere pecuniary gain: "Many of the churches, palaces, galleries and possibly the pyramids were created to make work for the people and none of these ventures were motivated for profit." It seems very likely that it was a perspective he would have placed before his fellow spenders in their frequent gatherings; it was one that Beardsley Ruml wisely placed before the president at Warm Springs. It was, as Herbert Stein has noted, an argument designed to resonate with FDR:

> It made the whole thing seem very elemental, rather than a complicated financial or economic technicality. It put the President in the picture as *an agent of a long historical process* [emphasis mine] and appealed to his pleasure in the role of prudent manager of the national domain—a role that he himself had said he enjoyed. Also, it was a democratic solution, not surrender to business.[107]

It worked. When Roosevelt returned to Washington from Warm Springs in early April he was determined to spend his way out of the recession. When he revealed his change of mind to his cabinet and congressional leaders, a distraught Henry Morgenthau threatened resignation, although he was dissuaded by the president. Meeting with his staff, the secretary revealed that FDR's spending proposals "just scared me to death."[108]

On April 14 the president disclosed his plan before a joint session of Congress. It consisted of essentially three measures. First, he suggested spending $1.5 billion in increased payments to the WPA, the Farm Security Administration, the National Youth Administration, and the Civilian Conservation Corps. He then offered another $1.5 billion for new public works and housing projects. In addition, he advocated a monetary stimulation by desterilizing $1.4 billion in gold and the lowering of bank reserve requirements.[109]

In his fireside chat to the American people that evening, FDR explained his spending proposals and provided a series of rationales for them. It amounted to nothing less than an unadulterated serving of Marriner Eccles's economic philosophy. He zeroed in—as Eccles had done so often in his memos—on the essential need to focus upon an increase in the national income. "This year you, the people of this country, are making about $12 billion less than last year." There was only one way to reduce the federal debt, said the president, conveying a point the Fed chairman had driven home time and again, and that was by obtaining a "vastly increased citizen income." If the national income could be raised to $80 billion, he continued, the government would be out of the red. "We must start again on a long, steady, upward incline in national income."

In making his proposal, FDR maintained that he was motivated not merely by the "immediate economic needs of the people" but by a profound concern for their "*personal liberties* [emphasis mine]." The alarming disappearance of democracies the world over was precipitated, he stated, not by the fact that the people of those nations disliked democracy, "but because they had grown tired of unemployment and insecurity, [and] of seeing their children hungry." They had wearied, he continued, of seeing their government confused, weak, and leaderless. "Finally, in desperation, they chose to sacrifice liberty in the hope of getting something to eat." The task before the American people now, he insisted, was to demonstrate by united action that the institutions of a democratic society were "equal to the task of protecting the security of the people."

The government initiatives he was placing before them, the president emphasized, were not fundamentally new:

> In the first century of our Republic we were short of capital, short of workers and short of industrial production, but we were rich in free land, free timber and free mineral wealth. The Federal Government rightly assumed the duty of promoting business and relieving depression by giving subsidies of land and other resources. Thus from our earliest days we have had a tradition of substantial government help to our system of private enterprise. But today the government no longer has vast tracts of land to give away and we have discovered that we must spend large sums to conserve our land from further erosion and our forests from further depletion.[110]

Addressing both his "friends" and "enemies," FDR then articulated what Marriner Eccles had long believed to be the New Deal's *raison d'être*: "In these great problems of government I try not to forget," he reflected, "that what really counts at the bottom of all is that men and women willing to work can have a decent job to take care of themselves and their homes and their children adequately."[111]

9

A DROP AT A TIME

John the Baptist

Eccles resumes his role as the oracle of compensatory economics and garners widespread attention—and FDR's gratitude—from a nationally broadcast debate with the fiscally conservative Senator Harry Byrd of Virginia.

Not long after his return to the spenders' fold, Eccles received a letter from Congressman and soon-to-be-senator David Worth Clark. The Idaho Democrat enclosed a letter written to President John Tyler in 1841 by a political advisor and professor of law, Nathaniel Beverly Tucker. Clark informed Eccles that he was struck by the advice Tucker had provided the president, observing that it contained the "germs of your theory of compensatory spending, even at the expense of deficit financing." The nation was then enduring what many consider the longest economic contraction (1837–1843) in its history. The chairman wrote back to the congressman that he had little doubt that such a suggestion was "befogged by politics, superstition and ignorance in those days just as it is now." He then cited for Clark, as he had for FDR, his favorite way of discrediting the fatuous claims of his budget-balancing detractors—Thomas Macaulay's refutation of debt hysteria in *The History of England*.[1]

It was among the countless examples of Eccles fulfilling his function—so Sidney Hyman has fairly assessed him—as "John the Baptist of the new dispensation." He rarely wasted an opportunity to proselytize on behalf of compensatory economics. He managed to slip a copy of a press release on Macaulay's assertions to Edsel Ford after he and his father toured the White House in April 1938. Eccles, who was one of the few "members" of the administration FDR invited to sit around the mahogany table in the Lincoln study to converse with the legendary carmaker, was forced to deny afterward that he and Henry

Ford had engaged in a bit of a verbal confrontation. Their exchange was, Eccles insisted, "a friendly affair."[2]

He rarely visited his home in Utah without scheduling speaking engagements while going and returning; on one occasion he spoke in St. Louis and Cincinnati while heading for Ogden and Chicago and Minneapolis upon his journey back to the Capital. In addition to such public appearances, the commandments of compensatory economics were revealed in letters to government and business leaders, radio addresses, interviews, and articles in newspapers and magazines. In 1937 Eccles began writing a yearly contribution on the subject of the Federal Reserve for the *Encyclopedia Britannica's* "Book of the Year." He managed, of course, to insert in the article his bleak assessment of monetary policy's ability to animate economic activity.

It was his highly competent—and, it appears, patient—staff that drafted most of what he sent out to the public. In crafting a spring 1937 article for *Fortune*, which appeared with the title "Controlling Booms and Depressions," Lauchlin Currie worked diligently with the magazine's editor, Eric Hodgins, only to have Eccles demand significant changes twenty-four hours before the press deadline.[3]

Eccles's views on what economic course the administration should pursue were consistently finding their way into public discourse. In April 1938, with the economy still very much stalled, he demonstrated yet again his absence of faith in mere monetary expansion. That month he informed the House Banking Committee that further desterilization of gold might "be psychologically inflationary," but he summarily dismissed the belief that the "fear of inflation" would foment increased spending. Desterilization would be desirable only in the event that the proceeds it generated were used by the government for "public purposes" and the "buying power" of the American consumer was increased.[4]

Eccles's comment may have been motivated by his sheer frustration with the pace of government spending. The chairman's testimony, moreover, was representative of the pedagogic tone of his exchanges with members of Congress and other government officials. Typical was his May 1939 reaction to a letter from the executive assistant to Commerce Secretary Daniel Roper. Secretary Roper had discovered from a *Wall Street Journal* article that taxes in fiscal 1938 had "absorbed" 22 percent of national income—the "highest percentage in history." With a clear sense of unease, the letter observed that this figure registered a mere 12 percent in the 1920s. Eccles's tutorial-like response noted that it was simply inaccurate to assert that "taxes absorbed" 22 percent. Such phraseology implies that tax collections represented a "withdrawal from national income" with no appreciation that the spending of such funds adds to national income. Additionally, the commerce secretary should be mindful, Eccles instructed, that Social Security taxes were collected not to pay the costs of government but to set aside unemployment insurance and old-age payments. If these costs are excluded from the tax receipts of 1938, its percentage of national income in 1938 would fall under 20 percent. It was also crucial to appreciate, he continued, that as national income increased between 1933 and 1938—excluding Social Security collections—taxes as a percentage of national income declined from 19 to 17 percent. Therefore, the increase in the percentage for 1938 was a "direct result of the fall in national income."[5]

Eccles's role as an explicator of compensatory economics may never have been more vital than in the aftermath of FDR's decision in the spring of 1938 to propose greater spending as an antidote to the recession. In its account of the president's speech to Congress—where he laid out his fiscal proposals—the *New York Times* denounced the proposal as a "rash gamble with the national credit" and cautioned that "observers predicted trouble ahead" for the president.[6] Determined to cause such trouble, and to spearhead opposition to the administration's fiscal policy, was yet another southern Democrat—Harry F. Byrd. Three days before FDR had revealed the details of his proposal to the nation, the junior senator from Virginia was already on the offensive. "Are we to embark again upon a policy," asked Byrd, "that has been proved by actual trial to be not only ineffectual but to create problems that will plague and harass generations of Americans to come?"[7]

Byrd's criticism of the administration intensified following the enactment of Roosevelt's budget proposals by Congress in June and culminated in a scathing speech before the Massachusetts Taxpayers Federation in December 1938. Byrd used the occasion to respond to an address that Eccles had delivered a week earlier before the New York chapter of the American Institute of Banking. In that speech Eccles defended the use of the budget as an instrument for moderating economic extremes. He appeared to have particularly irritated Byrd when he elaborated upon his conviction that reduced public spending had caused the 1937 recession. Eccles asserted in that speech that aggregate taxes in the United States in the previous three years had averaged 17.5 percent of national income. In Britain, he pointed out, it averaged 20 percent, and yet the national income in Britain—a fact he cited repeatedly—was at 110 percent of its 1929 level while the United States was at only 75 percent of its 1929 level. Taxation, he therefore reasoned, "does not necessarily impoverish a nation."[8]

Byrd used Eccles's address as the focal point of his attack. (His remarks were no doubt further animated by the prominently reported news, only days earlier, that the annual interest on the national debt had reached the $1 billion mark.) While acknowledging that he was a Democrat, he informed the Massachusetts Taxpayers Federation that he was a "yes, but, Senator," and not a "yes, yes, Senator." The nation, he stated, was "facing a perilous situation" so long as economic thinkers like Chairman Eccles influenced fiscal policies. The nation "faced disaster," in fact, if it turned away from balanced budgets. "We have tripled the public debt in five years," said Byrd, who calculated that the federal government was then spending $23 thousand every minute of every day and night—"including Sunday." That a public policy continued to be pursued after it had been proven a "tragic failure," he concluded, indicated "to what depths of false reasoning we have sunk in the crackpot legislative ideas of those holding important public positions."[9]

Eccles, not surprisingly, was incensed, not merely by the senator's words, which he would come to label "a blend of vitriol and popular aphorisms," but by the fact that the derisive sentiments made the front pages of many of the nation's leading newspapers. With FDR's blessing, and with the expressed intention of making the front pages himself, Eccles set out "with malice aforethought" to counter Byrd with a publicly released letter to him.[10] The senator, Eccles wrote on December 22, 1938, had "grossly misinterpreted" his views. The case for compensatory economics, he argued, deserved "consideration on its merits" devoid of ad hominem attacks and rancor. Was the senator aware, asked the chairman, that "while he lamented the loss of those time-old virtues of thrift, frugality, self-reliance, and industry" that the last of these could not exist in the face of the widespread practice of the first three? Was the senator aware that "the total of all domestic debts, both public and private, is no greater today than in 1929?" Was the government debt "evil" therefore while private debt was not? Moreover, Eccles insisted, the senator's expressions of concern for "the character of the individual citizen" and "the dignity and the rights of the individual" in no way exceeded his own. "I do not think," he went on, "that empty stomachs build character." In a country of such abundant wealth, however, the rights of its citizens should extend beyond the right to eat and work:

> I think the individual, whether rich or poor, has a right to a decent place to live. I think he has a right to security in old age and to protection

> against temporary unemployment. I think he has a right to adequate medical attention and to equal educational opportunities with the rest of his countrymen. The government expenditures which you condemn have in large part been the means of translating these basic rights into realities.[11]

In *Beckoning Frontiers* Eccles likened Byrd's reply to the erratic spraying of buckshot pellets—an insipid response fashioned "from *Poor Richard's Almanac* and *Bartlett's Quotations*." Byrd's letter dated January 14, 1939, however, was a good deal more focused and substantial and represents quite well the essential argument that Eccles and the spenders needed to address. "What you advocate is a direct repudiation of the Democratic platforms of 1932 and 1936," wrote Byrd, who quoted Secretary Morgenthau's characterization of Keynes as a "prophet without honor in his own country" and a seller of "seductive schemes." Did Eccles not state before Pat Harrison's committee in 1933 that a "gift" to the states of $3 billion would end the Depression? "We have expended that amount over and over again," insisted the senator. How would the chairman explain the fact, he asked, that in 1921 the national income fell from $73 billion to $53 billion as a consequence of a recession and yet managed to rise the following year to $60 billion, despite the fact that the federal government slashed its budget in 1922 from $5 billion to $3 billion? (The answer may have been an effective response by the Fed, which lowered the discount rate and made open-market purchases.) Government spending, Byrd concluded, cannot "be turned off and on like a spigot."[12]

Later in the month of January the National Broadcasting System invited both Byrd and Eccles to participate in a radio debate. Both men jumped at the opportunity to expound to a national audience. They continued the arguments that have been restated by Keynesians and fiscal conservatives on countless occasions since. Byrd took to the airwaves first, on January 16, 1939, and continued his diatribe against the enormous burden that he believed the government debt was placing upon future generations.

Eccles countered with an address a week later in which he patiently asserted that the actual dollar amount of the debt was of little consequence. Nor was it likely to be a burden to "our children and our children's children" as long as the national income increased. At least it would be no more burdensome to them "than was the reduction of nine billions of the war debt during the Twenties." While individuals and corporations could become bankrupt, he assured listeners, no nation as rich with human and material resources as the United States could become impoverished by borrowing from itself. He was emphatic, however, that the goal of a balanced budget was highly desirable when the time was right—after "purchasing power" had been sustained and the economy placed back on track. As for the fear of inflation, Eccles was striking the old chord: "I do not see how it would be possible to have a dangerous general inflation so long as we have a large amount of idle men and unused resources." Well before inflation could rear its ugly head, an increased "volume of business activity" would restore national income and allow the budget to be balanced.

Before Eccles could leave the studio that evening he received a call from Steve Early. "Marriner, I want you to know how much the boss appreciated your speech," said the press secretary. "Here you are, with much less reason to stand up for him than many others; yet you were the only one who did it." The following morning, FDR himself phoned to congratulate and thank him. "You made the problem so simple," the president praised him, "that even I was able to understand it."[13]

While Eccles claimed that he found the "uproar in the press" over his Harry Byrd debates "highly gratifying," he concluded that "hardly any editorial writers agreed with me." As he was well aware, however, it was not merely editorial writers who looked with disfavor upon deficit financing. Expectedly the conservative Republicans, led by Congressman Bruce Barton of New York, capitalized upon both the "astounding debt" and Eccles's justification of its existence to affirm that the New Deal made the "mistake of overestimating the patience and the dumbness of the middle class." While conceding that they still liked the president "personally," Barton asserted that those in the middle class "have made the sad discovery that it is their earnings which are being appropriated to pay for the extravagance of the New Deal."[14]

An indication that some of the conceptual aspects of compensatory economics were challenging ones to convey was reflected in an internal memo Eccles received from his advisor, Elliot Thurston. Following his American Banking Institute address in January, Thurston suggested that it might not be wise for the chairman to state publicly that the debt of the United States need never be repaid. (Of course, the federal government had run a debt since 1835, which, in fact, was the only year in U.S. history when there was no debt.) "I think you should show," Thurston further advised, "that you are aware that there are many loafers on relief."[15]

That the American people were dubious about the matter of deficits and debt was reflected in public-opinion polls. The month that Eccles and Byrd squared off on fiscal issues, George Gallup's relatively new—and, therefore, more questionably reliable—American Institute of Public Opinion, released figures that demonstrated that 61 percent of Americans answered "too much" when asked about their views on federal-government spending. Gallup specifically cited Marriner Eccles when he observed that these results came in spite of spirited defenses by some New Deal members. It was clear that many of the poll respondents were influenced by the economic slump of 1937–1938. That the recession struck at a time when the budget was, in fact, in cash surplus was an argument that Eccles rarely failed to make. And indeed by the end of April, Gallup's poll indicated the more nuanced sense of a citizenry that was "ideologically conservative" and "operationally progressive." When asked if they favored cutting spending on farm programs and old-age benefits, very large majorities responded no; the more nebulous category of "ordinary operating expenses" garnered large support for cutting.[16]

Eccles failed, of course, to significantly engender widespread acceptance for countercyclical measures in the 1930s. What is striking, however, is the degree to which he correctly understood the portents of economic developments. The scope of the nation's indebtedness was simply not a vital concern in the dynamic and growing economic prosperity that prevailed in the course of 1936 and the first quarter of 1937. (Indeed, historically it has never been an important issue when such economic conditions prevail.) The economic collapse that followed, however, cost the Democrats seven seats in the Senate and seventy in the House of Representatives, while enhancing the influence of conservative southerners. Had the administration stayed the course and maintained its high level of 1936 expenditures, the debt at the time of the 1938 elections would have been considerably larger, unemployment significantly lower, and the Democrats might possibly have added to their Congressional totals.

Despite the political losses in the 1938 elections, FDR held onto a sufficient degree of influence to continue his newfound advocacy of fiscal stimulus. In his 1939 State of the Union address, FDR spoke in the unmistakable vernacular of compensatory economics. "Many people have the idea that as a nation we are overburdened with debt and are spending more than we can afford," he informed the nation. "That is not so," he insisted, pointing out that the "entire debt of the national economic system, public and private together, is no larger today than it was in 1929, and the interest thereon is far less than it was in 1929." It did not seem "logical" that at a time the nation still sought an increase in production and consumption, it should consider "a drastic curtailment of its own investments." The nation had only lately discovered that "it is unsafe to make abrupt reductions at any time in our net expenditure program." Moreover, it was the "common sense action of resuming government activities last spring" that "reversed a recession and started a new rising tide of prosperity" that they were all presently enjoying. To further the continuation of wise "types of government *investment*"—not expenditures—the president then, with the value of "permanent long-range planning" firmly in mind, suggested the formation of an "agency" that would report on the "urgency" of such matters. (As explored below, Eccles would become a member of the Fiscal and Monetary Advisory Board that would emerge as a result.)

This 1939 State of the Union speech began and ended with reference to foreign affairs—"the enemies of our faith and humanity" that surrounded the nation and threatened to engulf the world in war. It was the duty of the United States to now reject the "false economy" of fiscal conservatives and demonstrate that it was not merely a "regimented" nation under the imposition of dictatorship that could offer a "solution of this problem of idle men and idle capital," but that the world's leading democracy could do so by wisely utilizing the "instrumentalities, like Federal investment, which are immediately available to us." As he so regularly did, FDR then connected his remarks to a venerable episode of past American greatness by concluding his address with a direct quotation of Lincoln's famous explication of the Emancipation in his 1862 State of the Union: "This generation will 'nobly save or meanly lose the last best hope of earth. . . . The way is plain, peaceful, generous, just—a way which if followed the world will forever applaud and God must forever bless.'"[17]

As FDR spoke about the state of the nation, private construction contracts in January showed a steep increase over the previous year, as did department store and automobile sales. The adjusted index of industrial production which had fallen to 79 in March 1938 had risen that month to 101; it would register 125 by November. From Eccles's perspective in early 1939, such progress was simply not sufficient. Throughout 1939 he would propose policies that he felt would accelerate the pace of recovery. He appeared to agree with Steve Early's assessment that the chairman was not sufficiently accompanied by enough other New Dealers in his defense of the president. He sent a letter to FDR a week following the State of the Union address. "It is of greatest importance . . . that others holding important positions in the government, particularly in the Cabinet," he insisted, "should participate in a program of presenting your case to the country." Eccles would come to maintain that such support never materialized in 1939 and that some men—he did not name names—who had urged a compensatory course upon the president had left him out to swing in the political wind. The irony was not lost upon him that "as a child of the Republican Party" he had become the Democratic president's chief defender.

Nothing More than Pawn Shops

Eccles makes yet another attempt to convince FDR and Congress that the regulation of the banking system should be centralized in the Federal Reserve and that it must apply supervisory authority as a countercyclical tool. His effort fails, but leads to the Uniform Agreement on Bank Supervisory Procedures.

Back in December of 1936, Carter Glass paid an urgent call upon the director of the Reconstruction Finance Corporation. After discovering that Jesse Jones had a short time before he left Washington for a trip to New York City, Glass left behind a "strictly confidential" missive for the influential Texas millionaire. He wished to caution Jones about the "desire of that adventurer Eccles to extend the jurisdiction of Federal Reserve Board over every other Federal agency." Glass reported that the head of the Federal Deposit Insurance Corporation, Leo T. Crowley, informed him that in a conversation with Eccles the Fed chairman "specifically" stated his conviction that all bank regulation should be consolidated under the aegis of the Federal Reserve. "In short," Glass continued, "the fellow is power-mad and wants to absorb all other Government agencies." The senator was planning to meet with the president soon and was confident that with Jones's backing he "could prevail with him against the wretched vagaries that Eccles proposes to propound to him." To encourage Jones's cooperation, Glass not so subtlety reminded him that the upcoming session of Congress would be taking up the matter of "a continuation of the R.F.C. to make loans for another year."[18]

As it happens, Eccles had a meeting with FDR the day before in which he hoped to discuss, yet again, the issue of "bank unification." To his dismay, however, the meeting that day was consumed with the issue of gold sterilization. The chairman expected that the president would respond to a memo that Eccles had left with him the previous month. If the policy that Eccles proposed in that memo seemed excessive to some observers of the American banking system, it was significantly modified from views he had earlier expressed. In his testimony on the Banking Act before the House Banking and Currency Committee in March of 1935, Eccles remarked: "It is my personal belief that State banking legislation ought to be abolished, but as a practical matter it is impossible to consider at the present time."[19]

The rationale that Eccles provided for the consolidation of banking regulation in 1935 was continually restated by him throughout his entire stewardship of the Federal Reserve. His first serious attempt to achieve this occurred when he left the above-mentioned memo for FDR in November of 1936, following a White House meeting where he verbally made his case to an attentive but noncommittal FDR. The thirty thousand banks that existed in the nation prior to the crash of 1929 had been reduced to some fifteen thousand at the beginning of 1936.

These institutions, Eccles believed, were subject to a labyrinth of regulatory oversight that was often disjointed, duplicative, and confusing. The Fed, the Treasury's comptroller of the currency, the Federal Deposit Insurance Corporation, and the Reconstruction Finance Corporation, all had field examiners descending upon the banks. (The RFC had the power to examine corporations' finances, as well as the right to control salaries and management decisions in the companies in which it had purchased preferred stock.) In addition, it was common for the Securities and Exchange Commission, the Department of Agriculture, and the Federal Housing Administration to require reports from banks; all of this coexisted with forty-eight state regulators.

A Federal Reserve study of the hybrid regulatory system that had developed in the United States reported on the "inability to agree upon uniform examining standards and the resulting application of different standards in the classification of assets; in the appraisal of real estate loans; in the treatment of depreciation in bonds and the values at which they should be carried; in the treatment of valuation reserves; and in the determination of losses." These agencies, moreover, used different standards to determine the overall soundness of banks. Even Leo T. Crowley, the chairman of the FDIC and a harsh critic of Eccles's designs on bank oversight, admitted to the House Committee on Banking and Currency that the "lack of uniformity" in the regulatory system produced significant confusion.[20]

It was particularly galling to Eccles that Crowley's FDIC regulated 7,500 banks that received deposit insurance but were not members of the Federal Reserve System. (The Banking Act of 1933 that required FDIC recipients to join the Fed had been rescinded. It remains so to this day.) Many of these institutions were unable to meet the capital requirements of member banks and were organized and led by officers who had little or no experience or competency. They amounted, he informed the president, to "nothing more than pawn shops." It was these "miscalled banks," he asserted, "which caused the greatest losses and misery among their depositors and brought a large share of discredit down upon the heads of bankers."[21]

Most importantly, the Fed simply could not manage the nation's currency—a crucial role in an economy off the gold standard—when half the banks were subject to the Fed's mechanisms while the other half were not. This, he emphasized to the president, was the essential aspect of bank reform. It was all fine and well to create efficiencies and eliminate redundancies, but the centralization of bank regulation under the guidance of the Fed would engender a regulatory framework that would operate in harmony with the principles of compensatory economics. The present regulatory system operated in a highly procyclical manner. The Comptroller's office "has repeatedly pursued a policy of restraint," the memo explained, "when correct central bank policy called for an easing of restraints, and conversely, has eased restraints when correct central bank policy called for a tightening of what would be acceptable in the credit structure of banks."[22]

It was a rather novel notion that bank oversight should concern itself, not merely with the general health and solvency of individual institutions, but with an expanded fiduciary responsibility that considered the overall health of the economy and the economic conditions in which its decisions on credit would play out. Eccles, however, had been making the case for such a regulatory scheme since the advent of the Depression. In March of 1936 the policy attained some degree of credibility when the notable economist, and fellow Treasury colleague in 1934, Jacob Viner endorsed the idea in the pages of the *American Economic Review*. This was a helpful development of which Eccles was well aware. At the same time the Treasury and the Fed are encouraging banks to loan, Viner observed, examiners, who had been blamed in the not-too-distant past for laxity, were "reacting in a perfectly natural manner" by becoming stricter and more exacting and pressuring banks to "liquidate loans and investments which the banks, if left to their own devices, would be happy to keep in their own portfolios." The directive often given to banks that they should "purge" themselves of "assets classed as 'doubtful' and 'slow'" was complicated, Viner wrote, by the fact that no two examiners could agree on what actually constituted such troublesome assets.[23]

Viner also took note of the curious irony that the American banking crisis that unfolded earlier in the decade occurred in spite of abundant oversight. "There is no other American industrial or commercial activity—outside of the prison workshops," he concluded, "which is so rigorously regulated and so closely supervised." Although he averred that the banking catastrophe in the United States would have been made worse with no regulation, he drew an interesting comparison with the Canadian and English banking structure which met the economic decline with few of the problems that beset the American system. "An English commercial bank is subject to no restriction which is not part of the body of commercial law to which all must comply." The problem in the United States, then, in his view, was a qualitative one. The "cure for this perverse effect of bank examination," he asserted, was a "unified control of bank supervision" and a "coordination of examination policy with credit control policy." Of course, to achieve this, he insisted, a nation must cultivate a highly trained cadre of bank examiners. The reason that an effort to correct these serious flaws has not yet been undertaken can be found, Viner believed, in the words of Marriner Eccles, whom he proceeded to quote: "'we cannot go faster than the people of the country are willing to let us go.'"[24]

Seven months later, however, Eccles was giving the president the assurance that the country was now ready to accept the significant banking reforms he was proposing. Written for FDR a week following the enormous political victory that both he and the Democratic Party received at the polls, and at the conclusion of the economically ebullient year of 1936, the memo stated that these banking revisions "will go down in history as among the outstanding achievements of the Administration." The opportunity was squandered—or so Eccles was convinced—when the president chose rather to use his political capital in 1937 in pursuit of a misbegotten attempt to reorganize the judiciary. His infamous "Court Packing Scheme" had engendered a climate in Congress, Eccles reflected, where any suggestion of "reorganization" was besmirched by accusations of aggrandizement of power and "dictatorship."[25]

In his memoir, however, Eccles conceded that the political setbacks of 1937—the court-packing attempt was followed by Hugo Black's controversial confirmation to the Court and then the recession—were really not at the heart of FDR's reluctance to pursue banking reform; it was rather a factor of the Brandeisian perspective he had upon American banking.

> The dual banking system in which part of the banks belonged to the Federal Reserve System and part to the state banking system alone was held in nostalgic affection by Roosevelt. In his view, the state nonmember banks represented the small, democratically controlled institution, responsive to local needs, with officers who had the welfare of the home folks at heart. For some curious reason the Federal Reserve, on the other hand, represented for him the banking giants, and in a way, he saw the Banking Act of 1935 as a means of curbing the giants. To unify the whole system, however, implied two things in Roosevelt's mind. First, it

> implied the end of the state banking system. And second, by forcing the small banks into the Reserve System, it implied a condition favorable to their destruction by the giants.[26]

It was a perspective that Eccles felt was at odds with reality. Only a quarter of the System's membership could be categorized as large banks, the rest were comprised of state and local banks that could be fairly classified as small. The chairman had abandoned any suggestion that state regulation be prohibited by the legislation. Under his proposal states could still examine banks—to what extent he was unclear—and still control the existence or extent of branch banking. (Of course, the law would require any bank receiving FDIC benefits to join the Fed.) His goal was to centralize the regulatory, supervisory, and investment policies of the federal government to achieve a coordinated and more effective monetary policy. Here Eccles failed to account for the fact that FDR, like so many other Americans, likely thought it counterintuitive to sanction more liberalized and riskier lending policies, when he largely perceived that such practices brought the financial roof crashing down upon the nation's head in the first place.

In his November 1936 banking memo on this matter Eccles also assured the president that "the program outlined would be welcomed enthusiastically by the most competent banking and business opinion throughout the nation." Despite his use of the qualifying adjective "competent," Eccles seemed surprised at the vituperative reaction of most banking institutions. This became apparent to him from the frosty reception he received when he set out to sell the idea to gatherings of bankers in various parts of the nation. He later explained the reaction against unification in rather Machiavellian terms: "based on the old principle of divide and conquer." A disjointed and uncoordinated supervisory structure militated against truly effective oversight. Eccles lamented that many bankers believed that this was the next best thing to no regulation whatsoever. ("Divided responsibility," commented the legendary German banker Ludwig Bamberger, "is no responsibility.") Thus, he believed, they shortsightedly rejected reform that in the long term would have generated improved economic growth and stability. (Indeed, some today believe that the Dodd-Frank Act contains a level of complexity—it stretches on for nearly nine hundred pages while the Glass-Steagall Act was all of thirty-seven—welcomed by the largest institutions as a means, as *The Economist* phrases it, "to game the system by exploiting loopholes.")[27]

The economic doldrums in which the nation found itself in 1938 served to inspire Eccles to revive the issue of bank unification as a costless form of private-sector business stimulation. This effort came despite a well-respected Brookings Institute study of the previous August that failed to support consolidation in the Federal Reserve. While the Brookings report favored eliminating the Comptroller's office, it stated that "it would be out of the question" to confer the FDIC's examination functions upon the Fed. It did urge "a close and harmonious relationship between the Board of Governors and the FDIC," and even suggested that the FDIC move into the Fed's newly constructed headquarters on Constitution Avenue. Moreover, it recommended that the Federal Reserve Bulletin become a joint publication, with the FDIC allocated space for its statistical data and research reports. Most significantly, the Brookings study recommended that cooperation between the agencies would be encouraged if the FDIC and the Fed were given a veto power over certain decisions of the other. A series of internal Fed memos critically analyzed the Brookings report, and as a consequence added to the chairman's litany of reasons why his reforms were necessary. From Eccles's perspective, placing the Comptroller's function in the FDIC would actually make matters worse. As the Fed memo explained, the FDIC "having its insurance at stake, as the Comptroller's office has never had, will apply standards still more severe." Nor, it was stated, did the Brookings study fully explore the way the present system "encourages the development of a mental attitude and tendency to ascribe the onus of failure or an unpopular action to the other agency."[28]

In 1937 James M. Landis offered a perspective that Eccles found helpfully persuasive. Soon to be the youngest-ever dean of Harvard Law School and the second head of the SEC, a position he was in the process of leaving, Landis was a leading crafter of New Deal legislation. A *Fortune* article titled "The Legend of Landis" was demonstrative of the high regard that many in public life had for the former student of Felix Frankfurter.

Landis's book, *The Administrative Process*, was based upon a series of talks he delivered—the Storrs Lectures—at Yale University in 1937. While his analysis might be viewed more unfavorably today as an overgeneralization supported by his brief and limited stint at the helm of the SEC, the work emerged at a time when the recession helped fuel accusations that Congress had delegated away far too much of its responsibility to government technocrats. The work was intended to provide the ideological support for New Deal administration and to assert that the true abusers of the governmental process were the uninformed court magistrates who struck down processes "developed by men bred to the facts" of modernity's mutational transitions.

There were, however, a few generalized principles that could be safely established. These included a strong emphasis on the benefit of centralizing bureaucratic responsibility, so that accusatory fingers could not be pointed in varied directions when any regulated entity went awry. It also asserted that doing so would enhance the attractiveness of government service for those highly effective individuals that the public sector badly needed. It was tailor made for Eccles's sensibilities; it is not surprising, therefore, that the following passage from the book found its way into a Fed report on bank unification.

> [A] finger can be publicly pointed at a particular man or men who are charged with the solution of a particular question. This localization of responsibility gives, in turn, to those positions a real attraction for men whose sole urge for public service is the opportunity that it affords for the satisfaction of achievement.[29]

This additional selling point—of pinpointing accountability—was made a part of the ongoing debate over unification that Eccles carried into the spring of 1938.

In the first week of April, FDR forwarded to Eccles a fretful letter he received from a twenty-five-year veteran of the New York Legislature, Nelson Cheney. The Republican state senator plaintively inquired why bank regulators cannot "be reasonable and let the small banks help our people." These institutions, attempting to loan to "the average or needy citizens," he wrote, were seeing their efforts thrown "out the window" by examiners who demanded unreasonable proof of financial stability. The president, as he had on other occasions, asked Eccles to draft a suggested reply. This, the chairman managed to do in swift fashion, returning to the White House on April 6 a highly sympathetic letter to Cheney. Attached to the letter was yet another memo in which he laid out the case for centralized, countercyclical bank supervision.[30]

That same week, Eccles would later claim in his memoir, FDR requested that he "draft paragraphs" to be inserted into a presidential message he was preparing to send to Congress, with proposals for extricating the nation from the recession. Eccles writes that these "paragraphs" appeared in the message sent to the Hill on April 14 (he inaccurately identifies the message as being sent on the thirteenth) "with but slight change." In fact, FDR made only the most tangential and noncommittal of references to the entire issue in his speech, stating merely that as part of "better administration" he had the "hope that Federal Banking supervision can be better coordinated."[31]

Although Eccles must have found this parenthetic allusion highly disappointing, he was successful in convincing the president to summon the heads of all the federal regulatory agencies to gather in May, with the directive to "co-ordinate and liberalize their examination policies." He directed them to arrive at a nonlegislative solution to these disagreements. Eccles later described what transpired in their early meetings as an "interfamily row" where nothing was agreed upon. It didn't help matters—at least from Eccles's view—that Henry Morgenthau was designated the chairman of this interdepartmental committee. He recalled in his memoir that FDR's sense of what was likely to emerge from it all was reflected in a comment he once made about the limits of executive authority: "Just because I'm President and order a thing done," he lamented, "doesn't mean it will be done." But, of course, the president had considerable influence with a handful of men who occupied positions at his discretion, and there is no evidence that he made any effort beyond broad semantics to alter their unanimity of opposition to Eccles's regulatory designs.[32]

While the "guerilla warfare"—as Eccles described it—within the administration continued against him, Eccles made what he termed the "distasteful" decision to reach out to the political opposition. In *Beckoning Frontiers* he framed his 1938 public exchange with Republican senator Arthur H. Vandenberg on the issue of bank unification as motivated by a blind determination to counter the nation's recessionary conditions. Of course, considerations of economic growth aside, by communicating to the possible Republican nominee in the next presidential contest that the administration's regulators were stifling financial transactions, he was lashing out at his rivals in the government and, it would appear, at the recalcitrant FDR himself. He later conceded that his fraternizing with the conservative Michigan senator "must have troubled the President."[33]

On June 16, 1938, Vandenberg stated on the Senate floor that he had just received an "amazingly interesting letter" from the chairman. The letter, he explained, was a response to an inquiry he had sent to Eccles concerning "certain fundamental questions" about the operation of the federal banking system. A longtime sufferer of Father Charles Coughlin's rants against privilege, Eccles suspected that the senator wished to have an official rejoinder to the Michigan-based radio-priest's broadcasts from the Shrine of the Little Flower which often challenged both the Fed's legality and efficacy. Considering the extensive public record that the chairman had already left in his wake on both issues, this seemed hardly necessary. Indeed, Eccles used the opportunity to furnish seemingly unsolicited advice on "why bank credit is not flowing adequately into productive business channels." It is entirely possible, of course, that this was the unstated purpose of both men, with the original request serving as a useful pretext, or "coverage," for Eccles to expound upon his favorite topic.[34]

"In my judgment," he wrote to Vandenberg, "banks are under too severe restrictions in their lending and investing operations." This is not particularly injurious to larger concerns, he argued, but rather to "sound local businesses" in need of working or fixed capital on terms that were too lengthy to satisfy the policies of state examiners and the regulations of the Comptroller's office. There is also, he pointed out, a commensurate difficulty placed before banks in terms of the investment securities that were deemed permissible. Local industries that were incapable of bearing the costs of registering with major rating firms to make public offerings, were unable to sell otherwise sound securities to banks. Thus, such companies—well known as creditworthy—were denied the ability to raise capital in this fashion.

Eccles also took aim at the fair value–oriented accounting practices then utilized by examiners. This practice, which would become better known as mark-to-market accounting, required banks to report the current or fair value of their assets rather than what many believed were more realistic historical prices that had been sustained over time. Bankers, he informed the senator, "cannot justly be held responsible" for a policy that confused "true worth with current depressed market values." He had long argued that such an accounting regimen, which compelled institutions to unwillingly sell off assets to avoid falling below solvency ratios, acted as a procyclical mechanism and assisted in furthering systemic risk in the field of banking. For all of these reasons, the chairman lamented that creation of "ample credit at reasonable rates" for American businesses was being "balked."[35]

"The controversy in print," Eccles later reflected, "ran for six days before it was ended." In fact, he kept clippings from scores of major American newspapers that carried headlines informing readers of a "ROW OVER BANKING POLICY" and a "SHOWDOWN SET ON RULES FOR BANK CONTROL." Not surprisingly, Eccles garnered words of praise from some of the New Deal's most consistent critics. "Now and then," wrote Glenn Frank, the conservative journalist and former University of Wisconsin president, "Mr. Eccles speaks with a refreshing realism out of the mist of alibi-manufacturing and face-saving pronouncements to which the New Deal has increasingly resorted." Capturing media attention just days before what was scheduled to be the concluding meeting of the interdepartmental banking committee was a masterful way for Eccles to highlight his positions in the timeliest of fashions.[36] It brought to the fore, however, yet another public conflict between the chairman and the treasury secretary. The front page of the *Los Angeles Times* carried adjacent photos of both men with the heading "Morgenthau and Eccles Clash over Bank Plan." Clearly annoyed that Eccles had furnished sustenance to the political opposition, Morgenthau informed the press that he and the comptroller were, as the AP phrased it, "guided solely by the interests of the depositors"; thus suggesting the perhaps politically unwise position that he was uninterested in adopting methods that would help to engender an economic upturn. Two days later all of the bank regulators convened to hammer out to what extent oversight would be liberalized. "The iron of compromise," reported the July issue of *Bankers' Magazine* on the committee's last gathering, "has smoothed out all difference of opinion between the Federal Reserve headed by Chairman Eccles and other government agencies on the matter of bank examination." While voicing slightly less confidence that a consensus had been amiably arrived at in the June 21 meeting, the *New York Times* reported that for "the first time in history" bank examiners had achieved an agreement that brought a good deal of uniformity to governmental supervision in the field of banking.[37]

To a significant degree, the accepted revisions—the "Uniform Agreement on Bank Supervisory Procedures"—were a near reflection of all that Eccles had been clamoring for. Beginning July 1 banks in the System could purchase securities of small local businesses that were of sound value without requiring they be readily marketable or listed on large exchanges. An eligible bond need merely be "salable under ordinary circumstances with reasonable promptness at a fair market value." In examination reports the terms "slow" and "doubtful" would be permanently replaced with numbered designations, with emphasis placed now on what the Fed termed "intrinsic value rather than upon liquidity or quick maturity."

Most crucially, the new policy acknowledged Eccles's insistence that the soundness of the banking system was tied to the overall health of the economy and should not be "measured by the precarious yardstick of current market quotations which often reflect speculative and not true appraisals of intrinsic worth." Portfolios would be valued at the average market price established in the course of the eighteen months prior to the examination date. Moreover, if any depreciation were required only 50 percent of such net depreciation would be applied in assessing a bank's capital viability. As a consequence, it was expected that the banking world would now purchase the securities of business and industrial concerns with "true worth" rather than speculation as an uppermost concern.[38]

It must surely have tempted those who championed the uniform agreement to ascribe the stunning economic output of 1939–1941, at least in part, to a more fluid credit channel: a corrective to a supply-side obstruction. As noted earlier, the 10 percent annual economic growth that the nation experienced from the early fall of 1938 through the year 1940 was unprecedented in the peacetime history of the United States. This take-off, however, was well established before the supervision agreement was activated and, as Christina Romer and others have pointed out, was proceeding well prior to the armament build-up that would send economic growth into the stratosphere. Studies have indicated that the pre–New Deal Recession years (1933 through mid-1936) witnessed economic growth despite the decline of loans as a percentage of earning assets. Banks eschewed the high costs of capital accumulation in these years and "scrambled" to reduce risk in their portfolios by "not replacing maturing loans."[39] While commercial and industrial loans seemed to have increased significantly by mid-1936, they fell precipitously a year later and thereafter; as Frank Steindl suggests, "the lending activity of banks was not sufficiently aggressive to promote recovery." As he further observes, "the growth of the economy was essentially independent of the lending activity of banks."[40]

Nonetheless, the abandonment of mark-to-market accounting would remain in place for nearly seven decades. Although a major alteration in the financial affairs of the nation, Eccles remained dissatisfied. The essential battle—for the consolidation of bank regulation in the Fed and the adoption of a policy of countercyclical oversight—had yet to be won. Eccles wasted little time in reinvigorating his advocacy of this position. Shortly after the 1938 election, FDR engaged in *what appeared to be* yet another of his inexplicable and pointless orchestrations by announcing, as noted earlier, that he had formed a committee to study how, as the Associated Press described it, "federal spending can be regulated to smooth out the peaks and valleys of public purchasing power." To study the effects of the administration's efforts at "pump priming," he assigned four men who had hitherto made their views on the matter emphatically and relentlessly clear: Henry Morgenthau and Budget Director Daniel Bell were to be paired with Frederic Delano and Marriner Eccles.[41]

A week later the AP reported that the Fed chairman was spending the weekend with the president at Warm Springs. Eccles refused to amplify the purpose of his visit to the mountain retreat, but the press speculated that the conversation was as likely to be about general economic conditions as it was any particular matter of banking. But, of course, Eccles considered them one and the same; indeed, this was the very point he was making to FDR in Georgia. He arrived with the inevitable memo in hand that essentially restated his case for the beneficent aspects of countercyclical regulation: it would further the cause of recovery and diminish the odds of any future catastrophic collapse. In Warm Springs, however, he illustrated for the president the intensity of his conviction on the issue by including in the memo his intention to leave "the Administration" and not accept reappointment in 1940 if unification were not pursued. This he later reflected was the "take-it-or-leave-it aspect of my memorandum."[42]

Eccles proposed, however, that the administration could remain publicly uncommitted to the proposal initially and allow sympathetic congressional leaders to champion the cause. Moreover, he informed the president that he would attempt to persuade the Federal Reserve Board to officially endorse the concept of supervisory concentration in its Annual Report of 1938. This strategy would allow hearings to be held and legislation pursued free of any taint either of them might bring to the endeavor. The president could then insert words of encouragement for the new Congress in January about the need for them to work out a legislative solution. While FDR consented to this idea, it was short-circuited when the *Wall Street Journal*, a week after the Warm Springs meeting, published what Eccles felt was a "planted" story identifying him as the moving force in the administration's advocacy of banking regulation revision. Thus was born, to his consternation, yet another "Eccles bill."

Only the night before, the chairman had addressed an assemblage of bankers and delivered his well-known caution about premature fiscal conservatism and the fact that the federal budget "will balance itself almost automatically if well timed federal expenditures increase national income." Despite this recitation of the basic tenets of compensatory economics, the press reported that he was "warmly received" by the conservative gathering. He spoke not a word that evening about regulatory consolidation and the preference of bankers to keep banking agencies "weak and divided." He was for a brief time merely the savior who had delivered them from the tortures of mark-to-market accounting. It was a honeymoon that would end with the *Wall Street Journal* article the following morning.[43]

The Federal Reserve's annual report for 1938 was released to the public on January 7, 1939. For the most part it elaborated on the points that Eccles and others had long asserted. It was true that the "crazy quilt of conflicting powers and jurisdictions" and of "overlapping authorities" had been diminished somewhat by the voluntary agreements reached the previous summer by the three principal federal supervisory agencies.

But these correctives depended upon the unlikely chance that future regulators would preserve the agreements and "points of view" so unofficially established. That the banking system continued to operate under a confusion of jurisdictions was graphically illustrated in a line chart inserted into the report that revealed a spider web of connections between banking entities and the agencies that oversaw the various activities in which they engaged. State member banks, for example, were chartered by their state government but licensed by the Treasury Department. While the Board of Governors determined the maximum permissible interest rate on time deposits for member banks, the FDIC set this rate for nonmember insured banks. Similarly, the prohibition on any bank with deposit insurance paying any interest on demand deposits (this would have constituted all but fifteen hundred of the nation's fifteen thousand banks) was complicated by the fact that determining what constituted the payment of interest was not always easily apparent. (Both of these restrictions were a result of "Regulation Q" which emerged from the Banking Act of 1933. Interest rate ceilings were phased out by March 1986; the prohibition on interest-paying demand deposits was repealed by the 2009 Dodd-Frank Act.) A bank might, for example, provide the equivalent of an interest payment on some accounts by taking on certain expenses and exchange charges as compensation for the maintenance of balances. This determination of when interest was in fact being paid, and the actual enforcement of the regulation, was yet another function where responsibility was diffused.[44]

Nor had the 1938 agreement hampered the practice of changing charters to avoid regulation. Throughout the year national banks converted to state status to benefit from their lower capital requirements demanded of branch banks. Others adopted state charters to escape federal restrictions on loans to officers. In addition, the efficacy of the Clayton Antitrust Act—to lessen concentrated banking power—was compromised by the fact that nonmember banks were not subject to its prohibitions on interlocking directorates. It should be reiterated that only 6,000 of the nation's 15,000 banks were in the System. Of that number only 1,000 were state chartered. While those banks in the System comprised 70 percent of total deposits, it still left a significant 30 percent outside its reach.

Eccles seems to suggest in his memoir that the Board endorsed the idea of countercyclical supervision. The annual report called upon Congress to consider how examination policy could be "so directed as to contribute to the protection of the general economy from the effects of undue expansion or contraction of credit." It further suggested that the degree to which examiners hasten and intensify downward spirals or accelerant inflationary conditions ought to be contemplated. While the report seemed to be sympathetic toward these ideas, it stopped short of a ringing endorsement for using supervision as a countercyclical tool. It posed, rather, a series of questions that Congress would be prudent to explore. But the report was mindful of its complexities.

> The bank examiner in the field deals with local situations. He attempts to appraise assets in the light of such information as is available to him and values must be determined in many cases by local conditions. These conditions may relate to the position of the particular bank being examined or of the particular community. It is a problem of great complexity to find means by which this local procedure, when multiplied by the thousands of banks throughout the country, can be brought into conformity with national policies.[45]

Eccles was heartened by Senator Robert Wagner's assumption of the chairmanship of the Senate Banking and Currency Committee in the new Congress. Wagner passed a resolution in mid-June, publically supported by FDR, which called for full-scale hearings to explore the whole concept. Now, however, the effort was inextricably tied to Eccles. This prompted his old enemies to emerge to engage him in public conflict once again. In the summer of 1939, Carter Glass wrote to Leo Crowley of the FDIC and requested a meeting with him "about Eccles's proposed reorganization of the banking system of the United States." The chairman, he wrote to Crowley, "does not know a damned thing about it and has been acting altogether, I am told, upon the whimsical misinformation supplied him by Currie, who has been taken into the circle of White House intriguers."[46]

While it is not difficult to believe that Currie exerted some influence with Eccles on the matter of regulation, it seems unlikely that with the chairman's extensive experience and expertise in banking that he was reliant upon the economist's tutorials on the subject. Glass was right about one thing, however: Currie had indeed become one of the "inside intriguers." FDR informed Eccles that he intended to "steal" Currie from him. In July of 1939, the Canadian economist went to work for the White House, thus becoming the first in his field to officially hold a position as economic advisor to the president. (It is Currie's White House role that would be constantly referenced when he became embroiled in the famous Communist-espionage accusations of Elizabeth Bentley.)[47]

Although Senator Wagner fought to acquire sufficient funds to support his inquiry, the condemnation of Eccles's proposals grew in vitriolic furor. In the fall of 1939, the National Association of Supervisors of State Banks unanimously endorsed a report that typified the criticism that was emerging. At their annual meeting held in Salt Lake City, the organization's president cited the report and cautioned that the creation of a single regulatory agency would effectively place a "dictatorship over our banking and monetary system." At the same gathering, an official of the American Institute of Banking sounded a more dire warning when he stated that such a proposal would mean "the destruction of everything typically American."[48]

Wagner's committee commenced its investigation in January of 1940. He had only managed to acquire a paltry $25,000 to sustain his efforts. It all became rather moot, however, when the Nazis overwhelmed Western Europe that spring. With Hitler posing for the cameras in front of the Eiffel Tower and London enduring terror from the air, banking reform seemed very unimportant indeed.[49]

How the adoption of a centralized overseer of the banking system would have altered financial history must, of course, remain merely speculative. In the 2011 update of their classic work *Manias, Panics, and Crashes*, Charles Kindleberger and Robert Aliber, after detailing the innovative mechanisms that banks devised to circumvent established capital requirements and other restrictions, suggest that the crisis of 2008 may have been, contrary to the premise of the Dodd-Frank legislation drafted to address it, less a factor of demand-side greed than supply-side overabundance of credit. "The banks," they write, "were one of the channels for the credit flows. The supply of credit would have been satisfied in some other way if the banks had been more cautious in buying mortgages and mortgage-related securities." They note earlier, however, that "a strong case can be made for stricter regulation and supervision of banks to forestall lending in euphoric periods that may end in financial crisis." They then immediately comment on the fragmented nature of bank examination in the United States and ramifications this could have in terms of "responsibility"—or the lack thereof.[50]

There is little doubt that Marriner Eccles believed that bank regulation could prove effective in establishing a sound financial sector, and just as little doubt that over time a divided regulatory structure would diminish that efficacy. One imagines that were he with us today he might assert that the remarkable financial stability that has distinguished the first three decades following the New Deal, and the turbulence that marked the years 2007 and 2008, has validated this conviction.

Americanized Keynesianism

In his typical penchant for strange bedfellows, FDR places Morgenthau and Eccles on a committee to improve economic life in the United States. What they propose, the Works Financing Bill, is a noble, if futile, attempt to bring the nation back to full employment.

It might be safely said that the president's appointment in November 1938 of a Fiscal and Monetary Committee to provide budgetary advice might truly have been an exercise in futility were it not for the expertise and stabilizing presence of Lauchlin Currie. Currie may possibly have been the only individual in the New Deal capable of bridging both the policy and personal divide between the chairman of the Fed and the secretary of the treasury.

Currie was aware that he needed to accommodate the political realities of 1939 as well as the budgetary priorities of Eccles and Morgenthau. It was certainly true that FDR had to some degree committed to a policy of fiscal stimulus. Not long after his 1939 State of the Union address, he acted upon Eccles's advice and—employing some of the chairman's more favored expressions—sent out a circular letter to his cabinet urging them to voice public support for "compensatory economics." Indeed, utilizing his assessment of stimulative impact, Currie calculated that the federal net contribution ($3.6 billion) came close to doubling in 1939. It was, in Currie's view at least, nearly the maximum that the American public and the newly elected Congress would allow. But it was insufficient.[51]

In November 1938 Currie and the Federal Reserve staff prepared a detailed memorandum for the Fiscal and Monetary Committee stating that even when full employment was achieved, it would necessitate both a continual level of public investment and improved methods to enhance private purchasing power, if it were to be sustained. Some ideas in this area were obvious. Revenue sources needed to become distinctly more progressive and, in the process, of course, achieve a meaningful redistribution of income. Scheduled increases in the payroll tax needed to be delayed—and at least part of the contribution to the retirement fund paid from general revenues—while scheduled payouts could be moved up. The expenditure side of things called for a bit more imaginative thinking. Throughout 1938 Currie and Eccles put forth various ideas designed to provide significant public investment with a minimal degree of federal spending. One such idea, for example, called for local governments to float bonds for public-works projects while the federal government agreed to pay off the interest. (This policy was achieved ten years later in 1948 when the federal government agreed to meet the interest and amortization charges on municipal-bond issues for the construction of public housing.) To win Morgenthau's and the public's approbation, however, it would be ideal if a fiscal measure had no budgetary cost whatsoever—or at least so appear.

Out of such necessity was born the Works Financing Bill, or, as it was officially introduced: "*The Self-liquidating Projects Act of 1939*." Its genesis was Currie's 1938 plan to have the federal government establish an entity that would call itself the Federal Railroad Equipment Corporation. The corporation would be authorized to issue debentures, enter into contracts for the construction of railroad cars and equipment, and allow the financially strapped railroads to lease them. Eccles received the idea with some enthusiasm and began an effort to sell the plan to various officials in the railroad industry.

Why some in the railroads looked with disfavor on the idea is a subject for speculation. Their public position was that they simply did not need the kind of assistance that the rail corporation offered. Reports that many lines were in desperate shape for new locomotives, railcars, and repair equipment left both Eccles and Currie incredulous. Was it possible, they reasoned, that some in the industry feared that such participation by government was a step down the slippery slope to state ownership and control?[52]

Undaunted by this reaction, Eccles and Currie put before the fiscal and monetary committee a vastly larger proposal in which the rail corporation was a small part. The basis of the proposal was the conviction that the increased level of savings in the American economy seemed a long-lasting phenomenon that could subject the nation to chronic deflationary gaps, unless a mechanism for "a continuing outlet" were created to "canalize" this saving into investment.[53] The idea they proposed was in most respects not entirely new or startling. By 1939 a number of state governments were distinguishing their budgetary outlays for capital—usually for public works and projects that would yield future revenue—from their operating expenditures; thus, theoretically at least, removing from the rancorous political process important investments in the long-term betterment of the commonweal. FDR's acceptance of the concept, writes economic historian William Barber, "appeared to signal that the administration had come to terms with an Americanized version of Keynesian aggregate demand management."[54]

When drafted, the legislation that became known as the "Works Financing Bill" and, more often than not, the "Lend-Spend Bill" by its detractors, failed to offer such lofty reasoning. Of course, it would hardly have been prudent for its authors to suggest that they were attempting to disjoin spending from public scrutiny. The stated purpose of the bill, rather, was to "provide a sound method of financing which, without burdening the national taxing power, will make it possible to increase employment through a self-liquidating improvement program." Under the direction of the president, the Reconstruction Finance Corporation (RFC) was authorized to issue bonds the proceeds from which would be funneled to various federal agencies who were in turn responsible for executing loans for a wide array of projects. While the law limited the maturity on RFC notes to five years, the Works Financing Bill would allow the agency to issue obligations for as long as forty years. The RFC could not have outstanding loans for this purpose in excess of $2.5 billion. After funds that were to be transferred to the program from previous appropriations were added, the program would command nearly $3 billion. The legislation stipulated that the maximum interest rate that could be charged to any project loan could not exceed the yield of the longest-term government security outstanding. The idea was to provide funds to borrowers at "the approximate cost to the Government of obtaining such funds." The bill, it was stated, was "designed to tap the annual stream of savings" and would therefore be utilizing "funds that otherwise would remain unused." Not only would the bill not increase the public debt, it would enhance the movement toward "balance between Federal expenditures and revenue" by lessening spending on relief and works projects such as the WPA. Best of all, touted its supporters, the program would yield "an economic return sufficient to pay the interest and principal." They were projects that were "self-liquidating."[55]

The funds were to be issued in the following ways:

> *$350 million to the Public Works Administration* to issue loans to state, local, and other public bodies for nonfederal projects. In the past the PWA made grants of 45 percent and loans of 55 percent. It was believed, as Senator Barkley testified, that "we have gotten far enough along to abandon the grant feature of these projects."
>
> *$500 million to the Rural Electrification Administration.* The enormous popularity of the REA of 1936 caused demands for new lines to far exceed the funds appropriated for electrification. Only one farm in five

was electrified by 1939. The program's aim was to bring electric line to 1,250,000 farm families and thereby spur the sales of electric appliances and increase the market for private utilities. The Department of Labor estimated that the program would add at least half a million direct and secondary jobs. It would require 9,200,000 poles, 1,150,000 meters, 1,000,000 transformers, and 400,000,000 pounds of copper, aluminum, and steel. It would result in the sale of 950,000 irons, 550,000 washing machines, 300,000 refrigerators, 270,000 toasters, 200,000 water pumps, and 200,000 vacuum cleaners.

$600 million to the Department of Agriculture for "rural security projects." The loans were to go to farm tenants, sharecroppers, and farm laborers. This was intended to further the program run by the Farm Security Program pursuant to the Bankhead-Jones Farm Act. There were twenty applications for every one loan. The program had issued loans to nearly 7,000 tenant families, who could not obtain credit from any other source, for the purchase of viable land assessed and approved by a local committee and government appraisers. The long-term amortized payments were often less than farmers had paid previously in rent. Remarkably, only one loan had defaulted in two years. The program would also issue small loans to 750,000 farm families for fencing, small water projects, and repair work. It was estimated that the program would increase the net worth of farm families $84 million by the following year. In addition to increasing the purchase of farm equipment and other durable goods, it would prevent farm families from drifting into cities for relief.

$500 million to the Reconstruction Finance Corporation to prepare plans and designs for the construction, rebuilding, and repair of railroad equipment, and to enter into contracts for railroads to lease, with or without the option to buy.

$100 million to the Export-Import Bank for financing of foreign trade. The bank was an extremely popular entity. In February of that year Congress overwhelmingly extended its life. Headed by Jesse Jones, it had been created by executive order in 1934. Its initial purpose was to finance and insure loans to credit risky foreign interests—essentially the Soviet Union—who wished to purchase from U.S. companies. By 1939 it

was backing loans to Latin America and was a central component of the Good Neighbor Policy. The bank already had an excellent track record having turned a profit of $1.7 million in fiscal 1939.

$750 million to the Public Roads Administration for highways, parkways, underpasses, overpasses, and tunnels. This funding would have gone a long way toward creating the national highway system built in the 1950s. In the testimony of the public roads administrator, Thomas McDonald, it is also clear that many of the contemplated highway projects were to be located "right in the heart of the cities." To install expressways through "diseased" areas of the inner cities he described as a "revolutionary idea." It presaged what many believe were the disastrous urban-renewal projects that began in the 1950s. The benefits, however, to interstate commerce were obvious. Its self-liquidating potential would come from eventual land sales and toll roads.[56]

The mechanism established for administering the law made it easy for its critics to make the accusation that it all amounted to mere budgetary sleight of hand. While the RFC issued the notes, the proceeds from those instruments were to be deposited with the Treasury. It was the Department of the Treasury that would then disburse the funds to the various agencies that were entrusted with running the programs. Any revenues derived from these projects were to be deposited in an account with the Treasury that the RFC would draw upon to pay back the interest and principal on their maturing bonds. While the law stated that no agency should issue a loan absent a "reasonable assurance" that it would be repaid, it also provided that the Treasury would pay the RFC the amount of all unrecoverable loans.[57]

The four days of Senate hearings before the Committee on Banking and Currency began in mid-July 1939 with Kentucky Senator Alben W. Barkley. It is commonplace for members of Congress to identify themselves as the "author" of a particular piece of legislation. It is rare, of course, that they actually engage in drafting the law. In Barkley's case this became readily apparent, and it did not bode well for the enactment of the bill. The senator was essentially uncertain of what time frame the law was to operate within. Under questioning from the committee's Republicans, he responded that the president was contemplating a seven-year period (which would have rendered the act virtually useless as a recovery measure in Eccles's view) and then concluded that he was uncertain about the period of duration. When asked by Robert Taft if the federal government was guaranteeing the loans, he responded that "in some respects" it was, before conceding that it was in all respects.[58]

The hearing did produce one of the rare occurrences of harmony between Morgenthau and Eccles. The secretary may have been the only budget hawk in Washington satisfied that the off-budget expenditures of the Lend-Spend Bill would operate, as he testified, "within the requirements of sound fiscal policy." The federal government, declared Morgenthau, must "act in these times" as a "catalytic agent."[59]

The central figure testifying in support of the Works Financing Bill was, of course, Marriner Eccles. He came before the committee, in his words, not as the Fed chairman, but as a member of the Fiscal and Monetary Advisory Board. He began with an extensive list of all the outlets for investment that no longer existed or were greatly curtailed. As always, he could hardly resist an attack on the structure of the social-security program. In England only 60 percent of their old-age pension revenue came from regressive payroll taxes, and in Sweden such sources amounted to a mere 22 percent. By December, he noted, the payroll tax would be responsible for sucking over $1.7 billion out of consumption. To restore the economy to full employment would require in excess of $18 billion. There must be either a "very considerable increase" in national consumption or new outlets for investment. It was his preference that both be achieved by adopting the Works Financing Bill and continuing a high level of expenditures on public-works projects.

In terms of the specifics of the legislation, Eccles's role at the hearings was to defend the need for the railroad equipment provisions. He attempted to allay fears of creeping socialism by emphasizing that, contrary to wide belief, the RFC was mandated to enter into contracts for railroad-related production only in cases where they would be satisfying an expressed need of a specific rail company. The federal government, he insisted, had no desire to enter the merchandising business. Moreover, he was quite familiar with railroad men who made it very clear that there was a desperate need for this kind of assistance. It was especially helpful, he said, to have the option of converting a lease into a purchase. Interestingly, many in the administration first became aware of this situation when the American Railroad Car Institute released figures at the beginning of 1938—prior to Currie's formulation of this kind of solution—that indicated that a large percentage of rail cars were over twenty-five years of age.

As was frequently the case, it was Robert Taft who offered the most trenchant observations. In light of the administration's efforts at superhighway construction, would there not be a shift in shipping preferences that would make it unwise for railroads to commit themselves to greater investments of this kind? As Alexander Field has observed, this was a development that only began to be appreciated in the 1930s. Trucking, it was generally believed, acted as an adjunct to rail shipping, by transferring cargo from the rail depots. This was beginning to change rapidly. In fact, rail mileage reached its apex in the United States in 1916, the same year that the first federal highway bill was enacted. The rail industry was only gradually waking up to the fact, Field writes, that the trucking industry "would eventually eat much of its lunch." Eccles, however, appeared to be prepared for the question, and pointed out that one of the kinds of contracts the RFC was prepared to engage was for the conversion of freight cars to accommodate passenger service. Those lines that wish to remain competitive, he cautioned, needed to act aggressively in this regard.[60]

Although the Works Financing Bill made it out of committee, there was only a remote chance that it would become law. The criticism of the proposed legislation intensified when Jesse Jones gave it a less-than-enthusiastic endorsement. The *Los Angeles Times* typified the attitude of much of the press when it wrote that had a private concern been operating under such procedures, the SEC "would put a stop order" on its activities. On August 1, 1939, in what the Associated Press called a "debacle" for the administration, the House of Representatives refused by a vote of 193 to 168 to take the issue up for debate. The Senate had already significantly pared back the bill to only $1.9 billion. A total of forty-seven House Democrats voted with nearly every Republican.[61]

The leader of the Republican opposition to the bill, Congressman Wolcott of Michigan, claimed a victory for constitutional rule and the Congress's power to control the nation's purse strings. At a press conference later that day, FDR was asked if the whole thing was not simply a way to circumvent the $45 billion debt ceiling. Was it "fair," he responded, to treat loans as expenditures? If it were fair to do so, he insisted, banks would be in perilous condition. FDR recollected that when the RFC was created it was attacked by many of the same critics, who asserted that the corporation would never get back the funds it was lending and investing in American banks and corporations. They were wrong, he said, because Jesse Jones was getting all of that money back. Had the bill been adopted, a discouraged president asserted, it would have had a significant benefit almost immediately. Certainly—and this may have been uppermost in his mind—the nation would have been in a far more favorable position to produce and transport armaments in the war years had the investments in railroads, highways, and electrical output that the bill called for been implemented.[62]

In August of 1939, shortly following the legislative demise of the Works Financing Bill, the Associated Press's Thomas E. Flanagan penned what must surely rank as one of the more fatuous contributions to the entire New Deal era—an inanity so stark in its dimensions that it elucidates, as few other comments could, the barriers that Eccles faced in his struggle to "reconstruct economic thinking." Flanagan informed his readers that the War Department had speeded expansion of air forces and awarded $85 million in contracts for the production of more than a thousand airplanes. The Army Ordinance Department meanwhile was on the verge of contractual agreements for the manufacture of over $100 million in munitions while $16 million was already being spent to assist other manufacturers in building up their plants and equipment to satisfy future orders for armaments. Moreover, the economy was poised to engage in such production on a much grander scale, with some "10,000 industrial concerns" already "given tentative wartime assignments." Flanagan reported that "business analysts" were expecting all of this to "boost" private industry. "Financial experts" on Wall Street were also heartened, he continued, by the defeat of the administration's Works Financing Bill and the appropriation of additional funds for the U.S. Housing Authority. "Most agreed," Flanagan concluded, without the slightest recognition of irony, "this meant a definite shift away from government spending of borrowed money as an experiment in stimulating business recovery."[63]

The Poison of Popular Politics

Through periods of despondency in the two years that followed the reemergence of economic growth in mid-1938, Eccles continued to push policies from a national health program to the elimination of excise taxes.

The Associated Press thought it "one of the most paradoxical situations in recent years." Testifying before a special Senate committee on silver legislation in March 1939, the chairman of the Federal Reserve stunned listeners by urging Congress to proceed immediately to balance the federal budget. First, he acknowledged the widely held belief that government deficits were "holding back private investment" and destroying "the moral fiber of our people," all the while "piling up a burden of debt that our children and grandchildren" will be forced to pay. Then he suggested that since "the regular establishments of government" absorbed a mere 10 percent of federal spending, lawmakers could proceed to the meaty parts of the budget and slash funds for CCC camps, and follow up by cutting veterans' benefits, relief payments, public-works projects, farm benefit payments, and by all means national defense. Since a majority of both the American people and Congress shared the conviction that this would restore "business confidence," then, reflected Eccles, the dictates of democracy required it be done. While the consequences would be "disastrous," the country, he pronounced from his prepared statement, "is entitled to a clear-cut and prompt determination of policy on this vital issue." Some members of the committee interpreted Eccles's comments as a way to put his congressional critics "on the spot." The reaction to his statement, he said, "took the form of a long sputter." So it has always been, he later reflected, when the challenge to cut expenditures moves from an abstraction to a realistic expectation. *The Nation* relished the hemming and hawing that Eccles's remarks drew from the "economy block" led by Senators Byrd and Harrison, who, the magazine observed, were loath to commit "themselves to anything so politically dangerous as specific proposals."[64]

After years of nearly continual struggle to achieve full employment through fiscal measures—with his plans blighted time and again with the same shibboleths—Eccles seemed, for this particular afternoon at least, to yield to a thinly disguised sense of cynicism. That this frustration should emerge in yet another hearing on monetary expansion seems fitting. The vitriol directed at him by the inflationists in Congress rivaled that of the fiscal conservatives. Both camps, interestingly, questioned why the head of the nation's central bank concerned himself so infrequently with the issues of monetary policy. Shortly following Eccles's display of testimonial artifice, Congressman James Oliver of Maine, who felt the refusal to flood the nation's money base with silver was tantamount to the "crime of 1873," demanded to know why the chairman felt content to "sit tight in this hour of the country's need and not demand constructive monetary action." Speaking on the floor of the House of Representatives, Oliver voiced the opinion that Eccles's nonfeasance was "criminal" and, in fact, amounted to "high treason."[65]

Anyone seeking to confirm that the chairman placed monetary affairs on the back burner will discover a degree of affirmation in his memoir. After the discussion of the reserve-ratio debate and its role in the onset of the 1937 recession, the affairs of the Fed and the mechanics of central banking are not discussed by him again until the nation was well into the Second World War. (And, true to form, Eccles relates how he locked horns with Morgenthau in 1943 over which agency should oversee the sale of war bonds.)[66] Inaction by the Federal Open Market Committee under Eccles's leadership was one of the principal reasons that Christina and David Romer have given him low marks as an effective Fed chairman. The error of instituting increased reserve requirements in 1936 was compounded, the Romers believe, by tepid monetary actions both prior to and after the adoption of that policy. And yet, other than the questionable wisdom of the hike in the reserve ratio—and it should be remembered he favored canceling the final increase—Eccles was certainly not leading the System in the wrong direction. It will be recalled, for example, that the Fed made sales in the spring of 1932 and raised the discount rate from 2 percent to 3.5 percent. While open-market purchases were slow in coming in the New Deal recession, they were made. In this regard Eccles should be credited for opposing the adoption of open-market sales favored by the FOMC in the summer of 1939—to "maintain orderly market conditions"—and for increasing purchases significantly in the still unemployment-plagued conditions that prevailed in the early fall of that year. Taken all in all, in the area of monetary affairs, Eccles might be as much sinned against as sinning.[67]

There can be slight doubt that "easy money" conditions prevailed for nearly the entirety of Eccles's tenure at the Fed in the 1930s. This had much more to do, of course, with the extraordinary increase in gold imports—the United States would house nearly 80 percent of the world's total by 1940—than any action promulgated by the Fed. Nonetheless, this supports Eccles's emphatic assertion that the true failing of the New Deal was a self-imposed fiscal sterility and not central banking malfeasance. Awash in a sea of monetary plenty, it made perfect sense in his view to maintain a constant assault on the real enemy: the disastrous pursuit of fiscal prudence. By 1939 the economy was making a significant recovery from the recession. Gross private domestic investment in 1939 was some 25 percent greater than the previous year. (It had increased by eight-fold between 1932 and 1937.) In August the Federal Reserve Board's index of industrial production had advanced 12 percent from May. Rather early in 1939, real GNP surpassed its 1937 high point. The unemployment rate, which had fallen to 9.2 percent in 1937 and had risen to 12.5 percent the following year, was now at 11.3.[68]

That the administration continued to tolerate such a high level of unemployment—a condition that could have been easily alleviated—he still found, as he had in 1933, "incomprehensible." The federal deficit for fiscal 1939 (concluding on June 30) stood at $3.2 billion. When contrasted with the $13.3 billion shortfall of 1919, this was indeed insubstantial. The 1939 deficit coincided, however, with a year of significant economic growth. This was in stark contrast to the substantially reduced deficit of fiscal 1938—which trimmed the $2.5 billion deficit of 1937 to a mere $486 million—which was accompanied by one of the sharpest economic declines in U.S. history.[69]

For Eccles these facts amounted to unimpeachable confirmation of the compensatory course of action that the spenders had long advocated. He had warned FDR in 1935 that "the safest policy was the boldest policy" and that half-way measures would simply increase the national debt and fail to fully restore economic health. To a significant degree this is what had materialized by 1939. A vigorous fiscal attack that could have been successfully sold to the American public in 1935 was now made considerably more difficult, if not impossible, by the accumulated debt, which, while entirely manageable, furnished fuel for the nation's many "calamity howlers."[70]

Writing to a friend in Utah that year, a discouraged Marriner Eccles excoriated the seventy-sixth Congress. It was a Congress that "business wanted and got," he said. Looking ahead to 1940, he entertained the thought that FDR would not be a candidate for reelection. Conservatives would seek to "reestablish in the White House an amiable stuffed shirt to hasten the day when our economic system falls into another perhaps worse collapse." They would soon have everything their way, he wrote. "In fact, they already have their way in producing, in effect, government paralysis." He dejectedly went on: "There is no sense, to my way of thinking, in continuing the New Deal after 1940 because that would only prolong the agony."[71] Still captivated by such sentiments, Eccles drafted a memo for the president in June 1939 forecasting that "there is little if any prospect for a marked recovery during the next two years."[72]

That Eccles felt rather isolated in 1939 can be explained in part by the fact that groups that had previously urged an all-out effort to revive the economy had gradually fallen by the wayside. As Herb Stein has written, the AFL and CIO were actively attempting to consolidate the many gains that the New Deal legislation had afforded them. They were less concerned with the unemployed than they were with the wages and working conditions of their membership. Gone from the national political stage by 1939, moreover, were the likes of Huey Long, Father Charles Coughlin, and Dr. Townsend who had forced the administration's hand and compelled progressive action. In addition, the intellectual forces on the left had drawn their gaze from domestic events to the international scene. This attention would become intensified with the actual outbreak of hostilities in September of that year.[73]

Nevertheless, despite moments of despondency, Eccles's memos calling for action continued. He had previously cited the fact that "the field of *public health*" was increasingly "coming to the fore and has not yet been exploited." He proposed to the president that grants-in-aid be utilized to establish a "National Health Program" that could be instituted in 1939. In addition to benefiting the "physical health of the nation," it would furnish outlays that would be "of major benefit to its economic health." In this matter Eccles had been encouraged by FDR's public letter to the American Medical Association in 1937 in which he stated that when he delivered his famous second inaugural address that focused upon the deprivations suffered by "one-third of the nation," he might have properly included the inability to "secure adequate medical and hospital care."[74]

The following July, the president called upon his previously created Interdepartmental Committee to Coordinate Health and Welfare Activities to sponsor a major conference of all involved parties to discuss the contours of a national health program. The committee, headed by Josephine Roache, who had replaced Eccles when he left the Treasury Department in 1934, presided over a three-day National Health Conference held in Washington. The committee was concerned that a health-care proposal be inclusive of the needs of the general public and not merely structured for the benefit of the indigent. The central idea discussed in the committee was a form of nonprofit, comprehensive system of "compulsory" insurance which, as scholar Daniel Hirshfield describes it, "would give considerable administrative power and freedom to the medical profession." The program would be financed from payroll deductions—of which Eccles may have disapproved—and would be created and run by the states with the federal government subsidizing the cost and establishing basic guidelines.[75] Roache telegrammed the president, who was away on a fishing trip, informing him that there was "amazing public support" for a "National Health Program."[76]

With Eccles's encouragement, and the apparent success of the Washington conference, it certainly looked like some meaningful legislation was on the horizon. A Gallup poll in January 1939 that indicated large public support for a program that would cover some 32 million Americans with a $3 monthly premium seemed to verify Roache's enthusiasm. In February 1939, Senator Robert Wagner introduced into Congress a National Health Bill. It was forcefully attacked by the American Medical Association on the grounds that it did "not specifically limit its benefits to those unable to pay for adequate medical care." The bill "insidiously promotes," one AMA witness asserted, "the development of a complete system of tax-supported government medical care, thus undermining and debasing present standards of medical services." Another witness said enacting the proposal would amount to accepting "complete totalitarianism."

Even before the onslaught of such criticisms, for reasons that may never be entirely clear, FDR subtly reduced his support for the idea. It is possible that the assumption of Walter George as the chairman of the powerful Senate Finance Committee convinced FDR he would be tilting at windmills. The president had actively campaigned against the conservative Georgian's reelection. The inability to maneuver something so "new" past the resentful George may have been the reason Roosevelt suggested that health care be held in abeyance until a presidential election year. In January 1940, the president proposed a widely scaled-back expenditure of $10 million for the construction of badly needed hospitals in neglected areas. While Eccles had long supported hospital construction, he must have been greatly disappointed over the meager amount of funds proposed in the program. The legislation, derisively deemed the "Forty Little Hospitals Bill," failed to make it out of the House of Representatives.[77]

The development and demise of the health care program in 1938 and 1939 lends credence to Alan Brinkley's assertion that the late 1930s witnessed the New Deal's "broad retreat from many of the commitments that had once defined their politics." It certainly adds resonance to the very last sentence of his work, *The End of Reform*, where he observes that the "New Deal's retreat from reform in the waning years is among the sources of American liberalism's present travails."[78]

Eccles continued, however, to offer suggestion after suggestion on ways to stimulate greater job creation. He put forward a plan to a Senate banking subcommittee in June 1939 that the Fed be given the authority to create a new corporation to make loans available to small businesses underserved by commercial banks. The financing could come—a suggestion that must have annoyed Henry Morgenthau—by tapping into the Treasury's languishing fund that it had accumulated from the gold content reduction.[79] A substantial boost to purchasing power could still be achieved, he believed, through a redistribution of the national income. In a November 1939 speech delivered in St. Louis to commemorate the twenty-fifth anniversary of that city's Federal Reserve bank, Eccles advocated major alterations in the tax structure. Regressive excise taxes on such things as automobiles, theater tickets, and gasoline, should be greatly reduced or eliminated entirely, he said. As would be expected, he made mention of the need to reduce payroll taxes and sounded the matter of sheer equity as preparations were made for the possibility that the country might be dragged into the European conflict which began that summer.

> In my opinion, it would be unfair and unsound economically to pass increased armaments cost on to those of the low-income groups who would profit the least out of foreign or domestic expenditures for armaments, who are the least able to bear the costs and whose increased purchasing power is essential to our economic welfare. . . . Accordingly additional taxation should be levied . . . upon those income groups now relatively undertaxed, among whom the greatest proportion of savings that are unable to find profitable outlet today are now accumulating.[80]

Specifically, Eccles called for increased taxation upon corporations and individuals earning between $5,000 and $50,000.[81] It seems hardly surprising that this speaking foray by the chairman set him at odds yet again with the Treasury Department. "Eccles Speech Reopens Feud" was the typical headline used in the Associated Press accounts published across the country. Observing that this was the "first serious break between the agencies" in nearly two months, the AP story reported that the Treasury stated emphatically that Eccles did not speak for the president, the department, or, for that matter, any known group in Congress. The robust economic growth in the past year, the statement read, and the anticipation of one of the best Christmas-sale seasons in memory might obviate any need to increase taxes upon any segment of Americans.[82]

A week later, however, FDR, behind the wheel of his touring car in Warm Springs, stopped to chat with reporters. Unfortunately, he informed them, "disturbed world conditions" would necessitate a record peacetime national defense program for the upcoming fiscal 1940 budget. Since he was considering slashing some $2 billion from that budget, it might require a "special defense tax." This might be preferable to borrowing the necessary funds since doing so would "put a burden on future generations." Nonetheless, he added, the American people would need to decide because it would have to be one thing or the other. The ostensibly impromptu news conference made its way to the front page of the *New York Times*.[83]

Slightly over a month later, in early January 1940, as the lull in the war in Europe continued—what the press had come to term "the phony war"—Eccles attended a luncheon meeting with the president. The economy had only recently regained the ground it had lost in the New Deal recession. With what the chairman once called the "disease of unemployment" still unacceptably high, he had come to argue, yet again, the case for continued appropriations for public works. In that meeting Eccles learned of, and strongly objected to, an administration proposal to cut relief spending by $500 million. FDR explained that this was necessitated by his request for a 50 percent increase in the military budget from $1 billion to $1.5 billion. When Eccles clamored for the administration to do both, the president patiently explained that that would be a political impossibility. "There is no pressure in the country for such [public works and relief] expenditures," FDR informed him. It would be all he could do, he said, to get the Congress to pass the military budget. He hoped to further ease unemployment with the expenditure of the military appropriation.[84]

By early May 1940, Roosevelt's military budget had yet to emerge from either the House or Senate committees. Within forty-eight hours of the Nazi penetration of the Maginot Line later that month, however, Congress passed the $1.5 billion military budget and further authorized an additional $2 billion in the event of military necessity. The comforting illusion that the war would replicate the stalemate conditions of 1916–1918, and thereby allow the United States to observe from the sidelines, was suddenly shattered. Eccles would lament that the Depression had been fought "a drop at a time" when what was needed was a "tidal wave." The tidal wave largely preceded the Pearl Harbor attack. In his January 1941 budget message, with the world at war and the country already spending 14 percent of the federal budget on defense expenditures, FDR requested a $25 billion defense appropriation, a level of spending that amounted to 62 percent of the budget. His January 1942 budget called for $53 billion for "a nation at war in a world at war." It would consume a full 90 percent of federal spending. Thus, in the first six months of the Second World War, the federal government would assume more debt than it had in the previous entirety of the New Deal. In the spring of 1942, for the first time in eleven years, the American economy achieved full employment. It was at the very least, Eccles believed, seven years too late in the making.[85]

Writing in the pages of the *New Republic* in July 1940, John Maynard Keynes, anticipating that the United States was on the verge of a "vast dissipation of resources in the preparation of arms," offered the hope that some good would come out of evil if the nation came away in the end having learned a "lesson that can be turned to account afterward to reconstruct a world which will understand the first principles governing the production of wealth and which can endeavor—a harder task—to put it to good use." He wondered, however, if it were "vain to suppose that a democracy can be wise and sensible? Must the poison of popular politics make impotent every free community?"[86]

Only a week before the attack on Pearl Harbor—with the country well on the way toward "military Keynesianism"—Marriner Eccles joined his economic ally in a similar rumination before the National Industrial Conference Board:

> It is, of course, tragic that the world thus far can only gear itself to full utilization of its manpower and material resources in the making of war or the implementation of war. It will be a world tragedy if, when peace is restored, we revert to the doctrine that we cannot afford to employ our human and material resources in full production.... Government [must be] prepared to assure useful employment to all who are able and willing to work who cannot find jobs in private activity.... The defeatists are those who say we can't afford it, that democracy can't achieve it. If that were so, then democracy could not and would not deserve to survive.[87]

AFTERWORD

Once, some years after his service in the Roosevelt administration, Rexford Tugwell was asked what he had accomplished in his stint as a government official. "I had," said Tugwell, after a moment of reflection, "annoyed a good many people who ought to have been annoyed."[1] Marriner Eccles, it might be said, achieved at least as much and, in the view of most New Deal scholars, considerably more. His penchant for vexing those he deemed in need of vexing continued for the remainder of his years at the Fed and, for that matter, the remainder of his life.

Characteristically, the entrance of the United States into the Second World War found Eccles engaged with nonmonetary affairs. When the Treasury announced on March 10, 1942, that the Federal Reserve of San Francisco would act as custodian of the property of soon-to-be-evacuated Japanese residents of the West Coast, Eccles had already dispatched Fed governor Menc Szymczak to San Francisco to oversee this process. The Fed found itself on familiar turf when challenging the authority of Eccles's old nemesis, Leo T. Crowley. The head of the Federal Deposit Insurance Corporation, Crowley had been designated the Alien Property Custodian. The Fed sought and obtained a clear directive from the War Department in early March, however, that Crowley's authority extended only to the frozen assets of aliens living abroad, and that all the property of Japanese residents in the United States would be handled by the Fed.[2]

Although Secretary Morgenthau described the Fed participation as a means to "hasten the evacuation," it appears that Eccles, and the Federal Reserve officials with whom he was in contact, viewed their role in somewhat more beneficent terms. The need for an agency to act in an ombudsman-like capacity became apparent in the immediate aftermath of President Roosevelt's infamous executive order 9066 which empowered the military to designate areas from which "any and all persons may be excluded."

The "voluntary" evacuation of some eight thousand Japanese residents in the weeks that followed demonstrated—as reports to Eccles indicated—their vulnerability to land sharks and racketeers of every variety. Even before the War

Relocation Authority was created in mid-March, the Fed was busy establishing offices throughout the West Coast to safeguard Japanese property interests. In a long phone conversation Eccles had with Szymczak on March 12, they discussed the welfare of the evacuees, including wariness about private banks acting as good-faith agents, since they were in many instances themselves creditors. The Fed is doing something, Szymczak announced, while everyone else is "just talking."

The Fed governor, who was then in Seattle, wrote to Eccles a few days later from Los Angeles to report that they had already opened nineteen offices in that city alone. By April the Fed had established seven storage facilities in California, where their records indicated that over 6,300 Japanese families had entrusted their property. They were, Szymczak assured Eccles, doing the job "without hesitation." (In fact, to get Treasury officials out of their way, he reported to the chairman that he arranged for them to take a tour of MGM studios.) Szymczak, who, along with other Fed representatives, had noted with distaste the callousness with which some other government agencies had dealt with Japanese residents, wrote Eccles that their efforts were something "that the Federal Reserve System can point to with pride."

It is clear that whatever perspective evacuees may have had of the Fed's efforts, Eccles and Szymczak considered that they were ameliorating rather punitive and uncaring treatment, and acting in the best interest of Japanese residents. Eccles may have been influenced by the sympathetic comments of his fellow Mormon Elbert Thomas. The Utah senator spent six years as an LDS missionary in Japan and spoke the language fluently. In the aftermath of Pearl Harbor, he cautioned the country against engaging in "Gestapo-like activities" and unfair actions against the "good Americans" of Japanese descent. The Fed's advocacy may have continued in the aftermath of the war. When Congress enacted the Japanese Claims Act in 1948 and distributed nearly $40 million in compensation to relocated Japanese, the San Francisco Fed is reported to have estimated the payment as insufficient to the tune of some $360 million.[3]

When a conference of government representatives from twelve western states convened with federal officials in Salt Lake City on April 7, 1942, there was grudging acceptance that the relocation camps to be erected in their territories were a "military necessity." It quickly became apparent, however, that agricultural interests in their states were quite eager to accept the Japanese as a badly needed source of labor. This was especially true of the sugar beet growers. Interestingly, it was Eccles's Amalgamated Sugar Company that was the first private concern to recruit Japanese workers when they were still residing in assembly centers on the West Coast. (Eccles was made the company's chairman of the board on December 10, 1941.) By the spring of 1942, several hundred Japanese were living in U.S. Department of Agriculture migrant labor camps in Oregon and Idaho, where they labored in fields owned by Amalgamated Sugar. Before the end of the year, the company would employ well over two thousand. When the Japanese agitated for higher pay in the summer of 1943, however, Amalgamated announced it was likely to turn to Mexican migrants the following season.[4]

Months before the attack at Pearl Harbor, Eccles laid before the nation a new rubric for compensatory economics. In an article in *Fortune* magazine, he sounded the warning that the inflation the calamity howlers had been spuriously forecasting for the past decade was at long last approaching the nation's doorstep. Titled "Price Fixing Is Not Enough," the article demonstrated that the chairman intended to be as resolute in demanding fiscal measures to counteract high prices as he had been in attacking high unemployment.[5]

As with depression, the use of monetary mechanisms was, in his view, of secondary importance in the battle against inflation. With prices rising above 10 percent by early November of 1941, Eccles was supportive of raising reserve requirements. However, with a great need for construction of manufacturing facilities, and the necessity of supporting the Treasury's bond sales, the Fed felt that keeping interest rates relatively low was its "primary duty."[6] And from Eccles's perspective, what difference did it make, when there was an abundance of policy options for halting rising inflation? Coming from the chairman now was a steady stream of suggestions. In addition to constant calls for increased taxes on excess profits and the corporate income tax was a variety of tax code revisions. Why not, for example, eliminate tax breaks for advertising expenditures? It was crucial to reduce consumption among average Americans. Why not lower credits for dependents and personal exemptions? The social-security tax that he had excoriated from its inception was now an important fiscal ally. Since the tax pulled $1 billion out of the economy in fiscal 1942, why not use it to extract $3 billion from the hands of consumers in 1943? In testimony before the Ways and Means Committee in the fall of that year, Eccles insisted that the $2 billion in new revenue they were proposing should be raised to $13.8 billion, with $6 billion placed in an account—as was done with a portion of the excess-profits tax—to be refunded when the war ended. Eccles's "super tax" was described in an unmistakably pejorative sense by the chairman of the committee as "amazing, fantastic and visionary." Thus Eccles had come full circle: his suggestions for taxes in 1943 seemed every bit as outlandish to most observers as his proposals for expenditures appeared in 1933.[7]

Yet another similarity with Eccles's public statements of the 1930s was his frequent invocation of British policies as proof of the viability of his ideas. The Brits, he liked to point out, were meeting well over half of their war costs through taxation. Moreover, they were doing a far better job, he maintained, in marketing their war bonds to common citizens rather than resorting to the far more inflationary utilization of the banking system. Britain sold only one-third of its war bonds to banks, while the United States resorted to those institutions for over two-thirds of such loans. In the end, the wise redirection of bond drives to encompass more individuals, and the greater utilization of taxes to fund the war, may arguably be attributed more to the efforts of Marriner Eccles than to those of any other individual. A full 40 percent of World War II was paid for in taxes, far more than any other conflict in U.S. history. Of course, Eccles maintained they should have, and could have, done far better.[8]

The exigencies of war production left what Eccles termed the "disease of unemployment" vanquished in its wake, and in the process generated widespread national acceptance of much of the spenders' creed. In December 1942 that bastion of free market thought, *Fortune* magazine, proclaimed that the government should dedicate itself to maintaining full employment once the winds of war had subsided. This goal, *Fortune* stated, should be realized if necessary by government spending. Thomas E. Dewey, the 1944 Republican candidate for the presidency, seconded this view. In his acceptance of his party's nomination, the New York governor spoke of the need for the federal government to function as a "necessary intervener" to guarantee full employment. "If at any time there are not sufficient jobs in the private employment to go around," insisted the Republican nominee, "then government must create additional job opportunities because there must be jobs for all in this country." In the course of the 1944 presidential campaign, 68 percent responded affirmatively in a national poll when asked if the "federal government should provide jobs for everyone able and willing to work but who cannot find a job in private employment."[9]

And yet, even before the war had ended, Eccles was one of the leading voices in the government calling for a modified commitment to the goal of "full employment." In June 1945, Senator Robert Wagner requested that the Fed chairman comment on a bill pending before his Banking Committee that called upon the federal government to maintain "continuing full employment." In a public letter to Wagner, Eccles sounded a note of caution over the inflationary possibilities of such a mandate. What was a more sensible statement of public policy, Eccles suggested, was a "general declaration that government action and policy should be directed toward the goal of stabilized economic progress, with the greatest possible encouragement to individual initiative and private enterprise and with the fullest sustainable employment of labor." He supported, therefore, the substitution of "policy" for "responsibility" in delineating the future role government would play in regard to the unemployed. The term "full employment" would be replaced with the need to foster "maximum employment, production and purchasing power." The wording of the Employment Act of 1946, Eccles believed, did not signal the abandonment of a higher standard on his part, but rather the enactment of a commitment he wanted attached to the Banking Act of 1935: a dual mandate to fight both high unemployment and high inflation.[10]

Eccles's letter to Wagner, however, reflected the increasing rejection—which by late 1945 had gained widespread acceptance—of what came to be termed the "secular stagnation thesis": the belief that the old stimuli of industrialization spurred on by railroads and western expansion had waned. This was a conviction that Eccles expressed in 1933. The clear potential for new avenues of investment and economic growth that could be sighted from the vantage of 1945, however, rendered a continual large-scale government commitment less essential, and, in Eccles's view at least, potentially inflationary. "The problem immediately ahead of us," Eccles informed a gathering of farm officials in October of 1946, "is controlling inflation." Speaking only weeks before President Truman lifted wartime price controls—an action that Eccles considered premature—the Fed chairman insisted that "on balance inflationary factors continue to outweigh deflationary factors."[11]

The use of fiscal policy to counter fluctuations in the economy rather than endemic stagnation may have made its use more acceptable to conservatives, as Herb Stein has written, but it also highlighted its imprecision in such an application. That fiscal policy constituted a blunt instrument in this regard was acknowledged by Eccles early on. "The difficulty is that government is not quite flexible enough," he informed Senator Wagner in 1937. "We are too slow stopping our spending," he recognized, "and we may be too slow in starting it."[12] However, in light of Eccles's firm conviction that the federal government now had in its power the ability to spare its citizens the ravages of severe economic collapse, this fact—referenced earlier in this work—might properly be considered: An American born in 1870 and who died in 1935 would, in the course of his sixty-five years, have lived through three catastrophic and prolonged depressions—over a quarter of his life—depressions which engendered a degree of human misery that economic statistics fail to quantify. That an American born in 1945 has yet to endure a single day of such conditions might be said to be the fulfillment of Marriner Eccles's fondest vision.

It seems more than passing strange that Marriner Eccles and John Maynard Keynes, two central bankers whose fidelity to that vision placed them both on the cover of *Time* magazine—albeit thirty years apart—never once met or exchanged any written communication throughout the entire span of the 1930s. Their first encounter in wartime Washington resulted in a few minutes of idle chatter. Only weeks following the end of the war, however, Keynes met with Eccles at the Federal Reserve offices. The famous economist had come to the Utah banker to borrow money. Few Americans were more desirous of providing financial aid to Britain than Eccles. Nonetheless, he understood that political realities required that Congress would only approve what Eccles called a "banker's loan" with well-established schedules of principal and interest payments. When Keynes balked at some of the conditions, he received a sharp Eccles-like retort: "Do you want the loan?" Eccles defended the loan before Congress—which in the end contained very favorable terms for Britain—as a matter of "values" and sound economic self-interest. It laid the groundwork for the massive Marshall Plan a few years subsequent.[13]

It was Eccles's entanglement with another banker, Transamerica Corporation's A. P. Giannini, that may well have brought his tenure as chairman to an end. In 1941, Eccles and the Fed Board attached conditions to the acceptance into the System of Peoples Bank of California. The bank was required to affirm that it was, and would remain, a "bona fide, local, independent institution" and that if Transamerica Corporation acquired any direct or indirect control of the bank it could be required to leave the Federal Reserve System. Five days before the bank applied for membership, where these conditions were attached, Eccles received a personal letter from Giannini. The Transamerica chairman assumed that a talented banker like Eccles would not wish to remain in the Washington environment forever and he might like to "get into the banking game out this way." Eccles's response to this apparent offer to assume a position with Transamerica seemed clear when the Fed Board rejected Peoples Bank's membership a few weeks later. While the decision of the Fed was upheld by a District Court and then affirmed in a United States Supreme Court ruling—written by Felix Frankfurter—in 1948, it was the decision of Eccles and the Board to consider antitrust action against Transamerica in late 1947 that may have pushed the envelope a bit too far.

The charge was that Giannini was creating a monopoly in five western states by gaining a controlling interest in some six hundred banks.

In his autobiography, Eccles takes note of the close ties that the Truman administration had with Giannini and clearly states that was why President Truman did not reappoint him to another four-year term as chairman in 1948. Truman refused to respond when asked by the press for his reasons. The Board, however, with Eccles abstaining because of his personal banking interests, voted unanimously to pursue action under the Clayton Act. After years of litigation, the case was eventually dropped.[14]

Eccles's decision to remain on the Board as a governor—he had, like all members, a fourteen-year appointment—surprised a good many people. It was hardly surprising, however, when he continued to voice strong opinions on a wide array of public-policy matters. He strongly opposed what he believed to be the premature lifting of price controls shortly after the end of the war and supported their return in 1948. (The Consumer Price Index rose 17.6 percent between June 1946 and June 1947 and 9.5 percent between June of 1947 and June of 1948. The economy then went into a recession in late 1948.) He was appalled that the excess-profits tax was lifted in 1946, and he campaigned for, and was pleased by, its reinstitution in 1951. As he did in the 1930s, Eccles continued to inveigh against what he believed to be unjustifiable price increases imposed by oligopolistic corporations and unreasonable wage increases granted to the more powerful segments of organized labor: a cost he felt was unfairly paid by the nonunionized workforce. Indeed, prior to Truman's decision to not reappoint him as chair, Eccles persuaded the entire Board to urge the president to sign the Taft-Hartley Bill. The law, passed over the president's veto, amended the National Labor Relations Act and weakened the power of unions. In his nationally broadcast veto message, Truman deemed Taft-Hartley a "shocking piece of legislation." Eccles's public endorsement of the act could not have pleased the president.[15]

Characteristically, the former Fed chairman exited Washington, D.C., as a leading figure in a crucial public-policy development. Throughout the Second World War, the Federal Open Market Committee had, as Eccles acknowledged, "merely executed Treasury decisions" in regard to interest rates. As Fed chairman, Eccles had established an official agreement with the Treasury that yields on government securities would be kept low—3/8 percent on ninety-day bills—through fed purchases. This, of course, acted to increase banking reserves and heighten inflationary pressures. By 1946 the Fed had made so many purchases of treasuries that its prewar portfolio of $2.5 billion had mushroomed to $20.5

billion. Eccles's eventual disenchantment with continuing the inflationary policy of supporting Treasury sales may also have been a contributing factor in President Truman's decision to not rename him to the chairmanship.

After the outbreak of the Korean War, the Treasury once again expected that the FOMC would adhere to an upper limit on the yields of government bonds. Following a public statement by Treasury Secretary John Snyder, on January 9, 1951, that the FOMC would continue to toe the line and keep long-term rates at 2.5 percent, Eccles went on the offensive. In testimony before Congress later that month he tangled with his old foe, Wright Patman, and pronounced that such a policy would make the Fed an "engine of inflation." The Fed, he stated, might just as well become a bureau of the Treasury. A few days later President Truman took the extraordinary action of summoning the entire FOMC to a meeting at the White House. In this unprecedented gathering, Truman informed them that the confrontation with world communism in which the nation was then engaged surpassed even the importance of World War II, and that he thought it crucial to show a united front to the world. After the president made his plea for the FOMC to support the Treasury's wishes, neither the new Fed chairman, Thomas McCabe, nor any other member, all of whom had listened politely, made any commitment other than to agree to keep in contact with the administration.

McCabe, in fact, made it clear that the Fed's primary concern was economic stability. When the White House soon thereafter issued a statement that an accord had been reached with the FOMC and that they had agreed to be supportive, Eccles without consultation with any other Fed member issued a statement contradicting the administration, and essentially accused it of issuing misleading information. Not surprisingly, the refutation made the front pages of the nation's newspapers. On March 4 an accord that the Fed reached with the Treasury effectively severed the practice of pegged prices on government bonds. One historian has proclaimed March 4 the Federal Reserve's "Independence Day." If so, it could be said that Marriner Eccles was its Thomas Jefferson. Shortly thereafter, Eccles announced he was resigning from the Federal Reserve.[16]

Eccles's position in this controversy—that interest rates kept low amounted to an engine of inflation—marked an interesting change in awareness. Allan Meltzer has traced Eccles's postwar statements about the ineffectiveness of open-market operations.[17] It seems likely that it was Eccles's strong distaste for the country's involvement in the Korean War that sparked his hesitancy to accommodate the conflict's funding. He found insufferable the notion that communism was a monolithic, coordinated menace against the West that needed to be confronted at every point on the compass. The best way of countering China's drift toward radicalism, he insisted, was to engage it in economic trade.

Eccles aired his views in an article in a November 1950 issue of *Fortune* magazine. While Eccles was asked to address the economic aspects of dealing with the war, he deviated from that assignment in part of the article to discuss his concerns about geopolitical affairs. Considering the McCarthy-driven hysteria of the day, it took more than a slight amount of gumption to be critical of U.S. involvement in that war. Eccles cautioned against the nation overextending itself in world affairs. He went on to state that the nationalist government of Chiang Kai-shek could not "speak for China" and that it was "difficult to justify our failure to recognize Communist China before the Korean War." The editor of *Fortune* called Eccles just before publication to request that they expunge the political aspects of what was intended as an economic analysis of the war effort. It is possible, of course, that it displeased the publisher, Henry Luce. Eccles insisted that the magazine could refrain from publishing the article altogether, but if they chose to publish, the comments about the war and China must remain in. Possibly because the magazine was on the eve of a printing deadline, it published it in full. It was yet another display of daring on Eccles's part, in those fearful days when such courage proved rare.[18]

Following his resignation from the Board in 1951, Eccles returned to Utah and made an unsuccessful attempt to win the Republican nomination for the U.S. Senate. (One suspects that Eccles was hoping that Utah's open-primary system might work in his favor with Democrats crossing over to vote for him.) His brand of unvarnished frankness was unsuited for the campaign trail. While resuming his career in private business, Eccles continued his involvement with public-policy issues. He became a member, and a large financial contributor, to the Planned Parenthood Association. He was one of the featured speakers at Margaret Sanger's testimonial dinner held at the Waldorf Astoria on May 11, 1961. Eccles took it upon himself that evening—and on numerous other occasions—to castigate what he believed to be the Catholic Church's foolish obstruction of world population control. Although the gathering was receptive that evening, Eccles never lost his penchant for delivering unpleasantries to an audience. In March 1962, he was invited to give an address at Brigham Young University on "Monetary Policy and Inflation." Without notifying the school's officials, he stepped to the lectern and announced that he was changing the topic; he would speak instead on the vital need to control world population growth. It would be the last invitation extended to him by the university.[19]

Eccles's distaste for the U.S. involvement in the Korean War naturally intensified as the country became increasingly embroiled in the affairs of Southeast Asia. In July of 1965, President Lyndon Johnson called upon business and labor leaders who had supported him in the 1964 election to attend a White House dinner. Marriner Eccles was among those invited. The purpose of the assemblage was to drum up support for the escalation of the war in Vietnam. One cabinet member after another rose to explain the administration's policy. When they concluded, the guests, seated at eight large, round tables were asked to express their views. Because of insufficient time it was explained that only one person from each table would be called upon to furnish a three-minute response. A card marked "speaker" had been placed next to the name of the guest chosen to comment. Someone had unwisely placed the "speaker" card at Eccles's place setting at the eighth table. After seven men in succession gave ringing endorsements of the administration's course of action, Eccles stood. "I take it, Mr. President," he said looking directly at LBJ, "that you want me to say what I think." President Johnson, who had little recourse, responded "of course." He could not, Eccles regretted to inform him, "subscribe in any sense" with the previous speakers. The administration's policy toward Vietnam was based upon "fatal errors" and the national interest could best be served by disentangling from "a course of action that is bound to be ruinous." He just happened to have, he went on to say—now far beyond his allotted three minutes—a resolution that he intended to discuss the following day with Senator William Fulbright calling for a complete reversal of the nation's policy in Vietnam. He then proceeded to read from the resolution. A stunned silence followed. It was the last time he would step foot in the White House.[20]

In the end, as in the beginning, Marriner Eccles was a man of business. Opposition to the war would be considerably more effective if it could be demonstrated to the nation that it was not merely long-haired students on America's college campuses who were clamoring for its end. Eccles sought to recruit as many business people as he could to the cause. Once again, his standing as a Mormon Republican—even if nominal—proved to be provocatively beneficial. Harold Williams, president of the Factory Equipment and Supply Corporation of Los Angeles, who stated that he was "inspired to action by Mr. Eccles' example," told reporters in the fall of 1967 that a Russian journalist expressed incredulity that "many big American businessmen" would speak out against the war. This was a man, Williams told the press, who needed to meet Marriner Eccles. Speaking to a sympathetic assemblage of three thousand businessmen in September 1967—only a few weeks after a fellow Mormon,

Governor George Romney, explained that he had been brainwashed to support the war by generals in Vietnam—Eccles was interrupted fourteen times by applause and given a rousing standing ovation following his conclusion:

> While the hour is late, it is not yet impossible to turn the page. Man and nations have made new beginnings before. And out of defeat there has often come victory—and what a victory it would be for this nation, so abundantly endowed—to reverse its image, make itself loved and admired and revered, so that it could stand forth before the globe, as an example of what they might wish to become.[21]

Writing to Eccles near the end of the former chairman's life, John Kenneth Galbraith mentioned a comment that Arthur Schlesinger once made "calling on the memory of somebody back in the early history of the Republic [that] the great thing in life was to stay the course. It's surprising how few manage to do so. . . . But you clearly qualify in any list of fifty cases in the last two hundred years."[22]

While Galbraith doubtlessly had more than economics in mind, there is little doubt that in regard to public policy, Eccles remained steadfast. In May 1972, in accepting an award bestowed by the World Trade Club of San Francisco, the eighty-two-year-old Marriner Eccles delivered his final public address. On that occasion he excoriated the Nixon administration for continuing the war and foisting upon the nation destructive and unnecessarily excessive budget deficits. How fitting that his last public utterance fused fiscal policy and national morality.[23]

In 1982, five years after his death, the Federal Reserve on Constitution Avenue was rededicated the Marriner S. Eccles Building. Back in 1937 the Fed chairman drafted a speech for FDR to deliver at the ceremonial opening of that building. He suggested that the president conclude his remarks with these words: "I would dedicate this building to the progress toward the ideal of an America in which every worker will be able to provide his family at all times with an ever rising standard of comfort." One suspects that the structure's namesake would continue to insist—and no doubt cantankerously—that the Fed remain in pursuit of that ideal.[24]

NOTES

NOTES TO INTRODUCTION

1. Marriner S. Eccles, *Beckoning Frontiers: Public and Personal Recollections* (New York: Alfred Knopf, 1951), 40.
2. Dwight Israelsen, "Marriner S. Eccles, Chairman of the Federal Reserve Board," *American Economic Review* (May 1985): 357, 362.
3. Marriner S. Eccles, The Papers of Marriner S. Eccles, Special Collections, J. Willard Marriott Library, University of Utah, Salt Lake City, 198:3 (hereafter Eccles Papers). Letter to Eccles from Galbraith dated June 18, 1976. Galbraith informed Eccles that it was while filming a documentary on the history of economic ideas in the Federal Reserve board room that he thought of Eccles as the leader of a "revolution." John Kenneth Galbraith, *Money: Whence It Came, Where It Went* (Boston: Houghton Mifflin Company, 1975), 276.
4. John Kenneth Galbraith, *A Life in Our Times* (Boston: Houghton Mifflin Company, 1981), 57–66. Galbraith describes in these pages the economic views of the businessman Henry Dennison. Dennison, like Eccles, espoused Keynesian ideas long before the publication of Keynes's *General Theory*. Sidney Hyman, *Marriner S. Eccles: Private Entrepreneur and Public Servant* (Stanford: Stanford University Graduate School of Business, 1976), 36, 237. Hyman states that Eccles "had completed three and one-half years of high school." He later states that Eccles "had not completed even a high school education."
5. It is rare for Eccles to be left completely uncommented upon in a New Deal history. Not uncommon, however, is for his role to be scarcely recognized. For example, in Michael Bernstein's *The Great Depression: Delayed Recovery and Economic Change in America, 1929–1959*, Eccles receives a mere two sentences on one page. Eccles is actually left undiscussed entirely in Charles Kindleberger's *The World in Depression*, despite the fact that he dedicates an entire chapter to the 1937 recession.
6. Robert E. Lucas, *Models of Business Cycles* (Oxford: Basil Blackwell, 1987), 1–3.
7. Christina D. Romer and David H. Romer, "Choosing the Federal Reserve Chair: Lessons from History," *Journal of Economic Perspectives* 18, no. 1 (Winter 2004): 129, 151–52. As noted below, Eccles's oversight of monetary policy is adjudged poorly by Allan Meltzer in his history of the Fed. For a similar view see Charles W. Calomiris and David Wheelock, "Was the Great Depression a Watershed for American Monetary Policy?," in *The Defining Moment: The Great Depression and the American Economy in the Twentieth Century*, ed. Michael Bordo, Claudia Goldin, and Eugene White (Chicago: University of Chicago Press, 1998), 23–65.
8. There are some notable exceptions. Alan Brinkley's *The End of Reform: New Deal Liberalism in Recession and War* makes significant mention of both men. William Barber's *Designs within Disorder: Franklin D. Roosevelt, the Economists, and the Shaping of American Economic Policy, 1933–1945* and Frank Steindl's *Understanding the Economic Recovery in the 1930s* cover the Eccles-Currie relationship rather well. An invaluable insight into Currie's monetary and fiscal views is to be found in the writings of Roger Sandilands, especially his *The Life and Political Economy of Lauchlin Currie*.
9. The dimensions of this controversy are, of course, beyond the scope of this study. Elizabeth Bentley, the self-identified one-time Soviet agent, in her initial testimony before the House Committee on Un-American Activities (HUAC) identified Currie as an unwitting supplier of information to Soviet agents in the 1930s but not a Communist himself. She later changed her opinion and named him as a participant in an espionage ring. On August 13, 1949, Currie requested an appearance before HUAC and vehemently denied the accusation. In the months preceding the publication of Eccles's memoir, *Beckoning Frontiers*, in June 1951, Currie's name resurfaced again with a different set of allegations. It speaks well of Eccles that in this highly charged atmosphere—the fall of China to the Communists, the emergence of Joseph McCarthy, and the outbreak of the Korean War—he wrote warmly

and admiringly of Currie and noted his (Eccles's) disappointment, and FDR's gain, when Currie left the Fed to work at the White House before the outbreak of World War II. In his biography of Currie, Roger Sandilands offers a strong defense of his innocence. A more detailed response can be found in his authorship with James M. Boughton of an article in the spring 2002 issue of *Intelligence and National Security*. An opposing view, and a discussion of the Venona transcripts, can be found in H-Net articles by John Hayes. Certainly, if Currie was a dedicated Communist, it seems odd indeed that he worked tirelessly throughout the New Deal to strengthen capitalism.

10. H. J. Cooke and M. Katzen, "The Public Debt Limit," *Journal of Finance* 9, no. 3 (September 1954): 299.
11. Barry Eichengreen, *Hall of Mirrors: The Great Depression, the Great Recession, and the Uses—and Misuses—of History* (New York: Oxford University Press, 2015), 328.
12. Eccles, *Beckoning Frontiers*, 81.
13. Edmund Morris, *Colonel Roosevelt* (New York: Random House, 2010), 93.
14. Keynes quote in Robert L. Heilbroner, *The Worldly Philosophers* (New York: Simon & Schuster, 1999), 14.
15. Bradford J. DeLong, "Review of Books," *Journal of Economic History* 48, no. 1 (March 1988): 239, 240. For a contemporary account of fiscal policy discussions in the Obama administration, see Michael Grunwald, *The New New Deal: The Hidden Story of Change in the Obama Era* (New York: Simon & Schuster, 2012), 336–39. The country was fortunate to have the two leading economic historians of the Great Depression in important government positions. Unfortunately, Christina Romer, unlike Ben Bernanke, did not have the power to implement the fiscal policy that would have complemented the Fed chairman's aggressive monetary measures. Obama quote in Grunwald, *The New New Deal*, 338.
16. George A. Akerlof and Robert J. Shiller, *Animal Spirits: How Human Psychology Drives the Economy, and Why It Matters for Global Capitalism* (Princeton: Princeton University Press, 2009), 96.
17. Gail Radford, *Modern Housing for America: Policy Struggles in the New Deal Era* (Chicago: University of Chicago Press, 1996), 194; Alexander James Field, "Uncontrolled Land Development and the Duration of the Depression in the United States," *Journal of Economic History* 52, no. 4 (December 1992): 803.
18. John Maynard Keynes, *General Theory of Employment, Interest and Money* (London: Palgrave Macmillan, 2007), 162; Hyman, *Marriner S. Eccles*, 378.
19. Hyman, *Marriner S. Eccles*, 238.
20. While this work accepts the view that economic growth was quite remarkable during the 1930s, it sympathizes with Eccles's view that it could have been much better had the New Deal been more forceful in its efforts and if it had not adopted anti-Keynesian policies in 1937. There is, of course, no shortage of studies that argue that the New Deal retarded economic recovery. Many of these are referenced throughout. Among the most prominent: Robert E. Lucas, *Models of Business Cycles*; Gary Dean Best, *Pride, Prejudice, and Politics: Roosevelt versus Recovery 1933–1938*; Harold Cole and Lee Ohanian, "New Deal Policies and the Persistence of the Great Depression: A General Equilibrium Analysis," *Journal of Political Economy* 112, no. 4 (2004): 779–816; Gene Smiley, *Rethinking the Great Depression*; and Robert Higgs, *Depression, War, and Cold War: Studies in Political Economy*. For information on the number of private-sector jobs created in 1936, see Allan H. Meltzer, *A History of the Federal Reserve* (Chicago: University of Chicago Press, 2003), 1:503.
21. Eccles Papers, 1:3.
22. Eccles, *Beckoning Frontiers*, 316.
23. Robert Skidelsky, *Keynes: The Return of the Master* (New York: Public Affairs, 2009), 81, 161.
24. Hyman, *Marriner S. Eccles*, 289, 290.

NOTES TO CHAPTER 1

1. Herbert Hoover and Calvin Coolidge, *Campaign Speeches of 1932* (New York: Doubleday, Doran & Company, 1933), 67, 76.
2. Ibid., 17, 67, 95.
3. Hugh S. Johnson, *The Blue Eagle from Egg to Earth* (New York: Greenwood Press, 1968), 123–27.
4. Conrad Black, *Franklin Delano Roosevelt: Champion of Freedom* (New York: Public Affairs, 2003), 247, 248.
5. William E. Leuchtenburg, *Franklin D. Roosevelt and the New Deal* (New York: Harper & Row, 1963), 11.
6. Hoover, *Campaign Speeches of 1932*, 110, 120.
7. *New York Times*, October 15, 1932.
8. *Los Angeles Examiner*, June 1, 1931.
9. Hoover, *Campaign Speeches of 1932*, 121, 122.
10. Peter Temin, *Lessons from the Great Depression* (Cambridge: MIT Press, 1993), 27.
11. Herbert Stein, *The Fiscal Revolution in America* (Chicago: University of Chicago Press, 1969), 16, 30. As Stein notes, the proposal to cut taxes resulted

in the loss of $160 million, or some 4 percent of annual federal revenues. President Herbert Hoover, State of Union Address, December 2, 1930, http://www.presidentialelection.com/state_of_theunion/index.htm.

12. Stein, *Fiscal Revolution*, 25.
13. Ibid., 4, 26.
14. Temin, *Lessons from the Great Depression*, 27, 28; Rosemary D. Marcuss and Richard E. Kane, "U.S. National Income and Product Statistics: Born of the Great Depression and World War II," Bureau of Economic Analysis, February 2007, https://www.bea.gov/.../0207_history_article.pdf, 32–40. Eccles used the term "national income" rather than Gross National Product. Until 1934 neither figure existed. In 1932, Senator Robert La Follette introduced a resolution that called upon the secretary of commerce to measure national income. By 1935 FDR—with Eccles's encouragement—was making frequent references to the "national income." The larger figure of GNP, which includes all government purchases, was not formulated until 1942. In other words, government was treated as a consumer or purchaser of goods and services rather than as an industry providing income to employees.
15. *New York Times*, October 14, 1932.
16. Adam Cohen, *Nothing to Fear: FDR's Inner Circle and the Hundred Days That Changed America* (New York: Penguin Books, 2009), 185.
17. Hoover, *Campaign Speeches of 1932*, 94; Jess Benhabib, George W. Evans, and Seppo Honkapohja, "Liquidity Traps and Expectation Dynamics: Fiscal Stimulus or Fiscal Austerity?," Working Paper No. 18114, National Bureau of Economic Research, May 2012, 1–20. The authors of this 2012 study suggest that "fiscal switching rules" that "automatically kick in without discretionary fine tuning" could be effective in preventing the creation of a liquidity trap.
18. Stein, *Fiscal Revolution*, 10–12.
19. Steven Fraser, *Labor Will Rule: Sidney Hillman and the Rise of American Labor* (Ithaca: Cornell University Press, 1991), 208. Fraser notes that the report was written by Leo Wolman, who served as an economic adviser to Hillman and the Amalgamated Clothing Workers of America. As Liaquat Ahamed stated in his recent book on the central banks of the 1920s, *Lords of Finance*, Hoover incurred the wrath of a number of officials in the Coolidge administration with his demand in late 1925 that something be done to curb dangerous speculation in real estate and stocks.
20. Harry L. Hopkins, *Spending to Save: The Complete Story of Relief* (New York: W. W. Norton, 1936), 18, 31; J. Ronnie Davis, *The New Economics and the Old Economics* (Iowa City: University of Iowa Press, 1971), 30; Stein, *Fiscal Revolution*, 14; for a typical critique of how Hoover interfered with what would have been a natural recovery, see Amity Shlaes, *The Forgotten Man: A New History of the Great Depression* (New York: Harper Collins, 2007), 92; for the case against the harmful nature of the Smoot-Hawley Act, see Temin, *Lessons from the Great Depression*, 46.
21. Ellis W. Hawley, *The Great War and the Search for a Modern Order: A History of the American People and Their Institutions, 1917–1933* (Prospect Heights, IL: Waveland Press, 1997), 188.
22. Roy G. Blakey and Gladys Blakey, "The Revenue Act of 1932," *American Economic Review* 22, no. 4 (December 1932): 620–40; Thomas M. Renaghan, "Distributional Effects of Federal Tax Policy, 1929–1939," *Explorations in Economic History* 21, no. 1 (January 1984): 43.
23. *New York Times*, October 15, 1932.
24. John A. Garraty, "The Big Picture of the Great Depression," in *Historical Viewpoints: Historical Articles from* American *Heritage*, ed. John A. Garraty (New York: Addison Wesley Longman, 1999), 193; Charles P. Kindleberger, *The World in Depression* (Berkeley: University of California Press, 1986), 179–80. Kindleberger notes that the public-debt increase in Sweden between 1932 and 1937 was quite modest.
25. *New York Times*, October 14, 1932.
26. Ibid., October 18, 1932.
27. Ibid., October 20, 1932.
28. Ibid.
29. *Evening Outlook* (Santa Monica, CA), October 20, 1932; *Hartford Courant*, October 20, 1932.
30. *New York Times*, October, 14, 1936. FDR was obliged to support some federal–state projects for unemployment insurance by the Democratic Party platform. He noted this in his radio address on the thirteenth of October.
31. Louis Pizzitola, *Hearst over Hollywood* (New York: Columbia University Press, 2002), 302.
32. Franklin D. Roosevelt, *Looking Forward* (New York: Simon & Schuster, 2009), 31, 90, 91, 207.
33. Ibid., 81, 107.
34. Pizzitola, *Hearst over Hollywood*, 297. Between the election and the inauguration, Hearst's newsreel service, Metrotone, made what amounted to a minidocumentary that portrayed the newly elected president in a favorable light.

35. Robert L. McConnell, "The Genesis and Ideology of *Gabriel Over the White House*," *Cinema Journal* 15, no. 2 (Spring 1976): 7–26.
36. *Gabriel Over the White House*, directed by Gregory La Cava (Metro-Goldwyn-Mayer, 1933).
37. Arthur M. Schlesinger Jr., *The Crisis of the Old Order: 1919–1933* (Boston: Houghton Mifflin Company, 1957), 457; Hyman, *Marriner S. Eccles*, 2, 3.
38. Margaret L. Coit, *Mr. Baruch* (Boston: Houghton Mifflin Company, 1957), 1, 68.
39. U.S. Senate Finance Committee, *Hearings on Causes and Cures for the Depression*, 73rd Cong., 2d sess., February 1933, 17, 18 (hereafter cited as Senate Finance Committee); Jordan A. Schwarz, *The New Dealers: Power Politics in the Age of Roosevelt* (New York: Vintage Books, 1993), 98, Baruch's use of war analogy.
40. Senate Finance Committee, 456.
41. Ibid., 248.
42. Ibid., 497. Litchfield favored limiting the work week to thirty hours for "fatigue jobs" and forty hours for "non-fatigue jobs."
43. Ibid., 219, 220.
44. Ibid., 273.
45. Ibid., 287. "This is not the first depression caused by reckless overexpansion." Houston then cited as evidence the fact that registered automobiles in the United States grew from roughly 2.5 million in 1915 to 26.5 million in 1929.
46. Ibid., 332, 126. While John Lewis, president of the United Mine Workers, scornfully ridiculed, in his testimony (p. 300), those who "utter ponderous platitudes about balancing the budget," his views were fashioned by humanitarian concerns rather than economic theory. The same could be said of Sidney Hillman (p. 873), president of the Amalgamated Clothing Workers of America. Both men fervently called, however, for increased government planning.
47. Ibid., 83, 102. Since half the people in the world still used silver as a standard, its remonetization, Arendtz claimed, would flood the United States with orders from the Orient for wheat, cotton, and copper.
48. Ibid., 704, 705.
49. Ibid., 704–33; *Ogden Standard-Examiner*, February 24, 1933. The paper printed the entirety of Eccles's statement.
50. *Ogden Standard-Examiner*, February 25, 1933; *New York Times*, February 25, 1933.

NOTES TO CHAPTER 2

1. Eccles Papers, 1:18.
2. Hyman, *Marriner S. Eccles*, 39.
3. Ibid., 12–14. Samuel Gompers, the future leader of the American Federation of Labor, also arrived at exactly this time, as an immigrant from Great Britain.
4. Eccles, *Beckoning Frontiers*, 32–45.
5. Hyman, *Marriner S. Eccles*, 30.
6. Ibid., 32.
7. Ibid., 22.
8. Eccles, *Beckoning Frontiers*, 37.
9. Leonard J. Arrington, *Great Basin Kingdom: An Economic History of the Latter-Day Saints, 1830–1900* (Urbana: University of Illinois Press, 2005), 295.
10. Ibid., 114–16.
11. Eccles Papers, 1:3; Master's thesis of William McKinley Merrill, University of Illinois, 1950; Lowell L. Bennion, "The Business Ethic of the World Religions and the Spirit of Capitalism," *International Journal of Politics, Culture, and Society* 6, no. 1 (Autumn 1992): 67–73.
12. Hyman, *Marriner S. Eccles*, 42.
13. *Collier's*, June 8, 1935; Eccles Papers, 1:1; Eccles, *Beckoning Frontiers*, 51, 53.
14. Eccles, *Beckoning Frontiers*, 51–53; Hyman, *Marriner S. Eccles*, 65.
15. Ibid.
16. *Ogden Standard American*, May 26, 1930. Proud of their native son, the paper printed a good deal of the *New York American* article.
17. Sidney Hyman, *Challenge and Response: The First Security Corporation First Fifty Years* (Salt Lake City: University of Utah Press, 1978), 28, 29, 185. George publicly defended the FHA and deficit financing throughout the Intermountain West.
18. Hyman, *Marriner S. Eccles*, 68, 69.
19. Eccles Papers, 4:2; Christina D. Romer, "What Ended the Great Depression?," *Journal of Economic History* 52, no. 4 (December 1992): 760; Benjamin S. Bernanke, *Essays on the Great Depression* (Princeton: Princeton University Press, 2004), 46.
20. Eccles, *Beckoning Frontiers*, 59.
21. Ibid., 62.
22. Ibid., 56–62.
23. Lauchlin Currie, "Lauchlin Currie's Memoirs, Chapter 3: The New Deal," *Journal of Economic Studies* 31, nos. 3 and 4 (2004): 205, 206.
24. Eccles, *Beckoning Frontiers*, 57.
25. Eccles Papers, 90:1; ibid., 1:4, comment of loan officer; *Fortune*, February 1935; *Time*, February 18, 1935. Eccles revealed these details in his Senate confirmation hearings cited below; Hyman, *Challenge and Response*, 97.
26. Hyman, *Marriner S. Eccles*, 76, 77.
27. Bernanke, *Essays on the Great Depression*, 47.

28. *New York Times*, January 1, 1931.
29. Ibid., 34, 35, 37.
30. Temin, *Lessons from the Great Depression*, 57–60. However, Christina Romer points out in "What Ended the Great Depression?" (p. 764) that government spending in 1920 did drop off sharply from the year before. The surplus/deficit-to-GDP ratio went from -8.3 in 1919 to 0.5 in 1920.
31. *Atlantic Monthly* 149 (May 1932): 538.
32. *Wall Street Journal*, January 2, 1931.
33. Meltzer, *A History of the Federal Reserve*, 329.
34. Akerlof and Shiller, *Animal Spirits*, 60. The duration of the depressions of the 1870s and the 1890s (described below) provide a response to the question posed by economic historian Michael Bernstein in his book *The Great Depression: Delayed Recovery and Economic Change in America, 1929–1939* (Cambridge: Cambridge University Press, 1989), and in Michael Bernstein, "The Great Depression as Historical Problem," *Magazine of History* 16, no. 1 (Fall 2001): 5. In challenging the notion that the Depression was prolonged by "policy failures," he asks: "Why were traditional policies that had seemingly worked in the past and that represented a theoretical consensus among generations of economists suddenly so perverse in the 1930s?"
35. O. V. Wells, "The Depression of 1873," *Agricultural History* 11, no. 3 (July 1937): 237–51. He notes the increase in bankruptcies after 1875; For an excellent article on the extent and duration of this Depression, see Samuel Rezneck, "Distress, Relief, and Discontent in the United States during the Depression of 1873–1878," *Journal of Political Economy* 58, no. 6 (December 1950): 494–512; John Steele Gordon, *Hamilton's Blessing: The Extraordinary Life and Times of Our National Debt* (New York: Penguin Books, 1997), 79.
36. Gordon, *Hamilton's Blessing*, 64; Stein, *Fiscal Revolution*, 15.
37. *New York Times*, April 13, 1931. Keynes made the broadcast over WABC of the Columbia Network. The *Times* identified him as John Murray Keynes.
38. Liaquat Ahamed, *Lords of Finance: The Bankers Who Broke the World* (New York: Penguin Press, 2009), 374.
39. Ibid., 384–88; Eichengreen, *Hall of Mirrors*, 129–31.
40. Bernanke, *Essays on the Great Depression*, 17; Ahamed, *Lords of Finance*, 384–90, 434, 435; George J. Benston, *The Separation of Commercial and Investment Banking: The Glass-Steagall Act Revisited* (New York: Macmillan Press, 1990), 30, 31. Milton Friedman and Rose Friedman, *Free to Choose: A Personal Statement* (New York: Harcourt Brace Jovanovich, 1979), 82, 83.
41. Senate Finance Committee, 1933, 71.
42. William Roger Biles, "The Urban South in the Great Depression," *The Journal of Southern History* 56, no. 1 (February 1990): 82.
43. Hopkins, *Spending to Save*, 79.
44. Eccles, *Beckoning Frontiers*, 54.
45. Ibid., 71.
46. *Ogden Standard-Examiner*, February 27 and May 14, 1932.
47. Hyman, *Marriner S. Eccles*, 71.
48. Ibid.; Stein, *Fiscal Revolution*, 148, 485; *New York Times*, June 19, 1931, New School talk.
49. *New York Times*, December 31, 1933; Skidelsky, *Keynes: The Return of the Master*, 78. In a section titled "The Neutrality of Money," he remarks on Keynes's belief: "If you doubled the quantity of money, everything was twice as expensive, but nothing changed."
50. John Maynard Keynes, *The Means to Prosperity* (Oxford: Oxford City Press, 2012).
51. Ibid., 20; *New York Times*, June 2, 1932. This issue mentions the publication that day of *Essays in Persuasion*, a collection of Keynes's essays from the previous twelve years.
52. Keynes, *Means to Prosperity*; *New York Times*, April 20 and 28 and May 8, 1933.
53. Galbraith, *A Life in Our Times*, 57–64.
54. Ibid.
55. Quoted in Heilbroner, *The Worldly Philosophers*, 291; Sandilands, *Life and Political Economy of Lauchlin Currie*, 25, 26. Quote on Schumpeter's salary.
56. Temin, *Lessons from the Great Depression*, 27.
57. Galbraith, *A Life in Our Times*, 57–64; David Laidler, *Fabricating the Keynesian Revolution: Studies in the Inter-War Literature on Money, the Cycle, and Unemployment* (Cambridge: Press Syndicate of the University of Cambridge, 1999), 3. In the phrase "engine of analysis," Laidler is quoting Alfred Marshall.
58. Galbraith, *Money: Whence It Came, Whence It Went*, 218, 219. As we shall see, Lauchlin Currie's teaching career at Harvard would be impeded for espousing such views. However, as we shall also see, Galbraith may have overstated this point, since a few of the leaders of the "New Economics" actually taught at Harvard at this time.
59. Keynes, *General Theory*, 378.
60. Ibid., 162, 163.
61. Galbraith, *A Life in Our Times*, 65, 66.
62. Davis, *The New Economics and the Old Economics*; Eccles, *Beckoning Frontiers*, 85; Hyman, *Marriner*

S. Eccles, 73, 93. Hyman states that in 1931 Eccles "seized upon the current writings" of Foster. The article he cites, however, was written for the *North American Review* in 1933. For a discussion of the influence of the University of Chicago in the formation of New Deal economics, see David Laidler, "Hawtrey, Harvard, and the Origins of the Chicago Tradition," *Journal of Political Economy* 101, no. 6 (December 1993): 1068–1103.

63. Waddill Catchings and William Trufant Foster, *The Road to Plenty* (Boston: Houghton Mifflin Company, 1928), iii, iv; Allan H. Gleason, "Foster and Catchings: A Reappraisal," *Journal of Political Economy* 67, no. 2 (April 1959): 156, 161, 162. The winner of the completion was an economist from New Zealand; Nicholas Wapshott, *Keynes Hayek: The Clash That Defined Modern Economics* (New York: W. W. Norton, 2011), 27, 28, 48, 49.
64. Catchings and Foster, *The Road to Plenty*, 20.
65. Ibid., 21.
66. Ibid., 68, 69.
67. Eccles Papers, 44:10.
68. Catchings and Foster, *The Road to Plenty*, 80.
69. Ibid., 189–96; Gleason, "Foster and Catchings: A Reappraisal," 169, 170.
70. Eccles Papers, 44:10; *Ogden Standard-Examiner*, February 19, 1933. This was one of the occasions when Foster visited Ogden. Story mentions how much they agreed and that he had been there on two previous occasions.
71. Eccles Papers, 90:10; Stanley Brice Frost, *The Man in the Ivory Tower* (Montreal and Kingston: McGill-Queen's University Press, 1991), 14, 15, 32–38. Interestingly James went on to become, later in the 1930s, the vice president of the Economists' National Committee on Monetary Policy which advocated a return to a gold standard.
72. Eccles Papers, 90:10. Both books, with Eccles underlines, are in the collection of his books housed in the special collections division of the J. Willard Marriott Library, University of Utah; *New York Times*, October 17, 1932; the *Times* noted that these six economists were "seldom in complete agreement"; *New York Times*, September, 10, 1933; Fraser, *Labor Will Rule*, 262; Callender observation.
73. Edward Filene, *Speaking of Change: A Selection of Speeches and Articles* (New York: Former Associates of Edward Filene, 1939), v. See also Filene, *The Way Out* (Garden City, NY: Doubleday, Page, 1924), 1–7. The book contains an inspirational chapter titled "The Liberal Business Man" which may have inspired many of the men of business discussed in the following paragraph.
74. Filene, *Speaking of Change*, 72; Fraser, *Labor Will Rule*, 128; Jill S. Quadagno, "Welfare Capitalism and the Social Security Act of 1935," *American Sociological Review* 49, no. 5 (October 1984): 636. The Wisconsin Plan was designed to reduce unemployment since employers would fund the program and their contribution would be based on unemployment experienced by each employer. This was to provide an incentive to hire.
75. Steven Fraser, *Every Man a Speculator: A History of Wall Street in American Life* (New York: Harper Perennial, 2005), 263, 265; Thomas Ferguson, "From Normalcy to New Deal: Industrial Structure, Party Competition, and American Public Policy in the Great Depression," *International Organization* 38, no. 1 (Winter 1984): 84–85, 91. Ferguson stresses the importance of the "multinational block" and its interest in free trade as a primary reason for supporting FDR; Schwarz, *The New Dealers*, 183, 184.
76. Mark A. Lutz, *Economics for the Common Good: Two Centuries of Social Economic Thought in the Humanistic Tradition* (London: Routledge, 1999), 70–72.
77. Ibid.; Heilbroner, *The Worldly Philosophers*, 193; Keynes, *General Theory*, 18, 19, 365, 366. Keynes makes mention in the footnote on page 19 that Hobson noted that Marshall did acknowledge as early as *Economics of Industry* in 1879 that in periods of "crisis," men who "might have the power to purchase . . . may not choose to use it." Hobson believes—and Keynes, who was a pupil of Marshall, agreed—that he never developed this idea.
78. Lutz, *Economics for the Common Good*, 75.
79. *Los Angeles Examiner*, June 3, 1931.
80. W. A. Swanberg, *Citizen Hearst* (New York: MacMillan, 1961), 509, 514.
81. Temin, *Did Monetary Forces Cause the Great Depression?* (New York: W. W. Norton, 1976), 32. He makes reference to the table on page 4.
82. Keynes, *General Theory*, 324, 325. Keynes added: "I should support at the same time all sorts of policies for increasing the propensity to consume"; Paul Krugman, *End This Depression Now* (New York: W. W. Norton, 2012), 83, 84.
83. *New York Times*, January 5, 1931. Among the economists and other professors that signed were Edwin R. A. Seligman, James T. Shotwell, James C. Bonbright, Samuel McCune Lindsay, Franklin H. Giddings and Joseph P. Chamberlain of Columbia, T. S. Adams of Yale, E. W. Kemmerer and Vernon A.

Mund of Princeton, Paul Douglas of the University of Chicago, John R. Commons of the University of Wisconsin, Willford I. King of New York University, and N. H. Comish of Oregon State College.

84. Paul H. Douglas, *In the Fullness of Time* (New York: Harcourt Brace Jovanovich, 1971), 71–77; Paul Samuelson, *Remembering the University of Chicago* (Chicago: University of Chicago Press, 1991), 533, 542. Douglas, writes Samuelson, taught "Marshallian economics." Douglas states, however, that he learned as much as he taught from Samuelson, in his modification of Marshall's ideas; Roger J. Sandilands, "The New Deal and 'Domestic Keynesianism' in America," chapter 12 in *Essays in Honor of John Kenneth Galbraith*, ed. Michael Keaney (London: Routledge, 2001). The book that the senior faculty published was titled *The Economics of the Recovery Program*.
85. Laidler, "Hawtrey, Harvard," 1068–99. Laidler states (footnote 12) that Friedman's mea culpa was contained in a letter that Friedman sent to him.
86. D. E. Moggridge and Susan Howson, "Keynes on Monetary Policy, 1910–1946," *Oxford Economic Papers, New Series* 26, no. 2 (July 1974): 233, 234.
87. J. Ronnie Davis, "Chicago Economists, Deficit Budgets, and the Early 1930s," Part 1, *American Economic Review* 58, no. 3 (June 1968): 476–81; Don Patinkin, "Keynes and Chicago," *Journal of Law and Economics* 22, no. 2 (October 1979): 213–21; Patinkin mentions that Keynes was asked if he thought the Fed should purchase industrial and public utility bonds as well as government securities. He responded negatively, stating that central bankers should not have such judgments "loaded on them." He goes on to state that the "Chicago School" of the 1930s also favored government deficit financing to deal with unemployment but that this was considered a short-run necessity which should be replaced by a surplus later in the cycle. Keynes, he states, "saw it as a necessary long-run feature of a full-employment capitalist economy"; Davis, *The New Economics*, 12, 19, 27. Chief among the "Chicagoans," in addition to Jacob Viner, were Simon E. LeLand, H. A. Millis, and Henry Simons; Stein, *Fiscal Revolution*, 145, 146; Moggridge and Howson, "Keynes on Monetary Policy," 247. See this article for a discussion of Keynes's willingness to let events alter his policy suggestions. Jacob Viner will be discussed below.
88. Senate Finance Committee, February 1933, 682, 683.
89. Hyman, *Marriner S. Eccles*, 77.
90. Eccles, *Beckoning Frontiers*, 82, 83.
91. Eccles Papers, 105:4. Speech before Utah Educational Association.
92. Ibid. It is worth noting that Eccles seemed to be influenced by Lawrence Dennis, a financial writer from New York City, who testified before the Senate Finance Committee in February of 1933 immediately after Eccles. Dennis made many of the points that Eccles would later incorporate into his speeches. That Dennis influenced Eccles seems likely since he would come to use much of the same language and references—at some points word for word; Stein, *Fiscal Revolution*, 175–76.
93. Senate Finance Committee, 698. W. Mont Ferry, vice president of the Silver King Coalition Mines of Salt Lake, represented the Utah mining interests before the committee. The Orient, it was argued, was using silver to undersell the West. Bimetalism or the purchasing of silver would combat this by boosting its price. Silver producers, he argued, did not really benefit from this increase since most silver (80 percent) produced is a by-product of copper, lead, and zinc. More silver production, therefore, would result in greater production of these metals and their prices would be greatly reduced.
94. Eccles Papers, 105:4.
95. Ibid.
96. Ibid.
97. Ibid.
98. Ibid., 92:1.
99. Eccles, *Beckoning Frontiers*, 85–87.
100. Stuart Chase, *A New Deal* (New York: MacMillan Company, 1932), 5. The first words of Chase's book are: "John Maynard Keynes tells us . . ." The last sentence of the book is equally interesting: "Why should the Russians have all the fun of remaking a world?"; Samuel I. Rosenman, *Working with Roosevelt* (New York: Harper & Brothers, 1952), 71.
101. Eccles, *Beckoning Frontiers*, 85–87; Hyman, *Marriner S. Eccles*, 101, 102.
102. Eccles, *Beckoning Frontiers*, 114, 115.
103. Ibid., 84, 104.
104. *New York Times*, February 25, 1933; Arthur M. Schlesinger Jr., *The Coming of the New Deal: 1933–1935* (Boston: Houghton Mifflin, 1958), 10; Schlesinger, *The Crisis of the Old Order*, 229.
105. Adam Cohen, *Nothing to Fear*, 99.
106. Raymond Moley, *After Seven Years* (New York: Harper & Brothers, 1939), 62; Raymond Moley, *The First New Deal* (New York: Harcourt, Brace & World, 1966), 200.
107. Rexford G. Tugwell, *In Search of Roosevelt* (Cambridge: Harvard University Press, 1972), 158–60. "He

is a wonder," FDR wrote of Hoover in 1920. "I wish we could make him President of the United States. There could not be a better one." It is interesting to note that Moley appeared to be unaware of this assessment of Hoover since he speculated in *The First New Deal* that the animus that developed between the two in later years had its origin in the Wilson administration; Rebecca Brooks Gruver, *An American History* (New York: Appleton-Century-Crofts, 1972), 889.

108. Adam Cohen, *Nothing to Fear*, 86, 87.
109. Franklin D. Roosevelt, *The Public Papers and Addresses of Franklin D. Roosevelt* (New York: Random House, 1938), 46, 49, 50.
110. *New York Times*, April 2, 1933; Adam Cohen, *Nothing to Fear*, 100, 106; Stephen R. Ortiz, "The 'New Deal' for Veterans: The Economy Act, the Veterans of Foreign Wars, and the Origins of the New Deal Dissent," *Journal of Military History* 70, no. 2 (April 2006): 421–23.
111. Eccles Papers, 105:1.
112. Ibid; *Utah History Encyclopedia*, http://historytogo.Utah.gov/GeorgeHenryDern; Eccles Papers, 1:3. Dern's religious affiliation is found in the thesis of William McKinley Merrill.
113. Eccles Papers, 105:1; Eccles, *Beckoning Frontiers*, 118; Hyman, *Marriner S. Eccles*, 120.
114. *Los Angeles Examiner*, June 1, 1931.
115. Eccles Papers, 105:1.
116. Ibid., 105:3.
117. Ibid., 105:1.
118. Eccles, *Beckoning Frontiers*, 122.
119. Bonnie Fox Schwartz, *The Civil Works Administration, 1933–1934* (Princeton: Princeton University Press, 1984), 21.
120. Eccles Papers, 92:1, 1:3. That Eccles was a director of the RFC is noted in the Merrill thesis. It is not an association that Eccles made much reference to. It is not stated in his memoir; Will Bagley, *Always a Cowboy: Judge Wilson McCarthy and the Rescue of the Denver & Rio Grande Western Railroad* (Logan: Utah State University Press, 2008), 114–20. As we shall see further on, although Eccles stated in his memoir that none of his twenty-six banks took RFC money, one of them did accept a loan and under FDR—who altered the RFC substantially—a number of his banks received a good deal of assistance in the form of RFC purchases of their preferred stock.
121. Eccles, *Beckoning Frontiers*, 119–21; Hyman, *Marriner S. Eccles*, 119. For information on Eccles's friendship with McCarthy, see Bagley, *Always a Cowboy*, 282.
122. Eccles, *Beckoning Frontiers*, 119–21; *New York Times*, January 28, 1934. The paper reported on Eccles's position in the Treasury and noted that his banks received no RFC loans.
123. Hyman, *Marriner S. Eccles*, 2, 6.
124. Schlaes, *The Forgotten Man*, 137.
125. Hopkins, *Spending to Save*, 97–100.
126. Eccles, *Beckoning Frontiers*, 119.
127. Nancy E. Rose, *Put to Work: The WPA and Public Employment in the Great Depression*, 2d ed. (New York: Monthly Review Press, 2009), 26–31. Rose points out that there was a good deal of local variation in the following of FERA regulations. Her book also provides an excellent account of the high level of racial and gender discrimination that occurred in virtually all of the work programs of the New Deal; Hopkins, *Spending to Save*, 100, 101.
128. Hopkins, *Spending to Save*, 101.
129. Ibid., 100; Eccles, *Beckoning Frontiers*, 121.
130. Eccles Papers, 105:3; Eccles, *Beckoning Frontiers*, 124.
131. Romer, "What Ended the Great Depression?," 759.
132. Schlesinger, *The Coming of the New Deal*, 222, 223; Ahamed, *Lords of Finance*, 469–71; Bernanke, *Essays on the Great Depression*, 78, 79.
133. Eccles, *Beckoning Frontiers*, 111, 112; Schlesinger, *The Coming of the New Deal*, 253.
134. Jose Alvarez and Leo L. Polopolus, "The Nature of Government Protection and Control in the U.S.," Staff Paper, SP 331, Department of Food and Resource Economics, University of Florida, Gainesville, June 1988; Hyman, *Marriner S. Eccles*, 90. The Jones-Costigan Act was passed as an amendment to the Agricultural Adjustment Act; Leonard J. Arrington, "Science, Government, and Enterprise in Economic Development: The Western Beet Sugar Industry," *Agricultural History* 41, no. 1 (January 1967): 1–3. Eccles's confirmation testimony before Senator Glass's committee is discussed in chapter 6; Jeremy Atack and Peter Passell, *A New Economic View of American History*, 2d ed. (New York: W. W. Norton, 1994), 600, figures on Smoot-Hawley increase, after citing the fact that U.S. exports amounted to $842 million in 1929 and fell to $225 by 1933. This decline, they write, was "modest by comparisons with the changes in consumption and investment expenditures that have already been discussed." Schwarz, *The New Dealers*, 37, 38, on alliance of "corn and cotton."
135. Douglas A. Irwin, "The Smoot-Hawley Tariff: A Quantitative Assessment," *The Review of Economics and Statistics* 80, no. 2 (May 1998): 326–34; Barry Eichengreen, "The Political Economy of the

Smoot-Hawley Tariff," *Research in Economic History* 12, no. 1 (1988): 1–43; Eichengreen, *Hall of Mirrors*, 122. For an excellent short examination of the tariff issue, see economist Anthony O'Brien at http://www.eh.net/encyclopedia/obrien.hawley-smoot.tariff; Bernstein, *The Great Depression*, 218–19.

136. Senate Finance Committee, 300.
137. Johnson, *The Blue Eagle*, 156, 157; Schwarz, *The New Dealers*, 33, 34, for Baruch's Supreme Court of Commerce.
138. Schwarz, *The New Dealers*; Schlesinger, *The Coming of the New Deal*, 88. The Chamber of Commerce, however, was highly critical of the fair labor provisions that Baruch championed.
139. Senate Finance Committee, 876.
140. Roosevelt, *Public Papers and Addresses*, 157, 160.
141. Schlesinger, *The Coming of the New Deal*, 114–16.
142. Eccles, *Beckoning Frontiers*, 125.
143. Johnson, *The Blue Eagle*, 164, 196; Schwarz, *The New Dealers*, 97–100. Sachs was considered a member of journalist Dorothy Thompson's "Brain Trust." She contributed a good deal of criticism of the administration thrice weekly in her nationally syndicated "On the Record" column. Sachs's most important role in history was, of course, the famous Albert Einstein letter he delivered in person to FDR warning of Nazi attempts at nuclear fission. Sachs was the one who actually composed the letter.
144. Hyman, *Marriner S. Eccles*, 123.
145. Ibid. The Bureau of Economic Research, employing various criteria, is generally credited with recording recessions and determining their duration. www.nber.org/cycles/cyclesmain.html http://www.nber.org/data/abc/abcq.html.
146. Eccles, *Beckoning Frontiers*, 125–27.
147. Gauti B. Eggertsson, "Was the New Deal Contractionary?," Federal Reserve Bank of New York (June 2008): 1–3, 31–33.
148. Moley, *The First New Deal*, 230, 295, 296; Adam Cohen, *Nothing to Fear*, 56, 60, 63.
149. Rexford G. Tugwell, *The Battle for Democracy* (New York: Columbia University Press, 1935), 6, 7.
150. Jordan A. Schwarz, *Liberal: Adolf A. Berle and the Vision of an American Era* (New York: Free Press, 1987), 18–21. Berle also gained from his Dominican experience—something else he shared with Eccles—a lifelong distaste for American interventionism.
151. Ibid.
152. Adolph Berle and Gardiner Means, *The Modern Corporation and Private Property* (New York: MacMillan Company, 1933), 356; Tugwell, *The Battle for Democracy*, 6, 7; Schwarz, *Liberal*, 18–21, 37, 53, 56, 57; Paddy Ireland, "Company Law and the Myth of Shareholder Ownership," *Modern Law Review* 62, no. 1 (January 1999): 55.
153. Richard Parker, *John Kenneth Galbraith: His Life, His Politics, His Economics* (New York: Farrar, Straus and Giroux, 2005), 73, 95; Schwarz, *The New Dealers*, 58–60.
154. Hyman, *Marriner S. Eccles*, 55, 56.
155. Schlesinger, *The Coming of the New Deal*, 433; Schwarz, *Liberal*, 66, 90.
156. Schwarz, *The New Dealers*, 62. Technically, the feds paid for only half the cost of the Houston project; however, they guaranteed the private bond purchases.
157. Schlesinger, *The Coming of the New Deal*, 429, 430; Schwarz, *The New Dealers*, 67.
158. Eccles, *Beckoning Frontiers*, 114.
159. Ibid., 128.
160. Eccles Papers, 105:4. Tugwell did write to him on October 10 following his August visit to Washington and Eccles responded on October 14. As mentioned above, however, the actual invitation to Eccles came in Tugwell's letter dated October 18.
161. John T. Flynn, *The Roosevelt Myth* (New York: Devin & Adair, 1948), 6.

NOTES TO CHAPTER 3

1. Louis Morton Hacker, "The New Deal Is No Revolution," *Harper's Magazine* (January 1934): 121–33; Louis Martin Sears, "The Roosevelt Foreign Policy," *Journal of Modern History* 15, no. 1 (March 1943): 47; H. G. Wells, *The New World Order*, 2:5, "unsalted Youth."
2. John Dewey, *Individualism, Old and New* (New York: Prometheus Books, 1999), 8, 9; http://www.fdrlibrary.marist.edu/_resources/images/msf/msf00667, Dutchess County speech, August 1933.
3. Frances Perkins, *The Roosevelt I Knew* (New York: Viking Press, 1946), 316; the quote about lack of a single ideological commitment comes from Julian E. Zelizer, "The Forgotten Legacy of the New Deal: Fiscal Conservatism and the Roosevelt Administration, 1933–1938," *Presidential Studies Quarterly* 30, no. 2 (June 2000): 333; Henry Feingold is the source of the "unencumbered and unenriched" quote. It can be found in his essay "'Courage First and Intelligence Second': The American Jewish Secular Elite, Roosevelt, and the Failure to Rescue," in *FDR and the Holocaust*, ed. Verne W. Newton (New York:

Palgrave McMillan, 1996), 75; Richard Hofstadter, "Franklin Roosevelt: The Patrician as Opportunist," in *The American Political Tradition and the Men Who Made It* (New York: Vintage Books, 1989), 411; Eliot Janeway, *The Struggle for Survival* (New York: Weybright and Talley, 1968), 5; Sidney M. Milkis, "Franklin D. Roosevelt and the Transcendence of Partisan Politics," *Political Science Quarterly* 100, no. 3 (Autumn 1985): 481. Milkis taught at Brandeis University.

4. Winthrop speech, Collections of Massachusetts Historical Society, https://history.hanover.edu/texts/winthmod.html; Fireside Chat, June 28, 1934, at http://millercenter.org/president/fdroosevelt/speeches/speech-3302.
5. William Clyde Dunn, "Adam Smith and Edmund Burke: Complementary Contemporaries," *Southern Economic Journal* 7, no. 3 (January 1941): 337, 339, 345.
6. Roosevelt, *Looking Forward*, 5, 6.
7. C. B. Macpherson, "Harrington's 'Opportunity State,'" *Past & Present* 17, no. 1 (April 1960): 45–70; J. G. A. Pocock, *The Machiavellian Moment* (Princeton: Princeton University Press, 1975), 387, 567; Richard Olson, *Science Deified & Science Defied: The Historical Significance of Science in Western* Culture (Berkeley: University of California Press), 2:61–72. There is, of course, a well-known disagreement between these two historians. Pocock took issue with Macpherson's belief that Harrington was quite aware of market forces and the rise of a bourgeois society.
8. Cass Sunstein, *The Second Bill of Rights* (New York: Basic Books, 2004), 116, Madison comments; James Morton Smith, *The Republic of Letters: The Correspondence between Thomas Jefferson and James Madison* (New York: W. W. Norton, 1995), 389–91, Jefferson's letter; Russell Kirk, *The Conservative Mind: From Burke to Elliott* (Washington, D.C.: Regnery Publishing, 1953), 76. Kirk discusses Hamilton's lack of concern for the problems that might accompany the emergence of a manufacturing society.
9. J. Bradford DeLong, *Slouching Towards Utopia?: The Economic History of the Twentieth Century*, vol. 38, *The Roaring Twenties* (University of California–Berkeley, http://econ161.berkeley.edu/TCEH/Slouch_roaring13.html), 11. There is little doubt that wealth in post-Revolutionary America was more evenly distributed than in the 1920s. However, Jackson Turner Main's study of Virginia in the 1790s reveals that a majority of the adult white male population were not landowners: "The Distribution of Property in Post-Revolutionary Virginia," *Mississippi Valley Historical Review* 41, no. 2 (September 1954): 243, 244. For an examination of this issue see James T. Lemon and Gary B. Nash, "The Distribution of Wealth in Eighteenth Century America," *Journal of Social History* 2, no. 19 (Autumn 1968): 1–24. That there was less inequality of wealth in the post-Revolutionary period is also found in Jeffery Williamson and Peter Lindert, *American Inequality: A Macroeconomic History* (Cambridge, MA: MIT Press, 1980). For an exploration of the problems encountered in such evaluations and an assertion that there was never a widespread distribution of wealth in the country, see Carole Shammas, "A New Look at Long-Term Trends in Wealth Inequality," *American Historical Review* 98, no. 2 (April 1993): 412–31; Joseph J. Ellis, *After the Revolution: Profiles of Early American Culture* (New York: W. W. Norton, 1979), 179–80. Noah Webster's views demonstrate that this belief in the merits of property distribution in America was bipartisan.
10. 1935 State of Union address,http://www.fdrlibrary.marist.edu/daybyday/resource/january-1935/; Roosevelt, *Looking Forward*, 6; Perkins, *The Roosevelt I Knew*, 318; Eccles, *Beckoning Frontiers*, 81; Hopkins, *Spending to Save*, 107.
11. 1935 State of Union address,http://www.fdrlibrary.marist.edu/daybyday/resource/january-1935/; Friedman and Friedman, *Free to Choose*, 134, 135.
12. Thanksgiving Day Proclamation, November, 21, 1933, http://www.presidency.ucsb.edu/ws/index.php?pid=15575; Roosevelt, *Looking Forward*, 5.
13. Jack N. Rakove, *Original Meanings: Politics and Ideas in the Making of the Constitution* (New York: Vintage Books, 1998), 366, 367; Joseph Ellis, *Founding Brothers: The Revolutionary Generation* (New York: Vintage Books, 2002), 16.
14. Arthur M. Schlesinger Jr., *The Politics of Upheaval: 1935–1936* (Cambridge: Houghton Mifflin, 1966), 581.
15. Herbert David Croly, *The Promise of American Life*, Project Gutenberg [EBook 14422], 5, http://www.gutenberg.org/files/14422/1422-h/1442-h-htm; Morris, *Colonel Roosevelt*, 109, 110. The letter was to Henry Cabot Lodge; for an insightful account of TR at Osawatomie, see Gary Gerstle, *American Crucible: Race and Nation in the Twentieth Century* (Princeton: Princeton University Press, 2001), 67–69.
16. FDR speech, June 27, 1936, http://millercenter.org/president/fdroosevelt/speeches/speech-3305.
17. Ibid.; Schlesinger, *Politics of Upheaval*, 585.

18. Croly, *The Promise of American Life*, 97–99. John Morton Blum, *The Republican Roosevelt* (Cambridge: Harvard University Press, 1977), ix; Morris, *Colonel Roosevelt*, 93, 251. For an exploration of the aspects of the Progressive Age that distinguish it from the New Deal, and even the administrations of TR and Wilson, see Eldon J. Eisenach, *The Lost Promise of Progressivism* (Lawrence: University Press of Kansas, 1994), 14, 254–58. Eisenach is right, of course, in pointing out that works like Charles Sheldon's *In His Steps*, or William Stead's *If Christ Came to Chicago*, found no counterpart in New Deal liberalism; Gabriel Kolko, *The Triumph of Conservatism: A Reinterpretation of American History, 1900–1916* (New York: Macmillan, 1963), 215, 216. Kolko's work will be discussed below. He does take a dim view of Croly's position on economic justice: "he defended inequality of a rather gross sort." He writes that Croly ended his career as a writer "in praise of Mussolini's corporate state."
19. Woodrow Wilson, *The State: Elements of Historical and Practical Politics* (Boston: D. C. Heath, 1898), 630–33; Scot J. Zenter, "Liberalism & Executive Power: Woodrow Wilson & the American Founders," *Polity* 26, no. 4 (Summer 1994): 579–83; George W. Ruiz, "The Ideological Convergence of Theodore Roosevelt and Woodrow Wilson," *Presidential Studies Quarterly* 19, no. 1 (Winter 1989): 159–68. The contrasts between the "New Nationalism" and the "New Freedom" often obscure this common ground on government's role in enhancing individualism. According to Ruiz, Wilson's activism in the cause of Progressivism did not commence until he became governor of New Jersey in 1910.
20. Hyman, *Marriner S. Eccles*, 220.
21. Eccles, *Beckoning Frontiers*, 3, 4; Joseph J. Spengler, "Adam Smith's Theory of Economic Growth," *Southern Economic Journal* 25 no. 4 (April 1959): 397–415.
22. Eccles, *Beckoning Frontiers*, 3, 4.
23. Adam Smith, *The Wealth of Nations*, ed. Edwin Cannan (New York: Bantam Dell, 2003), 5:1102, 1103; Henry Home's "general rules" can be found in Edwin Cannan's footnote on p. 1045 of this edition.
24. Friedman and Friedman, *Free to Choose*, 134–36. Moreover, it could be asserted that "fairness" comes as much from natural law as from "liberty."
25. Smith, *Wealth of Nations*, 1:195; Emma Rothschild, "Commerce and the State: Turgot, Condorcet and Smith," *Economic Journal* 102, no. 414 (September 1992): 1206; Stephen Copley and Kathryn Sutherland, eds., *Adam Smith's* Wealth of Nations: *New Interdisciplinary Essays* (Manchester: Manchester University Press, 1995), 79–83, for Smith's advocacy of education and arts exposure; Nick Taylor, *American-Made: The Enduring Legacy of the WPA* (New York: Bantam Dell, 2008), 424, for the questioning of Hallie Flanagan.
26. Emma Rothschild, *Economic Sentiments: Adam Smith, Condorcet, and the Enlightenment* (Cambridge: Harvard University Press, 2001), 61, 285; Adam Smith, *Wealth of Nations*, 1:111.
27. Sandilands, *The Life and Political Economy of Lauchlin Currie*, 56–60; Copley and Sutherland, *Adam Smith's* Wealth of Nations, 71.
28. Jacob Viner, "Adam Smith and Laissez Faire," *Journal of Political Economy* 35, no. 2 (April 1927): 221, 223; Peter Groenewegen, *Economics and Ethics?* (New York: Routledge, 1996), 61. In this chapter, Jeremy Shearmur writes: "At least since Viner" there is "no excuse" for viewing Adam Smith as a doctrinaire laissez-faire enthusiast. The new scholarship that has appeared in recent decades has seemed to satisfy the urge, he says, of many who have seen "one too many Adam Smith ties round the necks" of Thatcher and Reagan advisors, and now wish to "turn the ties into nooses."
29. Adam Smith, *Wealth of Nations*, 2:404; Viner, "Adam Smith and Laissez Faire," 241–56; Copley and Sutherland, *Adam Smith's* Wealth of Nations, 71–73; Roy C. Smith, *Adam Smith and the Origins of American Enterprise* (New York: Truman Talley Books, 2002), 14, 193.
30. Adam Smith, *Wealth of Nations*, 5:1065; Viner, "Adam Smith and Laissez Faire," 228, 229; Roy C. Smith, *Adam Smith and the Origins*, 193.
31. Viner, "Adam Smith and Laissez Faire," 228, 229.
32. Adam Smith, *Theory of Moral Sentiments* (Boston: Wells and Lilly, 1817), Book II, section II, 107.
33. Viner, "Adam Smith and Laissez Faire," 219; Stewart Davenport, *Friends of the Unrighteous Mammon: Northern Christians and Market Capitalism* (Chicago: University of Chicago Press, 2008), 26–28; Meltzer, *History of the Federal Reserve*, 466, for Viner on Eccles.
34. Rothschild, "Commerce and the State," 1197. In fact, both of these men, although associated with the physiocratic school of François Quesnay, had some differences with them.
35. Ibid., 1202, 1203, 1208. Rothschild, *Economic Sentiments*, 23, 79.
36. John Kenneth Galbraith, *Economics in Perspective* (Boston: Houghton Mifflin, 1987), 48, 49; Rothschild, *Economic Sentiments*, 22–23.

37. Peter Groenewegen, *Eighteenth Century Economics: Turgot, Becaria, Smith and Their Contemporaries* (New York: Routledge, 2002), 375; Rothschild, *Economic Sentiments*, 22; Rothschild, "Commerce and the State," 1209.
38. Jacob S. Hacker and Paul Pierson, *American Amnesia: How the War on Government Led Us to Forget What Made America Prosper* (New York: Simon & Schuster, 2016), 107. The authors note that "Jefferson wasn't that Jeffersonian" and that he and his followers "eventually embraced a large part of Hamilton's economic policy."
39. Tony Judt, *Ill Fares the Land* (New York: Penguin Books, 2010), 121.
40. Henry Steele Commager, *Lester Frank Ward and the Welfare State* (New York: Bobbs-Merrill, 1967), xv, xvi.
41. Francis Wayland, *The Elements of Political Economy* (New York: Sheldon & Company, 1886), 3–5. The publisher states in the introduction that the text is "now used in most schools in the country." Laurence M. Vance, "Francis Wayland: Preacher-Economist," *Independent Review* 10, no. 3 (Winter 2005): 401, 402, 406, 407; Davenport, *Friends of the Unrighteous Mammon*, 8, 35, 60.
42. Davenport, *Friends of the Unrighteous Mammon*, 20.
43. Ian Donnachie and George Hewitt, *Historical New Lanark* (Edinburgh: Edinburgh University Press, 1993), 25.
44. Robert Owen, *Report to the County of Lanark & a New View of Society* (Baltimore: Penguin Books, 1970), 94. The address "To the Superintendents of Manufactories" was included as a preface to all of the editions of *A New View of Society*; Peter Gordon, "Robert Owen," *Prospects: The Quarterly Review of Education* 24, no. 1 (March 1994): 1–4; David Carmony and Josephine Elliot, "New Harmony, Indiana: Robert Owen's Seedbed for Utopia," *Indiana Magazine of History* 76 (September 1980): 161–261.
45. Owen, *Report*, 194, 195. This publication contains a lengthy introduction by V. A. C. Gatrell, who discusses Owen's macroeconomic ideas (p. 68).
46. Ibid., 148; Margaret Cole, *Robert Owen of New Lanark* (New York: Oxford University Press, 1953), 224; Carmony and Elliot, "New Harmony, Indiana," 165–67.
47. Richard Olson, *Science and Scientism in Nineteenth-Century Europe* (Chicago: University of Illinois Press, 2008), 226, 238, 239, 252, 253.
48. Adam Smith, *Moral Sentiments*, 1, 9.
49. Olson, *Science and Scientism*, 240.
50. Adam Smith, *Moral Sentiments*, 178, 179, 253.
51. Commager, *Lester Frank Ward*, xxii; Sidney Fine, *Laissez Faire and the General Welfare State* (Ann Arbor: University of Michigan Press, 1956), 253.
52. Lester F. Ward, *Dynamic Sociology* (New York: D. Appleton and Company, 1883), 1:14, 15.
53. Ibid., 1:15, 40, 54, 60.
54. Miller Center, http://millercenter.org/president/speeches/speech-3307.
55. Miller Center,http://millercenter.org/president/wilson/speeches/speech-3566, Wilson Inaugural, March 4, 1913; Rebecca Edwards, *New Spirits: America in the "Gilded Age"* (New York: Oxford University Press, 2001), 145; Commager, *Lester Frank Ward*, xxxviii.
56. Fine, *Laissez Faire*, 278. FDR's "Crusade to restore America to its people" comes from his 1936 "I welcome their hatred" speech at Madison Square Garden.
57. Schlesinger, *The Politics of Upheaval*, 533, 534.
58. Kansaspedia, https://www.kshs.org/kansaspedia/alfred-landon-s-acceptance-speech/14501.
59. *Emporia Weekly Gazette*, September 17, 1908.
60. Cordell Hull, *The Memories of Cordell Hull* (New York: MacMillan, 1948), 1:49–53; Schlesinger, *The Coming of the New Deal*, 188, 189.
61. Jean Baptiste Say, *A Treatise on Political Economy; or, The Production, Distribution, and Consumption of Wealth* (Philadelphia: J. B. Lippincott, 1859), 133–35.
62. Ibid., 434–36.
63. Ibid., 454, 455.
64. Ibid., 411.

NOTES TO CHAPTER 4

1. *Federal Reserve Bulletin*, January 1940, 45; Frederick Lewis Allen, *Since Yesterday* (New York: Harper & Row, 1939), 162, 163.
2. *Time*, February 19, 1934; Eccles, *Beckoning Frontiers*, 134, 135; *Corpus Christi*, April 18, 1938. Pearson's syndicated "Merry Go-Round" appeared in this paper. This was not the first time he referred to "Big Spender" and "Little Spender" groups in his column; *Los Angeles Times*, August 12, 1934. The "protégé" comment is a good indication of how soon Eccles was receiving national attention.
3. June Hopkins, *Sudden Hero, Brash Reformer* (New York: St. Martin's Press, 1999), 1.
4. James Chance, *Acheson* (New York: Simon & Schuster, 1998), 62–68; Eccles, *Beckoning Frontiers*, 133, 134.

5. Robert D. Leighninger, *Long-Range Public Investment: The Forgotten Legacy of the New Deal* (Columbia: University of South Carolina Press, 2007), 37; Eccles, *Beckoning Frontiers*, 134.
6. Leighninger, *Long-Range Public Investment*, 39.
7. Eccles Papers, 5:5. Eccles would later suggest in this 1935 memo that federal money could be used to entice private interests to put up a portion of a project's cost; Leighninger, *Long-Range Public Investment*, 39, 42.
8. Eccles, *Beckoning Frontiers*, 134.
9. *Ogden Standard-Examiner*, November 13, 1933; United States Bureau of Reclamation, Ogden River–Pineview Dam, http://www.usbr. The Utah Construction Company shared the work with the Morrison-Knudsen Company of Boise, Idaho. The storing of water largely ended the perennial late-summer squabbling over primary access to water. Beets did indeed emerge as a significant crop in the region.
10. Rose, *Put to Work*, 39–41; Leighninger, *Long-Range Public Investment*, 46.
11. Schwartz, *The Civil Works Administration*, 36–40; Leuchtenberg, *Roosevelt and the New Deal*, 120, 121.
12. *New York Times*, November 16, 1933. That this assembly was held at the Mayflower Hotel is drawn from a source cited below.
13. Robert E. Sherwood, *Roosevelt and Hopkins* (New York: Harper and Brothers, 1948), 51; Schwartz, *The Civil Works Administration.*
14. Schwartz, *The Civil Works Administration*, 49.
15. *Salt Lake Tribune*, November 13, 1933; *The Ogden Standard-Examiner*, November 13, 1933; *Time*, February 19, 1934.
16. Schwartz, *The Civil Works Administration*, viii.
17. Ibid., 43.
18. Rose, *Put to Work*, 39, 97. For an excellent review of CWA, see Philip Harvey, "Learning from the New Deal," *Review of Black Political Economy* 39, no. 1 (March 2012): 87–105.
19. *Salt Lake Tribune*, November 20, 1933; *Ogden Standard-Examiner*, November 20, 1933.
20. Ibid.
21. *Salt Lake Tribune*, December 24, 1933; Ibid., January 14 and January 28, 1934; https://utahstatecapitol.utah.gov/explore/capitol-art/senate-chamber-murals.
22. Schwartz, *The Civil Works Administration*, 192, 193, 197.
23. Robert S. Lynd and Helen Merrell Lynd, *Middletown in Transition: A Study in Cultural Conflicts* (New York: Harcourt Brace Jovanovich, 1937), 120. The Lynds make reference to the fact that Muncie had few civic improvements during the boom years of the 1920s and "extensive improvements in the midst of depression."
24. *New York Times*, January 12, 1934.
25. Harry Hopkins, *Spending to Save*, 121–23; Leighninger, *Long-Range Public Investment*, 51–54; Harvey, "Learning from the New Deal"; *Sports Illustrated*, June 16, 2009. In an article titled "Going Public," the authors discuss how the game of golf in the United States was altered by the six hundred public courses that were renovated or built during the New Deal.
26. *Time*, January 1, 1934; Governor Talmadge called city dwellers who took federal relief "bums" and "chiselers." Talmadge and the state legislature's refusal to provide matching grants forced FDR to end all WPA and PWA funding for the Georgia. See Biles, "Urban South," 84.
27. *Ogden Standard-Examiner*, December 16, 1933; *Manitowoc Herald*, January 27, 1934. Carpenters protested when in late January the wage was reduced to 65 cents per hour.
28. Rose, *Put to Work*, 44.
29. *New York Times*, February 11, 1934; Schwartz, *The Civil Works Administration*, 214–16.
30. Forrest A. Walker, "Graft and the Civil Works Administration," *Southwestern Social Science Quarterly* 46, no. 2 (September 1965): 164–70.
31. *New York Times*, March 2, 1934, and May 8, 1935; Jim Powell, *FDR's Folly* (New York: Three Rivers Press, 2003), 95.
32. Eccles Papers, 107A:2.
33. Ibid.
34. Ibid. Letter to Hinckley dated February 17, 1934.
35. *New York Times*, February 8, 1934.
36. *Time*, February 19, 1934.
37. Walker, "Graft and the Civil Works Administration," 169, 170; William Roger Biles, "Mayor Edward J. Kelly of Chicago: Big City Boss in Depression and War" (PhD diss., University of Illinois, 1981), 51–54.
38. *New York Times*, April 5 and December 15, 1935; *Los Angeles Times*, June 10, 1935, advertisement for the Boondoggle hat appeared on p. 17; *Los Angeles Times*, November 13, 1935, reports on "Roosevelt the Waster"; Taylor, *American-Made*, 166, 167.
39. *Carrol Daily News*, July 37, 1935. Dutcher wrote for the Newspaper Enterprise Association. His column was widely published.
40. Eccles Papers, 107A: 2.
41. *Ogden Standard-Examiner*, January 21, 1934.
42. Ibid., January 19, 1934.

43. *Dallas Morning News*, May 30, 1934; *El Paso Herald*, February 9, 1934; *Time*, February 19, 1934; Texas Historical Association, https://www.tshaonline.org/handbook/online/articles/fte, 21, 40.
44. *New York Times*, January 22, 1934, rally at St. John the Divine; January 23, 1934; January 27, 1934, Governor Olson; February 8, 1934. Schlesinger, *The Coming of the New Deal*, 277, Landon quote; *Ogden Standard-Examiner*, January 14, 1934.
45. *New York Times*, March 25, 1934; Schwartz, *The Civil Works Administration*, 231–33.
46. *New York Times*, January 2, February 11, and March 4, 1934; *Altoona Mirror*, November 25, 1933, and April 17, 1934; Schwartz, *The Civil Works Administration*, 189–91; Leighninger, *Long-Range Public Investment*, 47; Biles, "Mayor Edward J. Kelly," 554.
47. *Federal Reserve Bulletin*, January 1940, 45. Schwartz, *The Civil Works Administration*, 190, 191.
48. Harvey, "Learning from the New Deal," 93.
49. *New York Times*, January 27, 1934; Zelizer, "The Forgotten Legacy of the New Deal"; Eccles, *Beckoning Frontiers*, 145.
50. Schwartz, *The Civil Works Administration*, 226. *Salt Lake Tribune*, March 24, 1934.

NOTES TO CHAPTER 5

1. Eccles, *Beckoning Frontiers*, 136, 137.
2. Ibid., 140, 141.
3. Flynn, *The Roosevelt Myth*, 55; *Ogden Standard-Examiner*, January 21, 1934. The skit was organized by Lawrence Clayton.
4. Moley, *After Seven Years*, 110, 111; Flynn, *The Roosevelt Myth*, 6; Tugwell, *In Search of Roosevelt*, 117; Rexford Tugwell, *Roosevelt's Revolution* (New York: Macmillan Publishing, 1977), 45; Joseph P. Lash, *Dealers and Dreamers* (New York: Doubleday, 1988), 138; Schlesinger, *The Coming of the New Deal*, 528; Leighninger, *Long-Range Public Investment*, 57.
5. Hyman, *Marriner S. Eccles*, 134. Both Eccles and Hyman suggest that Morgenthau was sensitive to conflict-of-interest issues since he had just experienced a controversy when a New York banker named Earl Bailey was denied congressional confirmation as assistant secretary.
6. Eccles, *Beckoning Frontiers*, 140, 141.
7. Eccles Papers, 2:4, Morgenthau letter; ibid., 107:A3, Clayton exchange; *Ogden Standard-Examiner*, December 1, 1934, article providing information on Clayton. He was a World War I vet and received an undergrad degree from Stanford and a LLD from Harvard.
8. Eccles Papers, 105:5.
9. "Mr. Roosevelt's Men," *Fortune*, April 1934.
10. John Morton Blum, *From the Morgenthau Diaries: Years of Crisis, 1928–1938* (Boston: Houghton Mifflin Company, 1970), 80.
11. Eccles Papers, 9:4; Hyman, *Marriner S. Eccles*, 148.
12. *New York Times*, August 7, 1934; Schlesinger, *The Coming of the New Deal*, 435–37, 457.
13. *New York Times*, February 17 and 28, March 5 and 14, 1934; Schlesinger, *The Coming of the New Deal*, 437, 438, 464.
14. *Lowell (MA) Sun*, March 3, 1934.
15. Eccles Papers, 105:4; Fraser, *Every Man a Speculator*, 461, 462.
16. *New York Times*, June 6 and 7, 1934.
17. H. D. M. Jr., "Banks and the Securities Act of 1933," *Virginia Law Review* 52, no. 1 (January 1966): 117–28.
18. Ibid., 122, 123. The 1933 and 1934 acts applied only to concerns listed on national stock exchanges, so some of the very largest banks may have been under its provisions. Eccles seemed to doubt the necessity of the Glass-Steagall separation. This is suggested in his testimony at his confirmation hearing before Carter Glass's subcommittee in 1935. It is cited below.
19. Eccles Papers, 107A:5. Letter from Richards dated March 7, 1934.
20. FDR Library, Morgenthau Diaries, February 9, 1934, http://www.fdrlibrary.marist.edu/_resources/images/morg/mdoo01.pdf.
21. *Ogden Standard-Examiner*, February 26, 1933.
22. Ibid., October 20, 1934.
23. Ibid., December 16, 1933; Eccles, *Beckoning Frontiers*, 138; Hyman, *Marriner S. Eccles*, 132, 133.
24. Brinkley, *The End of Reform*, 95.
25. Sandilands, *The Life and Political Economy of Lauchlin Currie*, 6–13, 385.
26. Meltzer, *A History of the Federal Reserve*, 467; Sandilands, *Life and Political Economy of Lauchlin Currie*, 32–35.
27. Lauchlin Currie, "The 'Leading Sector' Model of Growth in Developing Countries," *Journal of Economic Studies* 1, no. 1 (May 1974): 4–6. Currie elaborates on this: "And yet it is important to distinguish between an increase in overall demand arising from an increased rate of output in some sector, and an increase arising merely from monetary expansion. The essence of the distinction appears to be that in one case the increase in money demand is a consequence of an increase in real output; in the other,

it may occur in the first instance independently of any expansion in real output. In the first case the pattern of production-consumption in real terms is changed; in the second, it may not be. This distinction is vital to an understanding of the leading sector strategy of accelerating growth. If stable prices are to be maintained, an increase in output requires an offsetting increase in money incomes, but this is a consequence rather than a cause of increased output." While Currie is focusing in this article upon the particular circumstances that arise in developing countries, the passage above seems generally applicable.

28. Ibid.; Sandilands, *Life and Political Economy of Lauchlin Currie*, 244, 291–94, 299–302.
29. Sandilands, *Life and Political Economy of Lauchlin Currie*, 70–73.
30. Ibid.
31. Hyman, *Marriner S. Eccles*, 138.
32. Ibid., 61, 62.
33. Eccles Papers, 107A:3. Eccles's response, February 17, 1934.
34. Eccles Papers, 92:1; Eccles, *Beckoning Frontiers*, 144.
35. Eccles, *Beckoning Frontiers*, 144.
36. Ibid., 147, 148.
37. Eccles Papers, 28:1, memo about Fahey; John H. Fahey, "Competition and Mortgage Rates," *Journal of Land and Policy Economics* 15, no. 2 (May 1, 1939): 150–54.
38. Edith Elmer Wood, *The Housing of the Unskilled Wage Earner: America's Next Problem* (New York: MacMillan, 1919), 142–68, 252.
39. Eccles Papers, 27:6, memo from Matt Daiger to Eccles; *Fortune*, June 1935. The article draws upon a great deal of information from the Watson report. Bernanke, *Essays on the Great Depression*, 64; Radford, *Modern Housing for America*, 86.
40. U.S. Senate Committee on Banking, Hearings on National Housing Act, 73rd Cong., 2d sess. (hereafter Senate Committee, *National Housing Act*), May 16, 1934, 14, 15.
41. Radford, *Modern Housing for America*, 11–13, 22.
42. Ibid., 13; *Nation*, October 3, 1934, 381–83. The reference to "men of high standing" and the identification of Averell Harriman are noted in an earlier article in this issue under the headline "Guaranteed Mortgages."
43. Radford, *Modern Housing for America*, 16, 17.
44. Ibid., 45–48, 51, 52.
45. Morton Bodfish, "Government and Private Mortgage Loans on Real Estate," *Journal of Land and Public Utilities* 11, no. 4 (November 1935): 402–9; Hyman, *Marriner S. Eccles*, 145.
46. *President's Conference on Home Ownership* (Washington, D.C.: Government Printing Office, 1931), 2:16, 17, 20, 21; *New York Times*, November 2, 1934. This was a letter that was addressed to FHA administrator James Moffett, which will be referenced below.
47. *President's Conference on Home Ownership*, 2:16, 17, 20, 21.
48. Ibid., 2:11–13, 11:2, 4:vii.
49. U.S. House Committee on Banking and Currency, *Hearings on the National Housing Act*, 73rd Cong., 2d sess. (hereafter House Committee, *National Housing Act*), May 18, 1934, 8.; U.S. Senate Committee on Banking and Currency, *Hearings on Revision of the National Housing Act*, 75th Cong., 1st sess. (hereafter, Senate Committee, *Revision of National Housing Act*), December 8, 1937, 166. While Eccles made mention of the European mortgage structure in his 1934 testimony, he provided the statistics on Britain's system in testimony before this Senate Committee in 1937; Eccles Papers, 9:5. The reference to "the second mortgage racket" was made in an April 29, 1935, memo entitled "Towards a Uniform Home Financing System." For more information on the builder's-pool mortgages in Britain see Peter Michael Scott, *The Making of the Modern British Home* (Oxford: Oxford University Press, 2013).
50. House Committee, *National Housing Act*, 8; Arthur M. Weimer, "The Work of the Federal Housing Administration," *The Journal of Political Economy* 45, no. 4 (August 1937): 469, 470; *New York Times*, October 28, 1934.
51. House Committee, *National Housing Act*, 8.
52. Ibid.; *Fortune*, June 1935, 180, 181; Hyman, *Marriner S. Eccles*, 145; Weimer, "The Work of the Federal Housing Administration," 478.
53. Eccles, *Beckoning Frontiers*, 152–55; Hyman, *Marriner S. Eccles*, 146–48.
54. Eccles Papers, 27:4; Eccles, *Beckoning Frontiers*, 157, 158; *New York Times*, November 11, 1934.
55. Weimer, "The Work of the Federal Housing Administration," 469–72; Eccles, *Beckoning Frontiers*, 157–60.
56. Ronald C. Tobey, *Technology as Freedom: The New Deal and the Electrical Modernization of the American Home* (Los Angeles: University of California Press, 1996), 29.
57. Ibid., 29–31, 111, 139, 164. Title I modernization loans.
58. *Wall Street Journal*, July 12, 1935; "Ballyhoo Housing," *Ladies' Home Journal*, December 1934; *Fortune*, June

1935. Eccles, *Beckoning Frontiers*, 159–60; Radford, *Modern Housing for America*, 181–83.

59. Federal Housing Administration, *Second Annual Report of the United States Housing Administration* (Washington, D.C.: Government Printing Office, 1936), vi; Weimer, "The Work of the Federal Housing Administration," 476, 477, figures on percentage of new homes constructed under FHA.
60. Eccles Papers, 27:3.
61. Ibid., 28:1.
62. Alexander James Field, *A Great Leap Forward: 1930s Depression and U.S. Economic Growth* (New Haven: Yale University Press, 2011), 787.
63. Ibid., 788–800.
64. Eccles Papers, 27:1.
65. *Ogden Standard-Examiner*, December 16, 1933.
66. *Fortune*, June 1935, 77–79; Eccles Papers, 27:1.
67. Eccles Papers, 30:3.
68. Ibid., 28:5.
69. U.S. Senate Committee on Banking and Currency, *Hearings to Amend the National Housing Act*, 75th Cong., 1st sess. (hereafter Senate Committee, *Hearings to Amend National Housing Act*), April, May 1937, 173. Figures cited by Senator Byrnes.
70. U.S. Senate Special Committee on Unemployment Relief, *Hearings on Unemployment Relief*, 75th Cong., 2d sess. (hereafter Relief Committee Hearings), January 1938, 263. Figure cited by UAW president Homer Martin; *New York Times*, March 17, 1937, article on workers at Westinghouse.
71. Eccles Papers, 5:1. Memo dated November 11, 1934.
72. Ibid., 28:6. President of Turner Construction Company.
73. Ibid., 28:8. This is included in a letter Eccles wrote to Stewart McDonald at FHA. This file also contains a clipping from an article by John T. Flynn about corruption in the building trades that the AFL was not addressing.
74. Eccles Papers, 28:1, January 9, 1937, memo from Daiger describes mortgage moratoria in a number of states as "an extremely serious problem"; Robert H. Skilton, "Mortgage Moratoria since 1933," *University of Pennsylvania Law Review* 37, no. 8 (June 1939): 55–66; J. Douglass Poteat, "State Legislative Relief for the Mortgage Debtor during the Depression," *Law and Contemporary Problems* 5, no. 4 (Autumn 1938): 517–44.
75. Eccles Papers, 27:3; ibid., 28:1, reference to fear of real-estate bubble and inflation; Federal Housing Administration, *Third Annual Report of the United States Housing Administration* (Washington, D.C.: Government Printing Office, 1937), vii; Eccles Papers, 27:1; Eccles, *Beckoning Frontiers*, 160; *New York Times*, November 14, 1934, size of residential mortgage debt; *New York Times*, October 31, 1937, discussion of backlog of foreclosed properties; *Financial Crisis Inquiry Report: Final Report of the National Commission on the Causes of the Financial and Economic Crisis in the United States* (New York: Public Affairs, 2011).
76. *New York Times*, August 1, 1937; *New York Times*, October 31, 1937; Schwarz, *The New Dealers*, 87.
77. *New York Times*, December 1, 1937; *Annual Report to Congress in Fiscal Year 2011: Status of FHA Mutual Mortgage Insurance Fund*, November 15, 2011. While presenting his report to the Congressional Committee on Housing, Massachusetts congressman Mike Capuano responded to Republican criticism of the FHA by asking Secretary Donovan if it were true that prior to the creation of the FHA homeowners had to put down 50 percent of the price of a home and pay off the mortgage in less than five years. Secretary Donovan responded that that was his understanding. The congressman then reflected rhetorically on how many Americans would be capable of purchasing a home under such conditions.
78. David M. P. Freund, *Colored Property: State Policy & White Racial Politics in Suburban America* (Chicago: University of Chicago Press, 2007), 137; Eccles, *Beckoning Frontiers*, 160; James R. Hagerty, *The Fateful History of Fannie Mae: New Deal Birth to Mortgage Crisis Fall* (Charleston, SC: History Press, 2012), 21, 37–44.
79. Eccles Papers, 28:1. Daiger memo dated January 7, 1937.
80. Eccles Papers, 5:5, memo to FDR dated March 6, 1935; ibid., 84:7; ibid., 40:1, speech to New York Institute of Banking, December 1, 1938; *New York Times*, November 14, 1935. This article cited 300,000 units in the U.K. in 1934. The previous year the *New York Times* reported (October 24, 1934) that Great Britain, with one-third of the U.S. population, built 300,000 dwelling units in 1933 while the United States built 48,000. Great Britain, it was noted, had a National Mortgage banking system and a habit of regarding housing as an investment. Schlaes (*The Forgotten Man*, 339) cites an *Economist* editorial that references the change in per capita national income.
81. Temin, *Lessons from the Great Depression*, 117. For an excellent discussion of the 1930s comparison between the United States and Germany, see John Garraty, "The New Deal, National Socialism, and

the Great Depression," *American Historical Review* 78, no. 4 (October 1973): 907–44. Field, *A Great Leap Forward*, 802n63; Richard Harris and Chris Hammett, "The Myth of the Promised Land," *Annals of American Geographers* 77, no. 2 (June 1987): 180–82; according to the U.S. Census Bureau, homeownership was 43.6 percent in 1940; this figure was certainly lower in 1938. Skidelsky, *Keynes: The Return of the Master*, 70; Keynes, *Means to Prosperity*, 14. Keynes's conviction that "more than 90 percent of the depression in America was due to the falling off of construction" has been previously cited.

82. Eccles Papers, 28:2. Memo from George Terbourg. He cautions that building material costs would increase as well.
83. Eccles Papers, 5:4; ibid., 28:1, Daiger's letter to Mr. Rodgers, January 22, 1937; ibid., 27:6, Daiger and rent crisis; Weimer, "The Work of the Federal Housing Administration," 482–84; *Nation*, October 10, 1934, CWA surveys discussed; *New York Times*, November 19, 1936.
84. Eccles Papers, 5:5, 1935 memo to FDR, "A Suggested Works Program"; Eccles, *Beckoning Frontiers*, 302–4; *New York Times*, July 9, 1939; ibid., July 14, 1937, reference to 50 percent of income to rent; *Nation*, October 10, 1934.
85. Eccles Papers, 5:4, comments on Public Works; ibid., 28:2, memo from Daiger, March 18, 1937; Radford, *Modern Housing for America*, 100–102; *New York Times*, May 12, 1935.
86. Eccles Papers, 28:2. March 18 memo.
87. Radford, *Modern Housing for America*, 104–8.
88. *New York Times*, January 3, 1937.
89. Ibid., November 19, 1936.
90. Ibid., May 31, 1936.
91. Eccles Papers, 27:3, comment on "delusion and a snare"; ibid., 27:6, focus on cheap housing; ibid., 28:4. Eccles relied on Daiger's report dated August 17, 1937. Daiger was working at this time for the FHA. Ibid., 28:7. The suggestion that mortgage companies be allowed greater leverage was passed on to FDR by Jesse Jones in a letter dated November 23, 1937. Eccles, *Beckoning Frontiers*, 299–300.
92. Eccles, *Beckoning Frontiers*, 297–300; Radford, *Modern Housing for America*, 189–94.
93. David Levering Lewis, *When Harlem Was in Vogue* (New York: Penguin Books, 1997), 306; Lizabeth Cohen, *A Consumers' Republic: The Politics of Mass Consumption* (New York: Vintage Books, 2004), 171; Freund, *Colored Property*, 442.
94. *Chicago Defender*, September 1, 1934. Throughout the remainder of 1934 there were three more articles on the FHA including a question-and-answer format (October 27) that, like the others, dealt with home-repair loans; Freund, *Colored Property*, 153–59, 443.
95. *New York Times*, June 30, 1937.
96. *Time Magazine*, November 7, 1949. In the face of withering criticism, the school rejected Armstrong's offer and was flooded with smaller donations sent "with no strings attached." Eccles, *Beckoning Frontiers*, 92.
97. Eccles Papers, 90:1, *Forbes* article, February 1935; Michael Hiltzik, *Colossus: Hoover Dam and the Making of the American Century* (New York: Free Press, 2010), 315–18.
98. Radford, *Modern Housing for America*, 199–201.
99. *New York Times*, April 18, 1937, and January 7, 1940.
100. *Financial Crisis Inquiry Report: Final Report of the National Commission on the Causes and Financial and Economic Crisis in the United States* (New York: Public Affairs, 2011), 5.
101. Richard Green and Susan Wachter, "The American Mortgage in Historical and International Context," *Journal of Economic Perspectives* 19, no.4 (Autumn 2005): 94.
102. Eccles Papers, 28:2, memo dated March 18, 1937; Eccles, *Beckoning Frontiers*, 307, 308, on his concerns about relaxed lending terms after the war.

NOTES TO CHAPTER 6

1. *Los Angeles Times*, July 21, 1933; *New York Times*, September 2, 1934; Hyman, *Marriner S. Eccles*, 139; Ortiz, "The 'New Deal' for Veterans," 425–33. The Veterans of Foreign Wars led the attack against the pension cuts to vets. The much larger American Legion (one million members compared to 150,000) had a leadership that was friendlier to FDR. However, their rank and file joined the fray against the cuts.
2. *Ogden Standard-Examiner*, June 30, 1935.
3. Eccles Papers, 9:4.
4. *Collier's*, June 8, 1935, Flynn comment; Eccles Papers, 90:1, includes a *Fortune* article from February 18, 1935, that contains reference to an "occasional cocktail"; Tugwell, *In Search of Roosevelt*, 273; Hyman, *Marriner S. Eccles*, 129; Eccles, *Beckoning Frontiers*, 132, 133.
5. *Ogden Standard-Examiner*, August 7, 1934; Eccles, *Beckoning Frontiers*, 167, 168.
6. Blum, *Morgenthau Diaries*, 343; Hyman, *Marriner S. Eccles*, 155; Eccles, *Beckoning Frontiers*, 165, 166; Meltzer, *A History of the Federal Reserve*, 441.

7. Currie, "Lauchlin Currie's Memoirs," 203.
8. Sandilands, *Life and Political Economy of Lauchlin Currie*, 61, 62; Eccles Papers, 43:9. In a letter dated November 17, 1934, Currie requested a salary of $9,000.
9. Eccles Papers, 2:4.
10. *New York Times*, November 11, 1934.
11. Ibid.; ibid., January 28, 1934, "Out of beaten path" article; Hyman, *Marriner S. Eccles*, 161. Anna Schwartz and Milton Friedman may be responsible for the high regard many seem to still have for Benjamin Strong. Had he lived, it is believed, he would have sent interest rates in the right directions at the right times. As Peter Temin has argued, however, Strong's devotion to the gold standard was really the basis of the catastrophe that afflicted the world economy. See Temin, *Lessons from the Great Depression*, 38–39.
12. *Laredo Times*, February 8, 1935.
13. Ibid.; ibid., November 25, 1934, Kluckhorn article; ibid., February 17, 1935, Farnham's article; *Fortune*, February 18, 1935; ibid., May 5, 1935, Francis Brown article.
14. Eccles, *Beckoning Frontiers*, 102.
15. Schwarz, *New Dealers*, 298. This chapter discusses the elevation of Eccles's Hoover Dam partner Henry Kaiser as a New Deal icon of sorts. Kaiser was seriously considered as a vice-presidential running mate in 1944. Schwarz also discusses (pp. 35, 36) the fact that the South and the Farm Block were not always in alliance over tariff protection. As discussed earlier, the regions came to something of an understanding by 1927 that protection was needed. For Lippman's views, see Gary Dean Best, *Pride, Prejudice, and Politics: Roosevelt versus Recovery 1933–1938* (New York: Praeger Publishers, 1991), 4.
16. Sean Wilentz, *The Rise of American Democracy: Jefferson to Lincoln* (New York: W. W. Norton, 2005), 438–45. Jackson and his cabinet were under the influence of a very popular book, *A Short History of Paper Money and Banking in the United States*, published in 1833. In his book *Secrets of the Temple* (New York: Simon & Schuster, 1987), 258–60, William Greider discusses a somewhat contentious issue over the benefits that might have ensued from Jackson's bank policies. For a more involved exploration of this issue, see Bray Hammond, "Jackson, Biddle, and the Bank of the United States," *Journal of Economic History* 7, no. 1 (May 1947): 1–23; Marvin Myers, *The Jacksonian Persuasion: Politics and Belief* (Stanford: Stanford University Press, 1957).
17. H. Peers Brewer, "Eastern Money and Western Mortgages in the 1870s," *Business History Review* 50, no. 3 (Autumn 1976): 356–80; Atack and Passell, *A New Economic View*, 510, 511. The authors note that these interest-rate variations on commercial paper lessened in the twentieth century. The western sense of unfairness in this regard still registered with many as the accounts of Eccles's appointment demonstrate. The farm differentials are to be found in Edwards, *New Spirits*, 81; Eccles, *Beckoning Frontiers*, 102.
18. Atack and Passell, *A New Economic View*, 514–16; Jean Reith Schroedal, *Congress, the President, and Policymaking: A Historical Analysis* (New York: M. E. Sharpe, 1994), 70.
19. Robert F. Bruner and Sean D. Carr, *The Panic of 1907: Lessons Learned from the Market's Perfect Storm* (Hoboken: John Wiley & Sons, 2007), 58, 59.
20. Gabriel Kolko, *The Triumph of Conservatism: A Reinterpretation of American History, 1900–1916* (New York: Macmillan, 1963), 153–55; Bruner and Carr, *The Panic of 1907*, 136, 137, 165.
21. Kolko, *The Triumph of Conservatism*, 36, 37, 140, 153–56; Greider, *Secrets of the Temple*, 274–75.
22. Greider, *Secrets of the Temple*, 274–75. Perhaps John Morton Blum's perspective in his biography of Wilson (cited below) might serve as demonstrative of the 1913 Fed as an effective regulatory force. "It fulfilled in every respect," he wrote, "the relevant promises in Wilson's campaign and message to Congress. The regulatory authority of the Federal Reserve Board assured a larger degree of government control over banking than had ever existed before" (pp. 74, 75). The argument over what constituted a legitimate diminution of capitalist power was a common debate throughout the first decade of the century. See Richard W. Fox, "The Paradox of 'Progressive' Socialism: The Case of Morris Hillquit, 1901–1914," *American Quarterly* 26, no. 2 (May 1974): 127–40. Hillquit argued that Victor Berger's campaign for the government to purchase the large trusts and railroads would actually "strengthen rather than loosen the grip of capitalist governments on the people."
23. Schroedel, *Congress, the President, and Policymaking*, 68–70.
24. Bruner and Carr, *The Panic of 1907*, 148, 149; Greider, *Secrets of the Temple*, 275.
25. John Morton Blum, *Woodrow Wilson and the Politics of Morality* (Boston: Little, Brown, 1956), 72–75; Arthur Link, *Woodrow Wilson and the Progressive Era: 1910–1917* (New York: Harper & Row, 1954),

76–78; Kolko, *The Triumph of Conservatism*, 46, 47, 246. Here, too, Kolko points out that while International Harvester did sell 96 percent of all binders and 91 percent of all mowers at the turn of the century, it had lost a substantial amount of that market by 1912. There were other changes made to the enacted Federal Reserve legislation. The Aldrich plan called for the payment of 4 percent interest on stock in the Fed, while the act settled on 6 percent.

26. Meltzer, *A History of the Federal Reserve*, 138; Kolko, *The Triumph of Conservatism*, 252.
27. Bruner and Carr, *The Panic of 1907*, 145.
28. Laidler, "Origins of the Chicago Tradition," 1070, 1086–88, 1099. In footnote 12 Laidler mentions his correspondence with Friedman; the rest of the footnotes to this article are very useful as well. Frank G. Steindl, "The 'Oral Tradition' at Chicago in the 1930s," *Journal of Political Economy* 98, no. 2 (April 1990): 430–32.
29. *New York Times*, November 25, 1934; Meltzer, *A History of the Federal Reserve*, 465.
30. Eccles Papers, 99:5; the *New York Times* interview with Eccles, which appeared on November 25, stated that "the desire of Governor Eccles for another huge public works project seems to have met at least temporary defeat." It noted, however, that if the private sector stalled in the coming year, the president might reconsider.
31. Eccles Papers, 9:5. Memo dated November 16, 1934.
32. Eccles, *Beckoning Frontiers*, 258.
33. Meltzer, *A History of the Federal Reserve*, 457–59; *New York Times*, March 29, 1934. Sponsored by Carter Glass, the Industrial Advances Act was adopted prior to Eccles's arrival at the Fed. Allowing working-capital loans (work in progress or raw materials, etc., as opposed to fixed capital, or plant capital for bricks and mortar) was somewhat controversial. See *New York Times*, September 22, 1934. For a discussion of the history of section 13 of the Fed Act, see David Fettig, "The Lender of More Than Last Resort," *The Region* (September 2002), https://minneapolisfed.org/publications/the-region/lender-of-more-than-last-resort. Fettig notes that the idea that the discount window—and there literally was a discount window in Fed lobbies—should be open to everyone was a widely held belief when the Fed was established. The 1932 provision was employed on just 123 occasions between 1932 and 1936. The largest single loan was for $300,000. He speculates that the restrictions made an RFC loan preferable.
34. Eccles Papers, 1:1.
35. Ahamed, *Lords of Finance*, 318, 319; Eccles, *Beckoning Frontiers*, 178, 179.
36. Eichengreen, *Hall of Mirrors*, 114.
37. Eccles, *Beckoning Frontiers*, 191; Meltzer, *A History of the Federal Reserve*, 469–71.
38. Hyman, *Marriner S. Eccles*, 168, 169.
39. Ibid; Carl H. Moore, *The Federal Reserve System: A History of the First Seventy-Five Years* (Jefferson, NC: McFarland, 1990), 7; Schlesinger, *The Politics of Upheaval*, 296; Roger Lowenstein, *America's Bank: The Epic Struggle to Create the Federal Reserve* (New York: Penguin Press, 2015), 153.
40. Hyman, *Marriner S. Eccles*, 162.
41. Eccles, *Beckoning Frontiers*, 177, 178.
42. Eccles Papers, 56:4–18. The December 1934 correspondence between them is contained in these folders.
43. Eccles, *Beckoning Frontiers*, 194, 195.
44. *Los Angeles Times*, July 19, 1935; Flynn, *The Roosevelt Myth*, 85.
45. Moley, *After Seven Years*, 23.
46. Eccles Papers, 4:1. Memo to FDR.
47. Donald R. Stabile and Jeffrey A. Cantor, *A History of the Bureau of Public Debt* (Washington, D.C.: C. H. Associates, 1990); Meltzer, *A History of the Federal Reserve*, 141, 142. See also David Kinley, *Independent Treasury of the United States and Its Relations with the Banks of the Country* (Washington, D.C.: National Monetary Commission, Government Printing Office, 1910).
48. *Congressional Record*, 74th Cong., 1935, 11778. On the floor of the Senate, Carter Glass provided information on the status of government securities in 1913; Eccles Papers, 4:1.
49. Eccles, *Beckoning Frontiers*, 168–70; Meltzer, *A History of the Federal Reserve*, 429–34.
50. Eccles, *Beckoning Frontiers*, 175.
51. Letter from Lauchlin to Michael Whitehouse at Fed, written from Bogotá on August 16, 1984. Provided by Roger Sandilands to the author.
52. Burton A. Abrams and Russell F. Settle, "Pressure Group Influence and Institutional Change: Branch Banking Legislation during the Great Depression," *Public Choice* 77, no. 4 (1993): 687–705. This is an excellent discussion of the relaxation of laws on branch banking at the state level, the failure of so many banks in these years, and the intensified pressure-group interest associated with increased urbanization. Some twenty-two states, including Utah, changed laws; Charles Calomiris and Joseph Mason, "Consequences of Bank Distress during the Great Depression," *American Economic Review* 93, no. 5 (December 2003): 937–47.

53. Ferguson, "From Normalcy to New Deal," 81–83. Ferguson identifies a number of investment bankers as FDR supporters, including the previously mentioned Sidney Weinberg of Goldman, Sachs; Averell Harriman of Brown Brothers; James Forrestal of Dillon, Read; and "probably" John Milton Hancock of Lehman Brothers. On the Morgan vs. Rockefeller aspect to separation, see Alexander Tabarrok, "The Separation of Commercial and Investment Banking: The Morgans vs. the Rockefellers," *Quarterly Journal of Austrian Economics* 1, no. 1 (1998): 1–18. On wisdom of separation, see Carlos D. Ramirez, "Did Glass-Steagall Increase the Cost of External Finance for Corporate Investment? Evidence from Bank and Insurance Company Affiliations," *Journal of Economic History* 59, no. 2 (June 1999): 372–96; Benston, *Separation of Commercial and Investment Banking*, 20–27. This issue, of course, has been far from settled. Interestingly, Benston lists a number of potential abuses that might arise from the fusion of commercial and investment banking that appear significant. The series of financial crises since the 1980s, however, while demonstrating lax government oversight, may not prove the necessity of Glass-Steagall restrictions.
54. Meltzer, *A History of the Federal Reserve*, 432–35. Eccles's testimony before Senator Glass's hearing on the bill suggests his unfavorable view of Glass's commercial/investment banking separation.
55. Eccles Papers, 4:1. Memo to FDR.
56. Benston, *Separation of Commercial and Investment Banking*, 34, 35, 216, 217; Lauchlin Currie, "The Supply and Control of Money," *Journal of Economics* 49, no. 4 (August 1935): 700–704. The phrase "sweet and clean" comes from the testimony of Dr. Anderson before the Senate Banking Committee; Meltzer, *A History of the Federal Reserve*, 728; Greider, *Secrets of the Temple*, 282.
57. *Barrons*, May 27, 1935. Eccles authored this article in which he laid out a detailed defense of the act; Eccles, *Beckoning Frontiers*, 173–75; Meltzer, *A History of the Federal Reserve*, 476–77; Roger J. Sandilands, "New Light on Lauchlin Currie's Monetary Economics in the New Deal," *Journal of Economic Studies* 31, no. 3 (March 2004): 175.
58. Eccles, *Beckoning Frontiers*, 175; Hyman, *Marriner S. Eccles*, 185–87.
59. Hyman, *Marriner S. Eccles*, 171; Meltzer, *A History of the Federal Reserve*, 475, 476n126.
60. *New York Times*, February 8, 1935; *Time*, February 18, 1935; Meltzer, *A History of the Federal Reserve*, 475–77; Hyman, *Marriner S. Eccles*, 171.
61. *Time*, May 16, 1932; *New York Times*, March 21, 1938.
62. Eccles Papers, 4:2. The Patman bill is discussed here. It will be mentioned again further on; *New Republic*, February 20, 1935; *Nation*, June 26, 1935.
63. Schlesinger, *The Politics of Upheaval*, 296, 297; Eccles, *Beckoning Frontiers*, 202, 203.
64. Subcommittee of the Committee on Banking and Currency, United States Senate, 74th Cong., 1st Sess., *The Nomination of Marriner S. Eccles to Be a Member of the Federal Reserve Board*, April 15 and 19, 1935, 3–5 (hereafter *Senate Confirmation Hearing*).
65. *New York Times*, April 16, 1935.
66. *Senate Confirmation Hearing*, 11–13.
67. *New York Times*, April 23, 1935; *Time*, May 16, 1935.
68. *Congressional Record*, 74th Cong., 6717.
69. *Congressional Digest*, January 1935, 5, 31.
70. U.S. Senate Committee on Banking and Currency, *Subcommittee Hearings on Banking Act of 1935*, 74th Cong., 1st sess., 74 (hereafter *Subcommittee on Banking*).
71. Ibid., 76. Warburg had, of course, previously left his position in the administration. A strong anti-isolationist, however, he would patch things up with FDR later in the decade.
72. Ibid., 194, 195.
73. Ibid., 598–605. Eccles would later claim, somewhat condescendingly, that Glass never truly comprehended the workings or importance of the open-market operations.
74. Ibid., 674.
75. Ibid., 389, 423.
76. Schlesinger, *The Politics of Upheaval*, 296, 297.
77. *Subcommittee on Banking*, 280.
78. Ibid., 281.
79. Ibid., 282–83.
80. Ibid., 283, 284. In his testimony before the committee (938) David Stern presented these statistics: In 1860 cash in circulation was $9.76 per capita, demand deposits $9.85 or almost even. In 1880, cash per capita $13.90, deposits $44.80. In 1900, cash $17.10, deposits $111.57. In 1930, cash $29.76, deposits $485.57, or 16 to 1. *New York Times*, May 11, 1935. Although the tension between Eccles and Glass seems evident from merely reading the text, the newspaper accounts substantiate this. The story made the front page of the *New York Times* with the headline "Eccles and Glass Clash on Bank Bill."
81. *Subcommittee on Banking*, 292–96.
82. *Congressional Record*, 74th Cong., 6717. On the floor of the House, Representative Steagall elaborated upon what constituted eligible paper.
83. *Subcommittee on Banking*, 296, 297.

84. Ibid., 286.
85. Ibid., 287, 288.
86 Ibid., 674, 675. That banks were hesitant to buy government securities in 1929 when they seemed perfectly willing to indulge in any number of truly speculative investments seems hardly plausible.
87. Eccles, *Beckoning Frontiers*, 248.
88. *Ironwood (MI) Daily Globe*, May 13, 1935. Syndicates in "News behind the News." This was a syndicated column.
89. *Congressional Record*, 74th Cong., 8370. Eccles radio speech was introduced by Senator Fletcher; *New York Times*, May 26, 1935.
90. Eccles Papers, 90:1; *Barron's* article from May 19, 1935; *Time*, February 18, 1935; Hyman, *Marriner S. Eccles*, 181, 182.
91. *Congressional Record*, 74th Cong., 11826.
92. Ibid., 8372. Giannini's statement was placed in the *Congressional Record.*
93. *New York Times*, June 6, 1935; Eccles, *Beckoning Frontiers*, 202.
94. *New York Times*, May 25, 1935. Foster at New Jersey Bankers Association.
95. Morgenthau Diaries, meeting of April 29, at http://www.fdrlibraries.marist.edu/_resources/images/morg/md0009.pdf.
96. *Subcommittee on Banking*, 503–10; *New York Times*, May 18, 1935; Glass's reference to Eccles as "that Mormon missionary" was reported frequently, as in the "National Whirligig" in the *Abilene Morning Reporter–News* on July 28, 1935; Bernard Shull, *The Fourth Branch: The Federal Reserve's Unlikely Rise to Power and Influence* (Westport, CT: Praeger Publishers, 2005), 109.
97. *New York Times*, May 24, 1935; Meltzer, *A History of the Federal Reserve*, 483n141. The *New York Times* editorially opposed Title II on April 12, 1935.
98. *Provo Evening Herald*, July 10, 1932.
99. *New York Times*, July 2, 1935.
100. *Los Angeles Times*, June 30, 1935.
101. Ibid., July 9, 1935; *New York Times*, July 6, 1935.
102. *New York Times*, July 6, 1935.
103. Ibid., July 5 and 29, 1935.
104. Sandilands, "The New Deal and 'Domestic Keynesianism'"; *New York Times*, July 3, 1935, meeting with Kennedy; ibid., meeting with Harrison and Fisher.
105. William R. Allen, "Irving Fisher and the 100% Reserve Proposal," *Journal of Law and Economics* 36, no. 2 (October 1993): 704–6; Krugman, *End This Depression Now*, 44, 45.
106. Review of *100% Money*, *Journal of Royal Statistical Society* 99, no. 2 (1936): 386–90; E. A. Kincaid, Review of *100% Money*, *Accounting Review* 11, no. 2 (June 1936): 202–3.
107. Carter Glass Papers, August 9, 1935, Special Collections Library (The Roosevelt Vault), University of Virginia. FDR wrote to Glass on July 3 and 6 and on August 9; *(Elyria, OH) Chronicle-Telegram*, August 24, 1935. The letter was quoted in the popularly syndicated column called the "National Whirligig."
108. *Ogden Standard-Examiner*, December 16, 1933.
109. Ibid.
110. *New York Times*, August 24, 1935.
111. *Provo Evening Herald*, August 26, 1935; *Ogden Standard-Examiner*, August 17, 1935.
112. Eccles, *Beckoning Frontiers*, 225, Glass's wishes; Schlesinger, *The Politics of Upheaval*, 300, 301.
113. *New York Times*, August 17 and 24, 1935; *Ogden Standard-Examiner*, November 19, 1935, Fisher quoted on Banking Act.
114. Eccles Papers, 4:1. Memo dated August 18, given to the president on August 23, 1935.
115. Eccles Papers, 4:1. Second memo given to FDR on August 23, 1935.
116. *Subcommittee on Banking*, 290.
117. *Collier's*, June 25, 1935; *New Republic*, May 15, 1935, Flynn observation.
118. Hyman, *Marriner S. Eccles*, 181, 182.
119. *New Republic*, May 15, 1935.
120. *New York Times*, September 28, 1935.
121. *New York Times*, November 15, 1935. On the matter of banks requiring austerity from city governments, see Biles, "Urban South in the Great Depression," 82; Hyman, *Challenge and Response*, 105, 167, 187.
122. *New York Times*, November 15, 1935.

NOTES TO CHAPTER 7

1. *Subcommittee on Banking*, 282; Eccles quoted in Moore, *The Federal Reserve System*, 84, 85.
2. Eccles, *Beckoning Frontiers*, 279. On a number of occasions Eccles made reference to being in the administration. In this particular instance he spoke of his intent in 1940 to "leave the administration."
3. George Creel, "A Banker Who Can Talk," *Colliers*, June 25, 1935.
4. Eccles Papers, 4:1, letter from Early.
5. *New Republic*, December 22, 1937; Dean Lowe May, "New Deal to New Economics: The Response of Henry Morgenthau Jr. and Marriner S. Eccles to the Recession of 1937" (PhD diss., Brown University, June 1974), 99.

6. Eccles Papers, 105:10, letter from Brown; 105:17, letter from Eccles to E. G. Bennett. In this letter Eccles makes reference to a request that he raise money for the Democrats in Utah. Most of the people in Utah, he had protested, "are on the other side of the political fence."
7. Eccles Papers, 2:3; Meltzer, *A History of the Federal Reserve*, 500. Glass chose Ronald Ransom, John K. McKee, and Joseph Broderick. Ransom was a banker from Atlanta who had served as an official of the ABA. McKee came from the RFC where he was the chief examiner. Broderick was the New York state superintendent of banks.
8. Eccles, *Beckoning Frontiers*, 245–47.
9. *Big Springs (TX) Daily Herald*, June 16, 1936, Drew Pearson and Robert Allen; Meltzer, *A History of the Federal Reserve*, 460. The act committed the Treasury to purchase silver from foreign as well as domestic sources up to $1.29. This price was a sixteen-to-one ratio to gold at $20.67 per ounce.
10. Merry-Go-Round article by Drew Pearson cited in previous footnote; *Los Angeles Times*, May 22, 1936; *New York Times*, May 21, 1936.
11. Eccles, *Beckoning Frontiers*, 242–45.
12. *Ogden Standard-Examiner*, August 28, 1935, Eccles's comments on FDR's health; Currie, *Lauchlin Currie's Memoirs*, 209; Eccles, *Beckoning Frontiers*, 289; Hyman, *Marriner S. Eccles*, 213, Eccles's refusal to campaign directly for FDR in 1936; Sandilands, *The Life and Political Economy of Lauchlin Currie*, 81.
13. Eccles Papers, 2:3; Eccles, *Beckoning Frontiers*, 217. It is interesting to note that in September 1933, Jones spoke before the ABA and castigated them, in much the manner Eccles did two years later, for not taking advantage of New Deal offers to assist in recapitalization. This is mentioned in Michael Hiltzik, *The New Deal: A Modern History* (New York: Free Press, 2011), 331, 332.
14. Eccles Papers, 4:1, suggested Gridiron speech; *Syracuse Herald*, April 19, 1936.
15. Eccles Papers, 5:5. The term "lazy fairies" is cited by Hyman (*Marriner S. Eccles*, 93) as an expression used by William T. Foster. The term "lazy fairies" was not in this memo but it was a term that Eccles borrowed from Foster.
16. *Florence (SC) Morning News*, November 30, 1935. A survey of newspapers from Georgia and South Carolina reveals the details of the Atlanta address. A number of them also reported that Georgia governor Eugene Talmadge (FDR's harshest critic in the South) was hanged in effigy the morning of the Atlanta speech.
17. Eccles Papers: 4:2. Patman's letter to FDR.
18. Marriner Eccles, "Patman Federal Finance Dangers," *Bankers' Magazine* (May 1941): 440–44. The magazine published most of Eccles's letter to Patman.
19. *New York Times*, March 16, 1935.
20. Ibid., March 17, 1935. Of course, Eccles must have realized that the comparative cheapness of borrowing over printing would probably change if done on a very large scale.
21. *Ogden Standard-Examiner*, March 25, 1941, Eccles's quote about the "end of the capitalist system"; *New York Times*, May 8, 1938; William B. Harrison, "Annals of a Crusade: Wright Patman and the Federal Reserve System," *American Journal of Economics and Sociology* 40, no. 2 (July 1981): 317–20; Robert E. Weintraub, "Some Neglected Monetary Contributions: Congressman Wright Patman (1893–1976)," *Journal of Money, Credit and Banking* 9, no. 4 (November 1977): 517–28; Greider, *Secrets of the Temple*, 48–51; *New York Times*, March 16, 1935, Eccles's testimony in response to Congressman Cross's question about avoiding interest payments.
22. Eccles Papers, 4:2. Patman was viewed as the great champion of small retail businesses. In fact, the law was as supportive of the old wholesale system as it was small shops. A&P, which had only 200 stores circa 1900, had 15,000 by 1929. J.C. Penney had grown to 1,452. The Robinson-Patman Act amended the Clayton Anti-Trust Act to allow the FTC to safeguard against "predatory tactics" of chains. Eccles appeared to take no public position on this act. For more information, see Thomas W. Ross, "Winners and Losers under the Robinson-Patman Act," *Journal of Law and Economics* 27, no. 2 (October 1984): 243–71; Frederick Row, "The Evolution of the Robinson-Patman Act," *Columbia Law Review* 57, no. 8 (December 1957): 1059–88.
23. Biographical Directory of the United States Congress, Louis T. McFadden; Meltzer, *A History of the Federal Reserve*, 216–17; Greider, *Secrets of the Temple*, 276. Following McFadden's death in 1936 of an apparent heart attack, his followers claimed that he was murdered by people who feared his influence and his "encroaching" on the "powers of Judah." William Dudley Pelley's *Pelley's Weekly* reported on this. It is still part of the myth surrounding the Fed. For an insightful look at this world see Scott Beekman, *William Dudley Pelley: A Life in Right Wing Extremism and the Occult* (Syracuse: Syracuse University Press, 2005).
24. Eccles Papers, 4:1.

25. Ibid. "Confidential draft" on "the Patman Bill" dated March 7, 1938.
26. *New York Times*, May 8, 1938; Harrison, "Annals of a Crusade," 319.
27. *New York Times*, May 8, 1938.
28. *Ogden Standard-Examiner*, August 28, 1935.
29. *New York Times*, June 30, 1934; Perkins, *The Roosevelt I Knew*, 276.
30. Eccles Papers, 5:5, Eccles, *Beckoning Frontiers*, 185.
31. Eccles Papers, 5:5, "A Suggested Works Program"; Eccles, *Beckoning Frontiers*, 184, 185; *New York Times*, August 24, 1934, regarding rail pension requirements; Hiltzik, *The New Deal*, 206, 207. The "evil features" reference to public-utility holding companies is to be found in FDR's 1935 State of the Union address.
32. Eccles Papers, 5:5. Eccles did not refer to Gross National Product because that statistic would not be created until the Second World War. The matter of "national income" was discussed in an earlier footnote (see Marcuss and Kane). While the idea of measuring a nation's income goes back at least as far as William Petty's efforts in the early 1600s, it was not until the Great Depression that the Commerce Department and Simon Kuznets, on the National Bureau of Economic Research, formulated and presented these statistics to the Senate in January 1934. National income paid out was "the income from current production received by individuals as workers and owners of capital. It consisted of wages and salaries, income from unincorporated businesses, dividends, interest, and rental income. It was estimated using available data on industrial production, business payroll, and income tax returns."
33. Eccles Papers, 5:5; Eccles, *Beckoning Frontiers*, 185–87. The sentence that mentions "contract basis" comes from Eccles's recollection of his suggestion to the president in his memoir. It represents, however, the argument of the memo; Eccles Papers, 24:9. The file contains figures on the debt-per-capita figures. The report appears to be from 1938. *New York Times*, January 6, 1935, story on Britain's "Remarkable Recovery."
34. Eccles, *Beckoning Frontiers*, 185; Harvey, "U.S. Job Creation in the 1930s," 26, 27; George McJimsey, *Harry Hopkins* (Cambridge: Harvard University Press, 1987), 110–14. *New Republic*, December 22, 1937, mentions the three hundred thousand workers added for the winter of 1937–1938; Fireside Chat, April 1935.
35. Eccles Papers, 4:8, memo from Brimhall; *Salt Lake Tribune*, June 9, 1935. Brimhall was also president of Utah Pacific Airways and was related to Eccles by marriage; Eccles, *Beckoning Frontiers*, 186; Harvey, "U.S. Job Creation in the 1930s," 27; Rose, *Put to Work*, 78–80; *Ogden Standard-Examiner*, June 23, 1936. Hinckley resigned as western regional director in March of 1936 and took the position back in June after both FDR and Harry Hopkins made a personal appeal for him to do so. *New York Times*, October 13, 1940, information on Catherine Cleveland.
36. Dean Lowe May, "New Deal to New Economics: The Response of Henry Morgenthau Jr. and Marriner S. Eccles to the Recession of 1937" (PhD diss., Brown University, June 1974), 131.
37. *Fitchburg (MA) Sentinel*, March 7, 1935.
38. Eccles Papers, 5:5.
39. Mark Leff, *The Limits of Symbolic Reform: The New Deal and Taxation, 1933–1939* (Cambridge: Cambridge University Press, 2002), 81–83.
40. *Fortune*, April 1935.
41. Leff, *Limits of Symbolic Reform*, 36–40.
42. *Los Angeles Times*, May 4, 1935. The 1934 Revenue Act also partially restored the income-tax publicity provisions that were established in 1924 and repealed in 1926. It required taxpayers to publicly report their gross and taxable income and what they claimed as deductions, the theory being that it would discourage very wealthy individuals from claiming deductions that greatly reduced the percentage of income paid in taxes. It was repealed in 1935. The graduated tax on capital gains decreased the longer the security was held; Leff, *Limits of Symbolic Reform*, 61–65, 106, 107. Leff cites a phone conversation Eccles had with Fed economist Emmanuel Goldenweiser.
43. Schlesinger, *The Politics of Upheaval*, 325, 326; Stein, *Fiscal Revolution*, 81, 82; Leff, *Limits of Symbolic Reform*, 137, 138.
44. *Wall Street Journal*, June 20 and July 14, 1935; Schlesinger, *Politics of Upheaval*, 327; Leff, *Limits of Symbolic Reform*, 143.
45. Franklin Roosevelt, "Message to Congress on Tax Revision," June 19, 1935, online at American Presidency Project, http:// www.presidency.ucsb.edu.
46. *Fortune*, April 1935; Leff, *Limits of Symbolic Reform*, 145. Rockefeller was in the top bracket.
47. *Jefferson City Post-Tribune*, September 6, 1935, Associated Press coverage of FDR-Howard exchange; *Abilene Reporter News*, November 17, 1939, AP story on Eccles and exceptions; Stein, *Fiscal Revolution*, 80–85; Leff, *Limits of Symbolic Reform*, 93–95, 102.
48. T. H. Watkins, *Righteous Pilgrim: The Life and Times of Harold L. Ickes* (New York: Henry Holt, 1990),

424, 425, 438; Leff, *Limits of Symbolic Reform*, 144. The amount raised by the Revenue Act was $250 million, which amounted to less than half of one percent of the national income; no doubt tension in the administration mounted when the *Literary Digest*—which had successfully predicted the past four presidential elections—released a poll of its over one million readers that indicated an overwhelming Landon victory. FDR seemed unconcerned. See Frank Freidel, *Franklin D. Roosevelt: A Rendezvous with Destiny* (New York: Little, Brown, 1990), 196.

49. Eccles Papers, 5:5. Memo to the president, December 28, 1935.
50. Eccles Papers, 5:5; Blum, *Morgenthau Diaries*, 280.
51. FDR Library, Morgenthau Diaries, December 28, 1939, http://www.fdrlibrary.marist.edu/_resources/images/morg/md0063.pdf. In a phone conversation with the author, John Morton Blum agreed that a misfiling was a possibility.
52. Eccles Papers, 5:5; *Big Springs Daily Herald*, December 18, 1936. This Texas paper carried the AP story; Currie, "Lauchlin Currie's Memoirs," 209. Currie's sanguine views, however, seemed contingent upon a better level of housing construction than what actually occurred.
53. Stein, *Fiscal Revolution*, 93. Others who cite the "1936 memo" are Sidney Hyman, as mentioned above, Dean Lowe May, and Julian E. Zelizer. In this matter I have found no scholars who have taken note of this inaccuracy. There are many who have documented, as I do below, Eccles's change of heart on budget balancing and seem to have either been unaware of the claim of the December 1936 memo, or choose to ignore it as inconsistent with other facts.
54. Brinkley, *The End of Reform*, 28.
55. Schlesinger, *The Politics of Upheaval*, 503; http://millercenter.org/president/fdroosevelt/speeches/speech-3308, Roosevelt's message to Congress.
56. Zelizer, "The Forgotten Legacy of the New Deal," 346.
57. Luther Gulick, "Memorandum on Tax Conference with FDR," dated 1941, online at www.ssa.gov/history/gulick.html; Leff, *Limits of Symbolic Reform*, 45–46; Hiltzik, *The New Deal*, 248–50; Renaghan, "Distributional Effects of Federal Tax Policy," 43. That the payroll tax should not be considered a tax burden has been propounded by Martin Feldstein. Renaghan makes conclusions about the overall distributive effect of New Deal policies by presenting two variants of the 1939 tax burden—one factoring the tax as a burden and one where it is not.
58. Eccles Papers, 46:18, speech to Texas bankers; Eccles Papers, 5:9, memo to FDR; Eccles Papers, 9:6; Zelizer, "The Forgotten Legacy of the New Deal," 345, 346; Hiltzik, *The New Deal*, 248, 251.
59. Eccles, *Beckoning Frontiers*, 257, 258; Hyman, *Marriner S. Eccles*, 208.
60. Eccles Papers, 24:1; Leff, *Limits of Symbolic Reform*, 170–72.
61. Eccles Papers, 24:1, Currie memo dated July 23, 1935; Leff, *Limits of Symbolic Reform*, 172–75; Sandilands, *The Life and Political Economy of Lauchlin Currie*, 80, 81; Eccles, *Beckoning Frontiers*, 258, 259.
62. Eccles Papers, 24:2. Goldenweiser memo dated February 21, 1936.
63. Eccles Papers, 24:4. Vanderpoel column of May 18, 1936, in the *Chicago American*.
64. Eccles, *Beckoning Frontiers*, 257, 258; Stein, *Fiscal Revolution*, 85–87.
65. Eccles Papers, 9:8, "Eccles on the tax bill"; Eccles, *Beckoning Frontiers*, 260, 261; James G. Smith, "The Significance of the Undistributed Profits Tax," *American Economic Review* 26, no. 2 (June 1938): 307–9. Smith's favorable view of the tax is demonstrated in this article that makes the case for a number of popular conceptions about the act.
66. *New York Times*, April 3 and 7, 1936.
67. Eccles, *Beckoning Frontiers*, 264, 265.
68. *New York Times*, June 12, 1936. Text of the Revenue Act of 1936.
69. Leff, *Limits of Symbolic Reform*, 181–82; Eccles's files (24:5) contain a memo from Currie that informs Eccles of a story in the *Wall Street Journal* that Caterpillar Tractor Company was considering paying its dividends in preferred stock, which would be considered taxable income for the recipients and yet permit the company to retain earnings for expansion.
70. Francis McIntyre, "The Effect of the Undistributed Profits Tax," *Econometrica* 7, no. 4 (October 1939): 336–40; Harry G. Guthmann, "The Effect of Undistributed Profits Tax upon the Distribution of Corporate Earnings," *Econometrica* 8, no. 4 (October 1940): 354–56; Charles W. Carlumino and R. Glenn Hubbard, "Internal Finance and Investment: Evidence from the Undistributed Profits Tax of 1936–37," *Journal of Economic History* 68, no. 4 (October 1995): 443–48.

71. *New York Times*, April 3, 1936; Eccles, *Beckoning Frontiers*, 264, 265.

NOTES ON CHAPTER 8

1. Flynn, *The Roosevelt Myth*, 98; Robert H. Zieger, *The CIO: 1935–1955* (Chapel Hill: University of North Carolina Press, 1995), 52, 53.
2. *Federal Reserve Bulletin*, January 1940, 45.
3. Eccles Papers, 4:8 (*Chicago American* article dated January 24, 1938); *Federal Reserve Bulletin*, July 1937, 633; Hyman, *Challenge and Response*, 164.
4. *News-Palladium*, January 1, 1938. Babson comment. The AP was reviewing statements made the previous January; *New York Times*, January 4, 1937.
5. *Barron's*, January 4 and March 8, 1937; *The Economist*, February 27 and May 27, 1937.
6. Eccles Papers, 4:8. Vanderpoel column of January 1, 1938.
7. Ibid.
8. Romer, "What Ended the Great Depression?," 759; Meltzer, *A History of the Federal Reserve*, 490, 491.
9. *New York Times*, March 14, 1935. "I don't know much about you," Cross informed Eccles following his velocity explanation, "but Steagall [the chairman] says you are all right."
10. Eccles Papers, 9:4.
11. Meltzer, *A History of the Federal Reserve*, 492, 493.
12. Eccles Papers, 63:2, summary of statements on Banking Act of 1935; Meltzer, *A History of the Federal Reserve*, 493.
13. Eccles Papers, 63:2; Milton Friedman and Anna Jacobson Schwartz, *A Monetary History of the United States* (Princeton: Princeton University Press, 1963), 525; Meltzer, *A History of the Federal Reserve*, 499.
14. Eccles Papers, 46:3.
15. Ibid.
16. Eccles, *Beckoning Frontiers*, 287.
17. Eccles Papers, 92:5, press release dated November 22, 1935; *New York Times*, November 23, 1935.
18. Eccles Papers 92:5; Eccles, *Beckoning Frontiers*, 287; Meltzer, *A History of the Federal Reserve*, 499n171.
19. Eccles, *Beckoning Frontiers*, 251–54.
20. Meltzer, *A History of the Federal Reserve*, 498, 499.
21. *Oakland Tribune*, December 29, 1935; *New York Times*, December 29, 1935.
22. *Oakland Tribune*, December 29, 1935.
23. *Time*, February 10, 1936.
24. *Federal Reserve Bulletin*, February 1937, 96.
25. Eccles, *Beckoning Frontiers*, 290, 291; Blum, *Morgenthau Diaries*, 356–58; Hyman, *Marriner S. Eccles*, 216, 217.
26. *Federal Reserve Bulletin*, February 1937, 96.
27. Meltzer, *A History of the Federal Reserve*, 504.
28. Zelizer, "The Forgotten Legacy of the New Deal," 341–51.
29. Eccles Papers, 30:3; Irving Bernstein, *Turbulent Years: A History of the American Worker 1933–1941* (Boston: Houghton Mifflin, 1970), 463, 468, 471. Bernstein cites a memo written by Steve Early that mentions Eccles's memo to FDR.
30. Eccles Papers, 30:11.
31. *New Republic*, December 22, 1937.
32. Senate Committee, *Hearings to Amend National Housing Act* (1937), 174, 176.
33. Eccles Papers, 90:5, 92:5.
34. Ibid., 5:7, memo to FDR; *Charleston Daily Mail*, June 30, 1937, AP story; David Kennedy, *Freedom from Fear: The American People in Depression and War, 1929–1945* (New York: Oxford University Press, 1999), 289, 318.
35. Eccles Papers, 30:11.
36. Zieger, *The CIO*, 113–15. He adds that in the rest of the world the amenities enjoyed by American workers would be envied. "The possession of automobiles, for example, was beyond the dreams of the majority of British workers."
37. Ibid., 90.
38. *Nevada State Journal*, August 25, 1932; *Reno Evening Gazette*, August 20, 1932; Hiltzik, *Colossus*, 163, 224, 314. Hiltzik is no doubt correct when he writes that Eccles "held Utah Construction's purse strings in his hand."
39. *Nation*, March 27, 1937.
40. *New Republic*, March 31, 1937.
41. Eccles, *Beckoning Frontiers*, 255, 256; *New York Times*, March 17, 1935, for Eccles's statement that it was cheaper to borrow than to print money. The rejoinder to this eagerness to lend the government money was that it was an indication of the lack of confidence in the private sector. And, of course, the response to that charge was the primary need to boost aggregate demand without waiting upon the "lazy fairies of laissez faire." Meltzer, *A History of the Federal Reserve*, 84n43, for statistics on World War I debt; Eichengreen, *Hall of Mirrors*, 328, for stat on 1936 debt.
42. *Federal Reserve Bulletin*, February 1937, 96; Meltzer, *A History of the Federal Reserve*, 504–6; Douglas A.

Irwin, "Gold Sterilization and the Recession of 1937," NBER Working Paper 17595, September 9, 2011, online at http://economics.yale.edu/sites/default/files/files/Workshops-Seminars/Economic-History/irwin-110926.pdf.

43. Blum, *Morgenthau Diaries*, 363.
44. Eccles Papers, 43:2, letter marked "very confidential" from Currie, December, 12, 1936; May, "New Deal to New Economics," 97, 98.
45. Blum, *Morgenthau Diaries*, 363.
46. Eccles Papers, 9:8. Letter dated December 15, 1938, to Morgenthau. The conciliatory letter sent that day which is mentioned in the *Morgenthau Diaries* was not discovered by the author in Eccles's papers.
47. Eccles, *Beckoning Frontiers*, 291; Hyman, *Marriner S. Eccles*, 222, 223; Blum, *Morgenthau Diaries*, 364, 365; *New York Times*, December 22, 1936.
48. *Federal Reserve Bulletin*, December 1937, 1.
49. Eccles Papers, 43:10. Wood correspondence.
50. *Federal Reserve Bulletin*, February 1937, 95. There was not one uniform rate across the board. For example, the ratio of demand deposits in central reserve cities was increased from 19.5 percent to 26 percent and at "country" banks from 10.5 percent to 14 percent; on time deposits at all banks, from 4.5 percent to 6 percent.
51. Hyman, *Marriner S. Eccles*, 227.
52. Eccles Papers, 24:6, memo dated June 2, 1937, to Eccles from Currie. He mentions a conversation held previously with Wallace about cutting expenditures. Blum, *Morgenthau Diaries*, 382.
53. Blum, *Morgenthau Diaries*, 382, 383.
54. *Minutes of the Federal Reserve's Open Market Committee and Its Executive Committee*, 1937, 32(4). The meeting began in the Federal Reserve office and members of the Executive Committee walked to Morgenthau's office where the meeting was resumed.
55. Eccles Papers, 63:9, testimony before Senator Byrnes's committee on the causes of the recession of 1937; *New York Times*, December 19, 1936. The speaking engagement to Boston Bankers occurred "a month ago." The article concludes by cautioning that the "great boom of the Twenties occurred in a period when the national debt was being reduced rapidly." It is unclear, however, if this addendum was something that Eccles said that evening or the thoughts of the "Topics in Wall Street" article. Interestingly, both Eccles and Currie were careful not to overemphasize the extent of the 1920s "boom." Roger Sandilands has informed the author of D. H. Robertson's description of the 1920s as a "sloom followed by a bump." The assumption is that if there was a "great crash" there must have been a great boom. There was in the stock market, of course, but growth in the economy, Currie argued, was much more modest.
56. *New York Times*, May 6, 1936.
57. *Southwest Times*, November 13, 1936, U.P. reference; Friedman and Schwartz, *Monetary History*, 518, 519; Stein, *Fiscal Revolution*, 100.
58. Eccles Papers, 5:7, memo to FDR; Eccles, *Beckoning Frontiers*, 296–98.
59. Eccles Papers, 5:7. The statistics and charts that Eccles used in the memo were prepared for him by Isador Lubin.
60. Ibid.
61. Ibid., 24:6, Currie memo of April 1, 1937, and memo about Henry Wallace dated June 2, 1937; *New York Times*, April 25, 1937.
62. *Ogden Standard-Examiner*, February 8, 1937. Lippman comments.
63. *American Bankers' Magazine* (May 1937): 134; *Ogden Standard-Examiner*, February 8, 1937, Lippman remarks; *New York Times*, January 11, 1937, Brookings Institution report and "People's Lobby." All three spoke at assembly.
64. Eccles Papers, 92:5, press release dated March 16, 1937; Eccles, *Beckoning Frontiers*, 298, 299.
65. Eccles, *Beckoning Frontiers*, 299; Blum, *Morgenthau Diaries*, 282.
66. *Federal Reserve Bulletin*, May 1937, 385, 387; April 1937, 287; July 1937, 633.
67. Eccles Papers, 99:15, memo from Wood; *New York Times*, April 25, 1937.
68. *Federal Reserve Bulletin*, August 1937, 711; ibid., July 1937, 630; ibid., August 1937, 711.
69. Eccles Papers, 99:15. Memo to Eccles from Currie, August 12, 1937. The memo was written, it seems, with Arthur Gayer and Martin Krost. Eccles, *Beckoning Frontiers*, 295.
70. *Federal Reserve Bulletin*, January 1940, 4; Hyman, *Marriner S. Eccles*, 236; Blum, *Morgenthau Diaries*, 398. For figures on GDP decline, see NBER at http://www.nber.org/data/abc/. For decline in industrial production, see Fed at http://www.federalreserve.gov/releases/g17/iphist/iphist_sa.txt.
71. Eccles Papers, 43:10, Wood correspondence; *New York Times*, July 16, 1937, Eccles testimony before House Banking Committee. The *Times* stated that critics of increasing the tax called it "drastic." Meltzer, *A History of the Federal Reserve*, 522, stats on real GDP decline.
72. Blum, *Morgenthau Diaries*, xii, xiii.

73. Friedman and Schwartz, *Monetary History*, 524–28.
74. *Federal Reserve Bulletin*, April 1937, 284; Eccles, *Beckoning Frontiers*, 291; Meltzer, *A History of the Federal Reserve*, 514, 515; *New York Times*, September 10, 1937, "Topics in Wall Street" article on "paradoxical circumstances."
75. Eccles, *Beckoning Frontiers*, 292, 293; Meltzer, *A History of the Federal Reserve*, 514–17; Friedman and Schwartz, *Monetary History*, 526–28.
76. *Federal Reserve Bulletin*, September 1937, 819; *New York Times*, September 10, 1937; Meltzer, *A History of the Federal Reserve*, 523; *New York Times*, September 13, 1937.
77. *Federal Reserve Bulletin*, October 1937, 965–73.
78. Meltzer, *History of the Federal Reserve*, 522; Michael R. Darby, "Three-and-a-Half Million U.S. Employees Have Been Mislaid; or, An Explanation of Unemployment, 1934–41," *Journal of Political Economy* 84, no. 1 (February 1976): 7, 8.
79. James A. Farley, *Jim Farley's Story: The Roosevelt Years* (New York: McGraw Hill, 1948), 103–5; Blum, *Morgenthau Diaries*, 392.
80. Eccles, *Beckoning Frontiers*, 303–4; Sandilands, "New Light on Currie," 181, 182.
81. Eccles, *Beckoning Frontiers*, 304.
82. *Provo Evening Herald*, November 10, 1937, U.P. story; Eccles, *Beckoning Frontiers*, 303, 304.
83. *New York Times*, November 30, 1937; *Provo Evening Herald*, November 29, 1937; Eccles, *Beckoning Frontiers*, 304.
84. Eccles Papers, 9:8, copy of Morgenthau speech to Academy of Political Science; *New York Times*, September 29, 1937. FDR's speech was delivered at a ceremony at Bonneville Dam in Oregon. The comments about the joint statement of both men is contained at the end of this story on an inside page.
85. Eccles Papers, 5:8, October 31, 1937, memo to FDR; *New York Times*, November 2, 1937.
86. *Provo Evening Herald*, December 14, 1937, Merry-Go-Round.
87. *New York Times*, December 15, 1937.
88. Eccles, *Beckoning Frontiers*, 308, 309.
89. Ibid., 309, 310.
90. Relief Committee Hearings, 72–80. Eccles Papers, 63:9, folder contains testimony before the Byrnes committee; Blum, *Morgenthau Diaries*, 392, 393; Sandilands, "New Light on Currie," 185.
91. Relief Committee Hearings, 72–80; Eccles Papers, 63:9, testimony before committee; Leff, *Limits of Symbolic Reform*, 256–58.
92. Eccles, *Beckoning Frontiers*, 309; Eccles Papers, 63:9.
93. Sandilands, "New Light on Currie," 178, 182, 183; see L. G. Telser, "Higher Member Bank Reserve Ratios in 1936 and 1937 Did Not Cause the Relapse into Depression," *Journal of Post-Keynesian Economics* 24, no. 2 (Winter 2001): 205–16; Christina D. Romer and David H. Romer, "Does Monetary Policy Matter? A New Test in the Spirit of Friedman and Schwartz," *Macroeconomics Annual* 4 (January 1989): 123–32. They find that Friedman and Schwartz are selective about what years they choose to identify as examples of monetary shock.
94. Meltzer, *A History of the Federal Reserve*, 554.
95. Gene Smiley, *Rethinking the Great Depression* (Chicago: Ivan R. Dee, 2002), 120, 121; Christina Romer, "What Ended the Great Depression?," 763. For opposing view of Romer's, see Kenneth Roose, *The Economics of Recession and Revival* (New Haven: Yale University Press, 1954).
96. *Fortune*, October 20, 1939; Leff, *Limits of Symbolic Reform*, 227, 257, 273.
97. Meltzer, *A History of the Federal Reserve*, 515n201, 527, 528; Kindleberger, *World in Depression.*
98. Romer and Romer, "Choosing the Federal Reserve Chair," 151, 152. They note that gold inflows in the mid-1930s kept real interest rates "substantially negative"; Meltzer, *A History of the Federal Reserve*, 522, 525.
99. Irwin, "Gold Standardization and the Depression of 1937–1938." He makes reference to the fact that in Friedman and Schwartz's view, gold sterilization was "no less important" than increased reserve requirements for bringing on the recession.
100. Eccles letter, Securities and Exchange Historical Society Archive, http://www.sechistorical.org/museum/search/?q=Marriner+Eccles. Eccles wrote a letter to the SEC chairman dated March 12, 1938, in which he attached a letter he had previously written to Herbert Feis of the State Department where he voiced disapproval of a plan by State to set up an organization in London to "facilitate European transactions in American securities."
101. Field, *Great Leap Forward*, 275. The capital strike theorists that Field is making reference to are Robert Higgs, "Regime Uncertainty: Why the Great Depression Lasted So Long and Why Prosperity Resumed After the War," *Independent Review* 1, no. 4 (Spring 1997): 561–90; Harold Cole and Lee Ohanian, "The Great Depression in the United States from a Neoclassical Perspective," *Federal Reserve Bank of Minneapolis Quarterly Review* 23 (Winter 1999): 2–24.

102. Anthony Sutton, *Wall Street and FDR* (New York: Arlington House Publishers, 1975), 20, 21, 97; May, "New Deal to New Economics," 202; Stein, *Fiscal Revolution*, 102–3.
103. May, "New Deal to New Economics," 202. The person who made the observation about James's role was Paul Appleby, a newspaper editor who became an assistant to Henry Wallace.
104. Eccles Papers, 7:6.
105. *Oakland Tribune*, February 6, 1938; *News Palladium*, January 1, 1938; May, "New Deal to New Economics," 210, 211.
106. Stein, *Fiscal Revolution*, 108; Schlesinger, *Politics of Upheaval*, 405, 406.
107. Eccles Papers, 105:4, Eccles's "Reconstructing Economic Thinking" speech; Stein, *Fiscal Revolution*, 111.
108. May, "New Deal to New Economics," 218.
109. Roosevelt, *Public Papers*, 7:222–34.
110. Ibid., 7:237.
111. Ibid., 7:238–48; May, "New Deal to New Economics," 222–48.

NOTES TO CHAPTER 9

1. Eccles Papers, 56:13. Exchange with Congressman Clark. The political advisor to whom Clark referred, Nathaniel Beverly Tucker, was a prominent Virginian and strong states' rights advocate who penned the proslavery novel *George Balcombe*. In 1836 he authored a novel, *The Partisan Leader*, about a guerilla war in Virginia against a leviathan federal government under the dictatorship of Martin Van Buren. On January 5, 1938, Eccles sent his Macaulay letter to South Carolina senator James Byrnes; John Steele Gordon, *Hamilton's Blessing*, 64, 65. Gordon writes about the 1837–1843 depression. Macaulay's comments are still utilized to place fear of debt in perspective. See Samuel Brittan's reference in the March 13, 2009, issue of *Financial Times*.
2. *New York Times*, April 28 and May 4, 1938.
3. Eccles Papers, 90:4, Currie correspondence on *Fortune* article; *Ogden Standard-Examiner*, March 30 and April 15, 1936, Eccles's itinerary; Edsel Ford and Macaulay in Eccles Papers, 92:7.
4. Eccles Papers, 24:9.
5. Ibid. Response to Commerce Department.
6. *New York Times*, April 13, 1938.
7. Ibid., April 15, 1938.
8. Eccles Papers, 40:1. Eccles's speech to New York chapter of the American Institute of Banking and the text of Byrd's speech in Massachusetts.
9. Ibid.
10. Eccles, 312, 313. When Eccles did not promptly respond to Byrd, FDR inquired if he had suddenly gotten cold feet. Eccles explained that a commemorative plaque honoring Carter Glass was being unveiled for the twenty-fifth anniversary of the Fed's founding. Eccles told Roosevelt that he thought it imprudent to "assail the junior U.S. Senator from Virginia while immortalizing the senior one." He waited, therefore, until two days after the ceremony; Hyman, *Marriner S. Eccles*, 256. Malice aforethought quote.
11. Eccles Papers, 40:1.
12. Ibid.; Eccles, *Beckoning Frontiers*, 317.
13. Eccles Papers 83:3, National Broadcasting System speech; Eccles, *Beckoning Frontiers*, 320, 321; Atack and Passell, *New Economic View*, 566, response of the Fed in 1921.
14. Eccles, *Beckoning Frontiers*, 316; *New York Times*, January 28, 1939, Barton remarks.
15. Eccles Papers, 92:8.
16. *New York Times*, January 6 and April 21, 1939; Leff, *Limits of Symbolic Reform*, 252–54. Leff points out that a 1946 survey discovered that only half of those responding to such questions could accurately describe what a "balanced budget" was.
17. Roosevelt, State of the Union address, January 4, 1939, online at American Presidency Project, https://www.presidency project.ucsb.edu.
18. Carter Glass Papers, Special Collections Library, University of Virginia, Box 402, Jesse Jones Folder. Letter dated December 18, 1936.
19. *New York Times*, March 21, 1935.
20. Eccles Papers, 8:1. Report on "Improvement of Federal Supervision of Banks"; excerpt from Report of the Committee on Banking and Currency, June 6, 1934.
21. Ibid.; Hyman, *Marriner S. Eccles*, 218.
22. Eccles, *Beckoning Frontiers*, 267; Hyman, *Marriner S. Eccles*, 218.
23. Jacob Viner, "Recent Legislation and the Banking Situation," *American Economic Review* 26, no. 1 (March 1936): 107–12; Eccles Papers, 8:1, memo written by Ronal Ransom that discusses Viner's support for regulation that corresponds to economic conditions.
24. Viner, "Recent Legislation," 107–9.
25. Eccles, *Beckoning Frontiers*, 267, 268.
26. Ibid., 269.
27. Ibid., 270–73; *Economist*, "Too Big Not to Fail," March 12, 2012; Charles P. Kindleberger and Robert Z. Aliber, *Manias, Panics, and Crashes: A History of*

Financial Crises (New York: Palgrave Macmillan, 2011), 194, 332, German banker quote.

28. Eccles Papers: 8:1. Memo written by Ronald Ransom; "Critical Discussion of Report of Brookings Institute," by Mr. Wingfield.
29. Eccles Papers, 8:3, Fed report on unification, 6; Thomas K. McCraw, *Prophets of Regulation* (Cambridge: Harvard University Press, 1984), 153, 204–6, 212–16. See also on Landis, Donald A. Ritchie, *James M. Landis: Dean of the Regulators* (Cambridge, MA: Harvard University Press, 1980).
30. *Dunkirk (NY) Evening Observer*, September 21, 1938, details on Cheney; Eccles, *Beckoning Frontiers*, 271, 272.
31. *New York Times*, April 15, 1938, text of FDR's recovery program to Congress; Eccles, *Beckoning Frontiers*, 272.
32. Eccles, *Beckoning Frontiers*, 272, 273.
33. Ibid.
34. *The Congressional Record*, Senate, June 16, 1938, 9536.
35. Ibid., 9537.
36. *Los Angeles Times*, June 17, 1938. This article typified the attention Eccles comments received. Eccles, *Beckoning Frontiers*, 274, 275; *Los Angeles Times*, June 24, 1939, Glenn Frank comment. Frank was the author of one of the first scholarly attacks upon the New Deal with his 1934 work *America's Hour of Decision*. He was fired from his position at the University of Wisconsin despite his suspension of conservative students who raided groups of campus socialists.
37. *Bankers' Magazine*, July 1938, 89; *Los Angeles Times*, June 20, 1939; *New York Times*, June 21, 1938.
38. *Federal Reserve Bulletin*, July 1938, 563–65; *Bankers' Magazine*, July 1938, 89–91.
39. Romer, "What Ended the Great Depression?," 757, 758; Charles Calomiris and Berry Wilson, "Bank Capital and Portfolio Management: The 1930s 'Capital Crunch' and Scramble to Shed Risk," *Journal of Business* 77, no. 3 (July 2004): 421–50; Steindl, *Understanding Economic Recovery*, 137–39.
40. Steindl, *Understanding Economic Recovery*, 142.
41. *Salt Lake Tribune*, November 19, 1938; Eccles, *Beckoning Frontiers*, 278.
42. Eccles, *Beckoning Frontiers*, 279.
43. *Salt Lake Tribune*, December 2, 1938; *New York Times*, December 2, 1938; Eccles, *Beckoning Frontiers*, 280, 281.
44. *Annual Report of the Board of Governors of the Federal Reserve, 1938* (January 27, 1939), 1–4, 9, 13, https://fraser.stlouisfed.org/docs/publications/arfr_1938.pdf. For an exploration of Regulation Q, see Timothy Q. Cook, "Regulation Q and the Behavior of Savings and Small Time Deposits," *Economic Review*, Richmond Federal Reserve (November/December 1978): 14–17; Alton Gilbert, "Requiem for Regulation Q: What It Did and Why It Passed Away," *Federal Reserve Bank of St. Louis Review* (February 1986): 22–26, https://research.stlouisfed.org/publications/review/86/02/Requiem/Feb1986.pdf. In 1935 the Fed reduced the ceiling on time deposits from 3 percent to 2.5 percent. Most member banks paid average interest on these accounts of only 2.4 percent in 1934 and 1935.
45. *Annual Report of the Board of Governors*, 13, 17. The practice of countercyclical regulation seems to have at least some adherents. Financial historians Kindleberger and Aliber (*Manias, Panics, and Crashes*, 194) write: "A strong case can be made for stricter regulations and supervision of banks to forestall lending in euphoric periods that may end in financial crisis," thus endorsing at least half of Eccles's regulatory schema.
46. *Carter Glass Papers*. Crowley letter dated August 28, 1939.
47. Sandilands, *The Life and Political Economy of Lauchlin Currie*, 96. There seems to be no evidence that Currie was a major influence on the issue of bank unification during this period. He was directing his energy toward other matters that will be discussed below.
48. *New York Times*, August 5 and September 22, 1939.
49. Eccles, *Beckoning Frontiers*, 286.
50. Charles P. Kindleberger and Robert Z. Aliber, *Manias, Panics, and Crashes* (New York: Palgrave Macmillan, 2011), 193–95, 300, 301.
51. Barber, *Designs within Disorder*, 116; Sandilands, "The New Deal and 'Domestic Keynesianism,'" 22.
52. Currie, "Lauchlin Currie's Memoirs," 219. For a discussion of the housing legislation of 1948, see Douglas, *In the Fullness of Time*, 271.
53. Currie, "Lauchlin Currie's Memoirs," 220.
54 *Staff Paper Prepared for the President's Commission to Study Capital Budgeting* (Washington D.C.: U.S. Government Printing Office, October 1998), 1–4. See also J. Lisle Bozeman, "The Capital Budget History and Future Directions," *Public Budgeting and Finance* 4, no. 3 (September 1984): 18–30. In 1998 there were forty-two states that had capital budgets; Barber, *Designs within Disorder*, 116.
55. U.S. Senate Committee on Banking and Currency, *Report No. 896: To Provide for the Construction and Financing of Self-Liquidating Projects*, July 22, 1939,

76th Cong., 1st sess., 1–4 (hereafter *Senate Report on Works Financing*).

56. Ibid., 1–11; *Los Angeles Times*, February 23, 1939, popularity of Export-Import Bank; Office of the Historian, Bureau of Public Affairs, U.S. Department of State, https://history.state.govmilestones/1921-1936export-importbank; Schwarz, *The New Dealers*, 335, 336, Export-Import Bank.
57. *Senate Report on Works Financing*, 8–9; McDonald's testimony is found on page 35–50 of Committee Hearings listed below. As McDonald mentions, the Feds did not use power of eminent domain and relied upon state governments to acquire land in that way.
58. U.S. Senate Committee on Banking and Currency, *Hearings on Works Financing Bill, s.*2759, 76th Cong., 1st sess., 1939, 8–12; challenging Senator Barkley from the political left on the committee was the newly elected senator from California, Sheridan Downey. Downey was a Bull Moose Republican from Wyoming who moved to California and became a Democrat. In 1934 he ran as Upton Sinclair's lieutenant governor under the End Poverty in California (EPIC) banner. He felt resources dedicated to the plan were insufficient. See Greg Mitchell, *The Campaign of the Century: Upton Sinclair's Race for Governor of California and the Birth of Media Politics* (New York: Random House, 1992), 562, 572. For the bill's detractors, what must have been the most satisfying moment of Barkley's statement came when he revealed that he was unaware that the law encouraged the commissioner of public roads to engage in land speculation. In something of a Boss Tweed fashion, the commissioner of public roads—aside from the need to acquire necessary land through condemnation proceedings—was empowered to purchase additional land where a federal highway project was under consideration or planning. Land could only be purchased if the price was such that it was likely a profit could be realized as a result of appreciation. Indeed, this seemed an important resource in achieving self-liquidation. The absence of a well-informed defense of the acquisition provision allowed the political opposition to moralize a bit about the wisdom of the federal government entering the realm of real-estate speculation.
59. *Senate Report on Works Financing*, 2–5. The report quotes from Morgenthau's testimony before the committee.
60. *Senate Hearings on Works Financing Bill*, 176–87; Field, *A Great Leap Forward*, 76–77.
61. *Los Angeles Times*, July 16 and August 2, 1939.
62. Ibid., August 2, 1939; Sandilands, "The New Deal and 'Domestic Keynesianism,'" 23.
63. *Los Angeles Times*, August 13, 1939.
64. *New York Times*, March 24, 1939; *Los Angeles Times*, March 24, 1939; Eccles, *Beckoning Frontiers*, 321–23; *Nation*, April 1, 1939.
65. *Congressional Record, House of Representatives*, April 10, 1939, 4042–50.
66. Eccles, *Beckoning Frontiers*, 338.
67. Romer and Romer, "Choosing the Federal Reserve Chair," 129, 131–35; Meltzer, *A History of the Federal Reserve*, 357, 523, 524, 550. It is true, of course, that purchases were made in 1939 to support the Treasury. Meltzer notes that Morgenthau stated in a September meeting with the FOMC that he was about to sell some new issues and wanted "the market to reach bottom"; Christina Romer, "What Ended the Great Depression?," 773. Romer also is critical of the fact that the Fed stopped the practice of increasing credit to meet seasonal demands by the mid-1930s.
68. U.S. Department of Commerce, Bureau of Economic Analysis, National Income and Product Accounts Table, online at http://www.bea.gov; Darby, "Three-and-a-Half Million U.S. Employees," 8; *Federal Reserve Bulletin*, September 1939, 715; Meltzer, *A History of the Federal Reserve*, 547.
69. Office of Management and Budget, *The Budget for Fiscal Year 2012, Historical Tables*, 21, online at www.budget.gov.
70. Eccles Papers, 5:5.
71. Ibid., 105:11. Letter to S. J. Quinney, March 2, 1939.
72. Eccles Papers, 5:9.
73. Stein, *Fiscal Revolution*, 171.
74. Hyman, *Marriner S. Eccles*, 244; David Blumenthal and James A. Morone, *The Heart of Power: Health and Politics in the Oval Office* (Berkeley: University of California Press, 2009), 42.
75. Daniel S. Hirshfield, *The Lost Reform: The Campaign for Compulsory Health Insurance in the United States from 1932 to 1943* (Cambridge: Harvard University Press, 1970), 51–52.
76. *New York Times*, July 18, 1938; Blumenthal and Morone, *Heart of Power*, 44–45.
77. U.S. Senate Subcommittee on Education and Labor, *Hearings on Bill to Establish a National Health Program*, 76th Cong., 1st sess., May 25, 1939, 321, 322; *New York Times*, January 23, 1939; Blumenthal and Morone, *Heart of Power*, 45–49.
78. Brinkley, *The End of Reform*, 271.
79. *New York Times*, June 6, 1939.

80. Ibid., November 10, 1939.
81. Ibid.
82. *Abilene Reporter News*, November 17, 1939. The statement was issued by the acting secretary, John Hanes. Morgenthau was vacationing in Sweden.
83. *New York Times*, November 25, 1939.
84. Eccles, *Beckoning Frontiers*, 333, 334.
85. Marcuss and Kane, "U.S. National Income and Product Statistics," 37; Hyman, *Marriner S. Eccles*, 271.
86. Richard P. Adelstein, "'The Nation as an Economic Unit': Keynes, Roosevelt, and the Managerial Ideal," *Journal of American History* 78, no. 1 (June 1991): 187; *New Republic*, July 29, 1940.
87. Eccles Papers, 90:10.

NOTES TO AFTERWORD

1. Tugwell, *Roosevelt's Revolution*, 306.
2. Eccles Papers, 38:17; *New York Times*, March 12, 1942.
3. Eccles papers, 38:19, 38:17. One of the matters that concerned Fed officials, for example, was the fact that insurance companies were refusing to write fire policies for Japanese property. The accusation of callousness was made against a number of people, but especially Tom Clark who was representing the Justice Department as a special assistant to the U.S. attorney general. In the matter of the San Francisco Fed's much higher estimation of Japanese claims, the 1982 commission on wartime relocation and internment stated in chapter 4 that although the Fed figure is cited in numerous sources, there seems to be no official report extant; *Salt Lake Tribune*, December 26, 1941; ibid., January 25, 1942, Thomas comments.
4. *Salt Lake Tribune*, April 8, 1942; J. A. Krug and D. S. Myer, *The Relocation Program*, United States Department of the Interior and the War Relocation Authority (Washington D.C.: U.S. Government Printing Office, 1945); *Ogden Standard-Examiner*, May 20 and September 24, 1942. Also in the summer of 1942, the price administrator, Leon Henderson, denounced Amalgamated Sugar for engaging in a "propaganda campaign" against sugar rationing by circulating "grossly erroneous and misleading statements." See *New York Times*, July 7, 1942.
5. Hyman, *Marriner S. Eccles*, 279.
6. Meltzer, *A History of the Federal Reserve*, 579.
7. *Los Angeles Times*, October 5, 1943; Hyman, *Marriner S. Eccles*, 291.
8. Eccles, *Beckoning Frontiers*, 377. Meltzer, *A History of the Federal Reserve*, 580. Tax receipts increased from 7 percent of GNP in 1941 to 21 percent in 1945.
9. Stein, *Fiscal Revolution*, 173, 174.
10. *New York Times*, June 25, 1945; Eccles, *Beckoning Frontiers*, 228; Stein, *Fiscal Revolution*, 199–204. For an enlightening discussion of the adoption of the dual mandate, see Daniel L. Thornton, "The Dual Mandate: Has the Fed Changed Its Objective?," *Federal Reserve Bank of St. Louis Review* 94, no. 2 (March/April 2012): 117–34. Thornton studied the FOMC meetings and reports to Congress from 1979 through 2008 and noted that while the FOMC used "price stability" they never mentioned "maximum employment" as a policy objective; rather, they made reference to price stability and "economic growth." The first use of the Humphrey-Hawkins mandate of "maximum employment" that he could find was the FOMC statement from the meeting in December 2008. This seems to be a product of the Great Recession. Of course, the assumption had always been that economic growth brought a certain amount of employment with it. That this could be measured (Okun's Law, 1962) some feel has proven problematic—for example, if greater output comes from greater productivity it could leave unemployment stationary. For an exploration of the view that there was a costly obsession with full employment in the 1960s and 1970s that caused damaging inflation, see Robert J. Samuelson, *The Great Inflation and Its Aftermath: The Past and Future of American Affluence* (New York: Random House, 2008), 55. Arthur Okun and other Keynesians of the period were "public spirited engineers" who were unwilling to keep the brakes on long enough in the 1970s to end inflation that they had caused—until Paul Volker's efforts in 1979–1982.
11. *New York Times*, October 8, 1946; Stein, *Fiscal Revolution*, 175. Eccles may have been influenced by George Terborgh's 1945 work, *The Bogey of Economic Maturity.*
12. Senate Committee, *Revision of National Housing Act*, December 1937, 180.
13. Hyman, *Marriner S. Eccles*, 317–19. The conditions ended up quite lenient. The British were to have an interest-free loan for six years, after which the interest was to be 2 percent. Moreover, in a provision upon which Eccles was insistent, no interest would be charged in any year where British exports were insufficient.
14. *Peoples Bank v. Eccles et al.*, District Court of the United States for the District of Columbia, Civil

Action 32200, 111–15. The first application was rejected on February 14, 1942; *New York Times*, February 15, 1949, the details of Giannini's letter; *Eccles v. Peoples Bank*, 333US 426 (1948); Eccles, *Beckoning Frontiers*, 446–51. Eccles had a poor relationship with Fred Vinson who was appointed treasury secretary when Henry Morgenthau resigned in 1945. Nor did he get along with John Snyder who was appointed to the Treasury when Vinson was placed on the Supreme Court in 1946. Eccles felt that Snyder and California senator Sheridan Downey led the opposition to his reappointment.

15. Robert L. Hetzel and Ralph F. Leach, "The Treasury Accord: A New Narrative Account," *Federal Reserve Bank of Richmond Economic Quarterly* 87, no. 1 (Winter 2001): 34; Hyman, *Marriner S. Eccles*, 313, 314; Meltzer, *A History of the Federal Reserve*, 633n91, on Taft-Hartley.
16. Eccles, *Beckoning Frontiers*, 486–89, Hetzel and Leach, "The Treasury Accord," 44; Hyman, *Marriner S. Eccles*, 342; Meltzer, *A History of the Federal Reserve*, 704. McCabe also resigned that March. He was replaced by the assistant secretary of the treasury, William McChesney Martin. Martin would go on to serve nineteen years as chairman; Robert P. Bremner, *Chairman of the Fed: William McChesney Martin Jr. and the Modern American Financial System* (New Haven: Yale University Press, 2004), 72–75. Figures on Fed portfolio and view that Eccles opposition to supporting Treasury sales led to the end of his tenure as chairman.
17. Meltzer, *A History of the Federal Reserve*, 647–49.
18. Hyman, *Marriner S. Eccles*, 339–41. Eccles received a good number of firsthand accounts of the corruption surrounding Chiang Kai-shek and his entourage. Lauchlin Currie might possibly have been such a source. Currie had been FDR's personal emissary to China during the war. His insistence on trade with communist nations was made more fully in 1954 (see p. 375).
19. *New York Times*, May 12, 1961; Hyman, *Marriner S. Eccles*, 404.
20. Hyman, *Marriner S. Eccles*, 406–12.
21. *Salt Lake Tribune*, September 28, 1967.
22. Eccles Papers, 198:3. Galbraith letter dated June 18, 1976.
23. Eccles Papers, 130:7. Address to the World Trade Club.
24. Eccles Papers, 4:2. Speech for FDR at Fed opening.

BIBLIOGRAPHY

PRIMARY SOURCES

Government Publications and Documents

Congressional Digest, 1935–1937. Washington, D.C.: Government Printing Office.

Congressional Record, 1934–1938. Washington, D.C.: Government Printing Office.

Federal Housing Administration. *Fifth Annual Report of the United States Housing Administration*. Washington, D.C.: Government Printing Office, 1939.

Federal Housing Administration. *Second Annual Report of the United States Housing Administration*. Washington, D.C.: Government Printing Office, 1936.

Federal Housing Administration. *Third Annual Report of the United States Housing Administration*. Washington, D.C.: Government Printing Office, 1937.

Federal Reserve Board of Governors. *Annual Report of 1938*. Washington, D.C.: Government Printing Office, 1939.

Federal Reserve Board. *Minutes of the Federal Reserve Open Market Committee*. Washington, D.C.: Government Printing Office, 1937.

Federal Reserve Board. *Federal Reserve Bulletin*. Washington, D.C.: Government Printing Office, 1935–1940.

President's Commission to Study Capital Budgeting. Staff Paper, October 1988.

President's Conference on Home Ownership. Vols. 2, 4, and 11. Washington, D.C.: Government Printing Office, 1931.

U.S. House Committee on Banking and Currency. *Hearings on the National Housing Act*, 73rd Cong., 2d sess. May 1934.

U.S. House Committee on Banking and Currency. *Subcommittee Hearings on the Banking Act of 1935*, 74th Cong., 1st sess. April and May, 1935.

U.S. Senate Committee on Banking and Currency, *Hearings to Amend the National Housing Act*, 75th Cong., 1st sess. April, May 1937.

U.S. Senate Committee on Banking and Currency. *Hearings on Improvement of Federal Supervision of Banks*, 76th Cong., 1st sess. June 1939.

U.S. Senate Committee on Banking and Currency. *Hearings on the National Housing Act*, 73rd Cong., 2d sess. May 1934.

U.S. Senate Committee on Banking and Currency. *Hearings on the Revision of the National Housing Act*, 75th Cong, 1st sess. December 1937.

U.S. Senate Committee on Banking and Currency. *Hearings on Works Financing Bill*, 76th Cong., 1st sess. 1939.

U.S. Senate Committee on Banking and Currency. *Report No. 896. To Provide for the Construction and Financing of Self-Liquidating Projects*, 76th Cong., 1st sess. July 1939.

U.S. Senate Finance Committee. *Hearings on Causes and Cures for the Depression*. 73rd Cong., 2d sess. February 1933.

U.S. Senate Special Committee on Unemployment Relief. *Hearings on Unemployment Relief*, 75th Cong., 2d sess. January 1938.

U.S. Senate Subcommittee on Education and Labor. *Hearings on Bill to Establish a National Health Program*, 76th Cong., 1st sess. May 1939.

Personal Papers

Eccles, Marriner S. The Papers of Marriner S. Eccles, Special Collections, J. Willard Marriott Library, University of Utah, Salt Lake City.

Glass, Carter. The Papers of Carter Glass. Special Collections Library, University of Virginia, Charlottesville.

Frequently Cited Newspapers and Periodicals

Atlantic Monthly, 1932–1938.

Bankers' Magazine, 1937–1941.

Economist, 1937–2012.

Fortune, 1934–1935.

Los Angeles Times, 1931–1940.

Nation, 1933–1940.

New Republic, 1933–1940.

New York Times, 1932–1949.

Ogden Standard-Examiner, 1928–1951.

Salt Lake Tribune, 1928–1951.

Time, 1933–1940.

Wall Street Journal, 1932–1939.

SECONDARY SOURCES

Abrams, Burton A., and Russell F. Settle. "Pressure Group Influence and Institutional Change: Branch Banking Legislation during the Great Depression." *Public Choice* 77, no. 4 (1993): 687–705.

Adams, Charles. *For Good and Evil: The Impact of Taxes on the Course of Civilization.* New York: Madison Books, 1993.

Adelstein, Richard P. "'The Nation as an Economic Unit': Keynes, Roosevelt, and the Managerial Ideal." *Journal of American History* 78, no. 1 (June 1991): 180–87.

Ahamed, Liaquat. *Lords of Finance: The Bankers Who Broke the World.* New York: Penguin Press, 2009.

Akerlof, George A., and Robert J. Shiller. *Animal Spirits: How Human Psychology Drives the Economy, and Why It Matters for Global Capitalism.* Princeton: Princeton University Press, 2009.

Allen, Frederick Lewis. *Since Yesterday.* New York: Harper & Row, 1939.

Allen, William R. "Irving Fisher and the 100% Reserve Proposal." *Journal of Law and Economics* 36, no. 2 (October 1993): 704–6.

Alvarez, Jose, and Leo L. Polopolus. "The Nature of Government Protection and Control in the U.S." Staff Paper no. 331. Department of Food and Resource Economics, University of Florida, Gainesville, June 1988.

Appleby, Joyce. *The Relentless Revolution: A History of Capitalism.* New York: W. W. Norton, 2010.

Arrington, Leonard J. *Great Basin Kingdom: An Economic History of the Latter-Day Saints, 1830–1900.* Urbana: University of Illinois Press, 2005.

———. "Science, Government, and Enterprise in Economic Development: The Western Beet Sugar Industry." *Agricultural History* 41, no. 1 (January 1967): 1–3.

Atack, Jeremy, and Peter Passell. *A New Economic View of American History*, 2nd ed. New York: W. W. Norton, 1994.

Bagley, Will. *Always a Cowboy: Judge Wilson McCarthy and the Rescue of the Denver & Rio Grande Western Railroad.* Logan: Utah State University Press, 2008.

Barber, William J. *Designs within Disorder: Franklin D. Roosevelt, the Economists, and the Shaping of American Economic Policy, 1933–1945.* Cambridge: Cambridge University Press, 1996.

Barth, James R., Gerard Caprio, and Ross Levine. *Rethinking Bank Regulation: Till Angels Govern.* Cambridge: Cambridge University Press, 2007.

Beekman, Scott. *William Dudley Pelley: A Life in Right Wing Extremism and the Occult.* Syracuse: Syracuse University Press, 2005.

Bender, Thomas. *A Nation among Nations: America's Place in World History.* New York: Hill and Wang, 2006.

Benhabib, Jess, George W. Evans, and Seppo Honkapohja. "Liquidity Traps and Expectation Dynamics: Fiscal Stimulus or Fiscal Austerity?" Working Paper No. 18114, National Bureau of Economic Research, May 2012.

Bennion, Lowell L. "The Business Ethic of the World Religions and the Spirit of Capitalism." *International Journal of Politics, Culture, and Society* 6, no. 1 (Autumn 1992): 67–73.

Benston, George J. *The Separation of Commercial and Investment Banking: The Glass-Steagall Act Revisited.* New York: Macmillan Press, 1990.

Bergland, Per Gunnar, and Matias Vernengo. "A Debate on the Deficit." *Challenge* 47, no. 6 (February 2004): 5–45.

Berle, Adolf, and Gardiner Means. *The Modern Corporation and Private Property.* New York: MacMillan Company, 1933.

Bernanke, Benjamin S. *Essays on the Great Depression.* Princeton: Princeton University Press, 2004.

Bernanke, Ben S., and Harold James. "The Gold Standard, Deflation, and Financial Crisis in the Great Depression: An International Comparison." In *Financial Markets and Financial Crisis*, edited by R. Glen Hubbard, 33–68. Chicago: University of Chicago Press, 1991.

Bernstein, Irving. *Turbulent Years: A History of the American Worker, 1933–1941.* Boston: Houghton Mifflin, 1970.

Bernstein, Michael. *The Great Depression: Delayed Recovery and Economic Change in America, 1929–1939.* Cambridge: Cambridge University Press, 1989.

Best, Gary Dean. *Pride, Prejudice, and Politics: Roosevelt versus Recovery 1933–1938.* New York: Praeger Publishers, 1991.

Biles, William Roger. "Mayor Edward J. Kelly of Chicago: Big City Boss in Depression and War." PhD diss., University of Illinois, 1981.

———. "The Urban South in the Great Depression." *Journal of Southern History* 56, no. 1 (February 1990): 71–100.

Black, Conrad. *Franklin Delano Roosevelt: Champion of Freedom.* New York: Public Affairs, 2003.

Blakey, Roy G., and Gladys Blakey. "The Revenue Act of 1932." *The American Economic Review* 22, no. 4 (December 1932): 620–40.

Blum, John Morton. *From the Morgenthau Diaries: Years of Crisis, 1928–1938.* Boston: Houghton Mifflin Company, 1970.

———. *The Republican Roosevelt.* Cambridge: Harvard University Press, 1977.

———. *Roosevelt and Morgenthau.* Boston: Houghton Mifflin, 1970.

———. *Woodrow Wilson and the Politics of Morality.* Boston: Little, Brown, 1956.

Blumenthal, David, and James A. Morone. *The Heart of Power: Health and Politics in the Oval Office*. Berkeley: University of California Press, 2009.

Bodfish, Morton. "Government and Private Mortgage Loans on Real Estate." *Journal of Land and Public Utility Economics* 11, no. 4 (November 1935): 402–9.

Bozeman, J. Lisle. "The Capital Budget History and Future Directions." *Public Budgeting and Finance* 4, no. 3 (September 1984): 18–30.

Bremner, Robert P. *Chairman of the Fed: William McChesney Martin Jr. and the Creation of the Modern Financial System*. New Haven: Yale University Press, 2004.

Brewer, H. Peers. "Eastern Money and Western Mortgages in the 1870s." *Business History Review* 50, no. 3 (Autumn 1976): 356–80.

Brinkley, Alan. *The End of Reform: New Deal Liberalism in Recession and War*. New York: Vintage Books, 1996.

Bruner, Robert F., and Sean D. Carr. *The Panic of 1907: Lessons from the Market's Perfect Storm*. Hoboken: John Wiley & Sons, 2007.

Brunnermeier, Markus, et al. "The Fundamental Principles of Financial Regulation." *Geneva Reports on the World Economy* 11 (July 2009): 1–70.

Calomiris, Charles W. *U.S. Bank Deregulation in Historical Perspective*. Cambridge: Cambridge University Press, 2000.

———. "Reassessing the Regulatory Role of the Fed: Grappling with the Dual Mandate and More." Briefing Paper No. 10, PEW Charitable Trusts: Financial Reform Project, 2009.

Calomiris, Charles, and Joseph Mason. "Consequences of Bank Distress during the Great Depression." *American Economic Review* 93, no. 5 (December 2003): 937–47.

Calomiris, Charles W., and Berry Wilson. "Bank Capital and Portfolio Management: The 1930s 'Capital Crunch' and the Scramble to Shed Risk." *Journal of Business* 77, no. 3 (July 2004): 421–53.

Calomiris, Charles W., and David Wheelock. "Was the Great Depression a Watershed for American Monetary Policy?" In *The Defining Moment: The Great Depression and the American Economy in the Twentieth Century*, edited by Michael Bordo, Claudia Goldin, and Eugene White, 23–65. Chicago: University of Chicago Press, 1998.

Calomiris, Charles W., and R. Glenn Hubbard. "Internal Finance and Investment: Evidence from the Undistributed Profits Tax of 1936–37." *Journal of Economic History* 68, no. 4 (October 1995): 443–48.

Carmony, David, and Josephine Elliot. "New Harmony, Indiana: Robert Owen's Seedbed for Utopia." *Indiana Magazine of History* 76, no. 3 (September 1980): 161–261.

Catchings, Waddill, and William Trufant Foster. *The Road to Plenty*. Boston: Houghton Mifflin, 1928.

Chance, James. *Acheson*. New York: Simon & Schuster, 1998.

C. H. Associates. *A History of the Bureau of the Public Debt*. Washington, D.C.: Government Printing Office, 1990.

Chase, Stuart. *A New Deal*. New York: MacMillan, 1932.

Chernow, Ron. *Alexander Hamilton*. New York: Penguin Press, 2004.

Cohen, Adam. *Nothing to Fear: FDR's Inner Circle and the Hundred Days That Changed America*. New York: Penguin Books, 2009.

Cohen, Lizabeth. *A Consumers' Republic: The Politics of Mass Consumption*. New York: Vintage Books, 2004.

Cole, Harold, and Lee Ohanian. "The Great Depression in the United States from a Neoclassical Perspective." *Federal Reserve Bank of Minneapolis Quarterly Review* 2311 (Winter 1999): 2–24.

———. "New Deal Policies and the Persistence of the Great Depression: A General Equilibrium Analysis." *Journal of Political Economy* 112, no. 4 (August 2004): 779–816.

Cole, Margaret. *Robert Owen of New Lanark*. New York: Oxford University Press, 1953.

Coit, Margaret L. *Mr. Baruch*. Boston: Houghton Mifflin, 1957.

Commager, Henry Steele. *Lester Frank Ward and the Welfare State*. New York: Bobbs–Merrill, 1967.

Cooke, Blanche Wiesen. *Eleanor Roosevelt*. Vol. 2, *1933–1938*. New York: Penguin Putnam, 1999.

Cooke, H. J., and M. Katzen. "The Public Debt Limit." *Journal of Finance* 9, no. 3 (September 1954): 298–303.

Copley, Stephen, and Kathryn Sutherland, eds. *Adam Smith's* Wealth of Nations*: New Interdisciplinary Essays*. Manchester: Manchester University Press, 1995.

Croly, Herbert David. *The Promise of American Life*. New York: Macmillan, 1909. Project Gutenberg [EBook 14422]. http://www.gutenberg.org/files/14422/1422-h/1442-h.htm.

Currie, Lauchlin. "Lauchlin Currie's Memoirs, Chapter 3: The New Deal." *Journal of Economic Studies* 31, no. 3/4 (2004): 201–34.

———. "The 'Leading Sector' Model of Growth in Developing Countries." *Journal of Economic Studies* 1, no. 1 (May 1974): 1–16.

———. "The Supply and Control of Money." *Journal of Economics* 49, no. 4 (August 1935): 700–704.

Darby, Michael R. "Three-and-a-Half Million U.S. Employees Have Been Mislaid; or, An Explanation of Unemployment, 1934–41." *Journal of Political Economy* 84, no. 1 (February 1976): 1–16.

Davenport, Stewart. *Friends of the Unrighteous Mammon: Northern Christians and Market Capitalism*. Chicago: University of Chicago Press, 2008.

Davis, J. Ronnie. "Chicago Economists, Deficit Budgets and the Early 1930s." Part 1. *American Economic Review* 58, no. 3 (June 1968): 476–81.

———. *The New Economics and the Old Economics.* Iowa City: University of Iowa Press, 1971.

DeLong, J. Bradford. "Review of Books." *The Journal of Economic History* 48, no. 1 (March 1988): 239–40.

———. *Slouching Towards Utopia?: The Economic History of the Twentieth Century.* Vol. 38, *The Roaring Twenties.* University of California–Berkeley, http://econ161.berkeley.edu/TCEH/Slouch_roaring13.html.

Dewey, John. *Individualism, Old and New.* New York: Prometheus Books, 1999.

Donnachie, Ian, and George Hewitt. *Historical New Lanark.* Edinburgh: Edinburgh University Press, 1993.

Douglas, Paul H. *In the Fullness of Time.* New York: Harcourt Brace Jovanovich, 1971.

Dubofsky, Melvyn. "Not So Radical Years: Another Look at the 1930s." In Eileen Boris and Nelson Lichtenstein, *Major Problems in the History of American Workers,* 304–14. New York: Houghton Mifflin, 2003.

Dunn, William Clyde. "Adam Smith and Edmund Burke: Complementary Contemporaries." *Southern Economic Journal* 7, no. 3 (January 1941): 337–45.

Eccles, Marriner S. *Beckoning Frontiers: Public and Personal Recollections.* New York: Alfred A. Knopf, 1966.

———. "Patman Federal Finance Dangers." *Bankers' Magazine* (May 1941): 440–44.

Edwards, Rebecca. *New Spirits: America in the "Gilded Age."* New York: Oxford University Press, 2001.

Eggertsson, Gauti B. "Great Expectations and the End of the Depression." Staff report, Federal Reserve of New York, December 2005.

———. "Was the New Deal Contractionary?" Federal Reserve Bank of New York Staff Reports, June 2008.

Eichengreen, Barry. *Hall of Mirrors: The Great Depression, the Great Recession, and the Uses—and Misuses—of History.* New York: Oxford University Press, 2015.

———. "The Political Economy of the Smoot-Hawley Tariff." *Research in Economic History* 12, no. 1 (1988): 1–43.

Ellis, Joseph J. *After the Revolution: Profiles of Early American Culture.* New York: W. W. Norton, 1979.

———. *Founding Brothers: The Revolutionary Generation.* New York: Vintage Books, 2002.

Fahey, John H. "Competition and Mortgage Rates." *Journal of Land and Policy Economics* 15, no. 2 (May 1, 1939): 150–54.

Farley, James A. *Jim Farley's Story: The Roosevelt Years.* New York: McGraw Hill, 1948.

Feingold, Henry L. "'Courage First and Intelligence Second': The American Jewish Secular Elite, Roosevelt, and the Failure to Rescue." In *FDR and the Holocaust,* edited by Verne W. Newton, 51–87. New York: Palgrave McMillan, 1996.

Ferguson, Thomas. "From Normalcy to New Deal: Industrial Structure, Party Competition, and American Public Policy in the Great Depression." *International Organization* 38, no. 1 (Winter 1984): 84–91.

Field, Alexander James. *A Great Leap Forward: 1930s Depression and U.S. Economic Growth.* New Haven: Yale University Press, 2011.

———. "Uncontrolled Land Development and the Duration of the Depression in the United States." *The Journal of Economic History* 52, no. 4 (December 1992): 785–805.

Filene, Edward. *Speaking of Change: A Selection of Speeches and Articles.* New York: Former Associates of Edward Filene, 1939.

———. *The Way Out.* Garden City, NY: Doubleday, Page, 1924.

Fine, Sidney. *Laissez Faire and the General Welfare State.* Ann Arbor: University of Michigan Press, 1956.

Fishback, Price V., William C. Horrace, and Shawn Kantor. "Did New Deal Grant Programs Stimulate Local Economies? A Study of Federal Grants and Retail Sales during the Great Depression." *Journal of Economic History* 65, no. 1 (March 2005): 36–65.

Flynn, John T. *The Roosevelt Myth.* New York: Devin & Adair, 1948.

Foner, Eric. *Give Me Liberty: An American History.* New York: W. W. Norton, 2012.

Fraser, Steven. *Every Man a Speculator: A History of Wall Street in American Life.* New York: Harper Perennial, 2005.

———. *Labor Will Rule: Sidney Hillman and the Rise of American Labor.* Ithaca: Cornell University Press, 1991.

Freidel, Frank. *FDR: Launching the New Deal.* Boston: Little, Brown, 1973.

———. *Franklin D. Roosevelt: A Rendezvous with Destiny.* New York: Little, Brown, 1990.

Freund, David M. P. *Colored Property: State Policy & White Racial Politics in Suburban America.* Chicago: University of Chicago Press, 2007.

Friedman, Milton, and Rose Friedman. *Free to Choose: A Personal Statement.* New York: Harcourt Brace Jovanovich, 1979.

Friedman, Milton, and Anna Jacobson Schwartz. *A Monetary History of the United States.* Princeton: Princeton University Press, 1963.

Frost, Stanley Brice. *The Man in the Ivory Tower.* Montreal and Kingston: McGill-Queen's University Press, 1991.

Gabriel Over the White House. Directed by Gregory La Cava. Metro-Goldwyn-Mayer, 1933.

Galbraith, John Kenneth. *Economics in Perspective.* Boston: Houghton Mifflin, 1987.

———. *A Life in Our Times*. Boston: Houghton Mifflin, 1981.

———. *Money: Whence It Came, Where It Went*. Boston: Houghton Mifflin, 1975.

Garraty, John A. "The Big Picture of the Great Depression." In *Historical Viewpoints: Historical Articles from American Heritage*, edited by John A. Garraty, 188–98. New York: Addison Wesley Longman, 1999.

———. "The New Deal, National Socialism, and the Great Depression." *American Historical Review* 78, no. 4 (October 1973): 907–44.

Gleason, Alan H. "Foster and Catchings: A Reappraisal." *Journal of Political Economy* 67, no. 2 (April 1959): 156–72.

Glickman, Lawrence B. *A Living Wage: American Workers and the Making of Consumer Society*. Ithaca: Cornell University Press, 1997.

Golway, Terry. *Machine Made: Tammany Hall and the Creation of Modern American Politics*. New York: Liveright Publishing, 2014.

Gordon, John Steele. *Hamilton's Blessing: The Extraordinary Life and Times of Our National Debt*. New York: Penguin Books, 1997.

Gordon, Peter. "Robert Owen." *Prospects: The Quarterly Review of Education* 24, no. 1 (March 1994): 1–4.

Green, Richard, and Susan Wachter. "The American Mortgage in Historical and International Context." *Journal of Economic Perspectives* 19, no. 4 (Autumn 2005): 93–114.

Greider, William. *Secrets of the Temple*. New York: Simon & Schuster, 1987.

Groenewegen, Peter. *Economics and Ethics?* New York: Routledge, 1996.

———. *Eighteenth Century Economics: Turgot, Becaria, Smith and Their Contemporaries*. New York: Routledge, 2002.

Grunwald, Michael. *The New New Deal: The Hidden Story of Change in the Obama Era*. New York: Simon & Schuster, 2012.

Gruver, Rebecca Brooks. *An American History*. New York: Appleton-Century-Crofts, 1972.

Gulick, Luther. "Memorandum on Tax Conference with FDR," dated 1941. Online at www.ssa.gov/history/gulick.html.

Guthmann, Harry G. "The Effect of Undistributed Profits Tax upon the Distribution of Corporate Earnings." *Econometrica* 8, no. 4 (October 1940): 354–56.

Hacker, Jacob S., and Paul Pierson. *American Amnesia: How the War on Government Led Us to Forget What Made America Prosper*. New York: Simon & Schuster, 2016.

Hacker, Louis Morton. "The New Deal Is No Revolution." *Harper's Magazine* (January 1934): 121–33.

Hagerty, James R. *The Fateful History of Fannie Mae: New Deal Birth to Mortgage Crisis Fall*. Charleston, SC: History Press, 2012.

Hammond, Bray. "Jackson, Biddle, and the Bank of the United States." *Journal of Economic History* 7, no. 1 (May 1947): 1–23.

Hanson, Alvin. *A Guide to Keynes*. New York: McGraw-Hill, 1953.

Harris, Richard, and Chris Hammett. "The Myth of the Promised Land." *Annals of American Geographers* 77, no. 2 (June 1987): 180–82.

Harrison, William B. "Annals of a Crusade: Wright Patman and the Federal Reserve System." *American Journal of Economics and Sociology* 40, no. 2 (July 1981): 317–20.

Harvey, Philip. "Learning from the New Deal." *Review of Black Political Economy* 39, no. 1 (March 2012): 87–105.

Hawley, Ellis W. *The Great War and the Search for a Modern Order: A History of the American People and Their Institutions, 1917–1933*. Prospect Heights, IL: Waveland Press, 1997.

Hawtrey, R. G. Review of *100% Money*. *Journal of Royal Statistical Society* 99, no. 2 (1936): 386–90.

H. D. M. Jr. "Banks and the Securities Act of 1933." *Virginia Law Review* 52, no. 1 (January 1966): 117–28.

Heilbroner, Robert L. *21st Century Capitalism*. New York: W. W. Norton, 1993.

———. *The Worldly Philosophers*. New York: Simon & Schuster, 1999.

Hetzel, Robert L., and Ralph F. Leach. "The Treasury-Fed Accord: A New Narrative Account." *Federal Reserve Bank of Richmond Quarterly* 87, no. 1 (Winter 2001): 32–45.

Higgs, Robert. "Regime Uncertainty: Why the Great Depression Lasted So Long and Why Prosperity Resumed after the War." *Independent Review* 1, no. 4 (Spring 1997): 561–90.

Hiltzik, Michael. *Colossus: Hoover Dam and the Making of the American Century*. New York: Free Press, 2010.

———. *The New Deal: A Modern History*. New York: Free Press, 2011.

Hirshfield, Daniel S. *The Lost Reform: The Campaign for Compulsory Health Insurance in the United States from 1932 to 1943*. Cambridge: Harvard University Press, 1970.

Hofstadter, Richard. "Franklin Roosevelt: The Patrician as Opportunist." In *The American Political Tradition and the Men Who Made It*, 315–52. New York: Vintage Books, 1989.

Hoover, Herbert, and Calvin Coolidge. *Campaign Speeches of 1932*. New York: Doubleday, Doran, 1933.

Hopkins, Harry L. *Spending to Save: The Complete Story of Relief*. New York: W. W. Norton, 1936.

Hopkins, June. *Sudden Hero, Brash Reformer*. New York: St. Martin's Press, 1999.

Houck, Davis W. *FDR and Fear Itself: The First Inaugural Address*. College Station: Texas A&M University Press, 2002.

Hsieh, Chang-Tai, and Christina D. Romer. "Was the Federal Reserve Constrained by the Gold Standard during the Great Depression? Evidence from the 1932 Open Market Purchase Program." *Journal of Economic History* 66, no. 1 (March 2006): 140–56.

Hughes, Tony. "Economic Data Sharpen Credit Scores." *Moody's Regional Financial Review* (February 2010): 21–25.

Hull, Cordell. *The Memories of Cordell Hull*. Vol. 1. New York: MacMillan, 1948.

Huston, James L. "The American Revolutionaries, the Political Economy of Aristocracy, and the American Concept of the Distribution of Wealth, 1765–1900." *American Historical Review* 98, no. 4 (October 1993): 1079–105.

Hyman, Sidney. *Challenge and Response: The First Security Corporation First Fifty Years, 1928–78*. Salt Lake City: University of Utah Press, 1978.

———. *Marriner S. Eccles: Private Entrepreneur and Public Servant*. Stanford: Stanford University Graduate School of Business, 1976.

Ireland, Paddy. "Company Law and the Myth of Shareholder Ownership." *Modern Law Review* 62, no. 1 (January 1999): 32–57.

Irwin, Douglas A. "Gold Sterilization and the Recession of 1937." NBER Working Paper 17595, September 9, 2011.

———. "The Smoot-Hawley Tariff: A Quantitative Assessment." *Review of Economics and Statistics* 80, no. 2 (May 1998): 326–34.

Israelsen, Dwight. "Marriner S. Eccles, Chairman of the Federal Reserve Board." *American Economic Review* 75, no. 2 (May 1985): 357–62.

James, Harold. "1929: The New York Stock Market Crash." *Representations* 110, no. 1 (Spring 2010): 129–44.

Janeway, Eliot. *The Struggle for Survival*. New York: Weybright and Talley, 1968.

Johnson, Hugh S. *The Blue Eagle from Egg to Earth*. New York: Greenwood Press, 1968.

Judt, Tony. *Ill Fares the Land*. New York: Penguin Books, 2010.

Keaney, Michael, ed. *Economist with a Public Purpose: Essays in Honor of John Kenneth Galbraith*. New York: Routledge, 2001.

Kennedy, David. *Freedom from Fear: The American People in Depression and War, 1929–1945*. New York: Oxford University Press, 1999.

Keynes, John Maynard. *The General Theory of Employment, Interest and Money*. London: Palgrave Macmillan, 2007.

———. *The Means to Prosperity*. Oxford: Oxford City Press, 2012.

Kincaid, E. A. Review of *100% Money*. *Accounting Review* 11, no. 2 (June 1936): 202–3.

Kindleberger, Charles P. *The World in Depression*. Berkeley: University of California Press, 1986.

Kindleberger, Charles P., and Robert Z. Aliber. *Manias, Panics, and Crashes*. New York: Palgrave Macmillan, 2011.

Kirk, Russell. *The Conservative Mind: From Burke to Elliott*. Washington, D.C.: Regnery Publishing, 1995.

Kolko, Gabriel. *The Triumph of Conservatism: A Reinterpretation of American History, 1900–1916*. New York: Macmillan, 1963.

Krug, J. A., and D. S. Myer. *The Relocation Program*. United States Department of the Interior and the War Relocation Authority. Washington D.C.: U.S. Government Printing Office, 1945.

Krugman, Paul. *End This Depression Now*. New York: W. W. Norton, 2012.

———. "Introduction for the Royal Economic Society." In Keynes, *The General Theory of Employment, Interest and Money*.

———. *The Return of Depression Economics and the Crisis of 2008*. New York: W. W. Norton, 2009.

Laidler, David. *Fabricating the Keynesian Revolution: Studies in the Inter-War Literature on Money, the Cycle, and Unemployment*. Cambridge: Press Syndicate of the University of Cambridge, 1999.

———. "Hawtrey, Harvard, and the Origins of the Chicago Tradition." *Journal of Political Economy* 101, no. 6 (December 1993): 1068–99.

Lash, Joseph P. *Dealers and Dreamers*. New York: Doubleday, 1988.

Leff, Mark. *The Limits of Symbolic Reform: The New Deal and Taxation, 1933–1939*. Cambridge: Cambridge University Press, 2002.

Leighninger, Robert D. *Long-Range Public Investment: The Forgotten Legacy of the New Deal*. Columbia: University of South Carolina Press, 2007.

Leuchtenburg, William E. *Franklin D. Roosevelt and the New Deal*. New York: Harper & Row, 1963.

Lewis, David Levering. *When Harlem Was in Vogue*. New York: Penguin Books, 1997.

Link, Arthur S. *Woodrow Wilson and the Progressive Era: 1910–1917*. New York: Harper & Row, 1954.

Lowenstein, Roger. *America's Bank: The Epic Struggle to Create the Federal Reserve*. New York: Penguin Press, 2015.

Lucas, Robert E. *Models of Business Cycles*. Oxford: Basil Blackwell, 1987.

Lutz, Mark A. *Economics for the Common Good: Two Centuries of Social Economic Thought in the Humanistic Tradition*. London: Routledge, 1999.

Lynd, Robert S., and Helen Merrell Lynd. *Middletown in Transition: A Study in Cultural Conflicts*. New York: Harcourt Brace Jovanovich, 1937.

Macpherson, C. B. "Harrington's 'Opportunity State.'" *Past & Present* 17, no. 1 (April 1960): 34–70.

Main, Jackson Turner. "The Distribution of Property in Post-Revolutionary Virginia." *Mississippi Valley Historical Review* 41, no. 2 (September 1954): 241–58.

Marcuss, Rosemary D., and Richard E. Kane. "U.S. National Income and Product Statistics: Born of the Great Depression and World War II." Bureau of Economic Analysis, February 2007. https://www.bea.gov/.../0207_history_article.pdf.

Margo, Robert A. "Employment and Unemployment in the 1930s." *Journal of Economic Perspectives* 7, no. 2 (Spring 1993): 41–59.

Marmor, Theodore R., Jerry L. Mashaw, and Philip L. Harvey. *America's Misunderstood Welfare State*. New York: Basic Books, 1990.

May, Dean Lowe. "New Deal to New Economics: The Response of Henry Morgenthau Jr. and Marriner S. Eccles to the Recession of 1937." PhD diss., Brown University, June 1974.

McConnell, Robert L. "The Genesis and Ideology of *Gabriel Over the White House*." *Cinema Journal* 15, no. 2 (Spring 1976): 7–26.

McCraw, Thomas K. *Prophets of Regulation*. Cambridge: Harvard University Press, 1984.

McGinnis, John O. "The Partial Republican." *William and Mary Law Review* 35, no. 9 (Summer 1994): 1751–99.

McIntyre, Francis. "The Effect of the Undistributed Profits Tax." *Econometrica* 7, no. 4 (October 1939): 336–40.

McJimsey, George. *Harry Hopkins*. Cambridge: Harvard University Press, 1987.

M., H. D., Jr. [pseud.] "Banks and the Securities Act of 1933." *Virginia Law Review* 52, no. 1 (January 1966): 117–28.

Meltzer, Allan H. *A History of the Federal Reserve*. Vol. 1, *1913–1951*. Chicago: University of Chicago Press, 2003.

Milkis, Sidney M. "Franklin D. Roosevelt and the Transcendence of Partisan Politics." *Political Science Quarterly* 100, no. 3 (Autumn 1985): 479–504.

Mitchell, Greg. *The Campaign of the Century: Upton Sinclair's Race for Governor of California and the Birth of Media Politics*. New York: Random House, 1992.

Moggridge, D. E., and Susan Howson. "Keynes on Monetary Policy, 1910–1946." *Oxford Economic Papers, New Series* 26, no. 2 (July 1974): 226–47.

Moley, Raymond. *After Seven Years*. New York: Harper & Brothers, 1939.

———. *The First New Deal*. New York: Harcourt, Brace & World, 1966.

Moore, Carl H. *The Federal Reserve System: A History of the First Seventy-Five Years*. Jefferson, NC: McFarland, 1990.

Morris, Edmund. *Colonel Roosevelt*. New York: Random House, 2010.

"Mortgage Moratoria since 1933." *University of Pennsylvania Law Review* 37, no. 8 (June 1939): 55–66.

Myers, Marvin. *The Jacksonian Persuasion: Politics and Belief*. Stanford: Stanford University Press, 1957.

National Commission on the Causes and Financial and Economic Crisis in the United States. *Financial Crisis Inquiry Report*. New York: Public Affairs, 2011.

Olson, Richard. *Science Deified and Science Defied: The Historical Significance of Science in Western Culture*. Vol. 2. Berkeley: University of California Press, 1983.

———. *Science and Scientism in Nineteenth-Century Europe*. Chicago: University of Illinois Press, 2008.

Ortiz, Stephen R. "The 'New Deal' for Veterans: The Economy Act, the Veterans of Foreign Wars, and the Origins of the New Deal Dissent." *Journal of Military History* 70, no. 2 (April 2006): 415–38.

Owen, Robert. *Report to the County of Lanark & a New View of Society*. Baltimore: Penguin Books, 1970.

Parker, Richard. *John Kenneth Galbraith: His Life, His Politics, His Economics*. New York: Farrar, Straus and Giroux, 2005.

Patinkin, Don. "Keynes and Chicago." *Journal of Law and Economics* 22, no. 2 (October 1979): 213–21.

Pearson, Sidney A. "Thurman Arnold's Defense of the New Deal: The Folklore of Liberalism." In Thurman Arnold, *The Folklore of Capitalism*, ix–lvii. New Brunswick: Transaction Publishers, 2010.

Perkins, Francis. *The Roosevelt I Knew*. New York: Viking Press, 1946.

Pizzitola, Louis. *Hearst over Hollywood*. New York: Columbia University Press, 2002.

Pocock, J. G. A. *The Machiavellian Moment*. Princeton: Princeton University Press, 1975.

Powell, Jim. *FDR's Folly*. New York: Three Rivers Press, 2003.

President's Commission to Study Capital Budgeting. Staff Paper, October 1988. http://clinton.3.nara.gov/pcscb/index.html.

Poteat, J. Douglass. "State Legislative Relief for the Mortgage Debtor during the Depression." *Law and*

Contemporary Problems 5, no. 4 (Autumn 1938): 517–44.

Quadagno, Jill S. "Welfare Capitalism and the Social Security Act of 1935." *American Sociological Review* 49, no. 5 (October 1984): 632–47.

Radford, Gail. *Modern Housing for America: Policy Struggles in the New Deal Era.* Chicago: University of Chicago Press, 1996.

Rakove, Jack N. *Original Meanings: Politics and Ideas in the Making of the Constitution.* New York: Vintage Books, 1998.

Ramirez, Carlos D. "Did Glass-Steagall Increase the Cost of External Finance for Corporate Investment? Evidence from Bank and Insurance Company Affiliations." *Journal of Economic History* 59, no. 2 (June 1999): 372–96.

Renaghan, Thomas M. "Distributional Effects of Federal Tax Policy, 1929–1939." *Explorations in Economic History* 21, no. 1 (January 1984): 40–63.

Rezneck, Samuel. "Distress, Relief, and Discontent in the United States during the Depression of 1873–1878." *Journal of Political Economy* 58, no. 6 (December 1950): 494–512.

Ritchie, Donald A. *James M. Landis: Dean of the Regulators.* Cambridge, MA: Harvard University Press, 1980.

Romer, Christina D. "The Great Crash and the Onset of the Great Depression." *Quarterly Journal of Economics* 101, no. 3 (August 1990): 597–623.

———. "What Ended the Great Depression?" *Journal of Economic History* 52, no. 4 (December 1992): 757–84.

Romer, Christina D., and David H. Romer. "Choosing the Federal Reserve Chair: Lessons from History." *Journal of Economic Perspectives* 18, no. 1 (Winter 2004): 129–52.

———. "Does Monetary Policy Matter? A New Test in the Spirit of Friedman and Schwartz." *Macroeconomics Annual* 4 (January 1989), 121–70.

Roose, Kenneth. *The Economics of Recession and Revival.* New Haven: Yale University Press, 1954.

Roosevelt, Franklin D. *Looking Forward.* New York: Simon & Schuster, 2009.

———. *The Public Papers and Addresses of Franklin D. Roosevelt.* New York: Random House, 1938.

Rose, Nancy E. *Put to Work: The WPA and Public Employment in the Great Depression*, 2nd ed. New York: Monthly Review Press, 2009.

Rosenman, Samuel I. *Working with Roosevelt.* New York: Harper & Brothers, 1952.

Ross, Dorothy. "Socialism and American Liberalism: Academic Social Thought in the 1880s." *Perspectives in American History* 11 (1977–1978): 25.

Ross, Thomas W. "Winners and Losers under the Robinson-Patman Act." *Journal of Law and Economics* 27, no. 2 (October 1984): 243–71.

Rothschild, Emma. "Commerce and the State: Turgot, Condorcet and Smith." *Economic Journal* 102, no. 414 (September 1992): 1197–1210.

———. *Economic Sentiments: Adam Smith, Condorcet, and the Enlightenment.* Cambridge: Harvard University Press, 2001.

Row, Frederick. "The Resolution of the Robinson-Patman Act." *Columbia Law Review* 57, no. 8 (December 1957): 1059–88.

Ruiz, George W. "The Ideological Convergence of Theodore Roosevelt and Woodrow Wilson." *Presidential Studies Quarterly* 19, no. 1 (Winter 1989): 159–68.

Samuelson, Paul. *Remembering the University of Chicago.* Chicago: University of Chicago Press, 1991.

Samuelson, Robert J. *The Great Inflation and Its Aftermath: The Past and Future of American Affluence.* New York: Random House, 2008.

Sandilands, Roger J. *The Life and Political Economy of Lauchlin Currie: New Dealer, Presidential Advisor, and Development Economist.* Durham, NC: Duke University Press, 1990.

———. "The New Deal and 'Domestic Keynesianism' in America." Chapter 12 in Keaney, *Essays in Honor of John Kenneth Galbraith.*

———. "New Light on Lauchlin Currie's Monetary Economics in the New Deal." *Journal of Economic Studies* 31, no. 3 (March 2004): 175–85.

Say, Jean Baptiste. *A Treatise on Political Economy; or, The Production, Distribution, and Consumption of Wealth.* Philadelphia: J. B. Lippincott, 1859.

Schlaes, Amity. *The Forgotten Man: A New History of the Great Depression.* New York: Harper Collins, 2007.

Schlesinger, Arthur M., Jr. *The Coming of the New Deal: 1933–1935.* Boston: Houghton Mifflin, 1958.

———. *The Crisis of the Old Order: 1919–1933.* Boston: Houghton Mifflin Company, 1957.

———. *The Politics of Upheaval: 1935–1936.* Cambridge: Houghton Mifflin, 1966.

Schroedal, Jean Reith. *Congress, the President, and Policymaking: A Historical Analysis.* New York: M. E. Sharpe, 1994.

Schwartz, Bonnie Fox. *The Civil Works Administration, 1933–1944.* Princeton: Princeton University Press, 1984.

Schwarz, Jordan A. *Liberal: Adolf A. Berle and the Vision of an American Era.* New York: Free Press, 1987.

———. *The New Dealers: Power Politics in the Age of Roosevelt.* New York: Vintage Books, 1993.

Sears, Louis Martin. "The Roosevelt Foreign Policy." *Journal of Modern History* 15, no. 1 (March 1943): 47–53.

Sherwood, Robert E. *Roosevelt and Hopkins.* New York: Harper and Brothers, 1948.

Shull, Bernard. *The Fourth Branch: The Federal Reserve's Unlikely Rise to Power and Influence*. Westport, CT: Praeger Publishers, 2005.

Skidelsky, Robert. *Keynes: The Return of the Master*. New York: Public Affairs, 2009.

Skilton, Robert H. "Mortgage Moratoria since 1933." *University of Pennsylvania Law Review* 37, no. 8 (June 1939): 55–66.

Smiley, Gene. *Rethinking the Great Depression*. Chicago: Ivan R. Dee, 2002.

Smith, Adam. *Theory of Moral Sentiments*. Boston: Wells and Lilly, 1817.

———. *The Wealth of Nations*. Edited by Edwin Cannan. New York: Bantam Dell, 2003.

Smith, James G. "The Significance of the Undistributed Tax." *American Economic Review* 26, no. 2 (June 1938): 307–9.

Smith, James Morton. *The Republic of Letters: The Correspondence between Thomas Jefferson and James Madison*. New York: W. W. Norton, 1995.

Smith, Roy C. *Adam Smith and the Origins of American Enterprise*. New York: Truman Talley Books, 2002.

Spengler, Joseph J. "Adam Smith's Theory of Economic Growth." *Southern Economic Journal* 25, no. 4 (April 1959): 397–415.

Stabile, Donald R., and Jeffrey A. Cantor. *A History of the Bureau of Public Debt*. Washington, D.C.: C. H. Associates, 1990.

Steele, Richard W. "The Pulse of the People: Franklin D. Roosevelt and the Gauging of Public Opinion." *Journal of Contemporary History* 9, no. 4 (October 1975): 195–216.

Stein, Herbert. *The Fiscal Revolution in America*. Chicago: University of Chicago Press, 1969.

Steindl, Frank G. "The 'Oral Tradition' at Chicago in the 1930s." *Journal of Political Economy* 98, no. 2 (April 1990): 430–40.

———. *Understanding the Economic Recovery in the 1930s: Endogenous Propagation in the Great Depression*. Ann Arbor: University of Michigan Press, 2007.

Sunstein, Cass. *The Second Bill of Rights*. New York: Basic Books, 2004.

Sutton, Anthony. *Wall Street and FDR*. New York: Arlington House Publishers, 1975.

Swanberg, W. A. *Citizen Hearst*. New York: MacMillan, 1961. 03n80

Sweezy, Alan. "The Keynesians and Government Policy, 1933–1939." *American Economic Review Papers and Proceedings* (May 1972): 116–34.

Tabarrok, Alexander. "The Separation of Commercial and Investment Banking: The Morgans vs. the Rockefellers." *Quarterly Journal of Austrian Economics* 1, no. 1 (Spring 1998): 1–18.

Taylor, Nick. *American-Made: The Enduring Legacy of the WPA*. New York: Bantam Dell, 2008.

Telser, L. G. "Higher Member Bank Reserve Ratios in 1936 and 1937 Did Not Cause the Relapse into Depression." *Journal of Post-Keynesian Economics* 24, no. 2 (Winter 2001): 205–16.

Temin, Peter. *Did Monetary Forces Cause the Great Depression?* New York: W. W. Norton, 1976.

———. *Lessons from the Great Depression*. Cambridge: MIT Press, 1993.

Thornton, Daniel L. "The Dual Mandate: Has the Fed Changed Its Objective?" *Federal Reserve Bank of St. Louis Review* 94, no. 2 (March/April 2012): 117–34.

Tobey, Ronald C. *Technology as Freedom: The New Deal and the Electrical Modernization of the American Home*. Los Angeles: University of California Press, 1996.

Tugwell, Rexford G. *The Battle for Democracy*. New York: Columbia University Press, 1935.

———. *Roosevelt's Revolution*. New York: Macmillan, 1977.

———. *In Search of Roosevelt*. Cambridge: Harvard University Press, 1972.

———. "The Sources of New Deal Reformism." *Ethics* 64, no. 4 (July 1954): 249–76.

Vance, Laurence M. "Francis Wayland: Preacher-Economist." *Independent Review* 10, no. 3 (Winter 2005): 401–6.

Viner, Jacob. "Adam Smith and Laissez Faire." *Journal of Political Economy* 35, no. 2 (April 1927): 198–232.

———. "Recent Legislation and the Banking Situation." *American Economic Review* 26, no. 1 (March 1936): 107–12.

Walker, Forrest A. *The Civil Works Administration: An Experiment in Federal Work Relief*. New York: Garland Press, 1979.

———. "Graft and the Civil Works Administration." *Southwestern Social Science Quarterly* 46, no. 2 (September 1965): 164–70.

Wapshott, Nicholas. *Keynes Hayek: The Clash That Defined Modern Economics*. New York: W. W. Norton, 2011.

Ward, Lester F. *Dynamic Sociology*. Vol. 1. New York: D. Appleton and Company, 1883.

Watkins, T. H. *Righteous Pilgrim: The Life and Times of Harold L. Ickes*. New York: Henry Holt, 1990.

Wayland, Francis. *The Elements of Political Economy*. New York: Sheldon & Company, 1886.

Weimer, Arthur M. "The Work of the Federal Housing Administration." *Journal of Political Economy* 45, no. 4 (August 1937): 466–83.

Weintraub, Robert E. "Some Neglected Monetary Contributions: Congressman Wright Patman (1893–1976)." *Journal of Money, Credit and Banking* 9, no. 4 (November 1977): 517–28.

Wells, H. G. *The New World Order.* London: Secker and Warburg, 1940.

Wells, O. V. "The Depression of 1873." *Agricultural History* 11, no. 3 (July 1937): 237–51.

White, Joseph. "Making 'Common Sense' of Federal Budgeting." *Public Administration Review* 58, no. 2 (March–April 1998): 101–8.

Wilentz, Sean. *The Rise of American Democracy: Jefferson to Lincoln.* New York: W. W. Norton, 2005.

Williamson, Jeffery, and Peter Lindert. *American Inequality: A Macroeconomic History.* New York: Academic Press, 1980.

William Lasser, *Benjamin V. Cohen: Architect of the New Deal* (New Haven: Yale University Press, 2002), 50.

Wills, Garry. *Lincoln at Gettysburg: The Words That Remade America.* New York: Simon & Schuster, 1992.

Wilson, Woodrow. *The State: Elements of Historical and Practical Politics.* Boston: D. C. Heath, 1898.

Wood, Edith Elmer. *The Housing of the Unskilled Wage Earner: America's Next Problem.* New York: MacMillan, 1919.

Zelizer, Julian E. "The Forgotten Legacy of the New Deal: Fiscal Conservatism and the Roosevelt Administration, 1933–1938." *Presidential Studies Quarterly* 30, no. 2 (June 2000): 331–58.

Zenter, Scot J. "Liberalism & Executive Power: Woodrow Wilson & the American Founders." *Polity* 26, no. 4 (Summer 1994): 579–83.

Zieger, Robert H. *The CIO: 1935–1955.* Chapel Hill: University of North Carolina Press, 1995.

INDEX

Page numbers in *italics* indicate illustrations.